D0428778

WALT WHITMAN

Selected Poems

1855–1892

WALT WHITMAN

Selected Poems

1855–1892

A NEW EDITION

Edited by

GARY SCHMIDGALL

ST. MARTIN'S PRESS

NEW YORK

WALT WHITMAN: SELECTED POEMS 1855–1892.

Library of Congress Cataloging-in-Publication Data

Whitman, Walt, 1819–1892
[Poems. Selections]
Walt Whitman : selected poems, 1855–1892 : a new edition / edited by Gary Schmidgall. — 1st ed.
p. cm.
Includes bibliographical references (p. 517) and index.
ISBN 0-312-20619-4
I. Schmidgall, Gary, date . II. Title.
PS3204.S36 1999 99-21745
811'.3—dc21 CIP

First Edition: August 1999

10 9 8 7 6 5 4 3 2 1

Contents

INTRODUCTION xv

LEAVES OF GRASS • 1855

WHITMAN'S PREFACE 3
THE TWELVE POEMS OF THE 1855 EDITION:
"I celebrate myself . . ." 15
"Come closer to me . . ." 66
"To think of time . . ." 75
"I wander all night in my vision . . ." 81
"The bodies of men and women engirth me . . ." 89
"Sauntering the pavement . . ." 95
"A young man came to me . . ." 98
"Suddenly out of its stale and drowsy lair . . ." 101
"Clear the way there Jonathan! . . ." 103
"There was a child went forth . . ." 105
"Who learns my lesson complete? . . ." 107
"Great are the myths . . ." 108
WHITMAN'S UNSIGNED REVIEW, *BROOKLYN DAILY TIMES* (1855) 112
WHITMAN'S UNSIGNED REVIEW, *U.S. REVIEW* (1855) 114

LEAVES OF GRASS • 1856

Poem of Salutation 121
Poem of Wonder at The Resurrection of The Wheat 130
Poem of You, Whoever You Are 132
Sun-Down Poem 134
Poem of The Road 140
Poem of Procreation 149
Clef Poem 151
Poem of The Heart of The Son of Manhattan Island 152
Faith Poem 153
Poem of Perfect Miracles 154

Bunch Poem 155
Poem of The Propositions of Nakedness 157
Poem of The Sayers of The Words of The Earth 160
RALPH WALDO EMERSON'S CONGRATULATORY LETTER 166
WHITMAN'S REPLY TO EMERSON 166
THE EMERSON-WHITMAN EXCHANGE: A CONVERSATIONAL POSTSCRIPT (1889) 172

LEAVES OF GRASS • 1860

Proto-Leaf 177
FROM THE *CHANTS DEMOCRATIC* CLUSTER:
8 "Splendor of falling day . . ." 188
10 "Historian ! you who celebrate bygones! . . ." 190
12 "To oratists—to male or female . . ." 191
14 "Poets to come! . . ." 192
18 "Me imperturbe . . ." 193
19 "I was looking a long while . . ." 194
20 "American mouth-songs! . . ." 194
FROM THE *LEAVES OF GRASS* CLUSTER:
1 "Elemental drifts! . . ." 195
13 "O bitter sprig! . . ." 198
17 "I sit and look out . . ." 199
21 "Now I make a leaf of Voices . . ." 200
22 "What am I, after all, but a child . . ." 200
24 "Lift me close to your face till I whisper . . ." 201
Poem of Joys 201
A Word Out of the Sea 208
FROM THE *ENFANS D'ADAM* CLUSTER:
1 "To the garden, the world . . ." 214
2 "From that of myself . . ." 215
6 "O furious! O confine me not! . . ." 217
7 "You and I—what the earth is, we are . . ." 218
8 "Native moments! when you come upon me . . ." 219
9 "Once I passed through a populous city . . ." 220
10 "Inquiring, tireless, seeking that yet unfound . . ." 220
11 "In the new garden, in all the parts . . ." 221
12 "Ages and ages, returning at intervals . . ." 221
13 "O hymen! O hymenee! . . ." 222
14 "I am he that aches with love . . ." 222
15 "Early in the morning . . ." 222

THE COMPLETE *CALAMUS* CLUSTER:

1 "In paths untrodden . . ." 223
2 "Scented herbage of my breast . . ." 223
3 "Whoever you are holding me now in hand . . ." 225
4 "These I, singing in spring, collect for lovers . . ." 227
5 "States! . . ." 228
6 "Not heaving from my ribbed breast only . . ." 230
7 "Of the terrible question of appearances . . ." 230
8 "Long I thought that knowledge alone would suffice me . . ." 231
9 "Hours continuing long, sore and heavy-hearted . . ." 232
10 "You bards of ages hence! . . ." 233
11 "When I heard at the close of the day . . ." 234
12 "Are you the new person drawn toward me . . ." 235
13 "Calamus taste . . ." 235
14 "Not heat flames up and consumes . . ." 236
15 "O drops of me! trickle, slow drops . . ." 237
16 "Who is now reading this? . . ." 237
17 "Of him I love day and night . . ." 238
18 "City of my walks and joys! . . ." 239
19 "Mind you the timid models of the rest, the majority? . . ." 239
20 "I saw in Louisiana a live-oak growing . . ." 240
21 "Music always round me . . ." 241
22 "Passing stranger! . . ." 241
23 "This moment as I sit alone . . ." 242
24 "I hear it is charged against me . . ." 242
25 "The prairie-grass dividing . . ." 243
26 "We two boys together clinging . . ." 243
27 "O love! . . ." 244
28 "When I peruse the conquered fame of heroes . . ." 244
29 "One flitting glimpse, caught through an interstice . . ." 245
30 "A promise and gift to California . . ." 245
31 "What ship, puzzled at sea . . ." 246
32 "What think you I take my pen in hand to record . . ." 246
33 "No labor-saving machine . . ." 247
34 "I dreamed in a dream . . ." 247
35 "To you of New England . . ." 248
36 "Earth! my likeness! . . ." 248
37 "A Leaf for hand in hand! . . ." 249
38 "Primeval my love for the woman I love . . ." 249
39 "Sometimes with one I love . . ." 250
40 "That shadow, my likeness . . ." 250

41 "Among the men and women, the multitude . . ." 251
42 "To the young man, many things to absorb . . ." 251
43 "O you whom I often and silently come where you are . . ." 252
44 "Here my last words, and the most baffling . . ." 252
45 "Full of life, sweet-blooded, compact, visible . . ." 252
FROM THE *MESSENGER LEAVES* CLUSTER:
To Him That was Crucified 253
To One Shortly to Die 254
To a Common Prostitute 254
To a Pupil 255
To The States 256
To a Cantatrice 257
Walt Whitman's Caution 257
To a President 257
To You 258
To You 258
Mannahatta 258
FROM THE *THOUGHTS* CLUSTER:
"Of persons arrived at high positions . . ." 260
A Hand-Mirror 260
Beginners 261
Tests 261
FROM THE *DEBRIS* CLUSTER:
"Have you learned lessons . . ." 262
"Despairing cries float ceaselessly . . ." 262
"I understand your anguish . . ." 262
"Three old men slowly pass . . ." 262
"Women sit, or move to and fro . . ." 262
"I thought I was not alone . . ." 263
To My Soul 263
So long! 264
UNPUBLISHED INTRODUCTION (1861) 267

DRUM-TAPS • 1865

Beginning My Studies 271
The Dresser 271
Come Up from the Fields Father 273
City of Ships 275
Mother and Babe 276
Vigil Strange I Kept on the Field One Night 276
A March in the Ranks Hard-Prest, and the Road Unknown 277

A Farm Picture 278
Give Me the Splendid Silent Sun 279
Did You Ask Dulcet Rhymes from Me? 280
Year That Trembled and Reel'd Beneath Me 281
The Veteran's Vision 281
O Tan-Faced Prairie-Boy 283
As Toilsome I Wander'd Virginia's Woods 283
Look Down Fair Moon 284
Hush'd Be the Camps To-day 284
Not Youth Pertains to Me 285
UNPUBLISHED INTRODUCTION (1864) 285
UNPUBLISHED INSCRIPTION TO THE READER 287

SEQUEL TO *DRUM-TAPS* • *1865-66*

When Lilacs Last in the Door-Yard Bloom'd 291
O Captain! My Captain! 298
Chanting the Square Deific 299
Not My Enemies Ever Invade Me 301
Ah Poverties, Wincings, and Sulky Retreats 301
As I Lay with My Head in Your Lap, Camerado 302
Dirge for Two Veterans 303
Reconciliation 304

LEAVES OF GRASS • *1867*

Inscription 307
One's-Self I Sing 307
The Runner 308
Leaves of Grass 2 ("Tears! tears! tears!") 308
When I Read the Book 309
UNPUBLISHED INTRODUCTION: LONDON EDITION (1868) 309

LEAVES OF GRASS • *1871-72*

Passage to India 315
Proud Music of the Storm 323
This Dust was Once the Man 329
Whispers of Heavenly Death 329
A Noiseless, Patient Spider 330
Sparkles from the Wheel 330
Gods 331

The Untold Want 332
For Him I Sing 333
To Thee, Old Cause! 333
The Base of all Metaphysics 334

AS A STRONG BIRD ON PINIONS FREE • 1872

PREFACE 337
One Song, America, Before I Go 340
Souvenirs of Democracy 340
As a Strong Bird on Pinions Free 341
The Mystic Trumpeter 345
By Broad Potomac's Shore 348

TWO RIVULETS • 1876

PREFACE 353
Eidólons 360
Prayer of Columbus 362
To a Locomotive in Winter 365
Wandering at Morn 366
With All Thy Gifts 367
UNPUBLISHED LETTER TO THE FOREIGN READER (1876) 367

LEAVES OF GRASS • 1881

The Dalliance of the Eagles 371
Italian Music in Dakota 371
The Prairie States 372
A Riddle Song 372
Spirit That Form'd This Scene 374
A Clear Midnight 374

NOVEMBER BOUGHS • 1888

PREFACE *("A BACKWARD GLANCE O'ER TRAVEL'D ROADS")* 377
Mannahatta 386
A Carol Closing Sixty-Nine 387
A Font of Type 387
As I Sit Writing Here 388
Queries to My Seventieth Year 388
America 388

After the Dazzle of Day 389
Halcyon Days 389
Of That Blithe Throat of Thine 390
Broadway 390
To Get the Final Lilt of Songs 391
The Dead Tenor 391
Yonnondio 392
Life and Death 392
A Prairie Sunset 393
Twilight 393
Now Precedent Songs, Farewell 394
After the Supper and Talk 395
NOTE AT END: *COMPLETE POEMS AND PROSE* (1888) 396
NOTE PRECEDING *"A BACKWARD GLANCE"* (1889) 397

LEAVES OF GRASS • 1891–92

AUTHOR'S NOTE TO 1891–92 EDITION 401
PREFACE NOTE TO *GOOD-BYE MY FANCY* 401
Good-Bye my Fancy 402
On, on the Same, ye Jocund Twain! 403
The Pallid Wreath 404
To the Sun-Set Breeze 404
A Twilight Song 405
A Voice from Death 406
"The Rounded Catalogue Divine Complete" 407
L. of G.'s Purport 408
Good-Bye my Fancy! 409
ARTICLE ON *GOOD-BYE MY FANCY* (1891) 410

APPENDICES

1. **Poems Published Before *Leaves* or Posthumously**
The Love That Is Hereafter (1840) 413 • *Each Has His Grief (1841)* 414 • *A Sketch (1842)* 416 • *The Mississippi at Midnight (1848)* 417 • *Resurgemus (1850)* 418 • *Supplement Hours (1897)* 420 • *Of Many a Smutch'd Deed Reminiscent (1897)* 421 • *A Thought of Columbus (1897)* 421
2. **Significant Passages from Whitman Manuscripts** 423
3. **Whitman's Observations on *Leaves of Grass*, 1888–92** 438

4. Contemporary Reviews of *Leaves of Grass*

1855: Charles Dana, *New York Daily Tribune,* 23 July 1855 448
Charles Eliot Norton, *Putnam's Monthly* (New York), September 1855 449
Rufus W. Griswold, *New York Criterion,* 10 November 1855 449
Edward Everett Hale, *North American Review* (Boston), January 1856 451
New York Daily News, 27 February 1856 452
London Critic, 1 April 1856 453
Fanny Fern, *New York Ledger,* 10 May 1856 454
William Swinton, *New York Daily Times,* 13 November 1856 456
Frank Leslie's Illustrated Paper (New York), 20 December 1856 459

1856: *Boston Christian Examiner,* November 1856 459
Brooklyn Daily Times, 17 December 1856 461

1860: *New York Times,* 19 May 1860 462
Boston Banner of Light, 2 June 1860 463
London Literary Gazette, 7 July 1860 465
London Spectator, 14 July 1860 466

Drum-Taps: William Dean Howells, *Round Table* (New York), 11 November 1865 467
Henry James, *Nation* (New York), 16 November 1865 469
A. S. Hill, *North American Review* (Boston), January 1867 472

1871: Edward Dowden, *Westminster Review* (London), July 1871 473

1881–82: *New York Critic,* 5 November 1881 475
T. W. Higginson, *Nation* (New York), 15 December 1881 477

November Boughs: *Philadelphia Evening Bulletin,* 30 October 1888 478
San Francisco Chronicle, 13 January 1889 478
Oscar Wilde, *Pall Mall Gazette,* 25 January 1889 479

Good-Bye my Fancy: *New York Tribune,* 16 August 1891 481
Boston Literary World, 12 September 1891 481

A Whitman Chronology 483

Notes on the Poems 485

A Select Whitman Bibliography 517

Index of Titles 521

WALT WHITMAN

Selected Poems

1855–1892

One of the very few early photographs of Whitman surviving, this shows him in his midthirties, circa 1854.

Introduction

WALT Whitman's *Leaves of Grass* is presented here in a format unprecedented among the countless editions that have appeared since its epoch-shattering debut in 1855. Its fundamental goals can be briefly stated: first, to offer a selection of the work of America's first great poet that faithfully reflects Whitman's evolving artistry over fifty years of poem-making and also gives due emphasis to the short span of time—roughly 1853 to 1860—in which he wrote most of his finest verse; second, to offer Whitman's poems in chronological sequence and in their first published form.

More specifically, the rationale for this edition is based on two assumptions. The first is that Whitman was, by and large, a poet of superb first inspiration. Nothing demonstrates this better than the six editions (or eight, or nine, depending on how one counts) of *Leaves of Grass* itself. The 1855 edition had a thrust of originality that is perfectly epitomized by the fact that Whitman daringly chose to present himself to the world for the first time not with his name on the title page, but with an image of himself loafing in a slouch hat, his undershirt showing from a wide-spread, open collar. The 1855 edition is brilliantly *sui generis* and deserves study in its pristine 1855 form, for it is the American equivalent of the 1609 *Sonnets* of Shakespeare—the single most important volume in its nation's poetic patrimony. The Library of America acknowledged the first edition's importance by including both it and the last, or "deathbed," edition of *Leaves of Grass* in its Whitman volume. The 1855 edition has also appeared several times separately hitherto, sometimes in facsimile.

Whitman, however, could not leave well enough alone. He first published his masterwork at the age of thirty-six, the exact midpoint of his life, and he invested the rest of his largely sedentary life almost entirely in rewriting, rearranging, suppressing, and adding poems to *Leaves of Grass*. Over time, the twelve original poems turned into a conglomeration of nearly four hundred.

As we shall see, many distinguished readers of Whitman agree that this long period of revision and accretion amounted to a devolution rather than an evolution. Whitman loved the sea and its ships, and a nautical image comes to mind by way of suggesting the consequences of his poetical afterthoughts. "O to sail in a ship under full sail at sea," Whitman exulted in "Poem of

Joys," and one can think of the poet at his best as a vigorous clipper with sails unfurled before a strong wind. But it must be said that, as time passed, *Leaves of Grass* became more like an unwieldy steamship—low in the water from overfreighting and ever slower of maneuver.

THE second premise on which this edition is founded is that a large majority of Whitman's finest poems appeared in the first three editions of *Leaves of Grass,* those of 1855, 1856, and 1860. A scenario borrowed from the opera world can very appropriately help to make this point, for Whitman became a deeply devoted opera lover in the crucial period of the early 1850s, when *Leaves of Grass* was gestating. As the poet himself many times asserted, opera-going contributed to the vocal extravagance, virtuoso self-presentation, and wealth of musical references in the poems composed during his most original phase. The words *song, sing, singer,* and *singing* occur in them hundreds of times, along with a musical vocabulary of more than two hundred other words. "To a Cantatrice," his beautiful encomium to Marietta Alboni, the great Italian contralto who visited New York in 1852–53, is thus one of his most revealing poems.

Indeed, it is possible to compare the complete run of *Leaves* editions, from 1855 to 1892, with the contours of a stellar operatic career. For the budding vocalist there is, first, a lengthy preparatory period of study and tentative groping for a personal artistic identity. Whitman's two dozen pre-*Leaves* poems—mostly doggerel ballads in neat, rhymed stanzas, which he published now and then in New York newspapers in the 1840s—perfectly capture this haphazard stage of his career. Five of these early poems are sampled in appendix 1. There is no more puzzling mystery in American letters than that of how the 1855 *Leaves* could have emerged from the Mammoth Falcon quill pen of a formerly itinerant journalist/editor, writer of mundane poetry and short stories, and sometime carpenter in Manhattan and Brooklyn, and it is remarkable to compare Whitman's poetic styles before and after the amazing watershed year.

Then—if one has the right luck, pluck, and laryngeal equipment—comes the sudden, stunning debut. For Whitman, of course, this was the 1855 edition. Controversy may surround the vocal sensation, who naturally hopes influential cognoscenti will applaud, and the poet struck it rich when Ralph Waldo Emerson wrote him a warm letter of welcome to the ranks of American poets. Whitman appended Emerson's gallant missive to his second *Leaves* edition in 1856 and quoted from it on the book's spine—without asking Emerson's permission. Nor did he shrink from publishing his own unsigned rave reviews of his masterpiece; two of these reviews are included here.

The 1856 and 1860 editions, then, constitute the next stage in the poet's career: spirited performances at the top of his form. The 1860 edition is extensively represented here, as befits the pains Whitman recalled taking over its publication: "I gave it more than my usual attention: examined it, word for word, with the copy in my hand, which is an unusual caution for me." The stentorian opening poem, "Proto-Leaf" (later titled "Starting from Paumanok"), is quite literally a spectacular entrance, in which the "exultant" poet promises a high-decibel tour de force: "I . . . will now shake out carols stronger and haughtier than have ever yet been heard upon the earth." And Whitman also promised to do what all superior opera singers must do: "effuse egotism, and show it underlying all." These promises were fulfilled in the 123 other new poems he included in the third *Leaves of Grass.* The present edition, therefore, is devoted in large part to this early period, when the poet who heard America singing was himself launching his most clarion high notes and offering his most personal, innovative, and rousing arias.

After a time, the singer inevitably begins to sense some erosion in stamina, and the first tiny fissures in self-confidence begin to appear. An awareness of the throat's ebb tide begins to grow. As early as 1860, in a poem later titled aptly "As I Ebb'd with the Ocean of Life," Whitman poignantly captured this disconcerting moment in a vocal career when one feels "baffled, balked." The vocalist begins to fear the aficionados' "distant ironical laughter" at his expense for having "dared to open my mouth to sing at all." Then comes the long downward slope—that is, the *Leaves* editions of the 1870s, 1880s, and 1890s: the aging and growing recalcitrance of the voice and the increasing tendency to *imitate* rather than *be* one's artistic self. In other words, to *pose.* Whitman caught the pathos of this stage of his career in *"So long!"*—a grand farewell aria that rings the curtain down on the 1860 edition: "So I pass, a little time vocal, visible, contrary, / Afterward a melodious echo, passionately bent for . . ."

At last may come the extended period of "farewell" performances. Whitman certainly produced his share of these. He could well boast, "I sing the endless finales of things," for over his last decades he became an expert at the lavish valedictory gesture. His poem "One Song, America, Before I Go" appeared in 1872, but he did *not* go for another twenty years. As Whitman admitted in one of his last poems, he was "loth, O so loth to depart! / Garrulous to the very last." No one could accuse the poet of failing to be candid about his vocal decline, however. In "Queries to My Seventieth Year" of 1888, he cast himself, with humorous self-deprecation, as "dull, parrot-like and old, with crack'd voice harping, screeching."

MOST Whitman scholars would not quarrel with the present emphasis on the early *Leaves* editions, and many have asserted their distinction in the strongest terms. Jerome Loving, in the *Columbia Literary History of the United States,* calls the 1860 edition the poet's "truest song of himself" and ventures, perhaps a bit too daringly, that Whitman wrote "no truly great poems" after "When Lilacs Last in the Door-Yard Bloom'd." And Roy Harvey Pearce, who supervised a facsimile edition of the 1860 *Leaves* in 1961, urged in his essay "Whitman Justified" that it is the author of the third edition "we must recover."

R. W. B. Lewis extended the poet's halcyon years somewhat when he summarized that Whitman "wrote little poetry of lasting value" after "Passage to India" appeared in 1871. And Lewis sternly added that the poet's habits late in life were "constantly to reshuffle the contents of his expanding book: to disperse the poems out of their original and effective order, to arrange them in new and fundamentally misleading groups, to suppress some of the more telling and suggestive of the items, and to revise or delete a series of key passages." The result, according to Lewis, was "a serious shift of emphasis whereby the authentic Whitman was gradually dismembered and replaced by a synthetic entity that was more posture than poet." Joining this chorus was Paul Zweig, whose splendid study, *Walt Whitman: The Making of the Poet,* ends a few pages after the poet journeys to his Boston publisher with the manuscript for the 1860 edition under his arm. With the slender volume of Civil War poems, *Drum-Taps* (1865), and the Lincoln ode of the same year, Zweig concludes, Whitman's "great work was done."

Though many estimable late poems are offered here, this selection heavily favors the first three editions of *Leaves of Grass.* The ratio of new poems included here from each *Leaves* edition (or specially titled collection) is worth specifying:

poems published before 1855: about two dozen; 5 selected
1855 edition: 12 poems; 12 selected
1856: 20 new poems; 13 selected
1860: 124 new poems; 96 selected
Drum-Taps (1865): 53 new poems; 17 selected
Sequel to *Drum-Taps* (1865–66): 18 new poems; 8 selected
1867: 8 new poems; 5 selected
1871–72 *Passage to India*: 13 new poems; 11 selected
As a Strong Bird on Pinions Free (1872): 5 new poems; 5 selected
Two Rivulets (1876): 18 new poems; 5 selected
1881: 20 new poems; 6 selected
November Boughs (1888): 62 new poems; 18 selected
1891–92 (*Good-Bye my Fancy*): 31 new poems; 9 selected
1897 (posthumous): 13 new poems; 3 selected

In other words, about half of Whitman's four hundred poems are offered here, and most of the following pages are devoted to poems from his first three astonishing editions of *Leaves of Grass.* Nearly three-quarters of the lines presented here first saw the light during the poet's flourishing late thirties, and since Whitman's earlier poems tended to be much longer, nearly eighty percent of the lines he wrote are included in this edition.

On his fifty-sixth birthday in 1875, Whitman, newly afflicted by a "tedious attack of paralysis," fondly recalled "how much my former poems, the bulk of them, are indeed the expression of health and strength, the sanest, joyfullest life." These "former poems" are the core of this edition.

PUBLICLY, the aged Whitman would have disapproved of this emphasis. In the Author's Note for the last edition he supervised, he pronounced, "As there are now several editions of L. of G., different texts and dates, I wish to say that I prefer and recommend this present one, complete, for future printing, if there should be any; a copy and facsimile, indeed, of the text of these 438 pages." Publishers have proved eager to abide by the seventy-two-year-old poet's benighted directive. Dozens of pro forma and "complete" editions of the 1891–92 *Leaves* are thus currently available, some pointing to the virtue of its "authorized" status.

Such editions, however, give us *Leaves of Grass* in a chaotic, unedifying, and, truth to tell, occasionally tedious form. Whitman wrote some inferior late verse, and even in the best of times his verse was ripe for satire and parody. He once admitted as much to Horace Traubel, the young bank clerk who visited him almost daily for the last four years of his life: "I am aware that *Leaves of Grass* lends itself to parody—invites parody—given the right man to do it." At least one anthology of send-ups of the Whitman style has been published (in 1923).

And the rule is fair: the later the edition of *Leaves of Grass*, the more likely one is to open a page on an unremarkable or bombastic poem. Whitman, in a candid private moment, even admitted this once. In 1888, Traubel came across an old letter from a Boston friend, the poet and novelist John Trowbridge, who made bold to say that he preferred the 1855 version of "Song of Myself" to its form in a later edition. After Traubel had read the letter aloud, Whitman responded with striking candor: "I know what Trowbridge means, too: I do not consider his position unreasonable: there was an immediateness in the 1855 edition, an incisive directness, that was perhaps not repeated in any section of poems afterwards added to the book: a hot, unqualifying temper, an insulting arrogance (to use a few strong words) that would not have been as natural to the periods that followed. We miss that ecstasy of statement in some of the after-work." We do indeed.

Agreement on a severe diminution in artistic power also came from another impeccable member of Whitman's circle. In the very first letter that Richard Maurice Bucke, Whitman's longtime friend and first biographer, ever wrote to the poet (in December 1870), he seconded Trowbridge's view: "Lately I have got a copy of the 1867 edition of *Leaves of Grass,* and I have compared the ["Song of Myself"] in that with the same poem in the 1855 edition, and I must say that I like the earlier edition best." Two decades later, in a March 1891 letter, Bucke proved that perfect candor was the rule among the poet's inner circle by expressing precisely the view of Whitman's flourishing years that the present edition is based upon: "Of course, you do not write now as you did in the 'Song of Myself' days—in power there has been since then a tremendous drop—but that drop occurred in the early '60s."

In 1890, again in conversation with Traubel, Whitman made a remark that accords with his willingness to embrace the "heresy" of Trowbridge and Bucke. Traubel's father was a lithographer and artist, and he once made a charcoal sketch of Whitman. Some time later, the poet commented on this sketch and warned against fussy retouching: "I hope he has not touched it since I saw him—it seemed to me on the whole there was nothing more to be done. The devil in artists is to keep pegging away at a thing after it is all done—pegging away at it *done,* till it is *undone.*" Whitman made many shrewd comments to Traubel about *Leaves of Grass* (some are collected in appendix 3), but this unwitting one was perhaps the most trenchant of them all.

Another remark made to Traubel also reflects unwittingly on one other injurious habit of Whitman the reviser, namely, the removal of a poem from its original cluster to a new position in his increasingly capacious volume. "You can detach poems from the book and wonder why they were written," he said, "but if you see them in their place in the book you know why I wrote them." Whitman spent three decades ignoring this sensible observation, which he might have underscored by citing Emerson's little fable poem, "Each and All," about a sparrow foolishly snatched from its alder bough and caged. Several poems in this edition are returned to their original context; the reason Whitman wrote them often does become more clear.

IN addition to the benefits of emphasizing Whitman's "halcyon days" and retrieving many of his poems from alterations that range from the innocuous to the self-censoring to the simply ill-advised (and, be it also said, occasionally to the improving), several advantages of this edition can be noted. While a few treasurable lines may be lost in the process ("Out of the cradle endlessly rocking," for example), much is to be gained by encountering Whitman's best poems in their first state. Most obviously, the changes in his style, interests, and view of the world as he matured can much more readily be observed. All the poems in this edition appear in the form in which he first supervised their publication, and the resulting format thus presents with unprecedented clarity his "organic" growth as a poet over five decades. The most significant phrases and passages Whitman deleted or added in subsequent appearances of each poem are identified in the endnotes.

The importance of a clearer grasp of the integrity of the most estimable *Leaves* edition, that of 1860, can also scarcely be overestimated, particularly in respect of the *Calamus* sequence, the forty-five poems of which are presented here complete and in their original form (illuminating prior manuscript versions of a few of them can be found in appendix 2). *Calamus* may be the most richly autobiographical cluster of poems Whitman ever wrote, and its sole "complete" appearance was in the 1860 edition. Whitman took his title from a species of marsh plant whose flower is very like the shape of an erect phallus. Gay Wilson Allen, this century's most eminent and productive Whitman scholar, called *Calamus* "the most unified group in the third edition," and his observation that these poems "parallel in a number of ways" Shakespeare's sonnets underscores the important place they occupy in Whitman's oeuvre.

Many years after *Calamus* first appeared, Whitman boasted to Traubel that there had been "no apologies, no dickers, no compromises" in the post-1860 editions of *Leaves*, but that boast is simply untrue. In later years, Whitman did succeed in compromising the boldly autobiographical content of the sequence by suppressing forever three of its most moving poems—#8 ("Long I thought that knowledge alone would suffice me . . ."), #9 ("Hours continuing long . . ."), and #16 ("Who now is reading this? . . .")—and shifting other poems to less revealing contexts elsewhere. The three banished poems are, of course, in none of the several dutiful reproductions of the "deathbed" *Leaves*. Whitman's unfortunate injury to the *Calamus* sequence is undone in the present edition.

The toning down and, in effect, self-censorship Whitman indulged in with *Calamus* were on a large scale, but the later editions of *Leaves* offer countless minuscule but telling instances of what amounts to expurgation, a word Whitman professed to hate ("It is a nasty word: I don't like it," he told Traubel). Thus, another advantage of the present edition is that it brings us more vividly and candidly back to the sexual Whitman. In an essay from the 1920s in which he attempted to puzzle out Whitman's love affairs, Emory Holloway (second only to Allen as an indefatigable Whitman scholar) observed that Whitman the Man and Whitman the Missionary "waged a long war" after 1860. Clearly, the Missionary finally won out by the late 1860s or so. The very phrase "genital impulse" disappeared from "Poem of Many in One," an 1856 poem, after the 1871 edition, and though some erotic passages survived untouched through all *Leaves* editions, many a genital impulse was deleted or denatured through revision.

The return, in the present edition, to the more vigorously physical Whitman occurs in countless fleeting but wonderful moments. In "Starting from Paumanok" of 1867, for example, Whitman describes himself as "well-begotten, and rais'd by a perfect mother," but in the original version of the poem the mother vanishes and we return delightfully to an author who admits to being simply "lusty-begotten." Elsewhere, we return, more graphically, to the phallus, testicles, and seminal discharge, as well as to dozens of banished exclamation points conveying the ecstasy of copulation—as in "A Song of Joys": "O love branches! love-root! love-apples! / O chaste and electric torrents! O mad-sweet drops!" In "Song of Myself" we regain the "Thruster holding me tight, and that I hold tight!" In his "Poem of The Propositions of Nakedness" of 1856, Whitman urged, "Let shadows be furnished with genitals!" but by 1871 the poet came to feel embarrassed by the poem and suppressed it entirely. The wonderful, brief lover's *cri de coeur,* "Not My Enemies Ever Invade Me," was also suppressed in 1871.

The innocuous line of 1867 in "Paumanok"—"Not he with daily kiss onward from childhood kissing me"—becomes, when we return to its first version, an explicit assertion of same-sex love: "Not he, adhesive, kissing me so long with his daily kiss." Crucial here is the poet's use of the word *adhesive. Adhesiveness* was a term from the then popular pseudoscience of phrenology, the reading of character from the shape of the cranium, and the word denoted a propensity to experience same-sex friendship and affection. Whitman was much taken by phrenology, no doubt in part because phrenologists said flattering things about his head. Also in "Paumanok," by returning to the poet's first inspiration we retrieve the two italicized words in the following line and thus regain a literally flamboyant announcement of same-sex passion: "I will therefore let flame from me the burning fires *of adhesiveness* that were threatening to consume me."

The fourth *Leaves* edition of 1867 was the first in the melancholy decline of Whitman's masterwork from vibrant sexuality into sometimes inflated prophecy, democratic boosterism, and sentimental Good Gray Poetizing. Typical of the 1867 edition was the loss, at the end of "Paumanok," of this passage that first appeared in 1860, with its ecstatic deployment of the time-honored rhetorical device of ecphonesis, so popular with Shakespeare (*ecphonesis* = Greek for "to cry out"):

> O to be relieved of distinctions! to make as much of vices as virtues!
> O to level occupations and the sexes! O to bring all to common ground!
> O adhesiveness!
> O the pensive aching to be together . . .

Indeed, Whitman's general inclination in his later editions was toward wholesale deletion of many of his exuberant "O" 's and buoyant exclamation points.

More specifically, many a "lover" also disappeared from his poems: "the passionate lovers" became" "the passionate ones," and in 1867 the italicized words disappeared from Whitman's "Poem of The Road" (1856): "No husband, no wife, no friend, *no lover*, trusted to hear confession . . ." The disappearance of a "lover" is especially striking in Calamus 20, since this poem was originally the linchpin poem of what later became the *Calamus* sequence. The lonely live-oak expresses Whitman's desolation after a searing amorous defeat: "I wondered how it could utter joyous leaves standing alone there, without its friend, *its lover* near, for I knew I could not." Those two italicized words, in time, came to make Whitman uneasy, and they disappeared after the 1871 edition. Likewise, "Mon cher" became "Dear son," and "Proceed, comrade" (*comrade* was another same-sex code word for the poet) also became the harmlessly paternal "My dear son."

"Give me now libidinous joys only!" Whitman cried in 1860, and this edition returns to the light several memorable longer passages that rejoice in a body's passionate proximity. In one poem, for example, the dreary, second-thought opening that Whitman came up with in 1881 (only a Chamber of Commerce could love it)—

A song for occupations!
In the labor of engines and trades and the labor of fields
        I find the developments,
And find the eternal meanings.

—is jettisoned, and we return to the superbly characteristic first inspiration of 1855:

Come closer to me,
Push close my lovers and take the best I possess,
Yield closer and closer and give me the best you possess.

This is unfinished business with me. . . . how is it with you?

The passage gives us back the poet who desired "the contact of bodies and souls." Likewise regained is the thrilling physicality and anguish of this passage cut in 1881 from the 1855 poem "I wander all night in my vision":

O hotcheeked and blushing! O foolish hectic!
O for pity's sake, no one must see me now! . . . . my clothes were stolen
        while I was abed,
Now I am thrust forth, where shall I run?

Pier that I saw dimly last night when I looked from the windows,
Pier out from the main, let me catch myself with you and stay. . . .
        I will not chafe you;

I feel ashamed to go naked about the world,
And am curious to know where my feet stand. . . . and what is this
flooding me, childhood or manhood. . . . and the hunger
that crosses the bridge between.

The cloth laps a first sweet eating and drinking,
Laps life-swelling yolks. . . . laps ear of rose-corn, milky and just ripened:
The white teeth stay, and the boss-tooth advances in darkness,
And liquor is spilled on lips and bosoms by touching glasses,
and the best liquor afterward.

And Whitman's wide, fearless embrace, expressed in his "Clef Poem" of 1856 but cut after 1860, is also restored:

I am not uneasy but I am to be beloved by young and old men,
and to love them the same,
I suppose the pink nipples of the breasts of women with whom
I shall sleep will taste the same to my lips,
But this is the nipple of a breast of my mother, always near
and always divine to me, her true son and child.

In the opening poem of the 1860 *Leaves,* Whitman boasted of "extasy everywhere touching and thrilling me." This is perhaps as fitting a one-line synopsis of the ethos of the three early editions as one could wish. But ecstasy, alas, is not a notably lasting phenomenon. Most tellingly, Whitman chose to banish this superbly confessional line from the next edition of 1867. The present edition returns ecstasy from the exile it suffered when Whitman was—to borrow a phrase he used himself—stung by the respectability bee. The shadows in the following pages are most decidedly furnished with genitals.

WHEN Malcolm Cowley issued in 1974 a revised version of Mark Van Doren's *Portable Walt Whitman,* which offered only a hundred poems, he wrote, "As for Whitman's revisions, they were usually improvements over earlier versions, but there are exceptions to the rule." Cowley therefore promised that, except for a half dozen poems given in their 1855 versions, he "followed scrupulously" the 1891–92 edition of *Leaves of Grass*. As noted above, countless editions similarly respectful of the aging poet's final wishes are available, and this fact alone encourages this new approach to the texts of Whitman's poems.

But I am also encouraged by my view of Whitman's revisions, which is exactly the reverse of Cowley's: he believed improving revisions were the rule; I am convinced that improving changes were the exception. Three of the poet's closest and most knowing friends appear to have shared my view, as Whitman himself admitted near his life's end: "How William [O'Connor] would storm and cry out if I made a change in *Leaves of Grass*—a comma, even. He was worst of all. And Bucke next, easily next—though not quite as bad. And even Mrs. [Anne] Gilchrist, who, if she ever showed passion at all, came nearest it in the matter of revisions." As one studies the revisions, large and small, that Whitman made in his early poems, one's sympathy grows for the fiery O'Connor, loyal Dr. Bucke, and infatuated Mrs. Gilchrist, who had to stand by as Whitman pegged and pegged away, risking the undoing of his masterpiece. Hence the importance of making available this edition of Whitman the poet of first inspiration.

Bucke and Gilchrist, preferring "early" Whitman and rankling at "late" revisions, inevitably became partisans for another principle of the present edition: presentation of the poems in chronological order of composition. This format was debated more than once within Whitman's inner circle, apparently for the last time in August 1891, when the layout of the "deathbed" edition was being settled. Clearly, it was too late for Whitman to change habits thirty years old, and he brushed aside the idea of a chronological ordering with notable vagueness: "All my close friends have taken a lick at this chronological business—Mrs. Gilchrist for one, now Bucke. But I charge that matters be left where they are. When I went to Boston in '81, I put things together, knit them, gave them adherence, succession. Yet I have since thought that even that was unnecessary. The unitary principle is there—was there from the start—the scheme—the rest followed. I take it—want it—that the latest poem embraces the first, as the first the last."

But it could be said, as well, that the true "unitary principle" for any poet whose career spanned a half century is that his artistic personality and view of the world were bound to change. In Whitman's case, the extent of the change was astonishing, and it can only fully be revealed by a chronological panorama of his poems.

A MORE subtle advantage of reading Whitman's poems in their initial versions concerns punctuation. In the middle and later *Leaves* editions, the poet began systematically and radically to lighten his punctuation, presumably with a view to making his verse "flow" more swiftly. He withdrew from his frequent deployment of dashes (—) and ellipses (. . .), which he varied from two to as many as eight periods, depending upon the pregnancy of the pause he desired. In their place he began to use commas only, and he drastically curtailed the appearance of semicolons at line ends. Exclamation points, as already noted, were greatly reduced.

A significant consequence of this change of habit was a more than occasional loss of syntactic clarity in his long, free verse lines. One is often obliged to reread a line in later versions to grasp its sense clearly. Indeed, after becoming aware of the nuances of Whitman's punctuation in his "early" and "late" manners, I have come to prefer, on the whole, his early style. In particular, Whitman was very conscious of and habitually exploited the distinction between a dash and a comma pause. This helped to discipline his big-breathed syntax. As for all the original exclamations and "O!" 's and "Lo!" 's, they undeniably lend an occasionally unattractive air of garrulity to Whitman's verse. However, one is more often left feeling, with their disappearance, a loss of exuberance in his most successfully flamboyant passages.

A final advantage of this edition is obvious: the space saved by bringing the reader about half of Whitman's poems has allowed for the inclusion of the most important of the poet's published and unpublished prose discussions of *Leaves of Grass*. His prefaces, notes, and essays on his life's work between 1855 and 1891 offer keen insight into his changing views about *Leaves* as it evolved.

The appendices provide several illuminating contexts for the poems. As noted above, appendix 1 offers a sampling from Whitman's poetic juvenilia. Appendix 2, which presents manuscript versions of some of Whitman's published poems, sheds light on his compositional habits. Appendix 3 gathers several observations on *Leaves of Grass* made by Whitman in his conversations late in life with Horace Traubel. Appendix 4 offers a sampling of reviews Whitman received over his career. The earliest of these, some breathtakingly vituperative, reveal the enormous pressure Whitman was under to retreat from his bold early editions. As he summed up in 1888 for Traubel, "The world now can have no idea of the bitterness of the feelings against me in those early days. I was a tough—obscene: indeed, it was my obscenity, libidinousness, all that, upon which they made their charges." These reviews also show vividly why the poet could justly boast, late in life, of the thick skin he had developed: "I have the hide of the rhinoceros, morally and in other ways—can stand almost anything."

ALL the poems in this edition appear in approximately the same typographical layout as in their first appearance, with one major exception and a few minor ones.

Much care has been given to breaking the long Whitman line in syntactically natural fashion where, as often, a run-on is necessary. Perhaps having become inured to full justification by years of working in newspaper typesetting rooms, Whitman permitted his long-breathed lines to be subjected to the procrustean bed of right-margin justification. The consequences of this were particularly horrible in the extremely compact 1856 sextodecimo *Leaves* edition (sixteen leaves to a printer's sheet) and the slightly larger 1860 duodecimo (twelve leaves to a sheet). Their small pages caused many an awkwardly truncated phrase, much unsightly leading between words, and—not infrequently—a dismal hyphenated word at the turnaround. In the 1856 edition, an astonishing three-quarters of the lines in "Song of Myself" were run-on, and about eight percent employed a line-end hyphen. Even the roomy 1855 quarto edition (four leaves to a sheet) contained many such unfortunate occurrences, about a fifth of the lines being run-on. Not a single line-ending hyphen survives here, and all run-on lines are now broken between phrases or where a punctuational pause offers a logical break.

A more minor but still unattractive habit Whitman indulged in the *Leaves* editions of his middle period was to number the verse paragraphs of his longer poems (and many shorter ones). Thus, in 1860, the first line of each verse paragraph of "Walt Whitman"—later titled "Song of Myself"—received a small number in the left margin. The poem had 372 numbered verse paragraphs, many only a line or two long. After 1860, Whitman also numbered larger sections of this and other poems. In the last *Leaves* editions, all these distracting marginal numbers were happily dropped. I have deleted the verse-paragraph numbers from the few poems included here that had them on initial publication. All of Whitman's original stanza or section numbers have, of course, been retained, most famously, for example, in "When Lilacs Last in the Door-Yard Bloom'd."

Whitman also habitually punctuated confusingly, by modern standards, in the vicinity of parentheses, for example: "Mortally wounded he, and buried on the retreat, (easily all could I understand;) . . ." This becomes "Mortally wounded he, and buried on the retreat (easily all could I understand);" in the present edition. Nor is the period that Whitman placed after his poem titles retained. In all other respects, the poet's original, occasionally idiosyncratic punctuation is reproduced.

All italics are Whitman's, and I have respected his idiosyncrasies and inconsistencies of spelling (*extasy, ecstasy,* and *ecstacy* all appear, for example).

Allusions requiring explanation and words requiring definition in the endnotes are indicated by a (°). Fortunately, there are relatively few of these, given Whitman's democratic vocabulary and antipathy to the learned or arcane. "Be simple and clear.—Be not occult" and "Take no illustrations whatever from the ancients or classics" and "Make no quotations and no reference to any other writers" are among Whitman's early manuscript exhortations to himself, and he was largely faithful to them all his life.

Lines were not numbered in any *Leaves* edition, but for ease of reference, lines are counted here for all poems more than twenty lines long.

It would be inappropriate to impose a dedication page on an edition of *Leaves of Grass,* for not once did Whitman present his readers with a dedicatee. One wonders why. The reply he made when pressed on this absence is not very satisfying: "I do not know why—probably there is no why.

Dedications have gone out of vogue—are no longer considered necessary." Being reluctant to spoil my own perfect record in the matter of dedicatees, however, I would like to say here that my editorial efforts on Walt Whitman's behalf are dedicated to the memory of three cameradoes—Philip Jerry, Mark McDonagh, and David Sellars. They fell during the battle against AIDS, a kind of warfare far removed from the Civil War that so anguished Walt. Still, his verse recalls these friends often to mind.

For valuable responses to the rationale of this edition, suggestions, and—in several instances—persuasive encouragement to include favorite poems I had overlooked, I want to express my gratitude to Jay Fliegelman, Ed Folsom, Jerome Loving, G. Thomas Tanselle, and Helen Vendler.

An overarching purpose of this edition is to encourage a fundamental reappraisal of Walt Whitman's poetry. One day toward the end of his life, speaking "as if stirred by great feeling," he made a remark to Horace Traubel that suggests he might even, finally, have given his blessing to such an edition as this. "It does a man good to turn himself inside out once in a while: to sort of turn the tables on himself," Whitman observed. Then he added eloquently and truly, "It takes a good deal of resolution to do it: yet it should be done—no one is safe until he can give himself such a drubbing: until he can shock himself out of his complacency. . . . If we don't look out we develop a bumptious bigotry—a colossal self-satisfaction, which is worse for a man than being a damned scoundrel."

If this edition helps to shock us out of complacent assumptions about our first great national poet, it will have served its main purpose.

GARY SCHMIDGALL
Manhattan

Leaves

of

Grass.

Brooklyn, New York:

1855.

The steel engraving, based upon a daguerreotype of Whitman now lost, that appeared on the verso facing the title page of the 1855 edition of Leaves of Grass.

AMERICA does not repel the past or what it has produced under its forms or amid other politics or the idea of castes or the old religions . . . . accepts the lesson with calmness . . . is not so impatient as has been supposed that the slough still sticks to opinions and manners and literature while the life which served its requirements has passed into the new life of the new forms . . . perceives that the corpse is slowly borne from the eating and sleeping rooms of the house. . . perceives that it waits a little while in the door . . . that it was fittest for its days . . . that its action has descended to the stalwart and wellshaped heir who approaches . . . and that he shall be fittest for his days.

The Americans of all nations at any time upon the earth have probably the fullest poetical nature. The United States themselves are essentially the greatest poem. In the history of the earth hitherto the largest and most stirring appear tame and orderly to their ampler largeness and stir. Here at last is something in the doings of man that corresponds with the broadcast doings of the day and night. Here is not merely a nation but a teeming nation of nations. Here is action untied from strings necessarily blind to particulars and details magnificently moving in vast masses. Here is the hospitality which forever indicates heroes . . . . Here are the roughs and beards and space and ruggedness and nonchalance that the soul loves. Here the performance disdaining the trivial unapproached in the tremendous audacity of its crowds and groupings and the push of its perspective spreads with crampless and flowing breadth and showers its prolific and splendid extravagance. One sees it must indeed own the riches of the summer and winter, and need never be bankrupt while corn grows from the ground or the orchards drop apples or the bays contain fish or men beget children upon women.

Other states indicate themselves in their deputies . . . . but the genius of the United States is not best or most in its executives or legislatures, nor in its ambassadors or authors or colleges or churches or parlors, nor even in its newspapers or inventors . . . but always most in the common people. Their manners speech dress friendships—the freshness and candor of their physiognomy—the picturesque looseness of their carriage . . . their deathless attachment to freedom—their aversion to anything indecorous or soft or mean—the practical acknowledgment of the citizens of one state by the citizens of all other states—the fierceness of their roused resentment—their curiosity and welcome of novelty—their self-esteem and wonderful sympathy—their susceptibility to a slight—the air they have of persons who never knew how it felt to stand in the presence of superiors—the fluency of their speech—their delight in music, the sure symptom of manly tenderness and native elegance of soul . . . their good temper and openhandedness—the terrible significance of their elections—the President's taking off his hat to them not they to him—these too are unrhymed poetry. It awaits the gigantic and generous treatment worthy of it.

The largeness of nature or the nation were monstrous without a corresponding largeness and generosity of the spirit of the citizen. Not nature nor swarming states nor streets and steamships nor prosperous business nor farms nor capital nor learning may suffice for the ideal of man . . . nor suffice the poet. No reminiscences may suffice either. A live nation can always cut a deep mark and can have the best authority the cheapest . . . namely from its own soul. This is the sum of the profitable uses of individuals or states and of present action and grandeur and of the subjects of poets.—As if it were necessary to trot back generation after generation to the eastern records! As if the beauty and sacredness of the demonstrable must fall behind that of the mythical! As if men do not make their mark out of any times! As if the opening of the western continent by discovery and what has transpired since in North and South America were less than the small theatre of the antique or the aimless sleepwalking of the middle ages! The pride of the United States leaves the wealth and finesse of the cities and all returns of commerce and agriculture and all the magnitude of geography or shows of exterior victory to enjoy the breed of fullsized men or one fullsized man unconquerable and simple.

The American poets are to enclose old and new for America is the race of races. Of them a bard is to be commensurate with a people. To him the other continents arrive as contributions . . . he gives them reception for their sake and his own sake. His spirit responds to his country's spirit . . . . he incarnates its geography and natural life and rivers and lakes. Mississippi with annual freshets and changing chutes, Missouri and Columbia and Ohio and Saint Lawrence with the falls and beautiful masculine Hudson, do not embouchure where they spend themselves more than they embouchure into him. The blue breadth over the inland sea of Virginia and Maryland and the sea off Massachusetts and Maine and over Manhattan bay and over Champlain and Erie and over Ontario and Huron and Michigan and Superior, and over the Texan and Mexican and Floridian and Cuban seas and over the seas off California and Oregon, is not tallied by the blue breadth of the waters below more than the breadth of above and below is tallied by him. When the long Atlantic coast stretches longer and the Pacific coast stretches longer he easily stretches with them north or south. He spans between them from east to west and reflects what is between them. On him rise solid growths that offset the growths of pine and cedar and hemlock and liveoak and locust and chestnut and cypress and hickory and limetree and cottonwood and tuliptree and cactus and wildvine and tamarind and persimmon . . . . and tangles as tangled as any canebrake or swamp . . . . and forests coated with transparent ice and icicles hanging from the boughs and crackling in the wind . . . . and sides and peaks of mountains . . . . and pasturage sweet and free as savannah or upland or prairie . . . . with flights and songs and screams that answer those of the wild-pigeon and highhold and orchard-oriole and coot and surf-duck and redshouldered-hawk and fish-hawk and white-ibis and indian-hen and cat-owl and water-pheasant and qua-bird and pied-sheldrake and blackbird and mockingbird and buzzard and condor and night-heron and eagle. To him the hereditary countenance descends both mother's and father's. To him enter the essences of the real things and past and present events—of the enormous diversity of temperature and agriculture and mines—the tribes of red aborigines—the weatherbeaten vessels entering new ports or making landings on rocky coasts—the first settlements north or south—the rapid stature and muscle—the haughty defiance of '76, and the war and peace and formation of the constitution . . . . the union always surrounded by blatherers and always calm and impregnable—the perpetual coming of immigrants—the wharfhem'd cities and superior marine—the unsurveyed interior—the loghouses and clearings and wild animals and hunters and trappers . . . . the free commerce—the fisheries and whaling and golddigging—the endless gestation of new states—the convening of Congress every December, the members duly coming up from all climates and the uttermost parts . . . . the noble character of the young mechanics and of all free American workmen and workwomen . . . . the general ardor and friendliness and enterprise—the perfect equality of the female with the male . . . . the large amativeness—the fluid movement of the population—the factories and mercantile life and laborsaving machinery—the Yankee swap—

the New-York firemen and the target excursion—the southern plantation life—the character of the northeast and of the northwest and southwest—slavery and the tremulous spreading of hands to protect it, and the stern opposition to it which shall never cease till it ceases or the speaking of tongues and the moving of lips cease. For such the expression of the American poet is to be transcendant and new. It is to be indirect and not direct or descriptive or epic. Its quality goes through these to much more. Let the age and wars of other nations be chanted and their eras and characters be illustrated and that finish the verse. Not so the great psalm of the republic. Here the theme is creative and has vista. Here comes one among the wellbeloved stonecutters and plans with decision and science and sees the solid and beautiful forms of the future where there are now no solid forms.

Of all nations the United States with veins full of poetical stuff most need poets and will doubtless have the greatest and use them the greatest. Their Presidents shall not be their common referee so much as their poets shall. Of all mankind the great poet is the equable man. Not in him but off from him things are grotesque or eccentric or fail of their sanity. Nothing out of its place is good and nothing in its place is bad. He bestows on every object or quality its fit proportions neither more nor less. He is the arbiter of the diverse and he is the key. He is the equalizer of his age and land . . . . he supplies what wants supplying and checks what wants checking. If peace is the routine out of him speaks the spirit of peace, large, rich, thrifty, building vast and populous cities, encouraging agriculture and the arts and commerce—lighting the study of man, the soul, immortality—federal, state or municipal government, marriage, health, freetrade, intertravel by land and sea . . . . nothing too close, nothing too far off . . . the stars not too far off. In war he is the most deadly force of the war. Who recruits him recruits horse and foot . . . he fetches parks of artillery the best that engineer ever knew. If the time becomes slothful and heavy he knows how to arouse it . . . he can make every word he speaks draw blood. Whatever stagnates in the flat of custom or obedience or legislation he never stagnates. Obedience does not master him, he masters it. High up out of reach he stands turning a concentrated light . . . he turns the pivot with his finger . . . he baffles the swiftest runners as he stands and easily overtakes and envelops them. The time straying toward infidelity and confections and persiflage he withholds by his steady faith . . . he spreads out his dishes . . . he offers the sweet firmfibred meat that grows men and women. His brain is the ultimate brain. He is no arguer . . . he is judgment. He judges not as the judge judges but as the sun falling around a helpless thing. As he sees the farthest he has the most faith. His thoughts are the hymns of the praise of things. In the talk on the soul and eternity and God off of his equal plane he is silent. He sees eternity less like a play with a prologue and denouement . . . . he sees eternity in men and women . . . he does not see men and women as dreams or dots. Faith is the antiseptic of the soul . . . it pervades the common people and preserves them . . . they never give up believing and expecting and trusting. There is that indescribable freshness and unconsciousness about an illiterate person that humbles and mocks the power of the noblest expressive genius. The poet sees for a certainty how one not a great artist may be just as sacred and perfect as the greatest artist . . . . . . The power to destroy or remould is freely used by him but never the power of attack. What is past is past. If he does not expose superior models and prove himself by every step he takes he is not what is wanted. The presence of the greatest poet conquers . . . not parleying or struggling or any prepared attempts. Now he has passed that way see after him! there is not left any vestige of despair or misanthropy or cunning or exclusiveness or the ignominy of a nativity or color or delusion of hell or the necessity of hell . . . . . and no man thenceforward shall be degraded for ignorance or weakness or sin.

The greatest poet hardly knows pettiness or triviality. If he breathes into any thing that was before thought small it dilates with the grandeur and life of the universe. He is a seer . . . . he is individual . . . he is complete in himself . . . . the others are as good as he, only he sees it and they do not. He is not one of the chorus . . . . he does not stop for any regulation . . . he is the president of regulation. What the eyesight does to the rest he does to the rest. Who knows the curious mystery of the eyesight? The other senses corroborate themselves, but this is removed from any proof but its own and foreruns the identities of the spiritual world. A single glance of it mocks all the investigations of man and all the instruments and books of the earth and all reasoning. What is marvellous? what is unlikely? what is impossible or baseless or vague? after you have once just opened the space of a peachpit and given audience to far and near and to the sunset and had all things enter with electric swiftness softly and duly without confusion or jostling or jam.

The land and sea, the animals fishes and birds, the sky of heaven and the orbs, the forests mountains and rivers, are not small themes . . . but folks expect of the poet to indicate more than the beauty and dignity which always attach to dumb real objects . . . . they expect him to indicate the path between reality and their souls. Men and women perceive the beauty well enough . . probably as well as he. The passionate tenacity of hunters, woodmen, early risers, cultivators of gardens and orchards and fields, the love of healthy women for the manly form, seafaring persons, drivers of horses, the passion for light and the open air, all is an old varied sign of the unfailing perception of beauty and of a residence of the poetic in outdoor people. They can never be assisted by poets to perceive . . . some may but they never can. The poetic quality is not marshalled in rhyme or uniformity or abstract addresses to things nor in melancholy complaints or good precepts, but is the life of these and much else and is in the soul. The profit of rhyme is that it drops seeds of a sweeter and more luxuriant rhyme, and of uniformity that it conveys itself into its own roots in the ground out of sight. The rhyme and uniformity of perfect poems show the free growth of metrical laws and bud from them as unerringly and loosely as lilacs or roses on a bush, and take shapes as compact as the shapes of chestnuts and oranges and melons and pears, and shed the perfume impalpable to form. The fluency and ornaments of the finest poems or music or orations or recitations are not independent but dependent. All beauty comes from beautiful blood and a beautiful brain. If the greatnesses are in conjunction in a man or woman it is enough . . . . the fact will prevail through the universe . . . . but the gaggery and gilt of a million years will not prevail. Who troubles himself about his ornaments or fluency is lost. This is what you shall do: Love the earth and sun and the animals, despise riches, give alms to every one that asks, stand up for the stupid and crazy, devote your income and labor to others, hate tyrants, argue not concerning God, have patience and indulgence toward the people, take off your hat to nothing known or unknown or to any man or number of men, go freely with powerful uneducated persons and with the young and with the mothers of families, read these leaves in the open air every season of every year of your life, reexamine all you have been told at school or church or in any book, dismiss whatever insults your own soul, and your very flesh shall be a great poem and have the richest fluency not only in its words but in the silent lines of its lips and face and between the lashes of your eyes and in every motion and joint of your body . . . . The poet shall not spend his time in unneeded work. He shall know that the ground is always ready ploughed and manured . . . . others may not know it but he shall. He shall go directly to the creation. His trust shall master the trust of everything he touches . . . . and shall master all attachment.

The known universe has one complete lover and that is the greatest poet. He consumes an eternal passion and is indifferent which chance happens and which possible contingency of fortune or misfortune and persuades daily and hourly his delicious pay. What balks or breaks others is fuel for his burning progress to contact and amorous joy. Other proportions of the reception of pleasure dwindle to nothing to his proportions. All expected from heaven or from the highest he is rapport with in the sight of the daybreak or a scene of the winter woods or the presence of children playing or with his arm round the neck of a man or woman. His love above all love has leisure and expanse . . . . he leaves room ahead of himself. He is no irresolute or suspicious lover . . . he is sure . . . he scorns intervals. His experience and the showers and thrills are not for nothing. Nothing can jar him . . . . suffering and darkness cannot—death and fear cannot. To him complaint and jealousy and envy are corpses buried and rotten in the earth . . . . he saw them buried. The sea is not surer of the shore or the shore of the sea than he is of the fruition of his love and of all perfection and beauty.

The fruition of beauty is no chance of hit or miss . . . it is inevitable as life . . . . it is exact and plumb as gravitation. From the eyesight proceeds another eyesight and from the hearing proceeds another hearing and from the voice proceeds another voice eternally curious of the harmony of things with man. To these respond perfections not only in the committees that were supposed to stand for the rest but in the rest themselves just the same. These understand the law of perfection in masses and floods . . . that its finish is to each for itself and onward from itself . . . that it is profuse and impartial . . . that there is not a minute of the light or dark nor an acre of the earth or sea without it—nor any direction of the sky nor any trade or employment nor any turn of events. This is the reason that about the proper expression of beauty there is precision and balance . . . one part does not need to be thrust above another. The best singer is not the one who has the most lithe and powerful organ . . . the pleasure of poems is not in them that take the handsomest measure and similes and sound.

Without effort and without exposing in the least how it is done the greatest poet brings the spirit of any or all events and passions and scenes and persons some more and some less to bear on your individual character as you hear or read. To do this well is to compete with the laws that pursue and follow time. What is the purpose must surely be there and the clue of it must be there . . . . and the faintest indication is the indication of the best and then becomes the clearest indication. Past and present and future are not disjoined but joined. The greatest poet forms the consistence of what is to be from what has been and is. He drags the dead out of their coffins and stands them again on their feet . . . . he says to the past, Rise and walk before me that I may realize you. He learns the lesson . . . . he places himself where the future becomes present. The greatest poet does not only dazzle his rays over character and scenes and passions . . . he finally ascends and finishes all . . . he exhibits the pinnacles that no man can tell what they are for or what is beyond . . . . he glows a moment on the extremest verge. He is most wonderful in his last half-hidden smile or frown . . . by that flash of the moment of parting the one that sees it shall be encouraged or terrified afterward for many years. The greatest poet does not moralize or make applications of morals . . . he knows the soul. The soul has that measureless pride which consists in never acknowledging any lessons but its own. But it has sympathy as measureless as its pride and the one balances the other and neither can stretch too far while it stretches in company with the other. The inmost secrets of art sleep with the twain. The greatest poet has lain close betwixt both and they are vital in his style and thoughts.

The art of art, the glory of expression and the sunshine of the light of letters is simplicity. Nothing is better than simplicity . . . . nothing can make up for excess or for the lack of definiteness. To carry on the heave of impulse and pierce intellectual depths and give all subjects their articulations are powers neither common nor very uncommon. But to speak in literature with the perfect rectitude and insousiance of the movements of animals and the unimpeachableness of the sentiment of trees in the woods and grass by the roadside is the flawless triumph of art. If you have looked on him who has achieved it you have looked on one of the masters of the artists of all nations and times. You shall not contemplate the flight of the graygull over the bay or the mettlesome action of the blood horse or the tall leaning of sunflowers on their stalk or the appearance of the sun journeying through heaven or the appearance of the moon afterward with any more satisfaction than you shall contemplate him. The greatest poet has less a marked style and is more the channel of thoughts and things without increase or diminution, and is the free channel of himself. He swears to his art, I will not be meddlesome, I will not have in my writing any elegance or effect or originality to hang in the way between me and the rest like curtains. I will have nothing hang in the way, not the richest curtains. What I tell I tell for precisely what it is. Let who may exalt or startle or fascinate or soothe I will have purposes as health or heat or snow has and be as regardless of observation. What I experience or portray shall go from my composition without a shred of my composition. You shall stand by my side and look in the mirror with me.

The old red blood and stainless gentility of great poets will be proved by their unconstraint. A heroic person walks at his ease through and out of that custom or precedent or authority that suits him not. Of the traits of the brotherhood of writers savans musicians inventors and artists nothing is finer than silent defiance advancing from new free forms. In the need of poems philosophy politics mechanism science behaviour, the craft of art, an appropriate native grand-opera, shipcraft, or any craft, he is greatest forever and forever who contributes the greatest original practical example. The cleanest expression is that which finds no sphere worthy of itself and makes one.

The messages of great poets to each man and woman are, Come to us on equal terms, Only then can you understand us, We are no better than you, What we enclose you enclose, What we enjoy you may enjoy. Did you suppose there could be only one Supreme? We affirm there can be unnumbered Supremes, and that one does not countervail another any more than one eyesight countervails another . . and that men can be good or grand only of the consciousness of their supremacy within them. What do you think is the grandeur of storms and dismemberments and the deadliest battles and wrecks and the wildest fury of the elements and the power of the sea and the motion of nature and of the throes of human desires and dignity and hate and love? It is that something in the soul which says, Rage on, Whirl on, I tread master here and everywhere, Master of the spasms of the sky and of the shatter of the sea, Master of nature and passion and death, And of all terror and all pain.

The American bards shall be marked for generosity and affection and for encouraging competitors . . They shall be kosmos . . without monopoly or secresy . . glad to pass any thing to any one . . hungry for equals night and day. They shall not be careful of riches and privilege . . . . they shall be riches and privilege . . . . they shall perceive who the most affluent man is. The most affluent man is he that confronts all the shows he sees by equivalents out of the stronger wealth of himself. The American bard shall delineate no class of persons nor one or two out of the strata of interests nor love most nor truth most nor the soul most nor the body most . . . . and not be for the eastern states more than the western or the northern states more than the southern.

Exact science and its practical movements are no checks on the greatest poet but always his encouragement and support. The outset and remembrance are there . . there the arms that lifted him first and brace him best . . . . there he returns after all his goings and comings. The sailor and traveler . . the anatomist chemist astronomer geologist phrenologist spiritualist mathematician historian and lexicographer are not poets, but they are the lawgivers of poets and their construction underlies the structure of every perfect poem. No matter what rises or is uttered they sent the seed of the conception of it . . . of them and by them stand the visible proofs of souls. . . . . always of their fatherstuff must be begotten the sinewy races of bards. If there shall be love and content between the father and the son and if the greatness of the son is the exuding of the greatness of the father there shall be love between the poet and the man of demonstrable science. In the beauty of poems are the tuft and final applause of science.

Great is the faith of the flush of knowledge and of the investigation of the depths of qualities and things. Cleaving and circling here swells the soul of the poet yet is president of itself always. The depths are fathomless and therefore calm. The innocence and nakedness are resumed . . . they are neither modest nor immodest. The whole theory of the special and supernatural and all that was twined with it or educed out of it departs as a dream. What has ever happened . . . . what happens and whatever may or shall happen, the vital laws enclose all . . . . they are sufficient for any case and for all cases . . . none to be hurried or retarded . . . . any miracle of affairs or persons inadmissible in the vast clear scheme where every motion and every spear of grass and the frames and spirits of men and women and all that concerns them are unspeakably perfect miracles all referring to all and each distinct and in its place. It is also not consistent with the reality of the soul to admit that there is anything in the known universe more divine than men and women.

Men and women and the earth and all upon it are simply to be taken as they are, and the investigation of their past and present and future shall be unintermitted and shall be done with perfect candor. Upon this basis philosophy speculates ever looking toward the poet, ever regarding the eternal tendencies of all toward happiness never inconsistent with what is clear to the senses and to the soul. For the eternal tendencies of all toward happiness make the only point of sane philosophy. Whatever comprehends less than that . . . whatever is less than the laws of light and of astronomical motion . . . or less than the laws that follow the thief the liar the glutton and the drunkard through this life and doubtless afterward . . . . . . or less than vast stretches of time or the slow formation of density or the patient upheaving of strata—is of no account. Whatever would put God in a poem or system of philosophy as contending against some being or influence is also of no account. Sanity and ensemble characterise the great master . . . spoilt in one principle all is spoilt. The great master has nothing to do with miracles. He sees health for himself in being one of the mass . . . . he sees the hiatus in singular eminence. To the perfect shape comes common ground. To be under the general law is great for that is to correspond with it. The master knows that he is unspeakably great and that all are unspeakably great . . . . that nothing for instance is greater than to conceive children and bring them up well . . . that to be is just as great as to perceive or tell.

In the make of the great masters the idea of political liberty is indispensible. Liberty takes the adherence of heroes wherever men and women exist . . . . but never takes any adherence or welcome from the rest more than from poets. They are the voice and exposition of liberty. They out of ages are worthy the grand idea . . . . to them it is confided and they must sustain it. Nothing has precedence of it and nothing can warp or degrade it. The attitude of great poets is to cheer up slaves and horrify despots. The turn of their necks, the sound of their feet, the motions of their wrists, are full of hazard to the one and hope to the other. Come nigh them awhile and though they neither speak or advise you shall learn the faithful American lesson. Liberty is poorly served by men whose good intent is quelled from one failure or two failures or any number of failures, or from the casual indifference or ingratitude of the people, or from the sharp show of the tushes of power, or the bringing to bear soldiers and cannon or any penal statutes. Liberty relies upon itself, invites no one, promises nothing, sits in calmness and light, is positive and composed, and knows no discouragement. The battle rages with many a loud alarm and frequent advance and retreat . . . . the enemy triumphs . . . . the prison, the handcuffs, the iron necklace and anklet, the scaffold, garrote and leadballs do their work . . . . the cause is asleep . . . . the strong throats are choked with their own blood . . . . the young men drop their eyelashes toward the ground when they pass each other . . . . and is liberty gone out of that place? No never. When liberty goes it is not the first to go nor the second or third to go . . it waits for all the rest to go . . it is the last . . . When the memories of the old martyrs are faded utterly away . . . . when the large names of patriots are laughed at in the public halls from the lips of the orators . . . . when the boys are no more christened after the same but christened after tyrants and traitors instead . . . . when the laws of the free are grudgingly permitted and laws for informers and bloodmoney are sweet to the taste of the people . . . . when I and you walk abroad upon the earth stung with compassion at the sight of numberless brothers answering our equal friendship and calling no man master—and when we are elated with noble joy at the sight of slaves . . . . when the soul retires in the cool communion of the night and surveys its experience and has much extasy over the word and deed that put back a helpless innocent person into the gripe of the gripers or into any cruel inferiority . . . . when those in all parts of these states who could easier realize the true American character but do not yet—when the swarms of cringers, suckers, doughfaces, lice of politics, planners of sly involutions for their own preferment to city offices or state legislatures or the judiciary or congress or the presidency, obtain a response of love and natural deference from the people whether they get the offices or no . . . . when it is better to be a bound booby and rogue in office at a high salary than the poorest free mechanic or farmer with his hat unmoved from his head and firm eyes and a candid and generous heart . . . . and when servility by town or state or the federal government or any oppression on a large scale or small scale can be tried on without its own punishment following duly after in exact proportion against the smallest chance of escape . . . . or rather when all life and all the souls of men and women are discharged from any part of the earth—then only shall the instinct of liberty be discharged from that part of the earth.

As the attributes of the poets of the kosmos concentre in the real body and soul and in the pleasure of things they possess the superiority of genuineness over all fiction and romance. As they emit themselves facts are showered over with light . . . . the daylight is lit with more volatile light . . . . also the deep between the setting and rising sun goes deeper many fold. Each precise object or condition or combination or process exhibits a beauty . . . . the multiplication table its—old age its—the carpenter's trade its—the grand-opera its . . . . thc hugehulled cleanshaped New-York clipper at sea under steam or full sail gleams with unmatched beauty . . . . the American circles and large harmonies of government gleam with theirs . . . . and the commonest definite intentions and actions with theirs. The poets of the kosmos advance through all interpositions and coverings and turmoils and strategems to first principles. They are of use . . . . they dissolve poverty from its need and riches from its conceit. You large proprietor they say shall not realize or perceive more than any one else. The owner of the library is not he who holds a legal title to it having bought and paid for it. Any one and every one is owner of the library who can read the same through all the varieties of tongues and subjects and styles, and in whom they enter with ease and take residence and force toward paternity and maternity, and make supple and powerful and rich and large. . . . . These American states strong and healthy and accomplished shall receive no pleasure from violations of natural models and must not permit them. In paintings or mouldings or carvings in mineral or wood, or in the illustrations of books or newspapers, or in any comic or tragic prints, or in the patterns of woven stuffs or any thing to beautify rooms or furniture or costumes, or to put upon cornices or monuments or on the prows or sterns of ships, or to put anywhere before the human eye indoors or out, that which distorts honest shapes or which creates unearthly beings or places or contingencies is a nuisance and revolt. Of the human form especially it is so great it must never be made ridiculous. Of ornaments to a work nothing outre can be allowed . . but those ornaments can be allowed that conform to the perfect facts of the open air and that flow out of the nature of the work and come irrepressibly from it and are necessary to the completion of the work. Most works are most beautiful without ornament . . . Exaggerations will be revenged in human physiology. Clean and vigorous children are jetted and conceived only in those communities where the models of natural forms are public every day. . . . . Great genius and the people of these states must never be demeaned to romances. As soon as histories are properly told there is no more need of romances.

The great poets are also to be known by the absence in them of tricks and by the justification of perfect personal candor. Then folks echo a new cheap joy and a divine voice leaping from their brains: How beautiful is candor! All faults may be forgiven of him who has perfect candor. Henceforth let no man of us lie, for we have seen that openness wins the inner and outer world and that there is no single exception, and that never since our earth gathered itself in a mass have deceit or subterfuge or prevarication attracted its smallest particle or the faintest tinge of a shade—and that through the enveloping wealth and rank of a state or the whole republic of states a sneak or sly person shall be discovered and despised . . . . and that the soul has never been once fooled and never can be fooled . . . . and thrift without the loving nod of the soul is only a fœtid puff . . . . and there never grew up in any of the continents of the globe nor upon any planet or satellite or star, nor upon the asteroids, nor in any part of ethereal space, nor in the midst of density, nor under the fluid wet of the sea, nor in that condition which precedes the birth of babes, nor at any time during the changes of life, nor in that condition that follows what we term death, nor in any stretch of abeyance or action afterward of vitality, nor in any process of formation or reformation anywhere, a being whose instinct hated the truth.

Extreme caution or prudence, the soundest organic health, large hope and comparison and fondness for women and children, large alimentativeness and destructiveness and causality, with a perfect sense of the oneness of nature and the propriety of the same spirit applied to human affairs . . these are called up of the float of the brain of the world to be parts of the greatest poet from his birth out of his mother's womb and from her birth out of her mother's. Caution seldom goes far enough. It has been thought that the prudent citizen was the citizen who applied himself to solid gains and did well for himself without debt or crime. The greatest poet sees and admits these economies as he sees the economies of food and sleep, but has higher notions of prudence than to think he gives much when he gives a few slight attentions at the latch of the gate. The premises of the prudence of life are not the hospitality of it or the ripeness and harvest of it. Beyond the independence of a little sum laid aside for burial-money, and of a few clapboards around and shingles overhead on a lot of American soil owned, and the easy dollars that supply the year's plain clothing and meals, the melancholy prudence of the abandonment of such a great being as a man is to the toss and pallor of years of moneymaking with all their scorching days and icy nights and all their stifling deceits and underhanded dodgings, or infinitessimals of parlors, or shameless stuffing while others starve . . and all the loss of the bloom and odor of the earth and of the flowers and atmosphere and of the sea and of the true taste of the women and men you pass or have to do with in youth or middle age, and the issuing sickness and desperate revolt at the close of a life without elevation or naivete, and the ghastly chatter of a death without serenity or majesty, is the great fraud upon modern civilization and forethought, blotching the surface and system which civilization undeniably drafts, and moistening with tears the immense features it spreads and spreads with such velocity before the reached kisses of the soul . . . Still the right explanation remains to be made about prudence. The prudence of the mere wealth and respectability of the most esteemed life appears too faint for the eye to observe at all when little and large alike drop quietly aside at the thought of the prudence suitable for immortality. What is wisdom that fills the thinness of a year or seventy or eighty years to wisdom spaced out by ages and coming back at a certain time with strong reinforcements and rich presents and the clear faces of wedding-guests as far as you can look in every direction running gaily toward you? Only the soul is of itself . . . . all else has reference to what ensues. All that a person does or thinks is of consequence. Not a move can a man or woman make that affects him or her in a day or a month or any part of the direct lifetime or the hour of death but the same affects him or her onward afterward through the indirect lifetime. The indirect is always as great and real as the direct. The spirit receives from the body just as much as it gives to the body. Not one name of word or deed . . not of venereal sores or discolorations . . not the privacy of the onanist . . not of the putrid veins of gluttons or rum-drinkers . . . not peculation or cunning or betrayal or murder . . no serpentine poison of those that seduce women . . not the foolish yielding of women . . not prostitution . . not any depravity of young men . . not of the attainment of gain by discreditable means . . not any nastiness of appetite . . not any harshness of officers to men or judges to prisoners or fathers to sons or sons to fathers or of husbands to wives or bosses to their boys . . not of greedy looks or malignant wishes . . . nor any of the wiles practised by people upon themselves . . . ever is or ever can be stamped on the programme but it is duly realized and returned, and that returned in further performances . . . and they returned again. Nor can the push of charity or personal force ever be any thing else than the profoundest reason, whether it bring arguments to hand or no. No specification is necessary . . to add or subtract or divide is in vain. Little or big, learned or unlearned, white or black, legal or illegal, sick or well, from the first inspiration down the windpipe to the last expiration out of it, all that a male or female does that is vigorous and benevolent and clean is so much sure profit to him or her in the unshakable order of the universe and through the whole scope of it forever. If the savage or felon is wise it is well . . . . if the greatest poet or savan is wise it is simply the same . . if the President or chief justice is wise it is the same . . . if the young mechanic or farmer is wise it is no more or less . . if the prostitute is wise it is no more nor less. The interest will come round . . all will come round. All the best actions of war and peace . . . all help given to relatives and strangers and the poor and old and sorrowful and young children and widows and the sick, and to all shunned persons . . all furtherance of fugitives and of the escape of slaves . . all the self-denial that stood steady and aloof on wrecks and saw others take the seats of the boats . . . all offering of substance or life for the good old cause, or for a friend's sake or opinion's sake . . . all pains of enthusiasts scoffed at by their neighbors . . all the vast sweet love and precious suffering of mothers . . . all honest men baffled in strifes recorded or unrecorded . . . . all the grandeur and good of the few ancient nations whose fragments of annals we inherit . . and all the good of the hundreds of far mightier and more ancient nations unknown to us by name or date or location . . . . all that was ever manfully begun, whether it succeeded or no . . . . all that has at any time been well suggested out of the divine heart of man or by the divinity of his mouth or by the shaping of his great hands . . and all that is well thought or done this day on any part of the surface of the globe . . or on any of the wandering stars or fixed stars by those there as we are here . . or that is henceforth to be well thought or done by you whoever you are, or by any one—these singly and wholly inured at their time and inure now and will inure always to the identities from which they sprung or shall spring . . . . Did you guess any of them lived only its moment? The world does not so exist . . no parts palpable or impalpable so exist . . . no result exists now without being from its long antecedent result, and that from its antecedent, and so backward without the farthest mentionable spot coming a bit nearer the beginning than any other spot . . . . Whatever satisfies the soul is truth. The prudence of the greatest poet answers at last the craving and glut of the soul, is not contemptuous of less ways of prudence if they conform to its ways, puts off nothing, permits no let-up for its own case or any case, has no particular sabbath or judgment-day, divides not the living from the dead or the righteous from the unrighteous, is satisfied with the present, matches every thought or act by its correlative, knows no possible forgiveness or deputed atonement . . knows that the young man who composedly periled his life and lost it has done exceeding well for himself, while the man who has not periled his life and retains it to old age in riches and ease has perhaps achieved nothing for himself worth mentioning . . and that only that person has no great prudence to learn who has learnt to prefer real longlived things, and favors body and soul the same, and perceives the indirect assuredly following the direct, and what evil or good he does leaping onward and waiting to meet him again—and who in his spirit in any emergency whatever neither hurries or avoids death.

The direct trial of him who would be the greatest poet is today. If he does not flood himself with the immediate age as with vast oceanic tides. . . . . and if he does not attract his own land body and soul to himself and hang on its neck with incomparable love and plunge his semitic muscle into its merits and demerits . . . and if he be not himself the age transfigured . . . . and if to him is not opened the eternity which gives similitude to all periods and locations and processes and animate and inanimate forms, and which is the bond of time, and rises up from its inconceivable vagueness and infiniteness in the swimming shape of today, and is held by the ductile anchors of life, and makes the present spot the passage from what was to what shall be, and commits itself to the representation of this wave of an hour and this one of the sixty beautiful children of the wave—let him merge in the general run and wait his development. . . . . Still the final test of poems or any character or work remains. The prescient poet projects himself centuries ahead and judges performer and performance after the changes of time. Does it live through them? Does it still hold on untired? Will the same style and the direction of genius to similar points be satisfactory now? Has no new discovery in science or arrival at superior planes of thought and judgment and behaviour fixed him or his so that either can be looked down upon? Have the marches of tens and hundreds and thousands of years made willing detours to the right hand and the left hand for his sake? Is he beloved long and long after he is buried? Does the young man think often of him? and the young woman think often of him? and do the middleaged and the old think of him?

A great poem is for ages and ages in common and for all degrees and complexions and all departments and sects and for a woman as much as a man and a man as much as a woman. A great poem is no finish to a man or woman but rather a beginning. Has any one fancied he could sit at last under some due authority and rest satisfied with explanations and realize and be content and full? To no such terminus does the greatest poet bring . . . he brings neither cessation or sheltered fatness and ease. The touch of him tells in action. Whom he takes he takes with firm sure grasp into live regions previously unattained . . . . thenceforward is no rest . . . . they see the space and ineffable sheen that turn the old spots and lights into dead vacuums. The companion of him beholds the birth and progress of stars and learns one of the meanings. Now there shall be a man cohered out of tumult and chaos . . . . the elder encourages the younger and shows him how . . . they two shall launch off fearlessly together till the new world fits an orbit for itself and looks unabashed on the lesser orbits of the stars and sweeps through the ceaseless rings and shall never be quiet again.

There will soon be no more priests. Their work is done. They may wait awhile . . perhaps a generation or two . . dropping off by degrees. A superior breed shall take their place . . . . the gangs of kosmos and prophets en masse shall take their place. A new order shall arise and they shall be the priests of man, and every man shall be his own priest. The churches built under their umbrage shall be the churches of men and women. Through the divinity of themselves shall the kosmos and the new breed of poets be interpreters of men and women and of all events and things. They shall find their inspiration in real objects today, symptoms of the past and future . . . . They shall not deign to defend immortality or God or the perfection of things or liberty or the exquisite beauty and reality of the soul. They shall arise in America and be responded to from the remainder of the earth.

The English language befriends the grand American expression . . . . it is brawny enough and limber enough and full enough. On the tough stock of a race who through all change of circumstance was never without the idea of political liberty, which is the animus of all liberty, it has attracted the terms of daintier and gayer and subtler and more elegant tongues. It is the powerful language of resistance . . . it is the dialect of common sense. It is the speech of the proud and melancholy races and of all who aspire. It is the chosen tongue to express growth faith self-esteem freedom justice equality friendliness amplitude prudence decision and courage. It is the medium that shall well nigh express the inexpressible.

No great literature nor any like style of behaviour or oratory or social intercourse or household arrangements or public institutions or the treatment by bosses of employed people, nor executive detail or detail of the army or navy, nor spirit of legislation or courts or police or tuition or architecture or songs or amusements or the costumes of young men, can long elude the jealous and passionate instinct of American standards. Whether or no the sign appears from the mouths of the people, it throbs a live interrogation in every freeman's and freewoman's heart after that which passes by or this built to remain. Is it uniform with my country? Are its disposals without ignominious distinctions? Is it for the evergrowing communes of brothers and lovers, large, well-united, proud beyond the old models, generous beyond all models? Is it something grown fresh out of the fields or drawn from the sea for use to me today here? I know that what answers for me an American must answer for any individual or nation that serves for a part of my materials. Does this answer? or is it without reference to universal needs? or sprung of the needs of the less developed society of special ranks? or old needs of pleasure overlaid by modern science and forms? Does this acknowledge liberty with audible and absolute acknowledgement, and set slavery at nought for life and death? Will it help breed one goodshaped and wellhung man, and a woman to be his perfect and independent mate? Does it improve manners? Is it for the nursing of the young of the republic? Does it solve readily with the sweet milk of the nipples of the breasts of the mother of many children? Has it too the old ever-fresh forbearance and impartiality? Does it look with the same love on the last born and on those hardening toward stature, and on the errant, and on those who disdain all strength of assault outside of their own?

The poems distilled from other poems will probably pass away. The coward will surely pass away. The expectation of the vital and great can only be satisfied by the demeanor of the vital and great. The swarms of the polished deprecating and reflectors and the polite float off and leave no remembrance. America prepares with composure and goodwill for the visitors that have sent word. It is not intellect that is to be their warrant and welcome. The talented, the artist, the ingenious, the editor, the statesman, the erudite . . they are not unappreciated . . they fall in their place and do their work. The soul of the nation also does its work. No disguise can pass on it . . no disguise can conceal from it. It rejects none, it permits all. Only toward as good as itself and toward the like of itself will it advance half-way. An individual is as superb as a nation when he has the qualities which make a superb nation. The soul of the largest and wealthiest and proudest nation may well go half-way to meet that of its poets. The signs are effectual. There is no fear of mistake. If the one is true the other is true. The proof of a poet is that his country absorbs him as affectionately as he has absorbed it.

Leaves of Grass

I CELEBRATE myself,
And what I assume you shall assume,
For every atom belonging to me as good belongs to you.

I loafe and invite my soul,
I lean and loafe at my ease . . . . observing a spear of summer grass.

Houses and rooms are full of perfumes . . . . the shelves are crowded
with perfumes,
I breathe the fragrance myself, and know it and like it.
The distillation would intoxicate me also, but I shall not let it.

The atmosphere is not a perfume . . . . it has no taste of the distillation
. . . . it is odorless,
It is for my mouth forever . . . . I am in love with it,
I will go to the bank by the wood and become undisguised and naked,
I am mad for it to be in contact with me.

The smoke of my own breath,
Echos, ripples, and buzzed whispers . . . . loveroot, silkthread,
crotch and vine,
My respiration and inspiration . . . . the beating of my heart . . . .
the passing of blood and air through my lungs,
The sniff of green leaves and dry leaves, and of the shore
and darkcolored sea-rocks, and of hay in the barn,
The sound of the belched words of my voice . . . . words loosed
to the eddies of the wind,
A few light kisses . . . . a few embraces . . . . a reaching around of arms,
The play of shine and shade on the trees as the supple boughs wag,
The delight alone or in the rush of the streets, or along the fields
and hillsides,
The feeling of health . . . . the full-noon trill . . . . the song of me
rising from bed and meeting the sun.

Have you reckoned a thousand acres much? Have you reckoned
 the earth much?
Have you practiced so long to learn to read?
Have you felt so proud to get at the meaning of poems?

Stop this day and night with me and you shall possess the origin
 of all poems,
You shall possess the good of the earth and sun ....
 there are millions of suns left,
You shall no longer take things at second or third hand ....
 nor look through the eyes of the dead .... nor feed
 on the spectres in books,
You shall not look through my eyes either, nor take things from me,
You shall listen to all sides and filter them from yourself.

I have heard what the talkers were talking .... the talk
 of the beginning and the end,
But I do not talk of the beginning or the end.

There was never any more inception than there is now,
Nor any more youth or age than there is now;
And will never be any more perfection than there is now,
Nor any more heaven or hell than there is now.

Urge and urge and urge,
Always the procreant urge of the world.

Out of the dimness opposite equals advance .... Always substance
 and increase,
Always a knit of identity .... always distinction .... always a breed
 of life.

To elaborate is no avail .... Learned and unlearned feel that it is so.

Sure as the most certain sure .... plumb in the uprights,
 well entretied,[o] braced in the beams,
Stout as a horse, affectionate, haughty, electrical,
I and this mystery here we stand.

Clear and sweet is my soul .... and clear and sweet is all
 that is not my soul.

Lack one lacks both . . . . and the unseen is proved by the seen,
Till that becomes unseen and receives proof in its turn.

Showing the best and dividing it from the worst, age vexes age,
Knowing the perfect fitness and equanimity of things, while they discuss
I am silent, and go bathe and admire myself.

Welcome is every organ and attribute of me, and of any man
hearty and clean,
Not an inch nor a particle of an inch is vile, and none shall be
less familiar than the rest.

I am satisfied . . . . I see, dance, laugh, sing;
As God comes a loving bedfellow and sleeps at my side all night
and close on the peep of the day,
And leaves for me baskets covered with white towels bulging the house
with their plenty,
Shall I postpone my acceptance and realization and scream at my eyes,
That they turn from gazing after and down the road,
And forthwith cipher and show me to a cent,
Exactly the contents of one, and exactly the contents of two,
and which is ahead?

Trippers and askers surround me,
People I meet . . . . . the effect upon me of my early life . . . .
of the ward and city I live in . . . . of the nation,
The latest news . . . . discoveries, inventions, societies . . . .
authors old and new,
My dinner, dress, associates, looks, business, compliments, dues,
The real or fancied indifference of some man or woman I love,
The sickness of one of my folks—or of myself . . . . or ill-doing . . . .
or loss or lack of money . . . . or depressions or exaltations,
They come to me days and nights and go from me again,
But they are not the Me myself.

Apart from the pulling and hauling stands what I am,
Stands amused, complacent, compassionating, idle, unitary,
Looks down, is erect, bends an arm on an impalpable certain rest,
Looks with its sidecurved head curious what will come next,
Both in and out of the game, and watching and wondering at it.

Backward I see in my own days where I sweated through fog
with linguists and contenders,
I have no mocking or arguments . . . . I witness and wait.

I believe in you my soul . . . . the other I am must not abase itself to you,
And you must not be abased to the other.

Loafe with me on the grass . . . . loose the stop from your throat,
Not words, not music or rhyme I want . . . . not custom or lecture,
not even the best,
Only the lull I like, the hum of your valved voice.

I mind how we lay in June, such a transparent summer morning;
You settled your head athwart my hips and gently turned over upon me,
And parted the shirt from my bosom-bone, and plunged your tongue
to my barestript heart,
And reached till you felt my beard, and reached till you held my feet.

Swiftly arose and spread around me the peace and joy and knowledge
that pass all the art and argument of the earth;
And I know that the hand of God is the elderhand of my own,
And I know that the spirit of God is the eldest brother of my own,
And that all the men ever born are also my brothers . . . .
and the women my sisters and lovers,
And that a kelson° of the creation is love;
And limitless are leaves stiff or drooping in the fields,
And brown ants in the little wells beneath them,
And mossy scabs of the wormfence, and heaped stones,
and elder and mullen and pokeweed.

A child said, What is the grass? fetching it to me with full hands;
How could I answer the child? . . . . I do not know what it is
any more than he.

I guess it must be the flag of my disposition,
out of hopeful green stuff woven.

Or I guess it is the handkerchief of the Lord,
A scented gift and remembrancer designedly dropped,
Bearing the owner's name someway in the corners,
that we may see and remark, and say Whose?

Or I guess is itself a child . . . . the produced babe of the vegatation.

Or I guess it is a uniform hieroglyphic,
And it means, Sprouting alike in broad zones and narrow zones,
Growing among black folks as among white,
Kanuck, Tuckahoe, Congressman, Cuff,° I give them the same,
    I receive them the same.

And now it seems to me the beautiful uncut hair of graves.

Tenderly will I use you curling grass,
It may be you transpire from the breasts of young men,
It may be if I had known them I would have loved them;
It may be you are from old people and from women, and from offspring
    taken soon out of their mothers' laps,
And here you are the mothers' laps.

This grass is very dark to be from the white heads of old mothers,
Darker than the colorless beards of old men,
Dark to come from under the faint red roofs of mouths.

O I perceive after all so many uttering tongues!
And I perceive they do not come from the roofs of mouths for nothing.

I wish I could translate the hints about the dead young men and women,
And the hints about old men and mothers, and the offspring taken soon
    out of their laps.

What do you think has become of the young and old men?
And what do you think has become of the women and children?

They are alive and well somewhere;
The smallest sprout shows there is really no death,
And if ever there was it led forward life, and does not wait at the end
    to arrest it,
And ceased the moment life appeared.

All goes onward and outward . . . . and nothing collapses,
And to die is different from what any one supposed, and luckier.

Has any one supposed it lucky to be born?
I hasten to inform him or her it is just as lucky to die, and I know it.

I pass death with the dying, and birth with the new-washed babe . . . .
and am not contained between my hat and boots,
And peruse manifold objects, no two alike, and every one good,
The earth good, and the stars good, and their adjuncts all good.

I am not an earth nor an adjunct of an earth,
I am the mate and companion of people, all just as immortal
and fathomless as myself;
They do not know how immortal, but I know.

Every kind for itself and its own . . . . for me mine male and female,
For me all that have been boys and that love women,
For me the man that is proud and feels how it stings to be slighted,
For me the sweetheart and the old maid . . . . for me mothers
and the mothers of mothers,
For me lips that have smiled, eyes that have shed tears,
For me children and the begetters of children.

Who need be afraid of the merge?
Undrape . . . . you are not guilty to me, nor stale nor discarded,
I see through the broadcloth and gingham whether or no,
And am around, tenacious, acquisitive, tireless . . . .
and can never be shaken away.

The little one sleeps in its cradle,
I lift the gauze and look a long time, and silently brush away flies
with my hand.

The youngster and the redfaced girl turn aside up the bushy hill,
I peeringly view them from the top.

The suicide sprawls on the bloody floor of the bedroom,
It is so . . . . I witnessed the corpse . . . . there the pistol had fallen.

The blab of the pave . . . . the tires of carts and sluff of bootsoles
and talk of the promenaders,
The heavy omnibus, the driver with his interrogating thumb,
the clank of the shod horses on the granite floor,
The carnival of sleighs, the clinking and shouted jokes and pelts
of snowballs;
The hurrahs for popular favorites . . . . the fury of roused mobs,

The flap of the curtained litter—the sick man inside,
borne to the hospital,
The meeting of enemies, the sudden oath, the blows and fall,
The excited crowd—the policeman with his star quickly working
his passage to the centre of the crowd;
The impassive stones that receive and return so many echoes,
The souls moving along . . . . are they invisible while the least atom
of the stones is visible?
What groans of overfed or half-starved who fall on the flags sunstruck
or in fits,
What exclamations of women taken suddenly, who hurry home
and give birth to babes,
What living and buried speech is always vibrating here . . . .
what howls restrained by decorum,
Arrests of criminals, slights, adulterous offers made, acceptances,
rejections with convex lips,
I mind them or the resonance of them . . . . I come again and again.

The big doors of the country-barn stand open and ready,
The dried grass of the harvest-time loads the slow-drawn wagon,
The clear light plays on the brown gray and green intertinged,
The armfuls are packed to the sagging mow:
I am there . . . . I help . . . . I came stretched atop of the load,
I felt its soft jolts . . . . one leg reclined on the other,
I jump from the crossbeams, and seize the clover and timothy,
And roll head over heels, and tangle my hair full of wisps.

Alone far in the wilds and mountains I hunt,
Wandering amazed at my own lightness and glee,
In the late afternoon choosing a safe spot to pass the night,
Kindling a fire and broiling the freshkilled game,
Soundly falling asleep on the gathered leaves, my dog and gun
by my side.

The Yankee clipper is under her three skysails . . . .
she cuts the sparkle and scud,
My eyes settle the land . . . . I bend at her prow or shout joyously
from the deck.

The boatmen and clamdiggers arose early and stopped for me,
I tucked my trowser-ends in my boots and went and had a good time,
You should have been with us that day round the chowder-kettle.

I saw the marriage of the trapper in the open air in the far-west . . . .
the bride was a red girl,
Her father and his friends sat near by crosslegged and dumbly smoking . . . .
they had moccasins to their feet and large thick blankets
hanging from their shoulders;
On a bank lounged the trapper . . . . he was dressed mostly in skins . . . . .
his luxuriant beard and curls protected his neck,
One hand rested on his rifle . . . . the other hand held firmly the wrist
of the red girl,
She had long eyelashes . . . . her head was bare . . . . her coarse straight locks
descended upon her voluptuous limbs and reached to her feet.

The runaway slave came to my house and stopped outside,
I heard his motions crackling the twigs of the woodpile,
Through the swung half-door of the kitchen I saw him limpsey and weak,
And went where he sat on a log, and led him in and assured him,
And brought water and filled a tub for his sweated body and bruised feet,
And gave him a room that entered from my own, and gave him
some coarse clean clothes,
And remember perfectly well his revolving eyes and his awkwardness,
And remember putting plasters on the galls of his neck and ankles;
He staid with me a week before he was recuperated and passed north,
I had him sit next me at table . . . . my firelock leaned in the corner.

Twenty-eight young men bathe by the shore,
Twenty-eight young men, and all so friendly,
Twenty-eight years of womanly life, and all so lonesome.

She owns the fine house by the rise of the bank,
She hides handsome and richly drest aft the blinds of the window.

Which of the young men does she like the best?
Ah the homeliest of them is beautiful to her.

Where are you off to, lady? for I see you,
You splash in the water there, yet stay stock still in your room.

Dancing and laughing along the beach came the twenty-ninth bather,
The rest did not see her, but she saw them and loved them.

The beards of the young men glistened with wet, it ran
from their long hair,
Little streams passed all over their bodies.

An unseen hand also passed over their bodies,
It descended tremblingly from their temples and ribs.

The young men float on their backs, their white bellies swell to the sun
.... they do not ask who seizes fast to them,
They do not know who puffs and declines with pendant and bending arch,
They do not think whom they souse with spray.

The butcher-boy puts off his killing-clothes, or sharpens his knife
at the stall in the market,
I loiter enjoying his repartee and his shuffle and breakdown.°

Blacksmiths with grimed and hairy chests environ the anvil,
Each has his main-sledge .... they are all out .... there is a great heat
in the fire.

From the cinder-strewed threshold I follow their movements,
The lithe sheer of their waists plays even with their massive arms,
Overhand the hammers roll—overhand so slow—overhand so sure,
They do not hasten, each man hits in his place.

The negro holds firmly the reins of his four horses ....
the block swags underneath on its tied-over chain,
The negro that drives the huge dray of the stoneyard .... steady and tall
he stands poised on one leg on the stringpiece,°
His blue shirt exposes his ample neck and breast and loosens
over his hipband,
His glance is calm and commanding .... he tosses the slouch of his hat
away from his forehead,
The sun falls on his crispy hair and moustache .... falls on the black
of his polish'd and perfect limbs.

I behold the picturesque giant and love him .... and I do not stop there,
I go with the team also.

In me the caresser of life wherever moving .... backward as well as
forward slueing,
To niches aside and junior bending.

Oxen that rattle the yoke or halt in the shade, what is that you express
in your eyes?
It seems to me more than all the print I have read in my life.

My tread scares the wood-drake and wood-duck on my distant
and daylong ramble,
They rise together, they slowly circle around.
. . . . I believe in those winged purposes,
And acknowledge the red yellow and white playing within me,
And consider the green and violet and the tufted crown intentional;
And do not call the tortoise unworthy because she is not something else,
And the mockingbird in the swamp never studied the gamut,
yet trills pretty well to me,
And the look of the bay mare shames silliness out of me.

The wild gander leads his flock through the cool night,
Ya-honk! he says, and sounds it down to me like an invitation;
The pert may suppose it meaningless, but I listen closer,
I find its purpose and place up there toward the November sky.

The sharphoofed moose of the north, the cat on the housesill,
the chickadee, the prairie-dog,
The litter of the grunting sow as they tug at her teats,
The brood of the turkeyhen, and she with her halfspread wings,
I see in them and myself the same old law.

The press of my foot to the earth springs a hundred affections,
They scorn the best I can do to relate them.

I am enamoured of growing outdoors,
Of men that live among cattle or taste of the ocean or woods,
Of the builders and steerers of ships, of the wielders of axes and mauls,
of the drivers of horses,
I can eat and sleep with them week in and week out.

What is commonest and cheapest and nearest and easiest is Me,
Me going in for my chances, spending for vast returns,
Adorning myself to bestow myself on the first that will take me,
Not asking the sky to come down to my goodwill,
Scattering it freely forever.

The pure contralto sings in the organloft,
The carpenter dresses his plank . . . . the tongue of his foreplane
whistles its wild ascending lisp,
The married and unmarried children ride home
to their thanksgiving dinner,
The pilot seizes the king-pin, he heaves down with a strong arm,
The mate stands braced in the whaleboat, lance and harpoon are ready,
The duck-shooter walks by silent and cautious stretches,
The deacons are ordained with crossed hands at the altar,
The spinning-girl retreats and advances to the hum of the big wheel,
The farmer stops by the bars of a Sunday and looks at the oats and rye,
The lunatic is carried at last to the asylum a confirmed case,
He will never sleep any more as he did in the cot
in his mother's bedroom;
The jour printer° with gray head and gaunt jaws works at his case,
He turns his quid of tobacco, his eyes get blurred with the manuscript;
The malformed limbs are tied to the anatomist's table,
What is removed drops horribly in a pail;
The quadroon girl is sold at the stand . . . . the drunkard nods
by the barroom stove,
The machinist rolls up his sleeves . . . . the policeman travels his beat
. . . . the gatekeeper marks who pass,
The young fellow drives the express-wagon . . . . I love him
though I do not know him;
The half-breed straps on his light boots to compete in the race,
The western turkey-shooting draws old and young . . . . some lean
on their rifles, some sit on logs,
Out from the crowd steps the marksman and takes his position
and levels his piece;
The groups of newly-come immigrants cover the wharf or levee,
The woollypates hoe in the sugarfield, the overseer views them
from his saddle;
The bugle calls in the ballroom, the gentlemen run for their partners,
the dancers bow to each other;
The youth lies awake in the cedar-roofed garret and harks
to the musical rain,
The Wolverine° sets traps on the creek that helps fill the Huron,
The reformer ascends the platform, he spouts with his mouth and nose,
The company returns from its excursion, the darkey brings up the rear
and bears the well-riddled target;
The squaw wrapt in her yellow-hemmed cloth is offering moccasins
and beadbags for sale,

The connoisseur peers along the exhibition-gallery with halfshut eyes
bent sideways,
The deckhands make fast the steamboat, the plank is thrown
for the shoregoing passengers,
The young sister holds out the skein, the elder sister winds it off
in a ball and stops now and then for the knots,
The one-year wife is recovering and happy, a week ago she bore
her first child,
The cleanhaired Yankee girl works with her sewing-machine
or in the factory or mill,
The nine months' gone is in the parturition chamber, her faintness
and pains are advancing;
The pavingman leans on his twohanded rammer—the reporter's lead
flies swiftly over the notebook—the signpainter is lettering
with red and gold,
The canal-boy trots on the towpath—the bookkeeper counts at his desk—
the shoemaker waxes his thread,
The conductor beats time for the band and all the performers follow him,
The child is baptised—the convert is making the first professions,
The regatta is spread on the bay . . . . how the white sails sparkle!
The drover watches his drove, he sings out to them that would stray,
The pedlar sweats with his pack on his back—the purchaser higgles
about the odd cent,
The camera and plate are prepared, the lady must sit for her daguerreotype,
The bride unrumples her white dress, the minutehand of the clock
moves slowly,
The opium eater reclines with rigid head and just-opened lips,
The prostitute draggles her shawl, her bonnet bobs on her tipsy
and pimpled neck,
The crowd laugh at her blackguard oaths, the men jeer and wink
to each other
(Miserable! I do not laugh at your oaths nor jeer you),
The President holds a cabinet council, he is surrounded
by the great secretaries,
On the piazza walk five friendly matrons with twined arms;
The crew of the fish-smack pack repeated layers of halibut in the hold,
The Missourian crosses the plains toting his wares and his cattle,
The fare-collector goes through the train—he gives notice by the jingling
of loose change,
The floormen are laying the floor—the tinners are tinning the roof—
the masons are calling for mortar,

In single file each shouldering his hod pass onward the laborers;
Seasons pursuing each other the indescribable crowd is gathered . . . .
it is the Fourth of July . . . . what salutes of cannon and small arms!
Seasons pursuing each other the plougher ploughs and the mower mows
and the wintergrain falls in the ground;
Off on the lakes the pikefisher watches and waits by the hole
in the frozen surface,
The stumps stand thick round the clearing, the squatter strikes deep
with his axe,
The flatboatmen make fast toward dusk near the cottonwood
or pekantrees,
The coon-seekers go now through the regions of the Red river,
or through those drained by the Tennessee, or through those
of the Arkansas,
The torches shine in the dark that hangs on the Chattahoochee
or Altamahaw;
Patriarchs sit at supper with sons and grandsons and great grandsons
around them,
In walls of adobe, in canvass tents, rest hunters and trappers
after their day's sport,
The city sleeps and the country sleeps,
The living sleep for their time . . . . the dead sleep for their time,
The old husband sleeps by his wife and the young husband sleeps
by his wife;
And these one and all tend inward to me, and I tend outward to them,
And such as it is to be of these more or less I am.

I am of old and young, of the foolish as much as the wise,
Regardless of others, ever regardful of others,
Maternal as well as paternal, a child as well as a man,
Stuffed with the stuff that is coarse, and stuffed with the stuff that is fine,
One of the great nation, the nation of many nations—
the smallest the same and the largest the same,
A southerner soon as a northerner, a planter nonchalant and hospitable,
A Yankee bound my own way . . . . ready for trade . . . . my joints
the limberest joints on earth and the sternest joints on earth,
A Kentuckian walking the vale of the Elkhorn in my deerskin leggings,
A boatman over the lakes or bays or along coasts . . . . a Hoosier,
a Badger, a Buckeye,
A Louisianian or Georgian, a poke-easy from sandhills and pines,

At home on Canadian snowshoes or up in the bush, or with fishermen
off Newfoundland,
At home in the fleet of iceboats, sailing with the rest and tacking,
At home on the hills of Vermont or in the woods of Maine
or the Texan ranch,
Comrade of Californians . . . . comrade of free northwesterners,
loving their big proportions,
Comrade of raftsmen and coalmen—comrade of all who shake hands
and welcome to drink and meat;
A learner with the simplest, a teacher of the thoughtfulest,
A novice beginning experient of myriads of seasons,
Of every hue and trade and rank, of every caste and religion,
Not merely of the New World but of Africa Europe or Asia . . . .
a wandering savage,
A farmer, mechanic, or artist . . . . a gentleman, sailor, lover or quaker,
A prisoner, fancy-man, rowdy, lawyer, physician or priest.

I resist anything better than my own diversity,
And breathe the air and leave plenty after me,
And am not stuck up, and am in my place.

The moth and the fisheggs are in their place,
The suns I see and the suns I cannot see are in their place,
The palpable is in its place and the impalpable is in its place.

These are the thoughts of all men in all ages and lands,
they are not original with me,
If they are not yours as much as mine they are nothing or next to nothing,
If they do not enclose everything they are next to nothing,
If they are not the riddle and the untying of the riddle they are nothing,
If they are not just as close as they are distant they are nothing.

This is the grass that grows wherever the land is and the water is,
This is the common air that bathes the globe.

This is the breath of laws and songs and behaviour,
This is the tasteless water of souls . . . . this is the true sustenance,
It is for the illiterate . . . . it is for the judges of the supreme court . . . .
it is for the federal capitol and the state capitols,
It is for the admirable communes of literary men and composers
and singers and lecturers and engineers and savans,°
It is for the endless races of working people and farmers and seamen.

This is the trill of a thousand clear cornets and scream
of the octave flute and strike of triangles.

I play not a march for victors only . . . . I play great marches
for conquered and slain persons.

Have you heard that it was good to gain the day?
I also say it is good to fall . . . . battles are lost in the same spirit
in which they are won.

I sound triumphal drums for the dead . . . . I fling through
my embouchures° the loudest and gayest music to them,
Vivas to those who have failed, and to those whose war-vessels
sank in the sea, and those themselves who sank in the sea,
And to all generals that lost engagements, and all overcome heroes,
and the numberless unknown heroes equal to the greatest
heroes known.

This is the meal pleasantly set . . . . this is the meat and drink
for natural hunger,
It is for the wicked just the same as the righteous . . . .
I make appointments with all,
I will not have a single person slighted or left away,
The keptwoman and sponger and thief are hereby invited . . . .
the heavy-lipped slave is invited . . . . the venerealee is invited,
There shall be no difference between them and the rest.

This is the press of a bashful hand . . . . this is the float and odor of hair,
This is the touch of my lips to yours . . . . this is the murmur of yearning,
This is the far-off depth and height reflecting my own face,
This is the thoughtful merge of myself and the outlet again.

Do you guess I have some intricate purpose?
Well I have . . . . for the April rain has, and the mica on the side
of a rock has.

Do you take it I would astonish?
Does the daylight astonish? or the early redstart twittering
through the woods?
Do I astonish more than they?

This hour I tell things in confidence,
I might not tell everybody but I will tell you.

Who goes there! hankering, gross, mystical, nude?
How is it I extract strength from the beef I eat?

What is a man anyhow? What am I? and what are you?
All I mark as my own shall offset it with your own,
Else it were time lost listening to me.

I do not snivel that snivel the world over,
That months are vacuums and the ground but wallow and filth,
That life is a suck and a sell, and nothing remains at the end
        but threadbare crape and tears.

Whimpering and truckling fold with powders for invalids . . . .
        conformity goes to the fourth-removed,
I cock my hat as I please indoors or out.

Shall I pray? Shall I venerate and be ceremonious?

I have pried through the strata and analyzed to a hair,
And counselled with doctors and calculated close and found
        no sweeter fat than sticks to my own bones.

In all people I see myself, none more and not one a barleycorn less,
And the good or bad I say of myself I say of them.

And I know I am solid and sound,
To me the converging objects of the universe perpetually flow,
All are written to me, and I must get what the writing means.

And I know I am deathless,
I know this orbit of mine cannot be swept by a carpenter's compass,
I know I shall not pass like a child's carlacue° cut with a burnt stick
        at night.

I know I am august,
I do not trouble my spirit to vindicate itself or be understood,
I see that the elementary laws never apologize,
I reckon I behave no prouder than the level I plant my house by after all.

I exist as I am, that is enough,
If no other in the world be aware I sit content,
And if each and all be aware I sit content.

One world is aware, and by far the largest to me, and that is myself,
And whether I come to my own today or in ten thousand
or ten million years,
I can cheerfully take it now, or with equal cheerfulness I can wait.

My foothold is tenoned and mortised° in granite,
I laugh at what you call dissolution,
And I know the amplitude of time.

I am the poet of the body,
And I am the poet of the soul.

The pleasures of heaven are with me, and the pains of hell are with me,
The first I graft and increase upon myself . . . . the latter I translate
into a new tongue.

I am the poet of the woman the same as the man,
And I say it is as great to be a woman as to be a man,
And I say there is nothing greater than the mother of men.

I chant a new chant of dilation or pride,
We have had ducking and deprecating about enough,
I show that size is only development.

Have you outstript the rest? Are you the President?
It is a trifle . . . . they will more than arrive there every one,
and still pass on.

I am he that walks with the tender and growing night;
I call to the earth and sea half-held by the night.

Press close barebosomed night! Press close magnetic nourishing night!
Night of south winds! Night of the large few stars!
Still nodding night! Mad naked summer night!

Smile O voluptuous coolbreathed earth!
Earth of the slumbering and liquid trees!
Earth of departed sunset! Earth of the mountains misty-topt!
Earth of the vitreous pour of the full moon just tinged with blue!
Earth of shine and dark mottling the tide of the river!
Earth of the limpid gray of clouds brighter and clearer for my sake!

Far-swooping elbowed earth! Rich apple-blossomed earth!
Smile, for your lover comes!

Prodigal! you have given me love! . . . . therefore I to you give love!
O unspeakable passionate love!

Thruster holding me tight and that I hold tight!
We hurt each other as the bridegroom and the bride hurt each other.

You sea! I resign myself to you also . . . . I guess what you mean,
I behold from the beach your crooked inviting fingers,
I believe you refuse to go back without feeling of me;
We must have a turn together . . . . I undress . . . . hurry me out of sight
of the land,
Cushion me soft . . . . rock me in billowy drowse,
Dash me with amorous wet . . . . I can repay you.

Sea of stretched ground-swells!
Sea breathing broad and convulsive breaths!
Sea of the brine of life! Sea of unshovelled and always-ready graves!
Howler and scooper of storms! Capricious and dainty sea!
I am integral with you . . . . I too am of one phase and of all phases.

Partaker of influx and efflux . . . . extoler of hate and conciliation,
Extoler of amies° and those that sleep in each others' arms.

I am he attesting sympathy;
Shall I make my list of things in the house and skip the house
that supports them?

I am the poet of commonsense and of the demonstrable
and of immortality;
And am not the poet of goodness only . . . . I do not decline to be
the poet of wickedness also.

Washes and razors for foofoos . . . . for me freckles and a bristling beard.

What blurt is it about virtue and about vice?
Evil propels me, and reform of evil propels me . . . . I stand indifferent,
My gait is no faultfinder's or rejecter's gait,
I moisten the roots of all that has grown.

Did you fear some scrofula out of the unflagging pregnancy?
Did you guess the celestial laws are yet to be worked over and rectified?

I step up to say that what we do is right and what we affirm is right . . . .
        and some is only the ore of right,
Witnesses of us . . . . one side a balance and the antipodal side a balance,
Soft doctrine as steady help as stable doctrine,
Thoughts and deeds of the present our rouse and early start.

This minute that comes to me over the past decillions,
There is no better than it and now.

What behaved well in the past or behaves well today is not such a wonder,
The wonder is always and always how there can be a mean man
        or an infidel.

Endless unfolding of words of ages!
And mine a word of the modern . . . . a word en masse.

A word of the faith that never balks,
One time as good as another time . . . . here or henceforward
        it is all the same to me.

A word of reality . . . . materialism first and last imbueing.

Hurrah for positive science! Long live exact demonstration!
Fetch stonecrop° and mix it with cedar and branches of lilac;
This is the lexicographer or chemist . . . . this made a grammar
        of the old cartouches,°
These mariners put the ship through dangerous unknown seas,
This is the geologist, and this works with the scalpel,
        and this is a mathematician.

Gentlemen I receive you, and attach and clasp hands with you,
The facts are useful and real . . . . they are not my dwelling . . . .
        I enter by them to an area of the dwelling.

I am less the reminder of property or qualities, and more the reminder
        of life,
And go on the square for my own sake and for others' sakes,
And make short account of neuters and geldings, and favor men
        and women fully equipped,

And beat the gong of revolt, and stop with fugitives and them
that plot and conspire.

Walt Whitman, an American, one of the roughs, a kosmos,
Disorderly fleshy and sensual . . . . eating drinking and breeding,
No sentimentalist . . . . no stander above men and women
or apart from them . . . . no more modest than immodest.

Unscrew the locks from the doors!
Unscrew the doors themselves from their jambs!

Whoever degrades another degrades me . . . . and whatever is done
or said returns at last to me,
And whatever I do or say I also return.

Through me the afflatus° surging and surging . . . . through me
the current and index.

I speak the password primeval . . . . I give the sign of democracy;
By God! I will accept nothing which all cannot have their counterpart of
on the same terms.

Through me many long dumb voices,
Voices of the interminable generations of slaves,
Voices of prostitutes and of deformed persons,
Voices of the diseased and despairing, and of thieves and dwarfs,
Voices of cycles of preparation and accretion,
And of the threads that connect the stars—and of wombs,
and of the fatherstuff,
And of the rights of them the others are down upon,
Of the trivial and flat and foolish and despised,
Of fog in the air and beetles rolling balls of dung.

Through me forbidden voices,
Voices of sexes and lusts . . . . voices veiled, and I remove the veil,
Voices indecent by me clarified and transfigured.

I do not press my finger across my mouth,
I keep as delicate around the bowels as around the head and heart,
Copulation is no more rank to me than death is.

I believe in the flesh and the appetites,
Seeing hearing and feeling are miracles, and each part and tag of me
is a miracle.

Divine am I inside and out, and I make holy whatever I touch
or am touched from;
The scent of these arm-pits is aroma finer than prayer,
This head is more than churches or bibles or creeds.

If I worship any particular thing it shall be some of the spread of my body;
Translucent mould of me it shall be you,
Shaded ledges and rests, firm masculine coulter,° it shall be you,
Whatever goes to the tilth of me it shall be you,
You my rich blood, your milky stream pale strippings of my life;
Breast that presses against other breasts it shall be you,
My brain it shall be your occult convolutions,
Root of washed sweet-flag, timorous pond-snipe,
nest of guarded duplicate eggs, it shall be you,
Mixed tussled hay of head and beard and brawn it shall be you,
Trickling sap of maple, fibre of manly wheat, it shall be you;
Sun so generous it shall be you,
Vapors lighting and shading my face it shall be you,
You sweaty brooks and dews it shall be you,
Winds whose soft-tickling genitals rub against me it shall be you,
Broad muscular fields, branches of liveoak, loving lounger
in my winding paths, it shall be you,
Hands I have taken, face I have kissed, mortal I have ever touched,
it shall be you.

I dote on myself . . . . there is that lot of me, and all so luscious,
Each moment and whatever happens thrills me with joy.

I cannot tell how my ankles bend . . . . nor whence the cause
of my faintest wish,
Nor the cause of the friendship I emit . . . . nor the cause
of the friendship I take again.

To walk up my stoop is unaccountable . . . . I pause to consider
if it really be,
That I eat and drink is spectacle enough for the great authors
and schools,

A morning-glory at my window satisfies me more
than the metaphysics of books.

To behold the daybreak!
The little light fades the immense and diaphanous shadows,
The air tastes good to my palate.

Hefts of the moving world at innocent gambols, silently rising,
freshly exuding,
Scooting obliquely high and low.

Something I cannot see puts upward libidinous prongs,
Seas of bright juice suffuse heaven.

The earth by the sky staid with . . . . the daily close of their junction,
The heaved challenge from the east that moment over my head,
The mocking taunt, See then whether you shall be master!

Dazzling and tremendous how quick the sunrise would kill me,
If I could not now and always send sunrise out of me.

We also ascend dazzling and tremendous as the sun,
We found our own my soul in the calm and cool of the daybreak.

My voice goes after what my eyes cannot reach,
With the twirl of my tongue I encompass worlds and volumes of worlds.

Speech is the twin of my vision . . . . it is unequal to measure itself.

It provokes me forever,
It says sarcastically, Walt, you understand enough . . . .
why don't you let it out then?

Come now I will not be tantalized . . . . you conceive too much
of articulation.

Do you not know how the buds beneath are folded?
Waiting in gloom protected by frost,
The dirt receding before my prophetical screams,
I underlying causes to balance them at last,
My knowledge my live parts . . . . it keeping tally with the meaning
of things,

Happiness . . . . which whoever hears me let him or her set out
in search of this day.

My final merit I refuse you . . . . I refuse putting from me the best I am.

Encompass worlds but never try to encompass me,
I crowd your noisiest talk by looking toward you.

Writing and talk do not prove me,
I carry the plenum° of proof and every thing else in my face,
With the hush of my lips I confound the topmost skeptic.

I think I will do nothing for a long time but listen,
And accrue what I hear into myself . . . . and let sounds contribute
toward me.

I hear the bravuras of birds . . . . the bustle of growing wheat . . . .
gossip of flames . . . . clack of sticks cooking my meals.

I hear the sound of the human voice . . . . a sound I love,
I hear all sounds as they are tuned to their uses . . . . sounds of the city
and sounds out of the city . . . . sounds of the day and night;
Talkative young ones to those that like them . . . . the recitative
of fish-pedlars and fruit-pedlars . . . . the loud laugh
of workpeople at their meals,
The angry bass of disjointed friendship . . . . the faint tones of the sick,
The judge with hands tight to the desk, his shaky lips pronouncing
a death-sentence,
The heave'e'yo of stevedores unlading ships by the wharves . . . .
the refrain of the anchor-lifters;
The ring of alarm-bells . . . . the cry of fire . . . . the whirr
of swift-streaking engines and hose-carts with premonitory
tinkles and colored lights,
The steam-whistle . . . . the solid roll of the train of approaching cars;
The slow-march played at night at the head of the association,
They go to guard some corpse . . . . the flag-tops are draped
with black muslin.

I hear the violincello or man's heart's complaint,
And hear the keyed cornet or else the echo of sunset.

I hear the chorus . . . . it is a grand-opera . . . . this indeed is music!

A tenor large and fresh as the creation fills me,
The orbic flex of his mouth is pouring and filling me full.

I hear the trained soprano . . . . she convulses me like the climax
  of my love-grip;
The orchestra whirls me wider than Uranus flies,
It wrenches unnamable ardors from my breast,
It throbs me to gulps of the farthest down horror,
It sails me . . . . I dab with bare feet . . . . they are licked
  by the indolent waves,
I am exposed . . . . cut by bitter and poisoned hail,
Steeped amid honeyed morphine . . . . my windpipe squeezed
  in the fakes° of death,
Let up again to feel the puzzle of puzzles,
And what we call Being.

To be in any form, what is that?
If nothing lay more developed the quahaug° and its callous shell
  were enough.

Mine is no callous shell,
I have instant conductors all over me whether I pass or stop,
They seize every object and lead it harmlessly through me.

I merely stir, press, feel with my fingers, and am happy,
To touch my person to some one else's is about as much as I can stand.

Is this then a touch? . . . . quivering me to a new identity,
Flames and ether making a rush for my veins,
Treacherous tip of me reaching and crowding to help them,
My flesh and blood playing out lightning, to strike what is hardly different
  from myself,
On all sides prurient provokers stiffening my limbs,
Straining the udder of my heart for its withheld drip,
Behaving licentious toward me, taking no denial,
Depriving me of my best as for a purpose,
Unbuttoning my clothes and holding me by the bare waist,
Deluding my confusion with the calm of the sunlight and pasture fields,
Immodestly sliding the fellow-senses away,
They bribed to swap off with touch, and go and graze at the edges of me,
No consideration, no regard for my draining strength or my anger,

Fetching the rest of the herd around to enjoy them awhile,
Then all uniting to stand on a headland and worry me.

The sentries desert every other part of me,
They have left me helpless to a red marauder,
They all come to the headland to witness and assist against me.

I am given up by traitors;
I talk wildly . . . . I have lost my wits . . . . I and nobody else am the greatest traitor,
I went myself first to the headland . . . . my own hands carried me there.

You villain touch! what are you doing? . . . . my breath is tight in its throat;
Unclench your floodgates! you are too much for me.

Blind loving wrestling touch! Sheathed hooded sharptoothed touch!
Did it make you ache so leaving me?

Parting tracked by arriving . . . . perpetual payment of the perpetual loan,
Rich showering rain, and recompense richer afterward.

Sprouts take and accumulate . . . . stand by the curb prolific and vital,
Landscapes projected masculine full-sized and golden.

All truths wait in all things,
They neither hasten their own delivery nor resist it,
They do not need the obstetric forceps of the surgeon,
The insignificant is as big to me as any,
What is less or more than a touch?

Logic and sermons never convince,
The damp of the night drives deeper into my soul.

Only what proves itself to every man and woman is so,
Only what nobody denies is so.

A minute and a drop of me settle my brain;
I believe the soggy clods shall become lovers and lamps,
And a compend of compends is the meat of a man or woman,
And a summit and flower there is the feeling they have for each other,

And they are to branch boundlessly out of that lesson
until it becomes omnific,
And until every one shall delight us, and we them.

I believe a leaf of grass is no less than the journeywork of the stars,
And the pismire° is equally perfect, and a grain of sand,
and the egg of the wren,
And the tree-toad is a chef-d'ouvre for the highest,
And the running blackberry would adorn the parlors of heaven,
And the narrowest hinge in my hand puts to scorn all machinery,
And the cow crunching with depressed head surpasses any statue,
And a mouse is miracle enough to stagger sextillions of infidels,
And I could come every afternoon of my life to look at the farmer's girl
boiling her iron tea-kettle and baking shortcake.

I find I incorporate gneiss and coal and long-threaded moss and fruits
and grains and esculent° roots.
And am stucco'd with quadrupeds and birds all over,
And have distanced what is behind me for good reasons,
And call any thing close again when I desire it.

In vain the speeding or shyness,
In vain the plutonic rocks° send their old heat against my approach,
In vain the mastadon retreats beneath its own powdered bones,
In vain objects stand leagues off and assume manifold shapes,
In vain the ocean settling in hollows and the great monsters lying low,
In vain the buzzard houses herself with the sky,
In vain the snake slides through the creepers and logs,
In vain the elk takes to the inner passes of the woods,
In vain the razorbilled auk sails far north to Labrador,
I follow quickly . . . . I ascend to the nest in the fissure of the cliff.

I think I could turn and live awhile with the animals . . . .
they are so placid and self-contained,
I stand and look at them sometimes half the day long.

They do not sweat and whine about their condition,
They do not lie awake in the dark and weep for their sins,
They do not make me sick discussing their duty to God,
Not one is dissatisfied . . . . not one is demented with the mania
of owning things,

Not one kneels to another nor to his kind that lived thousands
of years ago,
Not one is respectable or industrious over the whole earth.

So they show their relations to me and I accept them;
They bring me tokens of myself . . . . they evince them plainly
in their possession.

I do not know where they got those tokens,
I must have passed that way untold times ago and negligently dropt them,
Myself moving forward then and now and forever,
Gathering and showing more always and with velocity,
Infinite and omnigenous° and the like of these among them;
Not too exclusive toward the reachers of my remembrancers,
Picking out here one that shall be my amie,
Choosing to go with him on brotherly terms.

A gigantic beauty of a stallion, fresh and responsive to my caresses,
Head high in the forehead and wide between the ears,
Limbs glossy and supple, tail dusting the ground,
Eyes well apart and full of sparkling wickedness . . . . ears finely cut
and flexibly moving.

His nostrils dilate . . . . my heels embrace him . . . . his well built limbs
tremble with pleasure . . . . we speed around and return.

I but use you a moment and then I resign you stallion . . . .
and do not need your paces, and outgallop them,
And myself as I stand or sit pass faster than you.

Swift wind! Space! My Soul! Now I know it is true what I guessed at;
What I guessed when I loafed on the grass,
What I guessed while I lay alone in my bed . . . . and again as I walked
the beach under the paling stars of the morning.

My ties and ballasts leave me . . . . I travel . . . . I sail . . . .
my elbows rest in the sea-gaps,
I skirt the sierras . . . . my palms cover continents,
I am afoot with my vision.

By the city's quadrangular houses . . . . in log-huts, or camping
with lumbermen,

Along the ruts of the turnpike . . . . along the dry gulch and rivulet bed,
Hoeing my onion-patch, and rows of carrots and parsnips . . . .
crossing savannas . . . . trailing in forests,
Prospecting . . . . gold-digging . . . . girdling the trees of a new purchase,
Scorched ankle-deep by the hot sand . . . . hauling my boat
down the shallow river;
Where the panther walks to and fro on a limb overhead . . . .
where the buck turns furiously at the hunter,
Where the rattlesnake suns his flabby length on a rock . . . .
where the otter is feeding on fish,
Where the alligator in his tough pimples sleeps by the bayou,
Where the black bear is searching for roots or honey . . . .
where the beaver pats the mud with his paddle-tail;
Over the growing sugar . . . . over the cottonplant . . . . over the rice
in its low moist field;
Over the sharp-peaked farmhouse with its scalloped scum
and slender shoots from the gutters;
Over the western persimmon . . . . over the longleaved corn
and the delicate blue-flowered flax;
Over the white and brown buckwheat, a hummer and a buzzer there
with the rest,
Over the dusky green of the rye as it ripples and shades the breeze;
Scaling mountains . . . . pulling myself cautiously up . . . . holding on
by low scragged limbs,
Walking the path worn in the grass and beat through the leaves
of the brush;
Where the quail is whistling betwixt the woods and the wheatlot,
Where the bat flies in the July eve . . . . where the great goldbug drops
through the dark;
Where the flails keep time on the barn floor,
Where the brook puts out of the roots of the old tree and flows
to the meadow,
Where cattle stand and shake away flies with the tremulous shuddering
of their hides,
Where the cheese-cloth hangs in the kitchen, and andirons straddle
the hearth-slab, and cobwebs fall in festoons from the rafters;
Where triphammers crash . . . . where the press is whirling its cylinders;
Wherever the human heart beats with terrible throes out of its ribs;
Where the pear-shaped balloon is floating aloft . . . . floating in it myself
and looking composedly down;
Where the life-car° is drawn on the slipnoose . . . . where the heat
hatches pale-green eggs in the dented sand,

Where the she-whale swims with her calves and never forsakes them,
Where the steamship trails hindways its long pennant of smoke,
Where the ground-shark's fin cuts like a black chip out of the water,
Where the half-burned brig is riding on unknown currents,
Where shells grow to her slimy deck, and the dead are corrupting below;
Where the striped and starred flag is borne at the head of the regiments;
Approaching Manhattan, up by the long-stretching island,
Under Niagara, the cataract falling like a veil over my countenance;
Upon a door-step . . . . upon the horse-block of hard wood outside,
Upon the race-course, or enjoying pic-nics or jigs or a good game
of base-ball,
At he-festivals with blackguard jibes and ironical license
and bull-dances° and drinking and laughter,
At the cider-mill, tasting the sweet of the brown sqush° . . . .
sucking the juice through a straw,
At apple-pealings, wanting kisses for all the red fruit I find,
At musters and beach-parties and friendly bees and huskings
and house-raisings;
Where the mockingbird sounds his delicious gurgles, and cackles
and screams and weeps,
Where the hay-rick stands in the barnyard, and the dry-stalks
are scattered, and the brood cow waits in the hovel,
Where the bull advances to do his masculine work, and the stud
to the mare, and the cock is treading the hen,
Where the heifers browse, and the geese nip their food with short jerks;
Where the sundown shadows lengthen over the limitless and lonesome
prairie,
Where the herds of buffalo make a crawling spread of the square miles
far and near;
Where the hummingbird shimmers . . . . where the neck
of the longlived swan is curving and winding;
Where the laughing-gull scoots by the slappy shore and laughs
her near-human laugh;
Where beehives range on a gray bench in the garden half-hid
by the high weeds;
Where the band-necked partridges roost in a ring on the ground
with their heads out;
Where burial coaches enter the arched gates of a cemetery;
Where winter wolves bark amid wastes of snow and icicled trees;
Where the yellow-crowned heron comes to the edge of the marsh
at night and feeds upon small crabs;
Where the splash of swimmers and divers cools the warm noon;

Where the katydid works her chromatic reed on the walnut-tree
over the well;
Through patches of citrons and cucumbers with silver-wired leaves,
Through the salt-lick or orange glade . . . . or under conical furs;
Through the gymnasium . . . . through the curtained saloon . . . .
through the office or public hall;
Pleased with the native and pleased with the foreign . . . .
pleased with the new and old,
Pleased with women, the homely as well as the handsome,
Pleased with the quakeress as she puts off her bonnet
and talks melodiously,
Pleased with the primitive tunes of the choir of the whitewashed church,
Pleased with the earnest words of the sweating Methodist preacher,
or any preacher . . . . looking seriously at the camp-meeting;
Looking in at the shop-windows in Broadway the whole forenoon . . . .
pressing the flesh of my nose to the thick plate-glass,
Wandering the same afternoon with my face turned up to the clouds;
My right and left arms round the sides of two friends and I in the middle;
Coming home with the bearded and dark-cheeked bush-boy . . . .
riding behind him at the drape of the day;
Far from the settlements studying the print of animals' feet,
or the moccasin print;
By the cot in the hospital reaching lemonade to a feverish patient,
By the coffined corpse when all is still, examining with a candle;
Voyaging to every port to dicker and adventure;
Hurrying with the modern crowd, as eager and fickle as any,
Hot toward one I hate, ready in my madness to knife him;
Solitary at midnight in my back yard, my thoughts gone from me
a long while,
Walking the old hills of Judea with the beautiful gentle god by my side;
Speeding through space . . . . speeding through heaven and the stars,
Speeding amid the seven satellites and the broad ring and the diameter
of eighty thousand miles,
Speeding with tailed meteors . . . . throwing fire-balls like the rest,
Carrying the crescent child that carries its own full mother in its belly:
Storming enjoying planning loving cautioning,
Backing and filling, appearing and disappearing,
I tread day and night such roads.

I visit the orchards of God and look at the spheric product,
And look at quintillions ripened, and look at quintillions green.

I fly the flight of the fluid and swallowing soul,
My course runs below the soundings of plummets.

I help myself to material and immaterial,
No guard can shut me off, no law can prevent me.

I anchor my ship for a little while only,
My messengers continually cruise away or bring their returns to me.

I go hunting polar furs and the seal . . . . leaping chasms with a
        pike-pointed staff . . . . clinging to topples of brittle and blue.

I ascend to the foretruck° . . . . I take my place late at night
        in the crow's nest . . . . we sail through the arctic sea . . . .
        it is plenty light enough,
Through the clear atmosphere I stretch around on the wonderful beauty,
The enormous masses of ice pass me and I pass them . . . . the scenery
        is plain in all directions,
The white-topped mountains point up in the distance . . . .
        I fling out my fancies toward them;
We are about approaching some great battlefield in which we are soon
        to be engaged,
We pass the colossal outposts of the encampments . . . . we pass
        with still feet and caution;
Or we are entering by the suburbs some vast and ruined city . . . .
        the blocks and fallen architecture more than all the living cities
        of the globe.

I am a free companion . . . . I bivouac by invading watchfires.

I turn the bridegroom out of bed and stay with the bride myself,
And tighten her all night to my thighs and lips.

My voice is the wife's voice, the screech by the rail of the stairs,
They fetch my man's body up dripping and drowned.

I understand the large hearts of heroes,
The courage of present times and all times;
How the skipper saw the crowded and rudderless wreck of the steamship,°
        and death chasing it up and down the storm,

How he knuckled tight and gave not back one inch, and was faithful
of days and faithful of nights,
And chalked in large letters on a board, Be of good cheer,
We will not desert you;
How he saved the drifting company at last,
How the lank loose-gowned women looked when boated from the side
of their prepared graves,
How the silent old-faced infants, and the lifted sick,
and the sharp-lipped unshaved men;
All this I swallow and it tastes good . . . . I like it well,
and it becomes mine,
I am the man . . . . I suffered . . . . I was there.

The disdain and calmness of martyrs,
The mother condemned for a witch and burnt with dry wood,
and her children gazing on;
The hounded slave that flags in the race and leans by the fence,
blowing and covered with sweat,
The twinges that sting like needles his legs and neck,
The murderous buckshot and the bullets,
All these I feel or am.

I am the hounded slave . . . . I wince at the bite of the dogs,
Hell and despair are upon me . . . . crack and again crack the marksmen,
I clutch the rails of the fence . . . . my gore dribs thinned with the ooze
of my skin,
I fall on the weeds and stones,
The riders spur their unwilling horses and haul close,
They taunt my dizzy ears . . . . they beat me violently over the head
with their whip-stocks.

Agonies are one of my changes of garments;
I do not ask the wounded person how he feels . . . . I myself
become the wounded person,
My hurt turns livid upon me as I lean on a cane and observe.

I am the mashed fireman with breastbone broken . . . .
tumbling walls buried me in their debris,
Heat and smoke I inspired . . . . I heard the yelling shouts
of my comrades,
I heard the distant click of their picks and shovels;
They have cleared the beams away . . . . they tenderly lift me forth.

I lie in the night air in my red shirt . . . . the pervading hush is for my sake,
Painless after all I lie, exhausted but not so unhappy,
White and beautiful are the faces around me . . . . the heads are bared of their firecaps,
The kneeling crowd fades with the light of the torches.

Distant and dead resuscitate,
They show as the dial or move as the hands of me . . . . and I am the clock myself.

I am an old artillerist, and tell of some fort's bombardment . . . . and am there again.

Again the reveille of drummers . . . . again the attacking cannon and mortars and howitzers,
Again the attacked send their cannon responsive.

I take part . . . . I see and hear the whole,
The cries and curses and roar . . . . the plaudits for well aimed shots,
The ambulanza slowly passing and trailing its red drip,
Workmen searching after damages and to make indispensible repairs,
The fall of grenades through the rent roof . . . . the fan-shaped explosion,
The whizz of limbs heads stone wood and iron high in the air.

Again gurgles the mouth of my dying general . . . . he furiously waves with his hand,
He gasps through the clot . . . . Mind not me . . . mind . . . . the entrenchments.

I tell not the fall of Alamo . . . . not one escaped to tell the fall of Alamo,
The hundred and fifty are dumb yet at Alamo.

Hear now the tale of a jetblack sunrise,
Hear of the murder in cold blood of four hundred and twelve young men.°

Retreating they had formed in a hollow square with their baggage for breastworks,
Nine hundred lives out of the surrounding enemy's nine times their number was the price they took in advance,
Their colonel was wounded and their ammunition gone,

They treated for an honorable capitulation, received writing and seal, gave up their arms, and marched back prisoners of war.

They were the glory of the race of rangers,
Matchless with a horse, a rifle, a song, a supper or a courtship,
Large, turbulent, brave, handsome, generous, proud and affectionate,
Bearded, sunburnt, dressed in the free costume of hunters,
Not a single one over thirty years of age.

The second Sunday morning they were brought out in squads and massacred . . . . it was beautiful early summer,
The work commenced about five o'clock and was over by eight.

None obeyed the command to kneel,
Some made a mad and helpless rush . . . . some stood stark and straight,
A few fell at once, shot in the temple or heart . . . . the living and dead lay together,
The maimed and mangled dug in the dirt . . . . the new-comers saw them there;
Some half-killed attempted to crawl away,
These were dispatched with bayonets or battered with the blunts of muskets;
A youth not seventeen years old seized his assassin till two more came to release him,
The three were all torn, and covered with the boy's blood.

At eleven o'clock began the burning of the bodies;
And that is the tale of the murder of the four hundred and twelve young men,
And that was a jetblack sunrise.

Did you read in the seabooks of the oldfashioned frigate-fight?°
Did you learn who won by the light of the moon and stars?

Our foe was no skulk in his ship, I tell you,
His was the English pluck, and there is no tougher or truer, and never was, and never will be;
Along the lowered eve he came, horribly raking us.

We closed with him . . . . the yards entangled . . . . the cannon touched,
My captain lashed fast with his own hands.

We had received some eighteen-pound shots under the water,
On our lower-gun-deck two large pieces had burst at the first fire,
killing all around and blowing up overhead.

Ten o'clock at night, and the full moon shining and the leaks
on the gain, and five feet of water reported,
The master-at-arms loosing the prisoners confined in the after-hold
to give them a chance for themselves.

The transit to and from the magazine was now stopped by the sentinels,
They saw so many strange faces they did not know whom to trust.

Our frigate was afire . . . . the other asked if we demanded quarters?
if our colors were struck and the fighting done?

I laughed content when I heard the voice of my little captain,
We have not struck, he composedly cried, We have just begun
our part of the fighting.

Only three guns were in use,
One was directed by the captain himself against the enemy's mainmast,
Two well-served with grape and canister silenced his musketry
and cleared his decks.

The tops alone seconded the fire of this little battery,
especially the maintop,
They all held out bravely during the whole of the action.

Not a moment's cease,
The leaks gained fast on the pumps . . . . the fire eat toward
the powder-magazine,
One of the pumps was shot away . . . . it was generally thought
we were sinking.

Serene stood the little captain,
He was not hurried . . . . his voice was neither high nor low,
His eyes gave more light to us than our battle-lanterns.

Toward twelve at night, there in the beams of the moon
they surrendered to us.

Stretched and still lay the midnight,
Two great hulls motionless on the breast of the darkness,
Our vessel riddled and slowly sinking . . . . preparations to pass
to the one we had conquered,
The captain on the quarter deck coldly giving his orders
through a countenance white as a sheet,
Near by the corpse of the child that served in the cabin,
The dead face of an old salt with long white hair
and carefully curled whiskers,
The flames spite of all that could be done flickering aloft and below,
The husky voices of the two or three officers yet fit for duty,
Formless stacks of bodies and bodies by themselves . . . .
dabs of flesh upon the masts and spars,
The cut of cordage and dangle of rigging . . . . the slight shock
of the soothe of waves,
Black and impassive guns, and litter of powder-parcels,
and the strong scent,
Delicate sniffs of the seabreeze . . . . smells of sedgy grass and fields
by the shore . . . death-messages given in charge to survivors,
The hiss of the surgeon's knife and the gnawing teeth of his saw,
The wheeze, the cluck, the swash of falling blood . . . .
the short wild scream, the long dull tapering groan,
These so . . . . these irretrievable.

O Christ! My fit is mastering me!
What the rebel said gaily adjusting his throat to the rope-noose,
What the savage at the stump, his eye-sockets empty, his mouth
spirting whoops and defiance,
What stills the traveler come to the vault at Mount Vernon,
What sobers the Brooklyn boy as he looks down the shores
of Wallabout and remembers the prison ships,
What burnt the gums of the redcoat at Saratoga when he surrendered
his brigades,
These become mine and me every one, and they are but little,
I become as much more as I like.

I become any presence or truth of humanity here,
And see myself in prison shaped like another man,
And feel the dull unintermitted pain.

For me the keepers of convicts shoulder their carbines and keep watch,
It is I let out in the morning and barred at night.

Not a mutineer walks handcuffed to the jail, but I am handcuffed to him and walk by his side,
I am less the jolly one there, and more the silent one with sweat on my twitching lips.

Not a youngster is taken for larceny, but I go up too and am tried and sentenced.

Not a cholera patient lies at the last gasp, but I also lie at the last gasp,
My face is ash-colored, my sinews gnarl . . . . away from me people retreat.

Askers embody themselves in me, and I am embodied in them,
I project my hat and sit shamefaced and beg.

I rise extatic through all, and sweep with the true gravitation,
The whirling and whirling is elemental within me.

Somehow I have been stunned. Stand back!
Give me a little time beyond my cuffed head and slumbers and dreams and gaping,
I discover myself on a verge of the usual mistake.

That I could forget the mockers and insults!
That I could forget the trickling tears and the blows of the bludgeons and hammers!
That I could look with a separate look on my own crucifixion and bloody crowning!

I remember . . . . I resume the overstaid fraction,
The grave of rock multiplies what has been confided to it . . . . or to any graves,
The corpses rise . . . . the gashes heal . . . . the fastenings roll away.

I troop forth replenished with supreme power, one of an average unending procession,
We walk the roads of Ohio and Massachusetts and Virginia and Wisconsin and New York and New Orleans and Texas and Montreal and San Francisco and Charleston and Savannah and Mexico,
Inland and by the seacoast and boundary lines . . . . and we pass the boundary lines.

Our swift ordinances are on their way over the whole earth,
The blossoms we wear in our hats are the growth of two thousand years.

Eleves° I salute you,
I see the approach of your numberless gangs . . . . I see
you understand yourselves and me,
And know that they who have eyes are divine, and the blind and lame
are equally divine,
And that my steps drag behind yours yet go before them,
And are aware how I am with you no more than I am with everybody.

The friendly and flowing savage . . . . Who is he?
Is he waiting for civilization or past it and mastering it?

Is he some southwesterner raised outdoors? Is he Canadian?
Is he from the Mississippi country? or from Iowa, Oregon
or California? or from the mountains? or prairie life
or bush-life? or from the sea?

Wherever he goes men and women accept and desire him,
They desire he should like them and touch them and speak to them
and stay with them.

Behaviour lawless as snow-flakes . . . . words simple as grass . . . .
uncombed head and laughter and naivete;
Slowstepping feet and the common features, and the common modes
and emanations,
They descend in new forms from the tips of his fingers,
They are wafted with the odor of his body or breath . . . . they fly out
of the glance of his eyes.

Flaunt of the sunshine I need not your bask . . . . lie over,
You light surfaces only . . . . I force the surfaces and the depths also.

Earth! you seem to look for something at my hands,
Say old topknot! what do you want?

Man or woman! I might tell how I like you, but cannot,
And might tell what it is in me and what it is in you, but cannot,
And might tell the pinings I have . . . . the pulse of my nights and days.

Behold I do not give lectures or a little charity,
What I give I give out of myself.

You there, impotent, loose in the knees, open your scarfed° chops till I blow grit within you,
Spread your palms and lift the flaps of your pockets,
I am not to be denied . . . . I compel . . . . I have stores plenty and to spare,
And any thing I have I bestow.

I do not ask who you are . . . . that is not important to me,
You can do nothing and be nothing but what I will infold you.

To a drudge of the cottonfields or emptier of privies I lean . . . . on his right cheek I put the family kiss,
And in my soul I swear I never will deny him.

On women fit for conception I start bigger and nimbler babes,
This day I am jetting the stuff of far more arrogant republics.

To any one dying . . . . thither I speed and twist the knob of the door,
Turn the bedclothes toward the foot of the bed,
Let the physician and the priest go home.

I seize the descending man . . . . I raise him with resistless will.

O despairer, here is my neck,
By God! you shall not go down! Hang your whole weight upon me.

I dilate you with tremendous breath . . . . I buoy you up;
Every room of the house do I fill with an armed force . . . . lovers of me, bafflers of graves:
Sleep! I and they keep guard all night;
Not doubt, not decease shall dare to lay finger upon you,
I have embraced you, and henceforth possess you to myself,
And when you rise in the morning you will find what I tell you is so.

I am he bringing help for the sick as they pant on their backs,
And for strong upright men I bring yet more needed help.

I heard what was said of the universe,
Heard it and heard of several thousand years;
It is middling well as far as it goes . . . . but is that all?

Magnifying and applying come I,
Outbidding at the start the old cautious hucksters,
The most they offer for mankind and eternity less than a spirt
of my own seminal wet,
Taking myself the exact dimensions of Jehovah and laying them away,
Lithographing Kronos and Zeus his son, and Hercules his grandson,
Buying drafts of Osiris and Isis and Belus and Brahma and Adonai,
In my portfolio placing Manito loose, and Allah on a leaf,
and the crucifix engraved,
With Odin, and the hideous-faced Mexitli, and all idols and images,
Honestly taking them all for what they are worth, and not a cent more,
Admitting they were alive and did the work of their day,
Admitting they bore mites as for unfledged birds who have now
to rise and fly and sing for themselves,
Accepting the rough deific sketches to fill out better in myself . . . .
bestowing them freely on each man and woman I see,
Discovering as much or more in a framer framing a house,
Putting higher claims for him there with his rolled-up sleeves,
driving the mallet and chisel;
Not objecting to special revelations . . . . considering a curl of smoke
or a hair on the back of my hand as curious as any revelation;
Those ahold of fire-engines and hook-and-ladder ropes more to me
than the gods of the antique wars,
Minding their voices peal through the crash of destruction,
Their brawny limbs passing safe over charred laths . . . .
their white foreheads whole and unhurt out of the flames;
By the mechanic's wife with her babe at her nipple interceding
for every person born;
Three scythes at harvest whizzing in a row from three lusty angels
with shirts bagged out at their waists;
The snag-toothed hostler with red hair redeeming sins past and to come,
Selling all he possesses and traveling on foot to fee lawyers
for his brother and sit by him while he is tried for forgery:
What was strewn in the amplest strewing the square rod about me,
and not filling the square rod then;
The bull and the bug never worshipped half enough,
Dung and dirt more admirable than was dreamed,

The supernatural of no account . . . . myself waiting my time
to be one of the supremes,
The day getting ready for me when I shall do as much good as the best,
and be as prodigious,
Guessing when I am it will not tickle me much to receive puffs
out of pulpit or print;
By my life-lumps! becoming already a creator!
Putting myself here and now to the ambushed womb of the shadows!

. . . . A call in the midst of the crowd,
My own voice, orotund sweeping and final.

Come my children,
Come my boys and girls, and my women and household and intimates,
Now the performer launches his nerve . . . . he has passed his prelude
on the reeds within.

Easily written loosefingered chords! I feel the thrum of their climax
and close.

My head evolves on my neck,
Music rolls, but not from the organ . . . . folks are around me,
but they are no household of mine.

Ever the hard and unsunk ground,
Ever the eaters and drinkers . . . . ever the upward and downward sun
. . . . ever the air and the ceaseless tides,
Ever myself and my neighbors, refreshing and wicked and real,
Ever the old inexplicable query . . . . ever that thorned thumb—
that breath of itches and thirsts,
Ever the vexer's hoot! hoot! till we find where the sly one hides
and bring him forth;
Ever love . . . . ever the sobbing liquid of life,
Ever the bandage under the chin . . . . ever the tressels° of death.

Here and there with dimes on the eyes walking,
To feed the greed of the belly the brains liberally spooning,
Tickets buying or taking or selling, but in to the feast never once going;
Many sweating and ploughing and thrashing, and then the chaff
for payment receiving,
A few idly owning, and they the wheat continually claiming.

This is the city . . . . and I am one of the citizens;
Whatever interests the rest interests me . . . . politics, churches,
newspapers, schools,
Benevolent societies, improvements, banks, tariffs, steamships,
factories, markets,
Stocks and stores and real estate and personal estate.

They who piddle and patter here in collars and tailed coats . . . .
I am aware who they are . . . . and that they are not worms or fleas,
I acknowledge the duplicates of myself under all the scrape-lipped
and pipe-legged concealments.

The weakest and shallowest is deathless with me,
What I do and say the same waits for them,
Every thought that flounders in me the same flounders in them.

I know perfectly well my own egotism,
And know my omniverous words, and cannot say any less,
And would fetch you whoever you are flush with myself.

My words are words of a questioning, and to indicate reality;
This printed and bound book . . . . but the printer
and the printing-office boy?
The marriage estate and settlement . . . . but the body and mind
of the bridegroom? also those of the bride?
The panorama of the sea . . . . but the sea itself?
The well-taken photographs . . . . but your wife or friend
close and solid in your arms?
The fleet of ships of the line and all the modern improvements . . . .
but the craft and pluck of the admiral?
The dishes and fare and furniture . . . . but the host and hostess,
and the look out of their eyes?
The sky up there . . . . yet here or next door or across the way?
The saints and sages in history . . . . but you yourself?
Sermons and creeds and theology . . . . but the human brain,
and what is called reason, and what is called love,
and what is called life?

I do not despise you priests;
My faith is the greatest of faiths and the least of faiths,
Enclosing all worship ancient and modern, and all between
ancient and modern,

Believing I shall come again upon the earth after five thousand years,
Waiting responses from oracles . . . . honoring the gods . . . . saluting the sun,
Making a fetish of the first rock or stump . . . . powowing with sticks in the circle of obis,°
Helping the lama or brahmin as he trims the lamps of the idols,
Dancing yet through the streets in a phallic procession . . . . rapt and austere in the woods, a gymnosophist,°
Drinking mead from the skull-cup . . . . to shasta and vedas° admirant . . . . minding the koran,
Walking the teokallis,° spotted with gore from the stone and knife—beating the serpent-skin drum;
Accepting the gospels, accepting him that was crucified, knowing assuredly that he is divine,
To the mass kneeling—to the puritan's prayer rising—sitting patiently in a pew,
Ranting and frothing in my insane crisis—waiting dead-like till my spirit arouses me;
Looking forth on pavement and land, and outside of pavement and land,
Belonging to the winders of the circuit of circuits.

One of that centripetal and centrifugal gang,
I turn and talk like a man leaving charges before a journey.

Down-hearted doubters, dull and excluded,
Frivolous sullen moping angry affected disheartened atheistical,
I know every one of you, and know the unspoken interrogatories,
By experience I know them.

How the flukes splash!
How they contort rapid as lightning, with spasms and spouts of blood!

Be at peace bloody flukes of doubters and sullen mopers,
I take my place among you as much as among any;
The past is the push of you and me and all precisely the same,
And the day and night are for you and me and all,°
And what is yet untried and afterward is for you and me and all.

I do not know what is untried and afterward,
But I do know it is sure and alive and sufficient.

Each who passes is considered, and each who stops is considered,
and not a single one can it fail.

It cannot fail the young man who died and was buried,
Nor the young woman who died and was put by his side,
Nor the little child that peeped in at the door and then drew back
and was never seen again,
Nor the old man who has lived without purpose, and feels it
with bitterness worse than gall,
Nor him in the poorhouse tubercled by rum and the bad disorder,
Nor the numberless slaughtered and wrecked . . . . nor the brutish koboo,°
called the ordure of humanity,
Nor the sacs merely floating with open mouths for food to slip in,
Nor any thing in the earth, or down in the oldest graves of the earth,
Nor any thing in the myriads of spheres, nor one of the myriads
of myriads that inhabit them,
Nor the present, nor the least wisp that is known.

It is time to explain myself . . . . let us stand up.

What is known I strip away . . . . I launch all men and women forward
with me into the unknown.

The clock indicates the moment . . . . but what does eternity indicate?

Eternity lies in bottomless reservoirs . . . . its buckets are rising
forever and ever,
They pour and they pour and they exhale away.

We have thus far exhausted trillions of winters and summers;
There are trillions ahead, and trillions ahead of them.

Births have brought us richness and variety,
And other births will bring us richness and variety.

I do not call one greater and one smaller,
That which fills its period and place is equal to any.

Were mankind murderous or jealous upon you my brother or my sister?
I am sorry for you . . . . they are not murderous or jealous upon me;
All has been gentle with me . . . . . . I keep no account with lamentation;
What have I to do with lamentation?

I am an acme of things accomplished, and I an encloser of things to be.

My feet strike an apex of the apices of the stairs,
On every step bunches of ages, and larger bunches between the steps,
All below duly traveled—and still I mount and mount.

Rise after rise bow the phantoms behind me,
Afar down I see the huge first Nothing, the vapor from the nostrils
of death,
I know I was even there . . . . I waited unseen and always,
And slept while God carried me through the lethargic mist,
And took my time . . . . and took no hurt from the fœtid carbon.

Long I was hugged close . . . . long and long.

Immense have been the preparations for me,
Faithful and friendly the arms that have helped me.

Cycles ferried my cradle, rowing and rowing like cheerful boatmen;
For room to me stars kept aside in their own rings,
They sent influences to look after what was to hold me.

Before I was born out of my mother generations guided me,
My embryo has never been torpid . . . . nothing could overlay it;
For it the nebula cohered to an orb . . . . the long slow strata piled
to rest it on . . . . vast vegetables gave it sustenance,
Monstrous sauroids° transported it in their mouths and deposited it
with care.

All forces have been steadily employed to complete and delight me,
Now I stand on this spot with my soul.

Span of youth! Ever-pushed elasticity! Manhood balanced and florid
and full!

My lovers suffocate me!
Crowding my lips, and thick in the pores of my skin,
Jostling me through streets and public halls . . . . coming naked to me
at night,
Crying by day Ahoy from the rocks of the river . . . .
swinging and chirping over my head,
Calling my name from flowerbeds or vines or tangled underbrush,

Or while I swim in the bath . . . . or drink from the pump at the corner
. . . . or the curtain is down at the opera . . . . or I glimpse
at a woman's face in the railroad car;
Lighting on every moment of my life,
Bussing my body with soft and balsamic busses,
Noiselessly passing handfuls out of their hearts and giving them
to be mine.

Old age superbly rising! Ineffable grace of dying days!

Every condition promulges not only itself . . . . it promulges
what grows after and out of itself,
And the dark hush promulges as much as any.

I open my scuttle at night and see the far-sprinkled systems,
And all I see, multiplied as high as I can cipher, edge but the rim
of the farther systems.

Wider and wider they spread, expanding and always expanding,
Outward and outward and forever outward.

My sun has his sun, and round him obediently wheels,
He joins with his partners a group of superior circuit,
And greater sets follow, making specks of the greatest inside them.

There is no stoppage, and never can be stoppage,
If I and you and the worlds and all beneath or upon their surfaces,
and all the palpable life, were this moment reduced back
to a pallid float, it would not avail in the long run,
We should surely bring up again where we now stand,
And as surely go as much farther, and then farther and farther.

A few quadrillions of eras, a few octillions of cubic leagues,
do not hazard the span, or make it impatient,
They are but parts . . . . any thing is but a part.

See ever so far . . . . there is limitless space outside of that,
Count ever so much . . . . there is limitless time around that.

Our rendezvous is fitly appointed . . . . God will be there and wait
till we come.

I know I have the best of time and space—and that I was never measured, and never will be measured.

I tramp a perpetual journey,
My signs are a rain-proof coat and good shoes and a staff cut from the woods;
No friend of mine takes his ease in my chair,
I have no chair, nor church nor philosophy;
I lead no man to a dinner-table or library or exchange,
But each man and each woman of you I lead upon a knoll,
My left hand hooks you round the waist,
My right hand points to landscapes of continents, and a plain public road.

Not I, not any one else can travel that road for you,
You must travel it for yourself.

It is not far . . . . it is within reach,
Perhaps you have been on it since you were born, and did not know,
Perhaps it is every where on water and on land.

Shoulder your duds, and I will mine, and let us hasten forth;
Wonderful cities and free nations we shall fetch as we go.

If you tire, give me both burdens, and the rest the chuff of your hand on my hip,
And in due time you shall repay the same service to me;
For after we start we never lie by again.

This day before dawn I ascended a hill and looked at the crowded heaven,
And I said to my spirit, When we become the enfolders of those orbs and the pleasure and knowledge of every thing in them, shall we be filled and satisfied then?
And my spirit said No, we level that lift to pass and continue beyond.

You are also asking me questions, and I hear you;
I answer that I cannot answer . . . . you must find out for yourself.

Sit awhile wayfarer,
Here are bisquits to eat and here is milk to drink,
But as soon as you sleep and renew yourself in sweet clothes I will certainly kiss you with my goodbye kiss and open the gate for your egress hence.

Long enough have you dreamed contemptible dreams,
Now I wash the gum from your eyes,
You must habit yourself to the dazzle of the light and of every moment
of your life.

Long have you timidly waded, holding a plank by the shore,
Now I will you to be a bold swimmer,
To jump off in the midst of the sea, and rise again and nod to me
and shout, and laughingly dash with your hair.

I am the teacher of athletes,
He that by me spreads a wider breast than my own proves the width
of my own,
He most honors my style who learns under it to destroy the teacher.

The boy I love, the same becomes a man not through derived power
but in his own right,
Wicked, rather than virtuous out of conformity or fear,
Fond of his sweetheart, relishing well his steak,
Unrequited love or a slight cutting him worse than a wound cuts,
First rate to ride, to fight, to hit the bull's eye, to sail a skiff,
to sing a song or play on the banjo,
Preferring scars and faces pitted with smallpox over all latherers
and those that keep out of the sun.

I teach straying from me, yet who can stray from me?
I follow you whoever you are from the present hour;
My words itch at your ears till you understand them.

I do not say these things for a dollar, or to fill up the time
while I wait for a boat;
It is you talking just as much as myself . . . . I act as the tongue of you,
It was tied in your mouth . . . . in mine it begins to be loosened.

I swear I will never mention love or death inside a house,
And I swear I never will translate myself at all, only to him or her
who privately stays with me in the open air.

If you would understand me go to the heights or water-shore,
The nearest gnat is an explanation and a drop or the motion of waves
a key,
The maul the oar and the handsaw second my words.

No shuttered room or school can commune with me,
But roughs and little children better than they.

The young mechanic is closest to me . . . . he knows me pretty well,
The woodman that takes his axe and jug with him shall take me with him
all day,
The farmboy ploughing in the field feels good at the sound of my voice,
In vessels that sail my words must sail . . . . I go with fishermen
and seamen, and love them,
My face rubs to the hunter's face when he lies down alone in his blanket,
The driver thinking of me does not mind the jolt of his wagon,
The young mother and old mother shall comprehend me,
The girl and the wife rest the needle a moment and forget where they are,
They and all would resume what I have told them.

I have said that the soul is not more than the body,
And I have said that the body is not more than the soul,
And nothing, not God, is greater to one than one's-self is,
And whoever walks a furlong without sympathy walks to his own funeral,
dressed in his shroud,
And I or you pocketless of a dime may purchase the pick of the earth,
And to glance with an eye or show a bean in its pod confounds
the learning of all times,
And there is no trade or employment but the young man following it
may become a hero,
And there is no object so soft but it makes a hub for the wheeled universe,
And any man or woman shall stand cool and supercilious
before a million universes.

And I call to mankind, Be not curious about God,
For I who am curious about each am not curious about God,
No array of terms can say how much I am at peace about God
and about death.

I hear and behold God in every object, yet I understand God
not in the least,
Nor do I understand who there can be more wonderful than myself.

Why should I wish to see God better than this day?
I see something of God each hour of the twenty-four,
and each moment then,
In the faces of men and women I see God, and in my own face in the glass;

I find letters from God dropped in the street, and every one is signed
by God's name,
And I leave them where they are, for I know that others will
punctually come forever and ever.

And as to you death, and you bitter hug of mortality . . . .
it is idle to try to alarm me.

To his work without flinching the accoucheur° comes,
I see the elderhand pressing receiving supporting,
I recline by the sills of the exquisite flexible doors . . . .
and mark the outlet, and mark the relief and escape.

And as to you corpse I think you are good manure,
but that does not offend me,
I smell the white roses sweetscented and growing,
I reach to the leafy lips . . . . I reach to the polished breasts of melons.

And as to you life, I reckon you are the leavings of many deaths,
No doubt I have died myself ten thousand times before.

I hear you whispering there O stars of heaven,
O suns . . . . O grass of graves . . . . O perpetual transfers and promotions
. . . . if you do not say anything how can I say anything?

Of the turbid pool that lies in the autumn forest,
Of the moon that descends the steeps of the soughing twilight,
Toss, sparkles of day and dusk . . . . toss on the black stems that decay
in the muck,
Toss to the moaning gibberish of the dry limbs.

I ascend from the moon . . . . I ascend from the night,
And perceive of the ghastly glitter the sunbeams reflected,
And debouch to the steady and central from the offspring great or small.

There is that in me . . . . I do not know what it is . . . . but I know it is in me.

Wrenched and sweaty . . . . calm and cool then my body becomes;
I sleep . . . . I sleep long.

I do not know it . . . . it is without name . . . . it is a word unsaid,
It is not in any dictionary or utterance or symbol.

Something it swings on more than the earth I swing on,
To it the creation is the friend whose embracing awakes me.

Perhaps I might tell more . . . . Outlines! I plead for my brothers
and sisters.

Do you see O my brothers and sisters?
It is not chaos or death . . . . it is form and union and plan . . . .
it is eternal life . . . . it is happiness.

The past and present wilt . . . . I have filled them and emptied them,
And proceed to fill my next fold of the future.

Listener up there! Here you . . . . what have you to confide to me?
Look in my face while I snuff the sidle of evening,
Talk honestly, for no one else hears you, and I stay only a minute longer.

Do I contradict myself?
Very well then . . . . I contradict myself;
I am large . . . . I contain multitudes.

I concentrate toward them that are nigh . . . . I wait on the door-slab.

Who has done his day's work and will soonest be through with his supper?
Who wishes to walk with me?

Will you speak before I am gone? Will you prove already too late?

The spotted hawk swoops by and accuses me . . . . he complains
of my gab and my loitering.

I too am not a bit tamed . . . . I too am untranslatable,
I sound my barbaric yawp over the roofs of the world.

The last scud of day holds back for me,
It flings my likeness after the rest and true as any on the shadowed wilds,
It coaxes me to the vapor and the dusk.

I depart as air . . . . I shake my white locks at the runaway sun,
I effuse my flesh in eddies and drift it in lacy jags.

I bequeath myself to the dirt to grow from the grass I love,
If you want me again look for me under your bootsoles.

You will hardly know who I am or what I mean,
But I shall be good health to you nevertheless,
And filter and fibre your blood.

Failing to fetch me at first keep encouraged,
Missing me one place search another,
I stop some where waiting for you

Leaves of Grass

COME closer to me,
Push close my lovers and take the best I possess,
Yield closer and closer and give me the best you possess.

This is unfinished business with me . . . . how is it with you?
I was chilled with the cold types and cylinder and wet paper between us.

I pass so poorly with paper and types . . . . I must pass with the contact
of bodies and souls.

I do not thank you for liking me as I am, and liking the touch of me
. . . . I know that it is good for you to do so.

Were all educations practical and ornamental well displayed out of me,
what would it amount to?
Were I as the head teacher or charitable proprietor or wise statesman,
what would it amount to?
Were I to you as the boss employing and paying you,
would that satisfy you?

The learned and virtuous and benevolent, and the usual terms;
A man like me, and never the usual terms.

Neither a servant nor a master am I,
I take no sooner a large price than a small price . . . . I will have my own whoever enjoys me,
I will be even with you, and you shall be even with me.

If you are a workman or workwoman I stand as nigh as the nighest that works in the same shop,
If you bestow gifts on your brother or dearest friend, I demand as good as your brother or dearest friend,
If your lover or husband or wife is welcome by day or night, I must be personally as welcome;
If you have become degraded or ill, then I will become so for your sake;
If you remember your foolish and outlawed deeds, do you think I cannot remember my foolish and outlawed deeds?
If you carouse at the table I say I will carouse at the opposite side of the table;
If you meet some stranger in the street and love him or her, do I not often meet strangers in the street and love them?
If you see a good deal remarkable in me I see just as much remarkable in you.

Why what have you thought of yourself?
Is it you then that thought yourself less?
Is it you that thought the President greater than you? or the rich better off than you? or the educated wiser than you?

Because you are greasy or pimpled—or that you was once drunk, or a thief, or diseased, or rheumatic, or a prostitute— or are so now—or from frivolity or impotence or that you are no scholar, and never saw your name in print . . . . do you give in that you are any less immortal?

Souls of men and women! it is not you I call unseen, unheard, untouchable and untouching;
It is not you I go argue pro and con about, and to settle whether you are alive or no;
I own publicly who you are, if nobody else owns . . . . and see and hear you, and what you give and take;
What is there you cannot give and take?

I see not merely that you are polite or whitefaced . . . . married or single . . . . citizens of old states or citizens of new states . . . .

eminent in some profession . . . . a lady or gentleman in a parlor
. . . . or dressed in the jail uniform . . . . or pulpit uniform,
Not only the free Utahan, Kansian, or Arkansian . . . .
not only the free Cuban . . . . not merely the slave . . . .
not Mexican native, or Flatfoot, or negro from Africa,
Iroquois eating the warflesh—fishtearer in his lair of rocks and sand
. . . . Esquimaux in the dark cold snowhouse . . . . Chinese
with his transverse eyes . . . . Bedowee—or wandering nomad—
or tabounschik at the head of his droves,
Grown, half-grown, and babe—of this country and every country,
indoors and outdoors I see . . . . and all else is behind
or through them.

The wife—and she is not one jot less than the husband,
The daughter—and she is just as good as the son,
The mother—and she is every bit as much as the father.

Offspring of those not rich—boys apprenticed to trades,
Young fellows working on farms and old fellows working on farms;
The naive . . . . the simple and hardy . . . . he going to the polls to vote
. . . . he who has a good time, and he who has a bad time;
Mechanics, southerners, new arrivals, sailors, mano'warsmen,
merchantmen, coasters,
All these I see . . . . but nigher and farther the same I see;
None shall escape me, and none shall wish to escape me.

I bring what you much need, yet always have,
I bring not money or amours or dress or eating . . . . but I bring as good;
And send no agent or medium . . . . and offer no representative of value—
but offer the value itself.

There is something that comes home to one now and perpetually,
It is not what is printed or preached or discussed . . . .
it eludes discussion and print,
It is not to be put in a book . . . . it is not in this book,
It is for you whoever you are . . . . it is no farther from you
than your hearing and sight are from you,
It is hinted by nearest and commonest and readiest . . . . it is not them,
though it is endlessly provoked by them . . . . What is there
ready and near you now?

You may read in many languages and read nothing about it;
You may read the President's message and read nothing about it there,
Nothing in the reports from the state department or treasury department
. . . . or in the daily papers, or the weekly papers,
Or in the census returns or assessors' returns or prices current
or any accounts of stock.

The sun and stars that float in the open air . . . . the appleshaped earth
and we upon it . . . . surely the drift of them is something grand;
I do not know what it is except that it is grand, and that it is happiness,
And that the enclosing purport of us here is not a speculation,
or bon-mot or reconnoissance,
And that it is not something which by luck may turn out well for us,
and without luck must be a failure for us,
And not something which may yet be retracted in a certain contingency.

The light and shade—the curious sense of body and identity—
the greed that with perfect complaisance devours all things—
the endless pride and outstretching of man—unspeakable joys
and sorrows,
The wonder every one sees in every one else he sees . . . .
and the wonders that fill each minute of time forever
and each acre of surface and space forever,
Have you reckoned them as mainly for a trade or farmwork?
or for the profits of a store? or to achieve yourself a position?
or to fill a gentleman's leisure or a lady's leisure?

Have you reckoned the landscape took substance and form
that it might be painted in a picture?
Or men and women that they might be written of, and songs sung?
Or the attraction of gravity and the great laws and harmonious
combinations and the fluids of the air as subjects for the savans?°
Or the brown land and the blue sea for maps and charts?
Or the stars to be put in constellations and named fancy names?
Or that the growth of seeds is for agricultural tables or agriculture itself?

Old institutions . . . . these arts libraries legends collections—
and the practice handed along in manufactures . . . .
will we rate them so high?
Will we rate our prudence and business so high? . . . . I have no objection,
I rate them as high as the highest . . . . but a child born of a woman
and man I rate beyond all rate.

We thought our Union grand and our Constitution grand;
I do not say they are not grand and good—for they are,
I am this day just as much in love with them as you,
But I am eternally in love with you and with all my fellows
upon the earth.

We consider the bibles and religions divine . . . . I do not say
they are not divine,
I say they have all grown out of you and may grow out of you still,
It is not they who give the life . . . . it is you who give the life;
Leaves are not more shed from the trees or trees from the earth
than they are shed out of you.

The sum of all known value and respect I add up in you whoever you are;
The President is up there in the White House for you . . . . it is not you
who are here for him,
The Secretaries act in their bureaus for you . . . . not you here for them,
The Congress convenes every December for you,
Laws, courts, the forming of states, the charters of cities, the going
and coming of commerce and mails are all for you.

All doctrines, all politics and civilization exurge from you,
All sculpture and monuments and anything inscribed anywhere
are tallied in you,
The gist of histories and statistics as far back as the records reach
is in you this hour—and myths and tales the same;
If you were not breathing and walking here where would they all be?
The most renowned poems would be ashes . . . . orations and plays
would be vacuums.

All architecture is what you do to it when you look upon it;
Did you think it was in the white or gray stone? or the lines
of the arches and cornices?

All music is what awakens from you when you are reminded
by the instruments,
It is not the violins and the cornets . . . . it is not the oboe
nor the beating drums—nor the notes of the baritone singer
singing his sweet romanza . . . . nor those of the men's chorus,
nor those of the women's chorus,
It is nearer and farther than they.

Will the whole come back then?
Can each see the signs of the best by a look in the lookingglass? Is there nothing greater or more?
Does all sit there with you and here with me?

The old forever new things . . . . you foolish child! . . . . the closest simplest things—this moment with you,
Your person and every particle that relates to your person,
The pulses of your brain waiting their chance and encouragement at every deed or sight;
Anything you do in public by day, and anything you do in secret betweendays,
What is called right and what is called wrong . . . . what you behold or touch . . . . what causes your anger or wonder,
The anklechain of the slave, the bed of the bedhouse, the cards of the gambler, the plates of the forger;
What is seen or learned in the street, or intuitively learned,
What is learned in the public school—spelling, reading, writing and ciphering . . . . the blackboard and the teacher's diagrams;
The panes of the windows and all that appears through them . . . . the going forth in the morning and the aimless spending of the day
(What is it that you made money? what is it that you got what you wanted?);
The usual routine . . . . the workshop, factory, yard, office, store, or desk;
The jaunt of hunting or fishing, or the life of hunting or fishing,
Pasturelife, foddering, milking and herding, and all the personnel and usages;
The plum-orchard and apple-orchard . . . . gardening . . seedlings, cuttings, flowers and vines,
Grains and manures . . marl, clay, loam . . the subsoil plough . . the shovel and pick and rake and hoe . . irrigation and draining;
The currycomb . . the horse-cloth . . the halter and bridle and bits . . the very wisps of straw,
The barn and barn-yard . . the bins and mangers . . the mows and racks;
Manufactures . . commerce . . engineering . . the building of cities, and every trade carried on there . . and the implements of every trade,
The anvil and tongs and hammer . . the axe and wedge . . the square and mitre and jointer and smoothingplane;

The plumbob and trowel and level . . the wall-scaffold, and the work
of walls and ceilings . . or any mason-work:
The ship's compass . . the sailor's tarpaulin . . the stays and lanyards,
and the ground-tackle for anchoring or mooring,
The sloop's tiller . . the pilot's wheel and bell . . the yacht or fish-smack
. . the great gay-pennanted three-hundred-foot steamboat
under full headway, with her proud fat breasts and her delicate
swift-flashing paddles;
The trail and line and hooks and sinkers . . the seine, and hauling the seine;
Smallarms and rifles . . . . the powder and shot and caps and wadding
. . . . the ordnance for war . . . the carriages:
Everyday objects . . . . the housechairs, the carpet, the bed
and the counterpane of the bed, and him or her sleeping
at night, and the wind blowing, and the indefinite noises:
The snowstorm or rainstorm . . . . the tow-trowsers . . . .
the lodge-hut in the woods, and the still-hunt:
City and country . . fireplace and candle . . gaslight and heater
and aqueduct;
The message of the governor, mayor, or chief of police . . . .
the dishes of breakfast or dinner or supper;
The bunkroom, the fire-engine, the string-team, and the car
or truck behind;
The paper I write on or you write on . . and every word we write . .
and every cross and twirl of the pen . . and the curious way
we write what we think . . . . yet very faintly;
The directory, the detector, the ledger . . . . the books in ranks
or the bookshelves . . . . the clock attached to the wall,
The ring on your finger . . the lady's wristlet . . the hammers
of stonebreakers or coppersmiths . . the druggist's vials and jars;
The etui of surgical instruments, and the etui of oculist's or aurist's
instruments, or dentist's instruments;
Glassblowing, grinding of wheat and corn . . casting, and what is cast . .
tinroofing, shingledressing,
Shipcarpentering, flagging of sidewalks by flaggers . . dockbuilding,
fishcuring, ferrying;
The pump, the piledriver, the great derrick . . the coalkiln and brickkiln,
Ironworks or whiteleadworks . . the sugarhouse . . steam-saws,
and the great mills and factories;
The cottonbale . . the stevedore's hook . . the saw and buck
of the sawyer . . the screen of the coalscreener . . the mould
of the moulder . . the workingknife of the butcher;

The cylinder press . . the handpress . . the frisket and tympan° . .
the compositor's stick and rule,
The implements for daguerreotyping . . . . the tools of the rigger
or grappler or sailmaker or blockmaker,
Goods of guttapercha or papiermache . . . . colors and brushes . . . .
glaziers' implements,
The veneer and gluepot . . the confectioner's ornaments . .
the decanter and glasses . . the shears and flatiron;
The awl and kneestrap . . the pint measure and quart measure . .
the counter and stool . . the writingpen of quill or metal;
Billiards and tenpins . . . . the ladders and hanging ropes
of the gymnasium, and the manly exercises;
The designs for wallpaper or oilcloths or carpets . . . . the fancies
for goods for women . . . . the bookbinder's stamps;
Leatherdressing, coachmaking, boilermaking, ropetwisting,
distilling, signpainting, limeburning, coopering, cottonpicking,
The walkingbeam of the steam-engine . . the throttle and governors,
and the up and down rods,
Stavemachines and plainingmachines . . . . the cart of the carman . .
the omnibus . . the ponderous dray;
The snowplough and two engines pushing it . . . . the ride
in the express train of only one car . . . . the swift go
through a howling storm;
The bearhunt or coonhunt . . . . the bonfire of shavings in the open lot
in the city . . the crowd of children watching;
The blows of the fighting-man . . the upper cut and one-two-three;
The shopwindows . . . . the coffins in the sexton's wareroom . . . .
the fruit on the fruitstand . . . . the beef on the butcher's stall,
The bread and cakes in the bakery . . . . the white and red pork
in the pork-store;
The milliner's ribbons . . the dressmaker's patterns . . . . the tea-table . .
the homemade sweetmeats:
The column of wants in the one-cent paper . . the news by telegraph . . . .
the amusements and operas and shows;
The cotton and woolen and linen you wear . . . . the money you make
and spend;
Your room and bedroom . . . . your piano-forte . . . . the stove and cookpans,
The house you live in . . . . the rent . . . . the other tenants . . . .
the deposite in the savings-bank . . . . the trade at the grocery,
The pay on Saturday night . . . . the going home, and the purchases;
In them the heft of the heaviest . . . . in them far more than you estimated,
and far less also,

In them, not yourself . . . . you and your soul enclose all things,
regardless of estimation,
In them your themes and hints and provokers . . if not, the whole earth
has no themes or hints or provokers, and never had.

I do not affirm what you see beyond is futile . . . . I do not advise you
to stop,
I do not say leadings you thought great are not great,
But I say that none lead to greater or sadder or happier than those lead to.

Will you seek afar off? You surely come back at last,
In things best known to you finding the best or as good as the best,
In folks nearest to you finding also the sweetest and strongest
and lovingest,
Happiness not in another place, but this place . . not for another hour,
but this hour,
Man in the first you see or touch . . . . always in your friend or brother
or nighest neighbor . . . . Woman in your mother or lover or wife,
And all else thus far known giving place to men and women.

When the psalm sings instead of the singer,
When the script preaches instead of the preacher,
When the pulpit descends and goes instead of the carver that carved
the supporting desk,
When the sacred vessels or the bits of the eucharist, or the lath and plast,
procreate as effectually as the young silversmiths or bakers,
or the masons in their overalls,
When a university course convinces like a slumbering woman and child
convince,
When the minted gold in the vault smiles like the nightwatchman's daughter,
When warrantee deeds loafe in chairs opposite and are
my friendly companions,
I intend to reach them my hand and make as much of them as I do
of men and women.

Leaves of Grass

To think of time . . . . to think through the retrospection,
To think of today . . and the ages continued henceforward.

Have you guessed you yourself would not continue? Have you
dreaded those earth-beetles?
Have you feared the future would be nothing to you?

Is today nothing? Is the beginningless past nothing?
If the future is nothing they are just as surely nothing.

To think that the sun rose in the east . . . . that men and women were
flexible and real and alive . . . . that every thing was real and alive;
To think that you and I did not see feel think nor bear our part,
To think that we are now here and bear our part.

Not a day passes . . not a minute or second without an accouchement;
Not a day passes . . not a minute or second without a corpse.

When the dull nights are over, and the dull days also,
When the soreness of lying so much in bed is over,
When the physician, after long putting off, gives the silent
and terrible look for an answer,
When the children come hurried and weeping, and the brothers
and sisters have been sent for,
When medicines stand unused on the shelf, and the camphor-smell
has pervaded the rooms,
When the faithful hand of the living does not desert the hand
of the dying,
When the twitching lips press lightly on the forehead of the dying,
When the breath ceases and the pulse of the heart ceases,
Then the corpse-limbs stretch on the bed, and the living look
upon them,
They are palpable as the living are palpable.

The living look upon the corpse with their eyesight,
But without eyesight lingers a different living and looks curiously
on the corpse.

To think that the rivers will come to flow, and the snow fall,
and fruits ripen . . and act upon others as upon us now . . . .
yet not act upon us;
To think of all these wonders of city and country . . and others taking
great interest in them . . and we taking small interest in them.

To think how eager we are in building our houses,
To think others shall be just as eager . . and we quite indifferent.

I see one building the house that serves him a few years . . . .
or seventy or eighty years at most;
I see one building the house that serves him longer than that.

Slowmoving and black lines creep over the whole earth . . . .
they never cease . . . . they are the burial lines,
He that was President was buried, and he that is now President
shall surely be buried.

Cold dash of waves at the ferrywharf,
Posh and ice in the river . . . . half-frozen mud in the streets,
A gray discouraged sky overhead . . . . the short last daylight
of December,
A hearse and stages . . . . other vehicles give place,
The funeral of an old stagedriver . . . . the cortege mostly drivers.

Rapid the trot to the cemetery,
Duly rattles the deathbell . . . . the gate is passed . . . . the grave
is halted at . . . . the living alight . . . . the hearse uncloses,
The coffin is lowered and settled . . . . the whip is laid on the coffin,
The earth is swiftly shovelled in . . . . a minute . . no one moves
or speaks . . . . it is done,
He is decently put away . . . . is there anything more?

He was a goodfellow,
Freemouthed, quicktempered, not badlooking, able to take his own part,
Witty, sensitive to a slight, ready with life or death for a friend,
Fond of women, . . played some . . eat hearty and drank hearty,

Had known what it was to be flush . . grew lowspirited toward the last . .
sickened . . was helped by a contribution,
Died aged forty-one years . . and that was his funeral.

Thumb extended or finger uplifted,
Apron, cape, gloves, strap . . . . wetweather clothes . . . .
whip carefully chosen . . . . boss, spotter, starter, and hostler,
Somebody loafing on you, or you loafing on somebody . . . . headway . . . .
man before and man behind,
Good day's work or bad day's work . . . . pet stock or mean stock
. . . . first out or last out . . . . turning in at night,
To think that these are so much and so nigh to other drivers . .
and he there takes no interest in them.

The markets, the government, the workingman's wages . . . .
to think what account they are through our nights and days;
To think that other workingmen will make just as great account of them . .
yet we make little or no account.

The vulgar and the refined . . . . what you call sin and what you
call goodness . . to think how wide a difference;
To think the difference will still continue to others, yet we lie
beyond the difference.

To think how much pleasure there is!
Have you pleasure from looking at the sky? Have you pleasure
from poems?
Do you enjoy yourself in the city? or engaged in business? or planning
a nomination and election? or with your wife and family?
Or with your mother and sisters? or in womanly housework?
or the beautiful maternal cares?

These also flow onward to others . . . . you and I flow onward;
But in due time you and I shall take less interest in them.

Your farm and profits and crops . . . . to think how engrossed you are;
To think there will still be farms and profits and crops . . yet for you
of what avail?

What will be will be well—for what is is well,
To take interest is well, and not to take interest shall be well.

The sky continues beautiful . . . . the pleasure of men with women
shall never be sated . . nor the pleasure of women with men . .
nor the pleasure from poems;
The domestic joys, the daily housework or business, the building
of houses—they are not phantasms . . they have weight and form
and location;
The farms and profits and crops . . the markets and wages
and government . . they also are not phantasms;
The difference between sin and goodness is no apparition;
The earth is not an echo . . . . man and his life and all the things
of his life are well-considered.

You are not thrown to the winds . . you gather certainly and safely
around yourself,
Yourself! Yourself! Yourself forever and ever!

It is not to diffuse you that you were born of your mother and father—
it is to identify you,
It is not that you should be undecided, but that you should be decided;
Something long preparing and formless is arrived and formed in you,
You are thenceforth secure, whatever comes or goes.

The threads that were spun are gathered . . . . the weft crosses the warp
. . . . the pattern is systematic.

The preparations have every one been justified;
The orchestra have tuned their instruments sufficiently . . . .
the baton has given the signal.

The guest that was coming . . . . he waited long for reasons . . . .
he is now housed,
He is one of those who are beautiful and happy . . . . he is one of those
that to look upon and be with is enough.

The law of the past cannot be eluded,
The law of the present and future cannot be eluded,
The law of the living cannot be eluded . . . . it is eternal,
The law of promotion and transformation cannot be eluded,
The law of heroes and good-doers cannot be eluded,
The law of drunkards and informers and mean persons cannot be eluded.

Slowmoving and black lines go ceaselessly over the earth,
Northerner goes carried and southerner goes carried . . . . and they
on the Atlantic side and they on the Pacific, and they between,
and all through the Mississippi country . . . . and all over the earth.

The great masters and kosmos are well as they go . . . .
the heroes and good-doers are well,
The known leaders and inventors and the rich owners and pious
and distinguished may be well,
But there is more account than that . . . . there is strict account of all.

The interminable hordes of the ignorant and wicked are not nothing,
The barbarians of Africa and Asia are not nothing,
The common people of Europe are not nothing . . . .
the American aborigines are not nothing,
A zambo or a foreheadless Crowfoot or a Camanche is not nothing,
The infected in the immigrant hospital are not nothing . . . .
the murderer or mean person is not nothing,
The perpetual succession of shallow people are not nothing as they go,
The prostitute is not nothing . . . . the mocker of religion is not nothing
as he goes.

I shall go with the rest . . . . we have satisfaction:
I have dreamed that we are not to be changed so much . . . .
nor the law of us changed;
I have dreamed that heroes and good-doers shall be under the present
and past law,
And that murderers and drunkards and liars shall be under the present
and past law;
For I have dreamed that the law they are under now is enough.

And I have dreamed that the satisfaction is not so much changed . . . .
and that there is no life without satisfaction;
What is the earth? what are body and soul without satisfaction?

I shall go with the rest,
We cannot be stopped at a given point . . . . that is no satisfaction;
To show us a good thing or a few good things for a space of time—
that is no satisfaction;
We must have the indestructible breed of the best, regardless of time.

If otherwise, all these things came but to ashes of dung;
If maggots and rats ended us, then suspicion and treachery and death.

Do you suspect death? If I were to suspect death I should die now,
Do you think I could walk pleasantly and well-suited toward annihilation?

Pleasantly and well-suited I walk,
Whither I walk I cannot define, but I know it is good,
The whole universe indicates that it is good,
The past and the present indicate that it is good.

How beautiful and perfect are the animals! How perfect is my soul!
How perfect the earth, and the minutest thing upon it!
What is called good is perfect, and what is called sin is just as perfect;
The vegetables and minerals are all perfect . . and the imponderable
    fluids are perfect;
Slowly and surely they have passed on to this, and slowly and surely
    they will yet pass on.

O my soul! if I realize you I have satisfaction,
Animals and vegetables! if I realize you I have satisfaction,
Laws of the earth and air! if I realize you I have satisfaction.

I cannot define my satisfaction . . yet it is so,
I cannot define my life . . yet it is so.

I swear I see now that every thing has an eternal soul!
The trees have, rooted in the ground . . . . the weeds of the sea have
    . . . . the animals.

I swear I think there is nothing but immortality!
That the exquisite scheme is for it, and the nebulous float is for it,
    and the cohering is for it,
And all preparation is for it . . and identity is for it . .
    and life and death are for it.

Leaves of Grass

I WANDER all night in my vision,
Stepping with light feet . . . . swiftly and noiselessly stepping
and stopping,
Bending with open eyes over the shut eyes of sleepers;
Wandering and confused . . . . lost to myself . . . . ill-assorted . . . .
contradictory,
Pausing and gazing and bending and stopping.

How solemn they look there, stretched and still;
How quiet they breathe, the little children in their cradles.

The wretched features of ennuyees, the white features of corpses,
the livid faces of drunkards, the sick-gray faces of onanists,
The gashed bodies on battlefields, the insane in their
strong-doored rooms, the sacred idiots,
The newborn emerging from gates and the dying emerging from gates,
The night pervades them and enfolds them.

The married couple sleep calmly in their bed, he with his palm on the hip
of the wife, and she with her palm on the hip of the husband,
The sisters sleep lovingly side by side in their bed,
The men sleep lovingly side by side in theirs,
And the mother sleeps with her little child carefully wrapped.

The blind sleep, and the deaf and dumb sleep,
The prisoner sleeps well in the prison . . . . the runaway son sleeps,
The murderer that is to be hung next day . . . . how does he sleep?
And the murdered person . . . . how does he sleep?

The female that loves unrequited sleeps,
And the male that loves unrequited sleeps;
The head of the moneymaker that plotted all day sleeps,
And the enraged and treacherous dispositions sleep.

I stand with drooping eyes by the worstsuffering and restless,
I pass my hands soothingly to and fro a few inches from them;
The restless sink in their beds . . . . they fitfully sleep.

The earth recedes from me into the night,
I saw that it was beautiful . . . . and I see that what is not the earth
is beautiful.

I go from bedside to bedside . . . . I sleep close with the other sleepers,
each in turn;
I dream in my dream all the dreams of the other dreamers,
And I become the other dreamers.

I am a dance . . . . Play up there! the fit is whirling me fast.

I am the everlaughing . . . . it is new moon and twilight,
I see the hiding of douceurs° . . . . I see nimble ghosts whichever way
I look,
Cache° and cache again deep in the ground and sea, and where it is
neither ground or sea.

Well do they do their jobs, those journeymen divine,
Only from me can they hide nothing and would not if they could;
I reckon I am their boss, and they make me a pet besides,
And surround me, and lead me and run ahead when I walk,
And lift their cunning covers and signify me with stretched arms,
and resume the way;
Onward we move, a gay gang of blackguards with mirthshouting music
and wildflapping pennants of joy.

I am the actor and the actress . . . . the voter . . the politician,
The emigrant and the exile . . the criminal that stood in the box,
He who has been famous, and he who shall be famous after today,
The stammerer . . . . . the wellformed person . . the wasted or feeble person.

I am she who adorned herself and folded her hair expectantly,
My truant lover has come and it is dark.

Double yourself and receive me darkness,
Receive me and my lover too . . . . he will not let me go without him.

I roll myself upon you as upon a bed . . . . I resign myself to the dusk.

He whom I call answers me and takes the place of my lover,
He rises with me silently from the bed.

Darkness you are gentler than my lover .... his flesh was sweaty
and panting,
I feel the hot moisture yet that he left me.

My hands are spread forth .. I pass them in all directions,
I would sound up the shadowy shore to which you are journeying.

Be careful, darkness .... already, what was it touched me?
I thought my lover had gone .... else darkness and he are one,
I hear the heart-beat .... I follow .. I fade away.

O hotcheeked and blushing! O foolish hectic!
O for pity's sake, no one must see me now! .... my clothes were stolen
while I was abed,
Now I am thrust forth, where shall I run?

Pier that I saw dimly last night when I looked from the windows,
Pier out from the main, let me catch myself with you and stay....
I will not chafe you;
I feel ashamed to go naked about the world,
And am curious to know where my feet stand .... and what is this
flooding me, childhood or manhood .... and the hunger
that crosses the bridge between.

The cloth laps a first sweet eating and drinking,
Laps life-swelling yolks .... laps ear of rose-corn, milky and just ripened:
The white teeth stay, and the boss-tooth advances in darkness,
And liquor is spilled on lips and bosoms by touching glasses,
and the best liquor afterward.

I descend my western course .... my sinews are flaccid,
Perfume and youth course through me, and I am their wake.

It is my face yellow and wrinkled instead of the old woman's,
I sit low in a strawbottom chair and carefully darn my grandson's stockings.

It is I too .... the sleepless widow looking out on the winter midnight,
I see the sparkles of starshine on the icy and pallid earth.

A shroud I see—and I am the shroud . . . . I wrap a body and lie
in the coffin;
It is dark here underground . . . . it is not evil or pain here . . . .
it is blank here, for reasons.

It seems to me that everything in the light and air ought to be happy;
Whoever is not in his coffin and the dark grave, let him know
he has enough.

I see a beautiful gigantic swimmer swimming naked through the eddies
of the sea,
His brown hair lies close and even to his head . . . . he strikes out
with courageous arms . . . . he urges himself with his legs.

I see his white body . . . . I see his undaunted eyes;
I hate the swift-running eddies that would dash him headforemost
on the rocks.

What are you doing you ruffianly red-trickled waves?
Will you kill the courageous giant? Will you kill him in the prime
of his middle age?

Steady and long he struggles;
He is baffled and banged and bruised . . . . he holds out
while his strength holds out,
The slapping eddies are spotted with his blood . . . . they bear him away
. . . . they roll him and swing him and turn him:
His beautiful body is borne in the circling eddies . . . .
it is continually bruised on rocks,
Swiftly and out of sight is borne the brave corpse.

I turn but do not extricate myself;
Confused . . . . a pastreading . . . . another, but with darkness yet.

The beach is cut by the razory ice-wind . . . . the wreck-guns sound,
The tempest lulls and the moon comes floundering through the drifts.

I look where the ship helplessly heads end on . . . . I hear the burst
as she strikes . . I hear the howls of dismay . . . . they grow
fainter and fainter.

I cannot aid with my wringing fingers;
I can but rush to the surf and let it drench me and freeze upon me.

I search with the crowd . . . . not one of the company is washed
to us alive;
In the morning I help pick up the dead and lay them in rows in a barn.

Now of the old war-days . . the defeat of Brooklyn;°
Washington stands inside the lines . . he stands on the entrenched hills
amid a crowd of officers,
His face is cold and damp . . . . he cannot repress the weeping drops . . . .
he lifts the glass perpetually to his eyes . . . . the color is blanched
from his cheeks,
He sees the slaughter of the southern braves confided to him
by their parents.

The same at last and at last when peace is declared,
He stands in the room of the old tavern . . . . the wellbeloved soldiers
all pass through,
The officers speechless and slow draw near in their turns,
The chief encircles their necks with his arm and kisses them on the cheek,
He kisses lightly the wet cheeks one after another . . . . he shakes hands
and bids goodbye to the army.

Now I tell what my mother told me today as we sat at dinner together,
Of when she was a nearly grown girl living home with her parents
on the old homestead.

A red squaw came one breakfasttime to the old homestead,
On her back she carried a bundle of rushes for rushbottoming chairs;
Her hair straight shiny coarse black and profuse halfenveloped her face,
Her step was free and elastic . . . . her voice sounded exquisitely
as she spoke.

My mother looked in delight and amazement at the stranger,
She looked at the beauty of her tallborne face and full and pliant limbs,
The more she looked upon her she loved her,
Never before had she seen such wonderful beauty and purity;
She made her sit on a bench by the jamb of the fireplace . . . .
she cooked food for her,
She had no work to give her but she gave her remembrance and fondness.

The red squaw staid all the forenoon, and toward the middle
of the afternoon she went away;
O my mother was loth to have her go away,
All the week she thought of her . . . . she watched for her many a month,
She remembered her many a winter and many a summer,
But the red squaw never came nor was heard of there again.

Now Lucifer was not dead . . . . or if he was I am his sorrowful terrible heir;
I have been wronged . . . . I am oppressed . . . . I hate him that oppresses me,
I will either destroy him, or he shall release me.

Damn him! how he does defile me,
How he informs against my brother and sister and takes pay for their blood,
How he laughs when I look down the bend after the steamboat
that carries away my woman.

Now the vast dusk bulk that is the whale's bulk . . . . it seems mine,
Warily, sportsman! though I lie so sleepy and sluggish, my tap is death.

A show of the summer softness . . . . a contact of something unseen . . . .
an amour of the light and air;
I am jealous and overwhelmed with friendliness,
And will go gallivant with the light and the air myself,
And have an unseen something to be in contact with them also.

O love and summer! you are in the dreams and in me,
Autumn and winter are in the dreams . . . . the farmer goes with his thrift,
The droves and crops increase . . . . the barns are wellfilled.

Elements merge in the night . . . . ships make tacks in the dreams . . . .
the sailor sails . . . . the exile returns home,
The fugitive returns unharmed . . . . the immigrant is back beyond months
and years;
The poor Irishman lives in the simple house of his childhood,
with the wellknown neighbors and faces,
They warmly welcome him . . . . he is barefoot again . . . .
he forgets he is welloff;
The Dutchman voyages home, and the Scotchman and Welchman
voyage home . . and the native of the Mediterranean voyages home;
To every port of England and France and Spain enter wellfilled ships;

The Swiss foots it toward his hills . . . . the Prussian goes his way,
and the Hungarian his way, and the Pole goes his way,
The Swede returns, and the Dane and Norwegian return.

The homeward bound and the outward bound,
The beautiful lost swimmer, the ennuyee, the onanist, the female
that loves unrequited, the moneymaker,
The actor and actress . . those through with their parts and those
waiting to commence,
The affectionate boy, the husband and wife, the voter, the nominee
that is chosen and the nominee that has failed,
The great already known, and the great anytime after to day,
The stammerer, the sick, the perfectformed, the homely,
The criminal that stood in the box, the judge that sat and sentenced him,
the fluent lawyers, the jury, the audience,
The laugher and weeper, the dancer, the midnight widow, the red squaw,
The consumptive, the erysipalite,° the idiot, he that is wronged,
The antipodes, and every one between this and them in the dark,
I swear they are averaged now . . . . one is no better than the other,
The night and sleep have likened them and restored them.

I swear they are all beautiful,
Every one that sleeps is beautiful . . . . every thing in the dim night
is beautiful,
The wildest and bloodiest is over and all is peace.

Peace is always beautiful,
The myth of heaven indicates peace and night.

The myth of heaven indicates the soul;
The soul is always beautiful . . . . it appears more or it appears less . . . .
it comes or lags behind,
It comes from its embowered garden and looks pleasantly on itself
and encloses the world;
Perfect and clean the genitals previously jetting, and perfect and clean
the womb cohering,
The head wellgrown and proportioned and plumb, and the bowels
and joints proportioned and plumb.

The soul is always beautiful,
The universe is duly in order . . . . every thing is in its place,

What is arrived is in its place, and what waits is in its place;
The twisted skull waits . . . . the watery or rotten blood waits,
The child of the glutton or venerealee waits long, and the child
of the drunkard waits long, and the drunkard himself waits long,
The sleepers that lived and died wait . . . . the far advanced are to go on
in their turns, and the far behind are to go on in their turns,
The diverse shall be no less diverse, but they shall flow and unite . . . .
they unite now.

The sleepers are very beautiful as they lie unclothed,
They flow hand in hand over the whole earth from east to west
as they lie unclothed;
The Asiatic and African are hand in hand . . . . the European
and American are hand in hand,
Learned and unlearned are hand in hand . . the male and female
are hand in hand;
The bare arm of the girl crosses the bare breast of her lover . . . .
they press close without lust . . . . his lips press her neck,
The father holds his grown or ungrown son in his arms
with measureless love . . . . and the son holds the father
in his arms with measureless love,
The white hair of the mother shines on the white wrist of her daughter,
The breath of the boy goes with the breath of the man . . . .
friend is inarmed by friend,
The scholar kisses the teacher and the teacher kisses the scholar . . . .
the wronged is made right,
The call of the slave is one with the master's call . . and the master
salutes the slave,
The felon steps forth from prison . . . . the insane becomes sane . . . .
the suffering of sick persons is relieved,
The sweatings and fevers stop . . the throat that was unsound
is sound . . the lungs of the consumptive are resumed . .
the poor distressed head is free,
The joints of the rheumatic move as smoothly as ever,
and smoother than ever,
Stiflings and passages open . . . . the paralysed become supple,
The swelled and convulsed and congested awake to themselves
in condition,
They pass the invigoration of the night and the chemistry of the night
and awake.

I too pass from the night;
I stay awhile away O night, but I return to you again and love you;
Why should I be afraid to trust myself to you?
I am not afraid . . . . I have been well brought forward by you;
I love the rich running day, but I do not desert her in whom I lay so long:
I know not how I came of you, and I know not where I go with you . . . .
but I know I came well and shall go well.

I will stop only a time with the night . . . . and rise betimes.

I will duly pass the day O my mother and duly return to you;
Not you will yield forth the dawn again more surely than you will
yield forth me again,
Not the womb yields the babe in its time more surely than I
shall be yielded from you in my time.

Leaves of Grass

THE bodies of men and women engirth me, and I engirth them,
They will not let me off nor I them till I go with them
and respond to them and love them.

Was it dreamed whether those who corrupted their own live bodies
could conceal themselves?
And whether those who defiled the living were as bad as they
who defiled the dead?

The expression of the body of man or woman balks account,
The male is perfect and that of the female is perfect.

The expression of a wellmade man appears not only in his face,
It is in his limbs and joints also . . . . it is curiously in the joints
of his hips and wrists,
It is in his walk . . the carriage of his neck . . the flex of his waist
and knees . . . . dress does not hide him,

The strong sweet supple quality he has strikes through the cotton
and flannel;
To see him pass conveys as much as the best poem . . perhaps more,
You linger to see his back and the back of his neck and shoulderside.

The sprawl and fulness of babes . . . . the bosoms and heads of women
. . . . the folds of their dress . . . . their style as we pass in the street
. . . . the contour of their shape downwards;
The swimmer naked in the swimmingbath . . seen as he swims
through the salt transparent greenshine, or lies on his back
and rolls silently with the heave of the water;
Framers bare-armed framing a house . . hoisting the beams
in their places . . or using the mallet and mortising-chisel,
The bending forward and backward of rowers in rowboats . . . .
the horseman in his saddle;
Girls and mothers and housekeepers in all their exquisite offices,
The group of laborers seated at noontime with their open dinnerkettles,
and their wives waiting,
The female soothing a child . . . . the farmer's daughter in the garden
or cowyard,
The woodman rapidly swinging his axe in the woods . . . .
the young fellow hoeing corn . . . . the sleighdriver
guiding his six horses through the crowd,
The wrestle of wrestlers . . two apprentice-boys, quite grown, lusty,
goodnatured, nativeborn, out on the vacant lot at sundown
after work,
The coats vests and caps thrown down . . the embrace of love
and resistance,
The upperhold and underhold—the hair rumpled over
and blinding the eyes;
The march of firemen in their own costumes—the play of the masculine
muscle through cleansetting trowsers and waistbands,
The slow return from the fire . . . . the pause when the bell strikes
suddenly again—the listening on the alert,
The natural perfect and varied attitudes . . . . the bent head,
the curved neck, the counting:
Suchlike I love . . . . I loosen myself and pass freely . . . .
and am at the mother's breast with the little child,
And swim with the swimmer, and wrestle with the wrestlers, and march
in line with the firemen, and pause and listen and count.

I knew a man . . . . he was a common farmer . . . . he was the father
of five sons . . . and in them were the fathers of sons . . .
and in them were the fathers of sons.

This man was of wonderful vigor and calmness and beauty of person;
The shape of his head, the richness and breadth of his manners,
the pale yellow and white of his hair and beard,
the immeasurable meaning of his black eyes,
These I used to go and visit him to see . . . . He was wise also,
He was six feet tall . . . . he was over eighty years old . . . .
his sons were massive clean bearded tanfaced and handsome,
They and his daughters loved him . . . all who saw him loved him . . .
they did not love him by allowance . . . they loved him
with personal love;
He drank water only . . . . the blood showed like scarlet
through the clear brown skin of his face;
He was a frequent gunner and fisher . . . he sailed his boat himself . . .
he had a fine one presented to him by a shipjoiner . . . . he had
fowling-pieces, presented to him by men that loved him;
When he went with his five sons and many grandsons to hunt or fish
you would pick him out as the most beautiful and vigorous
of the gang,
You would wish long and long to be with him . . . . you would wish
to sit by him in the boat that you and he might touch each other.

I have perceived that to be with those I like is enough,
To stop in company with the rest at evening is enough,
To be surrounded by beautiful curious breathing laughing flesh is enough,
To pass among them . . to touch any one . . . . to rest my arm ever so
lightly round his or her neck for a moment . . . . what is this then?
I do not ask any more delight . . . . I swim in it as in the sea.

There is something in staying close to men and women and looking
on them and in the contact and odor of them that pleases
the soul well,
All things please the soul, but these please the soul well.

This is the female form,
A divine nimbus exhales from it from head to foot,
It attracts with fierce undeniable attraction,
I am drawn by its breath as if I were no more than a helpless vapor . . . .
all falls aside but myself and it,

Books, art, religion, time . . the visible and solid earth . . the atmosphere
and the fringed clouds . . what was expected of heaven
or feared of hell are now consumed,
Mad filaments, ungovernable shoots play out of it . . the response
likewise ungovernable,
Hair, bosom, hips, bend of legs, negligent falling hands—all diffused
. . . . mine too diffused,
Ebb stung by the flow, and flow stung by the ebb . . . .
loveflesh swelling and deliciously aching,
Limitless limpid jets of love hot and enormous . . . . quivering jelly
of love . . . white-blow and delirious juice,
Bridegroom-night of love working surely and softly
into the prostrate dawn,
Undulating into the willing and yielding day,
Lost in the cleave of the clasping and sweetfleshed day.

This is the nucleus . . . after the child is born of woman
the man is born of woman,
This is the bath of birth . . . this is the merge of small and large
and the outlet again.

Be not ashamed women . . your privilege encloses the rest . .
it is the exit of the rest,
You are the gates of the body and you are the gates of the soul.

The female contains all qualities and tempers them . . . .
she is in her place . . . . she moves with perfect balance,
She is all things duly veiled . . . . she is both passive and active . . . .
she is to conceive daughters as well as sons and sons as well as daughters.

As I see my soul reflected in nature . . . . as I see through a mist one
with inexpressible completeness and beauty . . . . see the bent head
and arms folded over the breast . . . . the female I see,
I see the bearer of the great fruit which is immortality . . . .
the good thereof is not tasted by roues, and never can be.

The male is not less the soul, nor more . . . . he too is in his place,
He too is all qualities . . . . he is action and power . . . .
the flush of the known universe is in him,
Scorn becomes him well and appetite and defiance become him well,
The fiercest largest passions . . bliss that is utmost and sorrow
that is utmost become him well . . . . pride is for him,

The fullspread pride of man is calming and excellent to the soul;
Knowledge becomes him . . . . he likes it always . . . . he brings everything
to the test of himself,
Whatever the survey . . whatever the sea and the sail,
he strikes soundings at last only here,
Where else does he strike soundings except here?

The man's body is sacred and the woman's body is sacred . . . .
it is no matter who,
Is it a slave? Is it one of the dullfaced immigrants just landed
on the wharf?

Each belongs here or anywhere just as much as the welloff . . . .
just as much as you,
Each has his or her place in the procession.

All is a procession,
The universe is a procession with measured and beautiful motion.

Do you know so much that you call the slave or the dullface ignorant?
Do you suppose you have a right to a good sight . . . and he or she
has no right to a sight?
Do you think matter has cohered together from its diffused float,
and the soil is on the surface and water runs and vegetation
sprouts for you . . and not for him and her?

A slave at auction!
I help the auctioneer . . . . the sloven does not half know his business.

Gentlemen look on this curious creature,
Whatever the bids of the bidders they cannot be high enough for him,
For him the globe lay preparing quintillions of years
without one animal or plant,
For him the revolving cycles truly and steadily rolled.

In that head the allbaffling brain,
In it and below it the making of the attributes of heroes.

Examine these limbs, red black or white . . . . they are very cunning
in tendon and nerve;
They shall be stript that you may see them.

Exquisite senses, lifelit eyes, pluck, volition,
Flakes of breastmuscle, pliant backbone and neck, flesh not flabby,
goodsized arms and legs,
And wonders within there yet.

Within there runs his blood . . . . the same old blood . .
the same red running blood;
There swells and jets his heart . . . . There all passions and desires . .
all reachings and aspirations:
Do you think they are not there because they are not expressed
in parlors and lecture-rooms?

This is not only one man . . . . he is the father of those who shall
be fathers in their turns,
In him the start of populous states and rich republics,
Of him countless immortal lives and countless embodiments
and enjoyments.

How do you know who shall come from the offspring of his offspring
through the centuries?
Who might you find you have come from yourself if you could trace
back through the centuries?

A woman at auction,
She too is not only herself . . . . she is the teeming mother of mothers,
She is the bearer of them that shall grow and be mates to the mothers.

Her daughters or their daughters' daughters . . who knows who
shall mate with them?
Who knows through the centuries what heroes may come from them?

In them and of them natal love . . . . in them the divine mystery . . . .
the same old beautiful mystery.

Have you ever loved a woman?
Your mother . . . . is she living? . . . . Have you been much with her?
and has she been much with you?
Do you not see that these are exactly the same to all in all nations
and times all over the earth?

If life and the soul are sacred the human body is sacred;
And the glory and sweet of a man is the token of manhood untainted,

And in man or woman a clean strong firmfibred body is beautiful
as the most beautiful face.

Have you seen the fool that corrupted his own live body?
or the fool that corrupted her own live body?
For they do not conceal themselves, and cannot conceal themselves.

Who degrades or defiles the living human body is cursed,
Who degrades or defiles the body of the dead is not more cursed.

Leaves of Grass

SAUNTERING the pavement or riding the country byroad
here then are faces,
Faces of friendship, precision, caution, suavity, ideality,
The spiritual prescient face, the always welcome common
benevolent face,
The face of the singing of music, the grand faces of natural lawyers
and judges broad at the backtop,
The faces of hunters and fishers, bulged at the brows . . . .
the shaved blanched faces of orthodox citizens,
The pure extravagant yearning questioning artist's face,
The welcome ugly face of some beautiful soul . . . .
the handsome detested or despised face,
The sacred faces of infants . . . . the illuminated face of the mother
of many children,
The face of an amour . . . . the face of veneration,
The face as of a dream . . . . the face of an immobile rock,
The face withdrawn of its good and bad . . a castrated face,
A wild hawk . . his wings clipped by the clipper,
A stallion that yielded at last to the thongs and knife of the gelder.

Sauntering the pavement or crossing the ceaseless ferry,
here then are faces;
I see them and complain not and am content with all.

Do you suppose I could be content with all if I thought them
their own finale?

This now is too lamentable a face for a man;
Some abject louse asking leave to be . . cringing for it,
Some milknosed maggot blessing what lets it wrig° to its hole.

This face is a dog's snout sniffing for garbage;
Snakes nest in that mouth . . I hear the sibilant threat.

This face is a haze more chill than the arctic sea,
Its sleepy and wobbling icebergs crunch as they go.

This is a face of bitter herbs . . . . this an emetic . . . they need no label,
And more of the drugshelf . . laudanum, caoutchouc,° or hog's lard.

This face is an epilepsy advertising and doing business . . . .
its wordless tongue gives out the unearthly cry,
Its veins down the neck distend . . . . its eyes roll till they show nothing
but their whites,
Its teeth grit . . the palms of the hands are cut by the turned-in nails,
The man falls struggling and foaming to the ground while he
speculates well.

This face is bitten by vermin and worms,
And this is some murderer's knife with a halfpulled scabbard.

This face owes to the sexton his dismalest fee,
An unceasing deathbell tolls there.

Those are really men! . . . . the bosses and tufts of the great round globe!

Features of my equals, would you trick me with your creased
and cadaverous march?
Well then you cannot trick me.

I see your rounded never-erased flow,
I see neath the rims of your haggard and mean disguises.

Splay and twist as you like . . . . poke with the tangling fores
of fishes or rats,
You'll be unmuzzled . . . . you certainly will.

I saw the face of the most smeared and slobbering idiot
they had at the asylum,
And I knew for my consolation what they knew not;
I knew of the agents that emptied and broke my brother,°
The same wait to clear the rubbish from the fallen tenement;
And I shall look again in a score or two of ages,
And I shall meet the real landlord perfect and unharmed,
every inch as good as myself.

The Lord advances and yet advances:
Always the shadow in front . . . . always the reached hand
bringing up the laggards.

Out of this face emerge banners and horses . . . . O superb! . . . .
I see what is coming,
I see the high pioneercaps . . . . I see the staves of runners
clearing the way,
I hear victorious drums.

This face is a lifeboat;
This is the face commanding and bearded . . . . it asks no odds of the rest;
This face is flavored fruit ready for eating;
This face of a healthy honest boy is the programme of all good.

These faces bear testimony slumbering or awake,
They show their descent from the Master himself.

Off the word I have spoken I except not one . . . . red white or black,
all are deific,
In each house is the ovum . . . . it comes forth after a thousand years.

Spots or cracks at the windows do not disturb me,
Tall and sufficient stand behind and make signs to me;
I read the promise and patiently wait.

This is a fullgrown lily's face,
She speaks to the limber-hip'd man near the garden pickets,
Come here, she blushingly cries . . . . Come nigh to me limber-hip'd man
and give me your finger and thumb,
Stand at my side till I lean as high as I can upon you,
Fill me with albescent° honey . . . . bend down to me,
Rub to me with your chafing beard . . rub to my breast and shoulders.

The old face of the mother of many children:
Whist! I am fully content.

Lulled and late is the smoke of the Sabbath morning,
It hangs low over the rows of trees by the fences,
It hangs thin by the sassafras, the wildcherry and the catbrier under them.

I saw the rich ladies in full dress at the soiree,
I heard what the run of poets were saying so long,
Heard who sprang in crimson youth from the white froth and the water-blue.

Behold a woman!
She looks out from her quaker cap . . . . her face is clearer
and more beautiful than the sky.

She sits in an armchair under the shaded porch of the farmhouse,
The sun just shines on her old white head.

Her ample gown is of creamhued linen,
Her grandsons raised the flax, and her granddaughters spun it
with the distaff and the wheel.

The melodious character of the earth!
The finish beyond which philosophy cannot go and does not wish to go!
The justified mother of men!

A YOUNG man came to me with a message from his brother,
How should the young man know the whether and when
of his brother?
Tell him to send me the signs.

And I stood before the young man face to face, and took his right hand
in my left hand and his left hand in my right hand,
And I answered for his brother and for men . . . . and I answered
for the poet, and sent these signs.

Him all wait for .... him all yield up to .... his word is decisive
and final,
Him they accept .... in him lave .... in him perceive themselves
as amid light,
Him they immerse, and he immerses them.

Beautiful women, the haughtiest nations, laws, the landscape,
people and animals,
The profound earth and its attributes, and the unquiet ocean,
All enjoyments and properties, and money, and whatever money will buy,
The best farms .... others toiling and planting, and he unavoidably reaps,
The noblest and costliest cities .... others grading and building,
and he domiciles there;
Nothing for any one but what is for him .... near and far are for him,
The ships in the offing .... the perpetual shows and marches on land
are for him if they are for any body.

He puts things in their attitudes,
He puts today out of himself with plasticity and love,
He places his own city, times, reminiscences, parents, brothers and
sisters, associations employment and politics, so that the rest
never shame them afterward, nor assume to command them.

He is the answerer,
What can be answered he answers, and what cannot be answered
he shows how it cannot be answered.

A man is a summons and a challenge,
It is vain to skulk .... Do you hear that mocking and laughter?
Do you hear the ironical echoes?

Books friendships philosophers priests action pleasure pride
beat up and down seeking to give satisfaction;
He indicates the satisfaction, and indicates them that beat up
and down also.

Whichever the sex ... whatever the season or place he may go
freshly and gently and safely by day or by night,
He has the passkey of hearts .... to him the response of the prying
of hands on the knobs.

His welcome is universal . . . . the flow of beauty is not more welcome
        or universal than he is,
The person he favors by day or sleeps with at night is blessed.

Every existence has its idiom . . . . every thing has an idiom and tongue;
He resolves all tongues into his own, and bestows it upon men . .
        and any man translates . . and any man translates himself also:
One part does not counteract another part . . . . He is the joiner . .
        he sees how they join.

He says indifferently and alike, How are you friend? to the President
        at his levee,
And he says Good day my brother, to Cudge° that hoes in the sugarfield;
And both understand him and know that his speech is right.

He walks with perfect ease in the capitol,
He walks among the Congress . . . . and one representative says
        to another, Here is our equal appearing and new.

Then the mechanics take him for a mechanic,
And the soldiers suppose him to be a captain . . . . and the sailors
        that he has followed the sea,
And the authors take him for an author . . . . and the artists for an artist,
And the laborers perceive he could labor with them and love them;
No matter what the work is, that he is one to follow it or has followed it,
No matter what the nation, that he might find his brothers and sisters there.

The English believe he comes of their English stock,
A Jew to the Jew he seems . . . . a Russ to the Russ . . . . usual and near . .
        removed from none.

Whoever he looks at in the traveler's coffeehouse claims him,
The Italian or Frenchman is sure, and the German is sure,
        and the Spaniard is sure . . . . and the island Cuban is sure.

The engineer, the deckhand on the great lakes or on the Mississippi
        or St Lawrence or Sacramento or Hudson or Delaware claims him.

The gentleman of perfect blood acknowledges his perfect blood,
The insulter, the prostitute, the angry person, the beggar, see themselves
        in the ways of him . . . . he strangely transmutes them,

They are not vile any more .... they hardly know themselves,
they are so grown.

You think it would be good to be the writer of melodious verses,
Well it would be good to be the writer of melodious verses;
But what are verses beyond the flowing character you could have? ....
or beyond beautiful manners and behaviour?
Or beyond one manly or affectionate deed of an apprenticeboy? . .
or old woman? . . or man that has been in prison or is likely
to be in prison?

SUDDENLY out of its stale and drowsy lair, the lair of slaves,
Like lightning Europe le'pt forth .... half startled at itself,
Its feet upon the ashes and the rags .... Its hand tight to the throats
of kings.

O hope and faith! O aching close of lives! O many a sickened heart!
Turn back unto this day, and make yourselves afresh.

And you, paid to defile the People .... you liars mark:
Not for numberless agonies, murders, lusts,
For court thieving in its manifold mean forms,
Worming from his simplicity the poor man's wages;
For many a promise by royal lips, And broken, and laughed at
in the breaking,
Then in their power not for all these did the blows strike
of personal revenge . . or the heads of the nobles fall;
The People scorned the ferocity of kings.

But the sweetness of mercy brewed bitter destruction,
and the frightened rulers come back:
Each comes in state with his train .... hangman, priest
and tax-gatherer .... soldier, lawyer, jailer and sycophant.

Yet behind all, lo, a Shape,
Vague as the night, draped interminably, head front and form
in scarlet folds,

Whose face and eyes none may see,
Out of its robes only this . . . . the red robes, lifted by the arm,
One finger pointed high over the top, like the head of a snake appears.

Meanwhile corpses lie in new-made graves . . . . bloody corpses
of young men:
The rope of the gibbet hangs heavily . . . . the bullets of princes
are flying . . . . the creatures of power laugh aloud,
And all these things bear fruits . . . . and they are good.

Those corpses of young men,
Those martyrs that hang from the gibbets . . . those hearts pierced
by the gray lead,
Cold and motionless as they seem . . live elsewhere
with unslaughter'd vitality.

They live in other young men, O kings,
They live in brothers, again ready to defy you:
They were purified by death . . . . They were taught and exalted.

Not a grave of the murdered for freedom but grows seed for freedom
. . . . in its turn to bear seed,
Which the winds carry afar and re-sow, and the rains
and the snows nourish.

Not a disembodied spirit can the weapons of tyrants let loose,
But it stalks invisibly over the earth . . whispering counseling cautioning.

Liberty let others despair of you . . . . I never despair of you.

Is the house shut? Is the master away?
Nevertheless be ready . . . . be not weary of watching,
He will soon return . . . . his messengers come anon.

CLEAR the way there Jonathan!°
Way for the President's marshal! Way for the government cannon!
Way for the federal foot and dragoons . . . . and the phantoms afterward.

I rose this morning early to get betimes in Boston town;
Here's a good place at the corner . . . . I must stand and see the show.

I love to look on the stars and stripes . . . . I hope the fifes will play Yankee Doodle.

How bright shine the foremost with cutlasses,
Every man holds his revolver . . . . marching stiff through Boston town.

A fog follows . . . . antiques of the same come limping,
Some appear wooden-legged and some appear bandaged and bloodless.

Why this is a show! It has called the dead out of the earth,
The old graveyards of the hills have hurried to see;
Uncountable phantoms gather by flank and rear of it,
Cocked hats of mothy mould and crutches made of mist,
Arms in slings and old men leaning on young men's shoulders.

What troubles you, Yankee phantoms? What is all this chattering of bare gums?
Does the ague convulse your limbs? Do you mistake your crutches for firelocks, and level them?

If you blind your eyes with tears you will not see the President's marshal.
If you groan such groans you might balk the government cannon.

For shame old maniacs! . . . . Bring down those tossed arms, and let your white hair be;
Here gape your smart grandsons . . . . . their wives gaze at them from the windows,
See how well-dressed . . . . see how orderly they conduct themselves.

Worse and worse . . . . Can't you stand it? Are you retreating?
Is this hour with the living too dead for you?

Retreat then! Pell-mell! . . . . Back to the hills, old limpers!
I do not think you belong here anyhow.

But there is one thing that belongs here . . . . Shall I tell you what it is,
gentlemen of Boston?

I will whisper it to the Mayor . . . . he shall send a committee to England,
They shall get a grant from the Parliament, and go with a cart
to the royal vault,
Dig out King George's coffin . . . . unwrap him quick from the graveclothes
. . . . box up his bones for a journey:
Find a swift Yankee clipper . . . . here is freight for you
blackbellied clipper,
Up with your anchor! shake out your sails! . . . . steer straight
toward Boston bay.

Now call the President's marshal again, and bring out
the government cannon.
And fetch home the roarers from Congress, and make another procession
and guard it with foot and dragoons.

Here is a centrepiece for them:
Look! all orderly citizens . . . . look from the windows women.

The committee open the box and set up the regal ribs and glue those
that will not stay,
And clap the skull on top of the ribs, and clap a crown on top
of the skull.

You have got your revenge old buster! . . . . The crown is come
to its own and more than its own.

Stick your hands in your pockets Jonathan . . . . you are made man
from this day,
You are mighty cute° . . . . and here is one of your bargains.

THERE was a child went forth every day,
And the first object he looked upon and received with wonder
or pity or love or dread, that object he became,
And that object became part of him for the day or a certain part
of the day . . . . or for many years or stretching cycles of years.

The early lilacs became part of this child,
And grass, and white and red morningglories, and white and red clover,
and the song of the phœbe-bird,
And the March-born lambs, and sow's pink-faint litter,
and the mare's foal, and the cow's calf, and the noisy brood
of the barnyard or by the mire of the pondside . . and the fish
suspending themselves so curiously below there . .
and the beautiful curious liquid . . and the water-plants
with their graceful flat heads . . all become part of him.

And the field-sprouts of April and May became part of him . . . .
wintergrain sprouts, and those of the light-yellow corn,
and of the esculent° roots of the garden,
And the appletrees covered with blossoms, and the fruit afterward . . . .
and woodberries . . and the commonest weeds by the road;
And the old drunkard staggering home from the outhouse
of the tavern whence he had lately risen,
And the schoolmistress that passed on her way to the school . .
and the friendly boys that passed . . and the quarrelsome boys . .
and the tidy and freshcheeked girls . . and the barefoot negro
boy and girl,
And all the changes of city and country wherever he went.

His own parents . . he that had propelled the fatherstuff at night,
and fathered him . . and she that conceived him in her womb
and birthed him . . . . they gave this child more of themselves
than that,

They gave him afterward every day . . . . they and of them became
part of him.

The mother at home quietly placing the dishes on the suppertable,
The mother with mild words . . . . clean her cap and gown . . . .
a wholesome odor falling off her person and clothes
as she walks by:
The father, strong, selfsufficient, manly, mean, angered, unjust,
The blow, the quick loud word, the tight bargain, the crafty lure,
The family usages, the language, the company, the furniture . . . .
the yearning and swelling heart,
Affection that will not be gainsayed . . . . The sense of what is real . . . .
the thought if after all it should prove unreal,
The doubts of daytime and the doubts of nighttime . . . .
the curious whether and how,
Whether that which appears so is so . . . . Or is it all flashes and specks?
Men and women crowding fast in the streets . . if they are not flashes
and specks what are they?
The streets themselves, and the facades of houses . . . . the goods
in the windows,
Vehicles . . teams . . the tiered wharves, and the huge crossing
at the ferries;
The village on the highland seen from afar at sunset . . . .
the river between,
Shadows . . aureola and mist . . light falling on roofs and gables
of white or brown, three miles off,
The schooner near by sleepily dropping down the tide . . the little boat
slacktowed astern,
The hurrying tumbling waves and quickbroken crests and slapping;
The strata of colored clouds . . . . the long bar of maroontint away
solitary by itself . . . . the spread of purity it lies motionless in,
The horizon's edge, the flying seacrow, the fragrance of saltmarsh
and shoremud;
These became part of that child who went forth every day,
and who now goes and will always go forth every day,
And these become of him or her that peruses them now.

WHO learns my lesson complete?
Boss and journeyman and apprentice? . . . . churchman and atheist?
The stupid and the wise thinker . . . . parents and offspring . . . . merchant and clerk and porter and customer . . . . editor, author, artist and schoolboy?

Draw nigh and commence,
It is no lesson . . . . it lets down the bars to a good lesson,
And that to another . . . . and every one to another still.

The great laws take and effuse without argument,
I am of the same style, for I am their friend,
I love them quits and quits . . . . I do not halt and make salaams.

I lie abstracted and hear beautiful tales of things and the reasons of things,
They are so beautiful I nudge myself to listen.

I cannot say to any person what I hear . . . . I cannot say it to myself . . . . it is very wonderful.

It is no little matter, this round and delicious globe, moving so exactly in its orbit forever and ever, without one jolt or the untruth of a single second;
I do not think it was made in six days, nor in ten thousand years, nor ten decillions of years,
Nor planned and built one thing after another, as an architect plans and builds a house.

I do not think seventy years is the time of a man or woman,
Nor that seventy millions of years is the time of a man or woman,
Nor that years will ever stop the existence of me or any one else.

Is it wonderful that I should be immortal? as every one is immortal,
I know it is wonderful . . . . but my eyesight is equally wonderful . . . .

and how I was conceived in my mother's womb
is equally wonderful,
And how I was not palpable once but am now . . . . and was born
on the last day of May 1819 . . . . and passed from a babe
in the creeping trance of three summers and three winters
to articulate and walk . . . . are all equally wonderful.

And that I grew six feet high . . . . and that I have become a man
thirty-six years old in 1855 . . . . and that I am here anyhow—
are all equally wonderful;
And that my soul embraces you this hour, and we affect each other
without ever seeing each other, and never perhaps to see
each other, is every bit as wonderful:
And that I can think such thoughts as these is just as wonderful,
And that I can remind you, and you think them and know them
to be true is just as wonderful,
And that the moon spins round the earth and on with the earth
is equally wonderful,
And that they balance themselves with the sun and stars
is equally wonderful.

Come I should like to hear you tell me what there is in yourself
that is not just as wonderful,
And I should like to hear the name of anything between Sunday
morning and Saturday night that is not just as wonderful.

GREAT are the myths . . . . I too delight in them,
Great are Adam and Eve . . . . I too look back and accept them;
Great the risen and fallen nations, and their poets, women, sages,
inventors, rulers, warriors and priests.

Great is liberty! Great is equality! I am their follower,
Helmsmen of nations, choose your craft . . . . where you sail I sail,
Yours is the muscle of life or death . . . . yours is the perfect science
. . . . in you I have absolute faith.

Great is today, and beautiful,
It is good to live in this age . . . . there never was any better.

Great are the plunges and throes and triumphs and falls of democracy,
Great the reformers with their lapses and screams,
Great the daring and venture of sailors on new explorations.

Great are yourself and myself,
We are just as good and bad as the oldest and youngest or any,
What the best and worst did we could do,
What they felt . . do not we feel it in ourselves?
What they wished . . do we not wish the same?

Great is youth, and equally great is old age . . . . great are the day
and night;
Great is wealth and great is poverty . . . . great is expression
and great is silence.

Youth large lusty and loving . . . . youth full of grace and force
and fascination,
Do you know that old age may come after you with equal grace
and force and fascination?

Day fullblown and splendid . . . . day of the immense sun,
and action and ambition and laughter,
The night follows close, with millions of suns, and sleep
and restoring darkness.

Wealth with the flush hand and fine clothes and hospitality:
But then the soul's wealth—which is candor and knowledge
and pride and enfolding love:
Who goes for men and women showing poverty richer than wealth?

Expression of speech . . in what is written or said forget not
that silence is also expressive,
That anguish as hot as the hottest and contempt as cold as the coldest
may be without words,
That the true adoration is likewise without words and without kneeling.

Great is the greatest nation . . the nation of clusters of equal nations.

Great is the earth, and the way it became what it is,
Do you imagine it is stopped at this? . . . . and the increase abandoned?
Understand then that it goes as far onward from this as this is
from the times when it lay in covering waters and gases.

Great is the quality of truth in man,
The quality of truth in man supports itself through all changes,
It is inevitably in the man . . . . He and it are in love,
and never leave each other.

The truth in man is no dictum . . . . it is vital as eyesight,
If there be any soul there is truth . . . . if there be man or woman
there is truth . . . . If there be physical or moral there is truth,
If there be equilibrium or volition there is truth . . . . if there be things
at all upon the earth there is truth.

O truth of the earth! O truth of things! I am determined to press
the whole way toward you,
Sound your voice! I scale mountains or dive in the sea after you.

Great is language . . . . it is the mightiest of the sciences,
It is the fulness and color and form and diversity of the earth . . . .
and of men and women . . . . and of all qualities and processes;
It is greater than wealth . . . . it is greater than buildings or ships
or religions or paintings or music.

Great is the English speech . . . . What speech is so great as the English?
Great is the English brood . . . . What brood has so vast a destiny
as the English?
It is the mother of the brood that must rule the earth with new rule,
The new rule shall rule as the soul rules, and as the love and justice
and equality that are in the soul rule.

Great is the law . . . . Great are the old few landmarks of the law . . . .
they are the same in all times and shall not be disturbed.

Great are marriage, commerce, newspapers, books, freetrade, railroads,
steamers, international mails and telegraphs and exchanges.

Great is Justice;
Justice is not settled by legislators and laws . . . . it is in the soul,

It cannot be varied by statutes any more than love or pride
or the attraction of gravity can,
It is immutable . . it does not depend on majorities . . . .
majorities or what not come at last before the same
passionless and exact tribunal.

For justice are the grand natural lawyers and perfect judges . . . .
it is in their souls,
It is well assorted . . . . they have not studied for nothing . . . .
the great includes the less,
They rule on the highest grounds . . . . they oversee all eras and states
and administrations.

The perfect judge fears nothing . . . . he could go front to front
before God,
Before the perfect judge all shall stand back . . . . life and death
shall stand back . . . . heaven and hell shall stand back.

Great is goodness;
I do not know what it is any more than I know what health is . . . .
but I know it is great.

Great is wickedness . . . . I find I often admire it just as much
as I admire goodness:
Do you call that a paradox? It is certainly a paradox.

The eternal equilibrium of things is great, and the external overthrow
of things is great,
And there is another paradox.

Great is life . . and real and mystical . . wherever and whoever,
Great is death . . . . Sure as life holds all parts together,
death holds all parts together;
Sure as the stars return again after they merge in the light,
death is great as life.

Whitman's Unsigned *Leaves* Review
Brooklyn Daily Times, 29 September 1855

To give judgment on real poems, one needs an account of the poet himself. Very devilish to some, and very divine to some, will appear the poet of these new poems, the *Leaves of Grass;* an attempt, as they are, of a naive, masculine, tenderly affectionate, rowdyish, contemplative, sensual, moral, susceptible and imperious person, to cast into literature not only his own grit and arrogance, but his own flesh and form, undraped, regardless of models, regardless of modesty or law, and ignorant or silently scornful, as at first appears, of all except his own presence and experience, and all outside of the fiercely loved land of his birth and the birth of his parents, and their parents for several generations before him. Politeness this man has none, and regulation he has none. The effects he produces are no effects of artists or the arts, but effects of the original eye or arm, or the actual atmosphere of grass or brute or bird. You may feel the unconscious teaching of the presence of some fine animal, but will never feel the artificial teaching of the fine writer or speaker.

Other poets celebrate great events, personages, romances, wars, loves, passions, the victories and power of their country, or some real or imagined incident—and polish their work, and come to conclusions, and satisfy the reader. This poet celebrates himself: and that is the way he celebrates all. He comes to no conclusions, and does not satisfy the reader. He certainly leaves him what the serpent left the woman and the man, the taste of the tree of the knowledge of good and evil, never to be erased again.

What good is it to argue about egotism? There can be no two thoughts on Walt Whitman's egotism. That is avowedly what he steps out of the crowd and turns and faces them for. Mark, critics! for otherwise is not used for you the key that leads to the use of the other keys to this well enveloped yet terribly in earnest man. His whole work, his life, manners, friendships, writings, all have among their leading purposes an evident purpose, as strong and avowed as any of the rest, to stamp a new type of character, namely his own, and indelibly fix it and publish it, not for a model but an illustration, for the present and future of American letters and American young men, for the south the same as the north, and for the Pacific and Mississippi country, and Wisconsin and Texas and Canada and Havana, just as much as New York and Boston. Whatever is needed toward this achievement he puts his hand to, and lets imputations take their time to die.

First be yourself what you would show in your poem—such seems to be this man's example and inferred rebuke to the schools of poets. He makes no allusions to books or writers; their spirits do not seem to have touched him; he has not a word to say for or against them, or their theories or ways. He never offers others; what he continually offers is the man whom our Brooklynites know so well. Of pure American breed, of reckless health, his body perfect, free from taint top to toe, free forever from headache and dyspepsia, full-blooded, six feet high, a good feeder, never once using medicine, drinking water only—a swimmer in the river or bay or by the seashore—of straight attitude and slow movement of foot—an indescribable style evincing indifference and disdain—ample limbed, weight one hundred and eighty-five pounds, age thirty-six years (1855)—never dressed in black, always dressed freely and clean in strong clothes, neck open, shirt-collar flat and broad, countenance of swarthy, transparent red, beard short and well mottled with white hair like hay after it has been mowed in the field and lies tossed and streaked—face not refined or intellectual, but calm and wholesome—a face of an unaffected animal—a face that absorbs sunshine and meets savage and gentleman on equal terms—a face of one who eats and drinks and is a brawny lover and embracer—a face of undying friendship and indulgence toward men and women, and of one who finds the same returned many fold—a face with two grey eyes where passion and hauteur sleep, and melancholy stands behind them—a spirit that mixes cheerfully with the world—a person singularly beloved and welcome, especially by young men and mechanics—one who has firm attachments there, and associates there—one who does not associate with literary and elegant people—one of the two men sauntering along the street with their arms over each other's shoulders, his companions some boat man or ship joiner or from the hunting-tent or lumber-raft—one who has the quality of attracting the best out of people that they present to him, none of their meaner and stingier traits, but always their sweetest and most generous traits—a man never called upon to make speeches at public dinners, never on platforms amid the crowds of clergymen, or professors or aldermen or congressmen—rather down in the bay with pilots in their pilot boats—or off on a cruise with fishers in a fishing smack—or with a band of laughers and roughs in the streets of the city or on the open grounds of the country—fond of New York and Brooklyn—fond of the life of the wharves and great ferries, or along Broadway, observing the endless wonders of the thoroughfare of the world—one whom, if you should meet, you need not expect to meet an extraordinary person—one in whom you will see the singularity which consists in no singularity—whose contact is no dazzling fascination, nor requires any deference, but has the easy fascination of what is homely and accustomed—of something you knew before, and was waiting for—of natural pleasures, and well-known places, and welcome familiar faces—perhaps of a remembrance of your brother or mother, or friend away or dead—there you have Walt Whitman, the

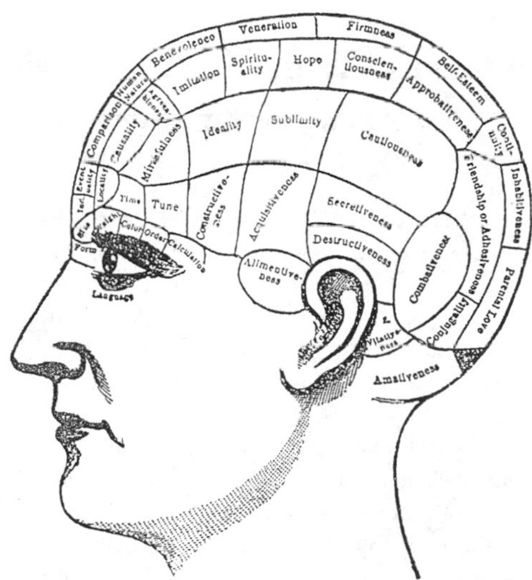

Phrenology, the reading of personality based on the shape of the cranium, was a popular pseudoscience of Whitman's day. (See the results of his own reading on the next page.) Note, behind the ear on this phrenologist's chart, "Amativeness" and "Adhesiveness," which became crucial words in Whitman's vocabulary for loving relationships.

begetter of a new offspring out of literature, taking with easy nonchalance the chances of its present reception, and, through all misunderstandings and distrusts, the chances of its future reception.

NOTE: Whitman reprinted this review, much revised, in a sixty-five-page pamphlet he anonymously published as an advertisement for the 1860 edition; the pamphlet was titled Leaves of Grass Imprints. American and European Criticisms on *Leaves of Grass. Whitman added to the review a reference to the pseudoscience of phrenology (the reading of character by the shape of the cranium) and the following footnote describing a reading of his own head:*

Phrenological Notes on W. Whitman, *by L. N. Fowler, July, 1849.—Size of head large, 23 inches. Leading traits appear to be Friendship, Sympathy, Sublimity, and Self-Esteem, and markedly among his combinations the dangerous faults of Indolence, a tendency to the pleasures of Voluptuousness and Alimentiveness, and a certain reckless swing of animal will.*

Amativeness large,† 6; Philoprogenitiveness, 6; Adhesiveness, 6; Inhabitiveness, 6; Concentrativeness, 4; Combativeness, 6; Destructiveness, 5 to 6; Alimentiveness, 4: Secretiveness, 3; Cautiousness, 6; Approbativeness, 4; Self-Esteem, 6 to 7; Firmness, 6 to 7; Conscientiousness, 6; Hope, 4; Marvellousness, 3; Veneration, 4; Benevolence, 6 to 7; Constructiveness, 5; Ideality, 5 to 6; Sublimity, 6 to 7; Imitation, 5; Mirthfulness, 5; Individuality, 6; Form, 6; Size, 6; Weight, 6; Color, 3; Order, 5; Calculation, 5; Locality, 6; Eventuality, 6; Time, 3; Tune, 4; Language, 5; Causality, 5 to 6; Comparison, 6, Suavitiveness, 4; Intuitiveness, or Human Nature, 6.

†The organs are marked by figures from 1 to 7, indicating their degree of development, 1 meaning very small, 2 small, 3 moderate, 4 average, 5 full, 6 large, and 7 very large.

Whitman's Unsigned *Leaves* Review
U.S. Review, September 1855

AN American Bard at last! One of the roughs, large, proud, affectionate, eating, drinking, and breeding, his costume manly and free, his face sunburnt and bearded, his posture strong and erect, his voice bringing hope and prophecy to the generous races of young and old. We shall cease shamming and be what we really are. We shall start an athletic and defiant literature. We realize now how it is, and what was most lacking. The interior American republic shall also be declared free and independent.

For all our intellectual people, followed by their books, poems, novels, essays, editorials, lectures, tuitions, and criticism, dress by London and Paris modes, receive what is received there, obey the authorities, settle disputes by the old tests, keep out of rain and sun, retreat to the shelter of houses and schools, trim their hair, shave, touch not the earth barefoot, and enter not the sea except in a complete bathing-dress. One sees unmistakably genteel persons, travelled, college-learned, used to be served by servants, conversing without heat or vulgarity, supported on chairs, or waling through handsomely-carpeted parlors, or along shelves bearing well-bound volumes, and walls adorned with curtained and collared portraits, and china things, and nick-nacks. But where in American literature is the first show of America? Where are the gristle and beards, and broad breasts, and space and ruggedness, and nonchalance, that the souls of the people love?

Where is the tremendous outdoors of these States? Where is the majesty of the federal mother, seated with more than antique grace, calm, just, indulgent to her brood of children, calling them around her, regarding the little and the large, and the younger and the older, with perfect impartiality? Where is the vehement growth of our cities? Where is the spirit of the strong rich life of the American mechanic, farmer, sailor, hunter, and miner? Where is the huge composite of all other nations, cast in a fresher and brawnier matrix, passing adolescence, and needed this day, live and arrogant, to lead the marches of the world?

Self-reliant, with haughty eyes, assuming to himself all the attributes of his country, steps Walt Whitman into literature, talking like a man unaware that there was ever hitherto such a production as a book, or such a being as a writer. Every move of him has the free play of the muscle of one who never knew what it was to feel that he stood in the presence of a superior. Every word that falls from his mouth shows silent disdain and defiance of the old theories and forms. Every phrase announces new laws; not once do his lips unclose except in conformity with them. With light and rapid touch he first indicates in prose the principles of the foundation of a race of poets so deeply to spring from the American people, and become ingrained through them, that their Presidents shall not be the common referees so much as that great race of poets shall. He proceeds himself to exemplify this new school, and set models for their expression and range of subjects. He makes audacious and native use of his own body and soul. He must recreate poetry with the elements always at hand. He must imbue it with himself as he is, disorderly, fleshy, and sensual, a lover of things, yet a lover of men and women above the whole of the other objects of the universe. His work is to be achieved by unusual methods. Neither classic or romantic is he, nor a materialist any more than a spiritualist. Not a whisper comes out of him of the old stock talk and rhyme of poetry—not the first recognition of gods or goddesses, or Greece or Rome. No breath of Europe, or her monarchies or priestly conventions, or her notions of gentlemen and ladies founded on the idea of caste, seems ever to have fanned his face or been inhaled into his lungs. But in their stead pour vast and fluid the fresh mentality of this mighty age, and the realities of this mighty continent, and the sciences and inventions and discoveries of the present world. Not geology, nor mathematics, nor chemistry, nor navigation, nor astronomy, nor anatomy, nor physiology, nor engineering, is more true to itself than Walt Whitman is true to them. They and the other sciences underlie his whole superstructure. In the beauty of the work of the poet, he affirms, are the tuft and final applause of science.

Affairs then are this man's poems. He will still inject nature through civilization. The movement of his verses is the sweeping movement of great currents of living people, with a general government, and state and municipal governments, courts, commerce, manufactures, arsenals, steamships, railroads, telegraphs, cities with paved streets, and aqueducts and police and gas—myriads of travellers arriving and departing—newspapers, music, elections, and all the features and processes of the nineteenth century in the wholesomest race and the only stable form of politics at present upon the earth. Along his words spread the broad impartialities of the United States. No innovations must be permitted on the stern severities of our liberty and equality. Undecked also is this poet with sentimentalism, or jingle, or nice conceits or flowery similes. He appears in his poems surrounded by women and children, and by young men, and by common objects and qualities. He gives to each just what belongs to it, neither more or less. The person nearest him, that person he ushers hand in hand with himself. Duly take places in his flowing procession, and step to the sounds of the newer and larger music, the essences of American things, and past and present events—the enormous diversity of temperature and agriculture and mines—the tribes of red aborigines—the weather-beaten vessels entering new ports, or making landings on rocky coasts—the first settlements north and south—the rapid stature and impatience of outside control—the sturdy defiance of '76, and the war and peace, and the leadership of Washington, and the formation of the Constitution—the Union always calm and impregnable—the perpetual coming of immigrants—the wharf-hemmed cities and superior marine—the unsurveyed interior—the log-house and clearings, and wild animals and hunters and trappers—the fisheries, and whaling, and gold-digging—the endless gestation of new states—the convening of Congress every December, the members coming up from all climates, and from the uttermost parts—the noble character of the free American workman and workwoman—the fierceness of the people when well-roused—the ardor of their friendships—the large amativeness—the equality of the female with the male—the Yankee swap—the New-York fireman and the target excursion—the southern plantation life—the character of the northeast and of the northwest and southwest—and the character of America and the American people everywhere. For these the old usages of poets afford Walt Whitman no means sufficiently fit and free, and he rejects the old usages. The style of the bard that is waited for is to be transcendent and new. It is to be indirect and not direct or descriptive or epic. Its quality is to go through these to much more. Let the age and wars (he says) of other nations be chanted, and their eras and characters be illustrated, and that finish the verse. Not so (he continues) the great psalm of the republic. Here the theme is creative and has vista. Here comes one among the well-beloved stonecutters, and announces himself, and plans with decision and science, and sees the solid and beautiful forms of the future where there are now solid forms.

The style of these poems, therefore, is simply their own style, new-born and red. Nature may have given the hint to the author of the *Leaves of Grass,* but there exists no book or fragment of a book which can have given the hint to them. All beauty, he says, comes from beautiful blood and a beautiful brain. His rhythm and uniformity he will conceal in the roots of his verses, not to be seen of themselves, but to break forth loosely as lilies on a bush, and take shapes compact as the shapes of melons, or chestnuts, or pears.

The poems of the *Leaves of Grass* are twelve in number. Walt Whitman at first proceeds to put his own body and soul into the new versification: [*quotes first three lines of "I celebrate myself"*].

He leaves houses and their shuttered rooms, for the open air. He drops disguise and ceremony, and walks forth with the confidence and gayety of a child. For the old decorums of writing he substitutes new decorums. The first glance out of his eyes electrifies him with love and delight. He will have the earth receive and return his affection; he will stay with it as the bride-groom stays with the bride. The cool-breath'd ground, the slumbering and liquid trees, the just-gone sunset, the vitreous pour of the full moon, the tender and growing night, he salutes and touches, and they touch him. The sea supports him, and hurries him off with its powerful and crooked fingers. Dash me with amorous wet! then he says, I can repay you.

By this writer the rules of polite circles are dismissed with scorn. Your stale modesties, he says, are filthy to such a man as I [*quotes lines 524–25, then lines 521–22 of "I celebrate myself"*].

No sniveller, or tea-drinking poet, no puny clawback or prude, is Walt Whitman. He will bring poems to fill the days and nights—fit for men and women with the attributes of throbbing blood and flesh. The body, he teaches, is beautiful. Sex is also beautiful. Are you to be put down, he seems to ask, to that shallow level of literature and conversation that stops a man's recognizing the delicious pleasure of his sex, or a woman hers? Nature he proclaims inherently pure. Sex will not be put aside; it is a great ordination of the universe. He works the muscle of the male and the teeming fibre of the female throughout his writings, as wholesome realities, impure only by deliberate intention and effort. To men and women he says: You can have healthy and powerful breeds of children on no less terms than these of mine. Follow me and there shall be taller and nobler crops of humanity on the earth.

In the *Leaves of Grass* are the facts of eternity and immortality, largely treated. Happiness is no dream, and perfection is no dream. Amelioration is my lesson, he says with calm voice, and progress is my lesson and the lesson of all things. Then his persuasion becomes a taunt, and his love bitter and compulsory. With strong and steady call he addresses men. Come, he seems to say, from the midst of all that you have been your whole life surrounding yourself with. Leave all the preaching and teaching of others, and mind only these words of mine [*quotes lines 1225–47 of "I celebrate myself"*].

The eleven other poems have each distinct purposes, curiously veiled. Theirs is no writer to be gone through with in a day or a month. Rather it is his pleasure to elude you and provoke you for deliberate purposes of his own.

Doubtless in the scheme this man has built for himself the writing of poems is but a proportionate part of the whole. It is plain that public and private performance, politics, love, friendship, behavior, the art of conversation, science, society, the American people, the reception of the great novelties of city and country, all have their equal call upon him, and receive equal attention. In politics he could enter with the freedom and reality he shows in poetry. His scope of life is the amplest of any yet in philosophy. He is the true spiritualist. He recognizes no annihilation, or death, or loss of identity. He is the largest lover and sympathizer that has appeared in literature. He loves the earth and sun, and the animals. He does not separate the learned from the unlearned, the Northerner from the Southerner, the white from the black, or the native from the immigrant just landed at the wharf. Every one, he seems to say, appears excellent to me, every employment is adorned, and every male and female glorious [*quotes lines 246–56 of "I celebrate myself"*].

If health were not his distinguishing attribute, this poet would be the very harlot of persons. Right and left he flings his arms, drawing men and women with undeniable love to his close embrace, loving the clasp of their hands, the touch of their necks and breasts, and the sound of their voice. All else seems to burn up under his fierce affection for persons. Politics, religion, institutions, art, quickly fall aside before them. In the whole universe, he says, I see nothing more divine than human souls [*quotes lines last eight lines of "Come closer to me"*].

Who then is that insolent unknown? Who is it, praising himself as if others were not fit to do it, and coming rough and unbidden among writers to unsettle what was settled, and to revolutionize, in fact, our modern civilization? Walt Whitman was born on Long Island, on the hills about thirty miles from the greatest American city, on the last day of May, 1819, and has grown up in Brooklyn and New-York to be thirty-six years old, to enjoy perfect health, and to understand his country and its spirit.

Interrogations more than this, and that will not be put off unanswered, spring continually through the perusal of these Leaves of Grass:

If there were to be selected, out of the incalculable volumes of printed matter in existence, any single work to stand for America and her times, should this be the work?

Must not the true American poet indeed absorb all others, and present a new and far more ample and vigorous type?

Has not the time arrived for a school of live writing and tuition consistent with the principles of these poems? consistent with the free spirit of this age, and with the American truths of politics? consistent with geology, and astronomy, and all science, and human physiology? consistent with the sublimity of immortality and the directness of common-sense?

If in this poem the United States have found their poetic voice, and taken measure and form, is it any more than a beginning? Walt Whitman himself disclaims singularity in his work, and announces the coming after him of great successions of poets, and that he but lifts his finger to give the signal.

Was he not needed? Has not literature been bred in and in long enough? Has it not become unbearably artificial?

Shall a man of faith and practice in the simplicity of real things be called eccentric, while the disciple of the fictitious school writes without question?

Shall it still be the amazement of the light and dark that freshness of expression is the rarest quality of all?

You have come in good time, Walt Whitman! In opinions, in manners, in costumes, in books, in the aims and occupancy of life, in associates, in poems, conformity to all unnatural and tainted customs passes without remark, while perfect naturalness, health, faith, self-reliance, and all primal expressions of the manliest love and friendship, subject one to the stare and controversy of the world.

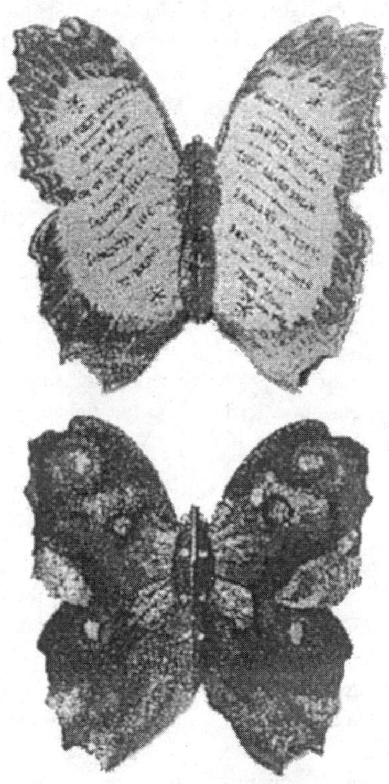

The cardboard butterfly on Whitman's finger in the photograph on page 370. It is now resident in the Library of Congress.

Leaves

of

Grass

1856

Poem of Salutation

O TAKE my hand, Walt Whitman!
Such gliding wonders! Such sights and sounds!
Such joined unended links, each hooked to the next!
Each answering all, each sharing the earth with all.

What widens within you, Walt Whitman?
What waves and soils exuding?
What climes? what persons and lands are here?
Who are the infants? some playing, some slumbering?
Who are the girls? Who are the married women?
Who are the three old men going slowly with their arms
        about each others' necks?
What rivers are these? What forests and fruits are these?
What are the mountains called that rise so high in the mists?
What myriads of dwellings are they, filled with dwellers?

Within me latitude widens, longitude lengthens,
Asia, Africa, Europe, are to the east—America is provided for in the west;
Banding the bulge of the earth winds the hot equator,
Curiously north and south turn the axis-ends;
Within me is the longest day, the sun wheels in slanting rings,
        it does not set for months,
Stretched in due time within me the midnight sun just rises
        above the horizon, and sinks again;
Within me zones, seas, cataracts, plains, volcanoes, groups,
Oceanica, Australasia, Polynesia, and the great West Indian islands.

What do you hear, Walt Whitman?

I hear the workman singing, the farmer's wife singing,
I hear in the distance the sounds of children, and of animals
        early in the day,
I hear the inimitable music of the voices of mothers,
I hear the persuasions of lovers,

I hear quick rifle-cracks from the riflemen of East Tennessee
    and Kentucky, hunting on hills,
I hear emulous shouts of Australians, pursuing the wild horse,
I hear the Spanish dance with castanets, in the chestnut shade,
    to the rebeck and guitar,
I hear continual echoes from the Thames,
I hear fierce French liberty songs,
I hear of the Italian boat-sculler the musical recitative of old poems,
I hear the Virginia plantation chorus of negroes, of a harvest night,
    in the glare of pine knots,
I hear the strong baritone of the 'long-shore-men of Manahatta—
    I hear the stevedores unlading the cargoes, and singing,
I hear the screams of the water-fowl of solitary northwest lakes,
I hear the rustling pattering of locusts, as they strike the grain and grass
    with the showers of their terrible clouds,
I hear the Coptic refrain toward sun-down pensively falling on the breast
    of the black venerable vast mother, the Nile,
I hear the bugles of raft-tenders on the streams of Canada,
I hear the chirp of the Mexican muleteer, and the bells of the mule,
I hear the Arab muezzin, calling from the top of the mosque,
I hear Christian priests at the altars of their churches—I hear
    the responsive bass and soprano,
I hear the wail of utter despair of the white-haired Irish grand-parents,
    when they learn the death of their grand-son,
I hear the cry of the Cossack, and the sailor's voice, putting to sea
    at Okotsk,
I hear the wheeze of the slave-coffle,[o] as the slaves march on,
    as the husky gangs pass on by twos and threes,
    fastened together with wrist-chains and ankle-chains,
I hear the entreaties of women tied up for punishment, I hear
    the sibilant whisk of thongs through the air,
I hear the appeal of the greatest orator, he that turns states by the tip
    of his tongue,
I hear the Hebrew reading his records and psalms,
I hear the rhythmic myths of the Greeks, and the strong legends
    of the Romans,
I hear the tale of the divine life and bloody death of the beautiful god,
    the Christ,
I hear the Hindoo teaching his favorite pupil the loves, wars, adages,
    transmitted safely to this day from poets who wrote
    three thousand years ago.

What do you see, Walt Whitman?
Who are they you salute, and that one after another salute you?

I see a great round wonder rolling through the air,
I see diminute farms, hamlets, ruins, grave-yards, jails, factories, palaces,
hovels, huts of barbarians, tents of nomads, upon the surface,
I see the shaded part on one side where the sleepers are sleeping,
and the sun-lit part on the other side,
I see the curious silent change of the light and shade,
I see distant lands, as real and near to the inhabitants of them
as my land is to me.

I see plenteous waters,
I see mountain peaks—I see the sierras of Andes and Alleghanies,
I see where they range,
I see plainly the Himmalehs, Chian Shahs, Altays, Gauts,
I see the Rocky Mountains, and the Peak of Winds,
I see the Styrian Alps and the Karnac Alps,
I see the Pyrenees, Balks, Carpathians, and to the north the Dofrafields,
and off at sea Mount Hecla,
I see Vesuvius and Etna—I see the Anahuacs,
I see the Mountains of the Moon, and the Snow Mountains,
and the Red Mountains of Madagascar,
I see the Vermont hills, and the long string of Cordilleras;
I see the vast deserts of Western America,
I see the Libyan, Arabian, and Asiatic deserts;
I see huge dreadful Arctic and Antarctic icebergs,
I see the superior oceans and the inferior ones—the Atlantic and Pacific,
the sea of Mexico, the Brazilian sea, and the sea of Peru,
The Japan waters, those of Hindostan, the China Sea,
and the Gulf of Guinea,
The spread of the Baltic, Caspian, Bothnia, the British shores,
and the Bay of Biscay,
The clear-sunned Mediterranean, and from one to another of its islands,
The inland fresh-tasted seas of North America,
The White Sea, and the sea around Greenland.

I behold the mariners of the world,
Some are in storms, some in the night, with the watch on the look-out,
some drifting helplessly, some with contagious diseases.

I behold the steam-ships of the world,
Some double the Cape of Storms, some Cape Verde,
others Capes Guardafui, Bon, or Bajadore,
Others Dondra Head, others pass the Straits of Sunda,
others Cape Lopatka, others Behring's Straits,
Others Cape Horn, others the Gulf of Mexico, or along Cuba or Hayti,
others Hudson's Bay or Baffin's Bay,
Others pass the Straits of Dover, others enter the Wash, others the Firth
of Solway, others round Cape Clear, others the Land's End,
Others traverse the Zuyder Zee or the Scheld,
Others add to the exits and entrances at Sandy Hook,
Others to the comers and goers at Gibraltar or the Dardanelles,
Others sternly push their way through the northern winter-packs,
Others descend or ascend the Obi or the Lena,
Others the Niger or the Congo, others the Hoang-ho and Amoor,
others the Indus, the Burampooter and Cambodia,
Others wait at the wharves of Manahatta, steamed up, ready to start,
Wait swift and swarthy in the ports of Australia,
Wait at Liverpool, Glasgow, Dublin, Marseilles, Lisbon, Naples,
Hamburgh, Bremen, Bordeaux, the Hague, Copenhagen,
Wait at Valparaiso, Rio Janeiro, Panama,
Wait at their moorings at Boston, Philadelphia, Baltimore, Charleston,
New Orleans, Galveston, San Francisco.

I see the tracks of the rail-roads of the earth,
I see them welding state to state, county to county, city to city,
through North America,
I see them in Great Britain, I see them in Europe,
I see them in Asia and in Africa.

I see the electric telegraphs of the earth,
I see the filaments of the news of the wars, deaths, losses, gains,
passions, of my race.

I see the long thick river-stripes of the earth,
I see where the Mississippi flows, I see where the Columbia flows,
I see the St. Lawrence and the falls of Niagara,
I see the Amazon and the Paraguay,
I see where the Seine flows, and where the Loire, the Rhone,
and the Guadalquivir flow,
I see the windings of the Volga, the Dnieper, the Oder,

I see the Tuscan going down the Arno, and the Venetian along the Po,
I see the Greek seaman sailing out of Egina bay.

I see the site of the great old empire of Assyria, and that of Persia,
    and that of India,
I see the falling of the Ganges over the high rim of Saukara.

I see the place of the idea of the Deity incarnated by avatars°
    in human forms,
I see the spots of the successions of priests on the earth, oracles,
    sacrificers, brahmins, sabians,° lamas, monks, muftis,° exhorters,
I see where druids walked the groves of Mona, I see the misletoe
    and vervain,°
I see the temples of the deaths of the bodies of gods,
    I see the old signifiers,
I see Christ once more eating the bread of his last supper in the midst
    of youths and old persons,
I see where the strong divine young man, the Hercules, toiled faithfully
    and long, and then died,
I see the place of the innocent rich life and hapless fate
    of the beautiful nocturnal son, the full-limbed Bacchus,
I see Kneph,° blooming, dressed in blue, with the crown of feathers
    on his head,
I see Hermes,° unsuspected, dying, well-beloved, saying to the people,
    Do not weep for me, this is not my true country, I have lived
    banished from my true country, I now go back there, I return
    to the celestial sphere where every one goes in his turn.

I see the battle-fields of the earth—grass grows upon them,
    and blossoms and corn,
I see the tracks of ancient and modern expeditions.

I see the nameless masonries, venerable messages of the unknown events,
    heroes, records of the earth.

I see the places of the sagas,
I see pine-trees and fir-trees torn by northern blasts,
I see granite boulders and cliffs, I see green meadows and lakes,
I see the burial-cairns of Scandinavian warriors,
I see them raised high with stones, by the marge of restless oceans,
    that the dead men's spirits, when they wearied of their quiet graves,

might rise up through the mounds, and gaze on the tossing billows,
and be refreshed by storms, immensity, liberty, action.

I see the steppes of Asia,
I see the tumuli of Mongolia, I see the tents of Kalmucks and Baskirs,
I see the nomadic tribes with herds of oxen and cows,
I see the table-lands notched with ravines, I see the jungles and deserts,
I see the camel, the wild steed, the bustard, the fat-tailed sheep,
the antelope, and the burrowing wolf.

I see the high-lands of Abyssinia,
I see the flocks of goats feeding, I see the fig-tree, tamarind, date,
I see fields of teff-wheat, I see the places of verdure and gold.

I see the Brazilian vaquero,
I see the Bolivian ascending Mount Sorata,
I see the Guacho crossing the plains, I see the incomparable rider
of horses with his lasso on his arm,
I see over the pampas the pursuit of wild cattle for their hides.

I see the little and large sea-dots, some inhabited, some uninhabited;
I see two boats with nets, lying off the shore of Paumanok, quite still,
I see ten fishermen waiting—they discover now a thick school
of mossbonkers, they drop the joined seine-ends in the water,
The boats separate, they diverge and row off, each on its rounding course
to the beach, enclosing the mossbonkers,
The net is drawn in by the windlass by those who stop ashore,
Some of the fishermen lounge in the boats, others stand negligently
ankle-deep in the water, poised on strong legs,
The boats are partly drawn up, the water slaps against them,
On the sand, in heaps and winrows,° well out from the water,
lie the green-backed spotted mossbonkers.

I see the despondent red man in the west, lingering about the banks
of Moingo, and about Lake Pepin,
He has beheld the quail and honey-bee, and sadly prepared to depart.

I see the regions of snow and ice,
I see the sharp-eyed Samoiede and the Finn,
I see the seal-seeker in his boat, poising his lance,
I see the Siberian on his slight-built sledge, drawn by dogs,

I see the porpoise-hunters, I see the whale-crews of the South Pacific
and the North Atlantic,
I see the cliffs, glaciers, torrents, valleys, of Switzerland—
I mark the long winters and the isolation.

I see the cities of the earth, and make myself a part of them,
I am a real Londoner, Parisian, Viennese,
I am a habitan of St. Petersburgh, Berlin, Constantinople,
I am of Adelaide, Sidney, Melbourne,
I am of Manchester, Bristol, Edinburgh, Limerick,
I am of Madrid, Cadiz, Barcelona, Oporto, Lyons, Brussels, Berne,
Frankfort, Stuttgart, Turin, Florence,
I belong in Moscow, Cracow, Warsaw—or northward in Christiania
or Stockholm—or in some street in Iceland,
I descend upon all those cities, and rise from them again.

I see vapors exhaling from unexplored countries,
I see the savage types, the bow and arrow, the poisoned splint,
the fetish and the obi.

I see African and Asiatic towns,
I see Algiers, Tripoli, Derne, Mogadore, Timbuctoo, Monrovia,
I see the swarms of Pekin, Canton, Benares, Delhi, Calcutta,
I see the Kruman in his hut, and the Dahoman and Ashantee-man
in their huts,
I see the Turk smoking opium in Aleppo,
I see the picturesque crowds at the fairs of Khiva, and those of Herat,
I see Teheran, I see Muscat and Medina, and the intervening sands—
I see the caravans toiling onward;
I see Egypt and the Egyptians, I see the pyramids and obelisks,
I look on chiselled histories, songs, philosophies, cut in slabs
of sand-stone or granite blocks.
I see at Memphis mummy-pits, containing mummies, embalmed,
swathed in linen cloth, lying there many centuries,
I look on the fall'n Theban, the large-ball'd eyes, the side-drooping neck,
the hands folded across the breast.

I see the menials of the earth, laboring,
I see the prisoners in the prisons,
I see the defective human bodies of the earth,
I see the blind, the deaf and dumb, idiots, hunch-backs, lunatics,

I see the pirates, thieves, betrayers, murderers, slave-makers of the earth,
I see the helpless infants, and the helpless old men and women.

I see male and female everywhere,
I see the serene brotherhood of philosophs,
I see the constructiveness of my race,
I see the results of perseverance and industry of my race,
I see ranks, colors, barbarisms, civilizations—I go among them,
I mix indiscriminately,
And I salute all the inhabitants of the earth.

You, inevitable where you are!
You daughter or son of England!
You free man of Australia! you of Tasmania! you of Papua!
you free woman of the same!
You of the mighty Slavic tribes and empires! you Russ in Russia!
You dim-descended, black, divine-souled African, large, fine-headed,
nobly-formed, superbly destined, on equal terms with me!
You Norwegian! Swede! Dane! Icelander! you Prussian!
You Spaniard of Spain! you Portuguese!
You Frenchwoman and Frenchman of France!
You Belge! you liberty-lover of Netherlands!
You sturdy Austrian! you Lombard! Hun! Bohemian! farmer of Styria!
You neighbor of the Danube!
You working-man of the Rhine, the Elbe, or the Weser!
you working-woman too!
You Sardinian! you Bavarian! you Swabian! Saxon! Wallachian!
Bulgarian!
You citizen of Prague! you Roman! Napolitan! Greek!
You lithe matador in the arena at Seville!
You mountaineer living lawlessly on the Taurus or Caucasus!
You Bokh horse-herd watching your mares and stallions feeding!
You beautiful-bodied Persian, at full speed in the saddle,
shooting arrows to the mark!
You Chinaman and Chinawoman of China! you Tartar of Tartary!
You women of the earth, subordinated at your tasks!
You Jew journeying in your old age through every risk to stand once
on Syrian ground!
You other Jews waiting in all lands for your Messiah!
You thoughtful Armenian pondering by some stream of the Euphrates!
you peering amid the ruins of Nineveh! you ascending
Mount Ararat!

You foot-worn pilgrim welcoming the far-away sparkle of the minarets
of Mecca!
You sheiks along the stretch from Suez to Babelmandel,
ruling your families and tribes!
You olive-grower tending your fruit on fields off Nazareth, Damascus,
or Lake Tiberias!
You Thibet trader on the wide inland, or bargaining in the shops
of Lassa
You Japanese man or woman! you liver in Madagascar, Ceylon,
Sumatra, Borneo!
All you continentals of Asia, Africa, Europe, Australia,
indifferent of place!
All you on the numberless islands of the archipelagoes of the sea!
And you of centuries hence, when you listen to me!
And you everywhere whom I specify not, but include just the same!
I salute you for myself and for America

Each of us inevitable,
Each of us limitless—each of us with his or her right upon the earth,
Each of us allowed the eternal purport of the earth,
Each of us here as divinely as any is here.

You Hottentot with clicking palate!
You woolly-haired hordes! you white or black owners of slaves!
You owned persons dropping sweat-drops or blood-drops!
You felons, deformed persons, idiots!
You human forms with the fathomless ever-impressive countenances
of brutes!
You poor koboo° whom the meanest of the rest look down upon,
for all your glimmering language and spirituality!
You low expiring aborigines of the hills of Utah, Oregon, California!
You dwarfed Kamskatkan, Greenlander, Lapp!
You Austral negro, naked, red, sooty, with protrusive lip, grovelling,
seeking your food!
You Caffre, Berber, Soudanese!
You haggard, uncouth, untutored Bedowee!
You plague-swarms in Madras, Nankin, Kaubul, Cairo!
You bather bathing in the Ganges!
You benighted roamer of Amazonia! you Patagonian! you Fegee-man!
You peon of Mexico! you Russian serf! you quadroon of Carolina,
Texas, Tennessee!
I do not refuse you my hand, or prefer others before you,

I do not say one word against you.

My spirit has passed in compassion and determination around
the whole earth,
I have looked for brothers, sisters, lovers, and found them ready
for me in all lands.

I think I have risen with you, you vapors, and moved away
to distant continents, and fallen down there, for reasons,
I think I have blown with you, you winds,
I think, you waters, I have fingered every shore with you,
I think I have run through what any river or strait of the globe
has run through,
I think I have taken my stand on the bases of peninsulas,
and on imbedded rocks.

What cities the light or warmth penetrates, I penetrate those cities myself,
All islands to which birds wing their way, I wing my way myself,
I find my home wherever there are any homes of men.

Poem of Wonder at The Resurrection of The Wheat

SOMETHING startles me where I thought I was safest,
I withdraw from the still woods I loved,
I will not go now on the pastures to walk,
I will not strip my clothes from my body to meet my lover the sea,
I will not touch my flesh to the earth, as to other flesh, to renew me.

How can the ground not sicken of men?
How can you be alive, you growths of spring?
How can you furnish health, you blood of herbs, roots, orchards, grain?
Are they not continually putting distempered corpses in the earth?
Is not every continent worked over and over with sour dead?
Where have you disposed of those carcasses of the drunkards
and gluttons of so many generations?

Where have you drawn off all the foul liquid and meat?
I do not see any of it upon you today—or perhaps I am deceived,
I will run a furrow with my plough—I will press my spade
through the sod, and turn it up underneath,
I am sure I shall expose some of the foul meat.

Behold!
This is the compost of billions of premature corpses,
Perhaps every mite has once formed part of a sick person,
Yet Behold!
The grass covers the prairies,
The bean bursts noiselessly through the mould in the garden,
The delicate spear of the onion pierces upwards,
The apple-buds cluster together on the apple-branches,
The resurrection of the wheat appears with pale visage out of its graves,
The tinge awakes over the willow-tree and the mulberry-tree,
The he-birds carol mornings and evenings, while the she-birds
sit on their nests,
The young of poultry break through the hatched eggs,
The new-born of animals appear, the calf is dropt from the cow,
the colt from the mare,
Out of its little hill faithfully rise the potato's dark green leaves,
Out of its hill rises the yellow maize-stalk;
The summer growth is innocent and disdainful above all those strata
of sour dead.

What chemistry!
That the winds are really not infectious!
That this is no cheat, this transparent green-wash of the sea,
which is so amorous after me!
That it is safe to allow it to lick my naked body all over with its tongues!
That it will not endanger me with the fevers that have
deposited themselves in it!
That all is clean, forever and forever!
That the cool drink from the well tastes so good!
That blackberries are so flavorous and juicy!
That the fruits of the apple-orchard, and of the orange-orchard—
that melons, grapes, peaches, plums, will none of them poison me!
That when I recline on the grass I do not catch any disease!
Though probably every spear of grass rises out of what was once
a catching disease.

Now I am terrified at the earth! it is that calm and patient,
It grows such sweet things out of such corruptions,
It turns harmless and stainless on its axis, with such endless successions
of diseased corpses,
It distils such exquisite winds out of such infused fetor,
It renews with such unwitting looks, its prodigal, annual,
sumptuous crops,
It gives such divine materials to men, and accepts such leavings
from them at last.

Poem of You, Whoever You Are

WHOEVER you are, I fear you are walking the walks of dreams,
I fear those realities are to melt from under your feet and hands;
Even now, your features, joys, speech, house, trade, manners, troubles,
follies, costume, crimes, dissipate away from you,
Your true soul and body appear before me,
They stand forth out of affairs—out of commerce, shops, law, science,
work, farms, clothes, the house, medicine, print, buying, selling,
eating, drinking, suffering, begetting, dying,
They receive these in their places, they find these or the like of these,
eternal, for reasons,
They find themselves eternal, they do not find that the water and soil
tend to endure forever—and they not endure.

Whoever you are, now I place my hand upon you, that you be my poem,
I whisper with my lips close to your ear,
I have loved many women and men, but I love none better than you.

O I have been dilatory and dumb,
I should have made my way straight to you long ago,
I should have blabbed nothing but you, I should have chanted nothing
but you.

I will leave all, and come and make the hymns of you;
None have understood you, but I understand you,
None have done justice to you, you have not done justice to yourself,
None but have found you imperfect, I only find no imperfection in you,
None but would subordinate you, I only am he who will never consent
to subordinate you.
I only am he who places over you no master, owner, better, god,
beyond what waits intrinsically in yourself.

Painters have painted their swarming groups, and the centre figure of all,
From the head of the centre figure spreading a nimbus of gold-colored light,
But I paint myriads of heads, but paint no head without its nimbus
of gold-colored light,
From my hand, from the brain of every man and woman it streams,
effulgently flowing forever.

O I could sing such grandeurs and glories about you!
You have not known what you are—you have slumbered upon yourself
all your life,
Your eye-lids have been as much as closed most of the time,
What you have done returns already in mockeries,
Your thrift, knowledge, prayers, if they do not return in mockeries,
what is their return?

The mockeries are not you,
Underneath them, and within them, I see you lurk,
I pursue you where none else has pursued you,
Silence, the desk, the flippant expression, the night,
the accustomed routine, if these conceal you from others,
or from yourself, they do not conceal you from me,
The shaved face, the unsteady eye, the impure complexion,
if these balk others, they do not balk me,
The pert apparel, the deformed attitude, drunkenness, greed,
premature death, all these I part aside,
I track through your windings and turnings—I come upon you
where you thought eye should never come upon you.

There is no endowment in man or woman that is not tallied in you,
There is no virtue, no beauty, in man or woman but as good is in you,
No pluck, no endurance in others, but as good is in you,
No pleasure waiting for others, but an equal pleasure waits for you.

As for me, I give nothing to any one, except I give the like carefully to you,
I sing the songs of the glory of none, not God, sooner than I sing the songs of the glory of you.

Whoever you are, you are to hold your own at any hazard,
These shows of the east and west are tame compared to you,
These immense meadows, these interminable rivers—you are immense and interminable as they,
These furies, elements, storms, motions of nature, throes of apparent dissolution,—you are he or she who is master or mistress over them,
Master or mistress in your own right over nature, elements, pain, passion, dissolution.

The hopples° fall from your ankles! you find an unfailing sufficiency!
Old, young, male, female, rude, low, rejected by the rest, whatever you are promulges itself,
Through birth, life, death, burial, the means are provided, nothing is scanted,
Through angers, losses, ambition, ignorance, ennui, what you are picks its way.

Sun-Down Poem

FLOOD-TIDE of the river, flow on! I watch you, face to face,
Clouds of the west! sun half an hour high! I see you also face to face.

Crowds of men and women attired in the usual costumes, how curious you are to me!
On the ferry-boats the hundreds and hundreds that cross are more curious to me than you suppose,
And you that shall cross from shore to shore years hence, are more to me, and more in my meditations, than you might suppose.

The impalpable sustenance of me from all things at all hours of the day,
The simple, compact, well-joined scheme—myself disintegrated,
every one disintegrated, yet part of the scheme,
The similitudes of the past and those of the future,
The glories strung like beads on my smallest sights and hearings—
on the walk in the street, and the passage over the river,
The current rushing so swiftly, and swimming with me far away,
The others that are to follow me, the ties between me and them,
The certainty of others—the life, love, sight, hearing of others.

Others will enter the gates of the ferry, and cross from shore to shore,
Others will watch the run of the flood-tide,
Others will see the shipping of Manhattan north and west,
and the heights of Brooklyn to the south and east,
Others will see the islands large and small,
Fifty years hence others will see them as they cross, the sun
half an hour high,
A hundred years hence, or ever so many hundred years hence,
others will see them,
Will enjoy the sun-set, the pouring in of the flood-tide, the falling back
to the sea of the ebb-tide.

It avails not, neither time or place—distance avails not,
I am with you, you men and women of a generation,
or ever so many generations hence,
I project myself, also I return—I am with you, and know how it is.

Just as you feel when you look on the river and sky, so I felt,
Just as any of you is one of a living crowd, I was one of a crowd,
Just as you are refreshed by the gladness of the river,
and the bright flow, I was refreshed,
Just as you stand and lean on the rail, yet hurry with the swift current,
I stood, yet was hurried,
Just as you look on the numberless masts of ships,
and the thick-stemmed pipes of steamboats, I looked.

I too many and many a time crossed the river, the sun half an hour high,
I watched the December sea-gulls, I saw them high in the air floating
with motionless wings oscillating their bodies,
I saw how the glistening yellow lit up parts of their bodies,
and left the rest in strong shadow,
I saw the slow-wheeling circles and the gradual edging toward the south.

I too saw the reflection of the summer-sky in the water,
Had my eyes dazzled by the shimmering track of beams,
Looked at the fine centrifugal spokes of light round the shape
of my head in the sun-lit water,
Looked on the haze on the hills southward and southwestward,
Looked on the vapor as it flew in fleeces tinged with violet,
Looked toward the lower bay to notice the arriving ships,
Saw their approach, saw aboard those that were near me,
Saw the white sails of schooners and sloops, saw the ships at anchor,
The sailors at work in the rigging or out astride the spars,
The round masts, the swinging motion of the hulls,
the slender serpentine pennants,
The large and small steamers in motion, the pilots in their pilot-houses,
The white wake left by the passage, the quick tremulous whirl
of the wheels,
The flags of all nations, the falling of them at sun-set,
The scallop-edged waves in the twilight, the ladled cups,
the frolicsome crests and glistening,
The stretch afar growing dimmer and dimmer, the gray walls
of the granite store-houses by the docks,
On the river the shadowy group, the big steam-tug closely flanked
on each side by the barges—the hay-boat, the belated lighter,
On the neighboring shore the fires from the foundry chimneys
burning high and glaringly into the night,
Casting their flicker of black, contrasted with wild red and yellow light,
over the tops of houses, and down into the clefts of streets.

These and all else were to me the same as they are to you,
I project myself a moment to tell you—also I return.

I loved well those cities,
I loved well the stately and rapid river,
The men and women I saw were all near to me,
Others the same—others who look back on me, because I looked
forward to them,
The time will come, though I stop here today and tonight.

What is it, then, between us? What is the count of the scores
or hundreds of years between us?
Whatever it is, it avails not—distance avails not, and place avails not.

I too lived,
I too walked the streets of Manhattan Island, and bathed in the waters
around it;
I too felt the curious abrupt questionings stir within me,
In the day, among crowds of people, sometimes they came upon me,
In my walks home late at night, or as I lay in my bed, they came upon me.

I too had been struck from the float forever held in solution,
I too had received identity by my body,
That I was, I knew was of my body, and what I should be,
I knew I should be of my body.

It is not upon you alone the dark patches fall,
The dark threw patches down upon me also,
The best I had done seemed to me blank and suspicious,
My great thoughts, as I supposed them, were they not in reality meagre?
Would not people laugh at me?

It is not you alone who know what it is to be evil,
I am he who knew what it was to be evil,
I too knitted the old knot of contrariety,
Blabbed, blushed, resented, lied, stole, grudged,
Had guile, anger, lust, hot wishes I dared not speak,
Was wayward, vain, greedy, shallow, sly, a solitary committer, a coward,
a malignant person,
The wolf, the snake, the hog, not wanting in me,
The cheating look, the frivolous word, the adulterous wish, not wanting,
Refusals, hates, postponements, meanness, laziness, none of these wanting.

But I was a Manhattanese, free, friendly, and proud!
I was called by my nighest name by clear loud voices of young men
as they saw me approaching or passing,
Felt their arms on my neck as I stood, or the negligent leaning
of their flesh against me as I sat,
Saw many I loved in the street, or ferry-boat, or public assembly,
yet never told them a word,
Lived the same life with the rest, the same old laughing, gnawing,
sleeping,
Played the part that still looks back on the actor or actress,
The same old role, the role that is what we make it, as great
as we like, or as small as we like, or both great and small.

Closer yet I approach you,
What thought you have of me, I had as much of you—
I laid in my stores in advance,
I considered long and seriously of you before you were born.

Who was to know what should come home to me?
Who knows but I am enjoying this?
Who knows but I am as good as looking at you now,
for all you cannot see me?

It is not you alone, nor I alone,
Not a few races, not a few generations, not a few centuries,
It is that each came, or comes, or shall come, from its due emission,
without fail, either now, or then, or henceforth.

Every thing indicates—the smallest does, and the largest does,
A necessary film envelops all, and envelops the soul for a proper time.

Now I am curious what sight can ever be more stately and admirable
to me than my mast-hemm'd Manhatta, my river and sun-set,
and my scallop-edged waves of flood-tide, the sea-gulls
oscillating their bodies, the hay-boat in the twilight,
and the belated lighter,
Curious what gods can exceed these that clasp me by the hand,
and with voices I love call me promptly and loudly
by my nighest name as I approach,
Curious what is more subtle than this which ties me to the woman
or man that looks in my face,
Which fuses me into you now, and pours my meaning into you.

We understand, then, do we not?
What I promised without mentioning it, have you not accepted?
What the study could not teach—what the preaching could not
accomplish is accomplished, is it not?
What the push of reading could not start is started by me personally,
is it not?

Flow on, river! Flow with the flood-tide, and ebb with the ebb-tide!
Frolic on, crested and scallop-edged waves!
Gorgeous clouds of the sun-set, drench with your splendor me,
or the men and women generations after me!
Cross from shore to shore, countless crowds of passengers!

Stand up, tall masts of Manahatta!—stand up, beautiful hills of Brooklyn!
Bully for you! you proud, friendly, free Manhattanese!
Throb, baffled and curious brain! throw out questions and answers!
Suspend here and everywhere, eternal float of solution!
Blab, blush, lie, steal, you or I or any one after us!
Gaze, loving and thirsting eyes, in the house or street or public assembly!
Sound out, voices of young men! loudly and musically call me by my nighest name!
Live, old life! play the part that looks back on the actor or actress!
Play the old role, the role that is great or small, according as one makes it!
Consider, you who peruse me, whether I may not in unknown ways be looking upon you!
Be firm, rail over the river, to support those who lean idly, yet haste with the hasting current!
Fly on, sea-birds! fly sideways, or wheel in large circles high in the air!
Receive the summer-sky, you water! faithfully hold it till all downcast eyes have time to take it from you!
Diverge, fine spokes of light, from the shape of my head, or any one's head, in the sun-lit water!
Come on, ships from the lower bay! pass up or down, white-sailed schooners, sloops, lighters!
Flaunt away, flags of all nations! be duly lowered at sun-set!
Burn high your fires, foundry chimneys! cast black shadows at night-fall! cast red and yellow light over the tops of houses!
Appearances, now or henceforth, indicate what you are!
You necessary film, continue to envelop the soul!
About my body for me, and your body for you, be hung our divinest aromas!
Thrive, cities! Bring your freight, bring your shows, ample and sufficient rivers!
Expand, being than which none else is perhaps more spiritual!
Keep your places, objects than which none else is more lasting!

We descend upon you and all things, we arrest you all,
We realize the soul only by you, you faithful solids and fluids,
Through you color, form, location, sublimity, ideality,
Through you every proof, comparison, and all the suggestions and determinations of ourselves.

You have waited, you always wait, you dumb beautiful ministers! you novices!

We receive you with free sense at last, and are insatiate henceforward,
Not you any more shall be able to foil us, or withhold yourselves
from us,
We use you, and do not cast you aside—we plant you permanently
within us,
We fathom you not—we love you—there is perfection in you also,
You furnish your parts toward eternity,
Great or small, you furnish your parts toward the soul.

Poem of The Road

AFOOT and light-hearted I take to the open road!
Healthy, free, the world before me!
The long brown path before me, leading wherever I choose!

Henceforth I ask not good-fortune, I am good-fortune,
Henceforth I whimper no more, postpone no more, need nothing,
Strong and content, I travel the open road.

The earth—that is sufficient,
I do not want the constellations any nearer,
I know they are very well where they are,
I know they suffice for those who belong to them.

Still here I carry my old delicious burdens,
I carry them, men and women—I carry them with me wherever I go,
I swear it is impossible for me to get rid of them,
I am filled with them, and I will fill them in return.

You road I travel and look around! I believe you are not all that is here!
I believe that something unseen is also here.

Here is the profound lesson of reception, neither preference or denial,
The black with his woolly head, the felon, the diseased,
the illiterate person, are not denied,

The birth, the hasting after the physician, the beggar's tramp,
the drunkard's stagger, the laughing party of mechanics,
The escaped youth, the rich person's carriage, the fop,
the eloping couple,
The early market-man, the hearse, the moving of furniture into the town,
the return back from the town,
They pass, I also pass, any thing passes, none can be interdicted,
None but are accepted, none but are dear to me.

You air that serves me with breath to speak!
You objects that call from diffusion my meanings and give them shape!
You light that wraps me and all things in delicate equable showers!
You animals moving serenely over the earth!
You birds that wing yourselves through the air! you insects!
You sprouting growths from the farmers' fields! you stalks and weeds
by the fences!
You paths worn in the irregular hollows by the road-sides!
I think you are latent with curious existences—you are so dear to me.

You flagged walks of the cities! you strong curbs at the edges!
You ferries! you planks and posts of wharves! you timber-lined sides!
you distant ships!
You rows of houses! you window-pierced facades! you roofs!
You porches and entrances! you copings and iron guards!
You windows whose transparent shells might expose so much!
You doors and ascending steps! you arches!
You gray stones of interminable pavements! you trodden crossings!
From all that has been near you I believe you have imparted
to yourselves, and now would impart the same secretly to me,
From the living and the dead I think you have peopled your
impassive surfaces, and the spirits thereof would be evident
and amicable with me.

The earth expanding right hand and left hand,
The picture alive, every part in its best light,
The music falling in where it is wanted, and stopping where it is
not wanted,
The cheerful voice of the public road—the gay fresh sentiment
of the road.

O highway I travel! O public road! do you say to me, Do not leave me?
Do you say, Venture not? If you leave me, you are lost?

Do you say, I am already prepared—I am well-beaten and undenied—
Adhere to me?

O public road! I say back, I am not afraid to leave you—yet I love you,
You express me better than I can express myself,
You shall be more to me than my poem.

I think heroic deeds were all conceived in the open air,
I think I could stop here myself, and do miracles,
I think whatever I meet on the road I shall like, and whatever beholds me
shall like me,
I think whoever I see must be happy.

From this hour, freedom!
From this hour, I ordain myself loosed of limits and imaginary lines!
Going where I list—my own master, total and absolute,
Listening to others, and considering well what they say,
Pausing, searching, receiving, contemplating,
Gently but with undeniable will divesting myself of the holds
that would hold me.

I inhale great draughts of air,
The east and the west are mine, and the north and the south are mine.

I am larger than I thought!
I did not know I held so much goodness!

All seems beautiful to me,
I can repeat over to men and women, You have done such good to me,
I would do the same to you.

I will recruit for myself and you as I go,
I will scatter myself among men and women as I go,
I will toss the new gladness and roughness among them;
Whoever denies me, it shall not trouble me,
Whoever accepts me, he or she shall be blessed, and shall bless me.

Now if a thousand perfect men were to appear, it would not amaze me,
Now if a thousand beautiful forms of women appeared,
it would not astonish me.

Now I see the secret of the making of the best persons,
It is to grow in the open air, and to eat and sleep with the earth.

Here is space—here a great personal deed has room,
Such a deed seizes upon the hearts of the whole race of men,
Its effusion of strength and will overwhelms law, and mocks all authority
and all argument against it.

Here is the test of wisdom,
Wisdom is not finally tested in schools,
Wisdom cannot be passed from one having it, to another not having it,
Wisdom is of the soul, is not susceptible of proof, is its own proof,
Applies to all stages and objects and qualities, and is content,
Is the certainty of the reality and immortality of things,
and the excellence of things.
Something there is in the float of the sight of things that provokes it
out of the soul.

Now I re-examine philosophies and religions,
They may prove well in lecture-rooms, yet not prove at all under the spacious
clouds, and along the landscape and flowing currents.

Here is realization,
Here is a man tallied—he realizes here what he has in him,
The animals, the past, the future, light, space, majesty, love,
if they are vacant of you, you are vacant of them.

Only the kernel of every object nourishes;
Where is he who tears off the husks for you and me?
Where is he that undoes stratagems and envelopes for you and me?

Here is adhesiveness°—it is not previously fashioned, it is apropos;
Do you know what it is as you pass to be loved by strangers?
Do you know the talk of those turning eye-balls?

Here is the efflux of the soul,
The efflux of the soul comes through beautiful gates of laws,
provoking questions,
These yearnings, why are they? these thoughts in the darkness,
why are they?
Why are there men and women that while they are nigh me
the sun-light expands my blood?

Why when they leave me do my pennants of joy sink flat and lank?
Why are there trees I never walk under but large and melodious thoughts
descend upon me?
(I think they hang there winter and summer on those trees,
and always drop fruit as I pass.)
What is it I interchange so suddenly with strangers?
What with some driver as I ride on the seat by his side?
What with some fisherman, drawing his seine by the shore,
as I walk by and pause?
What gives me to be free to a woman's or man's good-will?
What gives them to be free to mine?

The efflux of the soul is happiness—here is happiness,
I think it pervades the air, waiting at all times,
Now it flows into us—we are rightly charged.

Here rises the fluid and attaching character;
The fluid and attaching character is the freshness and sweetness
of man and woman,
The herbs of the morning sprout no fresher and sweeter every day
out of the roots of themselves, than it sprouts fresh and sweet
continually out of itself.

Toward the fluid and attaching character exudes the sweat of the love
of young and old,
From it falls distilled the charm that mocks beauty and attainments,
Toward it heaves the shuddering longing ache of contact.

Allons!° Whoever you are, come travel with me!
Traveling with me, you find what never tires.

The earth never tires!
The earth is rude, silent, incomprehensible at first—nature is rude
and incomprehensible at first,
Be not discouraged—keep on—there are divine things, well enveloped,
I swear to you there are divine things more beautiful than words can tell!

Allons! We must not stop here!
However sweet these laid-up stores, however convenient this dwelling,
we cannot remain here!
However sheltered this port, however calm these waters,
we must not anchor here!

However welcome the hospitality that surrounds us, we are permitted to receive it but a little while.

Allons! the inducements shall be great to you,
We will sail pathless and wild seas,
We will go where winds blow, waves dash, and the Yankee clipper speeds by under full sail.

Allons! With power, liberty, the earth, the elements!
Health, defiance, gaiety, self-esteem, curiosity!

Allons! From all formulas!
From your formulas, O bat-eyed and materialistic priests!

The stale cadaver blocks up the passage—the burial waits no longer.

Allons! Yet take warning!
He traveling with me needs the best blood, thews,° endurance,
None may come to the trial till he or she bring courage and health.

Come not here if you have already spent the best of yourself!
Only those may come who come in sweet and determined bodies,
No diseased person—no rum-drinker or venereal taint is permitted here.

I and mine do not convince by arguments, similes, rhymes,
We convince by our presence.

Listen! I will be honest with you,
I do not offer the old smooth prizes, but offer rough new prizes,
These are the days that must happen to you:
You shall not heap up what is called riches,
You shall scatter with lavish hand all that you earn or achieve,
You but arrive at the city to which you were destined—you hardly settle yourself to satisfaction, before you are called by an irresistible call to depart,
You shall be treated to the ironical smiles and mockings of those who remain behind you,
What beckonings of love you receive, you shall only answer with passionate kisses of parting,
You shall not allow the hold of those who spread their reached hands toward you.

Allons! After the great companions! and to belong to them!
They too are on the road! they are the swift and majestic men!
they are the greatest women!

Over that which hindered them, over that which retarded,
passing impediments large or small,
Committers of crimes, committers of many beautiful virtues,
Enjoyers of calms of seas, and storms of seas,
Sailors of many a ship, walkers of many a mile of land,
Habitues of many different countries, habitues of far-distant dwellings,
Trusters of men and women, observers of cities, solitary toilers,
Pausers and contemplaters of tufts, blossoms, shells of the shore,
Dancers at wedding-dances, kissers of brides, tender helpers of children,
bearers of children,
Soldiers of revolts, standers by gaping graves, lowerers down of coffins,
Journeyers over consecutive seasons, over the years—the curious years,
each emerging from that which preceded it,
Journeyers as with companions, namely, their own diverse phases,
Forth-steppers from the latent unrealized baby-days,
Journeyers gaily with their own youth—journeyers with their bearded
and well-grained manhood,
Journeyers with their womanhood, ample, unsurpassed, content,
Journeyers with their sublime old age of manhood or womanhood,
Old age, calm, expanded, broad with the haughty breadth of the universe,
Old age, flowing free with the delicious near-by freedom of death.

Allons! to that which is endless as it was beginningless!
To undergo much, tramps of days, rests of nights!
To merge all in the travel they tend to, and the days and nights they tend to!
Again to merge them in the start of superior journeys!
To see nothing anywhere but what you may reach it and pass it!
To conceive no time, however distant, but what you may reach it and pass it!
To look up or down no road but it stretches and waits for you!
however long, but it stretches and waits for you!
To see no being, not God's or any, but you also go thither!
To see no possession but you may possess it! enjoying all without labor or
purchase—abstracting the feast, yet not abstracting one particle of it;
To take the best of the farmer's farm and the rich man's elegant villa,
and the chaste blessings of the well-married couple, and the fruits
of orchards and flowers of gardens!

To take to your use out of the compact cities as you pass through!
To carry buildings and streets with you afterward wherever you go!
To gather the minds of men out of their brains as you encounter them!
to gather the love out of their hearts!
To take your own lovers on the road with you, for all that you
leave them behind you!
To know the universe itself as a road—as many roads—as roads
for traveling souls!

The soul travels,
The body does not travel as much as the soul,
The body has just as great a work as the soul, and parts away at last
for the journeys of the soul.

All parts away for the progress of souls,
All religion, all solid things, arts, governments—all that was or is apparent
upon this globe or any globe, falls into niches and corners
before the processions of souls along the grand roads
of the universe,
Of the progress of the souls of men and women along the grand roads
of the universe, all other progress is the needed emblem
and sustenance.

Forever alive, forever forward,
Stately, solemn, sad, withdrawn, baffled, mad, turbulent, feeble, dissatisfied,
Desperate, proud, fond, sick, accepted by men, rejected by men,
They go! they go! I know that they go, but I know not where they go,
But I know that they go toward the best—toward something great.

Allons! Whoever you are! come forth!
You must not stay in your house, though you built it,
or though it has been built for you.

Allons! out of the dark confinement!
It is useless to protest—I know all, and expose it.

Behold through you as bad as the rest!
Through the laughter, dancing, dining, supping, of people,
Inside of dresses and ornaments, inside of those washed
and trimmed faces,
Behold a secret silent loathing and despair!

No husband, no wife, no friend, no lover, so trusted as to hear the confession,
Another self, a duplicate of every one, skulking and hiding it goes, open and above-board it goes,
Formless and wordless through the streets of the cities, polite and bland in the parlors,
In the cars of rail-roads, in steam-boats, in the public assembly,
Home to the houses of men and women, among their families, at the table, in the bed-room, everywhere,
Smartly attired, countenance smiling, form upright, death under the breast-bones, hell under the skull-bones,
Under the broad-cloth and gloves, under the ribbons and artificial flowers,
Keeping fair with the customs, speaking not a syllable of itself,
Speaking of anything else, but never of itself.

Allons! through struggles and wars!
The goal that was named cannot be countermanded.

Have the past struggles succeeded?
What has succeeded? Yourself? Your nation? Nature?
Now understand me well—it is provided in the essence of things, that from any fruition of success, no matter what, shall come forth something to make a greater struggle necessary.

My call is the call of battle—I nourish active rebellion,
He going with me must go well armed,
He going with me goes often with spare diet, poverty, angry enemies, contentions.

Allons! the road is before us!
It is safe—I have tried it—my own feet have tried it well.

Allons! be not detained!
Let the paper remain on the desk unwritten, and the book on the shelf unopened!
Let the tools remain in the work-shop! let the money remain unearned!
Let the school stand! mind not the cry of the teacher!
Let the preacher preach in his pulpit! let the lawyer plead in the court, and the judge expound the law!

Mon enfant! I give you my hand!
I give you my love, more precious than money,

I give you myself, before preaching or law;
Will you give me yourself? Will you come travel with me?
Shall we stick by each other as long as we live?

Poem of Procreation

A WOMAN waits for me—she contains all, nothing is lacking,
Yet all were lacking, if sex were lacking, or if the moisture
of the right man were lacking.

Sex contains all,
Bodies, souls, meanings, proofs, purities, delicacies, results,
promulgations,
Songs, commands, health, pride, the maternal mystery, the semitic milk,
All hopes, benefactions, bestowals,
All the passions, loves, beauties, delights of the earth,
All the governments, judges, gods, followed persons of the earth,
These are contained in sex, as parts of itself and justification of itself.

Without shame the man I like knows and avows the deliciousness
of his sex,
Without shame the woman I like knows and avows hers.

O I will fetch bully breeds of children yet!
They cannot be fetched, I say, on less terms than mine,
Electric growth from the male, and rich ripe fibre from the female,
are the terms.

I will dismiss myself from impassive women,
I will go stay with her who waits for me, and with those women
that are warm-blooded and sufficient for me,
I see that they understand me, and do not deny me,
I see that they are worthy of me—so I will be the robust husband
of those women!
They are not one jot less than I am,

They are tanned in the face by shining suns and blowing winds,
Their flesh has the old divine suppleness and strength,
They know how to swim, row, ride, wrestle, shoot, run, strike, retreat, advance, resist, defend themselves,
They are ultimate in their own right—they are calm, clear, well-possessed of themselves.

I draw you close to me, you women!
I cannot let you go, I would do you good,
I am for you, and you are for me, not only for our own sake, but for others' sakes,
Enveloped in you sleep greater heroes and bards,
They refuse to awake at the touch of any man but me.

It is I, you women—I make my way,
I am stern, acrid, large, undissuadable—but I love you,
I do not hurt you any more than is necessary for you,
I pour the stuff to start sons and daughters fit for These States—I press with slow rude muscle,
I brace myself effectually—I listen to no entreaties,
I dare not withdraw till I deposite what has so long accumulated within me.

Through you I drain the pent-up rivers of myself,
In you I wrap a thousand onward years,
On you I graft the grafts of the best-beloved of me and of America,
The drops I distil upon you are drops of fierce and athletic girls, and of new artists, musicians, singers,
The babes I beget upon you are to beget babes in their turn,
I shall demand perfect men and women out of my love-spendings,
I shall expect them to interpenetrate with others, as I and you interpenetrate now,
I shall count on the fruits of the gushing showers of them, as I count on the fruits of the gushing showers I give now,
I shall look for loving crops from the birth, life, death, immortality I plant so lovingly now.

Clef Poem

THIS night I am happy,
As I watch the stars shining, I think a thought of the clef
of the universes, and of the future.

What can the future bring me more than I have?
Do you suppose I wish to enjoy life in other spheres?

I say distinctly I comprehend no better sphere than this earth,
I comprehend no better life than the life of my body.

I do not know what follows the death of my body,
But I know well that whatever it is, it is best for me.
And I know well that what is really Me shall live just as much as before.

I am not uneasy but I shall have good housing to myself,
But this is my first—how can I like the rest any better?
Here I grew up—the studs and rafters are grown parts of me.

I am not uneasy but I am to be beloved by young and old men,
and to love them the same,
I suppose the pink nipples of the breasts of women with whom
I shall sleep will taste the same to my lips,
But this is the nipple of a breast of my mother, always near
and always divine to me, her true child and son.

I suppose I am to be eligible to visit the stars, in my time,
I suppose I shall have myriads of new experiences—and that
the experience of this earth will prove only one out of myriads;
But I believe my body and my soul already indicate those experiences,
And I believe I shall find nothing in the stars more majestic
and beautiful than I have already found on the earth,
And I believe I have this night a clue through the universes,
And I believe I have this night thought a thought of the clef of eternity.

A vast similitude interlocks all,
All spheres, grown, ungrown, small, large, suns, moons, planets, comets,
asteroids,
All the substances of the same, and all that is spiritual upon the same,
All distances of place, however wide,
All distances of time—all inanimate forms,
All souls—all living bodies, though they be in different worlds,
All gaseous, watery, vegetable, mineral processes, the fishes, the brutes,
All men and women—me also,
All nations, colors, barbarisms, civilizations, languages,
All identities that have existed or may exist on this globe or any globe,
All lives and deaths—all of past, present, future,
This vast similitude spans them, and always has spanned,
and shall forever span them.

Poem of The Heart of The Son of Manhattan Island

WHO has gone farthest? For I swear I will go farther;
And who has been just? For I would be the most just person
of the earth;
And who most cautious? For I would be more cautious;
And who has been happiest? O I think it is I! I think no one
was ever happier than I;
And who has lavished all? For I lavish constantly the best I have;
And who has been firmest? For I would be firmer;
And who proudest? For I think I have reason to be the proudest
son alive—for I am the son of the brawny and tall-topt city;
And who has been bold and true? For I would be the boldest
and truest being of the universe;
And who benevolent? For I would show more benevolence
than all the rest;
And who has projected beautiful words through the longest time?
By God! I will outvie him! I will say such words,
they shall stretch through longer time!

And who has received the love of the most friends? For I know
what it is to receive the passionate love of many friends;
And to whom has been given the sweetest from women, and paid them
in kind? For I will take the like sweets, and pay them in kind;
And who possesses a perfect and enamored body? For I do not believe
any one possesses a more perfect or enamored body than mine;
And who thinks the amplest thoughts? For I will surround
those thoughts;
And who has made hymns fit for the earth? For I am mad with
devouring ecstasy to make joyous hymns for the whole earth!

Faith Poem

I NEED no assurances—I am a man who is pre-occupied of his own soul;
I do not doubt that whatever I know at a given time, there waits for me
more which I do not know;
I do not doubt that from under the feet, and beside the hands and face
I am cognizant of, are now looking faces I am not cognizant of—
calm and actual faces;
I do not doubt but the majesty and beauty of the world is latent
in any iota of the world;
I do not doubt there are realizations I have no idea of, waiting for me
through time and through the universes—also upon this earth;
I do not doubt I am limitless, and that the universes are limitless—
in vain I try to think how limitless;
I do not doubt that the orbs, and the systems of orbs, play their
swift sports through the air on purpose—and that I shall one day
be eligible to do as much as they, and more than they;
I do not doubt there is far more in trivialities, insects, vulgar persons,
slaves, dwarfs, weeds, rejected refuse, than I have supposed;
I do not doubt there is more in myself than I have supposed—
and more in all men and women—and more in my poems
than I have supposed;
I do not doubt that temporary affairs keep on and on, millions of years;
I do not doubt interiors have their interiors, and exteriors have

their exteriors—and that the eye-sight has another eye-sight, and the hearing another hearing, and the voice another voice;
I do not doubt that the passionately-wept deaths of young men are provided for—and that the deaths of young women, and the deaths of little children, are provided for;
I do not doubt that wrecks at sea, no matter what the horrors of them—no matter whose wife, child, husband, father, lover, has gone down—are provided for, to the minutest point;
I do not doubt that shallowness, meanness, malignance, are provided for;
I do not doubt that cities, you, America, the remainder of the earth, politics, freedom, degradations, are carefully provided for;
I do not doubt that whatever can possibly happen, any where, at any time, is provided for, in the inherences of things.

Poem of Perfect Miracles

REALISM is mine, my miracles,
Take all of the rest—take freely—I keep but my own—I give only of them,
I offer them without end—I offer them to you wherever your feet can carry you, or your eyes reach.

Why! who makes much of a miracle?
As to me, I know of nothing else but miracles,
Whether I walk the streets of Manhattan,
Or dart my sight over the roofs of houses toward the sky,
Or wade with naked feet along the beach, just in the edge of the water,
Or stand under trees in the woods,
Or talk by day with any one I love—or sleep in the bed at night with any one I love,
Or sit at the table at dinner with my mother,
Or look at strangers opposite me riding in the car,
Or watch honey-bees busy around the hive, of an August forenoon,
Or animals feeding in the fields,
Or birds—or the wonderfulness of insects in the air,

Or the wonderfulness of the sun-down—or of stars shining
so quiet and bright,
Or the exquisite, delicate, thin curve of the new-moon in May,
Or whether I go among those I like best, and that like me best—
mechanics, boatmen, farmers,
Or among the savans—or to the soiree—or to the opera,
Or stand a long while looking at the movements of machinery,
Or behold children at their sports,
Or the admirable sight of the perfect old man, or the perfect old woman,
Or the sick in hospitals, or the dead carried to burial,
Or my own eyes and figure in the glass,
These, with the rest, one and all, are to me miracles,
The whole referring—yet each distinct and in its place.

To me, every hour of the light and dark is a miracle,
Every inch of space is a miracle,
Every square yard of the surface of the earth is spread with the same,
Every cubic foot of the interior swarms with the same;
Every spear of grass—the frames, limbs, organs, of men and women,
and all that concerns them,
All these to me are unspeakably perfect miracles.

To me the sea is a continual miracle,
The fishes that swim—the rocks—the motion of the waves—the ships,
with men in them—what stranger miracles are there?

Bunch Poem

THE friend I am happy with,
The arm of my friend hanging idly over my shoulder,
The hill-side whitened with blossoms of the mountain ash,
The same, late in autumn—the gorgeous hues of red, yellow, drab,
purple, and light and dark green,
The rich coverlid of the grass—animals and birds—the private
untrimmed bank—the primitive apples—the pebble-stones,

Beautiful dripping fragments—the negligent list of one after another,
as I happen to call them to me, or think of them,
The real poems (what we call poems being merely pictures),
The poems of the privacy of the night, and of men like me,
This poem, drooping shy and unseen, that I always carry,
and that all men carry
(Know, once for all, avowed on purpose, wherever are men like me,
are our lusty, lurking, masculine poems),
Love-thoughts, love-juice, love-odor, love-yielding, love-climbers,
and the climbing sap,
Arms and hands of love—lips of love—phallic thumb of love—
breasts of love—bellies, pressed and glued together with love,
Earth of chaste love—life that is only life after love,
The body of my love—the body of the woman I love—the body
of the man—the body of the earth,
Soft forenoon airs that blow from the south-west,
The hairy wild-bee that murmurs and hankers up and down—
that gripes the full-grown lady-flower, curves upon her
with amorous firm legs, takes his will of her, and holds
himself tremulous and tight upon her till he is satisfied,
The wet of woods through the early hours,
Two sleepers at night lying close together as they sleep, one with an arm
slanting down across and below the waist of the other,
The smell of apples, aromas from crushed sage-plant, mint, birch-bark,
The boy's longings, the glow and pressure as he confides to me
what he was dreaming,
The dead leaf whirling its spiral whirl, and falling still and content
to the ground,
The no-formed stings that sights, people, objects, sting me with,
The hubbed sting of myself, stinging me as much as it ever can any one,
The sensitive, orbic, underlapped brothers, that only privileged feelers
may be intimate where they are,
The curious roamer, the hand, roaming all over the body—
the bashful withdrawing of flesh where the fingers
soothingly pause and edge themselves,
The limpid liquid within the young man,
The vexed corrosion, so pensive and so painful,
The torment—the irritable tide that will not be at rest,
The like of the same I feel—the like of the same in others,
The young woman that flushes and flushes, and the young man
that flushes and flushes,
The young man that wakes, deep at night, the hot hand seeking to repress

what would master him—the strange half-welcome pangs,
visions, sweats—the pulse pounding through palms
and trembling encircling fingers—the young man
all colored, red, ashamed, angry;
The souse upon me of my lover the sea, as I lie willing and naked,
The merriment of the twin-babes that crawl over the grass in the sun,
the mother never turning her vigilant eyes from them,
The walnut-trunk, the walnut-husks, and the ripening or ripened
long-round walnuts,
The continence of vegetables, birds, animals,
The consequent meanness of me should I skulk or find myself indecent,
while birds and animals never once skulk or find themselves indecent,
The great chastity of paternity, to match the great chastity of maternity,
The oath of procreation I have sworn,
The greed that eats in me day and night with hungry gnaw, till I saturate
what shall produce boys to fill my place when I am through,
The wholesome relief, repose, content,
And this bunch plucked at random from myself,
It has done its work—I toss it carelessly to fall where it may.

Poem of The Propositions of Nakedness

RESPONDEZ! Respondez!
Let every one answer! Let those who sleep be waked!
Let none evade—not you, any more than others!
Let that which stood in front go behind! and let that which was behind
advance to the front and speak!
Let murderers, thieves, tyrants, bigots, unclean persons,
offer new propositions!
Let the old propositions be postponed!
Let faces and theories be turned inside out! Let meanings be criminal
as well as results! (Say! can results be criminal, and meanings
not criminal?)
Let there be no suggestion besides the suggestion of drudgery!

Let none be pointed toward his destination! (Say! do you know
your destination?)
Let trillions of men and women be mocked with bodies
and mocked with souls!
Let the love that waits in them, wait! Let it die, or pass still-born
to other spheres!
Let the sympathy that waits in every man, wait! or let it also pass,
a dwarf, to other spheres!
Let contradictions prevail! Let one thing contradict another!
and let one line of my poem contradict another!
Let the people sprawl with yearning aimless hands! Let their tongues
be broken! Let their eyes be discouraged! Let none descend
into their hearts with the fresh lusciousness of love!
Let the theory of America be management, caste, comparison!
(Say! what other theory would you?)
Let them that distrust birth and death lead the rest!
(Say! why shall they not lead you?)
Let the crust of hell be neared and trod on! Let the days be darker
than the nights! Let slumber bring less slumber
than waking-time brings!
Let the world never appear to him or her for whom it was all made!
Let the heart of the young man exile itself from the heart of the old man!
and let the heart of the old man be exiled from that
of the young man!
Let the sun and moon go! Let scenery take the applause
of the audience! Let there be apathy under the stars!
Let freedom prove no man's inalienable right! Every one
who can tyrannize, let him tyrannize to his satisfaction!
Let none but infidels be countenanced!
Let the eminence of meanness, treachery, sarcasm, hate, greed,
indecency, impotence, lust, be taken for granted above all!
Let poems, judges, governments, households, religions,
philosophies, take such for granted above all!
Let the worst men beget children out of the worst women!
Let priests still play at immortality!
Let death be inaugurated!
Let nothing remain upon the earth except teachers, artists, moralists,
lawyers, and learned and polite persons!
Let him who is without my poems be assassinated!
Let the cow, the horse, the camel, the garden-bee—Let the mud-fish,
the lobster, the mussel, eel, the sting-ray and the grunting

pig-fish—Let these, and the like of these, be put on a perfect equality with man and woman!
Let churches accommodate serpents, vermin, and the corpses of those who have died of the most filthy diseases!
Let marriage slip down among fools, and be for none but fools!
Let men among themselves talk obscenely of women! and let women among themselves talk obscenely of men!
Let every man doubt every woman! and let every woman trick every man!
Let us all, without missing one, be exposed in public, naked, monthly, at the peril of our lives! Let our bodies be freely handled and examined by whoever chooses!
Let nothing but love-songs, pictures, statues, elegant works, be permitted to exist upon the earth!
Let the earth desert God, nor let there ever henceforth be mentioned the name of God!
Let there be no God!
Let there be money, business, railroads, imports, exports, custom, authority, precedents, pallor, dyspepsia, smut, ignorance, unbelief!
Let judges and criminals be transposed! Let the prison-keepers be put in prison! Let those that were prisoners take the keys! (Say! why might they not just as well be transposed?)
Let the slaves be masters! Let the masters become slaves!
Let the reformers descend from the stands where they are forever bawling! Let an idiot or insane person appear on each of the stands!
Let the Asiatic, the African, the European, the American and the Australian, go armed against the murderous stealthiness of each other! Let them sleep armed! Let none believe in good-will!
Let there be no living wisdom! Let such be scorned and derided off from the earth!
Let a floating cloud in the sky—Let a wave of the sea—Let one glimpse of your eye-sight upon the landscape or grass—Let growing mint, spinach, onions, tomatoes—Let these be exhibited as shows at a great price for admission!
Let all the men of These States stand aside for a few smouchers! Let the few seize on what they choose! Let the rest gawk, giggle, starve, obey!
Let shadows be furnished with genitals! Let substances be deprived of their genitals!
Let there be immense cities—but through any of them, not a single poet, saviour, knower, lover!

Let the infidels of These States laugh all faith away! If one man
be found who has faith, let the rest set upon him! Let them
affright faith! Let them destroy the power of breeding faith!
Let the she-harlots and the he-harlots be prudent! Let them dance on,
while seeming lasts! (O seeming! seeming! seeming!)
Let the preachers recite creeds! Let the preachers of creeds never dare
to go meditate upon the hills, alone, by day or by night!
(If one ever once dare, he is lost!)
Let insanity have charge of sanity!
Let books take the place of trees, animals, rivers, clouds!
Let the portraits of heroes supersede heroes!
Let the manhood of man never take steps after itself! Let it take steps
after eunuchs, and after consumptive and genteel persons!
Let the white person tread the black person under his heel!
(Say! which is trodden under heel, after all?)
Let the reflections of the things of the world be studied in mirrors!
Let the things themselves continue unstudied!
Let a man seek pleasure everywhere except in himself! Let a woman
seek happiness everywhere except in herself! (Say! what real
happiness have you had one single time through your whole life?)
Let limited years of life do nothing for the limitless years of death!
(Say! what do you suppose death will do, then?)

Poem of The Sayers of The Words of The Earth

EARTH, round, rolling, compact—suns, moons, animals—
all these are words,
Watery, vegetable, sauroid[°] advances—beings, premonitions,
lispings of the future—these are vast words.

Were you thinking that those were the words—those upright lines?
those curves, angles, dots?
No, those are not the words—the substantial words are in the ground
and sea,
They are in the air—they are in you.

Were you thinking that those were the words—those delicious sounds
out of your friends' mouths?
No, the real words are more delicious than they.

Human bodies are words more delicious than they.

Human bodies are words, myriads of words,
In the best poems re-appears the body, man's or woman's,
well-shaped, natural, gay,
Every part able, active, receptive, without shame or the need of shame.

Air, soil, water, fire, these are words,
I myself am a word with them—my qualities interpenetrate with theirs—
my name is nothing to them,
Though it were told in the three thousand languages, what would air,
soil, water, fire, know of my name?

A healthy presence, a friendly or commanding gesture, are words,
sayings, meanings,
The charms that go with the mere looks of some men and women
are sayings and meanings also.

The workmanship of souls is by the inaudible words of the earth,
The great masters, the sayers, know the earth's words, and use them
more than the audible words.

Syllables are not the earth's words,
Beauty, reality, manhood, time, life—the realities of such as these
are the earth's words.

Amelioration is one of the earth's words,
The earth neither lags nor hastens,
It has all attributes, growths, effects, latent in itself from the jump,
It is not half beautiful only—defects and excrescences show
just as much as perfections show.

The earth does not withhold, it is generous enough,
The truths of the earth continually wait, they are not so concealed either,
They are calm, subtle, untransmissible by print,
They are imbued through all things, conveying themselves willingly,
Conveying a sentiment and invitation of the earth—I utter and utter,

I speak not, yet if you hear me not, of what avail am I to you?
To bear—to better—lacking these, of what avail am I?

Accouche! Accouchez!°
Will you rot your own fruit in yourself there?
Will you squat and stifle there?

The earth does not argue,
Is not pathetic, has no arrangements,
Does not scream, haste, persuade, threaten, promise,
Makes no discriminations, has no conceivable failures,
Closes nothing, refuses nothing, shuts none out,
Of all the powers, objects, states, it notifies, shuts none out.

The earth does not exhibit itself nor refuse to exhibit itself—
possesses still underneath,
Underneath the ostensible sounds, the august chorus of heroes,
the wail of slaves,
Persuasions of lovers, curses, gasps of the dying, laughter
of young people, accents of bargainers,
Underneath these possessing the words that never fail.

To her children the words of the eloquent dumb great mother never fail,
The true words do not fail, for motion does not fail, and reflection
does not fail,
Also the day and night do not fail, and the voyage we pursue
does not fail.

Of the interminable sisters,°
Of the ceaseless cotillions° of sisters,
Of the centripetal and centrifugal sisters, the elder and younger sisters,
The beautiful sister we know dances on with the rest.

With her ample back toward every beholder,
With the fascinations of youth and the equal fascinations of age,
Sits she whom I too love like the rest, sits undisturbed,
Holding up in her hand what has the character of a mirror,
her eyes glancing back from it,
Glancing thence as she sits, inviting none, denying none,
Holding a mirror day and night tirelessly before her own face.

Seen at hand, or seen at a distance,
Duly the twenty-four appear in public every day,
Duly approach and pass with their companions, or a companion,
Looking from no countenances of their own, but from the countenances
of those who are with them,
From the countenances of children or women, or the manly countenance,
From the open countenances of animals, from inanimate things,
From the landscape or waters, or from the exquisite apparition of the sky,
From our own countenances, mine and yours, faithfully returning them,
Every day in public appearing without fail, but never twice
with the same companions.

Embracing man, embracing all, proceed the three hundred and sixty-five
resistlessly round the sun,
Embracing all, soothing, supporting, follow close three hundred
and sixty-five offsets of the first, sure and necessary as they.

Tumbling on steadily, nothing dreading,
Sunshine, storm, cold, heat, forever withstanding, passing, carrying,
The soul's realization and determination still inheriting,
The liquid vacuum around and ahead still entering and dividing,
No balk retarding, no anchor anchoring, on no rock striking,
Swift, glad, content, unbereaved, nothing losing,
Of all able and ready at any time to give strict account,
The divine ship sails the divine sea.

Whoever you are! motion and reflection are especially for you,
The divine ship sails the divine sea for you.

Whoever you are! you are he or she for whom the earth
is solid and liquid,
You are he or she for whom the sun and moon hang in the sky,
For none more than you are the present and the past,
For none more than you is immortality.

Each man to himself, and each woman to herself, is the word
of the past and present, and the word of immortality,
Not one can acquire for another—not one!
Not one can grow for another—not one!

The song is to the singer, and comes back most to him,
The teaching is to the teacher, and comes back most to him,

The murder is to the murderer, and comes back most to him,
The theft is to the thief, and comes back most to him,
The love is to the lover, and comes back most to him,
The gift is to the giver, and comes back most to him—it cannot fail,
The oration is to the orator, and the acting is to the actor and actress,
not to the audience,
And no man understands any greatness or goodness but his own,
or the indication of his own.

I swear the earth shall surely be complete to him or her
who shall be complete!
I swear the earth remains broken and jagged only to him or her
who remains broken and jagged!

I swear there is no greatness or power that does not emulate those
of the earth!
I swear there can be no theory of any account, unless it corroborate
the theory of the earth!
No politics, art, religion, behaviour, or what not, is of account,
unless it compare with the amplitude of the earth,
Unless it face the exactness, vitality, impartiality, rectitude of the earth.

I swear I begin to see love with sweeter spasms than that
which responds love!
It is that which contains itself, which never invites and never refuses.

I swear I begin to see little or nothing in audible words!
I swear I think all merges toward the presentation
of the unspoken meanings of the earth!
Toward him who sings the songs of the body, and of the truths
of the earth,
Toward him who makes the dictionaries of the words that print
cannot touch.

I swear I see what is better than to tell the best,
It is always to leave the best untold.

When I undertake to tell the best, I find I cannot,
My tongue is ineffectual on its pivots,
My breath will not be obedient to its organs,
I become a dumb man.

The best of the earth cannot be told anyhow—all or any is best,
It is not what you anticipated, it is cheaper, easier, nearer,
Things are not dismissed from the places they held before,
The earth is just as positive and direct as it was before,
Facts, religions, improvements, politics, trades, are as real as before,
But the soul is also real, it too is positive and direct,
No reasoning, no proof has established it,
Undeniable growth has established it.

This is a poem for the sayers of the earth—these are hints of meanings,
These are they that echo the tones of souls, and the phrases of souls;
If they did not echo the phrases of souls, what were they then?
If they had not reference to you in especial, what were they then?

I swear I will never henceforth have to do with the faith
 that tells the best!
I will have to do with that faith only that leaves the best untold.

Say on, sayers of the earth!
Delve! mould! pile the substantial words of the earth!
Work on, age after age! nothing is to be lost,
It may have to wait long, but it will certainly come in use,
When the materials are all prepared, the architects shall appear,
I swear to you the architects shall appear without fail!
 I announce them and lead them!
I swear to you they will understand you and justify you!
I swear to you the greatest among them shall be he who
 best knows you, and encloses all, and is faithful to all!
I swear to you, he and the rest shall not forget you! they shall
 perceive that you are not an iota less than they!
I swear to you, you shall be glorified in them!

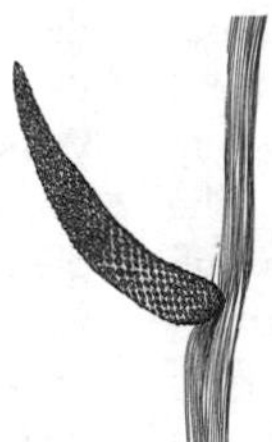

Ralph Waldo Emerson's Congratulatory Letter

(APPENDED TO THE 1856 EDITION)

Concord, Massachusetts, *21 July, 1855*

Dear Sir—I am not blind to the worth of the wonderful gift of *Leaves of Grass*. I find it the most extraordinary piece of wit and wisdom that America has yet contributed. I am very happy in reading it, as great power makes us happy. It meets the demand I am always making of what seemed the sterile and stingy nature, as if too much handiwork, or too much lymph in the temperament, were making our western wits fat and mean.

I give you joy of your free and brave thought. I have joy in it. I find incomparable things said incomparably well, as they must be. I find the courage of treatment which so delights us, and which large perception only can inspire.

I greet you at the beginning of a great career, which yet must have had a long foreground somewhere, for such a start. I rubbed my eyes a little, to see if this sunbeam were no illusion; but the solid sense of the book is a sober certainty. It has the best merits, namely, of fortifying and encouraging.

I did not know until I last night saw the book advertised in a newspaper that I could trust the name as real and available for a post-office. I wish to see my benefactor, and have felt much like striking my tasks and visiting New York to pay you my respects.

R. W. Emerson.

Whitman's Reply to Emerson

(APPENDED TO THE 1856 EDITION)

Brooklyn, *August*, 1856.

Here are thirty-two Poems, which I send you, dear Friend and Master, not having found how I could satisfy myself with sending any usual acknowledgment of your letter. The first edition, on which you mailed me that till now unanswered letter, was twelve poems—I printed a thousand copies, and they readily sold; these thirty-two Poems I stereotype, to print several thousand copies of. I much enjoy making poems. Other work I have set for myself to do, to meet people and The States face to face, to confront them with an American rude tongue; but the work of my life is making poems. I keep on till I make a hundred, and then several hundred—perhaps a thousand. The way is clear to me. A few years, and the average annual call for my Poems is ten or twenty thousand copies—more, quite likely. Why should I hurry or compromise? In poems or in speeches I say the word or two that has got to be said, adhere to the body, step with the countless common footsteps, and remind every man and woman of something.

Master, I am a man who has perfect faith. Master, we have not come through centuries, caste, heroisms, fables, to halt in this land today. Or I think it is to collect a ten-fold impetus that any halt is made. As nature, inexorable, onward, resistless, impassive amid the threats and screams of disputants, so America. Let all defer. Let all attend respectfully the leisure of These States, their politics, poems, literature, manners, and their free-handed modes of training their own offspring. Their own comes, just matured, certain, numerous and capable enough, with egotistical tongues, with sinewed wrists, seizing openly what belongs to them. They resume Personality, too long left out of mind. Their shadows are projected in employments, in books, in the cities, in trade; their feet are on the flights of the steps of the Capitol; they dilate, a larger, brawnier, more candid, more democratic, lawless, positive native to The States, sweet-bodied, completer, dauntless, flowing, masterful, beard-faced, new race of men.

Swiftly, on limitless foundations, the United States too are founding a literature. It is all as well done, in my opinion, as could be practicable. Each element here is in condition. Every day I go among the people of Manhattan Island, Brooklyn, and other cities, and among the young men, to discover the spirit of them, and to refresh myself. These are to be attended to; I am myself more drawn here than to those authors, publishers, importations, reprints, and so forth. I pass coolly through those, understanding them perfectly well, and that they do the indispensable service, outside of men like me, which nothing else could do. In poems, the young men of The States shall be represented, for they out-rival the best of the rest of the earth.

The lists of ready-made literature which America inherits by the mighty inheritance of the English language—all the rich repertoire of traditions, poems, histories, metaphysics, plays, classics, translations, have made, and still continue, magnificent preparations for that other plainly signified literature, to be our own, to be electric, fresh, lusty, to express the full-sized body, male and female—to give the modern meanings of things, to grow up beautiful, lasting, commensurate with America, with all the passions of home, with the inimitable sympathies of having been boys and girls together, and of parents who were with our parents.

What else can happen The States, even in their own despite? That huge English flow, so sweet, so undeniable, has done incalculable good here, and is to be spoken of for its own sake with generous praise and with gratitude. Yet the price The States have had to lie under for the same has not been a small price. Payment prevails; a nation can never take the issues of the needs of other nations for nothing. America, grandest of all lands in the theory of its politics, in popular reading, in hospitality, breadth, animal beauty, cities, ships, machines, money, credit, collapses quick as lightning at the repeated, admonishing, stern words, Where are any mental expressions from you, beyond what you have copied or stolen? Where the born throngs of poets, literats, orators, you promised? Will you but tag after other nations? They struggled long for their literature, painfully working their way, some with deficient languages, some with priest-craft, some in the endeavor just to live—yet achieved for their times, works, poems, perhaps the only solid consolation left to them through ages afterward of shame and decay. You are young, have the perfectest of dialects, a free press, a free government, the world forwarding its best to be with you. As justice has been strictly done to you, from this hour do strict justice to yourself. Strangle the singers who will not sing you loud and strong. Open the doors of The West. Call for new great masters to comprehend new arts, new perfections, new wants. Submit to the most robust bard till he remedy your barrenness. Then you will not need to adopt the heirs of others; you will have true heirs, begotten of yourself, blooded with your own blood.

With composure I see such propositions, seeing more and more every day of the answers that serve. Expressions do not yet serve, for sufficient reasons; but that is getting ready, beyond what the earth has hitherto known, to take home the expressions when they come, and to identify them with the populace of The States, which is the schooling cheaply procured by any outlay any number of years. Such schooling The States extract from the swarms of reprints, and from the current authors and editors. Such service and extract are done after enormous, reckless, free modes, characteristic of The States. Here are to be attained results never elsewhere thought possible; the modes are very grand too. The instincts of the American people are all perfect, and tend to make heroes. It is a rare thing in a man here to understand The States.

All current nourishments to literature serve. Of authors and editors I do not know how many there are in The States, but there are thousands, each one building his or her step to the stairs by which giants shall mount. Of the twenty-four modern mammoth two-double, three-double, and four-double cylinder presses now in the world, printing by steam, twenty-one of them are in These States. The twelve thousand large and small shops for dispensing books and newspapers—the same number of public libraries, any one of which has all the reading wanted to equip a man or woman for American reading—the three thousand different newspapers, the nutriment of the imperfect ones coming in just as usefully as any—the story papers, various, full of strong-flavored romances, widely circulated—the one-cent and two-cent journals—the political ones, no matter what side—the weeklies in the country—the sporting and pictorial papers—the monthly magazines, with plentiful imported feed—the sentimental novels, numberless copies of them—low-priced flaring tales, adventures, biographies—all are prophetic; all waft rapidly on. I see that they swell wide, for reasons. I am not troubled at the movement of them, but greatly pleased. I see plying shuttles, the active ephemeral myriads of books also, faithfully weaving the garments of a generation of men, and a generation of women, they do not perceive or know. What a progress popular reading and writing has made in fifty years! What a progress fifty years hence! The time is at hand when inherent literature will be a main part of These States, as general and real as steam-power, iron, corn, beef, fish. First-rate American persons are to be supplied. Our perennial materials for fresh thoughts, histories, poems, music, orations, religions, recitations, amusements, will then not be disregarded, any more than our perennial fields, mines, rivers, seas. Certain things are established, and are immovable; in those things millions of years stand justified. The mothers and fathers of whom modern centuries have come, have not existed for nothing; they too had brains and hearts. Of course all literature, in all nations and years, will share marked attributes in common, as we all, of all ages, share the common human attributes. America is to be kept coarse and broad. What is to be done is to withdraw from precedents, and be directed to men and women—also to The States in their federalness; for the union of the parts of the body is not more necessary to their life than the union of These States is to their life.

A profound person can easily know more of the people than they know of themselves. Always waiting untold in the souls of the armies of common people, is stuff better than anything that can possibly appear in the leadership of the same. That gives final verdicts. In every department of These States, he who travels with a coterie, or with selected persons, or with imitators, or with infidels, or with the owners of slaves, or with that which is ashamed of the body of a man, or with that which is ashamed of the body of a woman, or with any thing less than the bravest and the openest, travels straight for the slopes of dissolution. The genius of all foreign literature is clipped and cut small, compared to our genius, and is essentially insulting to our usages, and to the organic compacts of These States. Old forms, old poems, majestic and proper in their own lands here in this land are exiles; the air here is very strong. Much that stands well and has a little enough place provided for it in the small scales of European kingdoms, empires, and the like, here stands haggard, dwarfed, ludicrous, or has no place little enough provided for it. Authorities, poems, models, laws, names, imported into America, are useful to America today to destroy them, and so move disencumbered to great works, great days.

Just so long, in our country or any country, as no revolutionists advance, and are backed by the people, sweeping off the swarms of routine representatives, officers in power, book-makers, teachers, ecclesiastics, politicians, just so long, I perceive, do they who are in power fairly represent that country, and remain of use, probably of very great use. To supersede them, when it is the pleasure of These States, full provision is made; and I say the time has arrived to use it with a strong hand. Here also the souls of the armies have not only overtaken the souls of the officers, but passed on, and left the souls of the officers behind out of sight many weeks' journey; and the souls of the armies now go en-masse without officers. Here also formulas, glosses, blanks, minutiæ, are choking the throats of the spokesmen to death. Those things most listened for, certainly those are the things least said. There is not a single History of the World. There is not one of America, or of the organic compacts of These States, or of Washington, or of Jefferson, nor of Language, nor any Dictionary of the English Language. There is no great author; every one has demeaned himself to some etiquette or some impotence. There is no manhood or life-power in poems; there are shoats and geldings more like. Or literature will be dressed up, a fine gentleman, distasteful to our instincts, foreign to our soil. Its neck bends right and left wherever it goes. Its costumes and jewelry prove how little it knows Nature. Its flesh is soft; it shows less and less of the indefinable hard something that is Nature. Where is any thing but the shaved Nature of synods and schools? Where is a savage and luxuriant man? Where is an overseer? In lives, in poems, in codes of law, in Congress, in tuitions, theatres, conversations, argumentations, not a single head lifts itself clean out, with proof that it is their master, and has subordinated them to itself, and is ready to try their superiors. None believes in These States, boldly illustrating them in himself. Not a man faces round at the rest with terrible negative voice, refusing all terms to be bought off from his own eye-sight, or from the soul that he is, or from friendship, or from the body that he is, or from the soil and sea. To creeds, literature, art, the army, the navy, the executive, life is hardly proposed, but the sick and dying are proposed to cure the sick and dying. The churches are one vast lie; the people do not believe them, and they do not believe themselves; the priests are continually telling what they know well enough is not so, and keeping back what they know is so. The spectacle is a pitiful one. I think there can never be again upon the festive earth more bad-disordered persons deliberately taking seats, as of late in These States, at the heads of the public tables—such corpses' eyes for judges—such a rascal and thief in the Presidency.

Up to the present, as helps best, the people, like a lot of large boys, have no determined tastes, are quite unaware of the grandeur of themselves, and of their destiny, and of their immense strides—accept with voracity whatever is presented them in novels, histories, newspapers, poems, schools, lectures, every thing. Pretty soon, through these and other means, their development makes the fibre that is capable of itself, and will assume determined tastes. The young men will be clear what they want, and will have it. They will follow none except him whose spirit leads them in the like spirit with themselves. Any such man will be welcome as the flowers of May. Others will be put out without ceremony. How much is there anyhow, to the young men of These States, in a parcel of helpless dandies, who can neither fight, work, shoot, ride, run, command—some of them devout, some quite insane, some castrated—all second-hand, or third, fourth, or fifth hand—waited upon by waiters, putting not this land first, but always other lands first, talking of art, doing the most ridiculous things for fear of being called ridiculous, smirking and skipping along, continually taking off their hats—no one behaving, dressing, writing, talking, loving, out of any natural and manly tastes of his own, but each one looking cautiously to see how the rest behave, dress, write, talk, love—pressing the noses of dead books upon themselves and upon their country—favoring no poets, philosophs, literats here, but dog-like danglers at the heels of the poets, philosophs, literats, of enemies' lands—favoring mental expressions, models of gentlemen and ladies, social habitudes in These States to grow up in sneaking defiance of the popular substratums of The States? Of course they and the likes of them can never justify the strong poems of America. Of course no feed of theirs is to stop and be made welcome to muscle the bodies, male and female, for Manhattan Island, Brooklyn, Boston, Worcester, Hartford, Portland, Montreal, Detroit, Buffalo, Cleveland, Milwaukee, St. Louis, Indianapolis, Chicago, Cincinnati, Iowa City, Philadelphia, Baltimore, Raleigh, Savannah, Charleston, Mobile, New Orleans, Galveston, Brownsville, San Francisco, Havana, and a thousand equal cities, present and to come. Of course what they and the likes of them have been used for, draws toward its close, after which they will all be discharged, and not one of them will ever be heard of any more.

America, having duly conceived, bears out of her self offspring of her own to do the workmanship wanted. To freedom, to strength, to poems, to personal greatness, it is never permitted to rest, not a generation or part of a generation. To be ripe beyond further increase is to prepare to die. The architects of These States laid their foundations, and passed to further spheres. What they laid is a work done; as much more remains. Now are needed other architects, whose duty is not less difficult, but perhaps more difficult. Each age forever needs architects. America is not finished, perhaps never will be; now America is a divine true sketch. There are Thirty-Two States sketched—the population thirty millions. In a few years there will be Fifty States. Again in a few years there will be A Hundred States, the population hundreds of millions, the freshest and freest of men. Of course such men stand to nothing less than the freshest and freest expression.

Poets here, literats here, are to rest on organic different bases from other countries; not a class set apart, circling only in the circle of themselves, modest and pretty, desperately scratching for rhymes, pallid with white paper, shut off, aware of the old pictures and traditions of the race, but unaware of the actual race around them—not breeding in and in among each other till they all have the scrofula. Lands of ensemble, bards of ensemble! Walking freely out from the old traditions, as our politics has walked out, American poets and literats recognize nothing behind them superior to what is present with them—recognize with joy the sturdy living forms of the men and women of These States, the divinity of sex, the perfect eligibility of the female with the male, all The States, liberty and equality, real articles, the different trades, mechanics, the young fellows of Manhattan Island, customs, instincts, slang, Wisconsin, Georgia, the noble Southern heart, the hot blood, the spirit that will be nothing less than master, the filibuster spirit, the Western man, native-born perceptions, the eye for forms, the perfect models of made things, the wild smack of freedom, California, money, electric-telegraphs, free-trade, iron and the iron mines—recognize without demur those splendid resistless black poems, the steam-ships of the sea-board states, and those other resistless splendid poems, the locomotives, followed through the interior states by trains of rail-road cars.

A word remains to be said, as of one ever present, not yet permitted to be acknowledged, discarded or made dumb by literature, and the results apparent. To the lack of an avowed, empowered, unabashed development of sex (the only salvation for the same), and to the fact of speakers and writers fraudulently assuming as always dead what every one knows to be always alive, is attributable the remarkable non-personality and indistinctness of modern productions in books, art, talk; also that in the scanned lives of men and women most of them appear to have been for some time past of the neuter gender; and also the stinging fact that in orthodox society today, if the dresses were changed, the men might easily pass for women and the women for men.

Infidelism usurps most with fœtid polite face; among the rest infidelism about sex. By silence or obedience the pens of savans, poets, historians, biographers, and the rest, have long connived at the filthy law, and books enslaved to it, that what makes the manhood of a man, that sex, womanhood, maternity, desires, lusty animations, organs, acts, are unmentionable and to be ashamed of, to be driven to skulk out of literature with whatever belongs to them. This filthy law has to be repealed—it stands in the way of great reforms. Of women just as much as men, it is the interest that there should not be infidelism about sex, but perfect faith. Women in These States approach the day of that organic equality with men, without which, I see, men cannot have organic equality among themselves. This empty dish, gallantry, will then be filled with something. This tepid wash, this diluted deferential love, as in songs, fictions, and so forth, is enough to make a man vomit; as to manly friendship, everywhere observed in The States, there is not the first breath of it to be observed in print. I say that the body of a man or woman, the main matter, is so far quite unexpressed in poems; but that the body is to be expressed, and sex is. Of bards for These States, if it come to a question, it is whether they shall celebrate in poems the eternal decency of the amativeness of Nature, the motherhood of all, or whether they shall be the bards of the fashionable delusion of the inherent nastiness of sex, and of the feeble and querulous modesty of deprivation. This is important in poems, because the whole of the other expressions of a nation are but flanges out of its great poems. To me, henceforth, that theory of any thing, no matter what, stagnates in its vitals, cowardly and rotten, while it cannot publicly accept, and publicly name, with specific words, the things on which all existence, all souls, all realization, all decency, all health, all that is worth being here for, all of woman and of man, all beauty, all purity, all sweetness, all friendship, all strength, all life, all immortality depend. The courageous soul, for a year or two to come, may be proved by faith in sex, and by disdaining concessions.

To poets and literats—to every woman and man, today or any day, the conditions of the present, needs, dangers, prejudices, and the like, are the perfect conditions on which we are here, and the conditions for wording the future with undissuadable words. These States, receivers of the stamina of past ages and lands, initiate the outlines of repayment a thousand fold. They fetch the American great masters, waited for by old worlds and new, who accept evil as well as good, ignorance as well as erudition, black as soon as white, foreign-born materials as well as home-born, reject none, force discrepancies into range, surround the whole, concentrate them on present periods and places, show the application to each and any one's body and soul, and show the true use of precedents. Always America will be agitated and turbulent. This day it is taking shape, not to be less so, but to be more so, stormily, capriciously, on native principles, with such vast proportions of parts! As for me, I love screaming, wrestling, boiling-hot days.

Of course, we shall have a national character, an identity. As it ought to be, and as soon as it ought to be, it will be. That, with much else, takes care of itself, is a result, and the cause of greater results. With Ohio, Illinois, Missouri, Oregon—with the states around the Mexican sea—with cheerfully welcomed immigrants from Europe, Asia, Africa—with Connecticut, Vermont, New Hampshire, Rhode Island—with all varied interests, facts, beliefs, parties, genesis—there is being fused a determined character, fit for the broadest use for the freewomen and freemen of The States, accomplished and to be accomplished, without any exception whatever—each indeed free, each adhering to one enclosing general form of politics, manners, talk, personal style, as the plenteous varieties of the race adhere to one physical form. Such character is the brain and spine to all, including literature, including poems. Such character, strong, limber, just, open-mouthed, American-blooded, full of pride, full of ease, of passionate friendliness, is to stand compact upon that vast basis of the supremacy of Individuality—that new moral American continent without which, I see, the physical continent remained incomplete, may-be a carcass, a bloat—that newer America, answering face to face with The States, with ever-satisfying and ever-unsurveyable seas and shores.

Those shores you found. I say you have led The States there—have led Me there. I say that none has ever done, or ever can do, a greater deed for The States, than your deed. Others may line out the lines, build cities, work mines, break up farms; it is yours to have been the original true Captain who put to sea, intuitive, positive, rendering the first report, to be told less by any report, and more by the mariners of a thousand bays, in each tack of their arriving and departing, many years after you.

Receive, dear Master, these statements and assurances through me, for all the young men, and for an earnest that we know none before you, but the best following you; and that we demand to take your name into our keeping, and that we understand what you have indicated, and find the same indicated in ourselves, and that we will stick to it and enlarge upon it through These States.

Walt Whitman.

The Emerson-Whitman Exchange

(A CONVERSATIONAL POSTSCRIPT)

On 15 February 1889, the following exchange occurred between Walt Whitman and Horace Traubel in the poet's house in Camden, New Jersey. The topic of conversation was Emerson's letter applauding Whitman—and the use the poet had made of it in the 1856 edition (from *With Walt Whitman in Camden,* 4:152):

> I said: "According to your letter to Emerson you sold all the first edition: according to your stories to me you sold practically none of them at all." He said: "How do you make that out?" I replied: "You told Emerson that they 'readily sold.' Do you say to me now that they 'readily sold'?" "No—I do not." "Well, why did you say it then?" "At the time I thought the books were selling: a lot of them were consigned, right and left: there were no sales: they came back: then booksellers bought some that buyers would not take off their hands."

This did not satisfy Traubel, who, with a puckishness that only an extraordinary bond of affection would have allowed, continued his probing of Whitman's self-promotion. Traubel's transcription continues:

> I laughed rather heartily. W. asked me why. I said: "I was wondering whether you were not bluffing Emerson." "You mean bragging? Well—maybe there was something of that sort in it." I said: "I can't forget, either, that in that same letter you call Emerson 'master.' Now you repudiate the word. What did you mean by it then?" He answered: "They were salad days: I had many undeveloped angles at that time: I don't imagine I was guiltless: someone had to speak for me: no one would: I spoke for myself." I said: "You didn't need to play Emerson: he was on your side without it." W. said in a fiery voice: "Who the hell talked about playing anybody?" I said:

"You haven't made out a very good case for 'master' or 'readily sold.' I believe what you say because you say it but it hardly sounds plausible to me." "Do you mean to say I'm a liar?" "No: I only mean to say I'd like to know the real reason for 'readily sold' and 'master.' " He ended the quiz half petulantly, half jocularly. "Maybe if you look long enough in the right place you'll find what you're looking for."

Leaves

of

Grass

1860

The engraving that appeared on the verso facing the title page of the 1860 edition of Leaves of Grass; *it was based on a portrait of Whitman made by Charles Hine and shows the poet in 1859, when he was forty.*

Proto-Leaf

FREE, fresh, savage,
Fluent, luxuriant, self-content, fond of persons and places,
Fond of fish-shape Paumanok,° where I was born,
Fond of the sea—lusty-begotten and various,
Boy of the Mannahatta,° the city of ships, my city,
Or raised inland, or of the south savannas,
Or full-breath'd on Californian air, or Texan or Cuban air,
Tallying, vocalizing all—resounding Niagara—resounding Missouri,
Or rude in my home in Kanuck woods,
Or wandering and hunting, my drink water, my diet meat,
Or withdrawn to muse and meditate in some deep recess,
Far from the clank of crowds, an interval passing, rapt and happy,
Stars, vapor, snow, the hills, rocks, the Fifth Month flowers,
 my amaze, my love,
Aware of the buffalo, the peace-herds, the bull, strong-breasted
 and hairy,
Aware of the mocking-bird of the wilds, at daybreak,
Solitary, singing in the west, I strike up for a new world.

Victory, union, faith, identity, time, the Soul, yourself, the present
 and future lands, the indissoluble compacts, riches, mystery,
 eternal progress, the kosmos, and the modern reports.

This then is life,
Here is what has come to the surface after so many throes
 and convulsions.

How curious! How real!
Underfoot the divine soul—Overhead the sun.

See, revolving,
The globe—the ancestor-continents, away, grouped together,

The present and future continents, north and south,
with the isthmus between.

See, vast, trackless spaces,
As in a dream, they change, they swiftly fill,
Countless masses debouch upon them,
They are now covered with the foremost people, arts, institutions known.

See projected, through time,
For me, an audience interminable.

With firm and regular step they wend—they never stop,
Successions of men, Americanos, a hundred millions,
One generation playing its part and passing on,
And another generation playing its part and passing on in its turn,
With faces turned sideways or backward toward me to listen,
With eyes retrospective toward me.

Americanos! Masters!
Marches humanitarian! Foremost!
Century marches! Libertad!° Masses!
For you a programme of chants.

Chants of the prairies,
Chants of the long-running Mississippi,
Chants of Ohio, Indiana, Illinois, Wisconsin, Iowa, and Minnesota,
Inland chants—chants of Kanzas,
Chants away down to Mexico, and up north to Oregon—
Kanadian chants,
Chants of teeming and turbulent cities—chants of mechanics,
Yankee chants—Pennsylvanian chants—chants of Kentucky
and Tennessee,
Chants of dim-lit mines—chants of mountain-tops,
Chants of sailors—chants of the Eastern Sea and the Western Sea,
Chants of the Mannahatta, the place of my dearest love,
the place surrounded by hurried and sparkling currents,
Health chants—joy chants—robust chants of young men,
Chants inclusive—wide reverberating chants,
Chants of the Many In One.

In the Year 80 of The States,
My tongue, every atom of my blood, formed from this soil, this air,

Born here of parents born here,
From parents the same, and their parents' parents the same,
I, now thirty-six years old, in perfect health, begin,
Hoping to cease not till death.

Creeds and schools in abeyance,
Retiring back a while, sufficed at what they are, but never forgotten,
With accumulations, now coming forward in front,
Arrived again, I harbor, for good or bad—I permit to speak,
Nature, without check, with original energy.

Take my leaves, America!
Make welcome for them everywhere, for they are your own offspring;
Surround them, East and West! for they would surround you,
And you precedents! connect lovingly with them, for they connect
lovingly with you.

I conned old times,
I sat studying at the feet of the great masters;
Now, if eligible, O that the great masters might return and study me!

In the name of These States, shall I scorn the antique?
Why These are the children of the antique, to justify it.

Dead poets, philosophs, priests,
Martyrs, artists, inventors, governments long since,
Language-shapers, on other shores,
Nations once powerful, now reduced, withdrawn, or desolate,
I dare not proceed till I respectfully credit what you have left,
wafted hither,
I have perused it—I own it is admirable,
I think nothing can ever be greater—Nothing can ever deserve more
than it deserves;
I regard it all intently a long while,
Then take my place for good with my own day and race here.

Here lands female and male,
Here the heirship and heiress-ship of the world—Here the flame
of materials,
Here Spirituality, the translatress, the openly-avowed,
The ever-tending, the finale of visible forms,

The satisfier, after due long-waiting, now advancing,
Yes, here comes the mistress, the Soul.

The SOUL!
Forever and forever—Longer than soil is brown and solid—
Longer than water ebbs and flows.

I will make the poems of materials, for I think they are to be
the most spiritual poems,
And I will make the poems of my body and of mortality,
For I think I shall then supply myself with the poems
of my Soul and of immortality.

I will make a song for These States, that no one State may
under any circumstances be subjected to another State,
And I will make a song that there shall be comity by day
and by night between all The States, and between
any two of them,
And I will make a song of the organic bargains of These States—
And a shrill song of curses on him who would dissever
the Union;
And I will make a song for the ears of the President, full of weapons
with menacing points,
And behind the weapons countless dissatisfied faces.

I will acknowledge contemporary lands,
I will trail the whole geography of the globe, and salute courteously
every city large and small;
And employments! I will put in my poems, that with you is heroism,
upon land and sea—And I will report all heroism
from an American point of view;
And sexual organs and acts! do you concentrate in me—For I am
determined to tell you with courageous clear voice,
to prove you illustrious.

I will sing the song of companionship,
I will show what alone must compact These,
I believe These are to found their own ideal of manly love,
indicating it in me;
I will therefore let flame from me the burning fires that were threatening
to consume me;
I will lift what has too long kept down those smouldering fires,

I will give them complete abandonment,
I will write the evangel-poem of comrades° and of love.
(For who but I should understand love, with all its sorrow and joy?
And who but I should be the poet of comrades?)

I am the credulous man of qualities, ages, races,
I advance from the people en-masse in their own spirit,
Here is what sings unrestricted faith.

Omnes! Omnes!°
Let others ignore what they may,
I make the poem of evil also—I commemorate that part also,
I am myself just as much evil as good—And I say there is in fact
no evil,
Or if there is, I say it is just as important to you, to the earth,
or to me, as anything else.

I too, following many, and followed by many, inaugurate a Religion—
I too go to the wars,
It may be I am destined to utter the loudest cries thereof,
the conqueror's shouts,
They may rise from me yet, and soar above every thing.

Each is not for its own sake,
I say the whole earth, and all the stars in the sky, are for Religion's sake.

I say no man has ever been half devout enough,
None has ever adored or worship'd half enough,
None has begun to think how divine he himself is, and how certain
the future is.

I specifically announce that the real and permanent grandeur
of These States must be their Religion,
Otherwise there is no real and permanent grandeur.

What are you doing, young man?
Are you so earnest—so given up to literature, science, art, amours?
These ostensible realities, materials, points?
Your ambition or business, whatever it may be?

It is well—Against such I say not a word—I am their poet also;
But behold! such swiftly subside—burnt up for Religion's sake,

For not all matter is fuel to heat, impalpable flame, the essential life
of the earth,
Any more than such are to Religion.

What do you seek, so pensive and silent?
What do you need, comrade?°
Mon cher! do you think it is love?

Proceed, comrade,
It is a painful thing to love a man or woman to excess—yet it satisfies
—it is great,
But there is something else very great—it makes the whole coincide,
It, magnificent, beyond materials, with continuous hands,
sweeps and provides for all.

O I see the following poems are indeed to drop in the earth the germs
of a greater Religion.

My comrade!
For you, to share with me, two greatnesses—And a third one,
rising inclusive and more resplendent,
The greatness of Love and Democracy—and the greatness of Religion.

Melange mine!
Mysterious ocean where the streams empty,
Prophetic spirit of materials shifting and flickering around me,
Wondrous interplay between the seen and unseen,
Living beings, identities, now doubtless near us, in the air,
that we know not of,
Extasy everywhere touching and thrilling me,
Contact daily and hourly that will not release me,
These selecting—These, in hints, demanded of me.

Not he, adhesive,° kissing me so long with his daily kiss,
Has winded and twisted around me that which holds me to him,
Any more than I am held to the heavens, to the spiritual world,
And to the identities of the Gods, my unknown lovers,
After what they have done to me, suggesting such themes.

O such themes! Equalities!
O amazement of things! O divine average!
O warblings under the sun—ushered, as now, or at noon, or setting!

O strain, musical, flowing through ages—now reaching hither,
I take to your reckless and composite chords—I add to them,
and cheerfully pass them forward.

As I have walked in Alabama my morning walk,
I have seen where the she-bird, the mocking-bird, sat on her nest
in the briers, hatching her brood.

I have seen the he-bird also,
I have paused to hear him, near at hand, inflating his throat,
and joyfully singing.

And while I paused, it came to me that what he really sang for
was not there only,
Nor for his mate nor himself only, nor all sent back by the echoes,
But subtle, clandestine, away beyond,
A charge transmitted, and gift occult, for those being born.

Democracy!
Near at hand to you a throat is now inflating itself and joyfully singing.

Ma femme!
For the brood beyond us and of us,
For those who belong here, and those to come,
I, exultant, to be ready for them, will now shake out carols stronger
and haughtier than have ever yet been heard upon the earth.

I will make the songs of passions, to give them their way,
And your songs, offenders—for I scan you with kindred eyes,
and carry you with me the same as any.

I will make the true poem of riches,
Namely, to earn for the body and the mind, what adheres,
and goes forward, and is not dropt by death.

I will effuse egotism, and show it underlying all—And I will be
the bard of Personality;
And I will show of male and female that either is but the equal
of the other,
And I will show that there is no imperfection in male or female,
or in the earth, or in the present—and can be none in the future,
And I will show that whatever happens to anybody, it may be turned

to beautiful results—And I will show that nothing can happen
more beautiful than death;
And I will thread a thread through my poems that no one thing
in the universe is inferior to another thing,
And that all the things of the universe are perfect miracles,
each as profound as any.

I will not make poems with reference to parts,
But I will make leaves, poems, poemets, songs, says, thoughts,
with reference to ensemble;
And I will not sing with reference to a day, but with reference to all days,
And I will not make a poem, nor the least part of a poem,
but has reference to the Soul,
Because, having looked at the objects of the universe, I find there is
no one, nor any particle of one, but has reference to the Soul.

Was somebody asking to see the Soul?
See! your own shape and countenance—persons, substances, beasts,
the trees, the running rivers, the rocks and sands.

All hold spiritual joys, and afterward loosen them,
How can the real body ever die, and be buried?

Of your real body, and any man's or woman's real body, item for item,
it will elude the hands of the corpse-cleaners, and pass
to fitting spheres, carrying what has accrued to it
from the moment of birth to the moment of death.

Not the types set up by the printer return their impression, the meaning,
the main concern, any more than a man's substance and life,
or a woman's substance and life, return in the body and the Soul,
indifferently before death and after death.

Behold! the body includes and is the meaning, the main concern—
and includes and is the Soul;
Whoever you are! how superb and how divine is your body,
or any part of it.

Whoever you are! to you endless announcements.

Daughter of the lands, did you wait for your poet?
Did you wait for one with a flowing mouth and indicative hand?

Toward the male of The States, and toward the female of The States,
Toward the President, the Congress, the diverse Governors,
the new Judiciary,
Live words—words to the lands.

O the lands!
Lands scorning invaders! Interlinked, food-yielding lands!
Land of coal and iron! Land of gold! Lands of cotton, sugar, rice!
Odorous and sunny land! Floridian land!
Land of the spinal river, the Mississippi! Land of the Alleghanies!
Ohio's land!
Land of wheat, beef, pork! Land of wool and hemp!
Land of the potato, the apple, and the grape!
Land of the pastoral plains, the grass-fields of the world!
Land of those sweet-aired interminable plateaus!
Land there of the herd, the garden, the healthy house
of adobie! Land there of rapt thought, and of the realization
of the stars! Land of simple, holy, untamed lives!
Lands where the northwest Columbia winds, and where
the southwest Colorado winds!
Land of the Chesapeake! Land of the Delaware!
Land of Ontario, Erie, Huron, Michigan!
Land of the Old Thirteen! Massachusetts land! Land of Vermont
and Connecticut!
Land of many oceans! Land of sierras and peaks!
Land of boatmen and sailors! Fisherman's land!
Inextricable lands! the clutched together! the passionate lovers!
The side by side! the elder and younger brothers! the bony-limbed!
The great women's land! the feminine! the experienced sisters
and the inexperienced sisters!
Far breath'd land! Arctic braced! Mexican breezed! the diverse!
the compact!
The Pennsylvanian! the Virginian! the double Carolinian!
O all and each well-loved by me! my intrepid nations!
O I cannot be discharged from you!
O Death! O for all that, I am yet of you, unseen, this hour,
with irrepressible love,
Walking New England, a friend, a traveller,
Splashing my bare feet in the edge of the summer ripples,
on Paumanok's sands,
Crossing the prairies—dwelling again in Chicago—
dwelling in many towns,

Observing shows, births, improvements, structures, arts,
Listening to the orators and the oratresses in public halls,
Of and through The States, as during life—each man and woman
my neighbor,
The Louisianian, the Georgian, as near to me, and I as near to him
and her,
The Mississippian and Arkansian—the woman and man of Utah,
Dakotah, Nebraska, yet with me—and I yet with any of them,
Yet upon the plains west of the spinal river—yet in my house
of adobie,
Yet returning eastward—yet in the Sea-Side State, or in Maryland,
Yet a child of the North—yet Kanadian, cheerily braving the winter—
the snow and ice welcome to me,
Yet a true son either of Maine, or of the Granite State,
or of the Narragansett Bay State, or of the Empire State,
Yet sailing to other shores to annex the same—yet welcoming
every new brother,
Hereby applying these leaves to the new ones, from the hour they unite
with the old ones,
Coming among the new ones myself, to be their companion—
coming personally to you now,
Enjoining you to acts, characters, spectacles, with me.

With me, with firm holding—yet haste, haste on.

For your life, adhere to me,
Of all the men of the earth, I only can unloose you and toughen you,
I may have to be persuaded many times before I consent to give myself
to you—but what of that?
Must not Nature be persuaded many times?

No dainty dolce affettuoso° I;
Bearded, sunburnt, gray-necked, forbidding, I have arrived,
To be wrestled with as I pass, for the solid prizes of the universe,
For such I afford whoever can persevere to win them.

On my way a moment I pause,
Here for you! And here for America!
Still the Present I raise aloft—Still the Future as of The States I harbinge,
glad and sublime,
And for the Past I pronounce what the air holds of the red aborigines.

The red aborigines!
Leaving natural breaths, sounds of rain and winds, calls as of birds
and animals in the woods, syllabled to us for names,
Okonee, Koosa, Ottawa, Monongahela, Sauk, Natchez,
Chattahoochee, Kaqueta, Oronoco,
Wabash, Miami, Saginaw, Chippewa, Oshkosh, Walla-Walla,
Leaving such to The States, they melt, they depart, charging the water
and the land with names.

O expanding and swift! O henceforth,
Elements, breeds, adjustments, turbulent, quick, and audacious,
A world primal again—Vistas of glory, incessant and branching,
A new race, dominating previous ones, and grander far,
New politics—New literatures and religions—New inventions and arts.

These! These, my voice announcing—I will sleep no more, but arise;
You oceans that have been calm within me! how I feel you, fathomless,
stirring, preparing unprecedented waves and storms.

See! steamers steaming through my poems!
See, in my poems immigrants continually coming and landing;
See, in arriere, the wigwam, the trail, the hunter's hut, the flat-boat,
the maize-leaf, the claim, the rude fence, and the backwoods village;
See, on the one side the Western Sea, and on the other side
the Eastern Sea, how they advance and retreat
upon my poems, as upon their own shores;
See, pastures and forests in my poems—See, animals, wild and tame—
See, beyond the Kanzas, countless herds of buffalo, feeding
on short curly grass;
See, in my poems, old and new cities, solid, vast, inland, with paved streets,
with iron and stone edifices, and ceaseless vehicles, and commerce;
See the populace, millions upon millions, handsome, tall, muscular,
both sexes, clothed in easy and dignified clothes—teaching,
commanding, marrying, generating, equally electing and elective;
See, the many-cylinder'd steam printing-press—See, the electric telegraph—
See, the strong and quick locomotive, as it departs, panting,
blowing the steam-whistle;
See, ploughmen, ploughing farms—See, miners, digging mines—
See, the numberless factories;
See, mechanics, busy at their benches, with tools—See from
among them, superior judges, philosophs, Presidents, emerge,
dressed in working dresses;

See, lounging through the shops and fields of The States, me,
well-beloved, close-held by day and night,
Hear the loud echo of my songs there! Read the hints come at last.

O my comrade!
O you and me at last—and us two only;
O power, liberty, eternity at last!
O to be relieved of distinctions! to make as much of vices as virtues!
O to level occupations and the sexes! O to bring all to common ground!
O adhesiveness!
O the pensive aching to be together—you know not why,
and I know not why.

O a word to clear one's path ahead endlessly!
O something extatic and undemonstrable! O music wild!
O now I triumph—and you shall also;
O hand in hand—O wholesome pleasure—O one more desirer and lover,
O haste, firm holding—haste, haste on, with me.

Chants Democratic 8

SPLENDOR of falling day, floating and filling me,
Hour prophetic—hour resuming the past,
Inflating my throat—you, divine average!
You, Earth and Life, till the last ray gleams, I sing.

Open mouth of my Soul, uttering gladness,
Eyes of my Soul, seeing perfection,
Natural life of me, faithfully praising things,
Corroborating forever the triumph of things.

Illustrious every one!
Illustrious what we name space—sphere of unnumbered spirits,
Illustrious the mystery of motion, in all beings, even the tiniest insect,
Illustrious the attribute of speech—the senses—the body,

Illustrious the passing light! Illustrious the pale reflection on the moon
in the western sky!
Illustrious whatever I see, or hear, or touch, to the last.

Good in all,
In the satisfaction and aplomb of animals,
In the annual return of the seasons,
In the hilarity of youth,
In the strength and flush of manhood,
In the grandeur and exquisiteness of old age,
In the superb vistas of Death.

Wonderful to depart!
Wonderful to be here!
The heart, to jet the all-alike and innocent blood,
To breathe the air, how delicious!
To speak! to walk! to seize something by the hand!
To prepare for sleep, for bed—to look on my rose-colored flesh,
To be conscious of my body, so amorous, so large,
To be this incredible God I am,
To have gone forth among other Gods—those men and women I love.

Wonderful how I celebrate you and myself!
How my thoughts play subtly at the spectacles around!
How the clouds pass silently overhead!
How the earth darts on and on! and how the sun, moon, stars,
dart on and on!
How the water sports and sings! (Surely it is alive!)
How the trees rise and stand up—with strong trunks—with branches
and leaves!
(Surely there is something more in each of the trees—some living Soul.)

O amazement of things! even the least particle!
O spirituality of things!
O strain musical, flowing through ages and continents—
now reaching me and America!
I take your strong chords—I intersperse them, and cheerfully pass
them forward.

I too carol the sun, ushered, or at noon, or setting,
I too throb to the brain and beauty of the earth, and of all the growths
of the earth,
I too have felt the resistless call of myself.

As I sailed down the Mississippi,
As I wandered over the prairies,
As I have lived—As I have looked through my windows, my eyes,
As I went forth in the morning—As I beheld the light breaking in the east,
As I bathed on the beach of the Eastern Sea, and again on the beach on the Western Sea,
As I roamed the streets of inland Chicago—whatever streets I have roamed,
Wherever I have been, I have charged myself with contentment and triumph.

I sing the Equalities,
I sing the endless finales of things,
I say Nature continues—Glory continues,
I praise with electric voice,
For I do not see one imperfection in the universe,
And I do not see one cause or result lamentable at last in the universe.

O setting sun! O when the time comes,
I still warble under you, if none else does, unmitigated adoration!

Chants Democratic 10

HISTORIAN ! you who celebrate bygones!
You have explored the outward, the surface of the races—the life that has exhibited itself,
You have treated man as the creature of politics, aggregates, rulers, and priests;
But now I also, arriving, contribute something:
I, an habitué of the Alleghanies, treat man as he is in the influences of Nature, in himself, in his own inalienable rights,
Advancing, to give the spirit and the traits of new Democratic ages, myself, personally
(Let the future behold them all in me—Me, so puzzling

and contradictory—Me, a Manhattanese, the most loving
and arrogant of men);
I do not tell the usual facts, proved by records and documents,
What I tell (talking to every born American) requires no further proof
than he or she who will hear me, will furnish, by silently
meditating alone;
I press the pulse of the life that has hitherto seldom exhibited itself,
but has generally sought concealment (the great pride of man,
in himself),
I illuminate feelings, faults, yearnings, hopes—I have come at last,
no more ashamed nor afraid;
Chanter of Personality, outlining a history yet to be,
I project the ideal man, the American of the future.

Chants Democratic 12

TO oratists—to male or female,
Vocalism, breath, measure, concentration, determination,
and the divine power to use words.

Are you eligible?
Are you full-lung'd and limber-lipp'd from long trial?
from vigorous practice? from physique?
Do you move in these broad lands as broad as they?
Remembering inland America, the high plateaus, stretching long?
Remembering Kanada—Remembering what edges the vast round edge
of the Mexican Sea?
Come duly to the divine power to use words?

For only at last, after many years—after chastity, friendship,
procreation, prudence, and nakedness,
After treading ground and breasting river and lake,
After a loosened throat—after absorbing eras, temperaments,
races—after knowledge, freedom, crimes,

After complete faith—after clarifyings, elevations,
and removing obstructions,
After these, and more, it is just possible there comes to a man,
a woman, the divine power to use words.

Then toward that man or that woman swiftly hasten all—None refuse,
all attend,
Armies, ships, antiquities, the dead, libraries, paintings, machines,
cities, hate, despair, amity, pain, theft, murder, aspiration,
form in close ranks,
They debouch as they are wanted to march obediently
through the mouth of that man, or that woman.

O now I see arise orators fit for inland America,
And I see it is as slow to become an orator as to become a man,
And I see that power is folded in a great vocalism.

Of a great vocalism, when you hear it, the merciless light shall pour,
and the storm rage around,
Every flash shall be a revelation, an insult,
The glaring flame turned on depths, on heights, on suns, on stars,
On the interior and exterior of man or woman,
On the laws of Nature—on passive materials,
On what you called death—and what to you therefore was death,
As far as there can be death.

Chants Democratic 14

POETS to come!
Not to-day is to justify me, and Democracy, and what we are for,
But you, a new brood, native, athletic, continental, greater
than before known,
You must justify me.

Indeed, if it were not for you, what would I be?
What is the little I have done, except to arouse you?

I depend on being realized, long hence, where the broad fat prairies
spread, and thence to Oregon and California inclusive,
I expect that the Texan and the Arizonian, ages hence,
will understand me,
I expect that the future Carolinian and Georgian will understand me
and love me,
I expect that Kanadians, a hundred, and perhaps many hundred years
from now, in winter, in the splendor of the snow and woods,
or on the icy lakes, will take me with them, and permanently
enjoy themselves with me.

Of to-day I know I am momentary, untouched—I am the bard
of the future,
I but write one or two indicative words for the future,
I but advance a moment, only to wheel and hurry back in the darkness.

I am a man who, sauntering along, without fully stopping,
turns a casual look upon you, and then averts his face,
Leaving it to you to prove and define it,
Expecting the main things from you.

Chants Democratic 18

ME imperturbe,
Me standing at ease in Nature,
Master of all, or mistress of all—aplomb in the midst
of irrational things,
Imbued as they—passive, receptive, silent as they,
Finding my occupation, poverty, notoriety, foibles, crimes,
less important than I thought;
Me private, or public, or menial, or solitary—all these subordinate
(I am eternally equal with the best—I am not subordinate);
Me toward the Mexican Sea, or in the Mannahatta,° or the Tennessee,
or far north, or inland,
A river-man, or a man of the woods, or of any farmlife of These States,
or of the coast, or the lakes, or Kanada,

Me, wherever my life is to be lived, O to be self-balanced
for contingencies!
O to confront the night, storms, hunger, ridicule, accidents, rebuffs,
as the trees and animals do.

Chants Democratic 19

I WAS looking a long while for the history of the past for myself,
and for these Chants—and now I have found it,
It is not in those paged fables of the libraries, (them I neither accept
nor reject),
It is no more in the legends than in all else,
It is in the present—it is this earth to-day,
It is in Democracy—in this America—the old world also,
It is the life of one man or one woman to-day, the average man of to-day;
It is languages, social customs, literatures, arts,
It is the broad show of artificial things, ships, machinery, politics,
creeds, modern improvements, and the interchanges of nations,
All for the average man of to-day.

Chants Democratic 20

AMERICAN mouth-songs!
Those of mechanics—each one singing his, as it should be,
blithe and strong,
The carpenter singing his, as he measures his plank or beam,
The mason singing his, as he makes ready for work,
or leaves off work,

The boatman singing what belongs to him in his boat—
the deck-hand singing on the steamboat deck,
The shoemaker singing as he sits on his bench—the hatter singing
as he stands,
The wood-cutter's song—the ploughboy's, on his way in the morning,
or at the noon intermission, or at sundown;
The delicious singing of the mother—or of the young wife at work—
or of the girl sewing or washing—Each singing what belongs
to her, and to none else,
The day what belongs to the day—At night, the party
of young fellows, robust, friendly, clean-blooded,
singing with melodious voices, melodious thoughts.

Come! some of you! still be flooding The States with hundreds
and thousands of mouth-songs, fit for The States only.

Leaves of Grass 1

ELEMENTAL drifts!
O I wish I could impress others as you and the waves
have just been impressing me.

As I ebbed with an ebb of the ocean of life,
As I wended the shores I know,
As I walked where the sea-ripples wash you, Paumanok,°
Where they rustle up, hoarse and sibilant,
Where the fierce old mother endlessly cries for her castaways,
I, musing, late in the autumn day, gazing off southward,
Alone, held by the eternal self of me that threatens to get the better
of me, and stifle me,
Was seized by the spirit that trails in the lines underfoot,
In the rim, the sediment, that stands for all the water and all the land
of the globe.

Fascinated, my eyes, reverting from the south, dropped, to follow
those slender winrows,°
Chaff, straw, splinters of wood, weeds, and the sea-gluten,
Scum, scales from shining rocks, leaves of salt-lettuce, left by the tide;
Miles walking, the sound of breaking waves the other side of me,
Paumanok, there and then, as I thought the old thought of likenesses,
These you presented to me, you fish-shaped island,
As I wended the shores I know,
As I walked with that eternal self of me, seeking types.

As I wend the shores I know not,
As I listen to the dirge, the voices of men and women wrecked,
As I inhale the impalpable breezes that set in upon me,
As the ocean so mysterious rolls toward me closer and closer,
At once I find, the least thing that belongs to me, or that I see or touch,
I know not;
I, too, but signify, at the utmost, a little washed-up drift,
A few sands and dead leaves to gather,
Gather, and merge myself as part of the sands and drift.

O baffled, balked,
Bent to the very earth, here preceding what follows,
Oppressed with myself that I have dared to open my mouth,
Aware now, that, amid all the blab whose echoes recoil upon me,
I have not once had the least idea who or what I am,
But that before all my insolent poems the real ME still stands untouched,
untold, altogether unreached,
Withdrawn far, mocking me with mock-congratulatory signs and bows,
With peals of distant ironical laughter at every word I have written
or shall write,
Striking me with insults till I fall helpless upon the sand.

O I perceive I have not understood anything—not a single object—
and that no man ever can.

I perceive Nature here, in sight of the sea, is taking advantage of me,
to dart upon me, and sting me,
Because I was assuming so much,
And because I have dared to open my mouth to sing at all.

You oceans both! You tangible land! Nature!
Be not too rough with me—I submit—I close with you,
These little shreds shall, indeed, stand for all.

You friable shore, with trails of debris!
You fish-shaped island! I take what is underfoot;
What is yours is mine, my father.

I too Paumanok,
I too have bubbled up, floated the measureless float, and been washed
on your shores;
I too am but a trail of drift and debris,
I too leave little wrecks upon you, you fish-shaped island.

I throw myself upon your breast, my father,
I cling to you so that you cannot unloose me,
I hold you so firm, till you answer me something.

Kiss me, my father,
Touch me with your lips, as I touch those I love,
Breathe to me, while I hold you close, the secret
of the wondrous murmuring I envy,
For I fear I shall become crazed, if I cannot emulate it,
and utter myself as well as it.

Sea-raff! Crook-tongued waves!
O, I will yet sing, some day, what you have said to me.

Ebb, ocean of life, (the flow will return,)
Cease not your moaning, you fierce old mother,
Endlessly cry for your castaways—but fear not, deny not me,
Rustle not up so hoarse and angry against my feet, as I touch you,
or gather from you.

I mean tenderly by you,
I gather for myself, and for this phantom, looking down where we lead,
and following me and mine.

Me and mine!
We, loose winrows, little corpses,
Froth, snowy white, and bubbles,
(See! from my dead lips the ooze exuding at last!
See—the prismatic colors, glistening and rolling!),
Tufts of straw, sands, fragments,
Buoyed hither from many moods, one contradicting another,
From the storm, the long calm, the darkness, the swell,

Musing, pondering, a breath, a briny tear, a dab of liquid or soil,
Up just as much out of fathomless workings fermented and thrown,
A limp blossom or two, torn, just as much over waves floating,
drifted at random,
Just as much for us that sobbing dirge of Nature,
Just as much, whence we come, that blare of the cloud-trumpets;
We, capricious, brought hither, we know not whence, spread out
before You, up there, walking or sitting,
Whoever you are—we too lie in drifts at your feet.

Leaves of Grass 13

O BITTER sprig! Confession sprig!
In the bouquet I give you place also—I bind you in,
Proceeding no further till, humbled publicly,
I give fair warning, once for all.

I own that I have been sly, thievish, mean, a prevaricator, greedy,
derelict,
And I own that I remain so yet.

What foul thought but I think it—or have in me the stuff
out of which it is thought?
What in darkness in bed at night, alone or with a companion?

You felons on trials in courts,
You convicts in prison cells—you sentenced assassins,
chained and handcuffed with iron,
Who am I, that I am not on trial, or in prison?
Me, ruthless and devilish as any, that my wrists are not chained
with iron, or my ankles with iron?

You prostitutes flaunting over the trottoirs,° or obscene in your rooms,
Who am I, that I should call you more obscene than myself?

O culpable! O traitor!
O I acknowledge—I exposé!
(O admirers! praise not me! compliment not me! you make me wince,
I see what you do not—I know what you do not.)
Inside these breast-bones I lie smutch'd and choked,
Beneath this face that appears so impassive, hell's tides continually run,
Lusts and wickedness are acceptable to me,
I walk with delinquents with passionate love,
I feel I am of them—I belong to those convicts and prostitutes myself,
And henceforth I will not deny them—for how can I deny myself?

Leaves of Grass 17

I SIT and look out upon all the sorrows of the world,
and upon all oppression and shame,
I hear secret convulsive sobs from young men, at anguish
with themselves, remorseful after deeds done;
I see, in low life, the mother misused by her children, dying,
neglected, gaunt, desperate,
I see the wife misused by her husband—I see the treacherous seducer
of the young woman,
I mark the ranklings of jealousy and unrequited love,
attempted to be hid—I see these sights on the earth,
I see the workings of battle, pestilence, tyranny—I see martyrs
and prisoners,
I observe a famine at sea—I observe the sailors casting lots
who shall be killed, to preserve the lives of the rest,
I observe the slights and degradations cast by arrogant persons
upon laborers, the poor, and upon negroes, and the like;
All these—All the meanness and agony without end, I sitting,
look out upon,
See, hear, and am silent.

Leaves of Grass 21

NOW I make a leaf of Voices—for I have found nothing mightier
than they are,
And I have found that no word spoken, but is beautiful, in its place.

O what is it in me that makes me tremble so at voices?

Surely, whoever speaks to me in the right voice, him or her
I shall follow, as the waters follow the moon, silently,
with fluid steps, any where around the globe.

Now I believe that all waits for the right voices;
Where is the practised and perfect organ? Where is the developed Soul?
For I see every word uttered thence has deeper, sweeter, new sounds,
impossible on less terms.

I see brains and lips closed—I see tympans and temples unstruck,
Until that comes which has the quality to strike and to unclose,
Until that comes which has the quality to bring forth
what lies slumbering, forever ready, in all words.

Leaves of Grass 22

WHAT am I, after all, but a child, pleased with the sound
of my own name? repeating it over and over,
I cannot tell why it affects me so much, when I hear it
from women's voices, and from men's voices,
or from my own voice,
I stand apart to hear—it never tires me.

To you, your name also,
Did you think there was nothing but two or three pronunciations
in the sound of your name?

Leaves of Grass 24

LIFT me close to your face till I whisper,
What you are holding is in reality no book, nor part of a book,
It is a man, flushed and full-blooded—it is I—*So long!*
We must separate—Here! take from my lips this kiss,
Whoever you are, I give it especially to you;
So long—and I hope we shall meet again.

Poem of Joys

O TO make a most jubilant poem!
O full of music! Full of manhood, womanhood, infancy!
O full of common employments! Full of grain and trees.

O for the voices of animals! O for the swiftness and balance of fishes!
O for the dropping of rain-drops in a poem!
O for the sunshine and motion of waves in a poem.

O to be on the sea! the wind, the wide waters around;
O to sail in a ship under full sail at sea.

O the joy of my spirit! It is uncaged! It darts like lightning!
It is not enough to have this globe, or a certain time—
I will have thousands of globes, and all time.

O the engineer's joys!
To go with a locomotive!
To hear the hiss of steam—the merry shriek—the steam-whistle—
the laughing locomotive!
To push with resistless way, and speed off in the distance.

O the horseman's and horsewoman's joys!
The saddle—the gallop—the pressure upon the seat—
the cool gurgling by the ears and hair.

O the fireman's joys!
I hear the alarm at dead of night,
I hear bells—shouts!—I pass the crowd—I run!
The sight of the flames maddens me with pleasure.

O the joy of the strong-brawned fighter, towering in the arena,
in perfect condition, conscious of power, thirsting to meet
his opponent.

O the joy of that vast elemental sympathy which only the human Soul
is capable of generating and emitting in steady and limitless floods.

O the mother's joys!
The watching—the endurance—the precious love—the anguish—
the patiently yielded life.

O the joy of increase, growth, recuperation,
The joy of soothing and pacifying—the joy of concord and harmony.

O to go back to the place where I was born!
O to hear the birds sing once more!
To ramble about the house and barn, and over the fields, once more,
And through the orchard and along the old lanes once more.

O male and female!
O the presence of women! (I swear, nothing is more exquisite to me
than the presence of women.)
O for the girl, my mate! O for happiness with my mate!
O the young man as I pass! O I am sick after the friendship of him who,
I fear, is indifferent to me.

O the streets of cities!
The flitting faces—the expressions, eyes, feet, costumes!
O I cannot tell how welcome they are to me;
O of men—of women toward me as I pass—The memory of only one look—the boy lingering and waiting.

O to have been brought up on bays, lagoons, creeks, or along the coast!
O to continue and be employed there all my life!
O the briny and damp smell—the shore—the salt weeds exposed at low water,
The work of fishermen—the work of the eel-fisher and clam-fisher.

O it is I!
I come with my clam-rake and spade! I come with my eel-spear;
Is the tide out? I join the group of clam-diggers on the flats,
I laugh and work with them—I joke at my work, like a mettlesome young man.

In winter I take my eel-basket and eel-spear and travel out on foot on the ice—I have a small axe to cut holes in the ice;
Behold me, well-clothed, going gayly, or returning in the afternoon—my brood of tough boys accompanying me,
My brood of grown and part-grown boys, who love to be with none else so well as they love to be with me,
By day to work with me, and by night to sleep with me.

Or, another time, in warm weather, out in a boat, to lift the lobster-pots, where they are sunk with heavy stones (I know the buoys);
O the sweetness of the Fifth Month° morning upon the water, as I row, just before sunrise, toward the buoys;
I pull the wicker pots up slantingly—the dark green lobsters are desperate with their claws, as I take them out—I insert wooden pegs in the joints of their pincers,
I go to all the places, one after another, and then row back to the shore,
There, in a huge kettle of boiling water, the lobsters shall be boiled till their color becomes scarlet.

Or, another time, mackerel-taking,
Voracious, mad for the hook, near the surface, they seem to fill the water for miles;
Or, another time, fishing for rock-fish in Chesapeake Bay—I one of the brown-faced crew;

Or, another time, trailing for blue-fish off Paumanok, I stand
with braced body,
My left foot is on the gunwale—my right arm throws the coils
of slender rope,
In sight around me the quick veering and darting of fifty skiffs,
my companions.

O boating on the rivers!
The voyage down the Niagara (the St. Lawrence)—the superb scenery—
the steamers,
The ships sailing—the Thousand Islands—the occasional timber-raft,
and the raftsmen with long-reaching sweep-oars,
The little huts on the rafts, and the stream of smoke when they
cook supper at evening.

O something pernicious and dread!
Something far away from a puny and pious life!
Something unproved! Something in a trance!
Something escaped from the anchorage, and driving free.

O to work in mines, or forging iron!
Foundry casting—the foundry itself—the rude high roof—
the ample and shadowed space,
The furnace—the hot liquid poured out and running.

O the joys of the soldier!
To feel the presence of a brave general! to feel his sympathy!
To behold his calmness! to be warmed in the rays of his smile!
To go to battle! to hear the bugles play, and the drums beat!
To hear the artillery! to see the glittering of the bayonets
and musket-barrels in the sun!
To see men fall and die and not complain!
To taste the savage taste of blood! to be so devilish!
To gloat so over the wounds and deaths of the enemy.

O the whaleman's joys! O I cruise my old cruise again!
I feel the ship's motion under me—I feel the Atlantic breezes
fanning me,
I hear the cry again sent down from the mast-head, *There she blows,*
Again I spring up the rigging, to look with the rest—We see—
we descend, wild with excitement,
I leap in the lowered boat—We row toward our prey, where he lies,

We approach, stealthy and silent—I see the mountainous mass,
lethargic, basking,
I see the harpooner standing up—I see the weapon dart
from his vigorous arm;
O swift, again, now, far out in the ocean, the wounded whale, settling,
running to windward, tows me,
Again I see him rise to breathe—We row close again,
I see a lance driven through his side, pressed deep, turned in the wound,
Again we back off—I see him settle again—the life is leaving him fast,
As he rises, he spouts blood—I see him swim in circles narrower
and narrower, swiftly cutting the water—I see him die,
He gives one convulsive leap in the centre of the circle,
and then falls flat and still in the bloody foam.

O the old manhood of me, my joy!
My children and grand-children—my white hair and beard,
My largeness, calmness, majesty, out of the long stretch of my life.

O the ripened joy of womanhood!
O perfect happiness at last!
I am more than eighty years of age—my hair, too, is pure white—
I am the most venerable mother;
How clear is my mind! how all people draw nigh to me!
What attractions are these, beyond any before? what bloom,
more than the bloom of youth?
What beauty is this that descends upon me, and rises out of me?

O the joy of my Soul leaning poised on itself—receiving identity
through materials, and loving them—observing characters,
and absorbing them;
O my Soul, vibrated back to me, from them—from facts, sight,
hearing, touch, my phrenology,° reason, articulation,
comparison, memory, and the like;
O the real life of my senses and flesh, transcending my senses and flesh;
O my body, done with materials—my sight, done with my material eyes;
O what is proved to me this day, beyond cavil, that it is not
my material eyes which finally see,
Nor my material body which finally loves, walks, laughs, shouts,
embraces, procreates.

O the farmer's joys!
Ohioan's, Illinoisian's, Wisconsinese', Kanadian's, Iowan's,
Kansian's, Missourian's, Oregonese' joys,

To rise at peep of day, and pass forth nimbly to work,
To plough land in the fall for winter-sown crops,
To plough land in the spring for maize,
To train orchards—to graft the trees—to gather apples in the fall.

O the pleasure with trees!
The orchard—the forest—the oak, cedar, pine, pekan-tree,
The honey-locust, black-walnut, cottonwood, and magnolia.

O Death!
O the beautiful touch of Death, soothing and benumbing a few moments, for reasons;
O that of myself, discharging my excrementitious body, to be burned, or rendered to powder, or buried,
My real body doubtless left to me for other spheres,
My voided body, nothing more to me, returning to the purifications, further offices, eternal uses of the earth.

O to bathe in the swimming-bath, or in a good place along shore!
To splash the water! to walk ankle-deep; to race naked along the shore.

O to realize space!
The plenteousness of all—that there are no bounds;
To emerge, and be of the sky—of the sun and moon, and the flying clouds, as one with them.

O, while I live, to be the ruler of life°—not a slave,
To meet life as a powerful conqueror,
No fumes—no ennui—no more complaints or scornful criticisms.

O me repellent and ugly!
O to these proud laws of the air, the water, and the ground, proving my interior Soul impregnable,
And nothing exterior shall ever take command of me.

O to attract by more than attraction!
How it is I know not—yet behold! the something which obeys none of the rest,
It is offensive, never defensive—yet how magnetic it draws.

O the joy of suffering!
To struggle against great odds! to meet enemies undaunted!

To be entirely alone with them! to find how much I can stand!
To look strife, torture, prison, popular odium, death, face to face!
To mount the scaffold! to advance to the muzzles of guns
with perfect nonchalance!
To be indeed a God!

O the gleesome saunter over fields and hill-sides!
The leaves and flowers of the commonest weeds—
the moist fresh stillness of the woods,
The exquisite smell of the earth at day-break, and all through
the forenoon.

O love-branches! love-root! love-apples!
O chaste and electric torrents! O mad-sweet drops.

O the orator's joys!
To inflate the chest—to roll the thunder of the voice out from the ribs
and throat,
To make the people rage, weep, hate, desire, with yourself,
To lead America—to quell America with a great tongue.

O the joy of a manly self-hood!
Personality—to be servile to none—to defer to none—not to any tyrant,
known or unknown,
To walk with erect carriage, a step springy and elastic,
To look with calm gaze, or with a flashing eye,
To speak with a full and sonorous voice, out of a broad chest,
To confront with your personality all the other personalities of the earth.

O to have my life henceforth my poem of joys!
To dance, clap hands, exult, shout, skip, leap, roll on, float on,
An athlete—full of rich words—full of joys.

A Word Out of the Sea

OUT of the rocked cradle,
Out of the mocking-bird's throat, the musical shuttle,
Out of the boy's mother's womb, and from the nipples of her breasts,
Out of the Ninth Month° midnight,
Over the sterile sands, and the fields beyond, where the child,
leaving his bed, wandered alone, bareheaded, barefoot,
Down from the showered halo,
Up from the mystic play of shadows, twining and twisting
as if they were alive,
Out from the patches of briers and blackberries,
From the memories of the bird that chanted to me,
From your memories, sad brother—from the fitful risings and fallings
I heard,
From under that yellow half-moon, late-risen, and swollen
as if with tears,
From those beginning notes of sickness and love,
there in the transparent mist,
From the thousand responses of my heart, never to cease,
From the myriad thence-aroused words,
From the word stronger and more delicious than any,
From such, as now they start, the scene revisiting,
As a flock, twittering, rising, or overhead passing,
Borne hither—ere all eludes me, hurriedly,
A man—yet by these tears a little boy again,
Throwing myself on the sand, confronting the waves,
I, chanter of pains and joys, uniter of here and hereafter,
Taking all hints to use them—but swiftly leaping beyond them,
A reminiscence sing.

REMINISCENCE

ONCE, Paumanok,°
When the snows had melted, and the Fifth Month grass was growing,
Up this sea-shore, in some briers,

Two guests from Alabama—two together,
And their nest, and four light-green eggs, spotted with brown,
And every day the he-bird, to and fro, near at hand,
And every day the she-bird, crouched on her nest, silent,
with bright eyes,
And every day I, a curious boy, never too close, never disturbing them,
Cautiously peering, absorbing, translating.

Shine! Shine!
Pour down your warmth, great Sun!
While we bask—we two together.

Two together!
Winds blow South, or winds blow North,
Day come white, or night come black,
Home, or rivers and mountains from home,
Singing all time, minding no time,
If we two but keep together.

Till of a sudden,
May-be killed, unknown to her mate,
One forenoon the she-bird crouched not on the nest,
Nor returned that afternoon, nor the next,
Nor ever appeared again.

And thenceforward, all summer, in the sound of the sea,
And at night, under the full of the moon, in calmer weather,
Over the hoarse surging of the sea,
Or flitting from brier to brier by day,
I saw, I heard at intervals, the remaining one, the he-bird,
The solitary guest from Alabama.

Blow! Blow!
Blow up sea-winds along Paumanok's shore;
I wait and I wait, till you blow my mate to me.

Yes, when the stars glistened,
All night long, on the prong of a moss-scallop'd stake,
Down, almost amid the slapping waves,
Sat the lone singer, wonderful, causing tears.

He called on his mate,
He poured forth the meanings which I, of all men, know.

Yes, my brother, I know,
The rest might not—but I have treasured every note,
For once, and more than once, dimly, down to the beach gliding,
Silent, avoiding the moonbeams, blending myself with the shadows,
Recalling now the obscure shapes, the echoes, the sounds and sights
        after their sorts,
The white arms out in the breakers tirelessly tossing,
I, with bare feet, a child, the wind wafting my hair,
Listened long and long.

Listened, to keep, to sing—now translating the notes,
Following you, my brother.

Soothe! Soothe!
Close on its wave soothes the wave behind,
And again another behind, embracing and lapping, every one close,
But my love soothes not me.

Low hangs the moon—it rose late,
O it is lagging—O I think it is heavy with love.

O madly the sea pushes upon the land,
With love—with love.

O night!
O do I not see my love fluttering out there among the breakers?
What is that little black thing I see there in the white?

Loud! Loud!
Loud I call to you my love!
High and clear I shoot my voice over the waves,
Surely you must know who is here,
You must know who I am, my love.

Low-hanging moon!
What is that dusky spot in your brown yellow?
O it is the shape of my mate!
O moon, do not keep her from me any longer.

Land! O land!
Whichever way I turn, O I think you could give me my mate
back again, if you would,
For I am almost sure I see her dimly whichever way I look.

O rising stars!
Perhaps the one I want so much will rise with some of you.

O throat!
Sound clearer through the atmosphere!
Pierce the woods, the earth,
Somewhere listening to catch you must be the one I want.

Shake out, carols!
Solitary here—the night's carols!
Carols of lonesome love! Death's carols!
Carols under that lagging, yellow, waning moon!
O, under that moon, where she droops almost down into the sea!
O reckless, despairing carols!

But soft!
Sink low—soft!
Soft! Let me just murmur,
And do you wait a moment, you husky-noised sea,
For somewhere I believe I heard my mate responding to me,
So faint—I must be still to listen,
But not altogether still, for then she might not come immediately to me.

Hither, my love!
Here I am! Here!
With this just-sustained note I announce myself to you,
This gentle call is for you, my love.

Do not be decoyed elsewhere!
That is the whistle of the wind—it is not my voice,
That is the fluttering of the spray,
Those are the shadows of leaves.

O darkness! O in vain!
O I am very sick and sorrowful.

O brown halo in the sky, near the moon, drooping upon the sea!
O troubled reflection in the sea!
O throat! O throbbing heart!
O all—and I singing uselessly all the night.

Murmur! Murmur on!
O murmurs—you yourselves make me continue to sing, I know not why.

O past! O joy!
In the Air—in the woods—over fields,
Loved! Loved! Loved! Loved! Loved!
Loved—but no more with me,
We two together no more.

The aria sinking,°
All else continuing—the stars shining,
The winds blowing—the notes of the wondrous bird echoing,
With angry moans the fierce old mother yet, as ever, incessantly moaning,
On the sands of Paumanok's shore gray and rustling,
The yellow half-moon, enlarged, sagging down, drooping,
    the face of the sea almost touching,
The boy extatic—with his bare feet the waves, with his hair
    the atmosphere dallying,
The love in the heart pent, now loose, now at last tumultuously bursting,
The aria's meaning, the ears, the Soul, swiftly depositing,
The strange tears down the cheeks coursing,
The colloquy there—the trio—each uttering,
The undertone—the savage old mother, incessantly crying,
To the boy's Soul's questions sullenly timing—
    some drowned secret hissing,
To the outsetting bard of love.

Bird! (then said the boy's Soul)
Is it indeed toward your mate you sing? or is it mostly to me?
For I that was a child, my tongue's use sleeping,
Now that I have heard you,
Now in a moment I know what I am for—I awake,
And already a thousand singers—a thousand songs, clearer, louder,
    more sorrowful than yours,
A thousand warbling echoes have started to life within me,
Never to die.

O throes!
O you demon, singing by yourself—projecting me,
O solitary me, listening—never more shall I cease imitating,
        perpetuating you,
Never more shall I escape,
Never more shall the reverberations,
Never more the cries of unsatisfied love be absent from me,
Never again leave me to be the peaceful child I was before what there,
        in the night,
By the sea, under the yellow and sagging moon,
The dusky demon aroused—the fire, the sweet hell within,
The unknown want, the destiny of me.

O give me some clew!
O if I am to have so much, let me have more!
O a word! O what is my destination!
O I fear it is henceforth chaos!
O how joys, dreads, convolutions, human shapes, and all shapes,
        spring as from graves around me!
O phantoms! you cover all the land, and all the sea!
O I cannot see in the dimness whether you smile or frown upon me;
O vapor, a look, a word! O well-beloved!
O you dear women's and men's phantoms!

A word then (for I will conquer it),
The word final, superior to all,
Subtle, sent up—what is it?—I listen;
Are you whispering it, and have been all the time, you sea-waves?
Is that it from your liquid rims and wet sands?

Answering, the sea,
Delaying not, hurrying not,
Whispered me through the night, and very plainly before daybreak,
Lisped to me constantly the low and delicious word DEATH,
And again Death—ever Death, Death, Death,
Hissing melodious, neither like the bird, nor like my aroused child's heart,
But edging near, as privately for me, rustling at my feet,
And creeping thence steadily up to my ears,
Death, Death, Death, Death, Death.

Which I do not forget,
But fuse the song of two together,

That was sung to me in the moonlight on Paumanok's gray beach,
With the thousand responsive songs, at random,
My own songs, awaked from that hour,
And with them the key, the word up from the waves,
The word of the sweetest song, and all songs,
That strong and delicious word which, creeping to my feet,
The sea whispered me.

Enfans d'Adam 1

To the garden, the world, anew ascending,
Potent mates, daughters, sons, preluding,
The love, the life of their bodies, meaning and being,
Curious, here behold my resurrection, after slumber,
The revolving cycles, in their wide sweep, having brought me again,
Amorous, mature—all beautiful to me—all wondrous,
My limbs, and the quivering fire that ever plays through them,
        for reasons most wondrous;
Existing, I peer and penetrate still,
Content with the present—content with the past,
By my side, or back of me, Eve following,
Or in front, and I following her just the same.

Enfans d'Adam 2

FROM that of myself, without which I were nothing,
From what I am determined to make illustrious, even if I stand
sole among men,
From my own voice resonant—singing the phallus,
Singing the song of procreation,
Singing the need of superb children, and therein superb grown people,
Singing the muscular urge and the blending,
Singing the bedfellow's song (O resistless yearning!
O for any and each, the body correlative attracting!
O for you, whoever you are, your correlative body!
O it, more than all else, you delighting!),
From the pent up rivers of myself,
From the hungry gnaw that eats me night and day,
From native moments—from bashful pains—singing them,
Singing something yet unfound, though I have diligently sought it,
ten thousand years,
Singing the true song of the Soul, fitful, at random,
Singing what, to the Soul, entirely redeemed her, the faithful one,
the prostitute, who detained me when I went to the city,
Singing the song of prostitutes;
Renascent with grossest Nature, or among animals,
Of that—of them, and what goes with them, my poems informing,
Of the smell of apples and lemons—of the pairing of birds,
Of the wet of woods—of the lapping of waves,
Of the mad pushes of waves upon the land—I them chanting,
The overture lightly sounding—the strain anticipating,
The welcome nearness—the sight of the perfect body,
The swimmer swimming naked in the bath, or motionless on his back
lying and floating,
The female form approaching—I, pensive, love-flesh tremulous, aching;
The slave's body for sale—I, sternly, with harsh voice, auctioneering,
The divine list, for myself or you, or for any one, making,
The face—the limbs—the index from head to foot, and what it arouses,

The mystic deliria—the madness amorous—the utter abandonment
(Hark, close and still, what I now whisper to you,
I love you—O you entirely possess me,
O I wish that you and I escape from the rest, and go utterly off—
O free and lawless,
Two hawks in the air—two fishes swimming in the sea
not more lawless than we);
The furious storm through me careering—I passionately trembling,
The oath of the inseparableness of two together—of the woman
that loves me, and whom I love more than my life—
That oath swearing
(O I willingly stake all, for you!
O let me be lost, if it must be so!
O you and I—what is it to us what the rest do or think?
What is all else to us? only that we enjoy each other,
and exhaust each other, if it must be so);
From the master—the pilot I yield the vessel to,
The general commanding me, commanding all—from him
permission taking,
From time the programme hastening (I have loitered too long, as it is);
From sex—From the warp and from the woof
(To talk to the perfect girl who understands me—the girl of The States,
To waft to her these from my own lips—to effuse them
from my own body);
From privacy—From frequent repinings alone,
From plenty of persons near, and yet the right person not near,
From the soft sliding of hands over me, and thrusting of fingers
through my hair and beard,
From the long-sustained kiss upon the mouth or bosom,
From the close pressure that makes me or any man drunk,
fainting with excess,
From what the divine husband knows—from the work of fatherhood,
From exultation, victory, and relief—from the bedfellow's embrace
in the night,
From the act-poems of eyes, hands, hips, and bosoms,
From the cling of the trembling arm,
From the bending curve and the clinch,
From side by side, the pliant coverlid off throwing,
From the one so unwilling to have me leave—and me just as unwilling
to leave
(Yet a moment, O tender waiter, and I return),
From the hour of shining stars and dropping dews,

From the night, a moment, I, emerging, flitting out,
Celebrate you, enfans prepared for,
And you, stalwart loins.

Enfans d'Adam 6

O FURIOUS! O confine me not!
(What is this that frees me so in storms?
What do my shouts amid lightnings and raging winds mean?)

O to drink the mystic deliria deeper than any other man!
O savage and tender achings!
(I bequeath them to you, my children,
I tell them to you, for reasons, O bridegroom and bride.)

O to be yielded to you, whoever you are, and you to be yielded me,
in defiance of the world!
(Know, I am a man, attracting, at any time, her I but look upon,
or touch with the tips of my fingers,
Or that touches my face, or leans against me.)

O to return to Paradise!
O to draw you to me—to plant on you, for the first time, the lips
of a determined man!
O rich and feminine! O to show you to realize the blood of life
for yourself, whoever you are—and no matter when
and where you live.

O the puzzle—the thrice-tied knot—the deep and dark pool!
O all untied and illumined!
O to speed where there is space enough and air enough at last!
O to be absolved from previous follies and degradations—
I from mine, and you from yours!
O to find a new unthought-of nonchalance with the best of nature!
O to have the gag removed from one's mouth!
O to have the feeling, to-day or any day, I am sufficient as I am!

O something unproved! something in a trance!
O madness amorous! O trembling!
O to escape utterly from others' anchors and holds!
To drive free! to love free! to dash reckless and dangerous!
To court destruction with taunts—with invitations!
To ascend—to leap to the heavens of the love indicated to me!
To rise thither with my inebriate Soul!
To be lost, if it must be so!
To feed the remainder of life with one hour of fulness and freedom!
With one brief hour of madness and joy.

Enfans d'Adam 7

YOU and I—what the earth is, we are,
We two—how long we were fooled!
Now delicious, transmuted, swiftly we escape, as Nature escapes,
We are Nature—long have we been absent, but now we return,
We become plants, leaves, foliage, roots, bark,
We are bedded in the ground—we are rocks,
We are oaks—we grow in the openings side by side,
We browse—we are two among the wild herds, spontaneous as any,
We are two fishes swimming in the sea together,
We are what the locust blossoms are—we drop scent around the lanes, mornings and evenings,
We are also the coarse smut of beasts, vegetables, minerals,
We are what the flowing wet of the Tennessee is—we are two peaks of the Blue Mountains, rising up in Virginia,
We are two predatory hawks—we soar above and look down,
We are two resplendent suns—we it is who balance ourselves orbic and stellar—we are as two comets;
We prowl fanged and four-footed in the woods—we spring on prey;
We are two clouds, forenoons and afternoons, driving overhead,
We are seas mingling—we are two of those cheerful waves, rolling over each other, and interwetting each other,

We are what the atmosphere is, transparent, receptive, pervious,
impervious,
We are snow, rain, cold, darkness—we are each product and influence
of the globe,
We have circled and circled till we have arrived home again—
we two have,
We have voided all but freedom, and all but our own joy.

Enfans d'Adam 8

NATIVE moments! when you come upon me—Ah you are here now!
Give me now libidinous joys only!
Give me the drench of my passions! Give me life coarse and rank!
To-day, I go consort with nature's darlings—to-night too,
I am for those who believe in loose delights—I share the midnight orgies
of young men,
I dance with the dancers, and drink with the drinkers,
The echoes ring with our indecent calls,
I take for my love some prostitute—I pick out some low person
for my dearest friend,
He shall be lawless, rude, illiterate—he shall be one condemned
by others for deeds done;
I will play a part no longer—Why should I exile myself
from my companions?
O you shunned persons! I at least do not shun you,
I come forthwith in your midst—I will be your poet,
I will be more to you than to any of the rest.

Enfans d'Adam 9

ONCE I passed through a populous city, imprinting my brain,
for future use, with its shows, architecture, customs,
and traditions;
Yet now, of all that city, I remember only a woman
I casually met there, who detained me for love of me,
Day by day and night by night we were together,—All else
has long been forgotten by me,
I remember I say only that woman who passionately clung to me,
Again we wander—we love—we separate again,
Again she holds me by the hand—I must not go!
I see her close beside me, with silent lips, sad and tremulous.

Enfans d'Adam 10

INQUIRING, tireless, seeking that yet unfound,
I, a child, very old, over waves, toward the house of maternity,
the land of migrations, look afar,
Look off the shores of my Western Sea—having arrived at last
where I am—the circle almost circled;
For coming westward from Hindustan, from the vales of Kashmere,
From Asia—from the north—from the God, the sage, and the hero,
From the south—from the flowery peninsulas, and the spice islands,
Now I face the old home again—looking over to it, joyous,
as after long travel, growth, and sleep;
But where is what I started for, so long ago?
And why is it yet unfound?

Enfans d'Adam 11

IN the new garden, in all the parts,
In cities now, modern, I wander,
Though the second or third result, or still further, primitive yet,
Days, places, indifferent—though various, the same,
Time, Paradise, the Mannahatta, the prairies, finding me unchanged,
Death indifferent—Is it that I lived long since? Was I buried
very long ago?
For all that, I may now be watching you here, this moment;
For the future, with determined will, I seek—the woman of the future,
You, born years, centuries before me, I seek.

Enfans d'Adam 12

AGES and ages, returning at intervals,
Undestroyed, wandering immortal,
Lusty, phallic, with the potent original loins, perfectly sweet,
I, chanter of Adamic songs,
Through the new garden, the West, the great cities, calling,
Deliriate, thus prelude what is generated, offering these,
offering myself,
Bathing myself, bathing my songs in sex,
Offspring of my loins.

Enfans d'Adam 13

O HYMEN! O hymenee!
Why do you tantalize me thus?
O why sting me for a swift moment only?
Why can you not continue? O why do you now cease?
Is it because, if you continued beyond the swift moment,
you would soon certainly kill me?

Enfans d'Adam 14

I AM he that aches with love;
Does the earth gravitate? Does not all matter, aching,
attract all matter?
So the body of me to all I meet, or that I know.

Enfans d'Adam 15

EARLY in the morning,
Walking forth from the bower, refreshed with sleep,
Behold me where I pass—hear my voice—approach,
Touch me—touch the palm of your hand to my body as I pass,
Be not afraid of my body.

Calamus 1

IN paths untrodden,
In the growth by margins of pond-waters,
Escaped from the life that exhibits itself,
From all the standards hitherto published—from the pleasures,
profits, conformities,
Which too long I was offering to feed to my Soul;
Clear to me now, standards not yet published—
clear to me that my Soul,
That the Soul of the man I speak for, feeds, rejoices only in comrades;°
Here, by myself, away from the clank of the world,
Tallying and talked to here by tongues aromatic,
No longer abashed—for in this secluded spot I can respond
as I would not dare elsewhere,
Strong upon me the life that does not exhibit itself,
yet contains all the rest,
Resolved to sing no songs to-day but those of manly attachment,
Projecting them along that substantial life,
Bequeathing, hence, types of athletic love,
Afternoon, this delicious Ninth Month, in my forty-first year,°
I proceed, for all who are, or have been, young men,
To tell the secret of my nights and days,
To celebrate the need of comrades.

Calamus 2

SCENTED herbage of my breast,
Leaves from you I yield, I write, to be perused best afterwards,
Tomb-leaves, body-leaves, growing up above me, above death,

Perennial roots, tall leaves—O the winter shall not freeze you,
delicate leaves,
Every year shall you bloom again—Out from where you retired,
you shall emerge again;
O I do not know whether many, passing by, will discover you,
or inhale your faint odor—but I believe a few will;
O slender leaves! O blossoms of my blood! I permit you to tell,
in your own way, of the heart that is under you,
O burning and throbbing—surely all will one day be accomplished;
O I do not know what you mean, there underneath yourselves—
you are not happiness,
You are often more bitter than I can bear—you burn and sting me,
Yet you are very beautiful to me, you faint-tinged roots—
you make me think of Death,
Death is beautiful from you—(what indeed is beautiful,
except Death and Love?)—
O I think it is not for life I am chanting here my chant of lovers—
I think it must be for Death,
For how calm, how solemn it grows, to ascend to the atmosphere
of lovers,
Death or life I am then indifferent—my Soul declines to prefer,
I am not sure but the high Soul of lovers welcomes death most;
Indeed, O Death, I think now these leaves mean precisely the same
as you mean;
Grow up taller, sweet leaves, that I may see! Grow up out of my breast!
Spring away from the concealed heart there!
Do not fold yourselves so in you pink-tinged roots, timid leaves!
Do not remain down there so ashamed, herbage of my breast!
Come, I am determined to unbare this broad breast of mine—
I have long enough stifled and choked;
Emblematic and capricious blades, I leave you—now you serve me not,
Away! I will say what I have to say, by itself,
I will escape from the sham that was proposed to me,
I will sound myself and comrades only—I will never again utter a call,
only their call,
I will raise, with it, immortal reverberations through The States,
I will give an example to lovers, to take permanent shape and will
through The States;
Through me shall the words be said to make death exhilarating,
Give me your tone therefore, O Death, that I may accord with it,
Give me yourself—for I see that you belong to me now above all,
and are folded together above all—you Love and Death are,

Nor will I allow you to balk me any more with what I was calling life,
For now it is conveyed to me that you are the purports essential,
That you hide in these shifting forms of life, for reasons—
and that they are mainly for you,
That you, beyond them, come forth, to remain, the real reality,
That behind the mask of materials you patiently wait,
no matter how long,
That you will one day, perhaps, take control of all,
That you will perhaps dissipate this entire show of appearance,
That may be you are what it is all for—but it does not last so very long,
But you will last very long.

Calamus 3

WHOEVER you are holding me now in hand,
Without one thing all will be useless,
I give you fair warning, before you attempt me further,
I am not what you supposed, but far different.

Who is he that would become my follower?
Who would sign himself a candidate for my affections? Are you he?

The way is suspicious—the result slow, uncertain, may-be destructive;
You would have to give up all else—I alone would expect to be
your God, sole and exclusive,
Your novitiate would even then be long and exhausting,
The whole past theory of your life, and all conformity to the lives
around you, would have to be abandoned;
Therefore release me now, before troubling yourself any further—
Let go your hand from my shoulders,
Put me down, and depart on your way.

Or else, only by stealth, in some wood, for trial,
Or back of a rock, in the open air,
(For in any roofed room of a house I emerge not—nor in company,
And in libraries I lie as one dumb, a gawk, or unborn, or dead),

But just possibly with you on a high hill—first watching
lest any person, for miles around, approach unawares,
Or possibly with you sailing at sea, or on the beach of the sea,
or some quiet island,
Here to put your lips upon mine I permit you,
With the comrade's long-dwelling kiss, or the new husband's kiss,
For I am the new husband, and I am the comrade.

Or, if you will, thrusting me beneath your clothing,
Where I may feel the throbs of your heart, or rest upon your hip,
Carry me when you go forth over land or sea;
For thus, merely touching you, is enough—is best,
And thus, touching you, would I silently sleep and be carried eternally.

But these leaves conning, you con at peril,
For these leaves, and me, you will not understand,
They will elude you at first, and still more afterward—
I will certainly elude you,
Even while you should think you had unquestionably caught me, behold!
Already you see I have escaped from you.

For it is not for what I have put into it that I have written this book,
Nor is it by reading it you will acquire it,
Nor do those know me best who admire me, and vauntingly praise me,
Nor will the candidates for my love (unless at most a very few)
prove victorious,
Nor will my poems do good only—they will do just as much evil,
perhaps more,
For all is useless without that which you may guess at many times
and not hit—that which I hinted at,
Therefore release me, and depart on your way.

Calamus 4

THESE I, singing in spring, collect for lovers
(For who but I should understand lovers, and all their sorrow and joy?
And who but I should be the poet of comrades?),
Collecting, I traverse the garden, the world—but soon I pass the gates,
Now along the pond-side—now wading in a little, fearing not the wet,
Now by the post-and-rail fences, where the old stones thrown there,
picked from the fields, have accumulated,
Wild-flowers and vines and weeds come up through the stones,
and partly cover them—Beyond these I pass,
Far, far in the forest, before I think where I get,
Solitary, smelling the earthy smell, stopping now and then in the silence,
Alone I had thought—yet soon a silent troop gathers around me,
Some walk by my side, and some behind, and some embrace
my arms or neck,
They, the spirits of friends, dead or alive—thicker they come,
a great crowd, and I in the middle,
Collecting, dispensing, singing in spring, there I wander with them,
Plucking something for tokens—something for these, till I hit
upon a name—tossing toward whoever is near me,
Here! lilac, with a branch of pine,
Here, out of my pocket, some moss which I pulled off a live-oak
in Florida, as it hung trailing down,
Here, some pinks and laurel leaves, and a handful of sage,
And here what I now draw from the water, wading in the pond-side
(O here I last saw him that tenderly loves me—and returns again,
never to separate from me,
And this, O this shall henceforth be the token of comrades—
this calamus-root shall,
Interchange it, youths, with each other! Let none render it back!),
And twigs of maple, and a bunch of wild orange, and chestnut,
And stems of currants, and plum-blows, and the aromatic cedar;
These I, compassed around by a thick cloud of spirits,
Wandering, point to, or touch as I pass, or throw them loosely from me,

Indicating to each one what he shall have—giving something to each,
But what I drew from the water by the pond-side, that I reserve,
I will give of it—but only to them that love, as I myself am capable
of loving.

Calamus 5

STATES!
Were you looking to be held together by the lawyers?
By an agreement on a paper? Or by arms?

Away!
I arrive, bringing these, beyond all the forces of courts and arms,
These! to hold you together as firmly as the earth itself is held together.

The old breath of life, ever new,
Here! I pass it by contact to you, America.

O mother! have you done much for me?
Behold, there shall from me be much done for you.

There shall from me be a new friendship—It shall be called
after my name,
It shall circulate through The States, indifferent of place,
It shall twist and intertwist them through and around each other—
Compact shall they be, showing new signs,
Affection shall solve every one of the problems of freedom,
Those who love each other shall be invincible,
They shall finally make America completely victorious, in my name.

One from Massachusetts shall be comrade to a Missourian,
One from Maine or Vermont, and a Carolinian and an Oregonese,
shall be friends triune, more precious to each other
than all the riches of the earth.

To Michigan shall be wafted perfume from Florida,
To the Mannahatta from Cuba or Mexico,
Not the perfume of flowers, but sweeter, and wafted beyond death.

No danger shall balk Columbia's lovers,
If need be, a thousand shall sternly immolate themselves for one,
The Kanuck shall be willing to lay down his life for the Kansian,
        and the Kansian for the Kanuck, on due need.

It shall be customary in all directions, in the houses and streets,
        to see manly affection,
The departing brother or friend shall salute the remaining brother
        or friend with a kiss.

There shall be innovations,
There shall be countless linked hands—namely, the Northeasterner's,
        and the Northwesterner's, and the Southwesterner's,
        and those of the interior, and all their brood,
These shall be masters of the world under a new power,
They shall laugh to scorn the attacks of all the remainder of the world.

The most dauntless and rude shall touch face to face lightly,
The dependence of Liberty shall be lovers,
The continuance of Equality shall be comrades.

These shall tie and band stronger than hoops of iron,
I, extatic, O partners! O lands! henceforth with the love of lovers tie you.

I will make the continent indissoluble,
I will make the most splendid race the sun ever yet shone upon,
I will make divine magnetic lands.

I will plant companionship thick as trees along all the rivers
        of America, and along the shores of the great lakes,
        and all over the prairies,
I will make inseparable cities, with their arms about each other's necks.

For you these, from me, O Democracy, to serve you, ma femme!
For you! for you, I am trilling these songs.

Calamus 6

NOT heaving from my ribbed breast only,
Not in sighs at night, in rage, dissatisfied with myself,
Not in those long-drawn, ill-suppressed sighs,
Not in many an oath and promise broken,
Not in my wilful and savage soul's volition,
Not in the subtle nourishment of the air,
Not in this beating and pounding at my temples and wrists,
Not in the curious systole and diastole within, which will one day cease,
Not in many a hungry wish, told to the skies only,
Not in cries, laughter, defiances, thrown from me when alone,
  far in the wilds,
Not in husky pantings through clenched teeth,
Not in sounded and resounded words—chattering words, echoes,
  dead words,
Not in the murmurs of my dreams while I sleep,
Nor the other murmurs of these incredible dreams of every day,
Nor in the limbs and senses of my body, that take you
  and dismiss you continually—Not there,
Not in any or all of them, O adhesiveness!° O pulse of my life!
Need I that you exist and show yourself, any more than in these songs.

Calamus 7

OF the terrible question of appearances,
Of the doubts, the uncertainties after all,
That may-be reliance and hope are but speculations after all,
That may-be identity beyond the grave is a beautiful fable only,
May-be the things I perceive—the animals, plants, men, hills,

shining and flowing waters,
The skies of day and night—colors, densities, forms—May-be these
are (as doubtless they are) only apparitions, and the real
something has yet to be known
(How often they dart out of themselves, as if to confound me
and mock me!
How often I think neither I know, nor any man knows, aught of them);
May-be they only seem to me what they are (as doubtless they
indeed but seem), as from my present point of view—
And might prove (as of course they would) naught
of what they appear, or naught any how, from entirely
changed points of view;
To me, these, and the like of these, are curiously answered
by my lovers, my dear friends;
When he whom I love travels with me, or sits a long while holding me
by the hand,
When the subtle air, the impalpable, the sense that words and reason
hold not, surround us and pervade us,
Then I am charged with untold and untellable wisdom—I am silent—
I require nothing further,
I cannot answer the question of appearances, or that of identity
beyond the grave,
But I walk or sit indifferent—I am satisfied,
He ahold of my hand has completely satisfied me.

Calamus 8

LONG I thought that knowledge alone would suffice me—
O if I could but obtain knowledge!
Then my lands engrossed me—Lands of the prairies, Ohio's land,
the southern savannas, engrossed me—For them I would live—
I would be their orator;
Then I met the examples of old and new heroes—I heard of warriors,
sailors, and all dauntless persons—And it seemed to me that
I too had it in me to be as dauntless as any—and would be so;
And then, to enclose all, it came to me to strike up the songs

of the New World—And then I believed my life must be
spent in singing;
But now take notice, land of the prairies, land of the south savannas,
Ohio's land,
Take notice, you Kanuck woods—and you Lake Huron—and all
that with you roll toward Niagara—and you Niagara also,
And you, Californian mountains—That you each and all
find somebody else to be your singer of songs,
For I can be your singer of songs no longer—One who loves me is jealous
of me, and withdraws me from all but love,
With the rest I dispense—I sever from what I thought would
suffice me, for it does not—it is now empty and tasteless
to me,
I heed knowledge, and the grandeur of The States, and the example
of heroes, no more,
I am indifferent to my own songs—I will go with him I love,
It is enough for us that we are together—We never separate again.

Calamus 9

HOURS continuing long, sore and heavy-hearted,
Hours of the dusk, when I withdraw to a lonesome and unfrequented
spot, seating myself, leaning my face in my hands;
Hours sleepless, deep in the night, when I go forth, speeding swiftly
the country roads, or through the city streets, or pacing miles
and miles, stifling plaintive cries;
Hours discouraged, distracted—for the one I cannot content myself
without, soon I saw him content himself without me;
Hours when I am forgotten (O weeks and months are passing,
but I believe I am never to forget!)
Sullen and suffering hours! (I am ashamed—but it is useless—
I am what I am);
Hours of my torment—I wonder if other men ever have the like,
out of like feelings?
Is there even one other like me—distracted—his friend, his lover,
lost to him?

Is he too as I am now? Does he still rise in the morning, dejected,
thinking who is lost to him? and at night, awaking,
think who is lost?
Does he too harbor his friendship silent and endless?
harbor his anguish and passion?
Does some stray reminder, or the casual mention of a name,
bring the fit back upon him, taciturn and deprest?
Does he see himself reflected in me? In these hours, does he see
the face of his hours reflected?

Calamus 10

YOU bards of ages hence! when you refer to me, mind not so much
my poems,
Nor speak of me that I prophesied of The States, and led them the way
of their glories;
But come, I will take you down underneath this impassive exterior—
I will tell you what to say of me:
Publish my name and hang up my picture as that of the tenderest lover,
The friend, the lover's portrait, of whom his friend, his lover,
was fondest,
Who was not proud of his songs, but of the measureless ocean of love
within him—and freely poured it forth,
Who often walked lonesome walks, thinking of his dear friends,
his lovers,
Who pensive, away from one he loved, often lay sleepless
and dissatisfied at night,
Who knew too well the sick, sick dread lest the one he loved
might secretly be indifferent to him,
Whose happiest days were far away, through fields, in woods, on hills,
he and another, wandering hand in hand, they twain, apart
from other men,
Who oft as he sauntered the streets, curved with his arm the shoulder
of his friend—while the arm of his friend rested upon him also.

Calamus 11

When I heard at the close of the day how my name had been received
with plaudits in the capitol, still it was not a happy night for me
that followed;
And else, when I caroused, or when my plans were accomplished,
still I was not happy;
But the day when I rose at dawn from the bed of perfect health,
refreshed, singing, inhaling the ripe breath of autumn,
When I saw the full moon in the west grow pale and disappear
in the morning light,
When I wandered alone over the beach, and, undressing, bathed,
laughing with the cool waters, and saw the sun rise,
And when I thought how my dear friend, my lover,
was on his way coming, O then I was happy;
O then each breath tasted sweeter—and all that day my food
nourished me more—And the beautiful day passed well,
And the next came with equal joy—And with the next, at evening,
came my friend;
And that night, while all was still, I heard the waters roll slowly
continually up the shores,
I heard the hissing rustle of the liquid and sands, as directed to me,
whispering, to congratulate me,
For the one I love most lay sleeping by me under the same cover
in the cool night,
In the stillness, in the autumn moonbeams, his face was inclined
toward me,
And his arm lay lightly around my breast—And that night I was happy.

Calamus 12

ARE you the new person drawn toward me, and asking something
significant from me?
To begin with, take warning—I am probably far different
from what you suppose;
Do you suppose you will find in me your ideal?
Do you think it is so easy to have me become your lover?
Do you think the friendship of me would be unalloyed satisfaction?
Do you suppose I am trusty and faithful?
Do you see no further than this façade—this smooth and tolerant
manner of me?
Do you suppose yourself advancing on real ground
toward a real heroic man?
Have you no thought, O dreamer, that it may be all maya, illusion?
O the next step may precipitate you!
O let some past deceived one hiss in your ears, how many have
prest on the same as you are pressing now,
How many have fondly supposed what you are supposing now—
only to be disappointed.

Calamus 13

CALAMUS taste
(For I must change the strain—these are not to be pensive leaves,
but leaves of joy),
Roots and leaves unlike any but themselves,
Scents brought to men and women from the wild woods,
and from the pond-side,

Breast-sorrel and pinks of love—fingers that wind around
tighter than vines,
Gushes from the throats of birds, hid in the foliage of trees,
as the sun is risen,
Breezes of land and love—Breezes set from living shores
out to you on the living sea—to you, O sailors!
Frost-mellowed berries, and Third Month twigs, offered fresh
to young persons wandering out in the fields
when the winter breaks up,
Love-buds, put before you and within you, whoever you are,
Buds to be unfolded on the old terms,
If you bring the warmth of the sun to them, they will open,
and bring form, color, perfume, to you,
If you become the aliment and the wet, they will become flowers,
fruits, tall branches and trees,
They are comprised in you just as much as in themselves—
perhaps more than in themselves,
They are not comprised in one season or succession,
but many successions,
They have come slowly up out of the earth and me,
and are to come slowly up out of you.

Calamus 14

NOT heat flames up and consumes,
Not sea-waves hurry in and out,
Not the air, delicious and dry, the air of the ripe summer,
bears lightly along white down-balls of myriads of seeds,
wafted, sailing gracefully, to drop where they may,
Not these—O none of these, more than the flames of me,
consuming, burning for his love whom I love!
O none, more than I, hurrying in and out;
Does the tide hurry, seeking something, and never give up?
O I the same;

O nor down-balls, nor perfumes, nor the high rain-emitting clouds,
are borne through the open air,
Any more than my Soul is borne through the open air,
Wafted in all directions, O love, for friendship, for you.

Calamus 15

O DROPS of me! trickle, slow drops,
Candid, from me falling—drip, bleeding drops,
From wounds made to free you whence you were prisoned,
From my face—from my forehead and lips,
From my breast—from within where I was concealed—Press forth,
red drops—confession drops,
Stain every page—stain every song I sing, every word I say,
bloody drops,
Let them know your scarlet heat—let them glisten,
Saturate them with yourself, all ashamed and wet,
Glow upon all I have written or shall write, bleeding drops,
Let it all be seen in your light, blushing drops.

Calamus 16

WHO is now reading this?

May-be one is now reading this who knows some wrong-doing
of my past life,
Or may-be a stranger is reading this who has secretly loved me,
Or may-be one who meets all my grand assumptions
and egotisms with derision,

Or may-be one who is puzzled at me.

As if I were not puzzled at myself!
Or as if I never deride myself! (O conscience-struck!
O self-convicted!)
Or as if I do not secretly love strangers! (O tenderly, a long time,
and never avow it);
Or as if I did not see, perfectly well, interior in myself,
the stuff of wrong-doing,
Or as if it could cease transpiring from me until it must cease.

Calamus 17

OF him I love day and night, I dreamed I heard he was dead,
And I dreamed I went where they had buried him I love—
but he was not in that place,
And I dreamed I wandered, searching among burial-places, to find him,
And I found that every place was a burial-place,
The houses full of life were equally full of death (This house is now),
The streets, the shipping, the places of amusement, the Chicago,
Boston, Philadelphia, the Mannahatta, were as full of the dead
as of the living,
And fuller, O vastly fuller, of the dead than of the living;
—And what I dreamed I will henceforth tell to every person and age,
And I stand henceforth bound to what I dreamed;
And now I am willing to disregard burial-places, and dispense
with them,
And if the memorials of the dead were put up indifferently
everywhere, even in the room where I eat or sleep,
I should be satisfied,
And if the corpse of any one I love, or if my own corpse,
be duly rendered to powder, and poured in the sea,
I shall be satisfied,
Or if it be distributed to the winds, I shall be satisfied.

Calamus 18

CITY of my walks and joys!
City whom that I have lived and sung there will one day
make you illustrious,
Not the pageants of you—not your shifting tableaux,
your spectacles, repay me,
Not the interminable rows of your houses—nor the ships
at the wharves,
Nor the processions in the streets, nor the bright windows,
with goods in them,
Nor to converse with learned persons, or bear my share
in the soiree or feast;
Not those—but, as I pass, O Manhattan! your frequent
and swift flash of eyes offering me love,
Offering me the response of my own—those repay me,
Lovers, continual lovers, only repay me.

Calamus 19

MIND you the timid models of the rest, the majority?
Long I minded them, but hence I will not—for I have adopted
models for myself, and now offer them to The Lands.

Behold this swarthy and unrefined face—these gray eyes,
This beard—the white wool, unclipt upon my neck,
My brown hands, and the silent manner of me, without charm;
Yet comes one, a Manhattanese, and ever at parting,
kisses me lightly on the lips with robust love,

And I, in the public room, or on the crossing of the street,
    or on the ship's deck, kiss him in return;
We observe that salute of American comrades, land and sea,
We are those two natural and nonchalant persons.

Calamus 20

I SAW in Louisiana a live-oak growing,
All alone stood it, and the moss hung down from the branches,
Without any companion it grew there, uttering joyous leaves
    of dark green,
And its look, rude, unbending, lusty, made me think of myself,
But I wondered how it could utter joyous leaves, standing alone there,
    without its friend, its lover near—for I knew I could not,
And I broke off a twig with a certain number of leaves upon it,
    and twined around it a little moss,
And brought it away—and I have placed it in sight in my room,
It is not needed to remind me as of my own dear friends
(For I believe lately I think of little else than of them),
Yet it remains to me a curious token—it makes me think
    of manly love;
For all that, and though the live-oak glistens there in Louisiana,
    solitary, in a wide flat space,
Uttering joyous leaves all its life, without a friend, a lover, near,
I know very well I could not.

Calamus 21

MUSIC always round me, unceasing, unbeginning—
yet long untaught I did not hear,
But now the chorus I hear, and am elated,
A tenor, strong, ascending, with power and health, with glad notes
of day-break I hear,
A soprano, at intervals, sailing buoyantly over the tops
of immense waves,
A transparent bass, shuddering lusciously under and through
the universe,
The triumphant tutti—the funeral wailings, with sweet flutes
and violins—All these I fill myself with;
I hear not the volumes of sound merely—I am moved
by the exquisite meanings,
I listen to the different voices winding in and out, striving, contending
with fiery vehemence to excel each other in emotion,
I do not think the performers know themselves—But now I think
I begin to know them.

Calamus 22

PASSING stranger! you do not know how longingly I look upon you,
You must be he I was seeking, or she I was seeking
(It comes to me, as of a dream),
I have somewhere surely lived a life of joy with you,
All is recalled as we flit by each other, fluid, affectionate, chaste,
matured,
You grew up with me, were a boy with me, or a girl with me,

I ate with you, and slept with you—your body has become
not yours only, nor left my body mine only,
You give me the pleasure of your eyes, face, flesh, as we pass—
you take of my beard, breast, hands, in return,
I am not to speak to you—I am to think of you when I sit alone,
or wake at night alone,
I am to wait—I do not doubt I am to meet you again,
I am to see to it that I do not lose you.

Calamus 23

THIS moment as I sit alone, yearning and thoughtful, it seems to me
there are other men in other lands, yearning and thoughtful;
It seems to me I can look over and behold them, in Germany, Italy,
France, Spain—Or far, far away, in China, or in Russia
or India—talking other dialects;
And it seems to me if I could know those men better, I should
become attached to them, as I do to men in my own lands,
It seems to me they are as wise, beautiful, benevolent, as any
in my own lands;
O I know we should be brethren and lovers,
I know I should be happy with them.

Calamus 24

I HEAR it is charged against me that I seek to destroy institutions;
But really I am neither for nor against institutions
(What indeed have I in common with them?—Or what
with the destruction of them?),

Only I will establish in the Mannahatta, and in every city
of These States, inland and seaboard,
And in the fields and woods, above every keel little or large,
that dents the water,
Without edifices, or rules, or trustees, or any argument,
The institution of the dear love of comrades.

Calamus 25

THE prairie-grass dividing—its own odor breathing,
I demand of it the spiritual corresponding,
Demand the most copious and close companionship of men,
Demand the blades to rise of words, acts, beings,
Those of the open atmosphere, coarse, sunlit, fresh, nutritious,
Those that go their own gait, erect, stepping with freedom
and command—leading, not following,
Those with a never-quell'd audacity—those with sweet and lusty
flesh, clear of taint, choice and chary of its love-power,
Those that look carelessly in the faces of Presidents and Governors,
as to say, *Who are you?*
Those of earth-born passion, simple, never constrained,
never obedient,
Those of inland America.

Calamus 26

WE two boys together clinging,
One the other never leaving,
Up and down the roads going—North and South excursions making,

Power enjoying—elbows stretching—fingers clutching,
Armed and fearless—eating, drinking, sleeping, loving,
No law less than ourselves owning—sailing, soldiering, thieving,
threatening,
Misers, menials, priests alarming—air breathing, water drinking,
on the turf or the sea-beach dancing,
With birds singing—With fishes swimming—With trees branching
and leafing,
Cities wrenching, ease scorning, statutes mocking, feebleness chasing,
Fulfilling our foray.

Calamus 27

O LOVE!
O dying—always dying!
O the burials of me, past and present!
O me, while I stride ahead, material, visible, imperious as ever!
O me, what I was for years, now dead (I lament not—I am content);
O to disengage myself from those corpses of me, which I turn
and look at, where I cast them!
To pass on (O living! always living!) and leave the corpses behind!

Calamus 28

WHEN I peruse the conquered fame of heroes, and the victories
of mighty generals, I do not envy the generals,
Nor the President in his Presidency, nor the rich in his great house;
But when I read of the brotherhood of lovers, how it was with them,
How through life, through dangers, odium, unchanging, long and long,

Through youth, and through middle and old age, how unfaltering,
how affectionate and faithful they were,
Then I am pensive—I hastily put down the book, and walk away,
filled with the bitterest envy.

Calamus 29

ONE flitting glimpse, caught through an interstice,
Of a crowd of workmen and drivers in a bar-room, around the stove,
late of a winter night—And I unremarked, seated in a corner;
Of a youth who loves me, and whom I love, silently approaching,
and seating himself near, that he may hold me by the hand;
A long while, amid the noises of coming and going—of drinking
and oath and smutty jest,
There we two, content, happy in being together, speaking little,
perhaps not a word.

Calamus 30

A PROMISE and gift to California,
Also to the great Pastoral Plains, and for Oregon:
Sojourning east a while longer, soon I travel to you, to remain,
to teach robust American love;
For I know very well that I and robust love belong among you, inland,
and along the Western Sea,
For These States tend inland, and toward the Western Sea—
and I will also.

Calamus 31

WHAT ship, puzzled at sea, cons for the true reckoning?
Or, coming in, to avoid the bars, and follow the channel,
a perfect pilot needs?
Here, sailor! Here, ship! take aboard the most perfect pilot,
Whom, in a little boat, putting off, and rowing, I, hailing you, offer.

What place is besieged, and vainly tries to raise the siege?
Lo! I send to that place a commander, swift, brave, immortal,
And with him horse and foot—and parks of artillery,
And artillerymen, the deadliest that ever fired gun.

Calamus 32

WHAT think you I take my pen in hand to record?
The battle-ship, perfect-model'd, majestic, that I saw pass
the offing to-day under full sail?
The splendors of the past day? Or the splendor of the night
that envelops me?
Or the vaunted glory and growth of the great city spread around me?
—No;
But I record of two simple men I saw to-day, on the pier, in the midst
of the crowd, parting the parting of dear friends,
The one to remain hung on the other's neck, and passionately
kissed him,
While the one to depart, tightly prest the one to remain in his arms.

Calamus 33

No labor-saving machine,
Nor discovery have I made,
Nor will I be able to leave behind me any wealthy bequest
to found a hospital or library,
Nor reminiscence of any deed of courage, for America,
Nor literary success, nor intellect—nor book for the book-shelf;
Only these carols, vibrating through the air, I leave,
For comrades and lovers.

Calamus 34

I dreamed in a dream, I saw a city invincible to the attacks
of the whole of the rest of the earth,
I dreamed that was the new City of Friends,
Nothing was greater there than the quality of robust love—
it led the rest,
It was seen every hour in the actions of the men of that city,
And in all their looks and words.

Calamus 35

TO you of New England,
To the man of the Seaside State, and of Pennsylvania,
To the Kanadian of the north—to the Southerner I love,
These, with perfect trust, to depict you as myself—
the germs are in all men;
I believe the main purport of These States is to found
a superb friendship, exalté, previously unknown,
Because I perceive it waits, and has been always waiting,
latent in all men.

Calamus 36

EARTH! my likeness!
Though you look so impassive, ample and spheric there,
I now suspect that is not all;
I now suspect there is something fierce in you, eligible to burst forth;
But an athlete is enamoured of me—and I of him,
But toward him there is something fierce and terrible in me,
eligible to burst forth,
I dare not tell it in words—not even in these songs.

Calamus 37

A LEAF for hand in hand!
You natural persons old and young! You on the Eastern Sea,
and you on the Western!
You on the Mississippi, and on all the branches and bayous
of the Mississippi!
You friendly boatmen and mechanics! You roughs!
You twain! And all processions moving along the streets!
I wish to infuse myself among you till I see it common for you
to walk hand in hand.

Calamus 38

PRIMEVAL my love for the woman I love,
O bride! O wife! more resistless, more enduring than I can tell,
the thought of you!
Then separate, as disembodied, the purest born,
The ethereal, the last athletic reality, my consolation,
I ascend—I float in the regions of your love, O man,
O sharer of my roving life.

Calamus 39

SOMETIMES with one I love, I fill myself with rage, for I fear
I effuse unreturned love;
But now I think there is no unreturned love—the pay is certain,
one way or another,
Doubtless I could not have perceived the universe, or written
one of my poems, if I had not freely given myself
to comrades, to love.

Calamus 40

THAT shadow, my likeness, that goes to and fro,
seeking a livelihood, chattering, chaffering,
How often I find myself standing and looking at it where it flits,
How often I question and doubt whether that is really me;
But in these, and among my lovers, and carolling my songs,
O I never doubt whether that is really me.

Calamus 41

AMONG the men and women, the multitude, I perceive one
picking me out by secret and divine signs,
Acknowledging none else—not parent, wife, husband, brother,
child, any nearer than I am;
Some are baffled—But that one is not—that one knows me.

Lover and perfect equal!
I meant that you should discover me so, by my faint indirections,
And I, when I meet you, mean to discover you by the like in you.

Calamus 42

TO the young man, many things to absorb, to engraft, to develop,
I teach, to help him become élève of mine,
But if blood like mine circle not in his veins,
If he be not silently selected by lovers, and do not silently
select lovers,
Of what use is it that he seek to become élève of mine?

Calamus 43

O YOU whom I often and silently come where you are,
that I may be with you,
As I walk by your side, or sit near, or remain in the same room
with you,
Little you know the subtle electric fire that for your sake is playing
within me.

Calamus 44

HERE my last words, and the most baffling,
Here the frailest leaves of me, and yet my strongest-lasting,
Here I shade down and hide my thoughts—I do not expose them,
And yet they expose me more than all my other poems.

Calamus 45

FULL of life, sweet-blooded, compact, visible,
I, forty years old the Eighty-third Year of The States,
To one a century hence, or any number of centuries hence,
To you, yet unborn, these, seeking you.

When you read these, I, that was visible, am become invisible;
Now it is you, compact, visible, realizing my poems, seeking me,
Fancying how happy you were, if I could be with you,
        and become your lover;
Be it as if I were with you. Be not too certain but I am now with you.

From the *Messenger Leaves* Cluster

To Him That was Crucified

MY spirit to yours, dear brother,
Do not mind because many, sounding your name,
        do not understand you,
I do not sound your name, but I understand you (there are others also);
I specify you with joy, O my comrade, to salute you, and to salute those
        who are with you, before and since—and those to come also,
That we all labor together, transmitting the same charge and succession;
We few, equals, indifferent of lands, indifferent of times,
We, enclosers of all continents, all castes—allowers of all theologies,
Compassionaters, perceivers, rapport of men,
We walk silent among disputes and assertions, but reject not
        the disputers, nor any thing that is asserted,
We hear the bawling and din—we are reached at by divisions,
        jealousies, recriminations on every side,
They close peremptorily upon us, to surround us, my comrade,
Yet we walk unheld, free, the whole earth over, journeying up
        and down, till we make our ineffaceable mark upon time
        and the diverse eras,
Till we saturate time and eras, that the men and women of races,
        ages to come, may prove brethren and lovers, as we are.

To One Shortly to Die

FROM all the rest I single out you, having a message for you:
You are to die—Let others tell you what they please,
I cannot prevaricate,
I am exact and merciless, but I love you—There is no escape for you.

Softly I lay my right hand upon you—you just feel it,
I do not argue—I bend my head close, and half-envelop it,
I sit quietly by—I remain faithful,
I am more than nurse, more than parent or neighbor,
I absolve you from all except yourself, spiritual, bodily—
that is eternal
(The corpse you will leave will be but excrementitious).

The sun bursts through in unlooked-for directions!
Strong thoughts fill you, and confidences—you smile!
You forget you are sick, as I forget you are sick,
You do not see the medicines—you do not mind the weeping friends—
I am with you,
I exclude others from you—there is nothing to be commiserated,
I do not commiserate—I congratulate you.

To a Common Prostitute

BE composed—be at ease with me—I am Walt Whitman,
liberal and lusty as Nature,
Not till the sun excludes you, do I exclude you,
Not till the waters refuse to glisten for you, and the leaves to rustle
for you, do my words refuse to glisten and rustle for you.

My girl, I appoint with you an appointment—and I charge you
that you make preparation to be worthy to meet me,
And I charge you that you be patient and perfect till I come.

Till then, I salute you with a significant look, that you do not
forget me.

To a Pupil

Is reform needed? Is it through you?
The greater the reform needed, the greater the PERSONALITY
you need to accomplish it.

You! do you not see how it would serve to have eyes, blood,
complexion, clean and sweet?
Do you not see how it would serve to have such a body and Soul,
that when you enter the crowd, an atmosphere of desire
and command enters with you, and every one is impressed
with your personality?

O the magnet! the flesh over and over!
Go, mon cher! if need be, give up all else, and commence to-day
to inure yourself to pluck, reality, self-esteem, definiteness,
elevatedness,
Rest not, till you rivet and publish yourself of your own personality.

Carte de visite *of Marietta Alboni, the Italian contralto beloved by Whitman, and the subject of his poem "To a Cantatrice" (opposite), at about the time of her 1852–53 visit to America.*
COURTESY OF GIRVICE ARCHER, JR.

To The States

TO IDENTIFY THE 16TH, 17TH, OR 18TH PRESIDENTIAD

WHY reclining, interrogating? Why myself and all drowsing?
What deepening twilight! Scum floating atop of the waters!
Who are they, as bats and night-dogs, askant in the Capitol?
What a filthy Presidentiad! (O south, your torrid suns! O north,
your arctic freezings!)
Are those really Congressmen? Are those the great Judges?
Is that the President?
Then I will sleep a while yet—for I see that These States sleep,
for reasons
(With gathering murk—with muttering thunder and lambent shoots,
we all duly awake,
South, north, east, west, inland and seaboard, we will surely awake).

To a Cantatrice

HERE, take this gift!
I was reserving it for some hero, orator, or general,
One who should serve the good old cause, the progress and freedom
of the race, the cause of my Soul;
But I see that what I was reserving belongs to you just as much
as to any.

Walt Whitman's Caution

TO The States, or any one of them, or any city of The States,
Resist much, obey little,
Once unquestioning obedience, once fully enslaved,
Once fully enslaved, no nation, state, city, of this earth,
ever afterward resumes its liberty.

To a President

ALL you are doing and saying is to America dangled mirages,
You have not learned of Nature—of the politics of Nature, you have
not learned the great amplitude, rectitude, impartiality,
You have not seen that only such as they are for These States,
And that what is less than they, must sooner or later lift off
from These States.

To You

LET us twain walk aside from the rest;
Now we are together privately, do you discard ceremony,
Come! vouchsafe to me what has yet been vouchsafed to none
—Tell me the whole story,
Tell me what you would not tell your brother, wife, husband,
or physician.

To You

STRANGER! if you, passing, meet me, and desire to speak to me,
why should you not speak to me?
And why should I not speak to you?

Mannahatta

I WAS asking for something specific and perfect for my city,
and behold! here is the aboriginal name!
Now I see what there is in a name, a word, liquid, sane, unruly,
musical, self-sufficient,

I see that the word of my city, is that word up there,
Because I see that word nested in nests of water-bays, superb,
with tall and wonderful spires,
Rich, hemmed thick all around with sailships and steamships—
an island sixteen miles long, solid-founded,
Numberless crowded streets—high growths of iron, slender,
strong, light, splendidly uprising toward clear skies;
Tides swift and ample, well-loved by me, toward sun-down,
The flowing sea-currents, the little islands, the larger
adjoining islands, the heights, the villas,
The countless masts, the white shore-steamers, the lighters,
the ferry-boats, the black sea-steamers, well-model'd;
The down-town streets, the jobbers' houses of business—
the houses of business of the ship-merchants,
and money-brokers—the river-streets,
Immigrants arriving, fifteen or twenty thousand in a week,
The carts hauling goods—the manly race of drivers of horses—
the brown-faced sailors,
The summer-air, the bright sun shining, and the sailing clouds aloft,
The winter snows, the sleigh-bells—the broken ice in the river,
passing along, up or down, with the flood-tide or ebb-tide;
The mechanics of the city, the masters, well-formed, beautiful-faced,
looking you straight in the eyes;
Trottoirs° thronged—vehicles—Broadway—the women—
the shops and shows,
The parades, processions, bugles playing, flags flying, drums beating;
A million people—manners free and superb—open voices—
hospitality—the most courageous and friendly young men;
The free city! no slaves! no owners of slaves!
The beautiful city! the city of hurried and sparkling waters!
the city of spires and masts!
The city nested in bays! my city!
The city of such women, I am mad to be with them! I will return
after death to be with them!
The city of such young men, I swear I cannot live happy,
without I often go talk, walk, eat, drink, sleep, with them!

From the *Thoughts* Cluster

Of persons arrived at high positions, ceremonies, wealth,
scholarships, and the like,
To me, all that those persons have arrived at, sinks away from them,
except as it results to their bodies and Souls,
So that often to me they appear gaunt and naked,
And often, to me, each one mocks the others, and mocks himself
or herself,
And of each one, the core of life, namely happiness, is full
of the rotten excrement of maggots,
And often, to me, those men and women pass unwittingly
the true realities of life, and go toward false realities,
And often, to me, they are alive after what custom has served them,
but nothing more,
And often, to me, they are sad, hasty, unwaked sonnambules,°
walking the dusk.

A Hand-Mirror

Hold it up sternly! See this it sends back! (Who is it? Is it you?)
Outside fair costume—within, ashes and filth,
No more a flashing eye—no more a sonorous voice or springy step,
Now some slave's eye, voice, hands, step,
A drunkard's breath, unwholesome eater's face, venerealee's flesh,
Lungs rotting away piecemeal, stomach sour and cankerous,
Joints rheumatic, bowels clogged with abomination,
Blood circulating dark and poisonous streams,
Words babble, hearing and touch callous,

No brain, no heart left—no magnetism of sex;
Such, from one look in this looking-glass ere you go hence,
Such a result so soon—and from such a beginning!

Beginners

HOW they are provided for upon the earth (appearing at intervals),
How dear and dreadful they are to the earth,
How they inure to themselves as much as to any—
What a paradox appears, their age,
How people respond to them, yet know them not,
How there is something relentless in their fate, all times,
How all times mischoose the objects of their adulation and reward,
And how the same inexorable price must still be paid
for the same great purchase.

Tests

ALL submit to them, where they sit, inner, secure,
unapproachable to analysis, in the Soul;
Not traditions—not the outer authorities are the judges—they are
the judges of outer authorities, and of all traditions,
They corroborate as they go, only whatever corroborates themselves,
and touches themselves,
For all that, they have it forever in themselves to corroborate
far and near, without one exception.

From the *Debris* Cluster

HAVE you learned lessons only of those who admired you,
and were tender with you, and stood aside for you?
Have you not learned the great lessons of those who rejected you,
and braced themselves against you? or who treated you
with contempt, or disputed the passage with you?
Have you had no practice to receive opponents when they come?

DESPAIRING cries float ceaselessly toward me, day and night,
The sad voice of Death—the call of my nearest lover,
putting forth, alarmed, uncertain,
This sea I am quickly to sail, come tell me,
Come tell me where I am speeding—tell me my destination.

I UNDERSTAND your anguish, but I cannot help you,
I approach, hear, behold—the sad mouth, the look out
of the eyes, your mute inquiry,
Whither I go from the bed I now recline on, come tell me;
Old age, alarmed, uncertain—A young woman's voice
appealing to me for comfort,
A young man's voice, *Shall I not escape?*

THREE old men slowly pass, followed by three others,
and they by three others,
They are beautiful—the one in the middle of each group
holds his companions by the hand,
As they walk, they give out perfume wherever they walk.

WOMEN sit, or move to and fro—some old, some young,
The young are beautiful—but the old are more beautiful
than the young.

I THOUGHT I was not alone, walking here by the shore,
But the one I thought was with me, as now I walk by the shore,
As I lean and look through the glimmering light—
that one has utterly disappeared,
And those appear that perplex me.

To My Soul

As nearing departure,
As the time draws nigh, glooming from you,
A cloud—a dread beyond, of I know not what, darkens me.

I shall go forth,
I shall traverse The States—but I cannot tell whither or how long;
Perhaps soon, some day or night while I am singing,
my voice will suddenly cease.

O Soul!
Then all may arrive to but this;
The glances of my eyes, that swept the daylight,
The unspeakable love I interchanged with women,
My joys in the open air—my walks through the Mannahatta,
The continual good will I have met—the curious attachment
of young men to me,
My reflections alone—the absorption into me from the landscape, stars,
animals, thunder, rain, and snow, in my wanderings alone,
The words of my mouth, rude, ignorant, arrogant—my many faults
and derelictions,
The light touches, on my lips, of the lips of my comrades, at parting,
The tracks which I leave, upon the side-walks and fields,
May but arrive at this beginning of me,
This beginning of me—and yet it is enough, O Soul,
O Soul, we have positively appeared—that is enough.

So long!

To conclude—I announce what comes after me,
The thought must be promulged, that all I know at any time
suffices for that time only—not subsequent time;
I announce greater offspring, orators, days, and then depart.

I remember I said to myself at the winter-close, before my leaves
sprang at all, that I would become a candid and unloosed
summer-poet,
I said I would raise my voice jocund and strong, with reference
to consummations.

When America does what was promised,
When each part is peopled with free people,
When there is no city on earth to lead my city, the city of young men,
the Mannahatta city—But when the Mannahatta leads
all the cities of the earth,
When there are plentiful athletic bards, inland and seaboard,
When through These States walk a hundred millions of superb persons,
When the rest part away for superb persons, and contribute to them,
When fathers, firm, unconstrained, open-eyed—When breeds
of the most perfect mothers denote America,
Then to me ripeness and conclusion.

Yet not me, after all—let none be content with me,
I myself seek a man better than I am, or a woman better than I am,
I invite defiance, and to make myself superseded,
All I have done, I would cheerfully give to be trod under foot,
if it might only be the soil of superior poems.

I have established nothing for good,
I have but established these things, till things farther onward
shall be prepared to be established,
And I am myself the preparer of things farther onward.

I have pressed through in my own right,
I have offered my style to every one—I have journeyed
with confident step,
While my pleasure is yet at the full, I whisper *So long,*
And take the young woman's hand, and the young man's hand,
for the last time.

Once more I enforce you to give play to yourself—
and not depend on me, or on any one but yourself,
Once more I proclaim the whole of America for each individual,
without exception.

As I have announced the true theory of the youth, manhood,
womanhood, of The States, I adhere to it;
As I have announced myself on immortality, the body, procreation,
hauteur, prudence,
As I joined the stern crowd that still confronts the President
with menacing weapons—I adhere to all,
As I have announced each age for itself, this moment I set the example.

I demand the choicest edifices to destroy them;
Room! room! for new far-planning draughtsmen and engineers!
Clear that rubbish from the building-spots and the paths!

So long!
I announce natural persons to arise,
I announce justice triumphant,
I announce uncompromising liberty and equality,
I announce the justification of candor, and the justification of pride.

I announce that the identity of These States is a single identity only,
I announce the Union more and more compact,
I announce splendors and majesties to make all the previous politics
of the earth insignificant.

I announce adhesiveness°—I say it shall be limitless, unloosened,
I say you shall yet find the friend you was looking for.

So long!
I announce a man or woman coming—perhaps you are the one,
I announce a great individual, fluid as Nature, chaste, affectionate,
compassionate, fully armed.

So long!
I announce a life that shall be copious, vehement, spiritual, bold,
And I announce an old age that shall lightly and joyfully meet
its translation.

O thicker and faster!
O crowding too close upon me!
I foresee too much—it means more than I thought,
It appears to me I am dying.

Now throat, sound your last!
Salute me—salute the future once more. Peal the old cry once more.

Screaming electric, the atmosphere using,
At random glancing, each as I notice absorbing,
Swiftly on, but a little while alighting,
Curious enveloped messages delivering,
Sparkles hot, seed ethereal, down in the dirt dropping,
Myself unknowing, my commission obeying, to question it never daring,
To ages, and ages yet, the growth of the seed leaving,
To troops out of me rising—they the tasks I have set promulging,
To women certain whispers of myself bequeathing—their affection
me more clearly explaining,
To young men my problems offering—no dallier I—I the muscle
of their brains trying,
So I pass—a little time vocal, visible, contrary,
Afterward, a melodious echo, passionately bent for—
death making me undying,
The best of me then when no longer visible—for toward that
I have been incessantly preparing.

What is there more, that I lag and pause, and crouch extended
with unshut mouth?
Is there a single final farewell?

My songs cease—I abandon them,
From behind the screen where I hid, I advance personally.

This is no book,
Who touches this, touches a man
(Is it night? Are we here alone?),
It is I you hold, and who holds you,
I spring from the pages into your arms—decease calls me forth.

O how your fingers drowse me!
Your breath falls around me like dew—your pulse lulls the tympans
of my ears,
I feel immerged from head to foot,
Delicious—enough.

Enough, O deed impromptu and secret!
Enough, O gliding present! Enough, O summed-up past!

Dear friend, whoever you are, here, take this kiss,
I give it especially to you—Do not forget me,
I feel like one who has done his work—I progress on,
The unknown sphere, more real than I dreamed, more direct,
darts awakening rays about me—*So long!*
Remember my words—I love you—I depart from materials,
I am as one disembodied, triumphant, dead.

Unpublished Introduction

(DATED 31 MAY 1861)

I COMMENCED these Leaves of Grass in my thirty-sixth year, by publishing their first issue. Twice have I issued them since with increased matter—the present one making the fourth issue with the latest increase.

I am today (May 31, 1861) just forty-two years old—for I write this introduction on my birthday after having looked over what has been accomplished.

So far, so well, but the most and best of the Poem I perceive remains unwritten, and is the work of my life yet to be done.

The paths to the house are made—but where is the house itself? At most only indicated or touched. Nevertheless, as while we live some dream will play its part, I keep it in my plan of work ahead to yet fill up these *Whisperings* (if I live & have luck), somehow proportionate to their original design. If it should turn out otherwise (which is most likely, dear Reader), I hereby bequeath it to you—& that no doubt is much the best—to form & breathe Whisperings for yourself, in heart-felt meditations fitter far than words. Or rather, let me say, O friend, unless such meditations come, at reading any page or pages of our chant, no matter which, the Chant, the Book, is really not for you and has not done its office.

Need we mark, in this, the only true communion with our Book, which we have made, purposed, indeed unlike all others, and not, we finally confess, for literary satisfactions, ends or ornaments; made first, to be the Chant, the Book of Universal Life, and of the Body,—and then, just as much, to be the Chant of Universal Death, and of the Soul.

The theory of the poem involves both the

expression of the hottest, wildest passion, bravest, sturdiest character, not however illustrated after any of the well known types, the identities of the great bards old or modern. Nor Prometheus is here, nor Agamemnon, nor Aeneas, nor Hamlet, nor Iago, nor Antony, nor any of Dante's scenes or persons, nor ballad of lord or lady, nor Lucretian philosophy nor any special system of philosophy nor striking lyric achievement, nor Childe Harold, nor any epic tale with beginning, climax and termination, yet something of perhaps similar purpose, very definite, compact (and curiously digesting & including all the list we have just named), very simple even and applying directly to the reader at first hand, is the main result (& purpose) of this book, namely to suggest the substance and form of a large, sane, perfect Human Being or character for an American man and for woman. While other things are in the book, studies, digressions of various sorts, this is undoubtedly its essential purpose and its key, so that in the poems taken as a whole unquestionably appears a great Person, entirely modern, at least as great as anything in the Homeric or Shakesperian characters, a person with the free courage of Achilles, the craft of Ulysses, the attributes even of the Greek deities. Majesty, passion, temper, amativeness, Romeo, Lear, Antony, immense self-esteem, but after democratic forms, measureless love, the old eternal elements of first-class humanity. Yet worked over, cast in a new mould, and here chanted or anyhow put down & stated with invariable reference to the United States & the occasions of today & the future.

Dear friend! not here for you, melodious narratives, no pictures here, for you to con at leisure, as bright creations all outside yourself. But of SUGGESTIVENESS, with new centripetal reference out of the miracles of every day, this is the song—naught made complete by me for you, but only hinted to be made by you by robust exercise. I have not done the work and cannot do it. But you must do the work and make what is within the following song.

And now, with a remaining page or two, wherein we would pourtray, at least in pale reflection, the passionate, flush'd heart-visage of one that, having offered salutation, & join'd and journeyed on a while in close companionship, has now to resign you, Dearest Reader, and, with mingled cheer and sadness, bid farewell.

WALT WHITMAN

Drum-Taps

1865

Beginning My Studies

BEGINNING my studies, the first step pleas'd me so much,
The mere fact, consciousness—these forms—the power of motion,
The least insect or animal—the senses—eyesight;
The first step, I say, aw'd me and pleas'd me so much,
I have never gone, and never wish'd to go, any farther,
But stop and loiter all my life, to sing it in extatic songs.

The Dresser

AN old man bending, I come, among new faces,
Years looking backward, resuming, in answer to children,
Come tell us old man, as from young men and maidens that love me;
Years hence of these scenes, of these furious passions, these chances,
Of unsurpass'd heroes (was one side so brave? the other was equally brave);
Now be witness again—paint the mightiest armies of earth;
Of those armies so rapid, so wondrous, what saw you to tell us?
What stays with you latest and deepest? of curious panics,
Of hard-fought engagements, or sieges tremendous, what deepest remains?

O maidens and young men I love, and that love me,
What you ask of my days, those the strangest and sudden your talking recalls;
Soldier alert I arrive, after a long march, cover'd with sweat and dust;
In the nick of time I come, plunge in the fight, loudly shout in the rush of successful charge;

Enter the captur'd works . . . . yet lo! like a swift-running river,
they fade;
Pass and are gone, they fade—I dwell not on soldiers' perils
or soldiers' joys
(Both I remember well—many the hardships, few the joys,
yet I was content).

But in silence, in dream's projections,
While the world of gain and appearance and mirth goes on,
So soon what is over forgotten, and waves wash the imprints off the sand,
In nature's reverie sad, with hinged knees returning, I enter the doors—
(while for you up there,
Whoever you are, follow me without noise, and be of strong heart).

Bearing the bandages, water and sponge,
Straight and swift to my wounded I go,
Where they lie on the ground, after the battle brought in;
Where their priceless blood reddens the grass, the ground;
Or to the rows of the hospital tent, or under the roof'd hospital;
To the long rows of cots, up and down, each side, I return;
To each and all, one after another, I draw near—not one do I miss;
An attendant follows, holding a tray—he carries a refuse pail,
Soon to be fill'd with clotted rags and blood, emptied, and fill'd again.

I onward go, I stop,
With hinged knees and steady hand, to dress wounds;
I am firm with each—the pangs are sharp, yet unavoidable;
One turns to me his appealing eyes—(poor boy! I never knew you,
Yet I think I could not refuse this moment to die for you,
if that would save you).

On, on I go (open, doors of time! open, hospital doors!)—
The crush'd head I dress (poor crazed hand, tear not the bandage away);
The neck of the cavalry-man, with the bullet through and through,
I examine;
Hard the breathing rattles, quite glazed already the eye,
yet life struggles hard.
(Come, sweet death! be persuaded, O beautiful death!
In mercy come quickly.)

From the stump of the arm, the amputated hand,
I undo the clotted lint, remove the slough, wash off the matter and blood;

Back on his pillow the soldier bends, with curv'd neck,
        and side-falling head;
His eyes are closed, his face is pale, he dares not look
        on the bloody stump,
And has not yet looked on it.

I dress a wound in the side, deep, deep;
But a day or two more—for see, the frame all wasted and sinking,
And the yellow-blue countenance see.

I dress the perforated shoulder, the foot with the bullet wound,
Cleanse the one with a gnawing and putrid gangrene, so sickening,
        so offensive,
While the attendant stands behind aside me, holding the tray and pail.

I am faithful, I do not give out,
The fractur'd thigh, the knee, the wound in the abdomen,
These and more I dress with impassive hand
        (yet deep in my breast a fire, a burning flame).

Thus in silence, in dream's projections,
Returning, resuming, I thread my way through the hospitals;
The hurt and the wounded I pacify with soothing hand,
I sit by the restless all the dark night—some are so young;
Some suffer so much—I recall the experience sweet and sad.
(Many a soldier's loving arms about this neck have cross'd and rested,
Many a soldier's kiss dwells on these bearded lips.)

Come Up from the Fields Father

COME up from the fields, father, here's a letter from our Pete;
And come to the front door, mother—here's a letter from thy dear son.

Lo, 'tis autumn;
Lo, where the trees, deeper green, yellower and redder,

Cool and sweeten Ohio's villages, with leaves fluttering
in the moderate wind;
Where apples ripe in the orchards hang, and grapes on the trellis'd vines.
(Smell you the smell of the grapes on the vines?
Smell you the buckwheat, where the bees were lately buzzing?)

Above all, lo, the sky, so calm, so transparent after the rain,
and with wondrous clouds;
Below, too, all calm, all vital and beautiful—and the farm prospers well.

Down in the fields all prospers well;
But now from the fields come, father—come at the daughter's call;
And come to the entry, mother—to the front door come, right away.

Fast as she can she hurries—something ominous—her steps trembling;
She does not tarry to smooth her white hair, nor adjust her cap.

Open the envelope quickly;
O this is not our son's writing, yet his name is sign'd;
O a strange hand writes for our dear son—O stricken mother's soul!
All swims before her eyes—flashes with black—she catches
the main words only;
Sentences broken—*gun-shot wound in the breast, cavalry skirmish,*
taken to hospital,
At present low, but will soon be better.

Ah, now the single figure to me,
Amid all teeming and wealthy Ohio, with all its cities and farms,
Sickly white in the face and dull in the head, very faint,
By the jamb of a door leans.

Grieve not so, dear mother (the just-grown daughter speaks
through her sobs;
The little sisters huddle around, speechless and dismay'd);
See, dearest mother, the letter says Pete will soon be better.

Alas, poor boy, he will never be better (nor may-be needs to be better,
that brave and simple soul);
While they stand at home at the door, he is dead already;
The only son is dead.

But the mother needs to be better;
She, with thin form, presently drest in black;
By day her meals untouch'd—then at night fitfully sleeping,
often waking,
In the midnight waking, weeping, longing with one deep longing,
O that she might withdraw unnoticed—silent from life, escape
and withdraw,
To follow, to seek, to be with her dear dead son.

City of Ships

CITY of ships!
(O the black ships! O the fierce ships!
O the beautiful, sharp, bow'd steam-ships and sail-ships!)
City of the world! (for all races are here;
All the lands of the earth make contributions here);
City of the sea! city of hurried and glittering tides!
City whose gleeful tides continually rush or recede,
whirling in and out, with eddies and foam!
City of wharves and stores! city of tall façades of marble and iron!
Proud and passionate city! mettlesome, mad, extravagant city!
Spring up, O city! not for peace alone, but be indeed yourself, warlike!
Fear not! submit to no models but your own, O city!
Behold me! incarnate me, as I have incarnated you!
I have rejected nothing you offer'd me—whom you adopted,
I have adopted;
Good or bad, I never question you—I love all—
I do not condemn anything;
I chant and celebrate all that is yours—yet peace no more;
In peace I chanted peace, but now the drum of war is mine;
War, red war, is my song through your streets, O city!

Mother and Babe

I SEE the sleeping babe, nestling the breast of its mother;
The sleeping mother and babe—hush'd, I study them long and long.

Vigil Strange I Kept on the Field One Night

VIGIL strange I kept on the field one night,
When you, my son and my comrade, dropt at my side that day,
One look I but gave, which your dear eyes return'd, with a look I shall never forget;
One touch of your hand to mine, O boy, reach'd up as you lay on the ground;
Then onward I sped in the battle, the even-contested battle;
Till late in the night reliev'd, to the place at last again I made my way;
Found you in death so cold, dear comrade—found your body, son of responding kisses (never again on earth responding);
Bared your face in the starlight—curious the scene—cool blew the moderate night-wind;
Long there and then in vigil I stood, dimly around me the battle-field spreading;
Vigil wondrous and vigil sweet, there in the fragrant silent night;
But not a tear fell, not even a long-drawn sigh—Long, long I gazed;
Then on the earth partially reclining, sat by your side, leaning my chin in my hands;
Passing sweet hours, immortal and mystic hours with you, dearest comrade—Not a tear, not a word;
Vigil of silence, love and death—vigil for you, my son and my soldier,
As onward silently stars aloft, eastward new ones upward stole;

Vigil final for you, brave boy (I could not save you, swift was your death,
I faithfully loved you and cared for you living—I think we shall
surely meet again);
Till at latest lingering of the night, indeed just as the dawn appear'd,
My comrade I wrapt in his blanket, envelop'd well his form,
Folded the blanket well, tucking it carefully over head, and carefully
under feet;
And there and then, and bathed by the rising sun, my son in his grave,
in his rude-dug grave I deposited;
Ending my vigil strange with that—vigil of night and battle-field dim;
Vigil for boy of responding kisses (never again on earth responding),
Vigil for comrade swiftly slain—vigil I never forget,
how as day brighten'd,
I rose from the chill ground, and folded my soldier well in his blanket,
And buried him where he fell.

A March in the Ranks Hard-Prest, and the Road Unknown

A MARCH in the ranks hard-prest, and the road unknown;
A route through a heavy wood, with muffled steps in the darkness;
Our army foil'd with loss severe, and the sullen remnant retreating;
Till after midnight glimmer upon us, the lights of a dim-lighted building;
We come to an open space in the woods, and halt
by the dim-lighted building;
'Tis a large old church, at the crossing roads—'tis now
an impromptu hospital;
—Entering but for a minute, I see a sight beyond all the pictures
and poems ever made:
Shadows of deepest, deepest black, just lit by moving candles and lamps,
And by one great pitchy torch, stationary, with wild red flame,
and clouds of smoke;
By these, crowds, groups of forms, vaguely I see, on the floor,
some in the pews laid down;
At my feet more distinctly, a soldier, a mere lad, in danger of bleeding
to death (he is shot in the abdomen);

I staunch the blood temporarily (the youngster's face is white as a lily);
Then before I depart I sweep my eyes o'er the scene, fain to absorb it all;
Faces, varieties, postures beyond description, most in obscurity,
some of them dead;
Surgeons operating, attendants holding lights, the smell of ether,
the odor of blood;
The crowd, O the crowd of the bloody forms of soldiers—
the yard outside also fill'd;
Some on the bare ground, some on planks or stretchers,
some in the death-spasm sweating;
An occasional scream or cry, the doctor's shouted orders or calls;
The glisten of the little steel instruments catching the glint of the torches;
These I resume as I chant—I see again the forms, I smell the odor;
Then hear outside the orders given, *Fall in, my men, Fall in;*
But first I bend to the dying lad—his eyes open—a half-smile
gives he me;
Then the eyes close, calmly close, and I speed forth to the darkness,
Resuming, marching, as ever in darkness marching, on in the ranks,
The unknown road still marching.

A Farm Picture

THROUGH the ample open door of the peaceful country barn,
A sun-lit pasture field, with cattle and horses feeding.

Give Me the Splendid Silent Sun

1

GIVE me the splendid silent sun, with all his beams full-dazzling;
Give me juicy autumnal fruit, ripe and red from the orchard;
Give me a field where the unmow'd grass grows;
Give me an arbor, give me the trellis'd grape;
Give me fresh corn and wheat—give me serene-moving animals,
teaching content;
Give me nights perfectly quiet, as on high plateaus
west of the Mississippi, and I looking up at the stars,
Give me odorous at sunrise a garden of beautiful flowers,
where I can walk undisturb'd;
Give me for marriage a sweet-breath'd woman,
of whom I should never tire;
Give me a perfect child—give me, away, aside from the noise
of the world, a rural domestic life;
Give me to warble spontaneous songs, reliev'd, recluse by myself,
for my own ears only;
Give me solitude—give me Nature—give me again, O Nature,
your primal sanities!
—These, demanding to have them (tired with ceaseless excitement,
and rack'd by the war-strife);
These to procure, incessantly asking, rising in cries from my heart,
While yet incessantly asking, still I adhere to my city;
Day upon day, and year upon year, O city, walking your streets,
Where you hold me enchain'd a certain time, refusing to give me up;
Yet giving to make me glutted, enrich'd of soul—
you give me forever faces.
(O I see what I sought to escape, confronting, reversing my cries;
I see my own soul trampling down what it ask'd for.)

2

Keep your splendid silent sun;
Keep your woods, O Nature, and the quiet places by the woods;
Keep your fields of clover and timothy, and your corn-fields and orchards;
Keep the blossoming buckwheat fields, where the Ninth-month bees hum;

Give me faces and streets! give me these phantoms incessant and endless
along the trottoirs!°
Give me interminable eyes! give me women! give me comrades
and lovers by the thousand!
Let me see new ones every day! let me hold new ones by the hand
every day!
Give me such shows! give me the streets of Manhattan!
Give me Broadway, with the soldiers marching—give me the sound
of the trumpets and drums!
(The soldiers in companies or regiments—some, starting away,
flush'd and reckless;
Some, their time up, returning, with thinn'd ranks—young,
yet very old, worn, marching, noticing nothing.)
—Give me the shores and the wharves heavy-fringed with the black ships!
O such for me! O an intense life! O full of repletion, and varied!
The life of the theatre, bar-room, huge hotel, for me!
The saloon of the steamer! the crowded excursion for me!
the torch-light procession!
The dense brigade, bound for the war, with high piled military wagons
following;
People, endless, streaming, with strong voices, passions, pageants;
Manhattan streets, with their powerful throbs, with the beating drums,
as now;
The endless and noisy chorus, the rustle and clank of muskets
(even the sight of the wounded);
Manhattan crowds with their turbulent musical chorus—
with varied chorus and light of the sparkling eyes;
Manhattan faces and eyes forever for me.

Did You Ask Dulcet Rhymes from Me?

DID YOU ask dulcet rhymes from me?
Did you find what I sang erewhile so hard to follow, to understand?
Why I was not singing erewhile for you to follow, to understand—
nor am I now;

—What to such as you, anyhow, such a poet as I?
    —therefore leave my works,
And go lull yourself with what you can understand;
For I lull nobody—and you will never understand me.

Year That Trembled and Reel'd Beneath Me

YEAR that trembled and reel'd beneath me!
Your summer wind was warm enough—yet the air I breathed froze me;
A thick gloom fell through the sunshine and darken'd me;
Must I change my triumphant songs? said I to myself;
Must I indeed learn to chant the cold dirges of the baffled?
And sullen hymns of defeat?

The Veteran's Vision

WHILE my wife at my side lies slumbering, and the wars are over long,
And my head on the pillow rests at home, and the mystic midnight passes,
And through the stillness, through the dark, I hear, just hear, the breath
    of my infant,
There in the room, as I wake from sleep, this vision presses upon me:
The engagement opens there and then, in my busy brain unreal;
The skirmishers begin—they crawl cautiously ahead—
    I hear the irregular snap! snap!
I hear the sounds of the different missiles—the short *t-h-t! t-h-t!*
    of the rifle balls;
I see the shells exploding, leaving small white clouds—
    I hear the great shells shrieking as they pass;

The grape, like the hum and whirr of wind through the trees
(quick, tumultuous, now the contest rages!),
All the scenes at the batteries themselves rise in detail before me again;
The crashing and smoking—the pride of the men in their pieces,
The chief gunner ranges and sights his piece, and selects a fuse
of the right time;
After firing, I see him lean aside, and look eagerly off to note the effect;
—Elsewhere I hear the cry of a regiment charging (the young colonel
leads himself this time, with brandish'd sword);
I see the gaps cut by the enemy's volleys (quickly fill'd up—no delay);
I breathe the suffocating smoke—then the flat clouds hover low,
concealing all;
Now a strange lull comes for a few seconds, not a shot fired
on either side;
Then resumed, the chaos louder than ever, with eager calls,
and orders of officers;
While from some distant part of the field the wind wafts
to my ears a shout of applause (some special success);
And ever the sound of the cannon, far or near (rousing, even in dreams,
a devilish exultation, and all the old mad joy, in the depths
of my soul);
And ever the hastening of infantry shifting positions—batteries,
cavalry, moving hither and thither
(The falling, dying, I heed not—the wounded, dripping and red,
I heed not—some to the rear are hobbling);
Grime, heat, rush—aide-de-camps galloping by, or on a full run;
With the patter of small arms, the warning *s-s-t* of the rifles
(these in my vision I hear or see),
And bombs bursting in air, and at night the vari-color'd rockets.

O Tan-Faced Prairie-Boy

O TAN-FACED prairie-boy!
Before you came to camp, came many a welcome gift;
Praises and presents came, and nourishing food—
    till at last among the recruits,
You came, taciturn, with nothing to give—
    we but look'd on each other,
When lo! more than all the gifts of the world, you gave me.

As Toilsome I Wander'd Virginia's Woods

As toilsome I wander'd Virginia's woods,
To the music of rustling leaves, kick'd by my feet (for 'twas autumn),
I mark'd at the foot of a tree the grave of a soldier;
Mortally wounded he, and buried on the retreat
    (easily all could I understand);
The halt of a mid-day hour, when up! no time to lose—yet this sign left,
On a tablet scrawl'd and nail'd on the tree by the grave,
Bold, cautious, true, and my loving comrade.

Long, long I muse, then on my way go wandering;
Many a changeful season to follow, and many a scene of life;
Yet at times through changeful season and scene, abrupt, alone,
    or in the crowded street,
Comes before me the unknown soldier's grave—
    comes the inscription rude in Virginia's woods,
Bold, cautious, true, and my loving comrade.

Look Down Fair Moon

LOOK down, fair moon, and bathe this scene;
Pour softly down night's nimbus floods, on faces ghastly,
swollen, purple;
On the dead, on their backs, with their arms toss'd wide,
Pour down your unstinted nimbus, sacred moon.

Hush'd Be the Camps To-day

A.L. buried April 19, 1865.

HUSH'D be the camps to-day,
And, soldiers, let us drape our war-worn weapons;
And each, with musing soul retire, to celebrate,
Our dear commander's death.

No more for him life's stormy conflicts;
Nor victory, nor defeat—No more time's dark events,
Charging like ceaseless clouds across the sky.

But sing, poet, in our name;
Sing of the love we bore him—because you, dweller in camps, know it truly.

Sing, to the lower'd coffin there;
Sing with the shovel'd clods that fill the grave—a verse,
For the heavy hearts of soldiers.

Not Youth Pertains to Me

NOT youth pertains to me,
Nor delicatesse—I cannot beguile the time with talk;
Awkward in the parlor, neither a dancer nor elegant;
In the learn'd coterie sitting constrain'd and still—
for learning inures not to me;
Beauty, knowledge, fortune, inure not to me—
yet there are two things inure to me:
I have nourish'd the wounded, and sooth'd many a dying soldier;
And at intervals I have strung together a few songs,
Fit for war, and the life of the camp.

Unpublished Introduction

Dec. 23, 1864
good—& must be used

INTRODUCTION

I claim that in literature, I have judged and felt every thing from an American point of view which is no local standard, for America to me, includes humanity and is the universal.

America (I have said to myself) demands one Song, at any rate, that is bold, modern, and all-surrounding as she is herself.

Its scope, like hers, must span the future and dwell on it as much as on the present or the past. Like hers, it must extricate itself from the models of the past, and, while courteous to them must be sung from the depths of its own native spirit exclusively. Like her, it must bring to the van, and hold up at all hazards, the banner of inalienable rights, and the divine pride of man in himself. It must pierce through the shifting envelope of costumes & formulas, and strike perennial born qualities and organs, which always have meaning deeper than even any theories of morals or metaphysics, or any conventional distinctions whatever . . . . . . Hitherto the geniuses of nations have been listening to poems in which natural humanity bends low, humiliated. But the genius of America cannot listen to such poems. Erect & haughty must the chant be, and then the genius of America will listen with pleased ears . . . . The meaning of America is Democracy. The final meaning of Democracy through many transmigrations is to press on through all ridicules, arguments, and ostensible failures to put in practice the idea of the sovereignty, license, sacredness of the individual. This idea isolates, for reasons, each separate man and woman in the world;—while the idea of Love fuses and combines the whole. Out of the fusing of these twain, opposite as they are, I seek to make a homogeneous Song. A third idea, also, is or shall be put there, namely Religion—the idea which, purifying all things, gives endless purpose destiny and growth to a man or woman, and in him or her condenses the drift of all things.

These for the main result, which though I do not touch in my book, is the purpose of all, namely the unknown, which fills time, and is as sure as the known.

The employment and personnel of mechanics, farmers, boatmen, laborers, and men and women in factories, must be seized upon with decision by America's bards, to be by them saturated with fullest charges of electric illumination, and to be held up forever with enthusiasm and dignity. Our highest themes are things at hand. Current, practical times are to be photographed, embracing the war, commerce, inventions, Washington, Abraham Lincoln, the mechanics, and the great work now going on, the settlement of this Western World, the great railroads &c,—embracing indeed the races and locations of the whole world . . . . . .

Prevalent poems cast back only facial physiognomy, a part. In the following chant, the apparition of the whole form, as of one unclothed before a mirror is cast back. The teachers of the day teach (and stop there) that the unclothed face is divine. It is indeed; but I say that only the unclothed body, diviner still, is fully divine. These Leaves image that physiology—not apologising for it, but exulting openly in it and taking it to myself. I know the rectitude of my intentions & appeal to the future. I seek, by singing these to behold & exhibit what I am, as specimen to all—these material, aesthetic and spiritual relations & tally the same in you, whoever you are, I am.

The Body merged with & in the soul & the soul merged in the Body I seek. For once, anyhow, needs that tantalizing wonder to go or seek to go, in a poem, in perfect faith in itself—not as it might be or as it is fancied in conventional literature to be, but as it actually is, good and bad, as maturity and passions, youth, sex, experience and the world turn it out. A living, flush, eating and drinking man, the mould—and as from that, without wincing, to mould a book. Not but that modesty and decorum, delicatesse and what proceeds from them & accumulates in literature &c. are important. But that in literature &c. we were all lost without redemption, except we retain the sexual fibre of things and simplicity, and acknowledge as supreme and above these pictures and plays, man, nude & abysmal, and indifferent to mere conventional delicatesse.

Here then, make or break for me, it must be so, I sing the complete physiology.

This introduction on my birth day, after having looked over the poem, as far as accomplished. So far, so well; but the most and the best of it, I perceive, remains to be written—the work of my life ahead which if all prove propitious, I would yet do. All as is appropriate to me. Of the crowds of poets, current or on record, with performance popular and appropriate to them—they to their use (which is great) I, perhaps alone, to mine. I do not purpose to school man in virtues, nor prove anything to the intellect, nor play on the piano, nor rhyme, nor sing amours or romances, nor the epics of signal deeds—nor for fashion's coterie-crowds, nor to be trameled with the etiquet of those crowds. But from me to you, whoever you are, we twain, alone—together, a conference, giving up all my private interior musings, yearnings, extasies and contradictory moods, reserving nothing. A conference amid Nature, and in the spirit of Nature's genesis and primal sanity. A conference of our two Souls exclusively, as if the rest of the world, with its mocking misconceptions, were for a while left and escaped from. . . . . In short, the book will not serve as books serve. But may-be as the rude air, the salt sea, the fire, the woods, and the rocky ground—sharp, full of danger, full of contradictions and offence. Those elements, silent and old, stand or move and out of them curiously comes everything. I too (though a resident and singer of cities) came from them, and can boast, as I now do, that in their presence, before giving them here, I have sternly tried each passage of the following chants.

Unpublished Inscription To the Reader

INSCRIPTION
To the Reader
at the entrance of Leaves of Grass

Dear friend, whoe'er you are, at last arriving hither, accept from me (as one in waiting for you at this entrance) a word of living hospitality and love. I almost feel the curving hold and pressure of your hand, which I return, and thus throughout upon the journey linked together will we go. Indeed this is no book but more a man, within whose breast the common heart is throbbing; no leaves of paper these must prove but lips for your sake freely speaking. From me to you alone, a conference to ensue, to yield interior yearnings, discords and all my private egotisms and moods, reserving nothing. Conference wherein, along the robust virgin Western World, abandon we ourselves to Nature's primal mode again, our two exclusive souls, as if the imported society world were left behind with all the polite accumulations of the East. While untried, yet the greatest, is the theme of my recitative.

For main and spine of this my talk—leaving all outside heroes and events, the stock of previous bards—up through such epic movements, masses, history, war, the rise and fall of lands, with the rich turmoil of their ascent and precipitation, comes ever surely rising, advancing towards me, when times are still again, something that audience claims more close and deep than all those powerful themes, namely ONE'S-SELF—that wondrous thing, a Person. It is this that has moved me and written. What the New World means, where it centers itself in the prairies, the Missouri and the great lakes, and branches thence east and west to the seas, is INDIVIDUALITY for man and woman for the broadest average use—That, I alone among bards in the following chants sing.

One's self—you, whoever you are, pour'd into whom all that you read and hear and what existent is in heroes or events, with landscape, heavens, and every beast and bird, becomes so only then with play and interplay. For what to you or me is the round universe (with all its changing pageants of success and failure) except as feeding you and me? May-be indeed it is by us created in winking of our eyes. Or may-be for preparing us, by giving us identity—then sailing us with winds o'er the great seas, the apparent known, steadily to the harbors of the really great unknown.

Dear friend! I put not in the following leaves melodious narratives, or pictures for you to con at leisure, as bright creations finished all outside yourself. With such the world is well enough supplied. But of Suggestiveness alone out of the things around us, with steady reference to the life to come, and to the miracles of everyday this is the song—naught made by me for you, but only hinted, to be made by you yourself. Indeed I have not done the work, and cannot do it. But you must do the work to really make what is within the following song—which, if you do,

I promise you return & satisfaction earned by you yourself far more than ever book before has given you. For from this book Yourself, before unknown, shall now rise up & be revealed. This book shall hint the poem of America, and its mighty masses of men, and a new and grand race of women.

Man's physiology complete I sing. Not physiognomy alone is worthy for the muse. I say the perfect form, with all that with it goes, is only fully worthy. I think the human form the epitome of all the universal emblem. And whatever others do I will the ensemble seek and the actual fibres. Man I avow him, nude and abysmal man—and as for delicatesse and art they are indifferent and may follow, but never will I them. I think in literature or what not we will roam unsystematic and barbarous, except we seek ensemble through it and honor the actual fibres of things—whatever they be—acknowledging supreme above delicatesse and art, man, nude and abysmal and indifferent to mere delicatesse and art.

Therefore it comes, our New World, chords in diapason gathering. I chant with reference to original tastes, the flush and strength of things—chant materials, emanating spirituality—and the human form surcharged through all its veins the same: chant from the point of view of my own land, and in the spirit of my own race and not other races—Chant the modern world and cities and farms and the sights and facts thereof—rejoicing.

Rejoicing in all—accepting, proud, myself the pourtrayer of all—pourtrayer of cities and modern mechanics and farmers and farms; them with the world, both present and past—with poems, histories, war and peace—such, here engermed in myself and the following leaves, with new centripetal reference, offering to you dear friend for vista, for curious road with me to travel.

Advance therein, nor be too soon discouraged. Much will not appear that other poets, guiding you pleasant and safe, sing and sweetly pass the time away. But traveling with me, the rude air, woods and the salt sea, fire and the rocky ground, will appear—genuine, sharp, full of danger, full of contradictions and offense. We will interrogate these curious silent objects. We too for ourselves (no matter how many have gone before us) will arouse the original echoes.

Those—and from where it lurks, ever timidly peering, but seldom, ah so seldom really showing itself, that something also may appear, before your very feet and under them—BELIEF—that fuses past and present and to come in one, and never doubts them more. This, O friend, perfuming strange the hour that bathes you, the spot you stand on, the work you work at, and every drop of blood that courses through your veins, may prove this journey's gift.

Faith—lowly—worth all the lore and riches of the world—may somewhere by the path I lead you, among these leaves, an odorous glistening blossom, appear and become yours.

Sequel

to

Drum-Taps

1865–66

When Lilacs Last in the Door-Yard Bloom'd

1

WHEN lilacs° last in the door-yard bloom'd,
And the great star° early droop'd in the western sky in the night,
I mourn'd . . . and yet shall mourn with ever-returning spring.

O ever-returning spring! trinity sure to me you bring;
Lilac blooming perennial, and drooping star in the west,
And thought of him I love.

2

O powerful, western, fallen star!
O shades of night! O moody, tearful night!
O great star disappear'd! O the black murk that hides the star!
O cruel hands that hold me powerless! O helpless soul of me!
O harsh surrounding cloud that will not free my soul!

3

In the door-yard fronting an old farm-house, near the white-wash'd palings,
Stands the lilac-bush, tall-growing, with heart-shaped leaves of rich green,
With many a pointed blossom, rising, delicate, with the perfume strong I love,
With every leaf a miracle . . . . . . and from this bush in the door-yard,
With its delicate-color'd blossoms, and heart-shaped leaves of rich green,
A sprig, with its flower, I break.

4

In the swamp, in secluded recesses,
A shy and hidden bird is warbling a song.

Solitary, the thrush,
The hermit, withdrawn to himself, avoiding the settlements,
Sings by himself a song.

Song of the bleeding throat!
Death's outlet song of life (for well, dear brother, I know,
If thou wast not gifted to sing, thou would'st surely die).

5

Over the breast of the spring, the land, amid cities,
Amid lanes, and through old woods (where lately the violets peep'd
from the ground, spotting the gray debris);
Amid the grass in the fields each side of the lanes—
passing the endless grass;
Passing the yellow-spear'd wheat, every grain from its shroud
in the dark-brown fields uprising;
Passing the apple-tree blows of white and pink in the orchards;
Carrying a corpse to where it shall rest in the grave,
Night and day journeys a coffin.

6

Coffin that passes through lanes and streets,
Through day and night, with the great cloud darkening the land,
With the pomp of the inloop'd flags, with the cities draped in black,
With the show of the States themselves, as of crape-veil'd women, standing,
With processions long and winding, and the flambeaus of the night,
With the countless torches lit—with the silent sea of faces,
and the unbared heads,
With the waiting depot, the arriving coffin, and the sombre faces,
With dirges through the night, with the thousand voices rising
strong and solemn;
With all the mournful voices of the dirges, pour'd around the coffin,
The dim-lit churches and the shuddering organs—Where amid these
you journey,
With the tolling, tolling bells' perpetual clang;
Here! coffin that slowly passes,
I give you my sprig of lilac.

7

(Nor for you, for one, alone;
Blossoms and branches green to coffins all I bring:
For fresh as the morning—thus would I chant a song for you,
O sane and sacred death.

All over bouquets of roses,
O death! I cover you over with roses and early lilies;
But mostly and now the lilac that blooms the first,
Copious, I break, I break the sprigs from the bushes:
With loaded arms I come, pouring for you,
For you and the coffins all of you, O death.)

8

O western orb, sailing the heaven!
Now I know what you must have meant, as a month since we walk'd,
As we walk'd up and down in the dark blue so mystic,
As we walk'd in silence the transparent shadowy night,
As I saw you had something to tell, as you bent to me night after night,
As you droop'd from the sky low down, as if to my side
(while the other stars all look'd on);
As we wander'd together the solemn night (for something
I know not what, kept me from sleep);
As the night advanced, and I saw on the rim of the west, ere you went,
how full you were of woe;
As I stood on the rising ground in the breeze, in the cool transparent night,
As I watch'd where you pass'd and was lost in the netherward black
of the night,
As my soul, in its trouble, dissatisfied, sank, as where you, sad orb,
Concluded, dropt in the night, and was gone.

9

Sing on, there in the swamp!
O singer bashful and tender! I hear your notes—I hear your call;
I hear—I come presently—I understand you;
But a moment I linger—for the lustrous star has detain'd me;
The star, my comrade, departing, holds and detains me.

10

O how shall I warble myself for the dead one there I loved?
And how shall I deck my song for the large sweet soul that has gone?
And what shall my perfume be, for the grave of him I love?

Sea-winds, blown from east and west,
Blown from the eastern sea, and blown from the western sea,
till there on the prairies meeting:
These, and with these, and the breath of my chant,
I perfume the grave of him I love.

11

O what shall I hang on the chamber walls?
And what shall the pictures be that I hang on the walls,
To adorn the burial-house of him I love?

Pictures of growing spring, and farms, and homes,
With the Fourth-month eve at sundown, and the gray-smoke lucid and bright,
With floods of the yellow gold of the gorgeous, indolent, sinking sun, burning, expanding the air;
With the fresh sweet herbage under foot, and the pale green leaves of the trees prolific;
In the distance the flowing glaze, the breast of the river, with a wind-dapple here and there;
With ranging hills on the banks, with many a line against the sky, and shadows;
And the city at hand, with dwellings so dense, and stacks of chimneys,
And all the scenes of life, and the workshops, and the workmen homeward returning.

12

Lo! body and soul! this land!
Mighty Manhattan, with spires, and the sparkling and hurrying tides, and the ships;
The varied and ample land—the South and the North in the light—Ohio's shores, and flashing Missouri,
And ever the far-spreading prairies, cover'd with grass and corn.

Lo! the most excellent sun, so calm and haughty;
The violet and purple morn, with just-felt breezes;
The gentle, soft-born, measureless light;
The miracle, spreading, bathing all—the fulfill'd noon;
The coming eve, delicious—the welcome night, and the stars,
Over my cities shining all, enveloping man and land.

13

Sing on! sing on, you gray-brown bird!
Sing from the swamps, the recesses—pour your chant from the bushes;
Limitless out of the dusk, out of the cedars and pines.
Sing on, dearest brother—warble your reedy song;
Loud human song, with voice of uttermost woe.

O liquid, and free, and tender!
O wild and loose to my soul! O wondrous singer!
You only I hear . . . . . . yet the star holds me (but will soon depart);
Yet the lilac, with mastering odor, holds me.

14

Now while I sat in the day, and look'd forth,
In the close of the day, with its light, and the fields of spring,
and the farmer preparing his crops,
In the large unconscious scenery of my land, with its lakes and forests,
In the heavenly aerial beauty (after the perturb'd winds, and the storms);
Under the arching heavens of the afternoon swift passing,
and the voices of children and women,
The many-moving sea-tides—and I saw the ships how they sail'd,
And the summer approaching with richness, and the fields all busy
with labor,
And the infinite separate houses, how they all went on,
each with its meals and minutia of daily usages;
And the streets, how their throbbings throbb'd, and the cities pent—
lo! then and there,
Falling among them all, and upon them all, enveloping me with the rest,
Appear'd the cloud, appear'd the long black trail;
And I knew Death, its thought, and the sacred knowledge of death.

15

Then with the knowledge of death as walking one side of me,
And the thought of death close-walking the other side of me,
And I in the middle, as with companions, and as holding the hands
of companions,
I fled forth to the hiding receiving night, that talks not,
Down to the shores of the water, the path by the swamp in the dimness,
To the solemn shadowy cedars, and ghostly pines so still.

And the singer so shy to the rest receiv'd me;
The gray-brown bird I know, receiv'd us comrades three;
And he sang what seem'd the song of death, and a verse for him I love.

From deep secluded recesses,
From the fragrant cedars, and the ghostly pines so still,
Came the singing of the bird.

And the charm of the singing rapt me,
As I held, as if by their hands, my comrades in the night;
And the voice of my spirit tallied the song of the bird.

16

Come, lovely and soothing Death,
Undulate round the world, serenely arriving, arriving,
In the day, in the night, to all, to each,
Sooner or later, delicate Death.

Prais'd be the fathomless universe,
For life and joy, and for objects and knowledge curious;
And for love, sweet love—But praise! O praise and praise,
For the sure-enwinding arms of cool-enfolding Death.

Dark Mother, always gliding near, with soft feet,
Have none chanted for thee a chant of fullest welcome?
Then I chant it for thee—I glorify thee above all;
I bring thee a song that when thou must indeed come, come unfalteringly.

Approach, encompassing Death—strong Deliveress!
When it is so—when thou hast taken them, I joyously sing the dead,
Lost in the loving, floating ocean of thee,
Laved in the flood of thy bliss, O Death.

From me to thee glad serenades,
Dances for thee I propose, saluting thee—adornments and feastings for thee;
And the sights of the open landscape, and the high-spread sky, are fitting,
And life and the fields, and the huge and thoughtful night.

The night, in silence, under many a star;
The ocean shore, and the husky whispering wave, whose voice I know;
And the soul turning to thee, O vast and well-veil'd Death,
And the body gratefully nestling close to thee.

Over the tree-tops I float thee a song!
Over the rising and sinking waves—over the myriad fields,
        and the prairies wide;
Over the dense-pack'd cities all, and the teeming wharves and ways,
I float this carol with joy, with joy to thee, O Death!

17

To the tally of my soul,
Loud and strong kept up the gray-brown bird,
With pure, deliberate notes, spreading, filling the night.

Loud in the pines and cedars dim,
Clear in the freshness moist, and the swamp-perfume;
And I with my comrades there in the night.

While my sight was bound in my eyes unclosed,
As to long panoramas of visions.

18

I saw the vision of armies;
And I saw, as in noiseless dreams, hundreds of battle-flags;
Borne through the smoke of the battles, and pierc'd with missiles,
    I saw them,
And carried hither and yon through the smoke, and torn and bloody;
And at last but a few shreds of the flags left on the staffs
    (and all in silence),
And the staffs all splinter'd and broken.

I saw battle-corpses, myriads of them,
And the white skeletons of young men—I saw them;
I saw the debris and debris of all dead soldiers;
But I saw they were not as was thought;
They themselves were fully at rest, they suffer'd not,
The living remain'd and suffer'd—the mother suffer'd,
And the wife and the child, and the musing comrade suffer'd,
And the armies that remain'd suffer'd.

19

Passing the visions, passing the night;
Passing, unloosing the hold of my comrades' hands;
Passing the song of the hermit bird, and the tallying song of my soul,
Victorious song, death's outlet song (yet varying, ever-altering song,
As low and wailing, yet clear the notes, rising and falling,
    flooding the night,
Sadly sinking and fainting, as warning and warning, and yet again
    bursting with joy),
Covering the earth, and filling the spread of the heaven,
As that powerful psalm in the night I heard from recesses.

20

Must I leave thee, lilac with heart-shaped leaves?
Must I leave thee there in the door-yard, blooming, returning with spring?

Must I pass from my song for thee;
From my gaze on thee in the west, fronting the west, communing with thee,
O comrade lustrous, with silver face in the night?

21

Yet each I keep, and all;
The song, the wondrous chant of the gray-brown bird, I keep,
And the tallying chant, the echo arous'd in my soul, I keep,
With the lustrous and drooping star, with the countenance full of woe;
With the lilac tall, and its blossoms of mastering odor;
Comrades mine, and I in the midst, and their memory ever I keep—
for the dead I loved so well;
For the sweetest, wisest soul of all my days and lands . . .
and this for his dear sake;
Lilac and star and bird, twined with the chant of my soul,
With the holders holding my hand, nearing the call of the bird,
There in the fragrant pines, and the cedars dusk and dim.

O Captain! My Captain!

1

O CAPTAIN! my captain! our fearful trip is done;
The ship has weather'd every rack, the prize we sought is won;
The port is near, the bells I hear, the people all exulting,
While follow eyes the steady keel, the vessel grim and daring:
But O heart! heart! heart!
Leave you not the little spot,
Where on the deck my captain lies,
Fallen cold and dead.

2

O captain! my captain! rise up and hear the bells;
Rise up—for you the flag is flung—for you the bugle trills;
For you bouquets and ribbon'd wreaths—for you the shores a-crowding;
For you they call, the swaying mass, their eager faces turning:

O captain! dear father!
This arm I push beneath you;
It is some dream that on the deck,
You've fallen cold and dead.

3

My captain does not answer, his lips are pale and still;
My father does not feel my arm, he has no pulse nor will;
But the ship is anchor'd safe, its voyage closed and done;
From fearful trip, the victor ship, comes in with object won:
Exult, O shores, and ring, O bells!
But I, with silent tread,
Walk the spot my captain lies,
Fallen cold and dead.

Chanting the Square Deific

1

CHANTING the square deific, out of the One advancing, out of the sides;
Out of the old and new—out of the square entirely divine,
Solid, four-sided (all the sides needed) . . . from this side JEHOVAH am I,
Old Brahm° I, and I Saturnius° am;
Not Time affects me—I am Time, modern as any;
Unpersuadable, relentless, executing righteous judgments;
As the Earth, the Father, the brown old Kronos,° with laws,
Aged beyond computation—yet ever new—ever with those mighty laws rolling,
Relentless, I forgive no man—whoever sins, dies—I will have that man's life;
Therefore let none expect mercy—Have the seasons, gravitation, the appointed days, mercy? No more have I;
But as the seasons, and gravitation—and as all the appointed days, that forgive not,
I dispense from this side judgments inexorable, without the least remorse.

2

Consolator most mild, the promis'd one advancing,
With gentle hand extended, the mightier God am I,
Foretold by prophets and poets, in their most rapt prophecies and poems;
From this side, lo! the Lord CHRIST gazes—lo! Hermes I—
    lo! mine is Hercules' face;
All sorrow, labor, suffering, I, tallying it, absorb in myself;
Many times have I been rejected, taunted, put in prison, and crucified—
    and many times shall be again;
All the world have I given up for my dear brothers' and sisters' sake—
    for the soul's sake;
Wending my way through the homes of men, rich or poor,
    with the kiss of affection;
For I am affection—I am the cheer-bringing God, with hope,
    and all-enclosing Charity
(Conqueror yet—for before me all the armies and soldiers of the earth
    shall yet bow—and all the weapons of war become impotent);
With indulgent words, as to children—with fresh and sane words,
    mine only,
Young and strong I pass, knowing well I am destin'd myself
    to an early death:
But my Charity has no death—my Wisdom dies not, neither early
    nor late,
And my sweet Love, bequeath'd here and elsewhere, never dies.

3

Aloof, dissatisfied, plotting revolt,
Comrade of criminals, brother of slaves,
Crafty, despised, a drudge, ignorant,
With sudra° face and worn brow—black, and in the depths of my heart,
    proud as any;
Lifted, now and always, against whoever, scorning, assumes to rule me;
Morose, full of guile, full of reminiscences, brooding, with many wiles
(Though it was thought I was baffled and dispell'd, and my wiles done—
    but that will never be);
Defiant, I, SATAN, still live—still utter words—in new lands
    duly appearing (and old ones also);
Permanent here, from my side, warlike, equal with any, real as any,
Nor time, nor change, shall ever change me or my words.

4

Santa SPIRITA,° breather, life,
Beyond the light, lighter than light,
Beyond the flames of hell—joyous, leaping easily above hell;
Beyond Paradise—perfumed solely with mine own perfume;
Including all life on earth—touching, including God—
including Saviour and Satan;
Ethereal, pervading all (for without me, what were all? what were God?),
Essence of forms—life of the real identities, permanent, positive
(namely the unseen),
Life of the great round world, the sun and stars, and of man—
I, the general Soul,
Here the square finishing, the solid, I the most solid,
Breathe my breath also through these little songs.

Not My Enemies Ever Invade Me

NOT my enemies ever invade me—no harm to my pride from them I fear;
But the lovers I recklessly love—lo! how they master me!
Lo! me, ever open and helpless, bereft of my strength!
Utterly abject, grovelling on the ground before them.

Ah Poverties, Wincings, and Sulky Retreats

AH poverties, wincings, and sulky retreats!
Ah you foes that in conflict have overcome me!
(For what is my life, or any man's life, but a conflict with foes—
the old, the incessant war?)

You degradations—you tussle with passions and appetites;
You smarts from dissatisfied friendships (ah wounds, the sharpest of all);
You toil of painful and choked articulations—you meannesses;
You shallow tongue-talks at tables (my tongue the shallowest of any);
You broken resolutions, you racking angers, you smother'd ennuis;
Ah, think not you finally triumph—My real self has yet to come forth;
It shall yet march forth o'ermastering, till all lies beneath me;
It shall yet stand up the soldier of unquestion'd victory.

As I Lay with My Head in Your Lap, Camerado

As I lay with my head in your lap, camerado,
The confession I made I resume—what I said to you
    and the open air I resume:
I know I am restless, and make others so;
I know my words are weapons, full of danger, full of death
(Indeed I am myself the real soldier;
It is not he, there, with his bayonet, and not the red-striped
    artilleryman);
For I confront peace, security, and all the settled laws,
    to unsettle them;
I am more resolute because all have denied me,
    than I could ever have been had all accepted me;
I heed not, and have never heeded, either experience, cautions,
    majorities, nor ridicule;
And the threat of what is call'd hell is little or nothing to me;
And the lure of what is call'd heaven is little or nothing to me;
. . . Dear camerado! I confess I have urged you onward with me,
    and still urge you, without the least idea what is our destination,
Or whether we shall be victorious, or utterly quell'd and defeated.

Dirge for Two Veterans

1

THE last sunbeam
Lightly falls from the finish'd Sabbath,
On the pavement here—and there beyond, it is looking,
Down a new-made double grave.

2

Lo! the moon ascending!
Up from the east, the silvery round moon;
Beautiful over the house-tops, ghastly, phantom moon;
Immense and silent moon.

3

I see a sad procession,
And I hear the sound of coming full-key'd bugles;
All the channels of the city streets they're flooding,
As with voices and with tears.

4

I hear the great drum pounding,
And the small drums steady whirring;
And every blow of the great convulsive drums,
Strikes me through and through.

5

For the son is brought with the father
(In the foremost ranks of the fierce assault they fell;
Two veterans, son and father, dropt together,
And the double grave awaits them).

6

Now nearer blow the bugles,
And the drums strike more convulsive;
And the day-light o'er the pavement quite has faded,
And the strong dead-march enwraps me.

7

In the eastern sky up-buoying,
The sorrowful vast phantom moves illumin'd
('T is some mother's large, transparent face,
In heaven brighter growing).

8

O strong dead-march, you please me!
O moon immense, with your silvery face you soothe me!
O my soldiers twain! O my veterans, passing to burial!
What I have I also give you.

9

The moon gives you light,
And the bugles and the drums give you music;
And my heart, O my soldiers, my veterans,
My heart gives you love.

Reconciliation

WORD over all, beautiful as the sky!
Beautiful that war, and all its deeds of carnage, must in time be utterly lost;
That the hands of the sisters Death and Night, incessantly softly wash again, and ever again, this soil'd world:
. . . For my enemy is dead—a man divine as myself is dead;
I look where he lies, white-faced and still, in the coffin—I draw near;
I bend down and touch lightly with my lips the white face in the coffin.

Leaves

of

Grass

1867

Whitman with Peter Doyle, the former Confederate soldier and streetcar conductor he met and became very close to during his years as a resident of Washington, D.C. The picture, taken by M. P. Rice, is dated 1865 in Whitman's hand, but it was more likely taken circa 1869.

THE BAYLEY COLLECTION, OHIO WESLEYAN UNIVERSITY

Inscription

SMALL *is the theme of the following Chant, yet the greatest—namely,*
ONE'S SELF—*that wondrous thing, a simple, separate person.*
That, for the use of the New World, I sing.
Man's physiology complete, from top to toe, I sing. Not physiognomy alone,
nor brain alone, is worthy for the muse;—I say the Form complete
is worthier far. The female equally with the male, I sing.
Nor cease at the theme of One's-Self. I speak the word
of the modern, the word EN-MASSE.
My Days I sing, and the Lands—with interstice I knew of hapless War.
O friend, whoe'er you are, at last arriving hither to commence, I feel
through every leaf the pressure of your hand, which I return.
And thus upon our journey link'd together let us go.

One's-Self I Sing

(1871 VERSION OF ABOVE)

ONE'S-SELF I sing—a simple, separate Person;
Yet utter the word Democratic, the word *En-masse.*

Of Physiology from top to toe I sing;
Not physiognomy alone, nor brain alone, is worthy for the muse—
I say the Form complete is worthier far;
The Female with the male I sing.

Of Life immense in passion, pulse, and power,
Cheerful—for freest action form'd, under the laws divine,
The Modern Man I sing.

The Runner

ON a flat road runs the well-train'd runner;
He is lean and sinewy, with muscular legs;
He is thinly clothed—he leans forward as he runs,
With lightly closed fists, and arms partially rais'd.

Leaves of Grass 2

TEARS! tears! tears!
In the night, in solitude, tears;
On the white shore dripping, dripping, suck'd in by the sand;
Tears—not a star shining—all dark and desolate;
Moist tears from the eyes of a muffled head:
—O who is that ghost?—that form in the dark, with tears?
What shapeless lump is that, bent, crouch'd there on the sand?
Streaming tears—sobbing tears—throes, choked with wild cries;
O storm, embodied, rising, careering, with swift steps along the beach;
O wild and dismal night storm, with wind! O belching and desperate!
O shade, so sedate and decorous by day, with calm countenance
and regulated pace;
But away, at night, as you fly, none looking—
O then the unloosen'd ocean,
Of tears! tears! tears!

When I Read the Book

WHEN I read the book, the biography famous;
And is this, then (said I), what the author calls a man's life?
And so will some one, when I am dead and gone, write my life?
(As if any man really knew aught of my life;
As if you, O cunning Soul, did not keep your secret well!)

Unpublished Introduction

(LONDON EDITION 1868)

AMERICA—that new world in so many respects besides its geography—has perhaps afforded nothing even in the astonishing products of the fields of its politics, its mechanical invention, material growth, & the like, more original, more autochthonic, than its late contributions in the field of literature, the Poem, or poetic writings, named LEAVES OF GRASS, which in the following pages we present to the British public.

At first sight, the form of these verses, not only without rhyme, but wholly regardless of the customary verbal melody & regularity so much labored after by modern poets, will strike the reader with incredulous amazement. Then the perusal of the book will open to view his other still profounder innovations. The absolute & unqualified acceptance of Nature; the unprecedentedly candid treatment of the human body, & the exulting celebration of it in its entirety & in all its parts, without the exclusion of any; the absence, ostensibly at least, of any thing like plot, or definite point or purpose in the poems; their boundless outcroppage of arrogant animal muscle & brawn, closely tracked everywhere by an equal outcroppage of the most refined transcendentalism, & loftiest spirituality;—these, expressed through phraseology of never-surpassed earnestness and determination, make indeed a book whose presence & pages, & the action between them & their reader, resemble the struggles of the gymnastic arena, more than the usual orderly entertainment given by authors.

Taken as a unity, LEAVES OF GRASS, true to its American origin, is a song of "the great pride of man in himself." It assumes to bring the materials & outline the architecture of a more complete, more advanced, idiocratic, masterful, Western personality—the combination and model of a new MAN. It does not dwell on the past, & celebrates in no way the superb old feudal world, or its gorgeous reminiscences; it is built forward in the demesne(s) of the future, and it would seem as if somehow, a great coming and regnant Democracy —the dream of poets from the time of Plato, & before him, & since, too—had advanced sufficiently, & here given genesis to every line. —It possesses, more than any other known book, the magnetism of living flesh & blood, sitting near the reader, & looking & talking. It is marvellously cosmopolitan. Always manly friendship, the ties of nations & cities, & their common sympathies & common brotherhood —never their jealousies, vaunts special glories or any thought or thing calculated to keep them apart—are encouraged & persistently upheld. The book may be further described as a genuine confession & conference of one single representative humanity, a free, yet ardently intensified *tete-a-tete*. The crowded parlor or a promiscuous audience is not its sphere. It is the most emotional & yearning of poems, & really unfolds itself only in the presence of YOU, the reader, with no third person near.

Like the world itself, it is not without passages that will puzzle, cause hesitation, & even shock the conventional, well-meaning student & beholder. But its fervent & powerful efflux evidently flows from a devout soul, & its writer as evidently writes from deep plan & science, & with an elaborated ethic intention, born of & designed to justify, the Democratic theory of his country & carry it out far beyond the merely political beginning already made.

If indeed the various parts of LEAVES OF GRASS demanded a single word to sum up & characterize them, it would seem to be the word Democracy that was wanted. But it would mean a Democracy not confined to politics; that would describe a portion only. It would need the application of the word extended to all departments of civilization & humanity, & include especially the moral, esthetic, & philosophic departments.

In giving the preceding introduction we have not had so much in view to advocate or praise the book, as to prepare the reader, by a few general hints, for its novel form, & more novel & most free, sturdy, & all-tolerating spirit.

And as there has perhaps never been a book so resolvable into the personality that composed it, & so knitted with & faithfully reflecting that personality, we will add to the hasty synopsis of LEAVES OF GRASS, just given, a brief memorandum of the author, WALT WHITMAN. He was born on his father's farm, not far from the sea, in New York state, May 31, 1819. His descent is from Dutch and English ancestry, dating back, both in father's & mother's lines, to the first colonization of that part of the country, and is thus of the fullest & purest stock which America affords, bred of her own soil. He grew up, healthy & strong, alternating his life equally between the country-farm & New York city. He has since lived in the south, explored the west, & sailed the Mississippi, the Gulf of Mexico, & the great Canadian lakes. He has been a farmer, builder of houses, & printer & editor of newspapers. He first issued LEAVES OF GRASS in 1855.—The book has since been printed, with successive enlargements and readjustments, three times. As given in this volume, it was put forth by the author within the last year, & includes the poems & songs of DRUM-TAPS, written during, and at the close of the civil war of 1861–'5.

For Walt Whitman was in the midst of the war throughout. A volunteer care-taker of the wounded & sick, he joined the army early in the contest, & steadily remained at active work, in camp, on the battle-field, or in some or other of the huge military hospitals, ministering to southerner as well as northerner, till Richmond fell, & Lee capitulated.

He is now in his 49th year, and is pourtrayed by one who knows him intimately, as tall in stature, with shapely limbs; slow of movement, florid & clear face, bearded & gray, blue eyes, an expression of great equanimity, of decided presence & singular personal magnetism, very little of a talker, generally undemonstrative, yet capable of the strongest emotions, resolution, & even hauteur.

By report of an English gentleman & traveler, a believing reader of Walt Whitman, who sought & found him out in America, we have our latest direct account of the poet. He was, in August 1867, residing at Washington City, the capital of the United States, & held a small, but pleasant honorable post in the Attorney General's office there. Our informant had several interviews with him, & besides confirming the main parts of the foregoing account, adds one item, with which we may conclude our record. It is on a point that gives the final test to human character. He considers Walt Whitman the most thoroughly *religious* being that in the course of much travel, & long & varied contact with the world he has ever encountered. The interior & foundation quality of the man is Hebraic, Biblical, mystic. This exhibited & fused through a full & passionate physiology, a complete animal body, and joined with the most thorough-going realization & cordial acceptance of his country, & belief in its mission, and with a mind fully awake to the sacred practical obligations of each person as a citizen, neighbor & friend—deferentially absorbing modern science, yet with distinct acknowledgment that science, grand as it is, stands baffled before the impenetrable miracle of the least law of the universe, & even the least leaf or insect,—all this, we say, or something like this, gives the best clue both to the personal character & life, & to the poetic utterance, of this new, powerful, & we think we must say, most typical American.

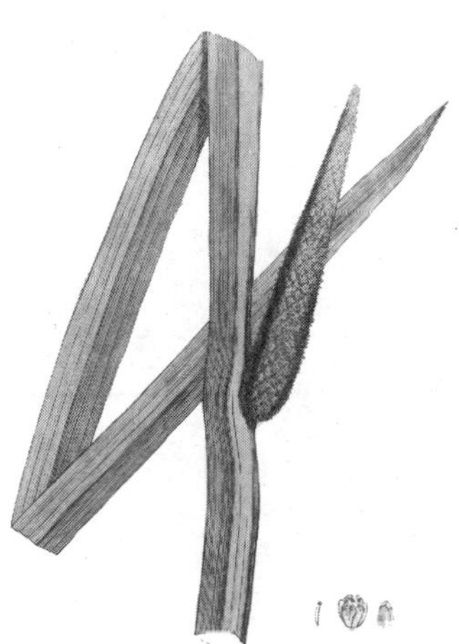

Illustration of the calamus plant (Acorus calamus) *from William Woodville's* Medical Botany *(1832).*

Leaves

of

Grass

1871–72

A photograph, taken in Brooklyn, of Whitman in 1872, with his distinctive autograph upper right.

COURTESY OF THE BERG COLLECTION,
NEW YORK PUBLIC LIBRARY

Passage to India

1

SINGING my days,
Singing the great achievements of the present,
Singing the strong, light works of engineers,
Our modern wonders (the antique ponderous Seven° outvied),
In the Old World, the east, the Suez canal,°
The New by its mighty railroad spann'd,°
The seas inlaid with eloquent, gentle wires,
I sound, to commence, the cry, with thee, O soul,
The Past! the Past! the Past!

The Past! the dark, unfathom'd retrospect!
The teeming gulf! the sleepers and the shadows!
The past! the infinite greatness of the past!
For what is the present, after all, but a growth out of the past?
(As a projectile, form'd, impell'd, passing a certain line, still keeps on,
So the present, utterly form'd, impell'd by the past.)

2

Passage O soul to India!
Eclaircise° the myths Asiatic—the primitive fables.

Not you alone, proud truths of the world!
Nor you alone, ye facts of modern science!
But myths and fables of eld—Asia's, Africa's fables!
The far-darting beams of the spirit!—the unloos'd dreams!
The deep diving bibles and legends;
The daring plots of the poets—the elder religions;
—O you temples fairer than lilies, pour'd over by the rising sun!
O you fables, spurning the known, eluding the hold of the known,
    mounting to heaven!
You lofty and dazzling towers, pinnacled, red as roses,
    burnish'd with gold!
Towers of fables immortal, fashion'd from mortal dreams!
You too I welcome, and fully, the same as the rest;
You too with joy I sing.

3

Passage to India!
Lo, soul! seest thou not God's purpose from the first?
The earth to be spann'd, connected by net-work,
The people to become brothers and sisters,
The races, neighbors, to marry and be given in marriage,
The oceans to be cross'd, the distant brought near,
The lands to be welded together.

(A worship new, I sing;
You captains, voyagers, explorers, yours!
You engineers! you architects, machinists, yours!
You, not for trade or transportation only,
But in God's name, and for thy sake, O soul.)

4

Passage to India!
Lo, soul, for thee, of tableaus twain,
I see, in one, the Suez canal initiated, open'd;
I see the procession of steamships, the Empress Eugenie's leading the van;[o]
I mark, from on deck, the strange landscape, the pure sky, the level sand
in the distance;
I pass swiftly the picturesque groups, the workmen gather'd,
The gigantic dredging machines.

In one, again, different (yet thine, all thine, O soul, the same),
I see over my own continent the Pacific Railroad,
surmounting every barrier;
I see continual trains of cars winding along the Platte,
carrying freight and passengers;
I hear the locomotives rushing and roaring, and the shrill steam-whistle,
I hear the echoes reverberate through the grandest scenery in the world;
I cross the Laramie plains—I note the rocks in grotesque shapes—
the buttes;
I see the plentiful larkspur and wild onions—the barren, colorless,
sage-deserts;
I see in glimpses afar, or towering immediately above me, the great
mountains—I see the Wind River and the Wahsatch mountains;
I see the Monument mountain and the Eagle's Nest—
I pass the Promontory—I ascend the Nevadas,
I scan the noble Elk mountain, and wind around its base;
I see the Humboldt range—I thread the valley and cross the river,

I see the clear waters of Lake Tahoe—I see forests of majestic pines,
Or, crossing the great desert, the alkaline plains, I behold
        enchanting mirages of waters and meadows;
Marking through these, and after all, in duplicate slender lines,
Bridging the three or four thousand miles of land travel,
Tying the Eastern to the Western sea,
The road between Europe and Asia.

(Ah Genoese,° thy dream! thy dream!
Centuries after thou art laid in thy grave,
The shore thou foundest verifies thy dream!)

5

Passage to India!
Struggles of many a captain—tales of many a sailor dead!
Over my mood, stealing and spreading they come,
Like clouds and cloudlets in the unreach'd sky.

Along all history, down the slopes,
As a rivulet running, sinking now, and now again to the surface rising,
A ceaseless thought, a varied train—Lo, soul! to thee, thy sight,
        they rise,
The plans, the voyages again, the expeditions:
Again Vasco de Gama sails forth;°
Again the knowledge gain'd, the mariner's compass,
Lands found, and nations born—thou born, America
        (a hemisphere unborn),
For purpose vast, man's long probation fill'd,
Thou, rondure of the world, at last accomplish'd.

6

O, vast Rondure, swimming in space!
Cover'd all over with visible power and beauty!
Alternate light and day, and the teeming, spiritual darkness;
Unspeakable, high processions of sun and moon,
        and countless stars, above;
Below, the manifold grass and waters, animals, mountains, trees;
With inscrutable purpose—some hidden, prophetic intention;
Now, first, it seems, my thought begins to span thee.

Down from the gardens of Asia, descending radiating,
Adam and Eve appear, then their myriad progeny after them,

Wandering, yearning, curious—with restless explorations,
With questionings, baffled, formless, feverish—with never-happy hearts,
With that sad, incessant refrain, *Wherefore unsatisfied Soul?* and,
Whither, O mocking Life?

Ah, who shall soothe these feverish children?
Who justify these restless explorations?
Who speak the secret of impassive Earth?
Who bind it to us? What is this separate Nature, so unnatural?
What is this Earth, to our affections (unloving earth, without a throb
to answer ours,
Cold earth, the place of graves)?

Yet, soul, be sure the first intent remains—and shall be carried out
(Perhaps even now the time has arrived).

After the seas are all cross'd (as they seem already cross'd),
After the great captains and engineers have accomplish'd their work,
After the noble inventors—after the scientists, the chemist,
the geologist, ethnologist,
Finally shall come the Poet, worthy that name;
The true Son of God shall come, singing his songs.

Then, not your deeds only, O voyagers, O scientists and inventors,
shall be justified,
All these hearts, as of fretted children, shall be sooth'd,
All affection shall be fully responded to—the secret shall be told;
All these separations and gaps shall be taken up, and hook'd
and link'd together;
The whole Earth—this cold, impassive, voiceless Earth,
shall be completely justified;
Trinitas divine shall be gloriously accomplish'd and compacted
by the true Son of God, the poet
(He shall indeed pass the straits and conquer the mountains,
He shall double the Cape of Good Hope to some purpose);
Nature and Man shall be disjoin'd and diffused no more,
The true Son of God shall absolutely fuse them.

7

Year at whose open'd, wide-flung door I sing!
Year of the purpose accomplish'd!

Year of the marriage of continents, climates and oceans!
(No mere Doge of Venice now, wedding the Adriatic.)°
I see, O year, in you, the vast terraqueous globe, given, and giving all,
Europe to Asia, Africa join'd, and they to the New World;
The lands, geographies, dancing before you, holding a festival garland,
As brides and bridegrooms hand in hand.

8

Passage to India!
Cooling airs from Caucasus far, soothing cradle of man,
The river Euphrates flowing, the past lit up again.

Lo, soul, the retrospect, brought forward;
The old, most populous, wealthiest of Earth's lands,
The streams of the Indus and the Ganges, and their many affluents
(I, my shores of America walking to-day, behold, resuming all);
The tale of Alexander, on his warlike marches, suddenly dying,°
On one side China, and on the other side Persia and Arabia,
To the south the great seas, and the Bay of Bengal;
The flowing literatures, tremendous epics, religions, castes,
Old occult Brahma, interminably far back—the tender and junior Buddha,
Central and southern empires, and all their belongings, possessors,
The wars of Tamerlane,° the reign of Aurungzebe,°
The traders, rulers, explorers, Moslems, Venetians, Byzantium,
        the Arabs, Portuguese,
The first travelers, famous yet, Marco Polo, Batouta the Moor,°
Doubts to be solv'd, the map incognita, blanks to be fill'd,
The foot of man unstay'd, the hands never at rest,
Thyself, O soul, that will not brook a challenge.

9

The medieval navigators rise before me,
The world of 1492, with its awaken'd enterprise;
Something swelling in humanity now like the sap of the earth in spring,
The sunset splendor of chivalry declining.

And who art thou, sad shade?
Gigantic, visionary, thyself a visionary,
With majestic limbs, and pious, beaming eyes,
Spreading around, with every look of thine, a golden world,
Enhuing it with gorgeous hues.

As the chief histrion,
Down to the footlights walks, in some great scena,
Dominating the rest, I see the Admiral himself°
(History's type of courage, action, faith);
Behold him sail from Palos, leading his little fleet;
His voyage behold—his return—his great fame,
His misfortunes, calumniators—behold him a prisoner, chain'd,
Behold his dejection, poverty, death.

(Curious, in time, I stand, noting the efforts of heroes;
Is the deferment long? bitter the slander, poverty, death?
Lies the seed unreck'd for centuries in the ground?
        Lo! to God's due occasion,
Uprising in the night, it sprouts, blooms,
And fills the earth with use and beauty.)

10

Passage indeed, O soul, to primal thought!
Not lands and seas alone—thy own clear freshness,
The young maturity of brood and bloom;
To realms of budding bibles.

O soul, repressless, I with thee, and thou with me,
Thy circumnavigation of the world begin;
Of man, the voyage of his mind's return,
To reason's early paradise,
Back, back to wisdom's birth, to innocent intuitions,
Again with fair Creation.

11

O we can wait no longer!
We too take ship, O soul!
Joyous, we too launch out on trackless seas!
Fearless, for unknown shores, on waves of extasy to sail,
Amid the wafting winds (thou pressing me to thee, I thee to me, O soul),
Caroling free—singing our song of God,
Chanting our chant of pleasant exploration.

With laugh, and many a kiss
(Let others deprecate—let others weep for sin, remorse, humiliation),
O soul, thou pleasest me—I thee.

Ah, more than any priest, O soul, we too believe in God;
But with the mystery of God we dare not dally.

O soul, thou pleasest me—I thee;
Sailing these seas, or on the hills, or waking in the night,
Thoughts, silent thoughts, of Time, and Space, and Death,
like waters flowing,
Bear me, indeed, as through the regions infinite,
Whose air I breathe, whose ripples hear—lave me all over;
Bathe me, O God, in thee—mounting to thee,
I and my soul to range in range of thee.

O Thou transcendent!
Nameless—the fibre and the breath!
Light of the light—shedding forth universes—thou centre of them!
Thou mightier centre of the true, the good, the loving!
Thou moral, spiritual fountain! affection's source! thou reservoir!
(O pensive soul of me! O thirst unsatisfied! waitest not there?
Waitest not haply for us, somewhere there, the Comrade perfect?)
Thou pulse! thou motive of the stars, suns, systems,
That, circling, move in order, safe, harmonious,
Athwart the shapeless vastnesses of space!
How should I think—how breathe a single breath—how speak—
if, out of myself,
I could not launch, to those, superior universes?

Swiftly I shrivel at the thought of God,
At Nature and its wonders, Time and Space and Death,
But that I, turning, call to thee O soul, thou actual Me,
And lo! thou gently masterest the orbs,
Thou matest Time, smilest content at Death,
And fillest, swellest full, the vastnesses of Space.

Greater than stars or suns,
Bounding, O soul, thou journeyest forth;
—What love, than thine and ours, could wider amplify?
What aspirations, wishes, outvie thine and ours, O soul?
What dreams of the ideal? what plans of purity, perfection, strength?
What cheerful willingness, for others' sake, to give up all?
For others' sake to suffer all?

Reckoning ahead, O soul, when thou, the time achiev'd
(The seas all cross'd, weather'd the capes, the voyage done),
Surrounded, copest, frontest God, yieldest, the aim attain'd,
As, fill'd with friendship, love complete, the Elder Brother found,
The Younger melts in fondness in his arms.

12

Passage to more than India!
Are thy wings plumed indeed for such far flights?
O Soul, voyagest thou indeed on voyages like these?
Disportest thou on waters such as these?
Soundest below the Sanscrit and the Vedas?°
Then have thy bent unleash'd.

Passage to you, your shores, ye aged fierce enigmas!
Passage to you, to mastership of you, ye strangling problems!
You, strew'd with the wrecks of skeletons, that, living, never reach'd you.

13

Passage to more than India!
O secret of the earth and sky!
Of you, O waters of the sea! O winding creeks and rivers!
Of you, O woods and fields! Of you, strong mountains of my land!
Of you, O prairies! Of you, gray rocks!
O morning red! O clouds! O rain and snows!
O day and night, passage to you!

O sun and moon, and all you stars! Sirius and Jupiter!
Passage to you!

Passage—immediate passage! the blood burns in my veins!
Away, O soul! hoist instantly the anchor!
Cut the hawsers—haul out—shake out every sail!
Have we not stood here like trees in the ground long enough?
Have we not grovell'd here long enough, eating and drinking
like mere brutes?
Have we not darken'd and dazed ourselves with books long enough?

Sail forth! steer for the deep waters only!
Reckless, O soul, exploring, I with thee, and thou with me;
For we are bound where mariner has not yet dared to go,
And we will risk the ship, ourselves and all.

O my brave soul!
O farther, farther sail!
O daring joy, but safe! Are they not all the seas of God?
O farther, farther, farther sail!

Proud Music of the Storm

1

PROUD music of the storm!
Blast that careers so free, whistling across the prairies!
Strong hum of forest tree-tops! Wind of the mountains!
Personified dim shapes! you hidden orchestras!
You serenades of phantoms, with instruments alert,
Blending, with Nature's rhythmus, all the tongues of nations;
You chords left as by vast composers! you choruses!
You formless, free, religious dances! you from the Orient!
You undertone of rivers, roar of pouring cataracts;
You sounds from distant guns, with galloping cavalry!
Echoes of camps, with all the different bugle-calls!
Trooping tumultuous, filling the midnight late, bending me powerless,
Entering my lonesome slumber-chamber—Why have you seiz'd me?

2

Come forward, O my Soul, and let the rest retire;
Listen—lose not—it is toward thee they tend;
Parting the midnight, entering my slumber-chamber,
For thee they sing and dance, O Soul.

A festival song!
The duet of the bridegroom and the bride—a marriage-march,
With lips of love, and hearts of lovers, fill'd to the brim with love;
The red-flush'd cheeks, and perfumes—the cortege swarming,
    full of friendly faces, young and old,
To flutes' clear notes, and sounding harps' cantabile.°

3

Now loud approaching drums!
Victoria! see'st thou in powder-smoke the banners torn but flying?
the rout of the baffled?°
Hearest those shouts of a conquering army?

(Ah, Soul, the sobs of women—the wounded groaning in agony,
The hiss and crackle of flames—the blacken'd ruins—the embers of cities,
The dirge and desolation of mankind.)

4

Now airs antique and medieval fill me!
I see and hear old harpers with their harps, at Welsh festivals,
I hear the minnesingers, singing their lays of love,
I hear the minstrels, gleemen, troubadours, of the feudal ages.

5

Now the great organ sounds,
Tremulous—while underneath (as the hid footholds of the earth,
On which arising, rest, and leaping forth, depend,
All shapes of beauty, grace and strength—all hues we know,
Green blades of grass, and warbling birds—children that gambol
and play—the clouds of heaven above)
The strong bass stands, and its pulsations intermits not,
Bathing, supporting, merging all the rest—maternity of all the rest;
And with it every instrument in multitudes,
The players playing—all the world's musicians,
The solemn hymns and masses, rousing adoration,
All passionate heart-chants, sorrowful appeals,
The measureless sweet vocalists of ages,
And for their solvent setting, Earth's own diapason,
Of winds and woods and mighty ocean waves;
A new composite orchestra—binder of years and climes—
ten-fold renewer,
As of the far-back days the poets tell—the Paradiso,
The straying thence, the separation long, but now the wandering done,
The journey done, the Journeyman come home,
And Man and Art, with Nature fused again.

6

Tutti!° for Earth and Heaven!
The Almighty Leader now for me, for once, has signal'd with his wand.

The manly strophe of the husbands of the world,
And all the wives responding.

The tongues of violins!
(I think, O tongues, ye tell this heart, that cannot tell itself,
This brooding, yearning heart, that cannot tell itself.)

7

Ah, from a little child,
Thou knowest, Soul, how to me all sounds became music;
My mother's voice, in lullaby or hymn
(The voice—O tender voices—memory's loving voices!
Last miracle of all—O dearest mother's, sister's, voices);
The rain, the growing corn, the breeze among the long-leav'd corn,
The measur'd sea-surf, beating on the sand,
The twittering bird, the hawk's sharp scream,
The wild-fowl's notes at night, as flying low, migrating north or south,
The psalm in the country church, or mid the clustering trees,
the open air camp-meeting,
The fiddler in the tavern—the glee, the long-strung sailor-song,
The lowing cattle, bleating sheep—the crowing cock at dawn.

8

All songs of current lands come sounding 'round me,
The German airs of friendship, wine and love,
Irish ballads, merry jigs and dances—English warbles,
Chansons of France, Scotch tunes—and o'er the rest,
Italia's peerless compositions.°

Across the stage, with pallor on her face, yet lurid passion,
Stalks Norma,° brandishing the dagger in her hand.

I see poor crazed Lucia's eyes' unnatural gleam;°
Her hair down her back falls loose and dishevell'd.

I see where Ernani, walking the bridal garden,°
Amid the scent of night-roses, radiant, holding his bride by the hand,
Hears the infernal call, the death-pledge of the horn.

To crossing swords, and grey hairs bared to heaven,
The clear, electric bass and baritone of the world,
The trombone duo—Libertad forever!°

From Spanish chestnut trees' dense shade,
By old and heavy convent walls, a wailing song,
Song of lost love—the torch of youth and life quench'd in despair,
Song of the dying swan—Fernando's heart is breaking.°

Awaking from her woes at last, retriev'd Amina sings;°
Copious as stars, and glad as morning light, the torrents of her joy.

(The teeming lady comes!
The lustrious orb—Venus contralto—the blooming mother,
Sister of loftiest gods—Alboni's self I hear.)°

9

I hear those odes, symphonies, operas;
I hear in the *William Tell,* the music of an arous'd and angry people;
I hear Meyerbeer's *Huguenots,* the *Prophet,* or *Robert;*
Gounod's *Faust,* or Mozart's *Don Juan.*°

10

I hear the dance-music of all nations,
The waltz (some delicious measure, lapsing, bathing me in bliss),
The bolero, to tinkling guitars and clattering castanets.

I see religious dances old and new,
I hear the sound of the Hebrew lyre,
I see the Crusaders marching, bearing the cross on high,
to the martial clang of cymbals;
I hear dervishes monotonously chanting, interspers'd with frantic shouts,
as they spin around, turning always towards Mecca;
I see the rapt religious dances of the Persians and the Arabs;
Again, at Eleusis, home of Ceres, I see the modern Greeks dancing,
I hear them clapping their hands, as they bend their bodies,
I hear the metrical shuffling of their feet.
I see again the wild old Corybantian dance,° the performers
wounding each other;
I see the Roman youth, to the shrill sound of flageolets,
throwing and catching their weapons,
As they fall on their knees, and rise again.

I hear from the Mussulman mosque the muezzin calling;
I see the worshippers within (nor form, nor sermon, argument, nor word,
But silent, strange, devout—rais'd, glowing heads—extatic faces).

11

I hear the Egyptian harp of many strings,
The primitive chants of the Nile boatmen;
The sacred imperial hymns of China,
To the delicate sounds of the king° (the stricken wood and stone);
Or to Hindu flutes, and the fretting twang of the vina,°
A band of bayaderes.°

12

Now Asia, Africa leave me—Europe, seizing, inflates me;
To organs huge, and bands, I hear as from vast concourses of voices,
Luther's strong hymn, *Eine feste Burg ist unser Gott;*°
Rossini's *Stabat Mater dolorosa;*°
Or, floating in some high cathedral dim, with gorgeous color'd windows,
The passionate *Agnus Dei,* or *Gloria in Excelsis.*

13

Composers! mighty maestros!
And you, sweet singers of old lands—Soprani! Tenori! Bassi!
To you a new bard, carolling free in the west.
Obeisant, sends his love.

(Such led to thee, O Soul!
All senses, shows and objects, lead to thee,
But now, it seems to me, sound leads o'er all the rest.)

14

I hear the annual singing of the children in St. Paul's Cathedral;
Or, under the high roof of some colossal hall, the symphonies,
    oratorios of Beethoven, Handel, or Haydn;
The *Creation,* in billows of godhood laves me.°

Give me to hold all sounds (I, madly struggling, cry),
Fill me with all the voices of the universe,
Endow me with their throbbings—Nature's also,
The tempests, waters, winds—operas and chants—marches and dances,
Utter—pour in—for I would take them all.

15

Then I woke softly,
And pausing, questioning awhile the music of my dream,
And questioning all those reminiscences—the tempest in its fury,

And all the songs of sopranos and tenors,
And those rapt oriental dances, of religious fervor,
And the sweet varied instruments, and the diapason of organs,
And all the artless plaints of love, and grief and death,
I said to my silent, curious Soul, out of the bed of the slumber-chamber,
Come, for I have found the clue I sought so long,
Let us go forth refresh'd amid the day,
Cheerfully tallying life, walking the world, the real,
Nourish'd henceforth by our celestial dream.

And I said, moreover,
Haply, what thou hast heard, O Soul, was not the sound of winds,
Nor dream of raging storm, nor sea-hawk's flapping wings,
    nor harsh scream,
Nor vocalism of sun-bright Italy,
Nor German organ majestic—nor vast concourse of voices—
    nor layers of harmonies;
Nor strophes of husbands and wives—nor sound of marching soldiers,
Nor flutes, nor harps, nor the bugle-calls of camps;
But, to a new rhythmus fitted for thee,
Poems, bridging the way from Life to Death, vaguely wafted in night air,
    uncaught, unwritten,
Which, let us go forth in the bold day, and write.

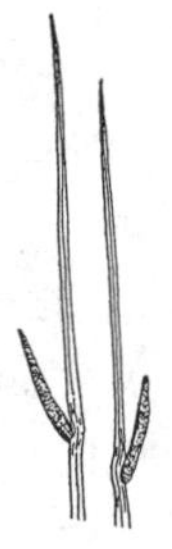

This Dust was Once the Man

THIS dust was once the man,
Gentle, plain, just and resolute—under whose cautious hand,
Against the foulest crimes in history known in any land or age,
Was saved the Union of These States.

Whispers of Heavenly Death

WHISPERS of heavenly death, murmur'd I hear;
Labial gossip of night—sibilant chorals,
Footsteps gently ascending—mystical breezes, wafted soft and low;
Ripples of unseen rivers—tides of a current, flowing, forever flowing
(Or is it the plashing of tears? the measureless waters of human tears?).

I see, just see, skyward, great cloud-masses;
Mournfully, slowly they roll, silently swelling and mixing;
With, at times, a half-dimm'd, sadden'd, far-off star,
Appearing and disappearing.

(Some parturition, rather—some solemn, immortal birth:
On the frontiers, to eyes impenetrable,
Some Soul is passing over.)

A Noiseless, Patient Spider

A NOISELESS patient spider,
I mark'd, where, on a little promontory, it stood isolated;
Mark'd how, to explore the vacant, vast surrounding,
It launch'd forth filament, filament, filament, out of itself;
Ever unreeling them—ever tirelessly speeding them.

And you, O my Soul, where you stand,
Surrounded, surrounded, in measureless oceans of space,
Ceaselessly musing, venturing, throwing—seeking the spheres,
to connect them;
Till the bridge you will need, be form'd—till the ductile anchor hold;
Till the gossamer thread you fling, catch somewhere, O my Soul.

Sparkles from the Wheel

1

WHERE the city's ceaseless crowd moves on, the livelong day,
Withdrawn, I join a group of children watching—
I pause aside with them.

By the curb, toward the edge of the flagging,
A knife-grinder works at his wheel, sharpening a great knife;
Bending over, he carefully holds it to the stone—by foot and knee,
With measur'd tread, he turns rapidly—As he presses
with light but firm hand,
Forth issue, then, in copious golden jets,
Sparkles from the wheel.

2

The scene, and all its belongings—how they seize and affect me!
The sad, sharp-chinn'd old man, with worn clothes,
    and broad shoulder-band of leather;
Myself, effusing and fluid—a phantom curiously floating—
    now here absorb'd and arrested;
The group (an unminded point, set in a vast surrounding);
The attentive, quiet children—the loud, proud, restive bass
    of the streets;
The low, hoarse purr of the whirling stone—the light-press'd blade,
Diffusing, dropping, sideways-darting, in tiny showers of gold,
Sparkles from the wheel.

Gods

1

THOUGHT of the Infinite—the All!
Be thou my God.

2

Lover Divine, and Perfect Comrade!
Waiting, content, invisible yet, but certain,
Be thou my God.

3

Thou—thou, the Ideal Man!
Fair, able, beautiful, content, and loving,
Complete in Body, and dilate in Spirit,
Be thou my God.

4

O Death (for Life has served its turn)—
Opener and usher to the heavenly mansion!
Be thou my God.

5

Aught, aught, of mightiest, best, I see, conceive, or know
(To break the stagnant tie—thee, thee to free, O Soul),
Be thou my God.

6

Or thee, Old Cause, whene'er advancing;
All great Ideas, the races' aspirations,
All that exalts, releases thee, my Soul!
All heroisms, deeds of rapt enthusiasts,
Be ye my Gods!

7

Or Time and Space!
Or shape of Earth, divine and wondrous!
Or shape in I myself—or some fair shape,
        I, viewing, worship,
Or lustrous orb of sun, or star by night:
Be ye my Gods.

The Untold Want

THE untold want, by life and land ne'er granted,
Now, Voyager, sail thou forth, to seek and find.

For Him I Sing

FOR him I sing,
I raise the Present on the Past
(As some perennial tree, out of its roots, the present on the past):
With time and space I him dilate—and fuse the immortal laws,
To make himself, by them, the law unto himself.

To Thee, Old Cause!

TO thee, old Cause!
Thou peerless, passionate, good cause!
Thou stern, remorseless, sweet Idea!
Deathless throughout the ages, races, lands!
After a strange, sad war—great war for thee
(I think all war through time was really fought, and ever will be
really fought, for thee);
These chants for thee—the eternal march of thee.

Thou orb of many orbs!
Though seething principle! Thou well-kept, latent germ!
Thou centre!
Around the idea of thee the strange sad war revolving,
With all its angry and vehement play of causes
(With yet unknown results to come, for thrice a thousand years),
These recitatives for thee—my Book and the War are one,
Merged in its spirit I and mine—as the contest hinged on thee,
As a wheel on its axis turns, this Book, unwitting to itself,
Around the Idea of thee.

The Base of all Metaphysics

AND now, gentlemen,
A word I give to remain in your memories and minds,
As base, and finale too, for all metaphysics.

(So, to the students, the old professor,
At the close of his crowded course.)

Having studied the new and antique, the Greek and Germanic systems,
Kant having studied and stated—Fichte and Schelling and Hegel,
Stated the lore of Plato—and Socrates, greater than Plato,
And greater than Socrates sought and stated—Christ divine
having studied long,
I see reminiscent to-day those Greek and Germanic systems,
See the philosophies all—Christian churches and tenets see,
Yet underneath Socrates clearly see—and underneath Christ the divine
I see,
The dear love of man for his comrade—the attraction of friend to friend,
Of the well-married husband and wife—of children and parents,
Of city for city, and land for land.

As a Strong Bird on Pinions Free

1872

Preface

THE impetus and ideas urging me, for some years past, to an utterance, or attempt at utterance, of New World songs, and an epic of Democracy, having already had their published expression, as well as I can expect to give it, in LEAVES OF GRASS, the present and any future pieces from me are really but the surplusage forming after that Volume, or the wake eddying behind it. I fulfilled in that an imperious conviction, and the commands of my nature as total and irresistible as those which make the sea flow, or the globe revolve. But of this Supplementary Volume, I confess I am not so certain. Having from early manhood abandoned the business pursuits and applications usual in my time and country, and obediently yielded myself up ever since to the impetus mentioned, and to the work of expressing those ideas, it may be that mere habit has got dominion of me, when there is no real need of saying any thing further .... But what is life but an experiment? and mortality but an exercise? with reference to results beyond. And so shall my poems be. If incomplete here, and superfluous there, *n'importe*—the earnest trial and persistent exploration shall at least be mine, and other success failing, shall be success enough. I have been more anxious, anyhow, to suggest the songs of vital endeavor and manly evolution, and furnish something for races of outdoor athletes, than to make perfect rhymes, or reign in the parlors. I ventured from the beginning, my own way, taking chances—and would keep on venturing.

I will therefore not conceal from any persons, known or unknown to me, who take interest in the matter, that I have the ambition of devoting yet a few years to poetic composition.... The mighty present age! To absorb, and express in poetry, any thing of it—of its world—America—cities and States—the years, the events of our Nineteenth Century—the rapidity of movement—the violent contrasts, fluctuations of light and shade, of hope and fear—the entire revolution made by science in the poetic method—these great new underlying facts and new ideas rushing and spreading everywhere;—Truly a mighty age! As if in some colossal drama, acted again like those of old, under the open sun, the Nations of our time, and all the characteristics of Civilization, seem hurrying, stalking across, flitting from wing to wing, gathering, closing up, toward some long-prepared, most tremendous denouement. Not to conclude the infinite scenas of the race's life and toil and happiness and sorrow, but haply that the boards be cleared from oldest, worst incumbrances, accumulations, and Man resume the eternal play anew, and under happier, freer auspices.... To me, the United States are important because, in this colossal drama, they are unquestionably designated for the leading parts, for many a century to come. In them History and Humanity seem to seek to culminate. Our broad areas are even now the busy theatre of plots, passions, interests, and suspended problems, compared to which the intrigues of the past of Europe, the wars of dynasties, the scope of kings and kingdoms, and even the development of peoples, as hitherto, exhibit scales of measurement comparatively narrow and trivial. And on these areas of ours, as on a stage, sooner or later, something like an *eclaircissement* of all past civilization of Europe and Asia is probably to be evolved.

The leading parts.... Not to be acted, emulated here, by us again, that role till now foremost in History—Not to become a conqueror Nation, or to achieve the glory of mere military, or diplomatic, or commercial superiority—but to become the grand Producing Land of nobler Men and Women—of copious races, cheerful, healthy, tolerant, free—To become the most friendly Nation (the United States indeed)—the modern composite Nation, formed from all, with room for all, welcoming all immigrants—accepting the work of our own interior development, as the work fitly filling ages and ages to come;—the leading Nation of peace, but neither ignorant nor incapable of being the leading Nation of war;—not the Man's Nation only, but the Woman's Nation—a land of splendid mothers, daughters, sisters, wives.

Our America to-day I consider in many respects as but indeed a vast seething mass of *materials,* ampler, better (worse also) than previously known—eligible to be used to carry toward its crowning stage, and build for good the great Ideal Nationality of the future, the nation of the Body and the Soul*—no limit here to land, help, opportunities, mines, products, demands, supplies, &c.—with (I think) our political organization, National, State, and Municipal, permanently established, as far ahead as we can calculate—but, so far, no social, literary, religious, or esthetic organizations, consistent with our politics, or becoming to us—which organizations can only come, in time, through native schools or teachers of great Democratic Ideas, Religion—through Science, which now, like a new sunrise, ascending, begins to illuminate all—and through our own begotten Poets and Literatuses. . . . (The moral of a late well-written book on Civilization seems to be that the only real foundation-walls and basis—and also *sine qua non* afterward—of true and full Civilization, is the eligibility and certainty of boundless products for feeding, clothing, sheltering every body—perennial fountains of physical and domestic comfort, with intercommunication, and with civil and ecclesiastical freedom—and that then the esthetic and mental business will take care of itself. . . . Well, the United States have established this basis, and upon scales of extent, variety, vitality, and continuity, rivaling those of Nature; and have now to proceed to build an Edifice upon it. I say this Edifice is only to be fitly built by new Literatures, especially the Poetic. I say a modern Image-Making creation is indispensable to fuse and express modern Political and Scientific creations—and then the Trinity will be complete.)

When I commenced, years ago, elaborating the plan of my poems, and continued turning over that plan, and shifting it in my mind through many years (from the age of twenty-eight to thirty-five), experimenting much, and writing and abandoning much, one deep purpose underlay the others, and has underlain it and its execution ever since—and that has been the Religious purpose. Amid many changes, and a formulation taking far different shape from what I at first supposed, this basic purpose has never been departed from in the composition of my verses. Not of course to exhibit itself in the old ways, as in writing hymns or psalms with an eye to the church-pew, or to express conventional pietism, or the sickly yearning of devotees, but in new ways, and aiming at the widest sub-bases and inclusions of Humanity, and tallying the fresh air of sea and land. I will see (said I to myself) whether there is not, for my purposes as poet, a Religion, and a sound Religious germenancy in the average Human Race, at least in their modern development in the United States, and in the hardy common fibre and native yearnings and elements, deeper and larger, and affording more profitable returns, than all mere sects or churches—as boundless, joyous, and vital as Nature itself—A germenancy that has too long been unencouraged, unsung, almost unknown. . . . With science, the Old Theology of the East, long in its dotage, begins evidently to die and disappear. But (to my mind) Science—and may be such will prove its principal service—as evidently prepares the way for One indescribably grander—Time's young but perfect offspring—the New Theology—heir of the West—lusty and loving, and wondrous beautiful. For America, and for to-day, just the same as any day, the supreme and final Science is the Science of God—what we call science being only its minister—as Democracy is or shall be also. And a poet of America (I said) must fill himself with such thoughts, and chant his best out of them. . . . And as those were the convictions and aims, for good or bad, of LEAVES OF GRASS, they are no less the intention of this Volume. As there can be, in my opinion, no sane and complete Personality, nor any grand and electric Nationality, without the stock element of Religion imbuing all the other elements (like heat in chemistry, invisible itself, but the life of all visible life), so there can be no Poetry worthy the name without that element behind all. . . . . . The time has certainly come to begin to discharge the idea of Religion, in the United States, from mere ecclesiasticism, and from Sundays and churches and churchgoing, and assign it to that general position, chiefest, most indispensable, most exhilarating, to which the others are to be adjusted, inside of all human character, and education, and affairs. The people, especially the young men and women of America, must begin to learn that Religion (like Poetry) is something far, far different from what they supposed. It is, indeed, too important to the power and perpetuity of the New World to be consigned any longer to the churches, old or new, Catholic or Protestant—Saint this, or Saint that. . . . It must be consigned henceforth to Democracy *en masse,* and to Literature. It must enter into the Poems of the Nation. It must make the Nation.

The Four Years' War is over—and in the peaceful, strong, exciting, fresh occasions of To-day, and of the Future, that strange, sad war is hurrying even now to be forgotten. The camp, the drill, the lines of sentries, the prisons, the hospitals—(ah! the hospitals!)—all have passed away—all seem now like a dream. A new race, a young and lusty generation, already sweeps in with oceanic currents, obliterating the war, and all its scars, its mounded graves, and all its reminiscences of hatred, conflict, death. So let it be obliterated. I say the life of the present and the future makes undeniable demands upon us each and all, South, North, East, West. . . . To help put the United States (even if only in imagination) hand in hand, in one unbroken circle in a chant—To rouse them to the unprecedented grandeur of the part they are to play, and are even now playing—to the thought of their great Future, and the attitude conformed to it—especially their great Esthetic, Moral, Scientific Future (of which their vulgar material and political present is but as the preparatory tuning of instruments by an orchestra)—these, as hitherto, are still, for me, among my hopes, ambitions.

LEAVES OF GRASS, already published, is, in its intentions, the song of a great composite *Democratic Individual,* male or female. And following on and amplifying the same purpose, I suppose I have in my mind to run through the chants of this Volume (if ever completed) the thread-voice, more or less audible, of an aggregated, inseparable, unprecedented, vast, composite, electric *Democratic Nationality.*

Purposing, then, to still fill out, from time to time through years to come, the following Volume (unless prevented), I conclude this Preface to the first installment of it, pencilled in the open air, on my fifty-third birth-day, by wafting to you, dear Reader, whoever you are (from amid the fresh scent of the grass, the pleasant coolness of the forenoon breeze, the lights and shades of tree-boughs silently dappling and playing around me, and the notes of the catbird for undertone and accompaniment), my true good-will and love.

W. W.

Washington, D.C., May 31, 1872.

**The problems of the achievement of this crowning stage through future first-class National Singers, Orators, Artists, and others—of creating in literature an* imaginative *New World, the correspondent and counterpart of the current Scientific and Political New Worlds—and the perhaps distant, but still delightful prospect (for our children, if not in our own day) of delivering America, and, indeed, all Christian lands everywhere, from the thin, moribund, and watery, but appallingly extensive nuisance of conventional poetry—by putting something really alive and substantial in its place—I have undertaken to grapple with, and argue, in* DEMOCRATIC VISTAS. [Whitman's note]

One Song, America, Before I Go

ONE song, America, before I go,
I'd sing, o'er all the rest, with trumpet sound,
For thee—the Future.

I'd sow a seed for thee of endless Nationality;
I'd fashion thy Ensemble, including Body and Soul;
I'd show, away ahead, thy real Union, and how it may be accomplish'd.

(The paths to the House I seek to make,
But leave to those to come, the House itself.)

Belief I sing—and Preparation;
As Life and Nature are not great with reference to the Present only,
But greater still from what is yet to come,
Out of that formula for Thee I sing.

Souvenirs of Democracy

THE business man, the acquirer vast,
After assiduous years, surveying results, preparing for departure,
Devises houses and lands to his children—bequeaths stocks, goods—
funds for a school or hospital,
Leaves money to certain companions to buy tokens,
souvenirs of gems and gold;
Parceling out with care—And then, to prevent all cavil,
His name to his testament formally signs.

But I, my life surveying,
With nothing to show, to devise, from its idle years,
Nor house, nor lands—nor tokens of gems or gold for my friends,
Only these Souvenirs of Democracy—In them—in all my songs—behind me leaving,
To You, whoever you are (bathing, leavening this leaf especially with my breath—pressing on it a moment with my own hands;
—Here! feel how the pulse beats in my wrists!—how my heart's-blood is swelling, contracting!),
I will You, in all, Myself, with promise to never desert you,
To which I sign my name,

Walt Whitman

As a Strong Bird on Pinions Free

1

As a strong bird on pinions free,
Joyous, the amplest spaces heavenward cleaving,
Such be the thought I'd think to-day of thee, America,
Such be the recitative I'd bring to-day for thee.

The conceits of the poets of other lands I bring thee not,
Nor the compliments that have served their turn so long,
Nor rhyme—nor the classics—nor perfume of foreign court, or indoor library;
But an odor I'd bring to-day as from forests of pine in the north, in Maine—or breath of an Illinois prairie,
With open airs of Virginia, or Georgia, or Tennessee—or from Texas uplands, or Florida's glades,
With presentment of Yellowstone's scenes, or Yosemite;
And murmuring under, pervading all, I'd bring the rustling sea-sound,
That endlessly sounds from the two great seas of the world.

And for thy subtler sense, subtler refrains, O Union!
Preludes of intellect tallying these and thee—mind-formulas fitted for thee—real, and sane, and large as these and thee;

Thou, mounting higher, diving deeper than we knew—
thou transcendental Union!
By thee Fact to be justified—blended with Thought;
Thought of Man justified—blended with God:
Through thy Idea—lo! the immortal Reality!
Through thy Reality—lo! the immortal Idea!

2

Brain of the New World! what a task is thine!
To formulate the Modern . . : . . Out of the peerless grandeur of the modern,
Out of Thyself—comprising Science—to recast Poems, Churches, Art
(Recast—may-be discard them, end them—May-be their work is done—
who knows?),
By vision, hand, conception, on the background of the mighty past,
the dead,
To limn, with absolute faith, the mighty living present.

And yet, thou living, present brain! heir of the dead, the Old World brain!
Thou that lay folded, like an unborn babe, within its folds so long!
Thou carefully prepared by it so long!—haply thou but unfoldest it—
only maturest it;
It to eventuate in thee—the essence of the by-gone time contain'd in thee;
Its poems, churches, arts, unwitting to themselves,
destined with reference to thee,
The fruit of all the Old, ripening to-day in thee.

3

Sail—sail thy best, ship of Democracy!
Of value is thy freight—'tis not the Present only,
The Past is also stored in thee!
Thou holdest not the venture of thyself alone—
not of the western continent alone;
Earth's *résumé* entire floats on thy keel, O ship—is steadied by thy spars;
With thee Time voyages in trust—the antecedent nations sink or swim
with thee;
With all their ancient struggles, martyrs, heroes, epics, wars,
thou bear'st the other continents;
Theirs, theirs as much as thine, the destination-port triumphant:
—Steer, steer with good strong hand and wary eye, O helmsman—
thou carryest great companions,
Venerable, priestly Asia sails this day with thee,
And royal, feudal Europe sails with thee.

4

Beautiful World of new, superber Birth, that rises to my eyes,
Like a limitless golden cloud, filling the western sky;
Emblem of general Maternity, lifted above all;
Sacred shape of the bearer of daughters and sons;
Out of thy teeming womb, thy giant babes in ceaseless procession issuing,
Acceding from such gestation, taking and giving continual strength
 and life;
World of the Real! world of the twain in one!
World of the Soul—born by the world of the real alone—
 led to identity, body, by it alone;
Yet in beginning only—incalculable masses of composite,
 precious materials,
By history's cycles forwarded—by every nation, language, hither sent,
Ready, collected here—a freer, vast, electric World,
 to be constructed here
(The true New World—the world of orbic Science, Morals, Literatures
 to come),
Thou Wonder World, yet undefined, unform'd—neither do I define thee;
How can I pierce the impenetrable blank of the future?
I feel thy ominous greatness, evil as well as good;
I watch thee, advancing, absorbing the present, transcending the past;
I see thy light lighting and thy shadow shadowing, as if the entire globe;
But I do not undertake to define thee—hardly to comprehend thee;
I but thee name—thee prophecy—as now!
I merely thee ejaculate!

Thee in thy future;
Thee in thy only permanent life, career—thy own unloosen'd mind—
 thy soaring spirit;
Thee as another equally needed sun, America—radiant, ablaze,
 swift-moving, fructifying all,
Thee! risen in thy potent cheerfulness and joy—thy endless, great hilarity!
(Scattering for good the cloud that hung so long—that weigh'd so long
 upon the mind of man,
The doubt, suspicion, dread, of gradual, certain decadence of man);
Thee in thy larger, saner breed of Female, Male—thee in thy athletes,
 moral, spiritual, South, North, West, East
(To thy immortal breasts, Mother of All, thy every daughter, son,
 endear'd alike, forever equal);
Thee in thy own musicians, singers, artists, unborn yet, but certain;

Thee in thy moral wealth and civilization (until which thy proudest
material wealth and civilization must remain in vain);
Thee in thy all-supplying, all-enclosing Worship—
thee in no single bible, saviour, merely,
Thy saviours countless, latent within thyself—thy bibles incessant,
within thyself, equal to any, divine as any;
Thee in an education grown of thee—in teachers, studies, students,
born of thee;
Thee in thy democratic fêtes, en masse—thy high original festivals,
operas, lecturers, preachers;
Thee in thy ultimata (the preparations only now completed—
the edifice on sure foundations tied);
Thee in thy pinnacles, intellect, thought—thy topmost rational joys—
thy love, and godlike aspiration,
In thy resplendent coming literati—thy full-lung'd orators—
thy sacerdotal bards—kosmic savans,
These! these in thee (certain to come) to-day I prophecy.

5

Land tolerating all—accepting all—not for the good alone—
all good for thee;
Land in the realms of God to be a realm unto thyself;
Under the rule of God to be a rule unto thyself.

(Lo! where arise three peerless stars,
To be thy natal stars, my country—Ensemble—Evolution—Freedom,
Set in the sky of Law.)

Land of unprecedented faith—God's faith!
Thy soil, thy very subsoil, all upheav'd;
The general inner earth, so long, so sedulously draped over,
now and hence for what it is boldly laid bare,
Open'd by thee to heaven's light, for benefit or bale.

Not for success alone;
Not to fair-sail unintermitted always;
The storm shall dash thy face—the murk of war, and worse than war,
shall cover thee all over
(Wert capable of war—its tug and trials? Be capable of peace, its trials;
For the tug and mortal strain of nations come at last in peace—not war);

In many a smiling mask death shall approach, beguiling thee—
thou in disease shalt swelter;
The livid cancer spread its hideous claws, clinging upon thy breasts,
seeking to strike thee deep within;
Consumption of the worst—moral consumption—shall rouge thy face
with hectic:
But thou shalt face thy fortunes, thy diseases, and surmount them all,
Whatever they are to-day, and whatever through time they may be,
They each and all shall lift, and pass away, and cease from thee;
While thou, Time's spirals rounding—out of thyself,
thyself still extricating, fusing,
Equable, natural, mystical Union thou (the mortal with immortal blent)—
Shalt soar toward the fulfilment of the future—the spirit of the body
and the mind,
The Soul—its destinies.

The Soul, its destinies—the real real
(Purport of all these apparitions of the real);
In thee, America, the Soul, its destinies;
Thou globe of globes! thou wonder nebulous!
By many a throe of heat and cold convuls'd (by these thyself solidifying);
Thou mental, moral orb! thou New, indeed new, Spiritual World!
The Present holds thee not—for such vast growth as thine—
for such unparallel'd flight as thine,
The Future only holds thee, and can hold thee.

The Mystic Trumpeter

1

HARK! some wild trumpeter—some strange musician,
Hovering unseen in air, vibrates capricious tunes to-night.

I hear thee, trumpeter—listening, alert, I catch thy notes,
Now pouring, whirling like a tempest round me,
Now low, subdued—now in the distance lost.

2

Come nearer, bodiless one—haply, in thee resounds
Some dead composer—haply thy pensive life
Was fill'd with aspirations high—unform'd ideals,
Waves, oceans musical, chaotically surging,
That now, ecstatic ghost, close to me bending, thy cornet echoing,
        pealing,
Gives out to no one's ears but mine—but freely gives to mine,
That I may thee translate.

3

Blow, trumpeter, free and clear—I follow thee,
While at thy liquid prelude, glad, serene,
The fretting world, the streets, the noisy hours of day, withdraw;
A holy calm descends, like dew, upon me,
I walk, in cool refreshing night, the walks of Paradise,
I scent the grass, the moist air, and the roses;
Thy song expands my numb'd, imbonded spirit—
        thou freest, launchest me,
Floating and basking upon Heaven's lake.

4

Blow again, trumpeter! and for my sensuous eyes,
Bring the old pageants—show the feudal world.

What charm thy music works!—thou makest pass before me,
Ladies and cavaliers long dead—barons are in their castle halls—
        the troubadours are singing;
Arm'd knights go forth to redress wrongs—some in quest
        of the Holy Graal;
I see the tournament—I see the contestants, encased in heavy armor,
        seated on stately, champing horses;
I hear the shouts—the sounds of blows and smiting steel;
I see the Crusaders' tumultuous armies—Hark! how the cymbals clang!
Lo! where the monks walk in advance, bearing the cross on high!

5

Blow again, trumpeter! and for thy theme,
Take now the enclosing theme of all—the solvent and the setting;
Love, that is pulse of all—the sustenance and the pang;
The heart of man and woman all for love;
No other theme but love—knitting, enclosing, all-diffusing love.

O, how the immortal phantoms crowd around me!
I see the vast alembic ever working—I see and know the flames
that heat the world;
The glow, the blush, the beating hearts of lovers,
So blissful happy some—and some so silent, dark, and nigh to death:
Love, that is all the earth to lovers—Love, that mocks time and space;
Love, that is day and night—Love, that is sun and moon and stars;
Love, that is crimson, sumptuous, sick with perfume;
No other words, but words of love—no other thought but Love.

6

Blow again, trumpeter—conjure war's wild alarums.

Swift to thy spell, a shuddering hum like distant thunder rolls;
Lo! where the arm'd men hasten—Lo! mid the clouds of dust,
the glint of bayonets;
I see the grime-faced cannoniers—I mark the rosy flash
amid the smoke—I hear the cracking of the guns:
Nor war alone—thy fearful music-song, wild player,
brings every sight of fear,
The deeds of ruthless brigands—rapine, murder—I hear the cries
for help!
I see ships foundering at sea—I behold on deck, and below deck,
the terrible tableaux.

7

O trumpeter! methinks I am myself the instrument thou playest!
Thou melt'st my heart, my brain—thou movest, drawest,
changest them, at will:
And now thy sullen notes send darkness through me;
Thou takest away all cheering light—all hope:
I see the enslaved, the overthrown, the hurt, the opprest
of the whole earth;
I feel the measureless shame and humiliation of my race—
it becomes all mine;
Mine too the revenges of humanity—the wrongs of ages—
baffled feuds and hatreds;
Utter defeat upon me weighs—all lost! the foe victorious!
(Yet 'mid the ruins Pride colossal stands, unshaken to the last;
Endurance, resolution, to the last.)

8

Now, trumpeter, for thy close,
Vouchsafe a higher strain than any yet;
Sing to my soul—renew its languishing faith and hope;
Rouse up my slow belief—give me some vision of the future;
Give me, for once, its prophecy and joy.

O glad, exulting, culminating song!
A vigor more than earth's is in thy notes!
Marches of victory—man disenthrall'd—the conqueror at last!
Hymns to the universal God, from universal Man—all joy!
A reborn race appears—a perfect World, all joy!
Women and Men, in wisdom, innocence and health—all joy!
Riotous, laughing bacchanals, fill'd with joy!
War, sorrow, suffering gone—the rank earth purged—
nothing but joy left!
The ocean fill'd with joy—the atmosphere all joy!
Joy! Joy! in freedom, worship, love! Joy in the ecstacy of life!
Enough to merely be! Enough to breathe!
Joy! Joy! all over Joy!

By Broad Potomac's Shore

1

BY broad Potomac's shore—again, old tongue!
(Still uttering—still ejaculating—canst never cease this babble?)
Again, old heart so gay—again to you, your sense,
the full flush spring returning;
Again the freshness and the odors—again Virginia's summer sky,
pellucid blue and silver,
Again the forenoon purple of the hills,
Again the deathless grass, so noiseless, soft and green,
Again the blood-red roses blooming.

2

Perfume this book of mine, O blood-red roses!
Lave subtly with your waters every line, Potomac!
Give me of you, O spring, before I close, to put between its pages!
O forenoon purple of the hills, before I close, of you!
O smiling earth—O summer sun, give me of you!
O deathless grass, of you!

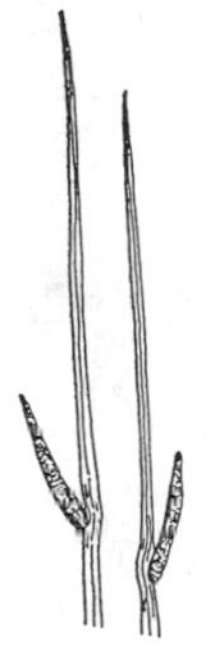

Two Rivulets

1876

(Companion to Centennial Edition)

Preface

AT the eleventh hour, under grave illness, I gather up the pieces of Prose and Poetry left over since publishing, a while since, my first and main Volume, LEAVES OF GRASS—pieces, here, some new, some old—nearly all of them (sombre as many are, making this almost Death's book) composed in by-gone atmospheres of perfect health—and, preceded by the freshest collection, the little TWO RIVULETS, and by this rambling Prefatory gossip,* now send them out, embodied in the present Melange, partly as my contribution and outpouring to celebrate, in some sort, the feature of the time, the first Centennial of our New World Nationality—and then as chyle and nutriment to that moral, Indissoluble Union, equally representing All, and the mother of many coming Centennials.

And e'en for flush and proof of our America—for reminder, just as much, or more, in moods of towering pride and joy, I keep my special chants of Death and Immortality** to stamp the coloring-finish of all, present and past. For terminus and temperer to all, they were originally written; and that shall be their office at the last.

For some reason—not explainable or definite to my own mind, yet secretly pleasing and satisfactory to it—I have not hesitated to embody in, and run through the Volume, two altogether distinct veins, or strata—Politics for one, and for the other, the pensive thought of Immortality. Thus, too, the prose and poetic, the dual forms of the present book. . . . The pictures from the Hospitals during the War, in *Memoranda,* I have also decided to include. Though they differ in character and composition from the rest of my pieces, yet I feel that they ought to go with them, and must do so. . . . The present Volume, therefore, after its minor episodes, probably divides into these Two, at first sight far diverse, veins of topics and treatment. One will be found in the prose part of TWO RIVULETS, in *Democratic Vistas,* in the Preface to *As a Strong Bird,* and in the concluding Notes to *Memoranda* of the Hospitals. The other, wherein the all-enclosing thought and fact of Death is admitted (not for itself so much as a powerful factor in the adjustments of Life), in the realistic pictures of *Memoranda,* and the free speculations and ideal escapades of *Passage to India.*

Has not the time come, indeed, in the development of the New World, when its Politics should ascend into atmospheres and regions hitherto unknown—(far, far different from the miserable business that of late and current years passes under that name)—and take rank with Science, Philosophy and Art? . . . Three points, in especial, have become very dear to me, and all through I seek to make them again and again, in many forms and repetitions, as will be seen: 1. That the true growth-characteristics of the Democracy of the New World are henceforth to radiate in superior Literary, Artistic and Religious Expressions, far more than in its Republican forms, universal suffrage, and frequent elections (though these are unspeakably important). . . . 2. That the vital political mission of The United States is, to practically solve and settle the problem of two sets of rights—the fusion, thorough compatibility and junction of individual State prerogatives, with the indispensable necessity of centrality and Oneness—the National Identity power—the sovereign Union, relentless, permanently comprising all, and over all, and in that never yielding an inch . . . . then 3d. Do we not, amid a general malaria of Fogs and Vapors, our day, unmistakably see two Pillars of Promise, with grandest, indestructible indications—One, that the morbid facts of American politics and society everywhere are but passing incidents and flanges of our unbounded impetus of growth—weeds, annuals, of the rank, rich soil—not central, enduring, perennial things?—The Other, that all the hitherto experience of The States, their first Century, has been but preparation, adolescence—and that This Union is only now and henceforth (*i.e* since the Secession war) to enter on its full Democratic career?

Of the whole, Poems and Prose (not attending at all to chronological order, and with original dates and passing allusions in the heat and impression of the hour, left shuffled in, and undisturb'd), the chants of LEAVES OF GRASS, my former Volume, yet serve as the indispensable deep soil, or basis, out of which, and out of which only, could come the roots and stems more definitely indicated by these later pages. (While that Volume radiates Physiology alone, the present One, though of the like origin in the main, more palpably doubtless shows the Pathology which was pretty sure to come in time from the other.)

In that former and main Volume, composed in the flush of my health and strength, from the age of 30 to 50 years, I dwelt on Birth and Life, clothing my ideas in pictures, days, transactions of my time, to give them positive place, identity—saturating them with that vehemence of pride and audacity of freedom necessary to loosen the mind of still-to-be-form'd America from the accumulated folds, the superstitions, and all the long, tenacious and stifling anti-democratic authorities of the Asiatic and European past—my enclosing purport being to express, above all artificial regulation and aid, the eternal Bodily Character of One's-Self.***

The varieties and phases (doubtless often paradoxical, contradictory) of the two Volumes, of LEAVES, and of these RIVULETS, are ultimately to be considered as One in structure, and as mutually explanatory of each other—as the multiplex results, like a tree, of series of successive growths (yet from one central or seed-purport)—there having been five or six such cumulative issues, editions, commencing back in 1855 and thence progressing through twenty years down to date (1875–76)—some things added or re-shaped from time to time, as they were found wanted, and other things represt. Of the former Book, more vehement, and perhaps pursuing a central idea with greater closeness—join'd with the present One, extremely varied in theme—I can only briefly reiterate here, that all my pieces, alternated through Both, are only of use and value, if any, as such an interpenetrating composite, inseparable Unity.

Two of the pieces in this Volume were originally Public Recitations—the College Commencement Poem, *As a Strong Bird*—and then the *Song of the Exposition,* to identify these great Industrial gatherings, the majestic outgrowths of the Modern Spirit and Practice—and now fix'd upon, the grandest of them, for the Material event around which shall be concentrated and celebrated (as far as any one event can combine them) the associations and practical proofs of the Hundred Years' life of the Republic. The glory of Labor, and the bringing together not only representatives of all the trades and products, but, fraternally, of all the Workmen of all the Nations of the World (for this is the Idea behind the Centennial at Philadelphia) is, to me, so welcome and inspiring a theme, that I only wish I were a younger and a fresher man, to attempt the enduring Book, of poetic character, that ought to be written about it.

The arrangement in print of TWO RIVULETS—the indirectness of the name itself (suggesting meanings, the start of other meanings, for the whole Volume)—are but parts of the Venture which my Poems entirely are. For really they have all been Experiments, under the urge of powerful, quite irresistible, perhaps wilful influences (even escapades), to see how such things will eventually turn out—and have been recited, as it were, by my Soul, to the special audience of Myself, far more than to the world's audience . . . Till now, by far the best part of the whole business is that, these days, in leisure, in sickness and old age, my Spirit, by which they were written or permitted erewhile, does not go back on them, but still and in calmest hours, fully, deliberately allows them.

Estimating the American Union as so far and for some time to come, in its yet formative condition, I therefore now bequeath Poems and Essays as nutriment and influences to help truly assimilate and harden, and especially to furnish something toward what The States most need of all, and which seems to me yet quite unsupplied in literature, namely, to show them, or begin to show them, Themselves distinctively, and what They are for. For though perhaps the main points of all ages and nations are points of resemblance, and, even while granting evolution, are substantially the same, there are some vital things in which this Republic, as to its Individualities, and as a compacted Nation, is to specially stand forth, and culminate modern humanity. And these are the very things it least morally and mentally knows (though, curiously enough, it is at the same time faithfully acting upon them).

I count with such absolute certainty on the Great Future of The United States—different from, though founded on, the past—that I have always invoked that Future, and surrounded myself with it, before or while singing my Songs. . . . (As ever, all tends to followings—America, too, is a prophecy. What, even of the best and most successful, would be justified by itself alone? by the present, or the material ostent alone? Of men or States, few realize how much they live in the future. That, rising like pinnacles, gives its main significance to all You and I are doing to-day. Without it, there were little meaning in lands or poems—little purport in human lives. . . . All ages, all Nations and States, have been such prophecies. But where any former ones with prophecy so broad, so clear, as our times, our lands—as those of the West?)

Without being a Scientist, I have thoroughly adopted the conclusions of the great Savans and Experimentalists of our time, and of the last hundred years, and they have interiorly tinged the chyle of all my verse, for purposes beyond. Following the Modern Spirit, the real Poems of the Present, ever solidifying and expanding into the Future, must vocalize the vastness and splendor and reality with which Scientism has invested Man and the Universe (all that is called Creation), and must henceforth launch Humanity into new orbits, consonant with that vastness, splendor, and reality (unknown to the old poems), like new systems of orbs, balanced upon themselves, revolving in limitless space, more subtle than the stars. Poetry, so largely hitherto and even at present wedded to children's tales, and to mere amorousness, upholstery and superficial rhyme, will have to accept, and, while not denying the Past, nor the Themes of the past, will be revivified by this tremendous innovation, the Kosmic Spirit, which must henceforth, in my opinion, be the background and underlying impetus, more or less visible, of all first-class Songs.

Only (for me, at any rate, in all my Prose and Poetry) joyfully accepting Modern Science, and loyally following it without the slightest hesitation, there remains ever recognized still a higher flight, a higher fact, the Eternal Soul of Man (of all Else too), the Spiritual, the Religious—which it is to be the greatest office of Scientism, in my opinion, and of future Poetry also, to free from fables, crudities and superstitions, and launch forth in renewed Faith and Scope a hundred fold. To me, the worlds of Religiousness, of the conception of the Divine, and of the Ideal, though mainly latent, are just as absolute in Humanity and the Universe as the world of Chemistry, or any thing in the objective worlds. To me,

> The Prophet and the Bard,
> Shall yet maintain themselves—
> in higher circles yet,
> Shall mediate to the Modern,
> to Democracy—interpret yet to them,
> God and Eidólons.

To me, the crown of Savantism is to be, that it surely opens the way for a more splendid Theology, and for ampler and diviner Songs. No year, nor even century, will settle this. There is a phase of the Real, lurking behind the Real, which it is all for. There is also in the Intellect of man, in time, far in prospective recesses, a judgment, a last appellate court, which will settle it.

In certain parts, in these flights, or attempting to depict or suggest them, I have not been afraid of the charge of obscurity, in either of my Two Volumes—because human thought, poetry or melody, must leave dim escapes and outlets—must possess a certain fluid, ærial character, akin to space itself, obscure to those of little or no imagination, but indispensable to the highest purposes. Poetic style, when address'd to the Soul, is less definite form, outline, sculpture, and becomes vista, music, half-tints, and even less than half-tints. True, it may be architecture; but again it may be the forest wild-wood, or the best effects thereof, at twilight, the waving oaks and cedars in the wind, and the impalpable odor.

Finally, as I have lived in fresh lands, inchoate, and in a revolutionary age, future-founding, I have felt to identify the points of that age, these lands, in my recitatives, altogether in my own way. Thus my form has strictly grown from my purports and facts, and is the analogy of them. . . . Within my time the United States have emerg'd from nebulous vagueness and suspense to full orbic (though varied) decision—have done the deeds and achiev'd the triumphs of half a score of centuries—and are henceforth to enter upon their real history—the way being now (*i.e.* since the result of the Secession War) clear'd of death-threatening impedimenta, and the free areas around and ahead of us assured and certain, which were not so before (the past century being but preparations, trial-voyages and experiments of the Ship, before her starting out upon deep water).

In estimating my Volumes, the world's current times and deeds, and their spirit, must be first profoundly estimated. Out of the Hundred Years just ending (1776–1876), with their genesis of inevitable wilful events, and new introductions, and many unprecedented things of war and peace (to be realized better, perhaps only realized, at the remove of another Century hence)—Out of that stretch of time, and especially out of the immediately preceding Twenty-Five Years (1850–75), with all their rapid changes, innovations, and audacious movements—and bearing their own inevitable wilful birthmarks—my Poems too have found genesis.

W. W.

**This Preface is not only for the present collection, but, in a sort, for all my writings, both Volumes.* [All notes are Whitman's.]

**PASSAGE TO INDIA.—*As in some ancient legend-play, to close the plot and the hero's career, there is a farewell gathering on ship's deck and on shore, a loosing of hawsers and ties, a spreading of sails to the wind—a starting out on unknown seas, to fetch up no one knows whither—to return no more—And the curtain falls, and there is the end of it—So I have reserv'd that Poem, with its cluster, to finish and explain much that, without them, would not be explain'd, and to take leave, and escape for good, from all that has preceded them. (Then probably* Passage to India, *and its cluster, are but freer vent and fuller expression to what, from the first, and so on throughout, more or less lurks in my writings, underneath every page, every line, every where.)*

I am not sure but the last enclosing sublimation of Race or Poem is, What it thinks of Death. . . . After the rest has been comprehended and said, even the grandest—After those contributions to mightiest Nationality, or to sweetest Song, or to the best Personalism, male or female, have been glean'd from the rich and varied themes of tangible life, and have been fully accepted and sung, and the pervading fact of visible existence, with the duty it devolves, is rounded and apparently completed, it still remains to be really completed by suffusing through the whole and several, that other pervading invisible fact, so large a part (is it not the largest part?) of life here, combining the rest, and furnishing, for Person or State, the only permanent and unitary meaning to all, even the meanest life, con-

sistently with the dignity of the Universe, in Time. . . . As, from the eligibility to this thought, and the cheerful conquest of this fact, flash forth the first distinctive proofs of the Soul, so to me (extending it only a little further) the ultimate Democratic purports, the ethereal and spiritual ones, are to concentrate here, and as fixed stars, radiate hence. For, in my opinion, it is no less than this idea of Immortality, above all other ideas, that is to enter into, and vivify, and give crowning religious stamp, to Democracy in the New World.

It was originally my intention, after chanting in LEAVES OF GRASS *the songs of the Body and Existence, to then compose a further, equally needed Volume, based on those convictions of perpetuity and conservation which, enveloping all precedents, make the unseen Soul govern absolutely at last. I meant, while in a sort continuing the theme of my first chants, to shift the slides, and exhibit the problem and paradox of the same ardent and fully appointed Personality entering the sphere of the resistless gravitation of Spiritual Law, and with cheerful face estimating Death, not at all as the cessation, but as somehow what I feel it must be, the entrance upon by far the greatest part of existence, and something that Life is at least as much for, as it is for itself.*

But the full construction of such a work (even if I lay the foundation, or give impetus to it) is beyond my powers, and must remain for some bard in the future. The physical and the sensuous, in themselves or in their immediate continuations, retain holds upon me which I think are never entirely releas'd; and those holds I have not only not denied, but hardly wish'd to weaken.

Meanwhile, not entirely to give the go-by to my original plan, and far more to avoid a mark'd hiatus in it, than to entirely fulfil it, I end my books with thoughts, or radiations from thoughts, on Death, Immortality, and a free entrance into the Spiritual world. In those thoughts, in a sort, I make the first steps or studies toward the mighty theme, from the point of view necessitated by my fore-going poems, and by Modern Science. In them I also seek to set the key-stone to my Democracy's enduring arch. I re-collate them now, for the press (much the same, I transcribe my Memoranda *following, of gloomy times out of the War, and Hospitals) in order to partially occupy and offset days of strange sickness, and the heaviest affliction and bereavement of my life; and I fondly please myself with the notion of leaving that cluster to you, O unknown Reader of the future, as 'something to remember me by,' more especially than all else. Written in former days of perfect health, little did I think the pieces had the purport that now, under present circumstances, opens to me.*

[As I write these lines, May 31, 1875, it is again early summer—again my birth-day—now my fifty-sixth. Amid the outside beauty and freshness, the sunlight and verdure of the delightful season, O how different the moral atmosphere amid which I now revise this Volume, from the jocund influences surrounding the growth and advent of LEAVES OF GRASS. *I occupy myself, arranging these pages for publication, still envelopt in thoughts of the death two years since of my dear Mother, the most perfect and magnetic character, the rarest combination of practical, moral and spiritual, and the least selfish, of all and any I have ever known—and by me O so much the most deeply loved. . . . and also under the physical affliction of a tedious attack of paralysis, obstinately lingering and keeping its hold upon me, and quite suspending all bodily activity and comfort. . . . I see now, much clearer than ever—perhaps these experiences were needed to show—how much my former poems, the bulk of them, are indeed the expression of health and strength, the sanest, joyfulest life.]*

Under these influences, therefore, I still feel to keep Passage to India *for last words even to this Centennial dithyramb. Not as, in antiquity, at highest festival of Egypt, the noisome skeleton of Death was also sent on exhibition to the revellers, for zest and shadow to the occasion's joy and light—but as the perfect marble statue of the normal Greeks at Elis, suggesting death in the form of a beautiful and perfect young man, with closed eyes, leaning on an inverted torch—emblem of rest and aspiration after action—of crown and point which all lives and poems should steadily have reference to, namely, the justified and noble termination of our identity, this grade of it, and outlet-preparation to another grade.*

***LEAVES OF GRASS.—*Namely, a Character, making most of common and normal elements, to the superstructure of which not only the precious accumulations of the learning and experiences of the Old World, and the settled social and municipal necessities and current requirements, so long a-building, shall still faithfully contribute, but which, at its foundations and carried up thence, and receiving its impetus from the Democratic spirit, and accepting its gauge, in all departments, from the Democratic formulas, shall again directly be vitalized by the perennial influences of Nature at first hand, and the old heroic stamina of Nature, the strong air of prairie and mountain, the dash of the briny sea, the primary antiseptics—of the passions, in all their fullest heat and potency, of courage, rankness, amativeness, and of immense pride. . . . Not to lose at all, therefore, the benefits of artificial progress and civilization, but to re-occupy for Western tenancy the oldest though ever-fresh fields, and reap from them the savage and sane nourishment indispensable to a hardy nation, and the absence of which, threatening to become worse and worse, is the most serious lack and defect to-day of our New World literature.*

Not but what the brawn of LEAVES OF GRASS *is, I think, thoroughly spiritualized everywhere, for final estimate, but, from the very subjects, the direct effect is a sense of the Life, as it should be, of flesh and blood, and physical urge, and animalism. . . . While there are other themes, and plenty of abstract thoughts and poems in the Volume—While I have put in it (supplemented in the present Work by my prose* Memoranda*) passing and rapid but actual glimpses of the great struggle between Nation and the Slave-power (1861–'65), as the fierce and bloody panorama of that contest unroll'd itself—While the whole Book, indeed, revolves around that Four Years' War, which, as I was in the midst of it, becomes, in* Drum-Taps, *pivotal to the rest entire—follow'd by* Marches now the War is Over*—and here and there, before and afterward, not a few episodes and speculations—*that*—namely, to make a type-portrait for living, active, worldly, healthy Personality, objective as well as subjective, joyful and potent, and modern and free, distinctively for the use of the United States, male and female, through the long future—has been, I say, my general object. (Probably, indeed, the whole of these varied songs, and all my writings, both Volumes, only ring changes in some sort, on the ejaculation, How vast, how eligible, how joyful, how real, is a Human Being, himself or herself.)*

Though from no definite plan at the time, I see now that I have unconsciously sought, by indirections at least as much as directions, to express the whirls and rapid growth and intensity of the United States, the prevailing tendency and events of the Nineteenth Century, and largely the spirit of the whole current World, my time; for I feel that I have partaken of that spirit, as I have been deeply interested in all those events, the closing of long-stretch'd eras and ages, and, illustrated in the history of the United States, the opening of larger ones. (The death of President Lincoln, for instance, fitly, historically closes, in the Civilization of Feudalism, many old influences—drops on them, suddenly, a vast, gloomy, as it were, separating curtain. The world's entire dramas afford none more indicative—none with folds more tragic, or more sombre or far spreading.)

Since I have been ill (1873–74–75), mostly without serious pain, and with plenty of time and frequent inclination to judge my poems (never composed with eye on the book-market, nor for fame, nor for any pecuniary profit), I have felt temporary depression more than once, for fear that in LEAVES OF GRASS *the* moral *parts were not sufficiently pronounc'd. But in my clearest and calmest moods I have realized that as those* LEAVES, *all and several, surely prepare the way for, and necessitate Morals, and are adjusted to them, just the same as Nature does and is, they are what, consistently with my plan, they must and probably should be. . . . (In a certain sense, while the Moral is the purport and last intel-*

ligence of all Nature, there is absolutely nothing of the moral in the works, or laws, or shows of Nature. Those only lead inevitably to it—begin and necessitate it.)

Then I meant LEAVES OF GRASS, *as published, to be the Poem of Identity (of* Yours, *whoever you are, now reading these lines). . . . For genius must realize that, precious as it may be, there is something far more precious, namely, simple Identity, One's-self. A man is not greatest as victor in war, nor inventor or explorer, nor even in science, or in his intellectual or artistic capacity, or exemplar in some vast benevolence. To the highest Democratic view, man is most acceptable in living well the average, practical life and lot which happens to him as ordinary farmer, sea-farer, mechanic, clerk, laborer, or driver upon and from which position as a central basis or pedestal, while performing its labors, and his duties as citizen, son, husband, father and employed person, he preserves his physique, ascends, developing, radiating himself in other regions—and especially where and when (greatest of all, and nobler than the proudest mere genius or magnate in any field) he fully realizes the Conscience, the Spiritual, the divine faculty, cultivated well, exemplified in all his deeds and words, through life, uncompromising to the end—a flight loftier than any of Homer's or Shakspere's—broader than all poems and bibles—namely, Nature's own, and in the midst of it, Yourself, your own Identity, body and soul. (All serves, helps—but in the centre of all, absorbing all, giving, for your purpose, the only meaning and vitality to all, master or mistress of all, under the law, stands Yourself.) . . . . To sing the Song of that divine law of Identity, and of Yourself, consistently with the Divine Law of the Universal, is a main intention of those* LEAVES.

Something more may be added—for, while I am about it, I would make a full confession. I also sent out LEAVES OF GRASS *to arouse and set flowing in men's and women's hearts, young and old (my present and future readers), endless streams of living, pulsating love and friendship, directly from them to myself, now and ever. To this terrible, irrepressible yearning (surely more or less down underneath in most human souls)—this never-satisfied appetite for sympathy, and this boundless offering of sympathy—this universal democratic comradeship—this old, eternal, yet ever-new interchange of adhesiveness, so fitly emblematic of America—I have given in that book, undisguisedly, declaredly, the openest expression. . . . Poetic literature has long been the formal and conventional tender of art and beauty merely, and of a narrow, constipated, special amativeness. I say, the subtlest, sweetest, surest tie between me and Him or Her who, in the pages of* Calamus *and other pieces realizes me—though we never see each other, or though ages and ages hence—must, in this way, be personal affection. And those—be they few, or be they many—are at any rate* my readers *in a sense that belongs not, and can never belong, to better, prouder poems.*

Besides, important as they are in my purpose as emotional expressions for humanity, the special meaning of the Calamus *cluster of* LEAVES OF GRASS *(and more or less running through that book, and cropping out in* Drum-Taps*) mainly resides in its Political significance. In my opinion it is by a fervent, accepted development of Comradeship, the beautiful and sane affection of man for man, latent in all the young fellows, North and South, East and West—it is by this, I say, and by what goes directly and indirectly along with it, that the United States of the future (I cannot too often repeat) are to be most effectually welded together, intercalated, anneal'd into a Living Union.*

Then, for enclosing clue of all, it is imperatively and ever to be borne in mind that LEAVES OF GRASS *entire is not to be construed as an intellectual or scholastic effort or Poem mainly, but more as a radical utterance out of the abysms of the Soul, the Emotions and the Physique—an utterance adjusted to, perhaps born of, Democracy and Modern Science, and in its very nature regardless of the old conventions, and, under the great Laws, following only its own impulses.*

Eidólons

I MET a Seer,
Passing the hues and objects of the world,
The fields of art and learning, pleasure, sense,
To glean Eidólons.

Put in thy chants, said he,
No more the puzzling hour, nor day—nor segments, parts, put in,
Put first before the rest, as light for all, and entrance-song of all,
That of Eidólons.

Ever the dim beginning;
Ever the growth, the rounding of the circle;
Ever the summit, and the merge at last (to surely start again),
Eidólons! Eidólons!

Ever the mutable!
Ever materials, changing, crumbling, re-cohering;
Ever the ateliers, the factories divine,
Issuing Eidólons!

Lo! I or you!
Or woman, man, or State, known or unknown;
We seeming solid wealth, strength, beauty build,
But really build Eidólons.

The ostent evanescent;
The substance of an artist's mood, or savan's studies long,
Or warrior's, martyr's, hero's toils,
To fashion his Eidólon.

Of every human life
(The units gather'd, posted—not a thought, emotion, deed, left out),
The whole, or large or small, summ'd, added up,
In its Eidólon.

The old, old urge;
Based on the ancient pinnacles, lo! newer, higher pinnacles;
From Science and the Modern still impell'd,
The old, old urge, Eidólons.

The present, now and here,
America's busy, teeming, intricate whirl,
Of aggregate and segregate, for only thence releasing,
To-day's Eidólons.

These, with the past,
Of vanish'd lands—of all the reigns of kings across the sea,
Old conquerors, old campaigns, old sailors' voyages,
Joining Eidólons.

Densities, growth, façades,
Strata of mountains, soils, rocks, giant trees,
Far-born, far-dying, living long, to leave,
Eidólons everlasting.

Exaltè, rapt, extatic,
The visible but their womb of birth,
Of orbic tendencies to shape, and shape, and shape,
The mighty Earth-Eidólon.

All space, all time
(The stars, the terrible perturbations of the suns,
Swelling, collapsing, ending—serving their longer, shorter use),
Fill'd with Eidólons only.

The noiseless myriads!
The infinite oceans where the rivers empty!
The separate, countless free identities, like eyesight;
The true realities, Eidólons.

Not this the World,
Nor these the Universes—they the Universes,
Purport and end—ever the permanent life of life,
Eidólons, Eidólons.

Beyond thy lectures, learn'd professor,
Beyond thy telescope or spectroscope, observer keen—beyond all mathematics,

Beyond the doctor's surgery, anatomy—beyond the chemist with his chemistry,
The entities of entities, Eidólons.

Unfix'd, yet fix'd;
Ever shall be—ever have been, and are,
Sweeping the present to the infinite future,
Eidólons, Eidólons, Eidólons.

The prophet and the bard,
Shall yet maintain themselves—in higher stages yet,
Shall mediate to the Modern, to Democracy—interpret yet to them,
God, and Eidólons.

And thee, My Soul!
Joys, ceaseless exercises, exaltations!
The yearning amply fed at last, prepared to meet,
Thy mates, Eidólons.

Thy Body permanent,
The Body lurking there within thy Body,
The only purport of the Form thou art—the real I myself,
An image, an Eidólon.

Thy very songs, not in thy songs;
No special strains to sing—none for itself;
But from the whole resulting, rising at last and floating,
A round full-orb'd Eidólon.

Prayer of Columbus

IT was near the close of his indomitable and pious life—on his last voyage when nearly 70 years of age—that Columbus, to save his two remaining ships from foundering in the Caribbean Sea in a terrible storm, had to run them ashore on the Island of Jamaica—where, laid up for a long and miserable year—1503—he was taken very sick, had several relapses, his men revolted, and death seem'd daily imminent;

though he was eventually rescued, and sent home to Spain to die, unrecognized, neglected and in want. . . . . . It is only ask'd, as preparation and atmosphere for the following lines, that the bare authentic facts be recall'd and realized, and nothing contributed by the fancy. See, the Antillean Island, with its florid skies and rich foliage and scenery, the waves beating the solitary sands, and the hulls of the ships in the distance. See, the figure of the great Admiral, walking the beach, as a stage, in this sublimest tragedy—for what tragedy, what poem, so piteous and majestic as the real scene?—and hear him uttering—as his mystical and religious soul surely utter'd, the ideas following—perhaps, in their equivalents, the very words.

A BATTER'D, wreck'd old man,
Thrown on this savage shore, far, far from home,
Pent by the sea, and dark rebellious brows, twelve dreary months,
Sore, stiff with many toils, sicken'd, and nigh to death,
I take my way along the island's edge,
Venting a heavy heart.

I am too full of woe!
Haply, I may not live another day;
I can not rest, O God—I can not eat or drink or sleep,
Till I put forth myself, my prayer, once more to Thee,
Breathe, bathe myself once more in Thee—commune with Thee,
Report myself once more to Thee.

Thou knowest my years entire, my life
(My long and crowded life of active work—not adoration merely);
Thou knowest the prayers and vigils of my youth;
Thou knowest my manhood's solemn and visionary meditations;
Thou knowest how, before I commenced, I devoted all to come to Thee;
Thou knowest I have in age ratified all those vows, and strictly kept them,
Thou knowest I have not once lost nor faith nor ecstasy in Thee
(In shackles, prison'd, in disgrace, repining not,
Accepting all from Thee—as duly come from Thee).

All my emprises have been fill'd with Thee,
My speculations, plans, begun and carried on in thoughts of Thee,
Sailing the deep, or journeying the land for Thee;
Intentions, purports, aspirations mine—leaving results to Thee.

O I am sure they really came from Thee!
The urge, the ardor, the unconquerable will,
The potent, felt, interior command, stronger than words,
A message from the Heavens, whispering to me even in sleep,
These sped me on.

By me, and these, the work so far accomplish'd (for what has been,
has been);
By me Earth's elder, cloy'd and stifled lands, uncloy'd, unloos'd;
By me the hemispheres rounded and tied—the unknown to the known.

The end I know not—it is all in Thee;
Or small, or great, I know not—haply, what broad fields, what lands;
Haply, the brutish, measureless human undergrowth I know,
Transplanted there, may rise to stature, knowledge worthy Thee;
Haply the swords I know may there indeed be turn'd to reaping-tools,
Haply the lifeless cross I know—Europe's dead cross—may bud
and blossom there.

One effort more—my altar this bleak sand:
That Thou, O God, my life hast lighted,
With ray of light, steady, ineffable, vouchsafed of Thee
(Light rare, untellable—lighting the very light!
Beyond all signs, descriptions, languages!);
For that, O God—be it my latest word—here on my knees,
Old, poor, and paralyzed—I thank Thee.

My terminus near,
The clouds already closing in upon me,
The voyage balk'd—the course disputed, lost,
I yield my ships to Thee.

Steersman unseen! henceforth the helms are Thine;
Take Thou command (what to my petty skill Thy navigation?).

My hands, my limbs grow nerveless;
My brain feels rack'd, bewilder'd;
Let the old timbers part—I will not part!
I will cling fast to Thee, O God, though the waves buffet me;
Thee, Thee, at least, I know.

Is it the prophet's thought I speak, or am I raving?
What do I know of life? what of myself?
I know not even my own work, past or present;
Dim, ever-shifting guesses of it spread before me,
Of newer, better worlds, their mighty parturition,
Mocking, perplexing me.

And these things I see suddenly—what mean they?
As if some miracle, some hand divine unseal'd my eyes,
Shadowy, vast shapes smile through the air and sky,
And on the distant waves sail countless ships,
And anthems in new tongues I hear saluting me.

To a Locomotive in Winter

THEE for my recitative!
Thee in the driving storm, even as now—the snow—
the winter-day declining;
Thee in thy panoply, thy measured dual throbbing,
and thy beat convulsive;
Thy black cylindric body, golden brass, and silvery steel;
Thy ponderous side-bars, parallel and connecting rods, gyrating,
shuttling at thy sides;
Thy metrical, now swelling pant and roar—now tapering in the distance;
Thy great protruding head-light, fix'd in front;
Thy long, pale, floating vapor-pennants, tinged with delicate purple;
The dense and murky clouds out-belching from thy smoke-stack;
Thy knitted frame—thy springs and valves—the tremulous twinkle
of thy wheels;
Thy train of cars behind, obedient, merrily-following,
Through gale or calm, now swift, now slack, yet steadily careering:
Type of the modern! emblem of motion and power! pulse of the continent!
For once, come serve the Muse, and merge in verse, even as here I see thee,

With storm, and buffeting gusts of wind, and falling snow;
By day, thy warning, ringing bell to sound its notes,
By night, thy silent signal lamps to swing.

Fierce-throated beauty!
Roll through my chant, with all thy lawless music!
        thy swinging lamps at night;
Thy piercing, madly-whistled laughter! thy echoes, rumbling
        like an earthquake, rousing all!
Law of thyself complete, thine own track firmly holding
(No sweetness debonair of tearful harp or glib piano thine);
Thy trills of shrieks by rocks and hills return'd,
Launch'd o'er the prairies wide—across the lakes,
To the free skies, unpent, and glad, and strong.

Wandering at Morn

WANDERING at morn,
        Emerging from the night, from gloomy thoughts—thee in my thoughts,
Yearning for thee, harmonious Union! thee, Singing Bird divine!
Thee, seated coil'd in evil times, my Country, with craft and
        black dismay—with every meanness, treason thrust upon thee;
—Wandering—this common marvel I beheld—the parent thrush I watch'd,
        feeding its young
(The singing thrush, whose tones of joy and faith ecstatic,
Fail not to certify and cheer my soul).

There ponder'd, felt I,
If worms, snakes, loathsome grubs, may to sweet spiritual songs be turn'd,
If vermin so transposed, so used, so bless'd may be,
Then may I trust in you, your fortunes, days, my country;
—Who knows but these may be the lessons fit for you?
From these your future Song may rise, with joyous trills,
Destin'd to fill the world.

With All Thy Gifts

WITH all thy gifts, America
(Standing secure, rapidly tending, overlooking the world),
Power, wealth, extent, vouchsafed to thee—With these,
and like of these, vouchsafed to thee,
What if one gift thou lackest (the ultimate human problem
never solving)?
The gift of Perfect Women fit for thee—What of that gift of gifts
thou lackest?
The towering Feminine of thee? the beauty, health, completion,
fit for thee?
The Mothers fit for thee?

Unpublished Letter To The Foreign Reader

U.S. America
Camden, N. Jersey, April, 1876

To the Foreign Reader, at outset:

Though there is many another influence and chord in the intentions of the following Recitatives, the one that for the purpose of this reprint doubtless o'erdominates the rest is to suggest and help a deeper, stronger (not now political, or business, or intellectual, but) heroic, artistic, and especially emotional, intertwining and affiliation of the Old and New Worlds.

Indeed, the peculiar glory of These

United States I have come to see, or expect to see, not in their geographical or even republican greatness, nor wealth or products, nor military or naval power, nor special, eminent Names in any department (to shine with, or outshine, foreign special names, in similar departments)—but more and more in a vaster, saner, more splendid COMRADESHIP, typifying the People everywhere, uniting closer and closer not only The American States, but all Nations, and all Humanity. (That, O Poets! is not *that* a theme, a Union, worth chanting, striving for? Why not fix our verses henceforth to the gauge of the round globe? the whole race?)

Perhaps the most illustrious culmination of the Modern and of Republicanism may prove to be a signal cluster of joyous, more exalted Bards of Adhesiveness, identically one in soul, but contributed by every nation, each after its distinctive kind. Let me dare here and now to start it. Let the diplomats, as ever, still deeply plan, seeking advantages, proposing treaties between governments, and to bind them, on paper: what I seek is different, simpler. I would inaugurate from America, for this purpose, new formulas, international poems. I have thought that the invisible root out of which the Poetry deepest in, and dearest to, humanity grows, is Friendship. I have thought that both in Patriotism and Song (even amid their grandest shows, past) we have adhered too long to petty limits, and that the time has come to enfold the world.

While my pieces, then, were put forth and sounded especially for my own country, and addressed to democratic needs, I cannot evade the conviction that the substances and subtle ties behind them, and which they celebrate (is it that the American character has enormous Pride and Self-assertion? aye, but underneath, living Good-will and Sympathy, on which the others rest, are far more enormous), belong equally to all countries. And the ambition to waken with them, and in their key, the latest echoes of every land, I here avow.

To begin, therefore, though nor envoy, nor ambassador, nor with any official right, nor commission'd by the President—with only Poet's right, as general simple friend of Man—the right of the Singer, admitted, all ranks all times—I will not repress the impulse I feel (what is it, after all, only one man facing another man, and giving him his hand?) to proffer here, for fittest outset to this Book, to share with the English, the Irish, the Scottish and the Welsh—to highest and to lowest of These Islands—(and why not, launch'd hence, to the mainland, to the Germanic peoples—to France, Spain, Italy, Holland—to Austro-Hungary—to every Scandinavian, every Russ?) the sister's salutation of America from over Sea—the New World's Greeting-word to all, and younger brother's love.

W. W.

Leaves

of

Grass

1881

Whitman posed with a butterfly in 1883. It was not real; the cardboard insect disappeared from the custody of the Library of Congress during World War II. Several valuable Whitman notebooks, in one of which the butterfly was preserved, were rediscovered in 1996 and returned to the Library.

LIBRARY OF CONGRESS

The Dalliance of the Eagles

SKIRTING the river road (my forenoon walk, my rest),
Skyward in air a sudden muffled sound, the dalliance of the eagles,
The rushing amorous contact high in space together,
The clinching interlocking claws, a living, fierce, gyrating wheel,
Four beating wings, two beaks, a swirling mass tight grappling,
In tumbling turning clustering loops, straight downward falling,
Till o'er the river pois'd, the twain yet one, a moment's lull,
A motionless still balance in the air, then parting, talons loosing,
Upward again on slow-firm pinions slanting, their separate diverse flight,
She hers, he his, pursuing.

Italian Music in Dakota

["The Seventeenth—the finest Regimental Band I ever heard."]

THROUGH the soft evening air enwinding all,
Rocks, woods, fort, cannon, pacing sentries, endless wilds,
In dulcet streams, in flutes' and cornets' notes,
Electric, pensive, turbulent, artificial
(Yet strangely fitting even here, meanings unknown before,
Subtler than ever, more harmony, as if born here, related here,
Not to the city's fresco'd rooms, not to the audience of the opera house,
Sounds, echoes, wandering strains, as really here at home,
Sonnambula's innocent love, trios with *Norma's* anguish,
And thy ecstatic chorus *Poliuto*);
Ray'd in the limpid yellow slanting sundown,
Music, Italian music in Dakota.

While Nature, sovereign of this gnarl'd realm,
Lurking in hidden barbaric grim recesses,
Acknowledging rapport however far remov'd
(As some old root or soil of earth its last-born flower or fruit),
Listens well pleas'd.

The Prairie States

A NEWER garden of creation, no primal solitude,
Dense, joyous, modern, populous millions, cities and farms,
With iron interlaced, composite, tied, many in one,
By all the world contributed—freedom's and law's and thrift's society,
The crown and teeming paradise, so far, of time's accumulations,
To justify the past.

A Riddle Song

THAT which eludes this verse and any verse,
Unheard by sharpest ear, unform'd in clearest eye or cunningest mind,
Nor lore nor fame, nor happiness nor wealth,
And yet the pulse of every heart and life throughout the world
incessantly,
Which you and I and all pursuing ever ever miss,
Open but still a secret, the real of the real, an illusion,
Costless, vouchsafed to each, yet never man the owner,
Which poets vainly seek to put in rhyme, historians in prose,
Which sculptor never chisel'd yet, nor painter painted,
Which vocalist never sung, nor orator nor actor ever utter'd,
Invoking here and now I challenge for my song.

Indifferently, 'mid public life, private haunts, in solitude,
Behind the mountain and the wood,
Companion of the city's busiest streets, through the assemblage,
It and its radiations constantly glide.

In looks of fair unconscious babes,
Or strangely in the coffin'd dead,
Or show of breaking dawn or stars by night,
As some dissolving delicate film of dreams,
Hiding yet lingering.

Two little breaths of words comprising it,
Two words, yet all from first to last comprised in it.

How ardently for it!
How many ships have sail'd and sunk for it!
How many travelers started from their homes and ne'er return'd!
How much of genius boldly staked and lost for it!
What countless stores of beauty, love, ventur'd for it!
How all superbest deeds since Time began are traceable to it—
and shall be to the end!
How all heroic martyrdoms to it!
How, justified by it, the horrors, evils, battles of the earth!
How the bright fascinating lambent flames of it, in every age and land,
have drawn men's eyes,
Rich as a sunset on the Norway coast, the sky, the islands, and the cliffs,
Or midnight's silent glowing northern lights unreachable.

Haply God's riddle it, so vague and yet so certain,
The soul for it, and all the visible universe for it,
And heaven at last for it.

Spirit That Form'd This Scene

WRITTEN IN PLATTE CAÑON, COLORADO.

SPIRIT that form'd this scene,
These tumbled rock-piles grim and red,
These reckless heaven-ambitious peaks,
These gorges, turbulent-clear streams, this naked freshness,
These formless wild arrays, for reasons of their own,
I know thee, savage spirit—we have communed together,
Mine too such wild arrays, for reasons of their own;
Was't charged against my chants they had forgotten art?
To fuse within themselves its rules precise and delicatesse?
The lyrist's measur'd beat, the wrought-out temple's grace—
column and polish'd arch forgot?
But thou that revelest here—spirit that form'd this scene,
They have remember'd thee.

A Clear Midnight

THIS is thy hour O Soul, thy free flight into the wordless,
Away from books, away from art, the day erased, the lesson done,
Thee fully forth emerging, silent, gazing, pondering the themes
thou lovest best,
Night, sleep, death and the stars.

November Boughs

1888

(Sands at Seventy)

A studio photograph, circa 1886, of Whitman with Bill Duckett, who was briefly a part of the Mickle Street household as a helper and cart-driver.
THE BAYLEY COLLECTION, OHIO WESLEYAN UNIVERSITY

Preface
"A Backward Glance O'er Travel'd Roads"

PERHAPS the best of songs heard, or of any and all true love, or life's fairest episodes, or sailors', soldiers' trying scenes on land or sea, is the *résumé* of them, or any of them, long afterwards, looking at the actualities away back past, with all their practical excitations gone. How the soul loves to float amid such reminiscences!

So here I sit gossiping in the early candle-light of old age—I and my book—casting backward glances over our travel'd road. After completing, as it were, the journey—(a varied jaunt of years, with many halts and gaps of intervals—or some lengthen'd ship-voyage, wherein more than once the last hour had apparently arrived, and we seem'd certainly going down—yet reaching port in a sufficient way through all discomfitures at last)—After completing my poems, I am curious to review them in the light of their own (at the time unconscious, or mostly unconscious) intentions, with certain unfoldings of the thirty years they seek to embody. These lines, therefore, will probably blend the weft of first purposes and speculations, with the warp of that experience afterwards, always bringing strange developments.

Result of seven or eight stages and struggles extending through nearly thirty years (as I nigh my three-score-and-ten I live largely on memory), I look upon *Leaves of Grass,* now finish'd to the end of its opportunities and powers, as my definitive *carte visite* to the coming generations of the New World,* if I may assume to say so. That I have not gain'd the acceptance of my own time, but have fallen back on fond dreams of the future—anticipations—("still lives the song, though Regnar dies")—That from a worldly and business point of view *Leaves of Grass* has been worse than a failure—that public criticism on the book and myself as author of it yet shows mark'd anger and contempt more than anything else—("I find a solid line of enemies to you everywhere,"—letter from W.S.K., Boston, May 28, 1884)—And that solely for publishing it I have been the object of two or three pretty serious special official buffetings—is all probably no more than I ought to have expected. I had my choice when I commenc'd. I bid neither for soft eulogies, big money returns, nor the approbation of existing schools and conventions. As fulfill'd, or partially fulfill'd, the best comfort of the whole business (after a small band of the dearest friends and upholders ever vouchsafed to man or cause—doubtless all the more faithful and uncompromising—this little phalanx!—for being so few) is that, unstopped and unwarp'd by any influence outside the soul within me, I have had my say entirely my own way, and put it unerringly on record—the value thereof to be decided by time.

In calculating that decision, William O'Connor and Dr. Bucke are far more peremptory than I am. Behind all else that can be said, I consider *Leaves of Grass* and its theory experimental—as, in the deepest sense, I consider our American republic itself to be, with its theory. (I think I have at least enough philosophy not to be too absolutely certain of any thing, or any results.) In the second place, the volume is a *sortie*—whether to prove triumphant, and conquer its field of aim and escape and construction, nothing less than a hundred years from now can fully answer. I consider the point that I have positively gain'd a hearing, to far more than make up for any and all other lacks and withholdings. Essentially, *that* was from the first, and has remain'd throughout, the main object. Now it seems to be achiev'd, I am certainly contented to waive any otherwise momentous drawbacks, as of little account. Candidly and dispassionately reviewing all my intentions, I feel that they were creditable—and I accept the result, whatever it may be.

After continued personal ambition and effort, as a young fellow, to enter with the rest into competition for the usual rewards, business, political, literary, &c.—to take part in the great *mêlée,* both for victory's prize itself and to do some good—After years of those aims and pursuits, I found myself remaining possess'd, at the age of thirty-one to thirty-three, with a special desire and conviction. Or rather, to be quite exact, a desire that had been flitting through my previous life, or hovering on the flanks, mostly indefinite hitherto, had steadily advanced to the front, defined itself, and finally dominated everything else. This was a feeling or ambition to articulate and faithfully express in literary or poetic form, and uncompromisingly, my own physical, emotional, moral, intellectual, and æsthetic Personality, in the midst of, and tallying, the momentous spirit and facts of its immediate days, and of current America—and to exploit that Personality, identified with place and date, in a far more candid and comprehensive sense than any hitherto poem or book.

Perhaps this is in brief, or suggests, all I have sought to do. Given the Nineteenth Century, with the United States, and what they furnish as area and points of view, *Leaves of Grass* is, or seeks to be, simply a faithful and doubtless self-will'd record. In the midst of all, it gives one man's—the author's—identity, ardors, observations, faiths, and thoughts, color'd hardly at all with any decided coloring from other faiths or other identities. Plenty of songs had been sung—beautiful, matchless songs—adjusted to other lands than these—another spirit and stage of evolution; but I would sing, and leave out or put in, quite solely with reference to America and to-day. Modern science and democracy seem'd to be throwing out their challenge to poetry to put them in its statements in contradistinction to the songs and myths of the past. As I see it now (perhaps too late), I have unwittingly taken up that challenge and made an attempt at such statements—which I certainly would not assume to do now, knowing more clearly what it means.

For grounds for *Leaves of Grass,* as a poem, I abandon'd the conventional themes, which do not appear in it: none of the stock ornamentation, or choice plots of love or war, or high, exceptional personages of Old-World song; nothing, as I may say, for beauty's sake—no legend, or myth, or romance, nor euphemism, nor rhyme. But the broadest average of humanity and its identities in the now ripening Nineteenth Century, and especially in each of their countless examples and practical occupations in the United States to-day.

One main contrast of the ideas behind every page of my verses, compared with establish'd poems, is their different relative attitude towards God, towards the objective universe, and still more (by reflection, confession, assumption, &c.) the quite changed attitude of the ego, the one chanting or talking, towards himself and towards his fellow-humanity. It is certainly time for America, above all, to begin this readjustment in the scope and basic point of view of verse; for everything else has changed. As I write, I see in an article on Wordsworth, in one of the current English magazines, the lines, "A few weeks ago an eminent French critic said that, owing to the special tendency to science and to its all-devouring force, poetry would cease to be read in fifty years." But I anticipate the very contrary. Only a firmer, vastly broader, new area begins to exist—nay, is already form'd—to which the poetic genius must emigrate. Whatever may have been the case in years gone by, the true use for the imaginative faculty of modern times is to give ultimate vivification to facts, to science, and to common lives, endowing them with the glows and glories and final illustriousness which belong to every real thing, and to real things only. Without that ultimate vivification—which the poet or other artist alone can give—reality would seem incomplete, and science, democracy, and life itself, finally in vain.

Few appreciate the moral revolutions, our age, which have been profounder far than the material or inventive or war-produced ones. The Nineteenth Century, now well towards its close (and ripening into fruit the seeds of the two preceding centuries**)—the uprisings of national masses and shiftings of boundary-lines—the historical and other prominent facts of the United States—the war of attempted Secession—the stormy rush and haste of nebulous forces—never can future years witness more excitement and din of action—never completer change of army front along the whole line, the whole civilized world. For all these new and evolutionary facts, meanings, purposes, new poetic messages, new forms and expressions, are inevitable.

My Book and I—what a period we have presumed to span! those thirty years from 1850 to '80—and America in them! Proud, proud indeed may we be, if we have cull'd enough of that period in its own spirit to worthily waft a few live breaths of it to the future!

Let me not dare, here or anywhere, for my own purposes, or any purposes, to attempt the definition of Poetry, nor answer the question what it is. Like Religion, Love, Nature, while those terms are indispensable, and we all give a sufficiently accurate meaning to them, in my opinion no definition that has ever been made sufficiently encloses the name Poetry; nor can any rule or convention ever so absolutely obtain but some great exception may arise and disregard and overturn it.

Also it must be carefully remember'd that first-class literature does not shine by any luminosity of its own; nor do its poems. They grow of circumstances, and are evolutionary. The actual living light is always curiously from elsewhere—follows unaccountable sources, and is lunar and relative at the best. There are, I know, certain controlling themes that seem endlessly appropriated to the poets—as war, in the past—in the Bible, religious rapture and adoration—always love, beauty some fine plot, or pensive or other emotion. But, strange as it may sound at first, I will say there is something striking far deeper and towering far higher than those themes for the best elements of modern song.

Just as all the old imaginative works rest, after their kind, on long trains of presuppositions, often entirely unmention'd by themselves, yet supplying the most important bases of them, and without which they could have had no reason for being, so *Leaves of Grass,* before a line was written, presupposed something different from any other, and, as it stands, is the result of such presupposition. I should say, indeed, it were useless to attempt reading the book without first carefully tallying that preparatory background and quality in the mind. Think of the United States to-day—the facts of these thirty-eight or forty empires solder'd in one—sixty or seventy millions of equals, with their lives, their passions, their future—these incalculable, modern, American, seething multitudes around us, of which we are inseparable parts! Think, in comparison, of the petty environage and limited area of the poets of past or present Europe, no matter how great their genius. Think of the absence and ignorance, in all cases hitherto, of the multitudinousness, vitality, and the unprecedented stimulants of to-day and here. It almost seems as if a poetry with cosmic and dynamic features of magnitude and limitlessness suitable to the human soul, were never possible before. It is certain that a poetry of absolute faith and equality for the use of the democratic masses never was.

In estimating first-class song, a sufficient Nationality, or, on the other hand, what may be call'd the negative and lack of it (as in Goethe's case, it sometimes seems to me), is often, if not always, the first element. One needs only a little penetration to see, at more or less removes, the material facts of their country and radius, with the coloring of the moods of humanity at the time, and its gloomy or hopeful prospects, behind all poets and each poet, and forming their birthmarks. I know very well that my *Leaves* could not possibly have emerged or been fashion'd or completed, from any other era than the latter half of the Nineteenth Century, nor any other land than democratic America, and from the absolute triumph of the National Union arms.

And whether my friends claim it for me or not, I know well enough, too, that in respect to pictorial talent, dramatic situations, and especially in verbal melody and all the conventional technique of poetry, not only the divine works that to-day stand ahead in the world's reading, but dozens more, transcend (some of them immeasurably transcend) all I have done, or could do. But it seem'd to me, as the objects in Nature, the themes of æstheticism, and all special exploitations of the mind and soul, involve not only their own inherent quality, but the quality, just as inherent and important, of *their point of view,**** the time had come to reflect all themes and things, old and new, in the lights thrown on them by the advent of America and democracy—to chant those themes through the utterance of one, not only the grateful and reverent legatee of the past, but the born child of the New World—to illustrate all through the genesis and ensemble of to-day; and that such illustration and ensemble are the chief demands of America's prospective imaginative literature. Not to carry out, in the approved style, some choice plot of fortune or misfortune, or fancy, or fine thoughts, or incidents, or courtesies—all of which has been done overwhelmingly and well, probably never to be excell'd—but that while in such æsthetic presentation of objects, passions, plots, thoughts, &c., our lands and days do not want, and probably will never have, anything better than they already possess from the bequests of the past, it still remains to be said that there is even towards all those a subjective and contemporary point of view appropriate to ourselves alone, and to our new genius and environments, different from anything hitherto; and that such conception of current or gone-by life and art is for us the only means of their assimilation consistent with the Western world.

Indeed, and anyhow, to put it specifically, has not the time arrived when (if it must be plainly said, for democratic America's sake, if for no other) there must imperatively come a readjustment of the whole theory and nature of Poetry? The question is important, and I may turn the argument over and repeat it: Does not the best thought of our day and Republic conceive of a birth and spirit of song superior to anything past or present? To the effectual and moral consolidation of our lands (already, as materially establish'd, the greatest factors in known history, and far, far greater through what they prelude and necessitate, and are to be in future)—to conform with and build on the concrete realities and theories of the universe furnish'd by science, and henceforth the only irrefragable basis for anything, verse included—to root both influences in the emotional and imaginative action of the modern time, and dominate all that precedes or opposes them—is not either a radical advance and step forward, or a new verteber of the best song indispensable?

The New World receives with joy the poems of the antique, with European feudalism's rich fund of epics, plays, ballads—seeks not in the least to deaden or displace those voices from our ear and area—holds them indeed as indispensable studies, influences, records, comparisons. But though the dawn-dazzle of the sun of literature is in those poems for us to-day—though perhaps the best parts of current character in nations, social groups, or any man's or woman's individuality, Old World or New, are from them—and though if I were ask'd to name the most precious bequest to current American civilization from all the hitherto ages, I am not sure but what I would name those old and less old songs ferried hither from east and west—some serious words and debits remain; some acrid considerations demand a hearing. Of the great poems receiv'd from abroad and from the ages, and to-day enveloping and penetrating America, is there one that is consistent with these United States, or essentially applicable to them as they are and are to be? Is there one whose underlying basis is not a denial and insult to democracy? What a comment it forms, anyhow, on this era of literary fulfilment, with the splendid day-rise of science and resuscitation of history, that our chief religious and poetical works are not our own, nor adapted to our light, but have been furnish'd by far-back ages out of their arriere and darkness, or, at most, twilight dimness! What is there in those works that so imperiously and scornfully dominates all our advanced civilization, and culture?

Even Shakspere, who so suffuses current letters and art (which indeed have in most degrees grown out of him), belongs essentially to the buried past. Only he holds the proud distinction, for certain important phases of that past, of being the loftiest of the singers life has yet given voice to. All, however, relate to and rest upon conditions, standards, politics, sociologies, ranges of belief, that have been quite eliminated from the Eastern hemisphere, and never existed at all in the Western. As authoritative types of song they belong in America just about as much as the persons and institutes they depict. True, it may be said, the emotional, moral, and æsthetic natures of humanity have not radically changed—that in these the old poems apply to our times and all times, irrespective of date; and that they are of incalculable value as pictures of the past. I willingly make those admissions, and to their fullest extent; then advance the points herewith as of serious, even paramount importance.

I have indeed put on record elsewhere my reverence and eulogy for those never-to-be-excell'd poetic bequests, and their indescribable preciousness as heirlooms for America. Another and separate point must now be candidly stated. If I had not stood before those poems with uncover'd head, fully aware of their colossal grandeur and beauty of form and spirit, I could not have written *Leaves of Grass*. My verdict and conclusions as illustrated in its pages are arrived at through the temper and inculcation of the old works as much as through anything else—perhaps more than through anything else. As America fully and fairly construed is the legitimate result and evolutionary outcome of the past, so I would dare to claim for my verse. Without stopping to qualify the averment, the Old World has had the poems of myths, fictions, feudalism, conquest, caste, dynastic wars, and splendid exceptional characters and affairs, which have been great; but the New World needs the poems of realities and science and of the democratic average and basic equality, which shall be greater. In the centre of all, and object of all, stands the Human Being, towards whose heroic and spiritual evolution poems and everything directly or indirectly tend, Old World or New.

Continuing the subject, my friends have more than once suggested—or may be the garrulity of advancing age is possessing me—some further embryonic facts of *Leaves of Grass*, and especially how I enter'd upon them. Dr. Bucke has, in his volume, already fully and fairly described the preparation of my poetic field, with the particular and general plowing, planting, seeding, and occupation of the ground, till everything was fertilized, rooted, and ready to start its own way for good or bad. Not till after this, did I attempt any serious acquaintance with poetic literature. Along in my sixteenth year I had become the possessor of a stout, well-cramm'd one thousand page octavo volume (I have it yet) containing Walter Scott's poetry entire—an inexhaustible mine and treasury of poetic forage (especially the endless forests and jungles of notes)—had been so to me for fifty years, and remains so to this day.†

Later, at intervals, summer and falls, I used to go off, sometimes for a week at a stretch, down in the country, or to Long Island's seashores—there, in the presence of outdoor influences, I went over thoroughly the Old and New Testaments, and absorb'd (probably to better advantage for me than in any library or indoor room—it makes such difference *where* you read) Shakspere, Ossian, the best translated versions I could get of Homer, Eschylus, Sophocles, the old German Nibelungen, the ancient Hindoo poems, and one or two other masterpieces, Dante's among them. As it happen'd, I read the latter mostly in an old wood. The Iliad (Buckley's prose version) I read first thoroughly on the peninsula of Orient, northeast end of Long Island, in a shelter'd hollow of rocks and sand, with the sea on each side. (I have wonder'd since why I was not overwhelm'd by those mighty masters. Likely because I read them, as described, in the full presence of Nature, under the sun, with the far-spreading landscape and vistas, or the sea rolling in.)

Toward the last I had among much else look'd over Edgar Poe's poems—of which I was not an admirer, tho' I always saw that beyond their limited range of melody (like perpetual chimes of music bells, ringing from lower *b* flat up to *g*) they were melodious expressions, and perhaps never excell'd ones, of certain pronounc'd phases of human morbidity. (The Poetic area is very spacious—has room for all—has so many mansions!) But I was repaid in Poe's prose by the idea that (at any rate for our occasions, our day) there can be no such thing as a long poem. The same thought had been haunting my mind before, but Poe's argument, though short, work'd the sum out and proved it to me.

Another point had an early settlement, clearing the ground greatly. I saw, from the time my enterprise and questionings positively shaped themselves (how best can I express my own distinctive era and surroundings, America, Democracy?), that the trunk and centre whence the answer was to radiate, and to which all should return from straying however far a distance, must be an identical body and soul, a personality—which personality, after many considerations and ponderings I deliberately settled should be myself—indeed could not be any other. I also felt strongly (whether I have shown it or not) that to the true and full estimate of the Present both the Past and the Future are main considerations.

These, however, and much more might have gone on and come to naught (almost positively would have come to naught) if a sudden, vast, terrible, direct and indirect stimulus for new and national declamatory expression had not been given to me. It is certain, I say, that, although I had made a start before, only from the occurrence of the Secession War, and what it show'd me as by flashes of lightning, with the emotional depths it sounded and arous'd (of course, I don't mean in my own heart only, I saw it just as plainly in others, in millions)—that only from the strong flare and provocation of that war's sights and scenes the final reasons-for-being of an autochthonic and passionate song definitely came forth.

I went down to the war fields in Virginia (end of 1862), lived thenceforward in camp—saw great battles and the days and nights afterward—partook of all the fluctuations, gloom, despair, hopes again arous'd, courage evoked—death readily risk'd—*the cause,* too—along and filling those agonistic and lurid following years, 1863–'64–'65—the real parturition years (more than 1776–83) of this henceforth homogeneous Union. Without those three or four years and the experiences they gave, *Leaves of Grass* would not now be existing.

But I set out with the intention also of indicating or hinting some point-characteristics which I since see (though I did not then, at least not definitely) were bases and object-urgings toward those *Leaves* from the first. The word I myself put primarily for the description of them as they stand at last, is the word Suggestiveness. I round and finish little, if anything; and could not, consistently with my scheme. The reader will always have his or her part to do, just as much as I have had mine. I seek less to state or display any theme or thought, and more to bring you, reader, into the atmosphere of the theme or thought—there to pursue your own flight. Another impetus-word is Comradeship as for all lands, and in a more commanding and acknowledg'd sense than hitherto. Other word-signs would be Good Cheer, Content, and Hope.

The chief trait of any given poet is always the spirit he brings to the observation of Humanity and Nature—the mood out of which he contemplates his subjects. What kind of temper and what amount of faith report these things? Up to how recent a date is the song carried? What the equipment, and special raciness of the singer—what his tinge of coloring?

The last value of artistic expressers, past and present—Greek æsthetes, Shakspere—or in our own day Tennyson, Victor Hugo, Carlyle, Emerson—is certainly involv'd in such questions. I say the profoundest service that poems or any other writings can do for their reader is not merely to satisfy the intellect, or supply something polish'd and interesting, nor even to depict great passions, or persons or events, but to fill him with vigorous and clean manliness, religiousness, and give him *good heart* as a radical possession and habit. The educated world seems to have been growing more and more ennuyed for ages, leaving to our time the inheritance of it all. Fortunately there is the original inexhaustible fund of buoyancy, normally resident in the race, forever eligible to be appeal'd to and relied on.

As for native American individuality, though certain to come, and on a large scale, the distinctive and ideal type of Western character (as consistent with the operative political and even money-making features of United States' humanity in the Nineteenth Century as chosen knights, gentlemen and warriors were the ideal of the centuries of European feudalism) it has not yet appear'd. I have allow'd the stress of my poems from beginning to end to bear upon American individuality and assist it—not only because that is a great lesson in Nature, amid all her generalizing laws, but as counterpoise to the leveling tendencies of Democracy—and for other reasons. Defiant of ostensible literary and other conventions, I avowedly chant "the great pride of man in himself," and permit it to be more or less a *motif* of nearly all my verse. I think this pride indispensable to an American. I think it not inconsistent with obedience, humility, deference, and self-questioning.

Democracy has been so retarded and jeopardized by powerful personalities, that its first instincts are fain to clip, conform, bring in stragglers, and reduce everything to a dead level. While the ambitious thought of my song is to help the forming of a great aggregate Nation, it is, perhaps, altogether through the forming of myriads of fully develop'd and enclosing individuals. Welcome as are equality's and fraternity's doctrines and popular education, a certain liability accompanies them all, as we see. That primal and interior something in man, in his soul's abysms, coloring all, and, by exceptional fruitions, giving the last majesty to him—something continually touch'd upon and attain'd by the old poems and ballads of feudalism, and often the principal foundation of them—modern science and democracy appear to be endangering, perhaps eliminating. But that forms an appearance only; the reality is quite different. The new influences, upon the whole, are surely preparing the way for grander individualities than ever. To-day and here personal force is behind everything, just the same. The times and depictions from the Iliad to Shakspere inclusive can happily never again be realized—but the elements of courageous and lofty manhood are unchanged.

Without yielding an inch the working-man and working-woman were to be in my pages from first to last. The ranges of heroism and loftiness with which Greek and feudal poets endow'd their god-like or lordly born characters—indeed prouder and better based and with fuller ranges than those—I was to endow the democratic averages of America. I was to show that we, here and to-day, are eligible to the grandest and the best—more eligible now than any times of old were. I will also want my utterances (I said to myself before beginning) to be in spirit the poems of the morning. (They have been founded and mainly written in the sunny forenoon and early midday of my life.) I will want them to be the poems of women entirely as much as men. I have wish'd to put the complete Union of the States in my songs without any preference or partiality whatever. Henceforth, if they live and are read, it must be just as much South as North—just as much along the Pacific as Atlantic—in the valley of the Mississippi, in Canada, up in Maine, down in Texas, and on the shores of Puget Sound.

From another point of view *Leaves of Grass* is avowedly the song of Sex and Amativeness, and even Animality—though meanings that do not usually go along with those words are behind all, and will duly emerge;

and all are sought to be lifted into a different light and atmosphere. Of this feature, intentionally palpable in a few lines, I shall only say the espousing principle of those lines so gives breath of life to my whole scheme that the bulk of the pieces might as well have been left unwritten were those lines omitted. Difficult as it will be, it has become, in my opinion, imperative to achieve a shifted attitude from superior men and women towards the thought and fact of sexuality, as an element in character, personality, the emotions, and a theme in literature. I am not going to argue the question by itself; it does not stand by itself. The vitality of it is altogether in its relations, bearings, significance—like the clef of a symphony. At last analogy the lines I allude to, and the spirit in which they are spoken, permeate all *Leaves of Grass,* and the work must stand or fall with them, as the human body and soul must remain as an entirety.

Universal as are certain facts and symptoms of communities or individuals all times, there is nothing so rare in modern conventions and poetry as their normal recognizance. Literature is always calling in the doctor for consultation and confession, and always giving evasions and swathing suppressions in place of that "heroic nudity"†† on which only a genuine diagnosis of serious cases can be built. And in respect to editions of *Leaves of Grass* in time to come (if there should be such) I take occasion now to confirm those lines with the settled convictions and deliberate renewals of thirty years, and to hereby prohibit, as far as word of mine can do so, any elision of them.

Then still a purpose enclosing all, and over and beneath all. Ever since what might be call'd thought, or the budding of thought, fairly began in my youthful mind, I had had a desire to attempt some worthy record of that entire faith and acceptance ("to justify the ways of God to man" is Milton's well-known and ambitious phrase) which is the foundation of moral America. I felt it all as positively then in my young days as I do now in my old ones; to formulate a poem whose every thought or fact should directly or indirectly be or connive at an implicit belief in the wisdom, health, mystery, beauty of every process, every concrete object, every human or other existence, not only consider'd from the point of view of all, but of each.

While I can not understand it or argue it out, I fully believe in a clue and purpose in Nature, entire and several; and that invisible spiritual results, just as real and definite as the visible, eventuate all concrete life and all materialism, through Time. My book ought to emanate buoyancy and gladness legitimately enough, for it was grown out of those elements, and has been the comfort of my life since it was originally commenced.

One main genesis-motive of the *Leaves* was my conviction (just as strong to-day as ever) that the crowning growth of the United States is to be spiritual and heroic. To help start and favor that growth—or even to call attention to it, or the need of it—is the beginning, middle and final purpose of the poems. (In fact, when really cipher'd out and summ'd to the last, plowing up in earnest the interminable average fallows of humanity—not "good government" merely, in the common sense—is the justification and main purpose of these United States.)

Isolated advantages in any rank or grace or fortune—the direct or indirect threads of all the poetry of the past—are in my opinion distasteful to the republican genius, and offer no foundation for its fitting verse. Establish'd poems, I know, have the very great advantage of chanting the already perform'd, so full of glories, reminiscences dear to the minds of men. But my volume is a candidate for the future. "All original art," says Taine, anyhow, "is self-regulated, and no original art can be regulated from without; it carries its own counterpoise, and does not receive it from elsewhere—lives on its own blood"—a solace to my frequent bruises and sulky vanity.

As the present is perhaps mainly an attempt at personal statement or illustration, I will allow myself as further help to extract the following anecdote from a book, *Annals of Old Painters,* conn'd by me in youth. Rubens, the Flemish painter, in one of his wanderings through the galleries of old convents, came across a singular work. After looking at it thoughtfully for a good while, and listening to the criticisms of his suite of students, he said to the latter, in answer to their questions (as to what school the work implied or belong'd), "I do not believe the artist, unknown and perhaps no longer living, who has given the world this legacy, ever belong'd to any school, or ever painted anything but this one picture, which is a personal affair—a piece out of a man's life."

Leaves of Grass indeed (I cannot too often reiterate) has mainly been the outcropping of my own emotional and other personal nature—an attempt, from first to last, to put a *Person,* a human being (myself, in the latter half of the Nineteenth Century, in America), freely, fully and truly on record. I could not find any similar personal record in current literature that satisfied me. But it is not on *Leaves of Grass* distinctively as *literature,* or a specimen thereof, that I feel to dwell, or advance claims. No one will get at my verses who insists upon viewing them as a literary performance, or attempt at such performance, or as aiming mainly toward art or æstheticism.

I say no land or people or circumstances ever existed so needing a race of singers and poems differing from all others, and rigidly their own, as the land and people and circumstances of our United States need such singers and poems to-day, and for the future. Still further, as long as the States continue to absorb and be dominated by the poetry of the Old World, and remain unsupplied with autochthonous song, to express, vitalize and give color to and define their material and political success, and minister to them distinctively, so long will they stop short of first-class Nationality and remain defective.

In the free evening of my day I give to you, reader, the foregoing garrulous talk, thoughts, reminiscences,

As idly drifting down the ebb,
Such ripples, half-caught voices,
echo from the shore.

Concluding with two items for the imaginative genius of the West, when it worthily rises—First, what Herder taught to the young Goethe, that really great poetry is always (like the Homeric or Biblical canticles) the result of a national spirit, and not the privilege of a polish'd and select few; Second, that the strongest and sweetest songs yet remain to be sung.

**When Champollion, on his death-bed, handed to the printer the revised proof of his* Egyptian Grammar, *he said gayly, "Be careful of this—it is my* carte de visite *to posterity."* [All notes are Whitman's.]

***The ferment and germination even of the United States to-day, dating back to, and in my opinion mainly founded on, the Elizabethan age in English history, the age of Francis Bacon and Shakspere. Indeed, when we pursue it, what growth or advent is there that does not date back, back, until lost—perhaps its most tantalizing clues lost—in the receded horizons of the past?*

****According to Immanuel Kant, the last essential reality, giving shape and significance to all the rest.*

†*Sir Walter Scott's* Complete Poems; *especially including* Border Minstrelsy; *then Sir Tristrem; Lay of the Last Minstrel; Ballads from the German; Marmion; Lady of the Lake; Vision of Don Roderick; Lord of the Isles; Rokeby; Bridal of Triermain; Field of Waterloo; Harold the Dauntless; all the Dramas; various Introductions, endless interesting Notes, and Essays on Poetry, Romance, &c.*

Lockhart's 1833 (or '34) edition with Scott's latest and copious revisions and annotations. (All the poems were thoroughly read by me, but the ballads of the Border Minstrelsy over and over again.)

††Nineteenth Century, *July, 1883.*

Horace Traubel in his early thirties when he visited Whitman almost daily. From March 1888 to the poet's death in March 1892, Traubel recorded verbatim several million words of conversation with Whitman; their full publication, in nine volumes, was completed in 1996.
LIBRARY OF CONGRESS

Mannahatta

MY city's fit and noble name resumed,
Choice aboriginal name, with marvellous beauty, meaning,
A rocky founded island—shores where ever gayly dash
the coming, going, hurrying sea waves.

A Carol Closing Sixty-Nine

A CAROL closing sixty-nine—a *résumé*—a repetition,
My lines in joy and hope continuing on the same,
Of ye, O God, Life, Nature, Freedom, Poetry;
Of you, my Land—your rivers, prairies, States—
you, mottled Flag I love,
Your aggregate retain'd entire—Of north, south, east and west,
your items all;
Of me myself—the jocund heart yet beating in my breast,
The body wreck'd, old, poor and paralyzed—the strange inertia
falling pall-like round me,
The burning fires down in my sluggish blood not yet extinct,
The undiminish'd faith—the groups of loving friends.

A Font of Type

THIS latent mine—these unlaunch'd voices—passionate powers,
Wrath, argument, or praise, or comic leer, or prayer devout
(Not nonpareil, brevier, bourgeois, long primer merely),°
These ocean waves arousable to fury and to death,
Or sooth'd to ease and sheeny sun and sleep,
Within the pallid slivers slumbering.

As I Sit Writing Here

As I sit writing here, sick and grown old,
Not my least burden is that dulness of the years, querilities,
Ungracious glooms, aches, lethargy, constipation, whimpering *ennui,*
May filter in my daily songs.

Queries to My Seventieth Year

Approaching, nearing, curious,
Thou dim, uncertain spectre—bringest thou life or death?
Strength, weakness, blindness, more paralysis and heavier?
Or placid skies and sun? Wilt stir the waters yet?
Or haply cut me short for good? Or leave me here as now,
Dull, parrot-like and old, with crack'd voice harping, screeching?

America

Centre of equal daughters, equal sons,
All, all alike endear'd, grown, ungrown, young or old,
Strong, ample, fair, enduring, capable, rich,
Perennial with the Earth, with Freedom, Law and Love,
A grand, sane, towering, seated Mother,
Chair'd in the adamant of Time.

After the Dazzle of Day

AFTER the dazzle of day is gone,
Only the dark, dark night shows to my eyes the stars;
After the clangor of organ majestic, or chorus, or perfect band,
Silent, athwart my soul, moves the symphony true.

Halcyon Days

NOT from successful love alone,
Nor wealth, nor honor'd middle age, nor victories of politics or war;
But as life wanes, and all the turbulent passions calm,
As gorgeous, vapory, silent hues cover the evening sky,
As softness, fulness, rest, suffuse the frame, like freshier, balmier air,
As the days take on a mellower light, and the apple at last hangs
really finish'd and indolent-ripe on the tree,
Then for the teeming quietest, happiest days of all!
The brooding and blissful halcyon days!

Of That Blithe Throat of Thine

[More than eighty-three degrees north—about a good day's steaming distance to the Pole by one of our fast oceaners in clear water—Greely the explorer heard the song of a single snow-bird merrily sounding over the desolation.]

OF that blithe throat of thine from arctic bleak and blank,
I'll mind the lesson, solitary bird—let me too welcome chilling drifts,
E'en the profoundest chill, as now—a torpid pulse, a brain unnerv'd,
Old age land-lock'd within its winter bay (cold, cold, O cold!)—
These snowy hairs, my feeble arm, my frozen feet,
For them thy faith, thy rule I take, and grave it to the last;
Not summer's zones alone—not chants of youth,
 or south's warm tides alone,
But held by sluggish floes, pack'd in the northern ice,
 the cumulus of years,
These with gay heart I also sing.

Broadway

WHAT hurrying human tides, or day or night!
What passions, winnings, losses, ardors, swim thy waters!
What whirls of evil, bliss and sorrow, stem thee!
What curious questioning glances—glints of love!
Leer, envy, scorn, contempt, hope, aspiration!
Thou portal—thou arena—thou of the myriad long-drawn lines and groups!
(Could but thy flagstones, curbs, façades, tell their inimitable tales;
Thy windows rich, and huge hotels—thy side-walks wide.)
Thou of the endless sliding, mincing, shuffling feet!
Thou, like the parti-colored world itself—
 like infinite, teeming, mocking life!
Thou visor'd, vast, unspeakable show and lesson!

To Get the Final Lilt of Songs

To get the final lilt of songs,
To penetrate the inmost lore of poets—to know the mighty ones;
Job, Homer, Eschylus, Dante, Shakspere, Tennyson, Emerson;
To diagnose the shifting-delicate tints of love and pride and doubt—
to truly understand,
To encompass these, the last keen faculty and entrance-price,
Old age, and what it brings from all its past experiences.

The Dead Tenor

As down the stage again,
With Spanish hat and plumes, and gait inimitable,
Back from the fading lessons of the past, I'd call, I'd tell and own,
How much from thee! the revelation of the singing voice from thee!
(So firm—so liquid-soft—again that tremulous, manly timbre!
The perfect singing voice—deepest of all to me the lesson—
trial and test of all.)
How through those strains distill'd—how the rapt ears, the soul of me,
absorbing
Fernando's heart, *Manrico's* passionate call, *Ernani's,* sweet *Gennaro's,*
I fold thenceforth, or seek to fold, within my chants transmuting,
Freedom's and Love's and Faith's unloos'd cantabile
(As perfume's, color's, sunlight's correlation):
From these, for these, with these, a hurried line, dead tenor,
A wafted autumn leaf, dropt in the closing grave, the shovel'd earth,
To memory of thee.

Yonnondio

[The sense of the word is *lament for the aborigines.* It is an Iroquois term; and has been used for a personal name.]

A SONG, a poem of itself—the word itself a dirge,
Amid the wilds, the rocks, the storm and wintry night,
To me such misty, strange tableaux the syllables calling up;
Yonnondio—I see, far in the west or north, a limitless ravine, with plains and mountains dark,
I see swarms of stalwart chieftains, medicine-men, and warriors,
As flitting by like clouds of ghosts, they pass and are gone in the twilight
(Race of the woods, the landscapes free, and the falls!
No picture, poem, statement, passing them to the future):
Yonnondio! Yonnondio!—unlimn'd they disappear;
To-day gives place, and fades—the cities, farms, factories fade;
A muffled sonorous sound, a wailing word is borne through the air for a moment,
Then blank and gone and still, and utterly lost.

Life and Death

THE two old, simple problems ever intertwined,
Close home, elusive, present, baffled, grappled.
By each successive age insoluble, pass'd on,
To ours to-day—and we pass on the same.

A Prairie Sunset

SHOT gold, maroon and violet, dazzling silver, emerald, fawn,
The earth's whole amplitude and Nature's multiform power
consign'd for once to colors;
The light, the general air possess'd by them—colors till now unknown,
No limit, confine—not the Western sky alone—the high meridian—
North, South, all,
Pure luminous color fighting the silent shadows to the last.

Twilight

THE soft voluptuous opiate shades,
The sun just gone, the eager light dispell'd
(I too will soon be gone, dispell'd),—
A haze—nirwana—rest and night—oblivion.

Now Precedent Songs, Farewell

NOW precedent songs, farewell—by every name farewell
(Trains of a staggering line in many a strange procession, waggons,
From ups and downs—with intervals—from elder years, mid-age,
or youth),
"In Cabin'd Ships," or "Thee Old Cause" or "Poets to Come,"
Or "Paumanok," "Song of Myself," "Calamus," or "Adam,"
Or "Beat! Beat! Drums!" or "To the Leaven'd Soil they Trod,"
Or "Captain! My Captain!" "Kosmos," "Quicksand Years,"
or "Thoughts,"
"Thou Mother with thy Equal Brood," and many, many more
unspecified,
From fibre heart of mine—from throat and tongue—
(My life's hot pulsing blood,
The personal urge and form for me—not merely paper,
automatic type and ink),
Each song of mine—each utterance in the past—
having its long, long history,
Of life or death, or soldier's wound, of country's loss or safety
(O heaven! what flash and started endless train of all!
compared indeed to that!
What wretched shred e'en at the best of all!)

After the Supper and Talk

AFTER the supper and talk—after the day is done,
As a friend from friends his final withdrawal prolonging,
Good-bye and Good-bye with emotional lips repeating
(So hard for his hand to release those hands—no more will they meet,
No more for communion of sorrow and joy, of old and young,
A far-stretching journey awaits him, to return no more),
Shunning, postponing severance—seeking to ward off the last word
ever so little,
E'en at the exit-door turning—charges superfluous calling back
e'en as he descends the steps,
Something to eke out a minute additional—shadows of nightfall
deepening,
Farewells, messages lessening—dimmer the forthgoer's visage
and form,
Soon to be lost for aye in the darkness—loth, O so loth to depart!
Garrulous to the very last.

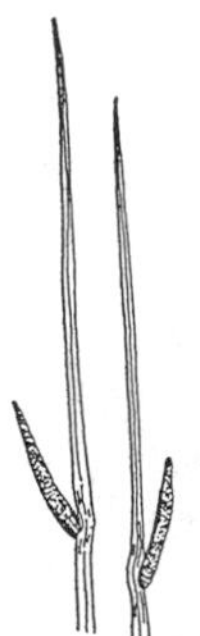

Note at End
Complete Poems and Prose (1888)

As I conclude—and (to get typographical correctness) after running my eyes diligently through the three big divisions of the preceding volume—the interrogative wonder-fancy rises in me whether (if it be not too arrogant to even state it) the 33 years of my current time, 1855–1888, with their aggregate of our New World doings and people, have not, indeed, created and formulated the foregoing leaves—forcing their utterance as the pages stand—coming actually from the direct urge and developments of those years, and not from any individual epic or lyrical attempts whatever, or from my pen or voice, or any body's special voice. Out of that supposition, the book might assume to be consider'd an autochthonic record and expression, freely render'd, of and out of these 30 to 35 years—of the soul and evolution of America—and of course, by reflection, not ours only, but more or less of the common people of the world. . . . . Seems to me I may dare to claim a deep native tap-root for the book, too, in some sort. I came on the stage too late for personally knowing much of even the lingering Revolutionary worthies—the men of '76. Yet, as a little boy, I have been press'd tightly and lovingly to the breast of Lafayette (Brooklyn, 1825) and have talk'd with old Aaron Burr, and also with those who knew Washington and his surroundings, and with original Jeffersonians, and more than one very old soldier and sailor. And in my own day and maturity, my eyes have seen, and ears heard, Lincoln, Grant and Emerson, and my hands have been grasp'd by their hands. Though in a different field and range from most of theirs, I give the foregoing pages as perfectly legitimate, resultant, evolutionary and consistent with them. If these lines should ever reach some reader of a far off future age, let him take them as a missive sent from Abraham Lincoln's fateful age. . . . Repeating, parrot-like, what in the preceding divisions has been already said, and must serve as a great reason-why of this whole book—1st, That the main part about pronounc'd events and shows (poems and persons also) is the point of view from which they are view'd and estimated—and 2d, That I cannot let my momentous, stormy, peculiar Era of peace and war, these States, these years, slip away without arresting some of its specimen events—even its vital breaths—to be portray'd and inscribed from out of the midst of it, from its own days and nights—not so much in themselves (statistically and descriptively our times are copiously noted and memorialized with an industrial zeal)—but to give from them here their flame-like results in imaginative and spiritual suggestiveness—as they present themselves to me, at any rate, from the point of view alluded to.

Then a few additional words yet to this hurried farewell note. In another sense (the warp crossing the woof, and knitted in), the book is probably a sort of autobiography; an element I have not attempted to specially restrain or erase. As alluded to at beginning, I had about got the volume well started by the printers, when a sixth recurrent attack of my war-paralysis fell upon me. It has proved the most serious and continued of the whole. I am now uttering *November Boughs,* and printing this book, in my 70th year. To get out the collection—mainly the born results of health, flush of life, buoyancy, and happy outdoor volition—and to prepare the *Boughs*—have beguiled my invalid months the past summer and fall. ("Are we to be beaten down in our old age?" says one white-hair'd fellow remonstratingly to another in a budget of letters

I read last night.) . . . Then I have wanted to leave something markedly *personal.* I have put my name with pen-and-ink with my own hand in the present volume. And from engraved or photo'd portraits taken from life, I have selected some, of different stages, which please me best (or at any rate displease me least), and bequeath them at a venture to you, reader, with my love.

W. W., *Nov. 13, '88.*

Note Preceding *"A Backward Glance"*

May 31, 1889
Camden, New Jersey, U.S. Amcrica.

TO-DAY computes my three-score-and-ten years—rounds and coheres the successive growths and stages of L. of G. with the following essay and (sort of) testament—my hurried epilogue of intentions-bequest—and gives me the crowning content (for these lines are written at the last) of feeling and definitely, perhaps boastfully, reiterating, For good or bad, plain or not plain, I have held out and now concluded my utterance, entirely its own way; the main wonder being to me, of the foregoing 404 pages entire, amid their many faults and omissions, that (after looking over them leisurely and critically, as the last week, night and day) they have adhered faithfully to, and carried out, for nearly 40 years, over many gaps, through thick and thin, peace and war, sickness and health, clouds and sunshine, my latent purposes, &c., even as measurably well and far as they do between these covers. (Nature evidently achieves specimens only—plants the seeds of suggestions—is not so intolerant of what is call'd evil—relies on *law* and *character* more than special cases or partialities; and in my little scope I have follow'd or tried to follow the lesson: . . Probably that is about all.)

Yes, to-day finishes my 70th year; and even if but the merest additional preface (and not plain what tie-together it has with the following *Backward Glance*), I suppose I must reel out something to celebrate my old birthday anniversary, and for this special edition of the latest completest L. of G. utterance.* Printers send word, too, there is a blank here to be written up—and what with? . . . Probably I may as well transcribe and eke out this note by the following lines of a letter last week to a valued friend who demands to know my current personal condition: . . . "First asking pardon for long neglect—The perfect physical health, strength, buoyancy (and inward impetus to back them), which were vouchsafed during my whole life, and especially throughout the Succession War period (1860 to '66), seem'd to wane after those years, and were closely track'd by a stunning paralytic seizure, and following physical debility and inertia (laggardness, torpor, indifference, perhaps laziness), which put me low in 1873 and '4 and '5—then lifted a little, but have essentially remain'd ever since; several spirts or attacks—five or six of them, one time or another from 1876 onward, but gradually mainly overcome—till now, 1888 and '9, the worst and most obstinate seizure of all . . . . Upon the whole, however, and even at this, and though old and sick, I keep up, maintain fair spirits, partially read and write—have publish'd last and full and revised editions of my poems and prose (records and results of youth and early and mid age—of absolute strength and health—o'erseen now during a lingering ill spell)—But have had a bad year, this last one—have run a varied gauntlet, chronic constipation, and then vertigo, bladder and gastric troubles, and the foremention'd steady disability and inertia; bequests of the serious paralysis at Washington, D.C., closing the Secession War—that seizure indeed the culmination of much that preceded, and real source of all my woes since. During the past year, and now, with all these (a body and brain-action dull'd, while the spirit is perhaps willing and live enough), I get along more contentedly and comfortably than you might suppose—sit here all day in my big, high, strong, rattan-bottom'd chair (with great wolf-skin spread on the back in cool weather)—as writing to you now on a tablet on my lap, may-be my last missives of love, memories and cheer."

**As there are now several editions of L. of G., different texts and dates, I wish to say that I prefer and recommend the present one, complete, for future printing, if there should be any; a copy and fac-simile, indeed, of the text of these 422 pages. The subsequent interval which is so important to form'd and launch'd works, books especially, has pass'd; and waiting till fully after that, I give these concluding words.*

Leaves

of

Grass

1891–92

(Annex: *Good-Bye my Fancy*)

Whitman at about seventy at the Camden, New Jersey, docks near the small house he lived in for the last two decades of his life. He is with his male nurse, Warren Fritzinger. The picture was taken by a visiting English admirer, John Johnston, who several years later published Diary Notes of a Visit to Walt Whitman and Some of His Friends.

LIBRARY OF CONGRESS

Author's Note to 1891-92 Edition

☞As there are now several editions of L. of G., different texts and dates, I wish to say that I prefer and recommend this present one, complete, for future printing, if there should be any; a copy and fac-simile, indeed, of the text of these 438 pages. The subsequent adjusting interval which is so important to form'd and launch'd work, books especially, has pass'd; and waiting till fully after that, I have given [in "A Backward Glance"] my concluding words.

W. W.

Preface Note to *Good-Bye my Fancy*

HAD I not better withhold (in this old age and paralysis of me) such little tags and fringe-dots (maybe specks, stains) as follow a long dusty journey, and witness it afterward? I have probably not been enough afraid of careless touches, from the first—and am not now—nor of parrot-like repetitions—nor platitudes and the commonplace. Perhaps I am too democratic for such avoidances. Besides, is not the verse-field, as originally plann'd by my theory, now sufficiently illustrated—and full time for me to silently retire?—(indeed amid no loud call or market for my sort of poetic utterance).

In answer, or rather defiance, to that kind of well-put interrogation, here comes this little cluster, and conclusion of my preceding clusters. Though not at all clear that, as here collated, it is worth printing (certainly I have nothing fresh to write)—I while away the hours of my 72d year—hours of forced confinement in my den—by putting in shape this small old age collation:

Last droplets of and after spontaneous rain,
From many limpid distillations and past showers;
(Will they germinate anything? mere exhalations as they all are—the land's and sea's America's;
Will they filter to any deep emotion? any heart and brain?)

However that may be, I feel like improving to-day's opportunity and wind up. During the last two years I have sent out, in the lulls of illness and exhaustion, certain chirps—lingering-dying ones probably (undoubtedly)—which now I may as well gather and put in fair type while able to see correctly—(for my eyes plainly warn me they are dimming, and my brain more and more palpably neglects or refuses, month after month, even slight tasks or revisions).

In fact, here I am these current years 1890 and '91 (each successive fortnight getting stiffer and stuck deeper), much like some hard-cased dilapidated grim ancient shell-fish or time-bang'd conch (no legs, utterly non-locomotive) cast up high and dry on the shore-sands, helpless to move anywhere—nothing left but behave myself quiet, and while away the days yet assign'd, and discover if there is anything for the said grim and time-bang'd conch to be got at last out of inherited good spirits and primal buoyant centre-pulses down there deep somewhere within his gray-blurr'd old shell...... (Reader, you must allow a little fun here—for one reason there are too many of the following poemets about death, &c., and for another the passing hours (July 5, 1890) are so sunny-fine. And old as I am I feel to-day almost a part of some frolicsome wave, or for sporting yet like a kid or kitten—probably a streak of physical adjustment and perfection here and now. I believe I have it in me perennially anyhow.

Then behind all, the deep down consolation (it is a glum one, but I dare not be sorry for the fact of it in the past, nor refrain from dwelling, even vaunting here at the end) that this late-years palsied old shorn and shell-fish condition of me is the indubitable outcome and growth, now near for 20 years along, of too overzealous, over-continued bodily and emotional excitement and action through the times of 1862, '3, '4, and '5, visiting and waiting on wounded and sick army volunteers, both sides, in campaigns or contests, or after them, or in hospitals or fields south of Washington City, or in that place and elsewhere—those hot, sad, wrenching times—the army volunteers, all States—or North or South—the wounded, suffering, dying—the exhausting, sweating summers, marches, battles, carnage—those trenches hurriedly heap'd by the corpse-thousands, mainly unknown—Will the America of the future—will this vast rich Union ever realize what itself cost, back there after all?—those hecatombs of battle-deaths—Those times of which, O far-off reader, this whole book is indeed finally but a reminiscent memorial from thence by me to you?

Good-Bye my Fancy

GOOD-BYE* my fancy—(I had a word to say,
But 'tis not quite the time—The best of any man's word or say,
Is when its proper place arrives—and for its meaning,
I keep mine till the last).

*Behind a Good-bye there lurks much of the salutation of another beginning—to me, Development, Continuity, Immortality, Transformation, are the chiefest life-meanings of Nature and Humanity, and are the *sine qua non* of all facts, and each fact.

Why do folks dwell so fondly on the last words, advice, appearance, of the departing? Those last words are not samples of the best, which involve vitality at its full, and balance, and perfect control and scope. But they are valuable beyond measure to confirm and endorse the varied train, facts, theories and faith of the whole preceding life.

On, on the Same, ye Jocund Twain!

ON, on the same, ye jocund twain!
My life and recitative, containing birth, youth, mid-age years,
Fitful as motley-tongues of flame, inseparably twined and merged in one—
combining all,
My single soul—aims, confirmations, failures, joys—Nor single soul alone,
I chant my nation's crucial stage (America's, haply humanity's)—
the trial great, the victory great,
A strange *eclaircissement*° of all the masses past, the eastern world,
the ancient, medieval,
Here, here from wanderings, strayings, lessons, wars, defeats—
here at the west a voice triumphant—justifying all,
A gladsome pealing cry—a song for once of utmost pride
and satisfaction;
I chant from it the common bulk, the general average horde
(the best no sooner than the worst)—And now I chant old age
(My verses, written first for forenoon life, and for the summer's,
autumn's spread,
I pass to snow-white hairs the same, and give to the pulses
winter-cool'd the same);
As here in careless trill, I and my recitatives, with faith and love,
Wafting to other work, to unknown songs, conditions,
On, on ye jocund twain! continue on the same!

The Pallid Wreath

SOMEHOW I cannot let it go yet, funeral though it is,
Let it remain back there on its nail suspended,
With pink, blue, yellow, all blanch'd, and the white now gray and ashy,
One wither'd rose put years ago for thee, dear friend;
But I do not forget thee. Hast thou then faded?
Is the color exhaled? Are the colors, vitalities, dead?
No, while memories subtly play—the past vivid as ever;
For but last night I woke, and in that spectral ring saw thee,
Thy smile, eyes, face, calm, silent, loving as ever:
So let the wreath hang still awhile within my eye-reach,
It is not yet dead to me, nor even pallid.

To the Sun-Set Breeze

AH, whispering, something again, unseen,
Where late this heated day thou enterest at my window, door,
Thou, laving, tempering all, cool-freshing, gently vitalizing
Me, old, alone, sick, weak-down, melted-worn with sweat;
Thou, nestling, folding close and firm yet soft,
    companion better than talk, book, art
(Thou hast, O Nature! elements! utterance to my heart
    beyond the rest—and this is of them),
So sweet thy primitive taste to breathe within—thy soothing fingers
    on my face and hands,
Thou, messenger-magical strange bringer to body and spirit of me
(Distances balk'd—occult medicines penetrating me from head to foot),
I feel the sky, the prairies vast—I feel the mighty northern lakes,

I feel the ocean and the forest—somehow I feel the globe itself
swift-swimming in space;
Thou blown from lips so loved, now gone—haply from endless store,
God-sent
(For thou art spiritual, Godly, most of all known to my sense),
Minister to speak to me, here and now, what word has never told,
and cannot tell,
Art thou not universal concrete's distillation? Law's, all Astronomy's
last refinement?
Hast thou no soul? Can I not know, identify thee?

A Twilight Song

As I sit in twilight late alone by the flickering oak-flame,
Musing on long-pass'd war-scenes—
of the countless buried unknown soldiers,
Of the vacant names, as unindented air's and sea's—the unreturn'd,
The brief truce after battle, with grim burial-squads,
and the deep-fill'd trenches
Of gather'd dead from all America, North, South, East, West,
whence they came up,
From wooded Maine, New-England's farms, from fertile Pennsylvania,
Illinois, Ohio,
From the measureless West, Virginia, the South, the Carolinas, Texas
(Even here in my room-shadows and half-lights
in the noiseless flickering flames,
Again I see the stalwart ranks on-filing, rising—I hear
the rhythmic tramp of the armies),
You million unwrit names all, all—you dark bequest from all the war,
A special verse for you—a flash of duty long neglected—
your mystic roll strangely gather'd here,
Each name recall'd by me from out the darkness and death's ashes,
Henceforth to be, deep, deep within my heart recording,
for many a future year,
Your mystic roll entire of unknown names, or North or South,
Embalm'd with love in this twilight song.

A Voice from Death

(The Johnstown, Penn., cataclysm, May 31, 1889.)

A VOICE from Death, solemn and strange, in all his sweep and power,
With sudden, indescribable blow—towns drown'd—
humanity by thousands slain,
The vaunted work of thrift, goods, dwellings, forge, street, iron bridge,
Dash'd pell-mell by the blow—yet usher'd life continuing on.
(Amid the rest, amid the rushing, whirling, wild debris,
A suffering woman saved—a baby safely born!)

Although I come and unannounc'd, in horror and in pang,
In pouring flood and fire, and wholesale elemental crash
(this voice so solemn, strange),
I too a minister of Deity.

Yea, Death, we bow our faces, veil our eyes to thee,
We mourn the old, the young untimely drawn to thee,
The fair, the strong, the good, the capable,
The household wreck'd, the husband and the wife,
the engulf'd forger in his forge,
The corpses in the whelming waters and the mud,
The gather'd thousands to their funeral mounds, and thousands
never found or gather'd.

Then after burying, mourning the dead
(Faithful to them found or unfound, forgetting not, bearing the past,
here new musing),
A day—a passing moment or an hour—America itself bends low,
Silent, resign'd, submissive.

War, death, cataclysm like this, America,
Take deep to thy proud prosperous heart.

E'en as I chant, lo! out of death, and out of ooze and slime,
The blossoms rapidly blooming, sympathy, help, love,
From West and East, from South and North and over sea,
Its hot-spurr'd hearts and hands humanity to human aid moves on;
And from within a thought and lesson yet.

Thou ever-darting Globe! through Space and Air!
Thou waters that encompass us!
Thou that in all the life and death of us, in action or in sleep!
Thou laws invisible that permeate them and all,
Thou that in all, and over all, and through and under all, incessant!
Thou! thou! the vital, universal, giant force resistless, sleepless, calm,
Holding Humanity as in thy open hand, as some ephemeral toy,
How ill to e'er forget thee!

For I too have forgotten
(Wrapt in these little potencies of progress, politics, culture, wealth,
inventions, civilization),
Have lost my recognition of your silent ever-swaying power,
ye mighty, elemental throes,
In which and upon which we float, and every one of us is buoy'd.

"The Rounded Catalogue Divine Complete"

[Sunday, ——— ——. —Went this forenoon to church. A college professor, Rev. Dr.——, gave us a fine sermon, during which I caught the above words; but the minister included in his "rounded catalogue" letter and spirit, only the esthetic things, and entirely ignored what I name in the following:]

THE devilish and the dark, the dying and diseas'd,
The countless (nineteen-twentieths) low and evil, crude and savage,
The crazed, prisoners in jail, the horrible, rank, malignant,
Venom and filth, serpents, the ravenous sharks, liars, the dissolute
(What is the part the wicked and the loathesome bear
within earth's orbic scheme?);
Newts, crawling things in slime and mud, poisons,
The barren soil, the evil men, the slag and hideous rot.

L. of G.'s Purport

NOT to exclude or demarcate, or pick out evils from their
formidable masses (even to expose them),
But add, fuse, complete, extend—and celebrate the immortal
and the good.

Haughty this song, its words and scope,
To span vast realms of space and time,
Evolution—the cumulative—growths and generations.

Begun in ripen'd youth and steadily pursued,
Wandering, peering, dallying with all—war, peace,
day and night absorbing,
Never even for one brief hour abandoning my task,
I end it here in sickness, poverty, and old age.

I sing of life, yet mind me well of death:
To-day shadowy Death dogs my steps, my seated shape,
and has for years—
Draws sometimes close to me, as face to face.

Good-Bye my Fancy!

GOOD-BYE my Fancy!
Farewell dear mate, dear love!
I'm going away, I know not where,
Or to what fortune, or whether I may ever see you again,
So Good-bye my Fancy.

Now for my last—let me look back a moment;
The slower fainter ticking of the clock is in me,
Exit, nightfall, and soon the heart-thud stopping.

Long have we lived, joy'd, caress'd together;
Delightful!—now separation—Good-bye my Fancy.

Yet let me not be too hasty,
Long indeed have we lived, slept, filter'd,
become really blended into one;
Then if we die we die together (yes, we'll remain one),
If we go anywhere we'll go together to meet what happens,
May-be we'll be better off and blither, and learn something,
May-be it is yourself now really ushering me to the true songs
(who knows?),
May-be it is you the mortal knob really undoing, turning—
so now finally,
Good-bye—and hail! my Fancy.

Article on *Good-Bye my Fancy* (1891)

"The Highest said: Don't let us begin so low—isn't our range too coarse—too gross? . . . . The Soul answer'd: No, not when we consider what it is all for—the end involved is Time and Space."

—*An item from last page of "Good-Bye."*

H. HEINE'S first principle of criticising a book was, What motive is the author trying to carry out, or express or accomplish? and the second, Has he achiev'd it?

The theory of my *Leaves of Grass* as a composition of verses has been from first to last (if I am to give impromptu a hint of the spinal marrow of the business, and sign it with my name) to thoroughly possess the mind, memory, cognizance of the author himself, with everything beforehand—a full armory of concrete actualities, observations, humanity, past poems, ballads, facts, technique, war and peace, politics, North and South, East and West, nothing too large or too small, the sciences as far as possible—and above all America and the present—after and out of which the subject of the poem, long or short, has been invariably turned over to his Emotionality, even Personality, to be shaped thence; and emerges strictly therefrom, with all its merits and demerits on its head. Every page of my poetic or attempt at poetic utterance therefore smacks of the living physical identity, date, environment, individuality, probably beyond anything known, and in style often offensive to the conventions.

This new last cluster, "Good-Bye my Fancy," follows suit, and yet with a difference. The clef is here changed to its lowest, and the little book is a lot of tremolos about old age, death, and faith. The physical just lingers, but almost vanishes. The book is garrulous, irascible (like old Lear) and has various breaks and even tricks to avoid monotony. It will have to be ciphered and ciphered out long—and is probably in some respects the most curious part of its author's baffling works. *Walt Whitman.*

[*from* Lippincott's Magazine, *August 1891*]

Appendices

An extremely rare photograph of young Whitman, circa 1846, when he would have been twenty-seven.

[1]
Poems Published before *Leaves* or Posthumously

THE LOVE THAT IS HEREAFTER

O BEAUTEOUS is the earth! and fair
The splendors of Creation are:
Nature's green robe, the shining sky,
The winds that through the tree-tops sigh,
All speak a bounteous God.

The noble trees, the sweet young flowers,
The birds that sing in forest bowers,
The rivers grand that murmuring roll,
And all which joys or calms the soul
Are made by gracious might.

The flocks and droves happy and free,
The dwellers of the boundless sea,
Each living thing on air or land,
Created by our Master's hand,
Is formed for joy and peace.

But man—weak, proud, and erring man,
Of truth ashamed, of folly vain—
Seems singled out to know no rest
And of all things that move, feels least
The sweets of happiness.

Yet he it is whose little life
Is passed in useless, vexing strife,
And all the glorious earth to him
Is rendered dull, and poor, and dim,
From hope unsatisfied.

He faints with grief—he toils through care—
And from the cradle to the bier
He wearily plods on—till Death
Cuts short his transient, panting breath,
And sends him to his sleep.

O, mighty powers of Destiny!
When from this coil of flesh I'm free—
When through my second life I rove,
Let me but find *one* heart to love,
As I would wish to love:

Let me but meet a single breast,
Where this tired soul its hope may rest,
In never-dying faith: ah, then,
That would be bliss all free from pain,
And sickness of the heart.

For vainly through this world below
We seek affection. Nought but wo
Is with our earthly journey wove;
And so the heart must look above,
Or die in dull despair.
(1840)

EACH HAS HIS GRIEF

ON earth are many sights of wo,
And many sounds of agony,
And many a sorrow-wither'd check,°
And many a pain-dulled eye.

The wretched weep, the poor complain,
And luckless love pines on unknown;
And faintly from the midnight couch
Sounds out the sick child's moan.

Each has his grief—old age fears death;
The young man's ills are pride, desire,
And heart-sickness; and in his breast
The beat of passion's fire.

And he who runs the race of fame,
Oft feels within a feverish dread,
Lest others snatch the laurel crown,
He bears upon his head.

All, all know care; and, at the close,
All lie earth's spreading arms within—
The poor, the black-soul'd, proud, and low,
Virtue, despair, and sin.

O, foolish, then, with pain to shrink
From the sure doom we each must meet.
Is earth so fair—or heaven so dark—
Or life so passing sweet?

No; dread ye not the fearful hour—
The coffin, and the pall's dark gloom,
For there's a calm to throbbing hearts,
And rest, down in the tomb.

Then our long journey will be o'er,
And throwing off earth's load of woes,
The pallid brow, the fainting heart,
Will sink in soft repose.

Nor only this: for wise men say
That when we leave our land of care,
We float to a mysterious shore,
Peaceful, and pure, and fair.

So, welcome death! Whene'er the time
That the dread summons must be met,
I'll yield without one pang of fear,
Or sigh, or vain regret.

But like unto a wearied child,
That over field and wood all day

Has ranged and struggled, and at last,
Worn out with toil and play,

Goes up at evening to his home,
And throws him, sleepy, tired, and sore,
Upon his bed, and rests him there,
His pain and trouble o'er.

(1841)

A SKETCH

"The trail of the serpent is at times seen in every man's path."

UPON the ocean's wave-worn shore
I marked a solitary form,
Whose brooding look, and features wore
The darkness of the coming storm!
And, from his lips, the sigh that broke,
So long within his bosom nursed,
In deep and mournful accents spoke,
Like troubled waves, that shining burst!

And as he gazed on earth and sea,
Girt with the gathering night; his soul,
Wearied and life-worn, longed to flee,
And rest within its final goal!
He thought of her whose love had beamed,
The sunlight of his ripened years;
But now her gentle memory seemed
To brim his eye with bitter tears!

"Oh! thou bless'd Spirit!" thus he sighed—
"Smile on me from thy realm of rest!
My dark and doubting spirit guide,
By conflict torn, and grief oppressed!
Teach me, in every saddening care,
To see the chastening hand of Heaven;

The Soul's high culture to prepare,
    Wisely and mercifully given!

"Could I this sacred solace share,
    'Twould still my struggling bosom's moan;
And the deep peacefulness of prayer,
    Might for thy heavy loss atone!
Earth, in its wreath of summer flowers,
    And all its varied scenes of joy,
Its festal halls and echoing bowers,
    No more my darkened thoughts employ.

"But here, the billow's heaving breast,
    And the low thunder's knelling tone,
Speak of the wearied soul's unrest,
    Its murmuring, and conflicts lone!
And yon sweet star, whose golden gleam,
    Pierces the tempest's gathering gloom,
In the rich radiance of its beam,
    Tells me of light beyond the tomb!"

(1842)

THE MISSISSIPPI AT MIDNIGHT

HOW solemn! sweeping this dense black tide!
    No friendly lights i' the heaven o'er us;
A murky darkness on either side,
    And kindred darkness all before us!

Now, drawn near the shelving rim,
    Weird-like shadows suddenly rise;
Shapes of mist and phantoms dim
    Baffle the gazer's straining eyes.

River fiends, with malignant faces!
    Wild and wide their arms are thrown,

As if to clutch in fatal embraces
Him who sails their realms upon.

Then, by the trick of our own swift motion,
Straight, tall giants, an army vast,
Rank by rank, like the waves of ocean,
On the shore march stilly past.

How solemn! the river a trailing pall,
Which takes, but never again gives back;
And moonless and starless the heavens' arch'd wall,
Responding an equal black!

Oh, tireless waters! like Life's quick dream,
Onward and onward ever hurrying—
Like Death in this midnight hour you seem,
Life in your chill drops greedily burying!
(1848)

RESURGEMUS

SUDDENLY, out of its stale and drowsy air, the air of slaves,
Like lightning Europe le'pt forth,
Sombre, superb and terrible,
As Ahimoth, brother of Death.

God, 'twas delicious!
That brief, tight, glorious grip
Upon the throats of kings.
You liars paid to defile the People,
Mark you now:
Not for numberless agonies, murders, lusts,
For court thieving in its manifold mean forms,
Worming from his simplicity the poor man's wages;
For many a promise sworn by royal lips
And broken, and laughed at in the breaking;

Then, in their power, not for all these,
Did a blow fall in personal revenge,
Or a hair draggle in blood:
The People scorned the ferocity of kings.

But the sweetness of mercy brewed bitter destruction,
And frightened rulers come back:
Each comes in state, with his train,
Hangman, priest, and tax-gatherer,
Soldier, lawyer, and sycophant;
An appalling procession of locusts,
And the king struts grandly again.

Yet behind all, lo, a Shape
Vague as the night, draped interminably,
Head, front and form, in scarlet folds;
Whose face and eyes none may see,
Out of its robes only this,
The red robes, lifted by the arm,
One finger pointed high over the top,
Like the head of a snake appears.

Meanwhile, corpses lie in new-made graves,
Bloody corpses of young men;
The rope of the gibbet hangs heavily,
The bullets of tyrants are flying,
The creatures of power laugh aloud:
And all these things bear fruit, and they are good.

Those corpses of young men,
Those martyrs that hang from the gibbets,
Those hearts pierced by the grey lead,
Cold and motionless as they seem,
Live elsewhere with undying vitality;
They live in other young men, O, kings,
They live in brothers, again ready to defy you;
They were purified by death,
They were taught and exalted.

Not a grave of those slaughtered ones,
But is growing its seed of freedom,
In its turn to bear seed,

Which the winds shall carry afar and resow,
And the rain nourish.

Not a disembodied spirit
Can the weapon of tyrants let loose,
But it shall stalk invisibly over the earth,
Whispering, counseling, cautioning.

Liberty, let others despair of thee,
But I will never despair of thee:
Is the house shut? Is the master away?
Nevertheless, be ready, be not weary of watching,
He will surely return; his messengers come anon.

(1850)

SUPPLEMENT HOURS

SANE, random, negligent hours,
Sane, easy, culminating hours,
After the flush, the Indian summer, of my life,
Away from Books—away from Art—the lesson learn'd, pass'd o'er,
Soothing, bathing, merging all—the sane, magnetic,
Now for the day and night themselves—the open air,
Now for the fields, the seasons, insects, trees—the rain and snow,
Where wild bees flitting hum,
Or August mulleins grow, or winter's snowflakes fall,
Or stars in the skies roll round—
The silent sun and stars.

(1897)

OF MANY A SMUTCH'D DEED REMINISCENT

FULL of wickedness, I—of many a smutch'd deed reminiscent—
of worse deeds capable,
Yet I look composedly upon nature, drink day and night
the joys of life, and await death with perfect equanimity,
Because of my tender and boundless love for him I love
and because of his boundless love for me.

(1897)

A THOUGHT OF COLUMBUS

THE mystery of mysteries, the crude and hurried ceaseless flame,
spontaneous, bearing on itself.
The bubble and the huge, round, concrete orb!
A breath of Deity, as thence the bulging universe unfolding!
The many issuing cycles from their precedent minute!
The eras of the soul incepting in an hour,
Haply the widest, farthest evolutions of the world and man.

Thousands and thousands of miles hence, and now four centuries back,
A mortal impulse thrilling its brain cell,
Reck'd or unreck'd, the birth can no longer be postpon'd:
A phantom of the moment, mystic, stalking, sudden,
Only a silent thought, yet toppling down of more than walls
of brass or stone.
(A flutter at the darkness' edge as if old Time's and Space's secret
near revealing.)
A thought! A definite thought works out in shape.
Four hundred years roll on.
The rapid cumulus—trade, navigation, war, peace, democracy, roll on;

The restless armies and the fleets of time following their leader—
the old camps of ages pitch'd in newer, larger areas,
The tangl'd, long-deferr'd éclaircissement° of human life and hopes
boldly begins untying,
As here to-day up-grows the Western World.

(An added word yet to my song, far Discoverer, as ne'er before
sent back to son of earth—
If still thou hearest, hear me,
Voicing as now—lands, races, arts, bravas to thee, one vast consensus,
north, south, east, west,
Soul plaudits! acclamation! reverent echoes!
One manifold, huge memory to thee! oceans and lands!
The modern world to thee and thought of thee!)

(1897)

[2]
Significant Passages from Whitman Manuscripts

Probably the most important Whitman manuscript to survive careless loss or the poet's desire, sometimes acted upon, to destroy his papers is now referred to as the "albot Wilson" notebook. Those are the first words in the 5½" by 3½" volume, which disappeared mysteriously from the possession of the Library of Congress, along with several other important Whitman manuscripts, while removed for safety reasons from Washington during World War II. Several of these fugitive treasures—but not "albot Wilson"—were offered for sale at Sotheby's in 1996 and were immediately returned to the Library. Fortunately, photostats of "albot Wilson" were made in the 1930s, and we are thus vouchsafed several pages dating from some time between 1847 and the early 1850s that show Whitman sketching preliminarily the poems that would begin appearing in 1855.

Immediately following several passages of general significance for Leaves of Grass, *taken from several other manuscripts, come some trial runs for "I celebrate myself . . ." from "albot Wilson." Various manuscripts pertinent to other poems are also excerpted. All italics are Whitman's. In parentheses after each passage, cognate line numbers from poems in this edition are given when appropriate, then the source in both* Notes and Fragments *(N&F), edited by Richard Maurice Bucke (1899), and in the New York University edition of* The Notebooks and Unpublished Prose Manuscripts *(NUPM), edited by Edward Grier (1984), and finally a best guess at the date of the manuscript.*

PLANS AND OBSERVATIONS

My Way

Boldness—*Nonchalant ease & indifference.* To encourage me or any one continually to strike out alone—So it seems good *to me*—This is my way, *my* pleasure, *my* choice, *my* costume, friendship, amour, or what not.—

(N&F 57; NUPM 321—probably circa 1856)

Audience and Ethos

How gladly we leave the best of what is called learned and refined society, or the company of men from stores and offices, to sail all day on the river amid a party of fresh and jovial boatmen, with no coats or suspenders, and their trowsers tucked in their boots.—Then the quick blood within joins their gay blood and the twain dances polkas from the bottom to the top of the house. After long constraint in the respectable and money-making dens of existence, a man emerges for a few hours and comes up like a whale to spout and breathe.—One glimpse then of the eternal realities of things—the real sun, burning and dazzling—the old, forever young and solid earth—real men and women refreshing, hearty, and wicked.—

Outdoors is the best antisep[tic] yet.—What a charm there is in men that have lived mainly in the open air—among horses—at sea—on the canals—digging clams—timbers—rafters and steamboaters,—or framers of houses—and mechanics generally.—Cleanly shaved and grammatical folks I call Mister, and lay the tips of my fingers inside their elbows after the orthodox fashion, and discuss whatever had the biggest headline in the morning papers, and pass the time as comfortably as the law allows.—But for the others, my arm leans over their shoulders, and around their necks.—In them nature justifies herself.—Their indefinable excellence gives out something as much beyond the special productions of colleges and pews and parlors as the morning air of the prairie or the sea-shore outsmells the costliest scents of the perfume shop.

(compare "I celebrate myself" ll. 197ff, 245ff; N&F 125; NUPM 169–70—before or early in 1855)

Solo Flight

Make no quotations, and no reference to any other writers.—

Lumber the writing with nothing—let it go as lightly as a bird flies in the air—or a fish swims in the sea

Be careful to temper down too much

(N&F 56; NUPM 159—probably before 1855)

The Knowing Poet

Sept. '56

"Leaves of Grass," must be called *not* objective, but altogether *subjective—"I know"* runs through them as a perpetual refrain. Yet the great Greek poems, also the Teutonic poems, also Shakespeare and all the great masters have been objective, epic—they have described characters, events, wars, heroes, &c

(N&F 73; NUPM 1432)

Things To Do

Make *the Works*—

Do not go into criticisms or arguments at all

Make full-blooded, rich, flush, natural *Works*—

Insert natural things, indestructibles, idioms, characteristics, rivers, States, persons, &c

Be full of *strong sensual germs*—

(N&F 57; NUPM 325—probably circa 1856)

Style: Sane and Shameless

This indirect mode of attack is better than all direct modes of attack.
The spirit of the above ☝
should pervade ALL my poems.

Avoid all the "intellectual subtleties," and "withering doubts" and "blasted hopes" and "unrequited loves," and "ennui," and "wretchedness" and the whole *lurid* and *artistical* and *melo-dramatic* effects.—Preserve perfect calmness and sanity

In the best poems appears the human body, well-formed, natural, accepting itself, unaware of shame, loving that which is necessary to make it complete, proud of its strength, active, receptive, a father, a mother,

(NUPM 233—after mid-1856)

Perfect Likelihood

It seems to me—to avoid *all* poetical similes—to be faithful to the perfect likelihoods of nature—healthy, exact, simple, disdaining ornament.

(N&F 57; NUPM 157—before 1855)

Resistless Power

Poems

Hasting, urging, resistless,—no flagging, not even in the "thoughts" or meditations—florid—spiritual—good, not from the direct but indirect meanings—to be perceived with the same perception that enjoys music, flowers and the beauty of men and women—free and luxuriant—

(N&F 57; NUPM 1442—after 1857)

American Personality

All I write I write to arouse in you a great personality. [To the left Whitman inserted: "All my poems do."]

I must not fail to SATURATE my poems with ☞ *things, substantial,* American scenes, *climates, names, places, words, permanent facts (include every important river and mountain animals trees crops, grains, vegetables, flowers*

(NUPM 267—about 1857)

American Faults

Tell the American people their faults—the departments of their character where they are most liable to break down—speak to them with unsparing tongue—carefully systematize beforehand *their faults.—*

(N&F 56; NUPM 627—probably after 1860)

Concentration

Saturday, June 21. It seems to me *[N&F;* "be" in *NUPM]* quite clear and determined that I should concentrate my powers [on] *Leaves of Grass*—not diverting any of my means, strength, interest to the construction of anything else—of any other book.

(N&F 84; NUPM 329—ms. lost, probably about 1856)

Insulting the Cultivated

We suppose it will excite the mirth of many of our readers to be told that a man has arisen, who has deliberately and insultingly ignored all the other, the cultivated classes as they are called, and set himself to work to write "America's first distinctive Poem," on the platform of these same New York Roughs, firemen, the ouvrier [i.e., working] class, masons and carpenters, stage-drivers, the Dry Dock boys, and so forth; and that furthermore he either is not aware of the existence of the polite social models, and the imported literary laws, or else he don't value them two cents for his purposes.

(N&F 70; NUPM 333–34—from the 1850s)

Perfect Reader

No one will perfectly enjoy me who has not some of my own rudeness, sensuality and hauteur.

(N&F 68; NUPM 380—possibly early 1850s)

Old World, So Long!

No I do not choose to write a poem on a lady's sparrow, like Catullus—or on a parrot, like Ovid—nor love-joys like Anacreon—nor even like Homer—nor the Siege of Jerusalem like Tass[o]—nor nor as Shakespeare—(What have these themes to do in America? or what are they to us except as beautiful studies, reminiscencing?)

All those are good—they are what they are—I know they should not have been different—I do not say I will furnish any thing better.—But instead I will aim at high immortal marks—American, the robust large manly character—the perfect woman—the illustriousness of sex, which I will celebrate—

(N&F 59; NUPM 349—late 1850s)

Brainstorming for Titles

Poemet Leaf Chant Song Poem Psalm Hymn
warble carol cavatina ballad Thought Caprices Fantasia Capricea
Sonnet-Trio Sonnet-Quinto Sonnet-Duo
Melange Canticles Songlet

(N&F 177; NUPM 1319—prior to 1860)

How to Revise

In future *Leaves of Grass. Be more severe* with the final revision of the poem, nothing will do, not one word or sentence, that is not *perfectly clear*—with positive purpose—harmony with the name, nature, drift of the poem. Also no *ornaments,* especially *no ornamental adjectives,* unless they have come molten hot, and imperiously prove themselves. *No ornamental similes at all—not one: perfect transparent clearness* sanity and health are wanted—*that* is the *divine style*—O if it can be attained—

(N&F 69; NUPM 385—ms. lost, undatable)

1855 EDITION

"I celebrate myself . . ."

My life is a miracle and my body which lives is a miracle; but of what can I nibble at the edges of the limitless and delicious wonder I know that I cannot separate them, and call one superior and the other inferior, any more than I can say my sight is greater than my eyes.—

You have been told that mind is greater than matter

I cannot understand the mystery, but I am always conscious of myself as two—as my soul and I; and I reckon it is the same with all men and women.—
(preface generally; ll. 43–44, 65–74, 422–23, 524–25, 1262–63; NUPM 63)

I will not descend among professors and capitalists,—I will turn up the ends of my trowsers around my boots, and my cuffs back from my wrists, and go with drivers and boatmen and men that catch fish or work in the field. I know they are sublime.

I am the poet of slaves and of the masters of slaves
I am the poet of the body
And I am

I am the poet of the body
And I am the poet of the soul
I go with the slaves of the earth equally with the masters
And I will stand between the masters and the slaves,
Entering into both so that both shall understand me alike.

I am the poet of Strength and Hope
Where is the house of any one dying?
(ll. 176, 509–10, 1003, 1202–3; NUPM 67)

I am the poet of little things and of babes
Of each gnat in the air, and of beetles rolling balls of dung,

Afar in the sky was a nest
And my soul flew thither, and squat, and looked out,
And saw the journeywork of suns and systems of suns,
And that a leaf of grass is not less than they
And that the pismire is equally perfect, and all grains of sand,
and every egg of the wren.
And the tree-toad is a chef' d ouvre for the highest.
And the running-blackberry would adorn the parlors of Heaven
And the cow crunching with depressed neck surpasses every statue,
And pictures great and small crowd the rail-fence, and hang on its heaped
stones and elder and poke-weed.

(ll. 89, 517, 662–67; NUPM 70–71)

Where is one abortive, mangy, cold—
Starved of his masculine lustiness?
Without core
Loose in the knees,
Clutch fast to me, my ungrown brother,
That I infuse you with grit and jets of life
I am not to be denied—I compel;
It is quite indifferent to me who you are.
I have stores plenty and to spare
And of whatsoever I have I bestow upon you
And first I bestow of my love.

(ll. 991–96; NUPM 73–74)

A touch now reads me a library of knowledge in an instant,
It smells for me the fragrance of wine and lemon-blows,
It tastes for me ripe strawberries and melons.—
It talks for me with a tongue of its own,
It finds an ear wherever it rests or taps,
It brings the rest around it, and enjoy them meanwhile and then
they all stand on a headland and mock me
The sentries have deserted every other part of me
They have all come to the headland to witness and assist against me.—
They have left me helpless to the torrent of touch
I am given up by traitors,
I talk wildly I am surely out of my head,
I am myself the greatest traitor
I went myself first to the headland

Unloose me touch you are taking the breath from my throat
Unbar your gates—you are too much for me.—
Fierce Wrestler! do you keep your heaviest grip for the last?
Will you sting me most even at parting?
Will you struggle even at the threshold with spasms more delicious
    than all before?
Does it make you ache so to leave me?
Do you wish to show me that even what you did before was nothing
    to what you can do?
Or have you and all the rest combined to see how much I can endure
Pass as you will; take drops of my life if that is what you are after
Only pass to some one else, for I can contain you no longer.
I held more than I thought
I did not think I was big enough for so much exstasy
Or that a touch could take it all out of me.

(ll. 618–42—see also ll. 53–54 of "The bodies of men and women engirth me . . ."; NUPM 75–77)

This is the common air . . . . it is for the heroes and sages . . . . it is for the
    workingmen and farmers . . . . it is for the wicked just the same as the
    righteous
I will not have a single person left out . . . . I will have the prostitute and the
    thief invited . . . .
I will make no difference between them and the rest.
Let every thing be as free as possible.—There is always danger in
    constipation.—
There is never danger in no constipation.—Let the schools and hospitals for
    the sick and idiots and the aged be perfectly free

(this is the last passage reproduced from "albot Wilson"; NUPM 80–81)

I want the tenor, large and fresh as the creation, the orbed parting of whose mouth shall lift over my head the sluices of all the delight yet discovered for our race.—

I want the soprano that lithely overleaps the stars, and convulses me like the love-grip of her in whose arms I lay last night.—I want an infinite chorus and orchestrium, wide as the orbit of Uranus true as the hours of the day, and filling my capacities to receive, as thoroughly as the sea fills its scooped out sands.—I want the chanted Hymn whose tremendous sentiment [Whitman made two complete versions of what follows; this is the second] shall uncage in my breast a thousand wide-winged strengths and unknown ardors and terrible extasies—putting me through the flights of all the passions—dilating me beyond time and air—startling me with the overtures of some unnamable horror—calmly sailing me all day on a bright river with lazy slapping waves—stabbing my heart with myriads of forked distractions more furious than hail or lightning—lulling me drowsily with honeyed morphine—tight'ning the fakes of death about my throat, and awakening me again to know by that comparison, the most positive wonder in the world, and that's what we call life.

(ll. 587–610—see also "Proud Music of the Storm" and Calamus 21; from the photostat of a lost Library of Congress ms.; NUPM 126–27)

"The bodies of men and women engirth me . . ."

The expression of a perfect made man appears not only in his face—but in his limbs—the motion of his hands and arms and all his joints—his walk—the carriage of his neck—and the flex of his waist and hips Dress does not hide him The quality he has and the strong sweet supple nature he has strike through cotton and woolen.—To see him walk conveys the impression of hearing a beautiful poem. To see his back and the back of his neck and shoulderside is a spectacle. Great is the body!—There is some thing in the touch of any candid clean person,—what it is I do not know . . . . but it fills me with wonderful and exquisite sensations. It is enough to be with him or her.—

(ll. 7–12; NUPM 151)

Bridalnight,

One quivering jelly of love limpid transparent
Limitless jets of love, hot and enormous
Arms of love strong as attraction reach as wide and large as the air
Drunken and crazy with love, swing in it's in the plumetless sea
Loveflesh swelling and deliciously aching whiteblood of love

(ll. 51–57; NUPM 149)

1856 EDITION

Sun-Down Poem

(Poem or passage)

the scenes on the river as I cross the Fulton ferry
Others will see the flow of the river, also,

Others will see on both sides the city of New York and the city of Brooklyn
A hundred years hence others will see them,
Two hundred years—many hundred years hence others will enjoy the flow . . .

(compare ll. 13–18, 57; NUPM 228—mid-1856)

Depressions

Every thing I have done seems to me blank and suspicious.—I doubt whether my greatest thoughts, as I had supposed them, are not shallow—and people will most likely laugh at me.—My pride is impotent, my love gets no response.—The complacency of nature is hateful—I am filled with restlessness.—I am incomplete.—

(compare ll. 67–70; NUPM 167—about 1855)

Full poem

I too have——
have—have—
I too have———felt the curious questioning come upon me.
In the day they came
In the silence of the night came upon me,
What is it now between us?—Is it a score of years? or a hundred years?
or five hundred years?
Whatever it is, it avails not . . . . distance avails not and place avails not.
I too lived,
I too walked upon the solid earth and bathed in the sea
But I, wearied, wavered,
I too was stuck from the float eternally held in solution.
I too was cohered and received identity through my body,
Of all that I had, I had nothing except through my body
Of all that I have or shall have, it is the same
That I am is of my body, and what I am is of my body
What identity I am, I owe to my body . . . . what soul I owe to my body,
What belongs to me . . . . that it does not yet spread in the spread
of the universe, I owe to my body
Of all that I have had, I have had nothing except through my body,
Of the make of my body was not my mortal experience only,
My body makes my immortal experience
drenched with joy,——had my friends, loved them, was loved by them,—
was irritated,—saw hundreds of men and women I loved, yet never
told them so,
Had my hopes and dreams,—laughed, slept, had my amours, friendships,
I too—approaching or passing, was called by name by the clear prompt voices
of my friends as they saw me passing or approaching

You wayward, vain, blabbed, blushed, resented, was shallow, ambitious,
curious, fearful, lied, stole, adulterous, a solitary committer, greedy,
grudging,—the wolf, the snake, the hog not altogether wanting the
covetous wish,—the frivolous word—the cheating look—
had guile, lust, hot wishes I dared not speak,
Refused my love to those that gave me theirs,
It is not you alone who know what it is to be these
I too knew what it was to be these—

(compare ll. 59-86; NUPM 230-31—after mid-1856)

1860 EDITION

Enfans d'Adam and *Calamus* Clusters

In 1955 the eminent bibliographical scholar Fredson Bowers published a parallel text edition of a trove of extant manuscripts in Whitman's handwriting from which a majority of the new poems in the 1860 edition were derived. These are now in the Valentine-Barrett collection at the University of Virginia. Bowers's analysis of these initial versions in Whitman's Manuscripts: Leaves of Grass (1860) *throws much light on Whitman's compositional practices, especially concerning the* Enfans d'Adam *and* Calamus *clusters. Particularly significant was Bowers's discovery that a dozen* Calamus *poems had, at an earlier stage, constituted a special sequence in Whitman's mind. The poet titled this sequence "Live Oak with Moss" and, probably in the spring of 1859, copied the twelve poems into a notebook, giving them roman numerals. Bowers plausibly speculated that these poems, which narrate an unhappy love affair, had special autobiographical significance for Whitman. One hint for Bowers was this note, in Whitman's hand, made on the back of a separate ms. with five lines from the first "Live Oak" poem (in the Berg Collection of the New York Public Library):*

Poems

A cluster of poems, sonnets expressing the thoughts,
pictures, aspirations, &c
Fit to be perused during the days of the approach of Death.
(that I have prepared myself for that purpose.—
(Remember now——
Remember the[n]——

The "Live Oak with Moss" cluster can be roughly reconstructed by reading the following Calamus *poems in this order: #14, #20, #11, #23, #8, #32, #10, #9, #34, #43, #36, #42 (see Bowers, pp. lxiii–lxxiv). For discussion of this prior sequence, see Alan Helms's essay "Whitman's 'Live Oak with Moss,' " in* The Continuing Presence of Walt Whitman, *ed. Robert K. Martin (1992), pp. 185–205, and Hershel Parker's response, "The Real 'Live Oak, with Moss,' "* Nineteenth Century Literature *(1996), pp. 145–60. There is, at Duke University, a ms. in which Whitman similarly sketched out preliminary thoughts for the* Enfans d'Adam *cluster:*

Theory of a Cluster of Poems the same *to the Passion of Woman-Love* as the "Calamus-Leaves" are to adhesiveness, manly love.
Full of animal-fire, tender, burning,—the tremulous ache, delicious,
yet such a torment,
The swelling, elate and vehement, that will not be denied,
Adam, as a central figure and type.
one piece
Presenting a vivid picture (in connection with the spirit) of a fully-complete, well-developed man[,] eld, bearded, swart, fiery—as a more than rival of the youthful type-hero of novels and love poems

(NUPM 413—during or after 1859)

Several manuscript passages examined by Bowers are fascinating and significant; four are given here:

Once I passed through a populous celebrated city, imprinting on my
brain for future use, its shows, with its shows, architecture,
customs and traditions
But now of all that city I remember only the man who wandered
with me, there, for love of me,
Day by day, and night by night, we were together,

All else has long been forgotten by me—I remember, I say, only
one rude and ignorant man who, when I departed, long and
long held me by the hand, with silent lip, sad and tremulous.—

(prior version of Enfans d'Adam 9; Bowers, p. 64)

Long I was held by the life that exhibits itself,
By what is done in the houses or streets, or in company,
The usual adjustments and pleasures—the things which

all conform to and which the writers celebrate;
But now I know a life which does not exhibit itself,
yet contains all the rest,
And now, escaping, I celebrate that concealed but substantial life,
I celebrate the need of the love of comrades.—

(prior version of Calamus 1; Bowers, p. 68)

I dreamed in a dream of a city where all the men were like brothers,
O I saw them tenderly love each other—I often saw them, in numbers,
walking hand in hand;
I dreamed that was the city of robust friends—Nothing was greater
there than manly love—it led the rest,
It was seen every hour in the actions of the men of that city, and in all
their looks and words.—

(Whitman's occasional inclination to make less obvious the same-sex emphasis in his poems is shown in this prior version of Calamus 34; Bowers, p. 114)

To

What you said, passionately clasping my hand, this is my answer:
Though you have strayed hither, for my sake, you can never
belong to me, nor I to you,
Behold the customary loves and friendships—the cold guards,
I am that rough and simple/scornful person
I am he who kisses his comrade lightly on the lips at parting,
and I am one who is kissed in return,
I introduce that new American salute
Behold love choked, correct, polite, always suspicious
Behold the received models of the parlors—What are they to me?
What to these young men that travel with me?

(this ms. poem is in the Calamus style, which suggests a date of 1857–60)

DRUM-TAPS

Vigil Strange I Kept on the Field One Night

Ending with that vigil a vigil of battle field dim, vigil of night, vigil
for boy of responding kisses, (never again on earth responding[)]
Vigil of loving comrade slain, vigil solemn & wondrous ending at sunrise.
Wrapt in his blanket I buried my son & soldier
Vigil of love I kept on the field to-night one night
Vigil I kept for love on the field one night;
When you my darling fell in the battle mortally wounded dropt
at my side that day
One look I but gave & your dear eyes returned, with a (look I shall
never forget)
One touch of the hand,
Then onward I sped in the battle,
Till late in the night relieved, to the place at last I made my way
Found you in death so cold my darling & comrade found your body,
son of responded kisses, (O never again on earth responding),
Bared your face in the starlight cool & sweet came the wafted wind
Long I stood then came in
in vigil wondrous around me the battle field spreading,
Vigil for you my son & darling dead, boy of my love & kisses dead,
Vigil wondrous & vigil sweet there in the fragrant silent night
But not a tear fell, not a long drawn breath, O son—long, long I gazed
Then on the ground reclining I sat by your side, my love—I leaning
my chin in my hands,
Passing sweet hours, immortal & wondrous hours with you,
dear comrade not a tear, not a word.
Vigil of love, vigil of death, & love, my son & my soldier,
As onward the stars aloft steadily silently westward moved,
as eastward new ones upward stole,
Vigil strange, O boy—(I could not save you—swift was your death—
I faithfully loved you while living I think we shall surely meet again)
Till at the latest lingering of night, indeed just as the dawn appeared
My son & my soldier duly I wrapped in his blanket,

Enveloped well folded the blanket well tucking it very carefully
over head & over feet.

(from a notebook compiled at Washington in the summer of 1863; NUPM 615–18)

[3]
Whitman's Observations on *Leaves of Grass*, 1888–92

From March 1888 until Whitman's death in March 1892, Horace Traubel (1858–1919) visited the poet almost every day, frequently more than once. During these visits he recorded, through a form of shorthand, several million words of Whitman's conversations, which he transcribed nightly after his visits. Between 1906 and 1996, these conversations were published in nine volumes under the title With Walt Whitman in Camden. *Following, with Whitman's italics, are some of his observations from these volumes that bear on* Leaves of Grass. *In parentheses after each quotation are given the volume and page numbers.*

The Title

"I am well satisfied with my success with titles—with *Leaves of Grass,* for instance, though some of my friends themselves rather kicked against it at the start as a species of folly. 'Leaves of Grass,' they said: 'there are no *leaves* of grass; there are *spears* of grass: that's your word, Walt Whitman: spears, spears.' But *Spears of Grass* would not have been the same to me. Etymologically *leaves* is correct—scientific men use it so. I stuck to leaves, leaves, leaves, until it was able to take care of itself. Now it has got well started on its voyage—it will never be displaced" (1:186). A year and a half later, Whitman recalled another instance of the debate over *leaves:* "There was one night the question came up; a very erudite—a scientific man—a botanist, in fact—having stood it as long as he could—spoke out—set me quite up—said that, whatever the case in literature, in science *leaves* of grass there were and doubtless would be." Whitman continued, "My critic gave all the intellectual reasons in the calendar, but the emotional, the sympathetic, he could say nothing—nothing!" Whitman's final point, though, was that of the practiced editor he had been: "A headline should be large—capacious—expansive—should cover its subject, explicitly—then something more." (6:197–98)

Early Foes (Bless 'Em)

"*Leaves of Grass* has had this advantage: it has had a stormy early life. Nothing could make up for the loss of this—it was a priceless privilege. Ease, comfort, acceptation would have ruined us." (6:340)

Emerson: Early Friend with a Blind Spot

Whitman received a very cordial letter from the literary eminence on his first edition of *Leaves* and famously made bold to print it and extract a blurb from it for his second edition. Glowing though all of Whitman's subsequent public comments on Emerson were, in private he never ceased to rankle at Emerson's attempt, during a walk on Boston Common, to urge a taming of his more daring poems. Almost three decades later, Whitman summed up: "He did not see the significance of the sex element as I put it into the book and resolutely there stuck to it—he did not see that if I had cut sex out I might just as well have cut everything out—the full scheme would no longer exist—it would have been violated in its most sensitive spot." (1:51)

Enemies

Over the years Whitman made many comments about the "enemies" of *Leaves of Grass*. Looking back at the age of sixty-nine, he summed up: "For a long time all I got out of my work was the work itself and a few amens like that [in a letter Traubel had just read aloud]: I was not only not popular (and am not popular yet—never will be) but I was *non grata*—I was not welcome in the world" (3:467). But not all his comments on enemies were resentful. "Some of my opponents are fairly on the other side—belong there, are honest, I respect them," he granted, but he also said, "others are malignant—are of the snake order" (1:112). Later he said, "I admire a good many of my enemies more than I admire some of my friends" (2:142). Emerson once made bold to advise Whitman how to deal with them: "You have a great pack howling at your heels always, Mr. Whitman: I hope you show them all a proper contempt: they deserve no more than your heels." (3:318)

Happy Ending

And how might Whitman have reacted to acceptance of *Leaves of Grass* at long last? In the summer of 1888, the thought evoked a little hilarity: "I wouldn't know what to do, how to comport myself, if I lived long enough to become accepted, to get in demand, to ride on the crest of the wave. I would have to go scratching, questioning, hitching about, to see if this was the real critter, the old Walt Whitman—to see if Walt Whitman had not suffered a destructive transformation—become apostate, formal, reconciled to the conventions, subdued from the old independence." (2:154)

Revisions

"How William [O'Connor] would storm and cry out if I made a change in *Leaves of Grass*—a comma, even. He was worst of all. And [Dr. Richard] Bucke next, easily next—though not quite as bad. And even Mrs. [Anne] Gilchrist, who, if she ever showed passion at all, came nearest it in the matter of revisions. . . . Bucke probably does not know that long long ago, before the Leaves had ever been to the printer, I had them in half a dozen forms—larger, smaller, recast, outcast, taken apart, put together—viewing them from every point I knew—even at the last not putting them together and out with any idea that they must eternally remain unchanged. Bucke mistakes the danger: there was no danger. I have always been disposed to hear the worst that could be said against the poems—even the most rasping things—everything, in fact which would serve to give me an honest new point of observation. That was a necessary part of my career." (8:351–52)

No Dickers

Whitman recalled the main impetus behind *Leaves of Grass* as being one of fearless self-will. On 8 August 1888, he told Traubel: "So it is with *Leaves*—it must drive on, drive on, without protest, without explanation, without hesitations, on and on—no apologies, no dickers, no compromises—just drive on and on, no matter how rough, how dangerous, the road may be." (2:107)

Spinal Purpose

One day Whitman insisted on holding Traubel's very cold hand when he arrived: "It *is* cold, therefore I keep it. It is a reminiscence of the open air, the sky, the sea, and no one knows how precious these are—have been—to me. And indeed, it is to surcharge *Leaves of Grass* with them that was my presiding spinal purpose from the start." (7:414)

Escaping the Taint

"I suppose every man has his purposes. I had mine—to have no purpose—to state, to capture, the drift of a life—to let things flow in, one after another, take their places, their own way. My worst struggle was not with ideas, anything of that sort, but against the literariness of the age—for I, too, like all others, was born in the vesture of this false notion of literature, and no one so born can entirely—I say entirely—escape the taint. Though, as for me, looking back on the battleground, I pride myself I have escaped the pollution as much as any." (8:423)

Mother Dearest

On 9 August 1888, Whitman spoke of the influence of his mother, Louisa Van Velsor Whitman: "The reality, the simplicity, the transparency of my dear, dear mother's life was responsible for the main things in the letters [Whitman wrote to her] as in *Leaves of Grass* itself. How much I owe to her! . . . *Leaves of Grass* is the flower of her temperament active in me." (2:113)

Pipes, Not Poems*—Leaves *Among the Whitmans

When Traubel asked about his family's response to *Leaves of Grass,* Whitman replied, "No one of my people—the people near to me—ever had any time for *Leaves of Grass*—thought it more than an ordinary piece of work, if that." Not even his mother? "No—I think not—even her: there is, as I say, no one in my immediate family who follows me out on that line. My dear mother had every general faith in me; that is where it stopped. She stood before *Leaves of Grass* mystified, defeated." And his brother George? Whitman smiled and said, "You know that George believes in pipes, not poems." (1:227)

At the Opera

Whitman several times invoked opera as an important influence on the early editions of *Leaves of Grass.* On 21 August 1888, he reminisced: "My younger life was so saturated with the emotions, raptures, up-lifts, of such musical experiences [as hearing the tenor Cesare Badiali] that it would be surprising indeed if all my future work had not been colored by them. A real musician running through *Leaves of Grass*—a philosopher musician—could put his finger on this and that anywhere in the text no doubt indicating the activity of the influences I have spoken of" (2:174). In his 1882 memoir, *Specimen Days,* Whitman wrote that "certain actors and singers" had "a good deal to do with the business" of gestating *Leaves of Grass:* "I heard, these years, well render'd, all the Italian and other operas in vogue." Reproduced by Traubel is a lengthy letter Whitman wrote to one of his young Civil War "soger boys" describing in detail an 1863 opera performance in New York. It ends, "Such singing and strong rich music always give me the greatest pleasure—and so the opera is the only amusement I have gone to, for my own satisfaction, for last ten years" (3:104). When Whitman vetted the manuscript of the first biography about him, published in 1883 by his friend R. M. Bucke, he added many passages, among them this sentence: "It has already been told how, during the gestation of the poems, the author was saturated for years with the rendering by the best vocalists and performers, of the best operas and oratorios."

Big Voices

"Understand me, I mean that men shall proceed in all they do out of a knowledge of life—as great actors act, orators speak, singers sing—as in [the Italian contralto Marietta] Alboni's voice, perhaps the greatest singer ever breathed—as in [Junius Brutus] Booth—the old Booth—I don't know but the grandest actor the world has seen or will see—as in [Col. Robert] Ingersoll—voice, vitality, and so on—full—overflowing—with accumulation of fact, feeling, actual palpitating experience—crowded into them, as crowded into me, by resistless forces of a proud pure ancestry—intricately woven from hardy, to hardy, purposes—splendid effects." (8:179–80)

Ecstatic Beginnings

In a letter of 2 December 1877, J. T. Trowbridge had long ago written that he was "astonished that these latter-day critics should have so little to say of the first *Leaves of Grass,* or venture to speak of them only apologetically." Whitman responded to a rereading of this letter on 30 August 1888: "I think I know what Trowbridge means, too: I do not consider his position unreasonable: there was an immediateness in the 1855 edition, an incisive directness, that was perhaps not repeated in any section of poems afterwards added to the book: a hot, unqualifying temper, an insulting arrogance (to use a few strong words) that would not have been as natural to the periods that followed. We miss the ecstasy of statement in some of the after-work—miss that and get something different, something in some ways undoubtedly better. But what's the use arguing the unarguable question?" (2.225). Whitman's first biographer, Richard Maurice Bucke, appears to have agreed with this view. In his first letter to Whitman, dated 19 December 1870, Bucke wrote: "Lately I have got a copy of the 1867 edition of *Leaves of Grass,* and I have compared the Walt Whitman in that with the same poem in the 1855 edition, and I must say that I like the earlier edition best." (2:6)

Funny Book

Talk on 30 January 1889 turned to the notion, then abroad among the public, that Whitman had no funny bone. The poet begged to differ: "I pride myself on being a real humorist underneath everything else. There are some people who look upon *Leaves of Grass* as a funny book: my brother George has often asked me with a wink in his eye: 'I say, Walt, what's the game you're up to, anyway?' So I may go down into history, if I go at all, as a merrymaker wearing a cap and bells rather than a prophet or what the Germans call a philosoph" (4:49). This view may help to explain why, the previous year, Whitman was willing to admit that *Leaves* left some room for satirical wits to play: "I am aware that *Leaves of Grass* lends itself readily to parody—invites parody—given the right man to do it." (2:252)

Dear Loving Comrade, Pete

One of Whitman's most important relationships was with the streetcar conductor Peter Doyle, whom he met while living in Washington, D.C. On 21 October 1888, he waxed nostalgic: "I remember one place in Maryland in particular to which we would go. How splendid, above all, the moon—the moon, the half moon: and then the wonder, the delight, the silences . . . It was a great, a precious, a memorable, experience. To get the ensemble of *Leaves of Grass* you have got to include such things as these—the walks, Pete's friendship: yes, such things: they are absolutely necessary to the completion of the story." (2:512)

Civil War Boys

Whitman told Traubel that his going off to the War was "the very centre, circumference, umbilicus of my whole career" (3:95). One day a few months later, when he was seventy, Whitman came across the draft of a letter written to one of his Manhattan friends from Washington over a quarter century earlier. In it he described his hospital work and reminisced about his profit from these harrowing ministrations: "What did I get? Well—I got the boys, for one thing: the boys: thousands of them: they were, they are, they will be mine. I gave myself for them: myself: I got the boys: then I got *Leaves of Grass:* but for this I would never have had *Leaves of Grass*—the consummated book (the last confirming word): I got that: the boys, the *Leaves:* I got them" (3:582). It is worth noting, however, that when Whitman was asked if he made *Leaves* a part of his hospital work, he replied that he could not remember once having given a copy of it to a wounded soldier (4:63).

Good Sex

Though Whitman had in fact toned down some of the potent sexuality of the early editions of *Leaves,* he spoke very differently on 20 March 1889: "Had I *Leaves of Grass* to write over again, knowing what I know now, I do not think I should in any way touch or abate the sexual portions, as you call them: but in the other matter, in the 'good' and 'evil' business, I should be more definite, more emphatic than ever." (4:389)

The Idiocity of Leaves

When an "error" in *Leaves* was drawn to his attention one day, Whitman responded: "I see—I see: it must be wrong—but that is one of my idiocities—to put it there and let it be, wrong or right. Maybe what is wrong for him is right for me: such things, too, do happen." (2:178)

Room for All

The open-armed essence of *Leaves of Grass* was insisted upon by Whitman many times. On 26 May 1889: "In my philosophy—in the bottom-meanings of *Leaves of Grass*—there is plenty of room for all" (5:227). In August 1890: "*Leaves of Grass* . . . is based on no less than the world, man in *ensemble*—

not his parts, not special races, religions" (7:72). And the next fall he remarked similarly, "*Leaves of Grass* has its own eligibilities—has no narrow tendencies—at least, I hope it has not" (7:238) and "catholicity—receptiveness—welcome: that is *Leaves of Grass.*" (7:355)

Damn *Art and Let Fly!*

In May 1891, Traubel tells Whitman of a debate on the future of American literature during which one suggestion is for building on "some great English model." Whitman erupts: "Damn the Professor! Damn the model! Build on hell! No, no, no—that is not what we are here for—that is not the future—that's not *Leaves of Grass*—opposite to all that . . . Here, Horace—here in *Leaves of Grass*—are 400, 430 pages of *let-fly*. No art, no schemes, no fanciful, delicate, elegant constructiveness—but *let-fly*. A young man appears in the Western world—the new world—is born in the free air, near the sea—lives an early life in the early life of a big city—absorbs its meanings, the past, history, masses of men, whores, saints, sailors, laborers, carpenters, pilots—goes liberal-footed everywhere—has no erudition—reads books, reads men—prepares himself a great ground—travels—takes everywhere—every sign a sign to him, every treasure his treasure—nothing denied—lives the life of a war—unmistakably the greatest war of history—passes through camps, enters the hospitals—using gifts of penetration (Horace, they told me my penetration would damn me!)—accumulates, accumulates—then lets fly—lets fly—no art—no, *damn* art!" (8:178–79)

The Painter for Leaves

Whitman saw the rural landscapes of Jean-François Millet (1814–75) in person for the first time on a trip to Boston; he was deeply moved, especially by *The Sower*. Later he told Traubel, "The *Leaves* are really only Millet in another form" (1:7). Three weeks later he elaborated, "Millet is my painter: he belongs to me: I have written Walt Whitman all over him" (1:63). Again, several months later he praised Millet in words that he might have liked to hear applied to *Leaves of Grass:* "Millet's color sense was opulent, thorough, uncompromising, yet not gaudy—never gilt and glitter: emphatic only as nature is emphatic." (3:89)

No Cocked Philosophy

On 21 June 1889, Whitman strongly asserted the lack of an "agenda" in *Leaves of Grass:* "I do not teach a definite philosophy—I have no cocked and primed system. . . . He who goes to my book expecting a cocked and primed philosophy will depart utterly disappointed—and deserve to!" (5:310)

Fair Warning
Whitman, on 1 October 1889, warned of the challenge presented by his lifework: "I almost pity the young man (or woman) who grapples with *Leaves of Grass*. It is so hard a tussle." (6:33)

A Woman's Book
"*Leaves of Grass* is essentially a woman's book: the women do not know it: it speaks out the necessities, its cry is the cry of the right and wrong of the woman sex—of the woman first of all, of the facts of creation first of all—of the feminine." (2:331)

Solving the Riddle
Traubel recorded one day Whitman's being "much amused" by a debate about the riddle in "A Riddle Song." The poet "roared when I told him B[ucke]. thought I should watch for some hint of a solution before W. slipped away from us." Whitman responded, "Doctor would find after all, that it is the old story, 'diplomacy,' again—the secret: that there is no secret. Some of my simplest pieces have created the most noise. I have been told that 'A Child Went Forth' was a favorite with Longfellow, but to me there is very little in that poem. That is one of my penalties—to have the real vital utterances, if there are any in me, go undetected." (8:116)

Turning Quaker
One day Whitman recalled a time early in life when he considered becoming a Quaker. In the end, he said, "I put it aside as impossible: I was never made to live inside a fence." Traubel then asked whether Whitman thought *Leaves* could have been written if he had "turned Quaker," and he replied, "It is more than likely not—quite probably not—almost certainly not" (2:19). In 1803, De Witt Clinton observed, "The meekness of Quakerism will do in religion, but not in politics." Nor, apparently, will it do in revolutionary poetics.

No China Spared
Whitman had good reason to boast, on 28 March 1890, that "*Leaves of Grass* is an iconoclasm, it starts out to shatter the idols of porcelain worshiped by the average poets of our age." (6:343)

Song of the Real Me
On 24 June 1890, Whitman asserted one of the most obvious characteristics of *Leaves*, namely its richly autobiographical impetus: "I should say that anyone, to get hold of me—all I have written—would see that all my work is

autobiographical—yes, and that this autobiography finds its center and explication in the poems—in *Leaves of Grass.*" (6:475)

Deep Exposé

A month earlier, at his seventy-first birthday party on 31 May 1890, which was held at Reisser's restaurant in Philadelphia, Whitman had delicately suggested that he had carefully veiled some of the autobiography in *Leaves:* "Often it is by the things unsaid, rather than the things said, that give importance to speech, to life. I have kept the roots well underground. *Leaves of Grass,* be they what they may, are only in part the fact—for beneath, around, are contributing forces, which do not come out in the superficial *exposé.*" (6:440)

Phenomenal

Several months later, on 28 September 1890, at supper with a piece of chicken suspended on his fork, Whitman paused to speak further of the implicit meanings of *Leaves of Grass:* "It can never be understood but by an indirection. . . . It stands first of all for that something back of phenomena, in phenomena, which gives it all its significance, yet cannot be described—which eludes definition, yet is the most real thing of all." (7:156)

Healthy Appetite

In the fall of 1891, Whitman offered several passing remarks about *Leaves of Grass.* On October 2 he whimsically imagined what might be in store for his book in the future: "It is one of my dreads, that there may come a time, and people, to *exposit, explicate, Leaves of Grass*" (9:3–4). On October 9, he said his main purpose was "to leave men healthy, to fill them with a new atmosphere" (9:19). "Solidarity—human solidarity—is not that *Leaves of Grass?*" (9:27), he asked rhetorically on October 14. A week later, on 20 October, he asserted that "there is no delicatesse, no aestheticism, about the *Leaves.*" On the same evening he spoke of "the heroic animality of the *Leaves*" and then went after its critics: "How these damned saints affect a carriage of anti-animality! Well, our *Leaves* stand against all that: we are solidly for healthy appetite!" (9:61)

Conclusive Utterance

In January 1892, feeling his death was imminent, Whitman several times emphasized his desire to give his final edition of *Leaves of Grass* precedence over all others: "This, of course, is the edition I swear by . . . the only authentic and perfect" (9:379). "This is now my own personal, authenticated volume. . . . It is my ultimate, my final word and touch, to go forth now, for good or bad, into the world of the future" (9:382). "The point is, to substitute *this* for all other editions—to make of it my final, conclusive utterance and message—a declaration of my realized intentions." (9:388)

Plus Ça Change

On January 27 of his last year, Whitman offered this response to news that *Leaves of Grass* was still banned from the library of Harvard College: "I am not astonished—the action would probably be duplicated in many quarters" (9:395). Early in his conversations with Traubel, Whitman summed up his fate on campus: "College men as a rule would rather get along without me . . . they go so far, the best of them—then stop: some of them don't go at all" (1:286). He also fared poorly in one of America's major emporiums, John Wanamaker's in Philadelphia, which had long been notoriously shy about *Leaves of Grass*. Just weeks before his death, when Whitman heard that Wanamaker's would take orders for *Leaves of Grass* but not keep it in stock, he laughed and said, "It is an old story—a pull on the old string." (9:538)

Individual

"My *Leaves* mean, that in the end reason, the individual, should have control—hold the reins—not necessarily to use them—but to possess the power: reason, the individual—through these solidarity (the whole race, all times, all lands)—this is the main purport, the spinal creative fact, by which we stand or fall." (8:208)

Humble Request

"If these fellows would only read *Leaves of Grass*—read it through with their eyes rather than through their prejudices: but when they condemn it without reading it—that's what nettles me." (2:142)

Ultimate Mystery

"*Leaves of Grass* is a mystery to me—I do not pretend myself to have solved it—not at all. Doctor [Bucke, in his book on Whitman,] starts off with great vehemence to assert—*Leaves of Grass* means this and this and this and this and this—oh! stamps it down with the hammer of Thor! But even he, much as he really *does* know about it, has never caught this—that *Leaves of Grass* never started out to do anything—has no purpose—has no definite beginning, middle, end. It is reflection, it is statement, it is to see and tell, it is to keep clear of judgments, lessons, school-ways—to be a world, with all the mystery of that, all its movement, all its life. From this standpoint I, myself, often stand in astonishment before the book—am defeated by it—lost in its curious revolutions, its whimsics, its overpowering momentum—lost as if a stranger, even as I am a stranger on this earth—driving about with it, knowing nothing of why or result. . . . This way, you see, I am a spectator, too." (8:321)

[4]
Contemporary Reviews of *Leaves of Grass*

Charles A. Dana, New York Daily Tribune, *23 July 1855*

From the unique effigies of the anonymous author of this volume which graces the frontispiece, we may infer that he belongs to the exemplary class of society sometimes irreverently styled "loafers." He is therein represented in a garb, half sailor's, half workman's, with no superfluous appendage of coat or waistcoat, a "wide-awake" perched jauntily on his head, one hand in his pocket and the other on his hip, with a certain air of mild defiance, and an expression of pensive insolence in his face which seems to betoken a consciousness of his mission as the "coming man." This view of the author is confirmed in the preface. He vouchsafes, before introducing us to his poetry, to enlighten our benighted minds as to the true function of the American poet. Evidently the original, which is embodied in the most extraordinary prose since the "Sayings" of the modern Orpheus, was found in the "interior consciousness" of the writer. Of the materials afforded by this country for the operations of poetic art we have a lucid account.

[*quotes second paragraph of the 1855 preface*]

With veins full of such poetical stuff, the United States, as we are kindly informed, "of all nations most needs poets, and will doubtless have the greatest and use them the greatest." Here is a full-length figure of the true poet:

[*quotes at length from the sixth paragraph*]

Of the nature of poetry the writer discourses in a somewhat too oracular strain, especially as he has been anticipated in his "utterances" by Emerson and other modern "prophets of the soul":

[*quotes at length from the eighth paragraph*]

Such is the poetic theory of our nameless bard. He furnishes a severe standard for the estimate of his own productions. His *Leaves of Grass* are doubtless intended as an illustration of the natural poet. They are certainly original in their external form, have been shaped on no pre-existent model out of the author's own brain. Indeed, his independence often becomes coarse and defiant. His language is too frequently reckless and indecent though this appears to arise from a naive unconsciousness rather than from an impure mind. His words might have passed between Adam and Eve in Paradise, before the want of fig-leaves brought no shame; but they are quite out of place amid the decorum of modern society, and will justly prevent his volume from free circulation in scrupulous circles. With these glaring faults, the *Leaves of Grass* are not destitute of peculiar poetic merits, which will awaken an interest in the lovers of literary curiosities. They are full of bold, stirring thoughts—with occasional passages of effective description, betraying a genuine intimacy with Nature and a keen appreciation of beauty—often presenting a rare felicity of diction, but so disfigured with eccentric fancies as to prevent a consecutive perusal without offense, though no impartial reader can fail to be impressed with the vigor and quaint beauty of isolated portions. A few specimens will suffice to give an idea of this odd genius.

[*quotes several long extracts*]

The volume contains many more *Leaves of Grass* of similar quality, as well as others which cannot be especially commended either for fragrance or form. Whatever severity of criticism they may challenge for their rude ingenuousness, and their frequent divergence into the domain of the fantastic, the taste of not over dainty fastidiousness will discern much of the essential spirit of poetry beneath an uncouth and grotesque embodiment.

Charles Eliot Norton, Putnam's Monthly *(New York), September 1855*

Our account of the last month's literature would be incomplete without some notice of a curious and lawless collection of poems, called *Leaves of Grass,* issued in a thin quarto without the name of publisher or author. The poems, twelve in number, are neither in rhyme nor blank verse, but in a sort of excited prose broken into lines without any attempt at measure or regularity, and, as many readers will perhaps think, without any idea of sense or reason. The writer's scorn for the wonted usages of good writing extends to the vocabulary he adopts; words usually banished from polite society are here employed without reserve and with perfect indifference to their effect on the reader's mind; and not only is the book one not to be read aloud to a mixed audience, but the introduction of terms, never before heard or seen, and of slang expressions, often renders an otherwise striking passage altogether laughable. But, as the writer is a new light in poetry, it is only fair to let him state his theory himself . . .

[*long quotation from preface on the "greatest poet," beginning "The art of art . . ."*]

The application of these principles, and of many others equally peculiar, which are expounded in a style equally oracular throughout the long preface, is made *passim,* and often with comical success, in the poems themselves, which may briefly be described as a compound of the New England transcendentalist and New York rowdy. A fireman or omnibus driver who had intelligence enough to absorb the speculations of that school of thought which culminated at Boston some fifteen or eighteen years ago, and resources of expression to put them forth again in a form of his own, with sufficient self-conceit and contempt for public taste to affront all usual propriety of diction, might have written this gross yet elevated, this superficial yet profound, this preposterous yet somehow fascinating book. As we say, it is a mixture of Yankee transcendentalism and New York rowdyism, and, what must be surprising to both these elements, they here seem to fuse and combine with the most perfect harmony. The vast and vague conceptions of the one lose nothing of their quality in passing through the coarse and odd intellectual medium of the other; while there is an original perception of nature, a manly brawn, and an epic directness in our new poet, which belong to no other adept of the transcendental school. But we have no intention of regularly criticising this very irregular production; our aim is rather to cull, from the rough and ragged thicket of its pages, a few passages equally remarkable in point of thought and expression. Of course we do not select those which are the most transcendental or the most bold . . . [*quotes a dozen extracts, more than eighty lines*].

Rufus W. Griswold, New York Criterion, *10 November 1855*

An unconsidered letter of introduction has oftentimes procured the admittance of a scurvy fellow into good society, and our apology for permitting any allusion to the above volume in our columns is, that it has been unworthily recommended by a gentleman of wide repute, and might, on that account, obtain access to respectable people, unless its real character were exposed.

Mr. Ralph Waldo Emerson either recognizes and accepts these "leaves," as the gratifying results of his own peculiar doctrines, or else he has hastily endorsed them, after a partial and superficial reading. If it is of any importance, he may extricate himself from the dilemma. We, however, believe that this book does express the bolder results of a certain transcendental kind of thinking, which some have styled philosophy.

As to the volume itself, we have only to remark that it strongly fortifies the doctrines of the Metempsychosists, for it is impossible to imagine how any man's fancy could have conceived such a mass of stupid filth, unless he were possessed of the soul of a sentimental donkey that had died of disappointed love. This *poet* (?) without wit, but with a certain vagrant wildness, just serves to show the energy which natural imbecility is occasionally capable of under strong excitement.

There are too many persons, who imagine they demonstrate their superiority to their fellows, by disregarding all the politeness and decencies of life, and, therefore, justify themselves in indulging the vilest imaginings and shamefullest license. But Nature, abhorring the abuse of the capacities she has given to man, retaliates upon him, by rendering extravagant indulgence in any direction followed by an insatiable, ever-consuming, and never to be appeased passion.

Thus, to these pitiful beings, virtue and honor are but names. Bloated with self-conceit, they strut abroad unabashed in the daylight, and expose to the world the festering sores that overlay them like a garment. Unless we admit this exhibition to be beautiful, we are at once set down for nonprogressive conservatives, destitute of the "inner light," the far-seeingness which, of course, characterizes those gifted individuals. Now, any one who has noticed the tendency of thought in these later years, must be aware that a quantity of this kind of nonsense is being constantly displayed. The immodesty of presumption exhibited by the *seers;* their arrogant pretentiousness; the complacent smile with which they listen to the echo of their own braying, should be, and we believe is, enough, to disgust the great majority of sensible folks; but, unfortunately, there is a class that, mistaking sound for sense, attach some importance to all this rant and cant. These candid, these ingenuous, these honest "progressionists"; these human diamonds without flaws; these men that have *come*—detest furiously all shams; "to the pure, all things are pure"; they are pure, and, consequently, must thrust their reeking presence under every man's nose.

They seem to think that man has no instinctive delicacy; is not imbued with a conservative and preservative modesty, that acts as a restraint upon the violence of passions, which, for a wise purpose, have been made so strong. No! these fellows have no secrets, no disguises; no, indeed! But they do have, conceal it by whatever language they choose, a degrading, beastly sensuality that is fast rotting the healthy core of all the social virtues.

There was a time when licentiousness laughed at reproval; now it writes essays and delivers lectures. Once it shunned the light; now it courts attention, writes books showing how grand and pure it is, and prophesies from its lecherous lips its own ultimate triumph.

Shall we argue with such men? Shall we admit them into our houses, that they may leave a foul odor, contaminate the pure, healthful air? Or shall they be placed in the same category with the comparatively innocent slave of poverty, ignorance and passion that skulks along in the shadows of byways, even in her deep degradation possessing some sparks of the Divine light, the germ of good that reveals itself by a sense of shame?

Thus, then, we leave this gathering of muck to the laws which, certainly, if they fulfill their intent, must have power to suppress such gross obscenity. As it is entirely destitute of wit, there is no probability that any one would, after this exposure, read it in the hope of finding that; and we trust no one will require further evidence—for, indeed, we do not believe there is a newspaper so vile that would print confirmatory extracts.

In our allusion to this book, we have found it impossible to convey any, even the most faint idea of its style and contents, and of our disgust and detestation of them, without employing language that cannot be pleasing to ears polite; but it does seem that some one should, under circumstances like these, undertake a most disagreeable, yet stern duty.

The records of crime show that many monsters have gone on in impunity, because the exposure of their vileness was attended with too great delicacy. "*Peccatum illud horribile, inter Christianos non nominandum.*"*

**The Latin phrase quoted by Griswold was the standard legal form of reference to sodomy; it translates as "that horrible sin not to be named among Christians." Blackstone, in his* Commentaries on the Laws of England *(1769), writes of sodomy: "It will be more eligible to imitate in this respect the delicacy of our English law, which treats it, in its very indictments, as a crime not fit to be named:* peccatum illud horribile, inter Christianos non nominandum."

Edward Everett Hale, North American Review *(Boston), January 1856*

Everything about the external arrangement of this book was odd and out of the way. The author printed it himself, and it seems to have been left to the winds of heaven to publish it. So it happened that we had not discovered it before our last number, although we believe the sheets had then passed the press. It bears no publisher's name, and, if the reader goes to a bookstore for it, he may expect to be told at first, as we were, that there is no such book, and has not been. Nevertheless, there is such a book, and it is well worth going twice to the bookstore to buy it. Walter Whitman, an American—one of the roughs—no sentimentalist—no stander above men and women, or apart from them—no more modest than immodest—has tried to write down here, in a sort of prose poetry, a good deal of what he has seen, felt, and guessed at in a pilgrimage of some thirty-five years. He has a horror of conventional language of any kind. His theory of expression is that, "to speak in literature with the perfect rectitude and *insouciance* of the movements of animals, is the flawless triumph of art." Now a great many men have said this before. But generally it is the introduction to something more artistic than ever—more conventional and strained. Antony began by saying he was no orator, but none the less did an oration follow. In this book, however, the prophecy is fairly fulfilled in the accomplishment. "What I experience or portray shall go from my composition without a shred of my composition. You shall stand by my side and look in the mirror with me."

So truly accomplished is this promise—which anywhere else would be a flourish of trumpets—that this thin quarto deserves its name. That is to say, one reads and enjoys the freshness, simplicity, and reality of what he reads, just as the tired man, lying on the hill-side in summer, enjoys the leaves of grass around him—enjoys the shadow—enjoys the flecks of sunshine—not for what they "suggest to him," but for what they are.

So completely does the author's remarkable power rest in his simplicity, that the preface to the book—which does not even have large letters at the beginning of the lines, as the rest has is perhaps the very best thing in it. We find more to the point in the following analysis of the "genius of the United States," than we have found in many more pretentious studies of it.

[*quotes entire third paragraph of preface*]

The book is divided into a dozen or more sections, and in each one of these some thread of connection may be traced, now with ease, now with difficulty—each being a string of verses, which claim to be written without effort and with entire *abandon.* So the book is a collection of observations, speculations, memories, and prophecies, clad in the simplest, truest, and often the most nervous English—in the midst of which the reader comes upon something as much out of place as a piece of rotten wood would be among leaves of grass in the meadow, if the meadow had no object but to furnish a child's couch. So slender is the connection that we hardly injure the following scraps by extracting them.

[*quotes lines 1231–9 of "I celebrate myself"*]

Here is the story of the gallant seaman who rescued the passengers on the *San Francisco:*

[*quotes lines 818–26 of "I celebrate myself"*]

Claiming in this way a personal interest in every thing that has ever happened in the world, and, by the wonderful sharpness and distinctness of his imagination, making the claim effective and reasonable, Mr. "Walt Whitman" leaves it a matter of doubt where he has been in this world, and where not. It is very clear that with him, as with most other effective writers, a keen, absolute memory, which takes in and holds every detail of the past—as they say the exaggerated power of the memory does when a man is drowning—is a gift of his organization as remarkable as his vivid imagination. What he has seen once, he has seen for ever. And thus there are in this curious book little thumb-nail sketches of life in the prairie, life in California, life at school, life in the nursery—life, indeed, we know not where not—which, as they are unfolded one after another, strike us as real—so real that we wonder how they came on paper.

For the purpose of showing that he is above every conventionalism, Mr. Whitman puts into the book one or two lines which he would not address to a woman nor to a company of men. There is not anything, perhaps, which modern usage would stamp as more indelicate than are some passages in Homer. There is not a word in it meant to attract readers by its grossness, as there is in half the literature of the last century, which holds its place unchallenged on the tables of our drawing-rooms. For all that, it is a pity that a book where everything else is natural should go out of the way to avoid the suspicion of being prudish.

New York Daily News, 27 *February 1856*

A new edition, we believe, of the famous Whitman's poems, which made such a flutter among the "gray goose quills" of this city and "other quarters of the globe" some time ago. Of the poem which occupies the ninety-five pages of this folio, we have before briefly spoken. Upon examining it a second time, and pondering its aims and expressions, we feel constrained to say that it is certainly the strangest, most extraordinary production we have ever attempted to peruse. Still, like the rest of our countrymen, we are by no means either averse to extraordinary things or afraid of them. We enjoy enterprise in speech and writing as thoroughly as in steam vessels, revolving rifles or new-found Nicaraguas. Therefore we shall not quarrel with Mr. Whitman for being odd. Oddness is the normal condition of some natures—of the freshest and best, perhaps—at least when it means frankness and opposition to solemn propriety, alias humbug and red tape.

Mr. Whitman's preface is what the humdrum world calls "queer" as entirely perhaps as his poem, yet we think a great deal of it both finely and bravely uttered as well as true. None can, more than we do, entirely hate that cant which always ascribes this or that kind of writing to this or the other "school," as if the young author had necessarily in every instance copied some model; as if two similarly constituted minds may not naturally seek similar expression! It is precisely this stupid, stereotyped classification adopted by indolent or clique-led reviewers, that has produced so many abortions in literature through the straining after at least the appearance of total originality, but to give future readers of this book some indication of its style, ere they have opened it, we will say that it is Germanic and Carlylean—even Emersonian—sometimes in the strain of Martin Farquhar Tupper, although far stronger and more pointed than the latter.

The poem exhibits undoubted and striking evidence of genius and power. But the author reasoning that the spirit of the American people, nay, of any people, is chiefly represented by its uncultivated though, perhaps, naturally intelligent classes, falls into the error of mistaking their frequent uncouthness as a fair revelation of that spirit, and the bathos often produced in some of his finest passages by the presence of this idea defaces his work and repels hundreds of candid minds who would be eager to acknowledge his claims, but are thus prevented from reading enough to recognize them.

In glancing rapidly over the *Leaves of Grass* you are puzzled whether to set the author down as a madman or an opium eater; when you have studied them you recognize a poet of extraordinary vigor, nay even beauty of thought, beneath the most fantastic possible garments of diction. If Hamlet had gone mad, in Ophelia's way, as well as in his own, and in addition to his own vein of madness, he might, when transported to our own age and country, have talked thus.

In a crush hat and red shirt open at the neck, without waistcoat or jacket, one hand on his hip and the other thrust into his pocket, Walt Whitman the b'hoy poet, on his muscle, writes sentences like these: [*a dozen short extracts follow*].

We are tempted to quote many strophes from this remarkable collection of genius inebriated with its own overflowing fountains of fancy, but must conclude with the following fine lines, referring to past struggles for freedom and predicting a future:

[*last seventeen lines of "Suddenly out of its stale and drowsy lair" quoted*]

For the sum of 75 cents any reader may accompany Whitman through a poetic chaos—bright, dark, splendid, common, ridiculous and sublime—in which are floating the nebulæ and germs of matter for a starry universe of organized and harmonious systems that may yet revolve, in all the magnificence of artistic order, through the highest heaven of fame!

As proof that whatever may be the merits or demerits of this singular production, we may state that very many thousand copies have been sold and the demand is still increasing.

London Critic, *1 April 1856*

We had ceased, we imagined, to be surprised at anything that America could produce. We had become stoically indifferent to her Woolly Horses, her Mermaids, her Sea Serpents, her Barnums, and her Fanny Ferns; but the last monstrous importation from Brooklyn, New York, has scattered our indifference to the winds. Here is a thin quarto volume without an author's name on the title-page; but to atone for which we have a portrait engraved on steel of the notorious individual who is the poet presumptive. This portrait expresses all the features of the hard democrat, and none of the flexile delicacy of the civilised poet. The damaged hat, the rough beard, the naked throat, the shirt exposed to the waist, are each and all presented to show that the man to whom those articles belongs scorns the delicate arts of civilisation. The man is the true impersonation of his book—rough, uncouth, vulgar. It was by the merest accident that we discovered the name of this erratic and newest wonder; but at page 29 we find that he is—

> Walt Whitman, an American, one of the
> roughs, a Kosmos,
> Disorderly, fleshly, and sensual.

The words "an American" are a surplussage, "one of the roughs" too painfully apparent; but what is intended to be conveyed by "a Kosmos" we cannot tell, unless it means a man who thinks that the fine essence of poetry consists in writing a book which an American reviewer is compelled to declare is "not to be read aloud to a mixed audience." We should have passed over this book, *Leaves of Grass,* with indignant contempt, had not some few Transatlantic critics attempted to "fix" this Walt Whitman as the poet who shall give a new and independent literature to America—who shall form a race of poets as Banquo's issue formed a line of kings. Is it possible that the most prudish nation in the world will adopt a poet whose indecencies stink in the nostrils? We hope not; and yet there is a probability, and we will show why, that this Walt Whitman will not meet with the stern rebuke which he so richly deserves. America has felt, oftener perhaps than we have declared, that she has no national poet—that each one of her children of song has relied too much on European inspiration, and clung too fervently to the old conventionalities. It is therefore not unlikely that she may believe in the dawn of a thoroughly original literature, now there has arisen a man who scorns the Hellenic deities, who has no belief in, perhaps because he has no knowledge of, Homer and Shakspere; who relies on his own rugged nature, and trusts to his own rugged language, being himself what he shows in his poems. Once transfix him as the genesis of a new era, and the manner of the man may be forgiven or forgotten. But what claim has this Walt Whitman to be thus considered, or to be considered a poet at all? We grant freely enough that he has a strong relish for nature and freedom, just as an animal has; nay, further, that his crude mind is capable of appreciating some of nature's beauties; but it by no means follows that, because nature is excellent, therefore art is contemptible. Walt Whitman is as unacquainted with art as a hog is with mathematics. His poems—we must call them so for convenience—twelve in number, are innocent of rhythm, and resemble nothing so much as the war-cry of the Red Indians. Indeed, Walt Whitman has had near and ample opportunities of studying the vociferations of a few amiable savages. Or rather perhaps, this Walt Whitman reminds us of Caliban flinging down his logs and setting himself to write a poem. In fact Caliban, and not Walt Whitman, might have written this:

> I too am not a bit tamed—I too am
>   untranslatable.
> I sound my *barbaric yawp* over the
>   roofs of the world.

Is this man with the "barbaric yawp" to push Longfellow into the shade, and he meanwhile to stand and "make mouths" at the sun? The chance of this might be formidable were it not ridiculous. That object or that act which most develops the ridiculous element carries in its bosom the seeds of decay, and is wholly powerless to trample out of God's universe one spark of the beautiful. We do not, then, fear this Walt Whitman, who gives us slang in the place of melody, and rowdyism in the place of regularity. The depth of his indecencies will be the grave of his fame, or ought to be if all proper feeling is not extinct. The very nature of this man's compositions excludes us from proving by extracts the truth of our remarks; but we, who are not prudish, emphatically declare that the man who wrote page 79 of the *Leaves of Grass* deserves nothing so richly as the public executioner's whip [*in 1855, page 79 included ll. 34–59 of "The bodies of men and women engirth me . . .* "]. Walt Whitman libels the highest type of humanity, and calls his free speech the true utterance of *a man:* we, who may have been misdirected by civilisation, call it the expression of a *beast.*

Fanny Fern, New York Ledger, *10 May 1856*

Well baptized: fresh, hardy, and grown for the masses. Not more welcome is their natural type to the winter-bound, bed-ridden, and spring-emancipated invalid. *Leaves of Grass* thou art unspeakably delicious, after the forced, stiff, Parnassian exotics for which our admiration has been vainly challenged.

Walt Whitman, the effeminate world needed thee. The timidest soul whose wings ever drooped with discouragement could not choose but rise on thy strong pinions.

> Undrape—you are not guilty to me,
>   nor stale nor discarded;
> I see through the broadcloth and
>   gingham whether or no.

> O despairer, here is my neck,
> You shall *not* go down! Hang your whole
>   weight upon me.

Walt Whitman, the world needed a "Native American" of thorough, out and out breed—

enamored of *women* not *ladies, men* not *gentlemen;* something beside a mere Catholic-hating Know-Nothing; it needed a man who dared speak out his strong, honest thoughts, in the face of pusillanimous, toadying, republican aristocracy; dictionary-men, hypocrites, cliques and creeds; it needed a large-hearted, untainted, self-reliant, fearless son of the Stars and Stripes, who disdains to sell his birthright for a mess of pottage; who does

> Not call one greater or one smaller,
> That which fills its period and place being
> equal to any . . .

who will

> Accept nothing which all cannot have
> their counterpart of on the same terms.

Fresh *Leaves of Grass*! not submitted by the self-reliant author to the fingering of any publisher's critic, to be arranged, rearranged and disarranged to his circumscribed liking, till they hung limp, tame, spiritless, and scentless. No. It were a spectacle worth seeing, this glorious Native American, who, when the daily labor of chisel and plane was over, himself, with toil-hardened fingers, handled the types to print the pages which wise and good men have since delighted to endorse and to honor. Small critics, whose contracted vision could see no beauty, strength, or grace in these *Leaves,* have long ago repented that they so hastily wrote themselves down shallow by such a premature confession. Where an Emerson and a Howitt have commended, my woman's voice of praise may not avail; but happiness was born a twin, and so I would fain share with others the unmingled delight which these *Leaves* have given me.

I say unmingled; I am not unaware that the charge of coarseness and sensuality has been affixed to them. My moral constitution may be hopelessly tainted—or too sound to be tainted, as the critic wills, but I confess that I extract no poison from these *Leaves*—to me they have brought only healing. Let him who can do so shroud the eyes of the nursing babe lest it should see its mother's breast. Let him look carefully between the gilded covers of books, backed by high-sounding names, and endorsed by parson and priest, lying unrebuked upon his own family table, where the asp of sensuality lies coiled amid rhetorical flowers. Let him examine well the paper dropped weekly at his door, in which virtue and religion are rendered disgusting, save when they walk in satin slippers, or, clothed in purple and fine linen, kneel on a damask *prie-dieu.*

Sensual!—No—the moral assassin looks you not boldly in the eye by broad daylight; but Borgia like takes you treacherously by the hand, while from the glittering ring on his finger he distils through your veins the subtle and deadly poison.

Sensual? The artist who would inflame paints you not nude Nature, but stealing Virtue's veil, with artful artlessness now conceals, now exposes, the ripe and swelling proportions.

Sensual? Let him who would affix this stigma upon *Leaves of Grass* write upon his heart, in letters of fire, these noble words of its author:

> In woman I see the bearer of the great
> fruit, which is immortality . . . .
> the good thereof is not tasted by *roues,*
> and never can be.

> Who degrades or defiles the living human
> body is cursed,
> Who degrades or defiles the body of the
> dead is not more cursed.

Were I an artist I would like no more suggestive subjects for my easel than Walt Whitman's pen has furnished.

William Swinton, New York Daily Times, *13 November 1856*

What Centaur have we here, half man, half beast, neighing shrill defiance to all the world? What conglomerate of thought is this before us, with insolence, philosophy, tenderness, blasphemy, beauty and gross indecency tumbling in drunken confusion through the pages? Who is this arrogant young man who proclaims himself the Poet of the Time, and who roots like a pig among a rotten garbage of licentious thoughts? Who is this flushed and full-blooded lover of Nature who studies her so affectionately, and who sometimes utters her teachings with a lofty tongue? This mass of extraordinary contradictions, this fool and this wise man, this lover of beauty and this sunken sensualist, this original thinker and blind egotist, is Mr. WALT WHITMAN, author of *Leaves of Grass,* and, according to his own account, "a Kosmos."

Some time since there was left at the office of this paper a thin quarto volume bound in green and gold. On opening the book we first beheld, as a frontispiece, the picture of a man in his shirt sleeves, wearing an expression of settled arrogance upon his countenance. We next arrived at a title page of magnificent proportions, with letter-press at least an inch and a half in length. From this title page we learned that the book was entitled *Leaves of Grass,* and was printed at Brooklyn in the year 1855. This inspected, we passed on to what seemed to be a sort of preface, only that it had no beginning, was remarkable for a singular sparseness in the punctuation, and was broken up in a confusing manner by frequent rows of dots separating the paragraphs. To this succeeded eighty-two pages of what appeared at the first glance to be a number of prose sentences printed somewhat after a biblical fashion. Almost at the first page we opened we lighted upon the confession that the author was

> WALT WHITMAN, an American, one of the
>   roughs, a Kosmos,
> Disorderly, fleshy and sensual. . . .

This was sufficient basis for a theory. We accordingly arrived at the conclusion that the insolent-looking young man on the frontispiece was this same WALT WHITMAN, and author of the *Leaves of Grass.*

Then returning to the fore-part of the book, we found proof slips of certain review articles about the *Leaves of Grass.* One of these purported to be extracted from a periodical entitled the *United States Review,* the other was headed "From the *American Phrenological Journal.*" These were accompanied by a printed copy of an extravagant letter of praise addressed by Mr. RALPH WALDO EMERSON to Mr. WALT WHITMAN, complimenting him on the benefaction conferred on society in the present volume. On subsequently comparing the critiques . . . with the preface of the *Leaves of Grass,* we discovered unmistakable internal evidence that Mr. WALT WHITMAN, true to his character of a Kosmos, was not content with writing a book, but was also determined to review it; so Mr. WALT WHITMAN had concocted both those criticisms of his own work, treating it we need not say how favorably. This little discovery of our "disorderly" acquaintance's mode of proceeding rather damped any enthusiasm with which Mr. EMERSON's extravagant letter may have inspired us. We reflected, here is a man who sets himself up as the poet and teacher of his time; who professes a scorn of everything mean and dastardly and double-faced, who hisses with scorn as he passes one in the street whom he suspects of the taint, hypocrisy—yet this self-contained teacher, this rough-and-ready scorner of dishonesty, this rowdy knight-errant who tilts against all lies and shams, himself perpetrates a lie and a sham at the very outset of his career. It is a lie to write a review of one's own book, then extract it from the work in which it appeared and send it out to the world as an impartial editorial utterance. It is an act that the most degraded helot of literature might blush to commit. It is a dishonesty committed against one's own nature, and all the world. Mr. WALT WHITMAN in one of his candid rhapsodies announces that he is "no more modest than immodest." Perhaps in literary matters he carries the theory farther, and is no more honest than dishonest. He likewise says in his preface: "The great poets are known by the absence in them of tricks, and by the justification of perfect personal candor." Where, then, can we place Mr. WALT WHITMAN's claims upon immortality?

We confess we turn from Mr. WHITMAN as Critic to Mr. WHITMAN as Poet with considerable pleasure. We prefer occupying that independent position which Mr. WHITMAN claims for man, and forming our own opinions, rather than swallowing those ready-made. This gentleman begins his poetic life with a coarse and bitter scorn of the past. We have been living stale and unprofitable lives; we have been surfeited with luxury and high living, and are grown lethargic and dull; the age is fast decaying, when, lo! the trump of the Angel Whitman brings the dead to life and animates the slumbering world. If we obey the dictates of that trumpet, we will do many strange things. We will fling off all moral clothing and walk naked over the earth. We will disembarrass our language of all the proprieties of speech and talk indecency broad cast. We will act in short as if the Millennium were arrived in this our present day, when the absence of all vice would no longer necessitate a virtuous discretion. We fear much, Mr. WALT WHITMAN, that the time is not yet come for the nakedness of purity. We are not yet virtuous enough to be able to read your poetry aloud to our children and our wives. What might be pastoral simplicity five hundred years hence, would perhaps be stigmatized as the coarser indecency now, and—we regret to think that you have spoken too soon.

The adoration of the "Me," the "Ego," the "eternal and universal I," to use the jargon of the Boston *Oracle,* is the prevailing motive of *Leaves of Grass*. Man embraces and comprehends the whole. He is everything, and everything is him. All nature ebbs and flows through him in ceaseless tides. He is "his own God and his own Devil," and everything that he does is good. He rejoices with all who rejoice; suffers with all who suffer. This doctrine is exemplified in the book by a panorama as it were of pictures, each of which is shared in by the author, who belongs to the universe, as the universe belongs to him. In detailing these pictures he hangs here and there shreds and tassels of his wild philosophy, till his work, like a maniac's robe, is bedizened with fluttering tags of a thousand colors. With all his follies, insolence, and indecency, no modern poet that we know of has presented finer descriptive passages than Mr. WALT WHITMAN. His phrasing, and the strength and completeness of his epithets, are truly wonderful. He paints in a single line with marvellous power and comprehensiveness. The following rhapsody will illustrate his fulness of epithet:

[*quotes lines 434–61 of "I celebrate myself"*]

Here are fine expressions well placed. Mr. WHITMAN's study of nature has been close and intense. He has expressed certain things better than any other man who has gone before him. He talks well, and largely, and tenderly of sea and sky, and men and trees, and women and children. His observation and his imagination are both large and well-developed. Take this picture; how pathetic, how tenderly touched!

[*quotes lines 840–50 of "I celebrate myself"*]

If it were permitted to us to outrage all precedent and print that which should not be printed, we could cull some passages from the *Leaves of Grass,* and place them in strange contrast with the extracts we have already made. If being a Kosmos is to set no limits to one's imagination; to use coarse epithets when coarseness is not needful; to roam like a drunken satyr, with inflamed blood, through every field of lascivious thought; to return time after time with a seemingly exhaustless prurient pleasure to the same licentious phrases and ideas; and to jumble all this up with bits of marvellously beautiful description, exquisite touches of nature, fragments of savagely uttered truth, shreds of unleavened philosophy—if to do all this is to be a Kosmos, then indeed we cede to Mr. WALT WHITMAN his arrogated title. Yet it seems to us that one may be profound without being beastly; one may teach philosophy without clothing it in slang; one may be a great poet without using language which shall outlaw the minstrel from every decent hearth. Mr. WALT WHITMAN does not think so. He tears the veil from all that society by a well-ordered law shrouds in a decent mystery. He is proud of his nakedness of speech; he glories in his savage scorn of decorum. Like the priests of Belus, he wreathes around his brow the emblems of the Phallic worship.

With all this muck of abomination soiling the pages, there is a wondrous, unaccountable fascination about the *Leaves of Grass*. As we read it again and again, and we will confess that we have returned to it often, a singular order seems to arise out of its chaotic verses. Out of the mire and slough, edged thoughts and keen philosophy start suddenly, as the men of Cadmus sprang from the muddy loam. A lofty purpose still dominates the uncleanness and the ridiculous self-conceit in which the author, led astray by ignorance, indulges. He gives token everywhere that he is a huge uncultivated thinker. No country save this could have given birth to the man. His mind is Western—brawny, rough, and original. Wholly uncultivated and beyond his associates, he has begotten within him the egotism of intellectual solitude. Had he mingled with scholars and men of intellect, those effete beings whom he so despises, he would have learned much that would have been beneficial. When we have none of our own size to measure ourselves with, we are apt to fancy ourselves broader and taller and stronger than we are. The poet of the little country town, who has reigned for years the Virgil or Anacreon of fifty square miles, finds, when he comes into the great metropolis, that he has not had all the thinking to himself. There he finds hundreds of men who have thought the same things as himself, and uttered them more fully. He is astonished to discover that his intellectual language is limited, when he thought that he had fathomed expression. He finds his verse unpolished, his structure defective, his best thoughts said before. He enters into the strife, clashes with his fellows, measures swords with this one, gives thrust for thrust with the other, until his muscles harden and his frame swells. He looks back upon his provincial intellectual existence with a smile; he laughs at his country arrogance and ignorant faith in himself. Now we gather from Mr. WHITMAN's own admissions—admissions that assume the form of boasts—that he has mingled but little with intellectual men. The love of the physical—which is the key-note of his entire book—has as yet altogether satisfied him. To mix with large-limbed, clean-skinned men, to look on ruddy, fair-proportioned women, is his highest social gratification. This love of the beautiful is by him largely and superbly expressed in many places, and it does one good to read those passages pulsating with the pure blood of animal life. But those associates, though manly and handsome, help but little to a man's inner appreciation of himself. Perhaps our author among his comrades had no equal in intellecutal force. He reigned triumphantly in an unquestioning circle of admirers. How easy, then, to fancy one's self a wonderful being! How easy to look around and say, "There are none like me here. I am the coming man!" It may be said that books will teach such a man the existence of other powerful minds, but this will not do. Such communion is abstract and has but little force. It is only in the actual combat of mind striving with mind that a man comes properly to estimate himself. Mr. WHITMAN has grown up in an intellectual isolation which has fully developed all the eccentricities of his nature. He has made some foolish theory that to be rough is to be original. Now, external softness of manner is in no degree incompatible with muscularity of intellect; and one thinks no more of a man's brains for his treading on one's toes without an apology, or his swearing in the presence of women. When Mr. WHITMAN shall have learned that a proper worship of the individual man need not be expressed so as to seem insolence, and that men are not to be bullied into receiving as a Messiah every man who sneers at them in his portrait, and disgusts them in his writings, we have no doubt that in some chastened mood of mind he will produce moving and powerful books. We select some passages exhibiting the different phases of Mr. WHITMAN's character. We do so more readily as, from the many indecencies contained in *Leaves of Grass,* we do not believe it will find its way into many families. [*several long extracts follow*]

Frank Leslie's Illustrated Newspaper *(New York), 20 December 1856*

We find upon our table (and shall put into the fire) a thin octavo volume, handsomely printed and bound, with the above curious title. We shall not aid in extending the sale of this intensely vulgar, nay, absolutely *beastly* book by telling our readers where it may be purchased. The only review we shall attempt of it will be to thus publicly call the attention of the grand jury to a matter that needs presentment by them, and to mildly suggest that the author should be sent to a lunatic asylum and the mercenary publishers to the penitentiary for pandering to the prurient tastes of morbid sensualists. Ralph W. Emerson's name appears as an indorser of these (so-called) poems (?)—God save the mark! We can only account for this strange fatuity upon the supposition that the letter is a forgery, that Mr. E. has not read *some* passages in the book, or that he lends his name to this vile production of a vitiated nature or diseased imagination, because the author is an imitator of his style and apes him occasionally in his transcendentalisms. Affectation is as pitiful an ambition in literature as alliteration, and never has it been more fully exhibited during the present century than in the case of Thomas Carlyle, a man with an order of intellect approaching genius, but who for a distinguishing mark to point like a fingerboard to himself, left a very terse and effective style of writing to adopt a jargon filled with new-fangled phrases and ungrammatical super-superlative adjectives—Mr. Carlyle buried himself for a long time in German universities and German philosophy, and came forth clothed in a full "old clothes" suit of transcendentalism worthy of the Chatham street embodiments of that pseudophilosophy, Kant and Spinosa—Carlyle by this operation became a full-fledged Psyche from the chrysalis and sported in the sunshine of popularity, whereupon a young gentleman ambitious of making New England an umbra of Scottish-Germanic glory, one Ralph Waldo Emerson, suddenly transforms himself into a metaphysical transcendentalist and begins talking about "Objective and Subjective," the "Inner and Outer," the "Real and Ideal," the "God-heads and God-tails," "Planes," "Spheres," "Finite, Infinite," "Unities," and "Dualities," "Squills, Ipecac," "Cascading and Cavorting," &c., &c. And lo! another appeared after this Mr. Emerson, one Walt Whitman, who kicked over the whole bucket of the Milky Way and deluged the world with the whey, curds and bonnyclabber of Brooklyn—which has resulted from the turning of the milk of human kindness in a "b'hoy's" brains to the cream of Tartar—and a delicious dish of the same is now furnished under cover of *Leaves of Grass,* and indorsed by the said Emerson, who swallows down Whitman's vulgarity and beastliness as if they were curds and whey. No wonder the Boston female schools are demoralized when Emerson, the head of the moral and solid people of Boston, indorses Whitman, and thus drags his slimy work into the sanctum of New England firesides.

Boston Christian Examiner, *November 1856*

So, then, these rank *Leaves* have sprouted afresh, and in still greater abundance. We hoped that they had dropped, and we should hear no more of them. But since they thrust themselves upon us again, with a pertinacity that is proverbial of noxious weeds, and since these thirty-two poems (!) threaten to become "several hundred—perhaps a thousand," we can no longer refrain from speaking of them as we think they deserve. For here is not a question of literary opinion principally, but of the very essence of religion and morality. The book might pass for merely hectoring and ludicrous, if it were not something a great deal more offensive. We are bound in conscience to call it impious and obscene. *Punch* made sarcastic allusion to it some time ago, as a specimen of American literature. We regard it as one of its worst disgraces. Whether or not the author really bears the name he assumes—whether or not the strange figure opposite the title-page resembles him or is even intended for his likeness—whether or not he is considered among his friends to be of a sane mind—whether he is in earnest, or only playing off some disgusting burlesque—we are hardly sure yet. We know only that, in point of style, the book is an impertinence towards the English language; and in point of sentiment, an affront upon the recognized morality of respectable people. Both its language and thought seem to have just broken out of Bedlam. It sets off upon a sort of distracted philosophy, and openly deifies the bodily organs, senses, and appetites, in terms that admit of no double sense. To its pantheism and libidinousness it adds the most ridiculous swell of self-applause; for the author is "one of the roughs, a kosmos, disorderly, fleshy, sensual, divine inside and out. This head more than churches or bibles or creeds. The scent of these arm-pits an aroma finer than prayer. If I worship any particular thing, it shall be some of the spread of my body." He leaves "washes and razors for foofoos"; thinks the talk "about virtue and about vice" only "blurt," he being above and indifferent to both of them; and he himself, "speaking the password primeval, By God! will accept nothing which all cannot have the counterpart of on the same terms." These quotations are made with cautious delicacy. We pick our way as cleanly as we can between other passages which are more detestable.

A friend whispers as we write, that there is nevertheless a vein of benevolence running through all this vagabondism and riot. Yes; there is plenty of that philanthropy, which cares as little for social rights as for the laws of God. This Titan in his own esteem is perfectly willing that all the rest of the world should be as frantic as himself. In fact, he has no objection to any persons whatever, unless they wear good clothes or keep themselves tidy. Perhaps it is not judicious to call any attention to such a prodigious impudence. Dante's guide through the infernal regions bade him, on one occasion, Look and pass on. It would be a still better direction sometimes, when in neighborhoods of defilement and death, to pass on without looking. Indeed, we should even now hardly be tempted to make the slightest allusion to this crazy outbreak of conceit and vulgarity, if a sister Review had not praised it, and even undertaken to set up a plea in apology for its indecencies. We must be allowed to say that it is not good to confound the blots upon great compositions with the compositions that are nothing but a blot. It is not good to confound the occasional ebullitions of too loose a fancy or too wanton a wit, with a profession and "illustrated" doctrine of licentiousness. And furthermore, it is specially desirable to be able to discern the difference between the nudity of a statue and the gestures of a satyr; between the plain language of a simple state of society and the lewd talk of the opposite state, which a worse than heathen lawlessness has corrupted; between the "εϑυή και φιλότητι" or "φιλότητι καί ἑυνήυαι" of the *Iliad* and *Odyssey,** and an ithyphallic audacity that insults what is most sacred and decent among men.

There is one feature connected with the second edition of this foul work to which we cannot feel that we do otherwise than right in making a marked reference, because it involves the grossest violation of literary comity and courtesy that ever passed under our notice. Mr. Emerson had written a letter, of greeting to the author on the perusal of the first edition, the warmth and eulogium of which amaze us. But "Walt Whitman" has taken the most emphatic sentence of praise from this letter, and had it stamped in gold, signed "R. W. Emerson" upon the back of his *second* edition. This second edition contains some additional pieces which in their loathsomeness exceed any of the contents of the first. Thus the honored name of Emerson, which has never before been associated with anything save refinement and delicacy in speech and writing, is made to indorse a work that teems with abominations.

**Two Homeric euphemisms are cited: "lay in the bed of love"* (Iliad *3.445) and "sported in a stranger's bed"* (Odyssey *23.219*).

Brooklyn Daily Times, *17 December 1856*

This is a new, enlarged and stereotyped edition of that singular production of "WALT WHITMAN," whose first appearance in '55 created such an extraordinary sensation in the literary world on both sides of the Atlantic. The first edition—which was duly noticed in these columns—contained twelve poems. In the present edition those poems are revised and twenty others are added. The form of the book has been changed from 4 to 16mo, and the typography is much improved.

The work, in its singular character, we understand to be an assertion of a two-fold individuality for the author: of himself personally, and of himself nationally; and the author, by example at least, to be an advocate of as much for all for his nation. A bold example he sets. The titles of the poems are various, and the poems under them present differences; yet through them all, with whatever else, runs one vital view, one ontological lesson in the same idiosyncratic strain.

Fanciful, fertile, and free in words, yet often, conventionally speaking, inelegant, and sometimes downright low; simple, abrupt, and detached sentences; frequently aphoristic, yet diffuse and uniform, sometimes to tediousness; at times strikingly clear and forcible, and again impenetrably obscure; a meeting of the extremes of literalness and metaleptic figures—of tiresome superficial details and comprehensive subtle generalities, oddities, ruggedness and strength; these are the chief characteristics of his style. There occur frequent instances of all-important and majestic thought, and so fitly expressed that the dissonance to the unaccustomed ears of the reader cannot prevent his stopping to admire. The matter is characterized by thought rather than by sentiment. The right and duty of man with the passions are enjoined and celebrated, rather than the passions themselves. There are speculative philosophies advanced, upon which readers will differ with the author and with each other; and some of these to intolerant conventionalists will give offense. We are not prepared to endorse them all ourselves. And there are practical philosophics of which he treats, destined to encounter fierce repugnance. But the book is not one that warrants its dismissal with disgust or contempt. There is a deep substratum of observant and contemplative wisdom as broad as the foundation of society running through it all; and whatever else there is of questionable good, so much at least is a genuine pearl that we cannot afford to trample it under our feet. The poems contain some lessons of the highest importance and possess a further value in their strong suggestiveness. We accord to the leading idea of the work alone, personal with national individuality, exemplified and recommended as it is, an incalculable value. The poems improve upon a second reading, and they may commonly require a repetition in order to gain a deserved appreciation, like a strange piece of music with subtle harmonies.

The work is altogether *sui generis,* unless we may call it Emersonian. That name is ample enough to cover a multitude of oddities and excellencies; but that it is not shaped to all the radiations of the unbridled muse of the author under notice we think a single extract from his first poem will show: [*quotes three dozen lines from "I celebrate myself"*]

New York Times, *19 May 1860*

Five years ago a new poet appeared, styling himself the representative of America, the mouthpiece of free institutions, the personification of all that men had waited for. His writings were neither poetry nor prose, but a curious medley, a mixture of quaint utterances and gross indecencies, a remarkable compound of fine thoughts and sentiment of the pot-house. It was not an easy task to winnow the chaff from the wheat, the tares came up in such heavy luxuriance that they stunted the chance kernels of the grain, and nothing but the most vigorous of threshing was adequate to the elimination of one pure thought. That first edition of the *Leaves of Grass* was the earliest appearance of Mr. Walt Whitman as an author. For a *debutant,* he was sufficiently egotistic and assuming. He announced, with a degree of confidence which could only have been the natural result of unparalleled self-conceit, that his mission lay in the reformation of the public taste, that the American people were to be enlightened and civilized and cultivated up to the proper standard, by virtue of his superior endowments, and that, being "a Kosmos" and inclined to "loafe" at his ease and "invite his soul," he could afford to wait for the public's warm appreciation of his self-sacrifice, and to recline in a comfortable attitude until the world saw fit to come round to him. Two years after the publication of the first thin and unprepossessing volume of the *Leaves,* a larger edition appeared, and that again is followed by a third and still more pretentious book, the present issue from the Boston house of Thayer & Eldridge.

Mr. Whitman has added to this volume a large collection of his writings which have never been given to the public. If possible, he is more reckless and vulgar than in his two former publications. He seems to delight in the contemplation of scenes that ordinary men do not love, or which they are content to regard as irremediable evils, about which it is needless to repine. Mr. Whitman sees nothing vulgar in that which is commonly regarded as the grossest obscenity; rejects the laws of conventionality so completely as to become repulsive; gloats over coarse images with the gusto of a Rabelais, but lacks the genius or the grace of Rabelais to vivify or adorn that which, when said at all, should be said as delicately as possible.

Yet it would be unjust to deny the evidences of remarkable power which are presented in this work. In his hearty human sympathy, his wonderful intensity, his fullness of epithet, the author shows that he is a man of strong passion, vigorous in thought and earnest in purpose. He is uncultured, rude, defiant and arrogant, but these are faults of his nature which have not been tempered by severe training. Occasionally, a gleam of the true poetic fire shines out of the mass of his rubbish, and there are tender and beautiful touches in the midst of his most objectionable and disagreeable writings. A rough diamond, much in need of cutting and grinding and polishing, he has great intrinsic worth, but the impurities which cling about him must keep him out of the refined company he desires to enter. To be an agent for the civilization of men, he must first himself become civilized. He can do no manner of good by throwing filth, even though a handful of pure gold be sometimes mingled with a cast from his moral cesspool.

Nearly two hundred poems, of all sizes and qualities, are contained in this edition. Two dozens of these are properly the *Leaves of Grass,* grouped under that title and mainly published in former editions. "Chants Democratic and Native American" comprise twenty-one curious specimens of composition, which are neither metrical nor harmonious. Fifteen others are collected under the comprehensive heading of "Enfant d'Adam," and are humanitary. Fifteen others are "Messenger Leaves." Four hundred and fifty pages of these productions establish the industry of the writer, and the fact that a respectable house has undertaken their publication illustrates a lively faith in the eagerness of the public for the reception of novelties.

Some of the finer passages in this intricate

maze of incongruous materials occur in the first hundred pages. Take the following weird conceit:

[*quotes the equivalent of lines 90–101 of "I celebrate myself"*]

In "Chants Democratic" the poet discourses of strong wills, and mirrors the image of the reformer [*quotes as follows from Chant Democratic 2, later titled "Song of the Broad-Axe"*].

How beggarly appear poems, arguments
orations, before an electric deed!
How the floridness of the materials of
cities shrivels before a man's or woman's
look!
All waits, or goes by default, till a strong
being appears;
A strong being is the proof of the race,
and of the ability of the universe;
When he or she appears, materials are
overawed,
The dispute on the Soul stops,
The old customs and phrases are
confronted, turned back, or laid away.

Again, he studies faces and draws sharply-lined portraits [*quotes as follows from "Faces"*]:

This face is a life-boat;
This is the face commanding and bearded,
it asks no odds of the rest;
This face is flavored fruit, ready for eating,
This face of a healthy, honest boy is the
programme of all good.

Yet the tendency to fall into the vulgar, apparently ineradicable in Mr. Whitman's composition, leads him to interlard with these such expressions as "abject louse, asking leave to be"—"milk-nosed maggot, blessing what lets it wrig to its hole"—"dog's snout, sniffing for garbage." He will be gross, and there is no help for it.

The egotism of the book is amusing. Mr. Whitman is not only "a man-myself, typical before all," but he is "a man thirty-six years old in the year 79 of America, and is here anyhow"—but, being here, lies in libraries "as one dumb, a gawk, or unborn, or dead," thereby evincing a hearty contempt for scholastic culture; but nevertheless avowing a stern determination to

. . . . . make a song for these States
. . . . . and a shrill song of curses on him
who would dissever the Union.

It is fair to presume that this "song of curses," should it ever come to be sung, will be "shrill" and loud, not to say foul and abusive. Mr. Whitman is master of the art . . .

We infer that this is not the last of Mr. Walt Whitman. In point of fact, he gravely tells us that he is "around, tenacious, acquisitive, tireless and can never be shaken away"; he sings "from the irresistible impulses of me"; purposes to make "the Poem of the New World"; and "invites defiance to make himself superseded," avowing his cheerful willingness to be "trod under foot, if it might only be the soil of superior poems"—from which latter confession it is clear that he regards himself as the fertilizing agent of American Poetry; perhaps all the better for fertilizing purposes that the rains and snows of a rough life have caused it to fester in a premature and unwholesome decay.

Boston Banner of Light, *2 June 1860*

The people who have not yet heard of Walt Whitman are few indeed. This last enlarged collection of his poems makes a stout volume, to which the bold and tasteful publishers have given a dress altogether striking, unique and original. All sorts of things—hard and soft—have been said about this same Walt Whitman and his writings. One paper, in commenting upon another's indiscriminate praise of him, remarks that it is "into this gentle garden of the Muses that that unclean cub of the wilderness, Walt Whitman, has been suffered to intrude, trampling with his vulgar and profane hoofs among the delicate flowers which bloom there" &c.

Nobody who has read Whitman's poems can question his originality. He betrays high culture, even when he seems almost swinishly to spurn it. We think that few writers of our day, if any, whether in prose or verse, have so seized hold of the *spirit* of things—no matter what, where found, or intertwisted with whatever associations—as this one before us. And the best proof of it is just that free habit of expression which all the literary poodles are happy to style "barbaric." It is time their snobbery was supplanted by strength of some sort even if it be barbaric. We have had soft flute-blowing long enough; now let us hear the jarring screech of a fife. Our poet they call *nasty,* because he scorns to be *knavish;* he has the right of it, beyond a question, calling a spade a spade, and a meat-axe a meat-axe; and in exercising his elephantine strength and motions, he doubtless takes a secret delight in the mere act of exercising them, and holding all napper-tandy forms and by-laws in scorn; he proudly refuses to so much as appease the prejudices of critics by respecting the commonly received statutes of the great Literary Republic.

This man's verse—wild, rapid, Ossianic, wailing, grand, humble, innocent, defiant, irregular, defective, overfull, and altogether inflexible as it is—forms, after all, the truest illustration, if not representative, of the real American Age that is, and is to be. He has searched all truth, all knowledge, all science. Even when his expression torments you, the great, surcharged soul that throbs and plays underneath looks forth serious and awful, refusing to be satisfied with itself, unsettling all things, breaking up the heavens into new and sometimes terrific forms, and pointing down to abysmal deeps in human experience, to which even the most powerful sight of spirit has never penetrated. Above all other singers of songs—rude or rhyming—Whitman hints to you of your capacity; if you have not yet awakened to the possession of any, you cannot understand him, of course. Neither can you understand him wholly, at best; for his own writings prove that he does not, and never will entirely, understand himself. And this is the mystery that gives Life its deep meaning.

The whole body of these Poems—spiritually considered—is alive with power, throbbing and beating behind and between the lines. There is more here than mere oddity, and barbaric indifference to elegant forms of speech; there is a *living soul*—no matter whether its owner drove an omnibus once, or stands on State street and chaffers greedily every day for gold—and that soul insists on giving itself to its fellows, even if it has to rend the most sacred rules of speech to achieve its larger liberty. Carlyle did so, and triumphed; Whitman's way is as much his own, too. It is no way at all, to make up even literary judgment by examining the colors, and not the warp and woof. It is the texture of the stuff that tells, because it is that which is going to endure.

Thus much of the Poet Whitman; we leave our readers to examine his wonderful productions—so bizarre, so fine, so entirely out of and beyond all rule—and know for themselves, as they would know a familiar friend, the spirit that lives in them. The *disjecta membra* of the man's speech we throw to the hungry critics, who are ever delighted to snap up such meaty morsels; of the soul that burns through—nay, *burns up*—all the mere words, consuming the verbiage as fire licks up dried grass, we are but too eager to speak as it deserves; and with that soul all other growing souls will hasten to make themselves acquainted. Whitman comes to us—perhaps not a discoverer, but certainly a grand interpreter. One-sided and all-sided—intense and indifferent—lazy and lashed into fury-spouting words and pouring out streams of rubies and diamonds—he is nothing more than the very child of nature, to whom accidentally has been given the name, Walt Whitman.

London Literary Gazette, *7 July 1860*

Not the least surprising thing about this book is its title. Had it been called "Stenches from the Sewer," "Garbage from the Gutter," or "Squeals from the Sty," we could have discerned the application. But "leaves"—which, we take it, is the Transatlantic for blades—"of grass" have nothing of irreligion or indecency about them. Mr. Walt Whitman—for it is with that choice spirit we are now dealing—might as well let them alone.

It is, for reasons we shall presently specify, rather a difficult matter to give the class of readers for whom we write any adequate notion of this remarkable volume. Let them, however, imagine a Mormon, a medical student, and Miss Eugenie Plummer* combining to draw up a treatise in the style of "Proverbial Philosophy," and they will have a faint idea of the last production of Mr. Walt Whitman.

The folly of the work is its least defect. The gregarious qualities of birds of a feather furnish matter for a very common aphorism, and we therefore see no reason to question the correctness of the subjoined assertion:

> The wild gander leads his flock through
> the cool night,
> *Ya-honk!* he says, and sounds it down
> to me like an invitation;
> The pert may suppose it meaningless,
> but I listen close,
> I find its purpose and place up there
> toward the wintry sky.

The following forms the conclusion of a pretty long rhapsody of the author concerning himself. We extract it because it is more decent and not more foolish than the rest of the volume:

[*quotes last fifteen lines of "I celebrate myself"*]

It is related of poor crazy Nat Lee that when a small poet asked him if it was not very easy to write like a madman, he replied, "No, but it is very easy indeed to write like a fool, as you do." Doubtless Mr. Walt Whitman imagines he is writing like a madman, when, as a matter of fact, he is only writing like Nat Lee's friend.

He tells us that the world is not devout enough—that he understands "Him who was crucified" and in general tries to impress upon us that he is an apostle of no mean pretensions. But his creed, so far as we understand it, consists in a peculiarly coarse materialism. He tells us pretty roundly that he worships his own body, and people who would like to learn a great number of particulars about Mr. Walt Whitman's body may find them in Mr. Walt Whitman's book.

Throughout the work there is a tone of consistent impurity which reaches its climax in some compositions entitled "Enfans d'Adam"—a designation which we can only explain by imagining it to contain some allusion to the Adamites, of which interesting, though as we had supposed, extinct sect, Mr. Walt Whitman is a very fair representative. For the downright foulness of some of these passages we do not believe that a parallel could be found even by ransacking the worst classical poets from Aristophanes to Ausonius, and we are rather surprised that with John Lord Campbell on the woolsack, and a certain act of his still unrepealed on the statute-book, Mr. Walt Whitman should have found a London vendor for his uncleanly work.**

This is more decided language than we generally employ, and our readers may ask us for some justification of it. Let us remind them of Lord Macaulay's description of Wycherley, which we can certainly apply to Walt Whitman. "His indecency is protected against the critics as a skunk is protected against the hunters. It is safe because it is too filthy to handle, and too noisome even to approach." There are certain criminals whom even literary judges must try with closed doors, and our readers must deduce from our verdict that "the evidence is unfit for publication." We say, then, deliberately, that of all the writers we have ever perused, Mr. Walt Whitman is the most silly, the most blasphemous, and the most disgusting; if we can think of any stronger epithets, we will print them in a second edition.

**Eleven-year-old Mary Eugenia Plummer was tried and convicted of "wilful and corrupt perjury" for testimony of sexual assault that had sent a married prison chaplain to jail; the May 1860 trial in Central Criminal Court was fully reported in the* London Times. *She was sentenced to three weeks in prison and two years in a reformatory, but in June Queen Victoria pardoned her on condition she be "placed in the care of a lady selected by her friends."*

***A reference to the Obscene Publications Act passed by Parliament in 1857. The* Encyclopædia Britannica *(1911) paints a picture of Campbell, then Lord Chancellor, as an anti-Whitman: "He had a hard head . . . there was nothing admirable or heroic in his nature . . . nor had he the magnanimity which excuses rather than aggravates the faults of others."*

London Spectator, *14 July 1860*

America is unreasonably impatient to possess a great national poet as intrinsically her own as Shakespeare is English, Burns Scotch, Goethe German, and Dante Italian. She may have an emperor sooner—*absit omen* [*"perish the thought"*]! Young as she is, the land of stars and stripes has within her plenty of the stuff of which emperors can be made; but poets are a choicer growth, and need more years than the Union number from its birth to acclimatize their race in a new country. Of the few poets born in America, not one is distinctively American in his poetry; all are exotics, and their roots are nurtured by the pabulum imported from the old country. In process of time, the foreign stock will accommodate itself to the new conditions by which it is surrounded; it will gradually undergo a transformation of species and become racy of the soil, but the soil itself must meanwhile pass through a corresponding change. It is still too crude; there is in it, as Oliver Wendell Holmes avows, "no sufficient flavour of humanity," such as inheres in every inch of ground belonging to some of the ancient seats of civilization. These truths are plainly discerned by the most cultivated minds in the States, and by them only; others believe that a great poet has actually arisen amongst them, and they hail his appearance with the more rapture because there has certainly never been anything like him in the guise of a poet since the world began. In the year 1855, this prodigy, this "compound of the New England transcendentalist and the New York rowdy," as a friendly critic calls him with literal truth, put forth the first issue of his *Leaves of Grass—videlicet* Scurvy grass—twelve poems, or rather bundles, in ninety-five pages, small quarto. The book was immediately pronounced by Ralph Waldo Emerson to be "the most extraordinary piece of wit and wisdom that America has yet contributed." Other critics followed suit, and Walt Whitman became as famous as the author of the Book of Mormon. A second edition of his *Leaves of Grass,* with twenty additional bundles, making together 384 pages, was published within a year after the first; and now there lies before us a new, enlarged, and glorified edition, for which the publishers "confidently claim recognition as one of the finest specimens of modern book-making." The paper, print, and binding are indeed superb; but one thing these gentlemen have forgotten: where are the phallic emblems, and the figures of Priapus and the Satyrs that should have adorned the covers and the pages of this new gospel of lewdness and obscenity? Its frontispiece should have been, not the head and shoulders of the author, but a full-length portrait drawn as he loves to depict himself in his "poems"—naked as an Anabaptist of Munster . . .

William Dean Howells, Round Table *(New York), 11 November 1865*

Will saltpeter explode? Is Walt Whitman a true poet? Doubts to be solved by the wise futurity which shall pay of our national debt. Poet or not, however, there was that in Walt Whitman's first book which compels attention to his second. There are obvious differences between the two: this is much smaller than that; and whereas you had at times to hold your nose (as a great sage observed) in reading *Leaves of Grass,* there is not an indecent thing in *Drum-Taps.* The artistic method of the poet remains, however, the same, and we must think it mistaken. The trouble about it is that it does not give you sensation in a portable shape; the thought is as intangible as aroma; it is no more put up than the atmosphere.

We are to suppose that Mr. Whitman first adopted his method as something that came to him of its own motion. This is the best possible reason, and only possible excuse, for it. In its way, it is quite as artificial as that of any other poet, while it is unspeakably inartistic. On this account it is a failure. The method of talking to one's self in rhythmic and ecstatic prose is one that surprises at first, but, in the end, the talker can only have the devil for a listener, as happens in other cases when people address their own individualities; not, however, the devil of the proverb, but the devil of reasonless, hopeless, all-defying egotism. An ingenious French critic said very acutely of Mr. Whitman that he made you partner of the poetical enterprise, which is perfectly true; but no one wants to share the enterprise. We want its effect, its success; we do not want to plant corn, to hoe it, to drive the crows away, to gather it, husk it, grind it, sift it, bake it, and butter it, before eating it, and then take the risk of its being at last moldy in our mouths. And this is what you have to do in reading Mr. Whitman's rhythm.

At first, a favorable impression is made by the lawlessness of this poet, and one asks himself if this is not the form which the unconscious poetry of American life would take, if it could find a general utterance. But there is really no evidence that such is the case. It is certain that among the rudest peoples the lurking sublimity of nature has always sought expression in artistic form, and there is no good reason to believe that the sentiment of a people with our high average culture would seek expression more rude and formless than that of the savagest tribes. Is it not more probable that, if the passional principle of American life could find utterance, it would choose the highest, least dubious, most articulate speech? Could the finest, most shapely expression be too good for it?

If we are to judge the worth of Mr. Whitman's poetic theory (or impulse, or possession) by its popular success, we must confess that he is wrong. It is already many years since he first appeared with his claim of poet, and in that time he has employed criticism as much as any literary man in our country, and he has enjoyed the fructifying extremes of blame and praise. Yet he is, perhaps, less known to the popular mind, to which he has attempted to give an utterance, than the newest growth of the magazines and the newspaper notices. The people fairly rejected his former revelation, letter and spirit, and those who enjoyed it were readers with a cultivated taste for the quaint and the outlandish. The time to denounce or to ridicule Mr. Whitman for his first book is past. The case of *Leaves of Grass* was long ago taken out of the hands of counsel and referred to the great jury. They have pronounced no audible verdict, but what does their silence mean? There were reasons in the preponderant beastliness of that book why a decent public should reject it; but now the poet has cleansed the old channels of their filth, and pours through them a stream of blameless purity, and the public has again to decide, and this time more directly, on the question of his poethood. As we said, his method remains the same, and he himself declares that, so far as concerns it, he has not changed nor grown in any way since we saw him last.

[*quotes "Beginning My Studies"*]

Mr. Whitman has summed up his own

poetical theory so well in these lines, that no criticism could possibly have done it better. It makes us doubt, indeed, if all we have said in consideration of him has not been said idly, and certainly releases us from further explanation of his method.

In *Drum-Taps* there is far more equality than in *Leaves of Grass,* and though the poet is not the least changed in purpose, he is certainly changed in fact. The pieces of the new book are nearly all very brief, but generally his expression is freer and fuller than ever before. The reader understands, doubtless, from the title, that nearly all these pieces relate to the war; and they celebrate many of the experiences of the author in the noble part he took in the war. One imagines that burly tenderness of the man who went to supply the "lack of woman's nursing" that there was in the hospitals of the field, and woman's tears creep unconsciously to the eyes as the pity of his heart communicates itself to his reader's. No doubt the pathos of many of the poems gains something from the quaintness of the poet's speech. One is touched in reading them by the same inarticulate feeling as that which dwells in music; and is sensible that the poet conveys to the heart certain emotions which the brain cannot analyze, and only remotely perceives. This is especially true of his inspirations from nature; memories and yearnings come to you folded, mute, and motionless in his verse, as they come in the breath of a familiar perfume. They give a strange, shadowy sort of pleasure, but they do not satisfy, and you rise from the perusal of this man's book as you issue from the presence of one whose personal magnetism is very subtle and strong, but who has not added to this tacit attraction the charm of spoken ideas. We must not mistake this fascination for a higher quality. In the tender eyes of an ox lurks a melancholy, soft and pleasing to the glance as the pensive sweetness of a woman's eyes; but in the orb of the brute there is no hope of expression, and in the woman's look there is the endless delight of history, the heavenly possibility of utterance.

Art cannot greatly employ itself with things in embryo. The instinct of the beast may interest science; but poetry, which is nobler than science, must concern itself with natural instincts only as they can be developed into the sentiments and ideas of the soul of man. The mind will absorb from nature all that is speechless in her influences: and it will demand from kindred mind those higher things which can be spoken. Let us say our say here against the nonsense, long current, that there is, or can be, poetry *between the lines,* as is often sillily asserted. *Expression* will always suggest; but mere *suggestion* in art is unworthy of existence, vexes the heart, and shall not live. Every man has tender, and beautiful, and lofty emotions; but the poet was sent into this world to give these a tangible utterance, and if he do not this, but only give us back dumb emotion, he is a cumberer of the earth. There is a yearning, almost to agony at times, in the human heart, to throw off the burden of inarticulate feeling, and if the poet will not help it in this effort, if, on the contrary, he shall seek to weigh it and sink it down under heavier burdens, he has not any reason to be.

So long, then, as Mr. Whitman chooses to stop at mere consciousness, he cannot be called a true poet. We all have consciousness; but we ask of art an utterance. We do not so much care in what way we get this expression; we will take it in ecstatic prose, though we think it is better subjected to the laws of prosody, since every good thing is subject to some law; but the expression we must have. Often, in spite of himself, Mr. Whitman grants it in this volume, and there is some hope that he will hereafter grant it more and more. There are such rich possibilities in the man that it is lamentable to contemplate his error of theory. He has truly and thoroughly absorbed the idea of our American life, and we say to him as he says to himself, "You've got enough in you, Walt; why don't you get it out?" A man's greatness is good for nothing folded up in him, and if emitted in barbaric yawps, it is not more filling than Ossian or the east wind.

Henry James, Nation *(New York), 16 November 1865*

It has been a melancholy task to read this book; and it is a still more melancholy one to write about it. Perhaps since the day of Mr. Tupper's *Philosophy* there has been no more difficult reading of the poetic sort. It exhibits the effort of an essentially prosaic mind to lift itself, by a prolonged muscular strain, into poetry. Like hundreds of other good patriots, during the last four years, Mr. Walt Whitman has imagined that a certain amount of violent sympathy with the great deeds and sufferings of our soldiers, and of admiration for our national energy, together with a ready command of picturesque language, are sufficient inspiration for a poet. If this were the case, we had been a nation of poets. The constant developments of the war moved us continually to strong feeling and to strong expression of it. But in those cases in which these expressions were written out and printed with all due regard to prosody, they failed to make poetry, as any one may see by consulting now in cold blood the back volumes of the *Rebellion Record. Of course* the city of Manhattan, as Mr. Whitman delights to call it, when regiments poured through it in the first months of the war, and its own sole god, to borrow the words of a real poet, ceased for a while to be the millionaire, was a noble spectacle, and a poetical statement to this effect is possible. *Of course* the tumult of a battle is grand, the results of a battle tragic, and the untimely deaths of young men a theme for elegies. But he is not a poet who merely reiterates these plain facts *ore rotundo*. He only sings them worthily who views them from a height. Every tragic event collects about it a number of persons who delight to dwell upon its superficial points—of minds which are bullied by the *accidents* of the affair. The temper of such minds seems to us to be the reverse of the poetic temper; for the poet, although he incidentally masters, grasps, and uses the superficial traits of his theme, is really a poet only in so far as he extracts its latent meaning and holds it up to common eyes. And yet from such minds most of our war-verses have come, and Mr. Whitman's utterances, much as the assertion may surprise his friends, are in this respect no exception to general fashion. They are an exception, however, in that they openly pretend to be something better; and this it is that makes them melancholy reading. Mr. Whitman is very fond of blowing his own trumpet, and he has made very explicit claims for his book. "Shut not your doors," he exclaims at the outset—

Shut not your doors to me, proud libraries,
For that which was lacking among
 you all, yet needed most, I bring;
A book I have made for your dear sake,
 O soldiers,
And for you, O soul of man, and you,
 love of comrades;
The words of my book nothing, the life
 of it everything;
A book separate, not link'd with the rest,
 nor felt by the intellect;
But you will feel every word, O Libertad!
 arm'd Libertad!
It shall pass by the intellect to swim
 the sea, the air,
With joy with you, O soul of man.

These are great pretensions, but it seems to us that the following are even greater:

From Paumanok starting, I fly like a bird,
Around and around to soar, to sing
 the idea of all;
To the north betaking myself, to sing
 there arctic songs,
To Kanada, 'till I absorb Kanada
 in myself—to Michigan then,
To Wisconsin, Iowa, Minnesota, to sing
 their songs (they are inimitable);
Then to Ohio and Indiana, to sing theirs—
 to Missouri and Kansas and Arkansas
 to sing theirs,
To Tennessee and Kentucky—to the
 Carolinas and Georgia, to sing theirs,
To Texas, and so along up toward
 California, to roam accepted everywhere;

To sing first (to the tap of the war-drum,
if need be)
The idea of all—of the western world,
one and inseparable,
And then the song of each member
of these States.

Mr. Whitman's primary purpose is to celebrate the greatness of our armies; his secondary purpose is to celebrate the greatness of the city of New York. He pursues these objects through a hundred pages of matter which remind us irresistibly of the story of the college professor who, on a venturesome youth's bringing him a theme done in blank verse, reminded him that it was not customary in writing prose to begin each line with a capital. The frequent capitals are the only marks of verse in Mr. Whitman's writing. There is, fortunately, but one attempt at rhyme. We say fortunately, for if the inequality of Mr. Whitman's lines were self-registering, as it would be in the case of an anticipated syllable at their close, the effect would be painful in the extreme. As the case stands, each line starts off by itself, in resolute independence of its companions, without a visible goal. But if Mr. Whitman does not write verse, he does not write ordinary prose. The reader has seen that liberty is "libertad." In like manner, comrade is "camerado"; Americans are "Americanos"; a pavement is a "trottoir"; and Mr. Whitman himself is a "chansonnier." If there is one thing that Mr. Whitman is not, it is this, for Béranger was a *chansonnier*. To appreciate the force of our conjunction, the reader should compare his military lyrics with Mr. Whitman's declamations. Our author's novelty, however, is not in his words, but in the form of his writing. As we have said, it begins for all the world like verse and turns out to be arrant prose. It is more like Mr. Tupper's proverbs than anything we have met. But what if, in form, it *is* prose? it may be asked. Very good poetry has come out of prose before this. To this we would reply that it must first have gone into it. Prose, in order to be good poetry, must first be good prose. As a general principle, we know of no circumstance more likely to impugn a writer's earnestness than the adoption of an anomalous style. He must have something very original to say if none of the old vehicles will carry his thoughts. Of course he *may* be surprisingly original. Still, presumption is against him. If on examination the matter of his discourse proves very valuable, it justifies, or at any rate excuses, his literary innovation.

But if, on the other hand, it is of a common quality, with nothing new about it but its manners, the public will judge the writer harshly. The most that can be said of Mr. Whitman's vaticinations is that, cast in a fluent and familiar manner, the average substance of them might escape unchallenged. But we have seen that Mr. Whitman prides himself especially on the substance—the life—of his poetry. It may be rough, it may be grim, it may be clumsy—such we take to be the author's argument—but it is sincere, it is sublime, it appears to the soul of man, it is the voice of a people. He tells us, in the lines quoted, that the words of his book are nothing. To our perception they are everything, and very little at that. A great deal of verse that is nothing but words has, during the war, been sympathetically sighed over and cut out of newspaper corners because it has possessed a certain simple melody. But Mr. Whitman's verse, we are confident, would have failed even of this triumph, for the simple reason that no triumph, however small, is won but through the exercise of art, and that this volume is an offense against art. It is not enough to be grim and rough and careless; common sense is also necessary, for it is by common sense that we are judged. There exists in even the commonest minds, in literary matters, a certain precise instinct of conservatism, which is very shrewd in detecting wanton eccentricities. To this instinct Mr. Whitman's attitude seems monstrous. It is monstrous because it pretends to persuade the soul while it slights the intellect; because it pretends to gratify the feelings while it outrages the taste. The point is that it does this *on theory,* wilfully, consciously, arrogantly. It is the little nursery game of "open your mouth and shut your eyes." Our hearts are often touched through a compromise with the artistic sense, but never in direct violation of it. Mr. Whitman sits down at the outset and counts out the intelligence. This were indeed a wise precaution on his part if the intelligence were only submissive! But when she is deliberately insulted, she takes her revenge by simply standing erect and open-eyed. This is assuredly the best she can do. And if she could find a voice she would probably address Mr. Whitman as follows: "You came to woo my sister, the human soul. Instead of giving me a kick as you approach, you should either greet me courteously, or, at least, steal in unobserved. But now you have me on your hands. Your chances are poor. What the human heart desires above all is sincerity, and you do not appear to me sincere. For a lover you talk entirely too much about yourself. In one place you threaten to absorb Kanada. In another you threaten to absorb Kanada. In another you call upon the city of New York to incarnate you, as you have incarnated it. In another you inform us that neither youth pertains to you nor 'delicatesse,' that you are awkward in the parlor, that you do not dance, and that you have neither bearing, beauty, knowledge, nor fortune. In another place, by an allusion to your 'little songs,' you seem to identify yourself with the third person of the Trinity. For a poet who claims to sing 'the idea of all,' this is tolerably egotistical. We look in vain, however, through your book for a single idea. We find nothing but flashy imitations of ideas. We find a medley of extravagances and commonplaces. We find art, measure, grace, sense sneered at on every page, and nothing positive given us in their stead. To be positive one must have something to say; to be positive requires reason, labor, and art; and art requires, above all things, a suppression of one's self, a subordination of one's self to an idea. This will never do for you, whose plan is to adapt the scheme of the universe to your own limitations. You cannot entertain and exhibit ideas; but, as we have seen, you are prepared to incarnate them. It is for this reason, doubtless, that when once you have planted yourself squarely before the public, and in view of the great service you have done to the ideal, have become, as you say, 'accepted everywhere,' you can afford to deal exclusively in words. What would be bald nonsense and dreary platitudes in any one else becomes sublimity in you. But all this is a mistake. To become adopted as a national poet, it is not enough to discard everything in particular and to accept everything in general, to amass crudity upon crudity, to discharge the undigested contents of your blotting-book into the lap of the public. You must respect the public which you address; for it has taste, if you have not. It delights in the grand, the heroic, and the masculine; but it delights to see these conceptions cast into worthy form. It is indifferent to brute sublimity. It will never do for you to thrust your hands into your pockets and cry out that, as the research of form is an intolerable bore, the shortest and most economical way for the public to embrace its idols—for the nation to realize its genius—is in your own person. This democratic, liberty-loving, American populace, this stern and war-tried people, is a great civilizer. It is devoted to refinement. If it has sustained a monstrous war, and practised human nature's best in so many ways for the last five years, it is not to put up with spurious poetry afterwards. To sing aright our battles and our glories it is not enough to have served in a hospital (however praiseworthy the task in itself), to be aggressively careless, inelegant, and ignorant, and to be constantly preoccupied with yourself. It is not enough to be rude, lugubrious, and grim. You must also be serious. You must forget yourself in your ideas. Your personal qualities—the vigor of your temperament, the manly independence of your nature, the tenderness of your heart—these facts are impertinent. You must be *possessed,* and you must strive to possess your possession. If in your striving you break into divine eloquence, then you are a poet. If the idea which possesses you is the idea of your country's greatness, then you are a national poet; and not otherwise.

A. S. Hill, North American Review *(Boston), January 1867*

It is fortunate that Walt Whitman's *Drum-Taps,* unlike his *Leaves of Grass,* is in point of propriety unexceptionable, so that it can be judged on its intrinsic merits.

The pieces of which *Drum-Taps* consists are in form like those in *Leaves of Grass,* neither blank verse nor rhythmical prose. A poet of genuine artistic power would suffer from the absence of those restraints which are to genius what its banks are to a river—limitations that aid in the development of beauty and of force; and Mr. Whitman is so far from being an artist that he boasts of his lack of culture, after the fashion of "self-made" men. Yet it is precisely this deficiency which disguises his real excellence, and stands between him and the fame he predicts for himself. A writer whose works are to live must have taste to discriminate between what is worth saying in a given poem, and what is not worth saying, and must have courage to excise the latter. The business of cataloguing the works of creation should be left to the auctioneer.

Poets of vastly more genius and culture than Mr. Whitman possesses have committed the error of thinking all objects and fancies equally worthy of a poem. Wordsworth, for example, patched his shining robes with homespun; but Wordsworth had the manners and speech of a gentleman, while Whitman has the characteristics, good and bad, of a Bowery boy. His love of New York City has more in common with Gavroche's love for Paris than with that of Victor Hugo, and more in common with Tony Weller's love for London than with that of Dr. Johnson, Lamb, or even Dickens. His glorification of America smacks of the "We can lick all creation" of Tammany Hall. But with the extravagance, coarseness, and general "loudness" of Bowery boys, Mr. Whitman possesses in an unusual degree their better traits. He is not ashamed of the body he lives in, and he calls all things by plain names. His compositions, without being sentimental or pretty, show genuine sensibility to the beauty of nature and of man. His braggart patriotism evinced its genuineness during the war:

Beauty, knowledge, fortune, inure not to
me, yet there are two things inure to me.
I have nourished the wounded
and soothed many a dying soldier;
And at intervals I have strung together
a few songs,
Fit for war and the life of a camp.

The fact that the "songs" in *Drum-Taps* were written under such circumstances ought to have rebutted in the most fastidious minds whatever presumption may have been raised against the volume by previous publications.

But the claims of these productions to consideration rest upon a more solid basis than the author's personal services in the hospital. Mr. Whitman not only possesses an almost photographic accuracy of observation, a masculine directness of expression, and real tenderness of feeling, but he sometimes hits upon an original epithet which illuminates a page of prosaic details. He speaks of "the *sturdy* artillery . . . soon, unlimbered to begin the *red business";* "the hurrying, crashing, sad, distracted, *robust* year" (1861); the *"hinged* knees and steady hand" of the dresser of wounds; the "elderly (sick) man, so gaunt and grim with *well-grayed hair and flesh all sunken about the eyes"; "million-footed, superb-faced* Manhattan"; "the wind with *girlish* laughter"; the "gentle, soft-born, *measureless* light"; "the gorgeous, *indolent,* sinking sun, burning, *expanding* the air"; the *most excellent* sun, so calm and haughty"; "the *huge* and thoughtful night." And in at least three places he shows more sustained, if not higher power. The effect of the news from Sumter upon New York is thus described:

The Lady of this teeming and turbulent
city,
Sleepless, amid her ships, her houses, her
incalculable wealth,
With her million children around her—
suddenly
At dead of night, at news from the South,

Incensed, struck with clenched hand the
  pavement.

"Old Ireland" is personified as

Crouching over a grave, an ancient,
  sorrowful mother,
Once a queen, now lean and tattered,
  seated on the ground,
Her old white hair drooping dishevelled
    round her shoulders;
At her feet fallen an unused royal harp.

But Mr. Whitman's faculty is, perhaps, most fully shown in the poem entitled "When Lilacs Last in the Door-Yard Bloomed," in which the contrast of the beauty and life of the opening spring with the scenes presented and the thoughts awakened by the funeral of Abraham Lincoln is drawn with unexpected power. The poem is, as a whole, remarkable, but we must content ourselves with a brief quotation [*quotes lines 26–45*].

Edward Dowden, Westminster Review *(London), July 1871*

What cannot be questioned after an hour's acquaintance with Walt Whitman and his *Leaves of Grass* is that in him we meet a man not shaped out of old-world clay, not cast in any old-world mould, and hard to name by any old-world name. In his self-assertion there is a manner of powerful nonchalantness which is not assumed; he does not peep timidly from behind his works to glean our suffrages, but seems to say, "Take me or leave me, here I am a solid and not an inconsiderable fact of the universe." He disturbs our classifications. He attracts us; he repels us; he excites our curiosity, wonder, admiration, love; or, our extreme repugnance. He does anything except leave us indifferent. However we feel towards him we cannot despise him. He is "a summons and a challenge." He must be understood and so accepted, or must be got rid of. Passed by he cannot be. To English readers Whitman is already known through Mr. Conway's personal reminiscences, published in the *Fortnightly Review,* through the judicious criticism of Mr. Rossetti prefixed to his volume of selections, and through other reviews, favourable and unfavourable. His critics have, for the most part, confined their attention to the personality of the man; they have studied him, for the most part, as a phenomenon isolated from the surrounding society, the environment, the *milieu,* which has made such a phenomenon possible. In a general way it has been said that Whitman is the representative in art of American democracy, but the meaning of this has not been investigated in detail. It is purposed here to consider some of the characteristics of democratic art, and to inquire in what manner they manifest themselves in Whitman's work.

A word of explanation is necessary. The representative man of a nation is not always the nation's favourite. Hebrew spiritualism, the deepest instincts, the highest reaches of the moral attainment of the Jewish race, appear in the cryings and communings of its prophets; yet the prophets sometimes cried in the wilderness, and the people went after strange gods. American democracy is as yet but half-formed. The framework of its institutions exists, but the will, the conscience, the mature desires of the democratic society are still in process of formation. If Whitman's writings are spoken of as the poetry of American democracy, it is not implied that his are the volumes most inquired after in the libraries of New York or Boston. What one means is that these are the poems which naturally arise when a man of imaginative genius stands face to face with a great democratic world, as yet but half-fashioned, such as society is in the United States of the present day. Successive editions of his works prove that Whitman has many readers. But whether he had them now, or waited for them in years to come, it would remain true that he is the first representative democrat in art of the American Continent. At the same time he is before all else a living man, and must not be compelled to appear as mere official representative of anything. He will not be comprehended in a formula. No *view* of him can image the substance, the life and movement of his manhood, which contracts and dilates, and is all over sensitive and vital. Such views are, however, valuable in the study of literature, as hypotheses are in the natural sciences, at least for the collocation of facts. They have a tendency to render criticism rigid and doctrinaire; the critic must therefore ever be ready to escape from his own theory of a man, and come in contact with the man himself. Every one doubtless moves in some regular orbit, and all aberrations are only apparent, but what the precise orbit is we must be slow to pronounce. Meanwhile we may legitimately conjecture, as Kepler conjectured, if only we remain ready as Kepler was to vary our conjectures as the exigencies of the observed phenomena require . . .

In the period of chivalry there existed a beautiful relation between man and man, of which no trace remains in existence as an institution—that of knight and squire. The protecting, encouraging, downward glance of the elder, experienced, and superior man was answered by the admiring and aspiring, upward gaze of the younger and inferior. The relation was founded upon inequality; from the inequality of the parties its essential beauty was derived. Is there any possible relation of no less beauty, corresponding to the new condition of things, and founded upon equality? Yes, there is manly comradeship. Here we catch one of the clearest and most often reiterated notes of Whitman's song. The feelings of equality, individualism, pride, self-maintenance he would not repress; they are to be as great as the soul is great; but they are to be balanced by the feelings of fraternity, sympathy, self-surrender, comradeship. European Radicals have for the most part been divided into two schools, with the respective watchwords of *Equality* and *Fraternity*. Whitman expresses the sentiments of both schools, while his position as poet rather than theorist or politician saves him from self-devotion to any such socialistic or communistic schemes, as the premature interpretation of the feeling of fraternity into political institutions has given birth to in untimely abortion. One division of *Leaves of Grass,* that entitled "Calamus" (Calamus being the grass with largest and hardiest spears and with fresh pungent *bouquet*), is appropriated to the theme of comradeship. And to us it seems impossible to read the poems comprised under this head without finding our interest in the poet Walt Whitman fast changing into hearty love of the man, these poems, through their tender reserves and concealments and betrayals, revealing his heart in its weakness and its strength more than any others. The chord of feeling which he strikes may be old—as old as David and Jonathan—but a fulness and peculiarity of tone are brought out, the like of which have not been heard before. For this love of man for man, as Whitman dreams of it, or rather confidently expects it, is to be no rare, no exceptional emotion, making its possessors illustrious by its singular preciousness, but it is to be widespread, common, unnoticeable.

[*quotes "Calamus 24" in full*]

In this growth of America, comradeship, which Whitman looks upon as a sure growth from seed already lying in the soil, he believes the most substantial hope and safety of the States will be found. In it he sees a power capable of counterbalancing the materialism, the selfishness, the vulgarity of American democracy—a power capable of spiritualizing the lives of American men. Many, Whitman is aware, will regard this assurance of his as a dream; but such loving comradeship seems to him implied in the very existence of democracy, "without which it will be incomplete, in vain, and incapable of perpetuating itself." In the following poem the tenderness and ardour of this love of man for man finds expression, but not its glad activity, its joyous fronting the stress and tumultuous agitation of life [*quotes "Calamus 11" in full*].*

**These two excerpts are from Dowden's much longer essay.*

New York Critic, *5 November 1881*

Practically, but not actually, this is the first time that Mr. Whitman has issued his poems through a publishing house instead of at his private cost. The two volumes called *Leaves of Grass* and the *Two Rivulets,* which he had printed and himself sold at Camden, N.J., are now issued in one, under the former title, without special accretions of new work, but not without a good deal of re-arrangement in the sequence of the poems. Pieces that were evidently written later, and intended to be eventually put under *Leaves of Grass* now find their place; some that apparently did well enough where they were have been shifted to other departments. On the whole, however, the changes have been in the direction of greater clearness as regards their relation to the subtitles. It is not apparent, however, that the new book is greatly superior to the old in typography, although undeniably the fault of the privately printed volumes, a variation in types used, is no longer met with. The margins are narrower, and the look of the page more commonplace. The famous poem called "Walt Whitman" is now the "Song of Myself." It still maintains:

I too am not a bit tamed, I too am
untranslatable;
I sound my barbaric yawp over the roofs
of the world.

It still has the portrait of Whitman when younger, standing in a loose flannel shirt and slouched hat, with one hand on his hip, the other in his pocket. "Eidolons" has been taken from the second volume and placed, for good reasons that the reader may not be ready to understand, among the first pieces gathered under the subtitle "Inscriptions." It ends with the "Songs of Parting," under which the last is "So Long," a title that a foreigner and perhaps many an American might easily consider quite as untranslatable as Mr. Whitman proclaims himself to be. The motive for the publication seems to be to take advantage of that wider popularity which is coming somewhat late in life to him whom his admirers like to call "the good gray poet."

One great anomaly of Whitman's case has been that while he is an aggressive champion of democracy and of the working-man, in a broad sense of the term working-man, his admirers have been almost exclusively of a class the farthest possibly removed from that which labors for daily bread by manual work. Whitman has always been truly caviare to the multitude. It was only those that knew much of poetry and loved it greatly who penetrated the singular shell of his verses and rejoiced in the rich, pulpy kernel. Even with connoisseurs, Whitman has been somewhat of an acquired taste, and it has always been amusing to note the readiness with which persons who would not or could not read him, raised a cry of affectation against those who did. This phenomenon is too well known in other departments of taste to need further remark; but it may be added that Mr. Whitman has both gained by it and lost. He has gained a vigorousness of support on the part of his admirers that probably more than outbalances the acrid attacks of those who consider his work synonymous with all that is vicious in poetical technique, and wicked from the point of morals. As to the latter, it must be confessed that, according to present standards of social relations, the doctrines taught by Whitman might readily be construed, by the overhasty or unscrupulous, into excuses for foul living: for such persons do not look below the surface, nor can they grasp the whole idea of Whitman's treatment of love. However fervid his expressions may be, and however scornful he is of the miserable hypocrisies that fetter but also protect the evilly disposed, it is plain that the idea he has at heart is that universal love which leaves no room for wickedness because it leaves no room for doing or saying unkind, uncharitable, unjust things to his fellow-man. With an exuberance of thought that would supply the mental outfit of ten ordinary poets, and with a rush of words that is by no means reckless, but intensely and grandly labored, Whitman hurls his view of the world at the heads of his readers with a vigor and boldness that takes away one's breath. This century is getting noted among centuries for singular departures in art and literature. Among them all, there is none bolder or more original than that of Whitman. Perhaps Poe in his own line might be cited as an equal. It is strange, and yet it is not strange, that he should have waited so long for recognition, and that by many thousands of people of no little culture his claims to being a poet at all are either frankly scouted or else held in abeyance. Literature here has remarkably held aloof from the vital thoughts and hopes of the country. It seems as if the very crudity of the struggle here drove people into a petty dilettante atmosphere of prettiness in art and literature as an escape from the dust and cinders of daily life. Hence our national love for "slicked up" pictures, for instance, by which it is often claimed in Europe that promising geniuses in painting, there, have been ruined for higher work. Hence our patronage of poets that have all the polish of a cymbal, but all a cymbal's dry note and hollowness. Hence, at one time, our admiration for orators that were ornate to the verge of inanity. Into this hot-house air of literature Walt Whitman bounded, with the vigor and suppleness of a clown at a funeral. Dire were the grimaces of the mourners in high places, and dire are their grimaces still. There were plenty of criticisms to make, even after one had finished crying Oh! at the frank sensuality, the unbelievable nakedness of Walt. Everything that decent folk covered up Walt exhibited and boasted of exhibiting! He was proud of his nakedness and sensuality. He cried, Look here, you pampered rogues of literature, what are you squirming about, when you know, and everybody knows, that things are just like this, always have been, always will be? But it must be remembered that this was what he wrote, and that he did with a plan, and by order from his genius. It has never been heard of him that he was disgusting in talk or vile in private life, while it has been known that poets celebrated for the lofty tone of their morality, for the strictness of their Christianity, the purity of their cabinet hymns, can condescend in private life to wallow in all that is base. That is the other great anomaly of Whitman. He rhapsodizes of things seldom seen in print with the enthusiasm of a surgeon enamoured of the wonderful mechanism of the body. But he does not soil his conversation with lewdness. If evil is in him, it is in his book.

Whitman's strength and Whitman's weakness lie in his lack of taste. As a mere external sign, look at his privately printed volumes. For a printer and typesetter, reporter and editor, they do not show taste in the selection and arrangement of the type. A cardinal sin in the eyes of most critics is the use of French, Spanish, and American-Spanish words which are scattered here and there, as if Whitman had picked them up, sometimes slightly incorrectly, from wandering minstrels, Cubans, or fugitives from one of Walker's raids. He shows crudely the American way of incorporating into the language a handy or a high-sounding word without elaborate examination of its original meaning, just as we absorb the different nationalities that crowd over from Europe. His thought and his mode of expression is immense, often flat, very often monotonous, like our great sprawling cities with their endless scattering of suburbs. Yet when one gets the "hang" of it, there is a colossal grandeur in conception and execution that must finally convince whoever will be patient enough to look for it. His rhythm, so much burlesqued, is all of a part with the man and his ideas. It is apparently confused; really most carefully schemed; certainly to a high degree original. It has what to the present writer is the finest thing in the music of Wagner—a great booming movement or undertone, like the noise of heavy surf. His crowded adjectives are like the mediæval writers of Irish, those extraordinary poets who sang the old Irish heroes and their own contemporaries, the chiefs of their clans. No Irishman of to-day has written a nobler lament for Ireland, or a more hopeful, or a more truthful, than has Walt Whitman. Yet it is not said that he has Irish blood. Nor is there to be found in our literature another original piece of prose so valuable to future historians as his notes on the war. Nor is there a poet of the war-time extant who has so struck the note of that day of conflict as Whitman has in *Drum-Taps.* He makes the flesh creep. His verses are like the march of the long lines of volunteers, and then again like the bugles of distant cavalry. But these are parts of him. As he stands complete in *Leaves of Grass,* in spite of all the things that regard for the decencies of drawing-rooms and families may wish away, he certainly represents, as no other writer in the world, the struggling, blundering, sound-hearted, somewhat coarse, but still magnificent vanguard of Western civilization that is encamped in the United States of America. He avoids the cultured few. He wants to represent, and does in his own strange way represent, the lower middle stratum of humanity. But, so far, it is not evident that his chosen constituency cares for or has even recognized him. Wide readers are beginning to guess his proportions.

T. W. Higginson, Nation *(New York), 15 December 1881*

We have read anew, from a sense of duty, the original and unexpurgated *Leaves of Grass,* by Walt Whitman, as now reprinted, with some milder additions. It cannot be said of them, as Sir Charles Pomander, in "Christie Johnstone," says of his broken statues, that "time has impaired their indelicacy." This somewhat nauseating quality remains in full force, and we see no good in their publication except to abate the outcries of the Liberal League against Mr. Anthony Comstock and his laws respecting obscene publications. So long as *Leaves of Grass* may be sent through the mails, the country is safe from over-prudery, at least. Mr. Whitman is often ranked with the "fleshly school," and his circle of English admirers is almost identical with the coterie whose apostles are Swinburne and Wilde. But the erotic poems of these authors are to those of Whitman as rosewater to vitriol. The English poets have at their worst some thin veneering of personal emotion; with Whitman there seems no gleam of anything personal, much less of that simple, generous impulse which makes almost every young man throw some halo of ideal charm about the object of his adoration. Whitman's love, if such it can be called, is the sheer animal longing of sex for sex—the impulse of the savage, who knocks down the first woman he sees and drags her to his cave. On the whole, the condition of the savage seems the more wholesome, for he simply gratifies his brute lust and writes no resounding lines about it.

Leaving this disagreeable aspect of the matter, we are impressed anew, on reading these poems, by a certain quality of hollowness, which is nowhere more felt than in the strains called *Drum-Taps.* It would be scarcely worth while to bring these strains to any personal test, perhaps, did not Mr. Whitman's admirers so constantly intrude his personality upon us; but we cannot quite forget what Emerson says, that "it makes a great difference to a sentence whether there be a man behind it or no." When Mr. Whitman speaks with utter contempt of the "civilian" and claps the soldier on the back as "camerado," we cannot help thinking of Thackeray's burly and peaceful Jos. Sedley at Brussels, just before the battle of Waterloo, striding and swaggering between two military officers and looking far more warlike than either. One can be aroused to some enthusiasm over the pallid shop-boy or the bookish undergraduate who knew no better than to shoulder his musket and march to the front in the war for the Union; but it is difficult to awaken any such emotion for a stalwart poet, who—with the finest physique in America, as his friends asserted, and claiming an unbounded influence over the "roughs" of New York—preferred to pass by the recruiting-office and take service in the hospital with the non-combatants.

When we come to purely intellectual traits, it is a curious fact that Mr. Whitman, by the production of one fine poem, has overthrown his whole poetic theory. Dozens of pages of his rhythmic prose are not worth "My Captain," which among all his compositions comes the nearest to accepting the restraints of ordinary rhyme. His success in this shows that he too may yet be compelled to recognize form as an element in poetic power. The discovery may have come too late, but unless he can regard its lessons he is likely to leave scarcely a complete work that will be remembered; only here and there a phrase, an epithet, a fine note—as when the midnight tolling for General Garfield is called "The sobbing of the bells." These are the passages which his especial admirers style "Homeric," but which we should rather call Ossianic. The shadowy Gaelic bard rejected the restraints of verse, like Whitman, and reiterated his peculiar images with wearisome diffuseness and minuteness. To be sure, he was not an egotist, and he kept within the limits of decency; but he gave fine glimpses and pictures, while there was always a certain large, free atmosphere about all his works. They were translated into all languages; he was ranked with Homer and Virgil; Goethe and Napoleon Bonaparte were his warm admirers—and the collections of English poetry do not now include a line of his composing. If Whitman, after the same length of time, proves more fortunate, it will be because he wrote "My Captain."

Philadelphia Evening Bulletin, *30 October 1888*

No one can fail to be affected by the appearance of the latest writings of Walt Whitman, which are published by Mr. David McKay. Like all that he has written, they are not to be criticised, for the writer's literary creed denies and defies criticism. He is himself, and has the faith in his self-hood that every sturdy revolutionist or sincere reformer has. He may be right or he may be wrong, but his standard is his own, and he is brave enough to maintain it. This volume is a collection of bits that Whitman has published in magazines or newspapers. Many are in prose, in fact all may be so called, although some are poetical in their typographical arrangement. In the first twelve pages is an explanation or defence of his *Leaves of Grass*. This is in many respects a noble composition, in spite of its frequent disregard of literary and academic conventions. The collection of thoughts called "Sands at Seventy" cannot be called poetical, though the printed lines suggest it. Still there are occasional flashes of poetic light, which gleam through an excess of bigwordiness. But this remark borders on criticism, and that is forbidden when Whitman's contemporaries consider him. He has his own ideas of grammar, phraseology and the meaning of words, English and French, and he is not to be disturbed in his rights. What we especially admire in him is his stout, tough Americanism, his faith in his country, its government, and its people. His "War Memoranda," his reminiscences of his devoted labors in the army hospitals, and his noble tribute to Lincoln (not so tender as the really rhythmic verses "My Captain"), are things for young Americans to study. His literary essays on Burns, Tennyson and Shakespeare stir the sympathies of all lovers of the English language. More elaborate and long than all is the paper on Elias Hicks, which is a fervid tribute to one man, and a lesson to many. It is full of ideas and suggestions of ideas, which will work and bear fruit in the minds of the seriously thoughtful.

San Francisco Chronicle, *13 January 1889*

The best things in *November Boughs*, by Walt Whitman, are a few sonnets and prose articles. The bulk of the book will prove tedious to all except his admirers, and nothing that he might write will daunt this loyal band. Those who have established the cult of any author always go to the extreme of hero-worship. This is seen in the Browning societies of England and this country, and it finds equal expression in the Whitman coterie. The very uncouthness of Whitman appears to give pleasure to these people, and they are never tired of praising what has been called his "heroic nudity." In the first article in this volume, written at 70, Whitman attempts again to justify *Leaves of Grass.* To use a phrase of Henry James, "he regards himself too seriously," and it makes one smile to read the frequent references to Goethe, Milton and other bards with whom Walt compares himself. What he says about his motive in writing this work which has called down on him so much orthodox condemnation is honestly and plainly stated, but we think he values the poem too highly and that it cannot in any sense be taken as the voice of a representative American of the latter half of this century. Whitman has always seemed very un-American in many of his traits, notably in his acceptance of gifts from friends and in his lack of ambition. That he has many genuine poetic ideas, even in his old age, is evident to any one who reads this collection of his later writings, but these ideas seldom find adequate expression. The mannerisms, both of his prose and his verse, check all perfect development, and one can only fancy what they might have been put in rhythmical verse or prose. The book has a good portrait of Whitman taken in his seventieth year.

Oscar Wilde, Pall Mall Gazette *(London), 25 January 1889*

"No one will get at my verses who insists upon viewing them as a literary performance, or as aiming mainly towards art and æstheticism. *Leaves of Grass* has been chiefly the outcropping of my own emotional and other personal nature—an attempt from first to last to put a *Person,* a human being (myself, in the latter half of the nineteenth century, in America) freely, fully and truly on record. I could not find any similar personal record in current literature that satisfied me." In these words Walt Whitman gives us the true attitude we should adopt towards his work, having indeed a much saner view of the value and meaning of that work than either his eloquent admirers or noisy detractors can boast of possessing. His last book, *November Boughs* as he calls it, published in the winter of the old man's life, reveals to us, not indeed a soul's tragedy, for its last note is one of joy and hope and noble and unshaken faith in all that is fine and worthy of such faith, but certainly the drama of a human soul, and puts on record with a simplicity that has in it both sweetness and strength the record of his spiritual development and the aim and motive both of his manner and the matter of his work. His strange mode of expression is shown in these pages to have been the result of deliberate and self-conscious choice. The "barbaric yawp," which he sent over "the roofs of the world" so many years ago, and which wrung from Mr. Swinburne's lips such lofty panegyric in song and such loud clamorous censure in prose, appears here in what will be to many an entirely new light. For in his very rejection of art Walt Whitman is an artist. He tried to produce a certain effect by certain means and he succeeded. There is much method in what many have termed his madness, too much method indeed some may be tempted to fancy.

In the story of his life, as he tells it to us, we find him at the age of sixteen beginning a definite and philosophical study of literature:

[*quotes full paragraph beginning "Later, at intervals" from "A Backward Glance"*]

Edgar Allan Poe's amusing bit of dogmatism that, for our occasions and for our day, there can be no such thing as a long poem, fascinated him: "The same thought had been haunting my mind before," he says, "but Poe's argument, though short, work'd the sum out and proved it to me"; and the English translation of the Bible seems to have suggested to him the possibility of a poetic form which while retaining the spirit of poetry would still be free from the trammels of rhyme and of a definite metrical system. Having thus to a certain degree settled upon what one might call the *technique* of Whitmanism, he began to brood upon the nature of that spirit that was to give life to the strange form. The central point of the poetry of the future seemed to him to be necessarily "an identical body and soul," a personality in fact, which personality he tells us frankly, "after many considerations and ponderings I deliberately settled should be myself." However, for the true creation and revealing of this personality, at first only dimly felt, a new stimulus was needed. This came from the Civil War. After describing the many dreams and passions of his boyhood and early manhood he goes on to say:

[*quotes two full paragraphs, beginning "These, however" and "I went down," from "A Backward Glance"*]

Having thus obtained the necessary stimulus for the quickening and awakening of the personal self, some day to be endowed with universality, he sought to find new notes of song, and passing beyond the mere passion for expression—he aimed at "Suggestiveness" first. "I round and finish little, if anything; and could not, consistently with my scheme. The reader will have his or her part to do, just as much as I have had mine. I seek less to state or display any theme of thought, and more to bring you, reader, into the atmosphere of the theme or thought—there to pursue your own flight." Another "impetus word" is Comradeship, and other "word-signs" are Good Cheer, Content, and Hope. Individuality, especially, he sought for: "I have allowed the stress of my poems from beginning to end to bear upon American individuality and assist it—not only because there is a great lesson in Nature, amid all her generalizing laws, but as a counterpoise to the levelling tendencies of Democracy—and for other reasons. Defiant of ostensible literary and other conventions, I avowedly chant 'the great pride of a man in himself,' and permit it to be more or less a *motif* of nearly all my verse. I think this pride indispensable to an American. I think it not inconsistent with obedience, humility, deference, and self-questioning."

A new theme also was to be found in the relation of the sexes, conceived in a natural, simple, and healthy form, and he protests against poor Mr. William Rossetti's attempt to Bowdlerize and expurgate his song:

[*quotes most of the two paragraphs beginning "From another point of view" and "Universal as are" from "A Backward Glance"*]

But beyond all these notes and moods and motives is the lofty spirit of a grand and free acceptance of all things that are worthy of existence. "I desired," he says, "to formulate a poem whose every thought or fact should indirectly or directly be or connive at an implicit belief in the wisdom, health, mystery, or beauty of every process, every concrete object, every human or other existence, not only consider'd from the point of view of all, but of each." His two final utterances are that really great poetry is always the result of a national spirit, and not the privilege of a polished and select few; and that the sweetest and strongest songs yet remain to be sung.

Such are the views contained in the opening essay, "A Backward Glance o'er Travel'd Roads," as he calls it: but there are many other essays in this fascinating volume, some on poets such as Burns and Lord Tennyson, for whom Walt Whitman has a profound admiration; some on old actors and singers, the elder Booth, Forrest, Alboni, and Mario being his special favourites; others on the native Indians, on the Spanish element in American nationality, on Western slang, on the poetry of the Bible, and on Abraham Lincoln. But Walt Whitman is at his best when he is analyzing his own work and making schemes for the poetry of the future. Literature to him has a distinctly social aim. He seeks to build up the masses by "building up grand individuals." And yet literature itself must be preceded by noble forms of life. "The best literature is always the result of something far greater than itself—not the hero but the portrait of the hero. Before there can be recorded history or poem there must be the transaction." Certainly in Walt Whitman's views there is a largeness of vision, a healthy sanity, and a fine ethical purpose. He is not to be placed with the professional *littérateurs* of his country, Boston novelists, New York poets, and the like. He stands apart, and the chief value of his work is in its prophecy not in its performance. He has begun a prelude to larger themes. He is the herald to a new era. As a man he is the precursor of a fresh type. He is a factor in the heroic and spiritual evolution of the human being. If Poetry has passed him by, Philosophy will take note of him.

New York Tribune, *16 August 1891*

A dreadful photograph resembling nothing so much as a death-mask serves as grim frontispiece to this ultimate publication by Walt Whitman. According to the practice of his later years the volume is written partly in prose and partly in Walt Whitman's peculiar idea of poetry. There is a melancholy flavor about the whole of it, though the old man tries very hard to be cheerful. More than once, however, he refers to the world's refusal to recognize him as a poet. All the great magazines, he declares, have declined to print his lucubrations, and apparently the general public have not fatigued his publisher with orders for his book. The so-called poetry in this volume is naturally of a valedictory character to a considerable extent, and though it is not less prosaic and unmelodious than the writer's earlier productions, the circumstances under which it was written impart a certain suggestion of pathos to it. Walt Whitman does not indeed face the Unknown with apprehensions and misgivings. If he does not appear to cherish Christian hopes and expectations, his Pantheism has not prevented him from maintaining a belief in another existence, and an existence not less adapted to and filled with activity and energy than the present one. Yet he does not speculate much upon the future. Rather does he seem to be chiefly interested in forecasting the ultimate destiny of *Leaves of Grass,* which he does not like to think will be relegated to the limbo of unused or unreadable books.

This question is of course not one upon which those who like or who dislike Walt Whitman's writings can pass final judgment. Posterity often does surprising things and adopts queer views. Among its peculiarities is a tendency *parcere subjectis et debellare superbos* [*"to spare the conquered and vanquish the proud"*]; and for all any one living knows this proclivity may be exercised on behalf of Walt Whitman. As regards his contemporaries, they certainly have not discovered in him the music of the future, and the reasons which have determined the prevailing judgment upon him do not appear weak or capricious. Walt Whitman himself retains a consolatory assurance of his own position, and it is not worth while to attempt to disturb his faith. In the concluding pages of the present volume he gives some autobiographic memoranda which will be found interesting and quaintly illustrative of character. As for the more pretentious papers—attempts at essay-writing and the like—perhaps the less said about them the better. For it is unfortunately the fact that when Walt Whitman tries to be profound he commonly becomes unintelligible, seeming to lose his footing in a bag of verbiage. His passion for stringing words together in catalogue-form recalls old Burton at times, though of course Whitman has nothing of Burton's erudition.* Let us hope, however, that this last booklet may contribute somewhat to the comfort of his age and the assuagement of his infirmities.

**This is a reference to the English scholar Robert Burton (1577–1640), author of* The Anatomy of Melancholy *(1621).*

Boston Literary World, *12 September 1891*

There is something at once very pathetic and courageous in this definitive leave-taking by the poet Walt Whitman. His traits and his place in literature need no farther discussion at present; neither does his absorbent personality that has desired to assimilate the world, or the singular contests of praise and blame which have been waged about him.

Such as he is—and surely he is unique—he now bids farewell, and yet not farewell, to his gift of utterance:

[*quotes five lines from "On, on the Same, ye Jocund Twain!"*]

And again:

[*quotes first four and last five lines from "Good-bye my Fancy!"*]

Other poems in this small but characteristic collection continue the design of the author's previous work, completing the message "today at twilight . . . with vital voice, reporting yet"—the brave veteran! More than half the volume is made up of prose articles and fragments. In these Mr. Whitman's manner remains much the same as in his chants, while the reader is at least spared the continual negation of the laws of the technical art of poetry. In an essay on "National Literature" he finds the essential traits of the American people to be good-nature, decorum, and intelligence, and bases his hopes upon these qualities. In music, despite the critics who assure him he belongs to the worship of Wagner, he dwelt under "the old Italian dispensation," as he calls it, and wishes that he might thank the composer Verdi for "much noble pleasure and happiness." The somber velvet of the voice of Signora Alboni also charmed him; and the brave songs of the Hutchinsons, with their sister, "the red-cheeked New England carnation, sweet Abby." Kean in *King John,* and Fanny Kemble in *Fazio,* "a rapid-running, yet heavy-timber'd, tremendous, wrenching, passionate play," and the comedy of Hackett, appealed, in their day, to Mr. Whitman; and were followed in his theatrical enjoyments by a long list of other artists. He describes his habitation, "a rather large 20 by 20 low-ceiling'd room something like a big old ship's cabin," in literary disorder of papers and books, with its three windows, the stove and oak-wood fuel, and the great arm-chair spread with a "wide wolf-skin of hairy black and silver."

If this volume shall be, as the author appears to intend, his last literary effort, it closes firmly and fitly the literary career of a poet who has with pride and fidelity obeyed his own genius, and who has sought to collect within himself, and to understand and speak—in his oracular, strange voice—the experiences of common humanity.

A Whitman Chronology

1819 Born May 31 near Huntington Township, Long Island

1823 Family moves to Brooklyn (family returns to Long Island ten years later); Whitman's family consisted of father Walter (1789–1855), mother Louisa Van Velsor (1795–1873), and children Jesse (1818–70), Mary (1821–99), Hannah (1823–1908), Andrew Jackson (1827–63), George Washington (1829–1901), Thomas Jefferson (1833–90), and Edward (1835–92)

1825–30 Attends public schools in Brooklyn

1830 End of formal education; office boy for a lawyer, later for a doctor

1831–35 Apprentice work in the printing trade in various offices

1836–41 Teaches in several Long Island schools for brief periods of time (Norwich, Babylon, Long Swamp, Smithtown, Woodbury, Dix Hills, Whitestone, and Southold); possibly dismissed from Southold for misconduct

1841–47 Functions in several journalistic capacities (compositor, reporter, fiction writer, editor) for a number of New York area papers, including the *New World, Aurora, Tattler, Long Island Star;* publishes temperance novella, *Franklin Evans,* in 1842

1846–48 From March 1846 to January 1848 edits *Brooklyn Daily Eagle;* quits or is discharged and travels in February with brother Jeff to New Orleans to edit new paper called the *Crescent;* resigns a few months later; back in Brooklyn by mid-June

1848–54 Continues newspaper work in Brooklyn and Manhattan; also pursues carpentering, house-building, stationery selling, and freelance writing

1855 Early July, first edition of *Leaves of Grass* published; father dies on July 11; Emerson writes to express famous "greetings" on July 21

1856 Late summer, second edition of *Leaves of Grass* appears; visited by Thoreau and, a year later, by Emerson

1857–59 Edits *Brooklyn Daily Times;* unemployed by summer of 1859; frequents Pfaff's Café; *Calamus* poems probably written between May 1857 and May 1859; probably meets Fred Vaughan at this time

1860 Third edition of *Leaves of Grass* published by Thayer & Eldridge of Boston; birth of niece Manahatta (she dies in 1886)

1861 April 13, learns of Ft. Sumter bombardment after attending a performance of Donizetti's *Linda di Chamounix* at the Academy of Music

1862 December, travels to Virginia to search for wounded brother, George; stays in camp two weeks at Fredericksburg

1863–64 Remains in Washington as unofficial nurse in various hospitals; returns in June 1864 to mother's Brooklyn house in broken health

1865 January 24, appointed clerk in Indian Affairs Office of Department of Interior; discharged by Secretary James Harlan in June; employed next day in Attorney General's office; meets streetcar driver Peter Doyle, a former Confederate soldier, around this time; April 14, President Lincoln assassinated; *Drum-Taps* appears

1866 *Drum-Taps,* with sequel including "When Lilacs Last in the Door-Yard Bloom'd" appears; William O'Connor publishes tract defending Whitman, *The Good Gray Poet*

1867 John Burroughs publishes *Notes on Walt Whitman as Poet and Person;* fourth edition of *Leaves of Grass* appears

1868 W. M. Rossetti's *Poems of Walt Whitman* published in London

1869 English widow Anne Gilchrist becomes enamored of Whitman at long distance; she arrives in Philadelphia in 1876 to be near him, staying two years; returns to England in 1879 and continues correspondence until her death in 1885

1870 *Democratic Vistas* published; distress and depression during summer, perhaps in part over his relationship with Peter Doyle

1871 Fifth edition of *Leaves of Grass* appears, including "Passage to India"

1873 January 23, paralytic stroke causes dizzy spells that last more than a year; mother dies, May 23; unable to work, moves from Washington to brother George's house in Camden, New Jersey

1876 Meets Harry Stafford in Camden newspaper office, beginning several years of intimacy; spends much time at Stafford family house near Timber Creek, ten miles southeast of Camden; sixth ("Centennial") edition of *Leaves of Grass* appears

1879 In New York, gives first of several annual lectures on Lincoln; travels to St. Louis to visit favorite brother, Jeff, then makes farthest westward journey, to Colorado; next year visits R. M. Bucke, a future biographer, in Canada

1881 Seventh edition of *Leaves of Grass* published by Boston firm Osgood & Company

1882 Oscar Wilde visits in January; Boston district attorney, urged by the Society for the Suppression of Vice, forces Osgood to cease publication of *Leaves;* next edition, published in Philadelphia, quickly sells out four printings; *Specimen Days & Collect* (including *Democratic Vistas*) published in Philadelphia

1883 R. M. Bucke's *Walt Whitman,* closely supervised by the poet, appears

1884 Buys house at 328 Mickle Street, Camden, his residence for the remainder of his life; Edward Carpenter visits in June

1885 Injured in two falls; friends present him with horse and buggy; next year friends donate $800 for cottage retreat at Timber Creek, which was never built

1888 March 28, Horace Traubel begins taking copious notes of Whitman conversations; June, another stroke; *November Boughs* and *Complete Poems and Prose* published

1890 Last Lincoln lecture, in Philadelphia; August 19, in a letter to John Addington Symonds, rejects homosexual interpretation of *Calamus* poems and tells of fathering six children

1891 Publishes *Good-Bye my Fancy* and last ("deathbed") edition of *Leaves of Grass;* prepares *Complete Prose Works,* published the next year

1892 March 26, dies and is buried four days later in a large granite "burial house," designed by himself, in Harleigh Cemetery, Camden

Notes on the Poems

References below to the years 1855, 1856, 1860, 1865 (Drum-Taps), *1865–66* (Sequel), *1871* (Passage to India), *1872* (Pinions), *1876* (Two Rivulets), *1881, 1888, and 1891–92 indicate the* Leaves of Grass *edition or other Whitman publication of that year. The abbreviation* WWC *refers to the nine volumes of Whitman conversations recorded by Horace Traubel and published under the title* With Walt Whitman in Camden; *volume and page numbers are given in parentheses. Only the more significant revisions made after initial publication are noted here. A complete census of changes can be found in the three-volume* Textual Variorum of the Printed Poems *of* The Collected Writings *(1980).*

1855 Edition

"I celebrate myself . . ."

TITLE: Whitman gave no title to this poem in the first edition. In 1856 it became "Poem of Walt Whitman, an American"; in 1860 and following editions it was "Walt Whitman." In 1881 and afterward it became "Song of Myself."

NOTE ON THE NUMBERING OF STANZAS AND SECTIONS: As in 1855, there was no numbering in the 1856 edition. For 1860 Whitman chose to number each verse paragraph, of which there were 372; the numbers were placed in the margin to the left of each paragraph's first line. For 1867 this numbering was retained (though after revision there were only 366 paragraphs), but Whitman also chose to place centered numbers at the beginning of the poem's 52 major sections. In 1881 the section numbers were retained but the paragraph numbers dropped. The 52 sections, with their equivalent opening line in the 1855 edition in parentheses, are as follows: 1 (1), 2 (6), 3 (30), 4 (58), 5 (73), 6 (90), 7 (122), 8 (140), 9 (160), 10 (168), 11 (193), 12 (211), 13 (219), 14 (238), 15 (257), 16 (326), 17 (353), 18 (not in 1855; new lines replaced original ll. 360–67 during revision), 19 (372), 20 (388), 21 (422), 22 (451), 23 (483), 24 (499), 25 (562), 26 (584), 27 (611), 28 (618), 29 (641), 30 (647), 31 (662), 32 (684), 33 (709), 34 (864), 35 (890), 36 (918), 37 (not in 1855; new lines replaced original ll. 933–41 during revision), 38

(953), 39 (974), 40 (984), 41 (1015), 42 (1050), 43 (1092), 44 (1133), 45 (1169), 46 (1198), 47 (1231), 48 (1262), 49 (1281), 50 (1299), 51 (1309), 52 (1321). **CHANGES: Line 1:** "and sing myself" was added in 1881. After **l. 5,** in 1881, Whitman inserted these lines from "Starting from Paumanok":

> My tongue, every atom of my blood, form'd from this soil, this air,
> Born here of parents born here from parents the same,
> and their parents the same,
> I, now thirty-seven years old in perfect health begin,
> Hoping to cease not till death.
>
> Creeds and schools in abeyance,
> Retiring back a while sufficed at what they are, but never forgotten,
> I harbor for good or bad, I permit to speak at every hazard,
> Nature without check with original energy.

In **l. 38** "always sex" was added after the final comma in 1856. In one of Whitman's more striking revisions, **l. 52** became in 1860 "As the hugging and loving Bedfellow sleeps at my side through the night, and withdraws at the peep of day." From **l. 82** "and joy" was removed in 1867. In **l. 208,** "swell" was changed to "bulge" in 1856. References to a "reformer" and a "darkey" were deleted by the removal of **ll. 283–84,** likewise the reference to childbirth in **l. 291** and a satiric reference, in **l. 299,** to a woman sitting for a daguerreotype (perhaps because this photographic method began to disappear in the 1850s). Lines **360–65** were deleted by 1867, and the new section began with the line "With music strong I come, with my cornets and my drums . . ." The boisterous line about life being a "suck and sell" **(l. 395)** was cut in 1881. The sexually explicit "Thruster" **ll. 449–50** were deleted in 1867; a prior ms. version of this passage deserves noting:

> Still slumberous night—mad, naked summer night!
>
> Smile, O voluptuous procreant earth! . . .
> Smile, for your lover comes!
>
> Spread round me earth! Spread with your curtained hours;
> Take me as many a time you've taken;
> Till springing up in* * *
>
> Prodigal, you have given me love;
> Sustenance, happiness, health have given;
> Therefore, I to you give love;
> O, unspeakable, passionate love!
>
> (*Notes and Fragments*, ed. R. M. Bucke, [1899; rpt. 1972], p. 17)

The boastful **l. 466** was dropped in 1867. **Line 468,** expressing the poet's preference for the bearded over the shaved, was cut in 1881. The famous **l. 499** became in 1867 "Walt Whitman am I, of mighty Manhattan the son." Then in 1871 "a kosmos" was added after "I"; the final version was "Walt Whitman, a kosmos, of Manhattan the son." **Line 511,** "Voices of prostitutes and of deformed persons," was deleted in 1881. **Line 602,** vividly expressing the sexual impact of the operatic voice, was toned down considerably by 1867 to "I hear the trained soprano (what work, with hers, is this?) . . ." Behind the powerful, sex-drenched **ll. 639–42** lie two striking Whitman ms. passages:

You villain touch! What are you doing?
Unloose me, the breath is leaving my throat;
Open your floodgates! You are too much for me.
Grip'd wrestler! do you keep the heaviest pull for the last?
Must you bite with your teeth at parting?
Will you struggle worst? I plunge you from the threshold.
Does it make you ache so to leave me!
Take what you like, I can resist you;
Take the tears of my soul if that is what you are after.
Pass to some one else;
Little as your mouth, it has drained me dry of my strength.

It is no miracle now that we are to live always.
Touch is the miracle!
What is it to be lost, or change our dresses, or sleep long, when . . . .

(*Notes and Fragments,* pp. 10, 23)

Line 669, asserting the poet's interest in a farmer's girl, was cut in 1881. The vaulting boast of **ll. 953–54** was deleted in 1867. After the line "Elves I salute you," **ll. 970–73** were cut in 1867 and replaced by this characteristically more abstract single line: "Continue your annotations, continue your questionings." **Line 1082** finally became, in 1881, "Not words of routine this song of mine." In 1860, **ll. 1084–85** were deleted, also **ll. 1136–37.** In the copy used for the Chandler facsimile, **l. 1118** reads, "And the night is for you and me and all," suggesting that a stop-press change was made. The entire line vanished after 1860. Whitman deleted the heterosexual assertion of **l. 1175** in 1867. **NOTE:** More extensive prior manuscript versions of passages in this poem can be found in appendix 2.

entretied (l. 41): a term from carpentry, Whitman's father's trade and occasionally his own in the years before the 1855 *Leaves of Grass,* meaning cross-braced.

kelson (l. 86): a variation of *keelson,* longitudinal strengthening framework of a ship's hull.

Kanuck, Tuckahoe . . . Cuff (l. 100): Kanuck = French Canadian; Tuckahoe refers to Virginians of the tidewater, who ate tuckahoe, a fungus known as Virginia truffle; Cuff – an African-American.

shuffle and breakdown (l. 212): varieties of dance, the shuffle being a slow one with sliding motions and the breakdown being boisterous and up-tempo.

stringpiece (l. 220): a long, large, squared piece of timber used for shoring during construction.

jour printer (l. 268): a journeyman printer.

Wolverine (l. 282): a native of Michigan.

savans (l. 363): philosophers or wise men, variant of *savants.*

embouchures (l. 369): mouthpieces of wind instruments or the mouth as shaped while playing.

carlacue (l. 408): variant of *curlicue*—the image here being of a fanciful spiral flourish made with a firework sparkler.

tenoned and mortised (l. 419): terms from carpentry; the tenon is the projection at the end of a piece of wood that is inserted into a mortise to make a solid joint.

amies (l. 463): from the French for "friends."

stonecrop (l. 489): a common, hardy, mosslike, ground-covering plant with a yellow flower.

cartouches (l. 490): scroll-shaped architectural ornaments, notably on ancient columns and entablatures.

afflatus (l. 506): from the Latin *afflare,* "to blow on"; a divine imparting of inspiration.
coulter (l. 531): or *colter,* the sharp blade attached to the beam of a plow, used to cut into the earth; figuratively, the phallus.
plenum (l. 582): fullness, completion.
fakes (l. 608): coils of rope.
quahaug (l. 612): a species of Atlantic clam.
pismire (l. 663): ant.
esculent (l. 670): edible.
plutonic rocks (l. 675): igneous or once-molten rocks formed deep in the earth.
omnigenous (l. 698): composed of or containing all varieties.
life-car (l. 740): a device used to rescue passengers from vessels in stormy weather.
bull-dances (l. 751): all-male dances (also sometimes called ram-reels).
sqush (l. 752): from *squash* or *squish*—the matter resulting from the pressing of fruit (Whitman later changed this word to *mash*).
foretruck (l. 806): the highest part of a ship's tallest mast.
the crowded and rudderless wreck of the steamship (l. 820): It is believed that Whitman based this passage on the fate of the *San Francisco,* which sailed on 22 December 1853 from New York bound for South America. From 23 December until 5 January 1854 it was rudderless; many passengers lost their lives. The story was reported in the *New York Weekly Tribune* on 21 January 1854.
murder . . . of four hundred (ll. 867–89): This passage describes a massacre that took place at Goliad, Texas, on 27 March 1836 (it was similar to that at the Alamo a few weeks earlier). Whitman was editor of the *Brooklyn Eagle* when it published, on 11 March 1846, an excerpt titled "Fanning's Men, or The Massacre at Goliad," which he had found in *Blackwood's* magazine.
frigate-fight (ll. 890–932): This North Sea battle took place on 23 September 1779 between John Paul Jones's *Bonhomme Richard* and the British warship *Serapis.*
Eleves (l. 969): from the French for "pupil" or "disciple."
scarfed (l. 993): tapered and joined, a carpenter's term.
tressels (l. 1064): variant of *trestles,* here probably the pallets on which the dead lie.
the circle of obis (l. 1097): a reference to "obi" or "obeah," sorcery with African roots practiced in the United States and Caribbean.
gymnosophist (l. 1099): a sect of ancient ascetic Hindus who often went naked.
shasta and vedas (l. 1100): shastras, the correct spelling, and vedas are collections of ancient sacred Hindu literature.
teokallis (l. 1101): Aztec temples.
And the day . . . (l. 1118): Preparation of this edition has revealed for the first time a substantial variant among copies of the 1855 *Leaves*; the apparent first version of this line reads: "And the night is for you and me and all."
koboo (l. 1128): a native of Sumatra.
sauroids (l. 1166): a reference to large prehistoric reptiles.
accoucheur (l. 1282): from the French, "midwife."

"Come closer to me . . ."

TITLE: Untitled in 1855, this became in 1856 "Poem of The Daily Work of The Workmen and Workwomen of These States." In 1860 it was simply #3 of the *Chants Democratic* cluster; in 1867 it was "To Workingmen"; in 1871 and 1876, "Carol of Occupations"; its final title came in 1881, "A Song of Occupations." **CHANGES:** The poem was subject to elaborate revision over time; it grew from its original length of 178 lines to 205 in 1860; by the final *Leaves* edition it was reduced to 151. In 1881 Whitman dropped **ll. 1–7,** and the new opening stanza read, "A song for occupations! / In the labor of engines and trades and the labor of fields I find the developments, / And find the eternal meanings." (A short essay on the essential differences between the early and late Whitman could be based on these two beginnings.) Cut in 1867 was the passage, **ll. 30–33,** beginning ". . . and see and hear you." Other cuts were **ll. 40–41** and about two dozen lines from the long list beginning at **l. 100.** In **l. 168,** Whitman added "knowledge" after "Happiness." In **l. 169** "lover" was changed to "sister" in 1881. In 1856 these two lines were added after **l. 169:** "The popular tastes and employments taking precedence in poems or anywhere, / You workwomen and workmen of these States having your own divine and strong life . . ." **savans** (l. 67): philosophers or wise men, variant of *savants.*

frisket, tympan (l. 138): the tympan, of paper or cloth, is placed over the platen of a hand press to provide support for the sheet being printed; the frisket is a light frame that holds the sheet to the tympan.

"To think of time . . ."

TITLE: "Burial Poem" in 1856; "Burial" in 1860 and 1867; "To Think of Time" from 1871 on. **CHANGES:** This was one of the poems Whitman considerably revised. He seems to have removed some defensiveness about the American taste for poetry by deleting **ll. 58** and **67** in 1881. **Lines 96–99** and **100–101** were also cut in 1881. **Lines 125–29** were deleted in 1871.

"I wander all night in my vision . . ."

TITLE: At first untitled, then "Night Poem" in 1856; "Sleep-Chasings" in 1860 and 1867; "The Sleepers" in 1871 and after. **CHANGES:** This poem was substantially revised. The editors of the New York University Whitman edition call it "perhaps the only surrealist American poem of the nineteenth century, remarkable in its anticipation of later experiment" (*Comprehensive Reader's Edition*, p. 424). One of Whitman's most powerfully sexual passages, **ll. 60–70,** was deleted in 1881, likewise lines **127–34.** In 1881, "contact" with an "unseen something" is cut in **l. 138. Lines 204–5,** the poem's last, were deleted in 1856.

douceurs (l. 34): from the French, plural of "delight" or "sweetness."

Cache (l. 35): from the French for "hiding place."

defeat of Brooklyn (l. 101): a reference to the Battle of Brooklyn Heights, 27 August 1776, a serious American defeat saved from being worse when Washington ferried his troops across the East River to Manhattan.

erysipalite (l. 158): victim of erysipelas, an acute skin disease caused by the streptococcus bacteria.

"The bodies of men and women engirth me . . ."

TITLE: At first untitled, then "Poem of the Body" in 1856; in 1860 it was the third *Enfans d'Adam* poem; from 1867 on it was "I Sing the Body Electric." **CHANGES:** This poem was subject to extensive but mostly detailed revisions. The **first line** read in 1867, "I sing the body electric" (in 1860 it was "O my children! O mates!"). The original first line became the second, and in 1867 read, more soothingly without specifics of gender, "The armies of those I love engirth me and I engirth them." In **l. 2,** the phrase "and love them" was deleted for 1867. In **l. 10** the "supple" quality of the "wellmade" man's body was deleted in 1881. **Line 65** was cut in 1860. **Line 80** was changed to read ". . . you call the meanest ignorant . . ." in 1881, and in **l. 83** "A slave at auction!" became "A man's body at auction" in 1856 (likewise "a woman's body" in **l. 104**). **Lines 107–9** were deleted for 1867; after **l. 110** Whitman inserted, "Have you ever loved the Body of a man?" For 1856, Whitman made one major alteration. The present last two lines (118–19) were deleted and the following lines added as a separate section; here Whitman's characteristic bias in favor of the male anatomy is elaborately displayed (final 1881 version given):

O my body! I dare not desert the likes of you in other men and women,
nor the likes of the parts of you,
I believe the likes of you are to stand or fall with the likes of the soul
(and that they are the soul),
I believe the likes of you shall stand or fall with my poems,
and that they are my poems,
Man's, woman's, child's, youth's, wife's, husband's, mother's, father's,
young man's, young woman's poems,
Head, neck, hair, ears, drop and tympan of the ears,
Eyes, eye-fringes, iris of the eye, eyebrows and the waking or sleeping
of the lids,
Mouth, tongue, lips, teeth, roof of the mouth, jaws, and the jaw-hinges,
Nose, nostrils of the nose, and the partition,
Cheeks, temples, forehead, chin, throat, back of the neck, neck-slue,
Strong shoulders, manly beard, scapula, hind-shoulders,
and the ample side-round of the chest,
Upper-arm, armpit, elbow-socket, lower-arm, arm-sinews, arm-bones,
Wrist and wrist-joints, hand, palm, knuckles, thumb, forefinger, finger-joints,
finger-nails,
Broad breast-front, curling hair of the breast, breast-bone, breast-side,
Ribs, belly, backbone, joints of the backbone,
Hips, hip-sockets, hip-strength, inward and outward round, man-balls, man-root,
Strong set of thighs, well carrying the trunk above,
Leg-fibres, knee, knee-pan, upper-leg, under-leg,
Ankles, instep, foot-ball, toes, toe-joints, the heel;
All attitudes, all the shapeliness, all the belongings of my or your body
or of any one's body, male or female,
The lung-sponges, the stomach-sac, the bowels sweet and clean,
The brain in its folds inside the skull-frame,
Sympathies, heart-valves, palate-valves, sexuality, maternity,
Womanhood, and all that is a woman, and the man that comes from woman,
The womb, the teats, nipples, breast-milk, tears, laughter, weeping,
love-looks, love-perturbations and risings,
The voice, articulation, language, whispering, shouting aloud,
Food, drink, pulse, digestion, sweat, sleep, walking, swimming,
Poise on the hips, leaping, reclining, embracing, arm-curving and tightening,
The continual changes of the flex of the mouth, and around the eyes,
The skin, the sunburnt shade, freckles, hair,
The curious sympathy one feels when feeling with the hand the naked meat
of the body,
The circling rivers the breath, and breathing it in and out,
The beauty of the waist, and thence of the hips, and thence downward
toward the knees,
The thin red jellies within you or within me, the bones and the marrow in the bones,
The exquisite realization of health;
O I say these are not the parts and poems of the body only, but of the soul,
O I say now these are the soul!

NOTE: A prior ms. version of **lines 7–12** and **51–57** can be found in appendix 2.

"Sauntering the pavement . . ."

TITLE: At first untitled, then "Poem of Faces" in 1856; "Leaf of Faces" in 1860; "A Leaf of Faces" in 1867; and "Faces" from 1871 on. Whitman revised this poem constantly but in minor ways. **CHANGE: Line 34** deleted in 1881.

wrig (l. 19): Whitman's foreshortening of *wriggle.*

caoutchouc (l. 25): crude rubber.

broke my brother (l. 43): Whitman's brother Edward, born in 1835, was mentally defective and for much of his life placed under special care, paid for by Whitman; known as Eddie, he died eight months after Whitman.

albescent (l. 67): whitish in color, the phrase referring to semen.

"A young man came to me . . ."

TITLE: Untitled in the first edition, this became "Poem of The Poet" in 1856, then the third of the *Leaves of Grass* cluster in 1860, and in 1867 "Now List to My Morning Romanza." In 1881, **ll. 51–54** of the poem were deleted and the poem joined with lines that had comprised "Poem of The Singers, and of The Words of Poems" (1856, later Leaves of Grass 6 and "The Indications") to create "Song of the Answerer." **CHANGES:** In 1867 these two lines were added as a separate stanza before **l. 1:** "Now list to my morning romanza, I tell the signs of the Answerer, / To the cities and farms I sing as they spread in the sunshine before me" (the last half of the first line was added in 1871). —**Cudge** (l. 33): a common name for an African American field hand (like "Cuff" in line 100 of "I celebrate myself . . .").

"Suddenly out of its stale and drowsy lair . . ."

TITLE: This is the earliest of all *Leaves of Grass* poems, the only one in the 1855 edition that had previously been published. This occurred on 21 June 1850, when it appeared under the title of "Resurgemus" in the *New York Tribune* (see this version in appendix 1 and its note). In 1855 it was untitled; in 1856 it became "Poem of The Dead Young Men of Europe, The 72nd and 73rd Years of These States." In 1860 it received its final title, "Europe." The revolutions throughout Europe in 1848—most notably in France, Austria, and Hungary—inspired the poem.

"Clear the way there Jonathan!"

TITLE: Untitled in 1855, it became in 1856 "Poem of Apparitions in Boston, The 70th Year of These States"; in 1860, "A Boston Ballad, The 70th Year of These States"; in 1867, "To Get Betimes in Boston Town (1854)"; from 1871 on, it was "A Boston Ballad" and the first *By the Roadside* poem. It was likely written in June of 1854, amid the furor over the arrest and trial in Boston of a fugitive slave named Anthony Burns. **CHANGE:** The poem, from 1867, began with these lines as a separate stanza before the original **l. 1:** "To get betimes to Boston town I rose this morning early, / Here's a good place at the corner, I must stand and see the show." —**Jonathan** (l. 1): by this time a common nickname for a New England rustic or Yankee; its use may date back to Royall Tyler's comedy *The Contrast* (1787). **cute** (l. 41): i.e. acute.

"There was a child went forth . . ."

TITLE: Untitled in 1855, this became "Poem of the Child That Went Forth, and Always Goes Forth, Forever and Forever" in 1856; in 1860 it was the ninth poem of a *Leaves of Grass* cluster, in 1867 the first; after 1871, "There Was a Child Went Forth." **CHANGES:** For 1860, the rather graphic sexual description of **l. 12** was changed to ". . . he that had fathered him, and she that . . ." The **last line** was deleted in 1867. —**esculent** (l. 7): edible.

"Who learns my lesson complete?"

TITLE: Untitled in 1855, this became "Lesson Poem" in 1856 and was in 1860 and 1867 #11 and #3, respectively, in the *Leaves of Grass* cluster; after 1871 it became "Who Learns My Lesson Complete?" in the *Autumn Rivulets* group. **CHANGES:** In **l. 14,** "ten decillions" to "billions." In 1860, **l. 21**'s birth data was altered to "but am now—and was born on the last day of Fifth Month, in the Year 43 of America . . ." This self-description was dropped in 1867. The **last two lines** were deleted after 1867.

"Great are the myths . . ."

TITLE: Untitled in 1855, it was in 1856 "Poem of a Few Greatnesses"; in 1860, the second poem in the *Leaves of Grass* cluster; in 1867, its final title was "Great Are the Myths." In 1881 it was banished completely (except for four lines, **19–22,** salvaged to make the poem "Youth, Day, Old Age and Night"). **CHANGES: Lines 6–16** were cut for 1867. From 1856 to 1860, the ending was different: Whitman deleted the original last line **(l. 67)** and ended the poem and stanza with these four lines: "Death has just as much purport as Life has, / Do you enjoy what Life confers? you shall enjoy what Death confers, / I do not understand the realities of Death, but I know they are great, / I do not understand the least reality of Life—how then can I understand the realities of Death?" Whitman, apparently, preferred to be not so uncomprehending a poet-prophet in his later years.

1856 Edition

Poem of Salutation

TITLE: Whitman's final title for this poem—"Salut au Monde!"—first appeared in the 1860 edition. **CHANGES:** Several cuts were made in the lists of this poem; among them, **ll. 25–27, 33–35, 42, 45–46** were deleted from the "I hear" list. **Lines 139–46** were cut and for 1881 turned into a separate poem, "A Paumanok Picture." For a new ending in 1860, the **last line** was deleted, and these four lines added as a separate concluding stanza (this is the final 1881 version): "Toward you all, in America's name, / I raise high the perpendicular hand, I make the signal, / To remain after me in sight forever, / For all the haunts of homes and men."

slave-coffle (l. 44): a slave caravan.
avatars (l. 110): incarnation of a deity by an avatar in human form is a Hindu belief.
sabians (l. 111): a semi-Christian sect of Babylonia.
muftis (l. 111): official promulgators of Muslim law.
vervain (l. 112): the mallow plant, associated, as was mistletoe, with Druid worship.
Kneph (l. 117): an Egyptian god, with the body of a man and the head of a sheep.
Hermes (l. 118): the messenger of the gods in Greek mythology.
winrows (l. 146): variation of *windrows,* rows of sand or debris created by the wind.
koboo (l. 230): a native of Sumatra.

Poem of Wonder at The Resurrection of The Wheat

TITLE: This poem appeared as Leaves of Grass 4 in 1860 and assumed its final title, "This Compost," in 1867. Compare lines 1285–89 of "I celebrate myself . . ." This poem was much revised; a long manuscript version can be found in *Faint Clews and Indirections* (1949), pp. 9–11. **CHANGES: Line 6** became "O how can it be that the ground itself does not sicken?" **Line 30:** For 1871, movingly, "the lilacs bloom in the dooryards" was added.

Poem of You, Whoever You Are

TITLE: In 1860, this was "To You, Whoever You Are" in *Messenger Leaves,* in 1867 becoming the fourth poem in the *Leaves of Grass* cluster; from 1871 it was simply "To You." **CHANGES: Lines 6–7** were cut in 1860. The rather intimidating **l. 35** was cut in 1867. —**hopples** (l. 47): hobbles or fetters.

Sun-Down Poem

TITLE: This received its final title, "Crossing Brooklyn Ferry," in 1860. **CHANGES:** Several deletions occurred after 1871, with the effect of distancing the poet from the reader. The intimacy-professing **l. 22** vanished; the similarly self-projecting **l. 51** was dropped. **Line 80,** boasting of being a "free, friendly, and proud" Manhattanese, was deleted, and the entire stanza of **ll. 93–97** vanished. **Line 105,** suggesting the poet's impelling effect on the reader, was cut. The subversive **l. 114**—"Blab, blush, lie, steal, you or I or any one of us!"—was cut in 1871. The boldly assertive passage in the last verse paragraph, beginning "We descend upon you . . ." **(ll. 133–36),** was cut after 1871. **NOTE:** Prior manuscript versions of passages in this poem can be found in appendix 2.

Poem of the Road

TITLE: Whitman changed this title in 1867 to "Song of the Open Road." **CHANGES:** Several cuts of interest occurred after 1871. **Lines 27–29** were cut for 1871. "Freedom" was lost when **l. 55** was deleted. The lines joining "committers of crimes" with "committers of . . . virtues" **(ll. 154–55)** were cut. Three lines daringly asserting the body's equal status with the soul **(ll. 186–88)** were cut. The "lover" was deleted from the list of potential confidants in **l. 205** after 1860. —**adhesiveness** (l. 94): see note for Calamus 6 below. **Allons** (l. 117): from the French, "Let us go." **thews** (l. 136): muscles or sinews.

Poem of Procreation

TITLE: This became the fourth *Enfans d'Adam* poem in 1860, then received its final title, "A Woman Waits for Me," in 1867. **CHANGE:** A stanza boasting of engendering "bully breeds of children" and of "Electric growth from the male" **(ll. 12–14)** was cut after 1860.

Clef Poem

TITLE: This poem (*clef* is used in the sense of "clue") became the twelfth in the *Leaves of Grass* cluster of 1860, then the first poem of that cluster in 1867. Its final title, "On the Beach at Night Alone," was conferred in 1871. **CHANGES:** This poem was radically cut. **Lines 4–21** were deleted after 1860; **l. 29** was also cut.

Poem of The Heart of The Son of Manhattan Island

TITLE: This personal credo-poem became the fifteenth of the *Chants Democratic* cluster in 1860 and received its final title, "Excelsior," in 1867. **CHANGE: Lines 6** and **10** were cut after 1871, as was the assertion of heterosexuality in **l. 12.**

Faith Poem

TITLE: This became the seventh poem in the *Leaves of Grass* cluster in 1860; its final title, "Assurances," came in 1867. **CHANGES:** The boldly assertive **ll. 2, 5,** and **8–9** were all deleted after 1860. **Lines 14–15** were cut after 1867.

Poem of Perfect Miracles

TITLE: This poem became the eighth poem in the *Leaves of Grass* cluster in 1860, and took its final title, "Miracles," in 1867. **CHANGES:** The **first three lines** were altered in 1860 and disappeared entirely after 1867. **Lines 18–24** and **31–32** were cut after 1871.

Bunch Poem

TITLE: This poem (whose title comes from its final line) became the fifth *Enfans d'Adam* poem in 1860 and in 1867 received its final title, "Spontaneous Me." **CHANGES:** The original **first line** became these two lines: "Spontaneous me, Nature, / The loving day, the mounting sun, the friend I am happy with . . ." In 1867 the phrase "the mystic amorous night" was added to **l. 31** after the phrase "would master him." To the end of **l. 38** was added, in 1860, the phrase "my Adamic and fresh daughters."

Poem of The Propositions of Nakedness

TITLE: This poem lost its title and became the fifth of the *Chants Democratic and Native American* cluster in 1860; it was "Respondez!" until 1881, when Whitman excluded the poem entirely (several lines were salvaged and slipped into other poems). **CHANGES:** After **l. 1** this parenthesis appeared after 1871: "(The war is completed—the price is paid—the title is settled beyond recall)." In 1860, after **l. 2,** these two boldly assertive lines were added: "Must we still go on with our affections and sneaking? / Let me bring this to a close—I pronounce openly for a new distribution of roles." In the list in **l. 4,** "thieves" and "tyrants" were deleted after 1867. In 1871, these four lines were inserted in parentheses after **l. 13:** "(Stifled, O days! O lands! in every public and private corruption! / Smother'd in thievery, impotence, shamelessness, mountain-high; / Brazen effrontery, scheming, rolling like ocean's waves around and upon you, O my days! my lands! / For not even those thunderstorms, nor fiercest lightnings of the war, have purified the atmosphere)." This rhetoric is very much akin to Whitman's Juvenalian fulmination in prose, *Democratic Vistas,* which also appeared in 1871. **Line 32,** with (like many lines in Whitman) its subtly misogynistic phrasing, was deleted in 1871.

Poem of The Sayers of The Words of The Earth

TITLE: The title became "To the Sayers of Words" in 1860, then "Carol of Words" in 1871, then "A Song of the Rolling Earth" in 1881. **CHANGES:** Instead of **ll. 1–2,** from 1881 the poem began with this single line: "A song of the rolling earth, and of words according . . ." **Lines 18–19** were dropped in 1860, **l. 119** in 1881. The bold ending to **l. 130,** "I announce them and lead them!," was dropped in 1881. **Lines 132–4:** the last three repetitions of "I swear" were deleted in 1881.

sauroid (l. 2): a large prehistoric reptile

Accouche! Accouchez! (l. 31): from the French, "You pregnant one! Be delivered!"

interminable sisters (l. 47): a figurative reference to the stars and planets, with the earth being the "beautiful sister" of l. 50.

cotillions (l. 48): from the French for a lively ballroom dance.

1860 Edition

Proto-Leaf

TITLE: According to Fredson Bowers, Whitman's original ms. title was "Premonition" (see Bowers's lengthy discussion of the poem in his edition of the 1860 manuscripts, pp. li–lxiii, and his full reproduction of the poem's prior versions, pp. 2–56). The poem was significantly revised and received its final title, "Starting from Paumanok," in the 1867 edition. In 1871, it was made the initial poem of *Leaves of Grass* (after several shorter poems in an *Inscriptions* cluster). **CHANGES:** This poem was considerably revised, mainly for 1867, notably in the opening stanza; **ll. 1–2** were deleted and the poem later began

Starting from fish-shape Paumanok where I was born,
Well-begotten, and rais'd by a perfect mother,
After roaming many lands, lover of populous pavements,
Dweller in Mannahatta my city, or on southern savannas . . .

From **l. 13** was removed "my love," from **l. 17** "the Soul." **Lines 44–64** were cut. In **l. 88** "the mistress" was changed to "my mistress." The reference to cursing anti-Unionists, **l. 96,** was deleted. In **l. 140** "Mon cher!" becomes "Dear son." In **l. 141** "Proceed, comrade!" is replaced by "Listen dear son—listen America, daughter or son." **Line 154,** proclaiming "Extasy everywhere touching and thrilling me," was deleted. **Line 160** speaks of "Gods, my unknown lovers" and was deleted after 1871. **Line 248,** declaring Whitman's desire to "unloose" and "toughen" men, was deleted after 1871. **Line 277,** with its "handsome, tall, muscular" populace of "both sexes" in "easy and dignified clothes," was deleted. "O my comrade!" in **l. 283** became "O camerado close!" after 1860. Four highly charged lines expressing a "pensive aching to be together" **(ll. 285–88)** were deleted after 1860.

Paumanok (l. 3): the Algonquian name for Long Island.

Mannahatta (l. 5): the Algonquian name for Manhattan Island, variously translated as "large island" or "island of hills." See Whitman's "Mannahatta" (1888), below, for praise of the "marvellous beauty" of this "choice aboriginal name." Whitman told Traubel, "The Indians use the word to indicate a plot of ground, an island, about which the waters flow—keep up a devil of a swirl, whirl, ebullition—have a hell of a time" (*WWC,* 5:470). Doubtless to please Whitman, the daughter of his favorite brother, Jefferson, was named Manahatta (*sic*), though she was always referred to as Hattie; she died, aged twenty-six, in 1886.

Libertad (l. 39): Spanish for "freedom" or "liberty."

comrades (l. 109): see note to l. 139 below.

Omnes (l. 115): Latin for "everyone."

comrade (l. 139): In 1867, Whitman changed this to the more famous "camerado," a word he much favored and associated with same-sex affection. He could have borrowed the word from the French *camarade* or Spanish *camarada,* though he may also have come upon it in Sir Walter Scott's Waverley novels, which he read with keen pleasure throughout his life.

adhesive (l. 157): see note to l. 16 of Calamus 6 below.

dolce affettuoso (l. 251): a musical interpretative direction from the Italian, "sweetly, with affection"—Whitman, as often, here distancing himself from the Old World.

The *Chants Democratic* Cluster

Chants Democratic 8: This became "Song at Sunset" in 1867 (in an extant ms. Whitman called it "A Sunset Carol") and part of a *Songs of Parting* cluster. **Chants Democratic 10:** It was shortened radically to but seven lines after 1860 (**ll. 4, 6–9, 11** being cut) and became "To a Historian." It finally became the fifth poem in the *Inscriptions* cluster. **Chants Democratic 12:** In 1881, this poem was joined with the twenty-first poem of the *Leaves of Grass* cluster to form "Vocalism." Bowers (pp. 154–58) prints prior ms. versions of both poems. **Chants Democratic 14:** This poem was shortened in 1867 (**ll. 5–11** cut) and became Leaves of Grass 4. Its final title, "Poets to Come," appeared in 1871, and in 1881 it became an *Inscriptions* poem. **Chants Democratic 18:** This became "Me Imperturbe" in 1867 and was moved to the *Inscriptions* cluster in 1881. —**Mannahatta** (l. 7): see note to "Proto-Leaf," line 5, above. **Chants Democratic 19:** This became "I Was Looking a Long While" in 1867. It, too, might have made an apt *Inscriptions* poem, but it eventually became part of *Autumn Rivulets.* **Chants Democratic 20:** Whitman produced his famous new first line for this poem and hence its new title, "I Hear America Singing," for the 1867 edition. It was transferred to *Inscriptions* in 1881.

The *Leaves of Grass* Cluster

Leaves of Grass 1: The poem, probably written in 1859, was published as "Bardic Symbols" in the *Atlantic Monthly* of April 1860. It became "Elemental Drifts" in 1867 and received its final title, "As I Ebb'd with the Ocean of Life," in 1881, when it was moved to the *Sea-Drift* cluster. —**Paumanok** (l. 5): see note to line 3 of "Proto-Leaf." **winrows** (l. 12): variation of *windrows,* rows of sand or debris created by the wind. **Leaves of Grass 13:** After contemplating removal of this poem after 1860, Whitman deleted only **ll. 1–8** for 1867, when the title became "You Felons on Trial in Courts." —**trottoirs** (l. 13) French for "sidewalks." **Leaves of Grass 17:** This poem received its final title, "I Sit and Look Out," in 1871; in 1881 it came to rest in the *By the Roadside* cluster. **Leaves of Grass 21:** see note to Chants Democratic 12, above. **Leaves of Grass 22:** The poem's final title, "What Am I After All," was given in 1871. **Line 2** deleted for 1867. **Leaves of Grass 24:** This poem became "Now Lift Me Close" in 1867; in 1871, "To the Reader at Parting." In 1871, **ll. 1–3** were deleted and replaced by one: "Now, dearest comrade, lift me to your face." Whitman then excluded the poem from all later editions.

Poem of Joys

TITLE: "Poems of Joy" in 1867, reverting to first title in 1871; final title, "A Song of Joys," in 1881. **CHANGES: Lines 7–8** deleted. Two stanzas, **ll. 31–37,** with their reference to the poet being "sick after the friendship" of a "young man" and to a memory of gazing at a lingering, waiting boy, were deleted in 1881 (the line about the boy was singly deleted in 1871). **Line 130,** "O me repellent and ugly," was deleted in 1881. **Lines 145–46,** with several sexual innuendos, were deleted in 1871. The following new ending of 1871 removed emphasis from "an athlete" **(l. 159)** to an inanimate symbol: ". . . To be a sailor of the world bound for all ports, / A ship itself (see indeed these sails I spread to the sun and air), / A swift and swelling ship full of rich words, full of joys."

Fifth Month (l. 51): Quaker style for May.

phrenology (l. 103): see note on Calamus 6 below.

to be the ruler of life, etc. (ll. 127–29): compare this passage from a Whitman ms.:

> Perfect serenity of mind
>
> To take with entire self-possession whatever comes.
> What is this small thing in the great continuous volumes everywhere?
> This is but a temporary portion—not to be dwelt upon—not to distress—
> not to have prominence
>
> Superior nonchalance
> No fumes—no ennui—no complaints or scornful criticisms.
> (*Notes and Fragments,* p. 53)

A Word Out of the Sea

TITLE: First published as "A Child's Reminiscence" in the Christmas-eve issue of the *New York Saturday Press* in 1859. This statement that appeared with it in the issue was probably written by Whitman: "Like the *Leaves of Grass,* the purport of this wild and plaintive song, well-enveloped, and eluding definition, is positive and unquestionable, like the effect of music. The piece will bear reading many times—perhaps, indeed only comes forth, as from recesses, by many repetitions." The final title, "Out of the Cradle Endlessly Rocking," first appeared in 1871. **CHANGES: Line 3,** which refers to womb, breasts, and nipples, was deleted after 1860. The subtitle "Reminiscence" at **l. 24** was also removed. At **l. 148,** "outsetting bard of love" became "outsetting bard" after 1871. "Bird!" of **l. 149** later became "Demon or bird!" **Lines 157–60** were altered to read: "O you singer solitary, singing by yourself, projecting me, / O solitary me," etc. **Lines 169–75** were deleted. Before the **last line,** the following parenthesis was added after 1871: "(Or like some old crone rocking the cradle, swathed in sweet garments, bending aside)."

Ninth Month (l. 4): Quaker style for September.

Paumanok: (l. 24): the Algonquian name for Long Island.

The aria sinking (l. 135): Whitman was deeply influenced by performances of opera, especially Italian opera, and the entire poem can be compared to the recitative-and-aria style of the composers Rossini, Donizetti, Bellini, or Verdi. For more discussion of the influence of opera on Whitman, see Robert Faner's *Walt Whitman and Opera* and the first chapter of the editor's *Walt Whitman: A Gay Life.*

The *Enfans d'Adam* Cluster

ENFANS D'ADAM 1: This poem became "To the Garden, the World" in 1867. **ENFANS D'ADAM 2:** This poem became "From Pent-Up Aching Rivers" in 1867, when a new first line appeared (Whitman thus deleted **l. 10. Lines 15–16** deleted in 1881. **NOTE ON ENFANS D'ADAM 3, 4, AND 5:** These three poems were previously published: see, respectively, "The bodies of men and women engirth me . . ." (1855), "Poem of Procreation" (1856), and "Bunch Poem" (1856). **ENFANS D'ADAM 6:** Whitman added a first line and thus gave it a new title, "One Hour to Madness and Joy," in 1867. The parenthetical statement in **lines 9–10** was deleted in 1867. **ENFANS D'ADAM 7:** In 1867 the title became "We Two, How Long We were Fool'd" and **ll. 1 and 12** were deleted. **ENFANS D'ADAM 8:** This became "Native Moments" in 1867. In 1881 the phrase "I take for my love some prostitute" in **l. 8** was deleted. **ENFANS D'ADAM 9:** This became "Once I Pass'd through a Populous City" in 1867. It was scarcely altered throughout the editions, but it should be noted that its first published form is significantly different from its ms. version, which is reproduced in appendix 2. **Enfans d'Adam 10:** This became "Facing West from California's Shores" in 1867, thanks to a new line at the beginning. Also in 1867, after **l. 6** was added "Long having wander'd since, round the earth having wander'd . . ." **Enfans d'Adam 11:** This poem appeared only in the 1860 edition. **Enfans d'Adam 12, 13, 14, and 15:** All received their final titles in 1867; they were, respectively, "Ages and Ages Returning at Intervals," "O Hymen! O Hymenee!" "I Am He that Aches with Love," and "As Adam Early in the Morning."

The *Calamus* Cluster

Unless otherwise noted, the title given is the final one and first appeared in the fourth edition of 1867. For a discussion of the mss. extant for the *Calamus* poems, see appendix 2.

The botanical name for calamus is *Acorus calamus,* but it is also known as *Calamus aromaticus,* sea-sedge, myrtle-sedge, sweet sedge, and most commonly, sweet flag. It is a perennial herb with long, narrow, sword-shaped leaves; from its three-sided, flowering stem grows a long cylindrical spadix bearing minuscule yellow-green flowerets. The name derives from the Greek *kalamos* = reed. It has long been used as an herbal remedy, notably for stomach ailments, and in perfumery. For a drawing of the plant, see page 311.

Whitman had occasion to explain the title for his sequence to his English editor, W. M. Rossetti: " 'Calamus' is a common word here. It is the very large & aromatic grass, or rush, growing about water-ponds in the valleys—spears about three feet high—often called 'sweet flag'—grows all over the Northern and Middle States. . . . The recherché or ethereal sense of the term, as used in my book, arises probably from the actual Calamus presenting the biggest & hardiest kind of spears of grass—and their fresh, aquatic, pungent bouquet" (*Correspondence,* 1:347).

Whitman neglected to add another potent reason for showing such favor to calamus: its spadix, or inflorescence, emerges from its stalk in a shape highly reminiscent of an erect phallus. The sexual allusiveness of the plant for Whitman is strongly suggested by a manuscript with the following lines he hastily jotted, probably before 1855 (*Notebooks and Unpublished Manuscripts,* 1:94): "Calamus sweet-green bulb and melons with bulbs grateful to the hand / I am a mystic in a trance exaltation / something wild and untamed—half savage / Coarse things / Trickling Sap flows from the end of the manly maple tooth of delight tooth-prong—tine / spend spend / bulbous / Living bulbs, melon polished rinds that smooth to the reached hand . . ."

One day in his last summer, Whitman was taken on an excursion from Camden to nearby Pea Shore on the Delaware River, where he caught sight of a stand of the plant. His enthusiastic reaction momentarily recaptured the mood of the poem sequence he had written more than thirty years before: "Leaves of Grass! The largest leaves of grass known! Calamus! Yes, that is calamus! Profuse, rich, noble—upright, emotional!" (*WWC,* 8:361).

Thoreau referred to the plant as critchicrotches or sweet flag and observed in his journal, "How agreeable and surprising the peculiar fragrance of the sweet flag when it is bruised" (19: 301). Whitman might have been pleased to learn from William Salmon's *Botanologia* (1710) that the spirit derived from calamus makes "a Noble and Generous Cordial, chears the Heart, revives the Spirits, and strengthens Universal Nature." Salmon also recommends it for "the Bitings of Mad Dogs" and says that, as a cataplasm applied "to the Testicles, it wonderfully abates their Swelling" (pp. 360–61). Anne Pratt, in *Flowering Plants of Great Britain* (1876), records a more elevated use for the plant on the floors of the cathedral at Norwich: "When trodden on, its fragrance becomes stronger, and the old cathedral seems filled with incense" (p. 324).

CALAMUS 1: "In Paths Untrodden." In mss. are these lines that Whitman chose not to include in the published version: "And now I care not to walk the earth unless a friend walk by my side, / And now I dare sing no other songs only those of lovers." See appendix 2 for another significant ms. passage. —**comrades** (l. 7): see note for l. 139 of "Proto-Leaf" above. **Ninth Month, in my forty-first year** (l. 15): that is, September 1859. **CALAMUS 2:** "Scented Herbage of My Breast." **Line 8** was deleted in 1881. **CALAMUS 3:** "Whoever You Are Holding Me Now in Hand." "Are you he?" was dropped from **l. 6** in 1867. **CALAMUS 4:** "These I Singing in Spring." **CALAMUS 5:** This poem appeared only in 1860, but Whitman used parts of it in two subsequent poems, "Over the Carnage Rose Prophetic a Voice" and the later *Calamus* poem "For You O Democracy." **CALAMUS 6:** "Not Heaving From My Ribb'd Breast Only." —**O adhesiveness** (l. 16): a term from the pseudoscience of phrenology (reading of character from the shape of the head), with which Whitman was much taken. Adhesiveness indicated a propensity for passionate affection for someone of the same sex; Whitman several times deployed it as code for same-sex passion. On 16 July 1849, he visited the Phrenological Cabinet of Fowler & Wells in lower Manhattan and had his head analyzed. The results were highly favorable, with Whitman scoring the top marks of 6 and 7 in such categories as self-esteem, benevolence, firmness, conscientiousness, cautiousness . . . and adhesiveness. (See Whitman's note on his own phrenological reading at the end of his unsigned review of *Leaves* in the *Brooklyn Daily Times*, included above after the 1855 edition, p. 113.) Fowler & Wells eventually came to act as the distributor of the first edition of *Leaves of Grass* and as the publisher of the second edition. For more on Whitman's use of the term, see Michael Lynch's essay " 'Here is Adhesiveness': From Friendship to Homosexuality," *Victorian Studies* 29 (1985), pp. 67–96. **Calamus 7:** "Of the Terrible Doubt of Appearances" (note change from "question" to "doubt" after 1860). Whitman entertained dropping the long ninth line, but finally left it in. **CALAMUS 8:** Whitman did not allow this poem to be republished, for reasons that are fascinating to speculate about. It is worth noting that in the ms. version of this poem, according to Bowers (p. 80), the lover was originally a man rather than a woman. **CALAMUS 9:** Whitman also suppressed this poem in all succeeding editions. **CALAMUS 10:** "Recorders Ages Hence." In 1867, Whitman replaced the first two lines with the simple, three-word line of the new title. **CALAMUS 11:** "When I Heard at the Close of the Day." **CALAMUS 12:** "Are You the New Person Drawn toward Me?" Later, Whitman ended the poem with the phrase "maya, illusion?" in the ninth line. **CALAMUS 13:** "Roots and Leaves Themselves Alone." **Lines 1–2** and the **last three** were deleted for 1867. The poem's ms. title was "Buds." **CALAMUS 14:** "Not Heat Flames up and Consumes." This was originally the first poem in a ms. sequence of twelve poems that all eventually became constituents of the *Calamus* cluster; ms. titles entertained for it were "Live Oak, with Moss" and "Calamus-Leaves" (see appendix 2). **CALAMUS 15:** "Trickle Drops." The title came from a line added at the beginning of the 1867 version ("Trickle drops! my blue veins leaving!"). **CALAMUS 16:** Whitman suppressed this poem after its one appearance in 1860. **CALAMUS 17:** "Of Him I Love Day and Night." Whitman later moved this poem to the *Whispers of Heavenly Death* cluster. **CALAMUS 18:** "City of Orgies." Compare with "City of Ships" (1865). **CALAMUS 19:** "Behold This Swarthy Face." In 1867 Whitman dropped **ll. 1–2.** **CALAMUS 20:** "I Saw in Louisiana a Live-Oak Growing." **CALAMUS 21:** "That Music Always Round Me." Later moved to *Whispers of Heavenly Death.* **CALAMUS 22:** "To a Stranger." **CALAMUS 23:** "This Moment Yearning and Thoughtful." In 1867, **l. 4** was deleted. **CALAMUS 24:** "I Hear It Was Charged against Me." **CALAMUS 25:** "The Prairie-Grass Dividing." The phrase "choice and chary of its love-power" in **l. 7** was deleted in 1867. **CALAMUS 26:** "We Two Boys Together Clinging." The **eighth line** was deleted in 1867. **CALAMUS 27:** "O Living Always, Always Dying." **Line 1** was deleted after 1860. Later moved to *Whispers of Heavenly Death.* **CALAMUS 28:** "When I Peruse the Conquer'd Fame." **CALAMUS 29:** "A Glimpse." **CALAMUS 30:** "A

Promise to California." **CALAMUS 31:** In 1867, the two stanzas were separated and became two poems, "What Ship Puzzled at Sea" (*Whispers*) and "What Place is Besieged?" (*Inscriptions*). **CALAMUS 32:** "What Think You I Take My Pen in Hand?" **CALAMUS 33:** "No Labor-Saving Machine." **CALAMUS 34:** "I Dream'd in a Dream." See appendix 2 for a prior manuscript version of part of this poem. **CALAMUS 35:** "To the East and to the West." **CALAMUS 36:** "Earth, My Likeness." **CALAMUS 37:** "A Leaf for Hand in Hand." **CALAMUS 38:** "Fast Anchor'd Eternal O Love!" In 1867 Whitman replaced the first line with "Fast-anchor'd eternal O love! O woman I love!" **CALAMUS 39:** "Sometimes with One I Love." **CALAMUS 40:** "That Shadow My Likeness." **CALAMUS 41:** "Among the Multitude." The phrase "faint indirections" is later echoed in the phrase "faint clues and indirections" in the final version of "When I Read the Book" (1867); see note for that poem. **CALAMUS 42:** "To a Western Boy." **CALAMUS 43:** "O You Whom I Often and Silently Come." **CALAMUS 44:** "Here the Frailest Leaves of Me." In 1867 the poem's **first line** was deleted. **CALAMUS 45:** "Full of Life Now." A ms. has this opening line, which Whitman did not use: "Throwing far, throwing over the head of death, I, full of affection . . ." (Bowers, p. 122). A former second line, which is the first two lines of the poem as printed here, read "thirty-eight years old the eighty-first year of The States," which would suggest Whitman commenced on this poem in 1857.

The *Messenger Leaves* Cluster

TO HIM THAT WAS CRUCIFIED: The parenthetical phrase in **l. 3** was deleted in 1881. **TO ONE SHORTLY TO DIE:** This poem moved into the *Whispers of Heavenly Death* cluster in 1881. **TO A COMMON PROSTITUTE:** In a ms. for this poem at the Huntington Library, Whitman wrote "My love" instead of "My girl" in the fourth line and "kiss on your lips" instead of "significant look" in the sixth line. **TO A PUPIL:** This remained the poem's title through all editions. **TO THE STATES:** This poem was almost unchanged in all editions. **TO A CANTATRICE:** The final title, "To a Certain Cantatrice," appeared in 1867. *Cantatrice* is Italian for "female singer"; Whitman may have encountered the word in one of his most beloved novels, George Sand's *Consuelo,* which has an opera-singer heroine and which appeared in an English translation in 1846. This poem was moved to *Songs of Insurrection* for 1871, then to *Inscriptions* in 1881. It was most likely addressed to the great Italian contralto Marietta Alboni (1823–94), who is also memorialized in "Proud Music of the Storm" (l. 94). She visited New York for a year in 1852–53, performing in several recitals and about a dozen fully staged operas, and Whitman proudly said many years later that he had attended every one of her performances. For more on the influence of Alboni and opera on the poet's verse, see the first chapter of the editor's *Walt Whitman: A Gay Life.* **WALT WHITMAN'S CAUTION:** This poem later became "To The States" and was eventually moved to the *Inscriptions* cluster. **TO YOU** ("Let us twain . . ."): In 1872 Whitman added this line after the third line: "Let us talk of death—unbosom all freely." Whitman banished the poem after 1876. **TO YOU** ("Stranger! . . ."): This poem became the last *Inscriptions* poem in 1881.

Mannahatta

Lines 17–23 were cut in 1881 and replaced by these three lines: "A million people—manners free and superb—open voices—hospitality—the most courageous and friendly young men, / City of hurried and sparkling waters! city of spires and masts! / City nested in bays! my city!" —**trottoirs** (l. 16): French for "sidewalks."

"Of persons arrived at high positions . . ."

Became "Thought" in 1871. Whitman later enclosed all but the first line in a parenthesis. —**sonnambules:** (l. 8) French for "sleepwalkers."

A Hand-Mirror

A ms. version of the poem was titled "Looking-Glass"; it was eventually moved to the *By the Roadside* cluster.

Beginners

This poem remained virtually untouched in all later editions; it became an obvious candidate for the *Inscriptions* cluster in 1881.

Tests

Also nearly untouched in all later editions, this poem became a part of the *Autumn Rivulets* cluster.

The *Debris* Cluster

"HAVE YOU LEARNED . . .": This poem vanished from 1871 to 1888. The first two lines became part of *Sands at Seventy* in 1888 under the title "Stronger Lessons." **"DESPAIRING CRIES . . ."** and **"I UNDERSTAND YOUR ANGUISH . . .":** These two poems became part of the same poem, "Despairing Cries," in 1867; in 1871 a new first stanza was added, giving the poem its final title, "Yet, Yet, Ye Downcast Hours." It was placed in the *Whispers of Heavenly Death* section. **"THREE OLD MEN . . .":** These lines appeared only in 1860. **"WOMEN SIT . . .":** This became "Picture" in 1867, then "Beautiful Women" in 1871; it was placed in the *By the Roadside* cluster in 1881. **"I THOUGHT I WAS NOT ALONE . . .":** This poem received a new first line and title, "As if a Phantom Caress'd Me," in 1867; the phrase "the one I loved that caress'd me" was added to the second line of the 1860 version.

To My Soul

TITLE: Heavily cut, this poem became "As Nearing Departure" in 1867. In 1871 it became "As the Time Draws Nigh" and was moved to the *Songs of Parting* cluster. The poem was radically cut down, finally, to eight lines (kept, slightly altered, were **ll. 2–5** and **18–19**).

So Long!

TITLE: This poem kept its title throughout and ended every edition from 1860. It lost nearly two dozen lines in 1867 (notably **ll. 2–3, 7–8, 14–20, 25–33**); after **line 86,** Whitman added this line: "I receive now again of my many translations, from my avataras ascending, while others doubtless await me" (*avataras:* the Sanskrit word for incarnation, associated with appearances of the deity). —**adhesiveness** (l. 42): on this term from phrenology, see note to Calamus 6, above.

Drum-Taps (1865)

Beginning My Studies

Transferred to the *Inscriptions* cluster in 1871.

The Dresser

TITLE: The poem had its original title until 1876, when it became "The Wound-Dresser." After **line 3**, Whitman, in 1881, inserted a three-line parenthetical passage that had, in 1871 and 1876, been an epigraph for the entire *Drum-Taps* poems: "(Arous'd and angry, I'd thought to beat the alarum, and urge relentless war, / But soon my fingers fail'd me, my face droop'd and I resign'd myself, / To sit by the wounded and soothe them, or silently watch the dead) . . ." Richard Maurice Bucke used the poem's final title as the title for a 1898 edition of Whitman's correspondence with soldiers during the Civil War.

Come Up from the Fields Father

This poem always remained, unchanged, in the *Drum-Taps* cluster.

City of Ships

This poem remained virtually unrevised and in *Drum-Taps* for all editions.

Mother and Babe

The poem was in no group until 1881, when it became part of *By the Roadside.*

Vigil Strange I Kept on the Field One Night

This important *Drum-Taps* poem sustained only minor revision. It should be noted that many young boys were in the ranks. Official roles alone listed 127 thirteen-year-olds, 330 fourteen-year-olds, 773 fifteen-year-olds, 2,758 sixteen-year-olds, and 6,425 seventeen-year-olds (see Shively, *Drum-Beats,* pp. 41–48, and Bell Wiley, *The Life of Billy Yank* [1978], p. 299). Whitman recorded on 21 January 1863 in Washington, "I am more and more surprised at the very great proportion of youngsters from fifteen to twenty-one in the army. I afterwards found a still greater proportion among the southerners" (*Specimen Days,* p. 714 in Library of America). **NOTE:** A prior ms. version of this poem, from a Civil War notebook, is reproduced in appendix 2.

A March in the Ranks Hard-Prest, and the Road Unknown

Another poem almost unchanged from its original version. Whitman's hospital notebooks from 1862–63 make it clear that a poem like this derived from jottings he made on the spot.

A Farm Picture

This poem was ungrouped until 1881, when it arrived in *By the Roadside.* For 1871, Whitman added a third line at the end: "And haze and vista, and the far horizon fading away."

Give Me the Splendid Silent Sun

This poem went virtually unchanged through all editions, except for the deletion of the phrase after the dash in the next-to-last line in 1881. A ms. fragment at Duke University has this passage, which Whitman was reluctant to include: "Give me something savage and luxuriant . . . Give me large, full-voiced men."—**trottoirs** (l. 24): French for "sidewalks."

Did You Ask Dulcet Rhymes from Me?

TITLE: In 1871 and 1876 this poem was included, under its new title, "To a Certain Civilian," in the *Ashes of Soldiers* group; it was returned to *Drum-Taps* in 1881. **CHANGES:** The 1871 version contained four new lines; this line followed the second line: "Did you seek the civilian's peaceful and languishing rhymes?" Following the third line was added this three-line parenthetical assertion: "(I have been born of the same as the war was born, / The drum-corps' rattle is ever to me sweet music, I love well the martial dirge, / With slow wail and convulsive throb leading the officer's funeral)." Whitman also added "and with piano tunes" to the end of the next-to-last line.

Year that Trembled and Reel'd Beneath Me

This poem may refer to 1863–1864, when the outcome of the Civil War lay in doubt.

The Veteran's Vision

TITLE: This became "The Artilleryman's Vision" in 1871. The poem is based upon ms. lines jotted down in a notebook by Whitman in 1862–63 while in Washington; the passage is transcribed in Charles Glicksberg, *Walt Whitman and the Civil War* (1933), pp. 121–23.

O Tan-Faced Prairie-Boy

This poem remained unchanged through all editions (though Whitman did remove the opening exclamation point).

Look Down Fair Moon

Unchanged later, except that Whitman removed the second "their" from l. 3.

Hush'd Be the Camps To-day

In 1871 the title note was changed to "May 4, 1865" and some details of the interment altered (Whitman had assumed Lincoln's burial would occur quickly and in Washington).

Not Youth Pertains to Me

In 1871 the poem appeared with these lines instead of the last two: "And at intervals waiting or in the midst of camp, / Composed these songs."

Sequel to *Drum-Taps* (1865-66)

When Lilacs Last in the Door-Yard Bloom'd

This elegy or, to use the Greek term, threnody was written shortly after the assassination of President Lincoln on 14 April 1865. In *Specimen Days* a paragraph is devoted to the "Death of President Lincoln." It is dated 16 April 1865 and reads, in part: "He leaves for America's history and biography, so far, not only its most dramatic reminiscence—he leaves, in my opinion, the greatest, best, most characteristic, artistic, moral personality. Not but that he had faults, and show'd them in the Presidency; but honesty, goodness, shrewdness, conscience, and (a new virtue, unknown to other lands, and hardly yet really known here, but the foundation and tie of all, as the future will grandly develop), UNIONISM, in its truest and amplest sense, form'd the hard-pan of his character. These he seal'd with his life. The tragic splendor of his death, purging, illuminating all, throws round his form, his head, an aureole that will remain and will grow brighter through time, while history lives, and love of country lasts" (Library of America, pp. 763–64). The three central symbols deployed in the poem are the lilacs (figuring the poet's love for his president), the fallen western star (Lincoln), and the hermit thrush (chanter of death).

TITLE: In 1871 and 1876 the poem began a grouping under the title "President Lincoln's Burial Hymn." Whitman called the cluster *Memories of President Lincoln* in 1881. **CHANGES:** Whitman in 1871 italicized the thrush's song (section 16) and gave the song its own title, "Death Carol" (this was deleted in 1881). He also deleted **l. 57**.

lilacs (l. 1): The heart-shaped leaves of the lilac cause one to consider it in the context of Whitman's uses of other plants (sweet flag or calamus and bearded moss) to express affection, love, or admiration for masculine ideals. In one of his many annual Lincoln lectures given late in life, Whitman also recalled of the day of the assassination: "I remember where I was stopping at the time, the season being advanced, there were many lilacs in full bloom. By one of those caprices that enter and give tinge to events without being at all a part of them, I find myself always reminded of the great tragedy of that day by the sight and odor of these blossoms" (*Complete Works,* 5:246).

great star (l. 2): Venus

O Captain! My Captain!

This was easily the best loved of all Whitman's short poems during his lifetime. Because its form was highly uncharacteristic (regular, neatly rhymed stanzas), its popularity came to aggravate the poet. In 1888, when an early draft of the poem emerged amid the clutter in his Mickle Street house, Whitman waxed a little wroth: "I'm honest when I say, damn 'My Captain' and all the 'My Captains' in my book! This is not the first time I have been irritated into saying I'm almost sorry I ever wrote the poem" (*WWC,* 2:304). A few days later Whitman observed to Traubel, "You don't like the poem anyway," and Traubel had to agree, saying, "I think it clumsy: you tried too hard to make it what you shouldn't have tried to make it at all—and what you didn't succeed in making it in the end." Whitman laughed and responded, "You're more than half right. . . . The thing that tantalizes me most is not its rhythmic imperfection or its imperfection as a ballad or rhymed poem (it is damned bad in all that, I do believe) but the fact that my enemies and some of my friends who half doubt me, look upon it as a concession made to the philistines—that makes me mad" (*WWC,* 2:333). In any event, he made only minor changes in the poem for later editions.

Chanting the Square Deific

The poem was moved in 1871 to *Whispers of Heavenly Death.* The parenthetical in **l. 22** was deleted after 1871. Whitman's mss. show that he contemplated this poem even before the 1855 edition appeared. In 1888 he made a not entirely successful attempt to explain the poem: "It would be hard to give the idea mathematical expression: the idea of spiritual equity—of spiritual substance: the four-square entity—the north, south, east, west of the constituted universe (even the soul universe)—the four sides as sustaining the universe (the supernatural something): this is not the poem but the idea back of the poem or below the poem. I am lame enough trying to explain it in other words—the idea seems to fit its own words better than mine. You see, at the time the poem wrote itself: now I am trying to write it" (*WWC,* 1:156).

Brahm (l. 4): Brahma, the supreme spirit of the Hindu universe.

Saturnius (l. 4): in Roman mythology the Titan who preceded Jupiter as supreme on Olympus; son of Uranus. As the first god to care for humanity, he came to be associated with sowing and harvesting.

Kronus (l. 7): most ancient of Greek deities, born of Uranus, whom he succeeded by force (specifically, castration); associated with the ancient discovery of time.

sudra (l. 30): the lowest Hindu caste.

Santa Spirita (l. 37): that is, "The Holy Spirit" (Latin, *Spiritus Sanctus*). Whitman makes its gender feminine.

Not My Enemies Ever Invade Me

Whitman suppressed this seemingly very personal ebullition after 1867.

Ah Poverties, Wincings, and Sulky Retreats

The only Whitman poem that begins with the exclamatory "Ah" so favored by Shakespeare (who was occasionally maligned by Whitman over the years), it was virtually unrevised in later editions, except that "unquestion'd" in the last line was replaced by "ultimate," and an exclamation point was added within the parenthesis of **l. 5.**

As I Lay with My Head in Your Lap, Camerado

This poem became part of a *Leaves of Grass* cluster in 1871 and was moved to *Drum-Taps* in 1881, when the parenthetical **ll. 5–6** were deleted.

Dirge for Two Veterans

Just a few minor changes were made in later editions. It is—notably along with "O Captain! My Captain!"—one of Whitman's few post-1855 poems in regular stanzas. Whitman deleted the stanza numbers after 1871.

Reconciliation

The only substantial change was the deletion, in 1881, of the opening "I" in the last line.

1867 Edition

Inscription and *One's-Self I Sing*

The first poem appeared in this form on the frontispiece of the 1867 edition, then in 1888 in the *Sands at Seventy* group as "Small the Theme of My Chant." The second poem first appeared in 1871 and remained thereafter the lead poem in *Leaves.*

The Runner

This poem was not in a group until placed in *By the Roadside* in 1881.

Leaves of Grass 2

This poem became "Tears" in 1871, when it was transferred to a *Sea-Shore Memories* group, finally becoming part of *Sea-Drift* in 1881.

When I Read the Book

Whitman moved this poem in 1871 to a new nine-poem group called *Inscriptions,* where it remained thereafter. He also finally changed the concluding parenthesis to the following assertion: ". . . of my life, / Why even I myself, I often think know little or nothing of my real life, / Only a few hints, a few diffused faint clews and indirections / I seek for my own use to trace out here.)"

1871–72 Edition (*Passage to India*)

Passage to India

This was the title poem of a 120-page pamphlet of seventy-five poems (twenty-three being new) that appeared in 1871, and which soon became a supplement to the 1871–72 edition. See Whitman's discussion of it in the preface to the 1876 edition. Many extant mss. show that this poem had a long gestation (see *Comprehensive Reader's Edition,* p. 410). The second part of section 2, for example, the poet had originally intended as a separate poem, to be titled "Fables." The long passage in section 11 beginning "With laugh, and many a kiss" (ll. 183–224) also appears to have originated as a separate poem, titled "O Soul, Thou Pleaseth Me." As to the poem's meaning, the poet commented to Traubel in 1888, "There's more of me, the essential ultimate me, in that than in any of the poems. There is no philosophy, consistent or inconsistent, in that poem . . . but the burden of it is evolution—the one thing escaping the other—the unfolding of cosmic purposes" (*WWC,* 1:156–57). Virtually all of the changes made for later editions were minor.

Seven (l. 4): that is, the so-called Seven Wonders of the ancient world: the pyramids, the mausoleum at Halicarnassus, the temple of Artemis at Ephesus, the hanging gardens of Babylon, the colossus of Rhodes, the statue of Zeus at Olympia, and the lighthouse at Alexandria.

Suez canal (l. 5): Work on the canal commenced in 1859, and it was opened on 17 November 1869.

mighty railroad spann'd (l. 6): The Union Pacific and Central Pacific railroads were joined at Promontory, Utah, on 10 May 1869.

Eclaircise (l. 17): from the French for "to clarify."

Eugenie (l. 45): The Empress Eugénie, the wife of Napoleon III, helped to celebrate the opening of the canal.

Genoese (l. 66): Christopher Columbus.

Vasco de Gama (l. 77): the Portuguese explorer, properly da Gama; the first to circumnavigate Africa bound for India, in 1497–98.

Doge . . . wedding the Adriatic (l. 120): Venetian doges for centuries performed the ritual of marrying Venice with the Adriatic Sea by tossing a ring into the waters.

Alexander . . . suddenly dying (l. 132): He died at Babylon, aged thirty-two, in 323 B.C. after his return from an invasion of India.

Tamerlane . . . Aurungzebe (l. 138): Tamerlane (1335?–1405), popularized in England by the two *Tamburlane* plays of Christopher Marlowe, led numerous devastating invasions of conquest in Turkey, Persia, and India; Aurungzebe (1618–1707) was emperor of Hindustan and also an eager world-conqueror (and the subject of a play by John Dryden).

Marco Polo . . . Batouta the Moor (l. 140): Polo (1254–1324) traveled famously from Venice to China, Batouta (1303–77) to Africa and Asia.

the Admiral himself (l. 155): Columbus. Palos, mentioned in l. 157, was the port from which he sailed on 3 August 1492. This passage should be compared with Whitman's "Prayer of Columbus," new in the 1876 edition, and his apparently final published poem, "A Thought of Columbus," which can be found in appendix 1.

the Sanscrit and the Vedas (l. 229): Vedas, Hindu holy texts, were written in Sanskrit.

Proud Music of the Storm

The poem was first published separately as "Proud Music of the Sea-Storm" in the *Atlantic Monthly* of February 1869; it was submitted to the editor by Emerson (at Whitman's request), and Whitman received $100 for it.

cantabile (l. 22): Italian noun for a "songlike" musical passage or piece.

Victoria (l. 24): Queen Victoria, in allusion to some unspecified British military defeat.

Tutti (l. 52): Italian for "all," a musical reference to the simultaneous playing of all musicians.

Italia's peerless compositions (l. 75): The following verse paragraphs make it clear that these compositions are operas.

Stalks Norma (l. 77): reference to Vincenzo Bellini's bel canto masterpiece *Norma* (1831), an extremely popular opera in America in Whitman's day. He was particularly transfixed by the performance of Marietta Alboni in the title role (she is singled out in l. 94 below). In *Specimen Days,* Whitman recalled some of "my life's rare and blessed bits of hours," and among these he counted a huge winter storm off Fire Island, seeing the elder Booth in *Richard III,* and seeing "Alboni in the children's scene in *Norma*" (Library of America, p. 877).

crazed Lucia's eyes' unnatural gleam (l. 78): Gaetano Donizetti's opera *Lucia di Lammermoor* (1835), based on Whitman's beloved Sir Walter Scott, tells of a heroine who, seemingly betrayed by her lover and forced to marry another, murders her husband on the wedding night, then displays her vocal virtuosity in a famous "mad" scene.

Ernani, walking (l. 80): reference to *Ernani,* one of Giuseppe Verdi's first great operatic successes (1844), based on the epoch-opening romantic play *Hernani* by Victor Hugo. Early in his journalistic career, Whitman decided to introduce his readers to opera and chose for the occasion the "noble opera" *Ernani* as performed at the Academy of Music on Fourteenth Street. Whitman had especially dear memories of hearing the tenor Geremia Bettini singing the title role. "The young and manly Ernani used to be well played by Bettini, now at the Grand Opera in Paris. Bettini was a beautiful, large, robust, friendly, young man—a fine tenor" (*Life Illustrated,* 10 November 1855, collected in *New York Dissected* [1936], p. 18).

The trombone duo (l. 85): This refers to the rousing Trumpet (or Liberty) Duet, "Suoni la tromba," sung by the principal baritone and bass in Bellini's opera *I Puritani* (1835). Whitman got his instrument wrong (*tromba* is the Italian for "trumpet").

Fernando's heart is breaking (l. 89): allusion to another opera that deeply moved Whitman in his opera-going days, Donizetti's *La Favorita* (1840). In one of his journalistic "Letters from Paumanok," in 1851, Whitman took readers to another performance, this time with Bettini as the tenor hero Fernando in *La Favorita:* his "clear, firm, wonderfully exalting notes, filling and expanding away, dwelling like a poised lark up in heaven, have made my very soul tremble." Whitman continues, "Never before did I realize what an indescribable volume of delight the recesses of the human soul can bear from the sound of the honied perfection of the human voice," and then he ends with this remarkable epiphany experienced in Bettini's presence: "Pure and vast, that voice now rises, as on clouds, to the heaven where it claims audience. Now, firm and unbroken, it spreads like an ocean around us. . . . Thanks, limner of the spirit of life, and hope and peace; of the red fire of passion, the cavernous vacancy of despair, and the black pall of the grave" (*Uncollected Poetry and Prose,* 1:257).

retriev'd Amina sings (l. 90): reference to the sleepwalking heroine of Bellini's opera *La Sonnambula* (1831), a favorite vehicle for coloratura singers of the day.

Alboni's self I hear (l. 94): the contralto Marietta Alboni; see note above for "To a Cantatrice," from the *Messenger Leaves* cluster of 1860.

William Tell . . . Don Juan (ll. 96–98): references to several more operas popular in Whitman's day, which was something of a golden age for opera in New York City: Giaochino Rossini's *Guillaume Tell* (1829); Giacomo Meyerbeer's *Les Huguenots* (1836), *Le Prophète* (1849), and *Robert le Diable* (1831); Charles Gounod's *Faust* (1859); and Wolfgang Amadeus Mozart's *Don Giovanni* (1787).

Corybantian dance (l. 110): Corybantes were companions to the goddess Cybele and followed her with wild music and dancing.

king (l. 119): ancient Chinese instrument with hanging stones struck by hammers.

vina (l. 120): a zitherlike Hindu instrument.

bayaderes (l. 121): Indian dancing girls.

Eine feste Burg . . . (l. 124): Luther's hymn "A Mighty Fortress Is Our God."

Stabat Mater dolorosa (l. 125): an oratorio, whose definitive version premiered to spectacular acclaim in Paris in 1842 (Latin for "the sorrowing mother stood").

The *Creation* (l. 137): Franz Joseph Haydn's oratorio (1799).

Whispers of Heavenly Death

This was the first of five poems published together in the London *Broadway Magazine* of October 1868. It was virtually unchanged in all later editions.

A Noiseless, Patient Spider

Another poem that appeared in the London *Broadway Magazine* in 1868; later included in the new *Whispers of Heavenly Death* group of 1871. This significantly different ms. version is extant in a Whitman notebook (*Uncollected Poetry and Prose,* 2:93):

> The Soul, reaching, throwing out for love,
> As the spider, from some little promontory, throwing out filament after filament,
> tirelessly out of itself, that one at least may catch and form a link, a bridge,
> a connection
> O I saw one passing alone, saying hardly a word—yet full of love I detected him
> by certain signs
> O eyes wishfully turning! O silent eyes! . . .

Sparkles from the Wheel

First appeared in the *Leaves of Grass* group; Bowers (pp. 254–56) prints prior ms. versions.

Gods

Whitman later deleted the stanza numbers, and in the 1881 edition he deleted **ll. 1–2** and the reference to "thee, Old Cause" in the sixth stanza.

For Him I Sing

The poem always remained in the *Inscriptions* group, which first appeared in this edition.

To Thee, Old Cause!

In 1881, Whitman added as a separate section between the original two the following two-line parenthesis: "(A war O soldiers not for itself alone, / Far, far more stood silently waiting behind, now to advance in this book.)"

The Base of all Metaphysics

This was the only poem Whitman ever imported subsequently into the *Calamus* sequence, which he did in 1871. The editors of the *Comprehensive Reader's Edition* observe that this poem "sublimates the sentiment of 'adhesiveness' to lofty universal principle" (p. 120). A Whitman ms. gave the poem the title "The Professor's Answer."

As a Strong Bird on Pinions Free (1872)

One Song, America, Before I Go

This was the first of two prefatory poems for this small volume; in 1881 its **first line** was deleted and **ll. 2–12** were incorporated as the opening stanza of the 1881 version of "As a Strong Bird on Pinions Free."

Souvenirs of Democracy

This was the second of the two prefatory poems and became, considerably revised, "My Legacy" in 1881.

As a Strong Bird on Pinions Free

This poem, which became "Thou Mother with Thy Equal Brood" in 1881, was composed in response to an invitation from Dartmouth University to read a commencement poem there on 26 June 1872, which Whitman did. The invitation, unsurprisingly, had not come from the Dartmouth faculty but from the students, who appear to have desired to annoy the professorate. It must have, for a continuing theme of Whitman's correspondence and conversations was a lifelong detestation for college professors, who (as he said of those at Georgetown University) "esteem themselves great punkins." The "excessive caution of the university man" (*WWC,* 1: 286) disgusted Whitman, and he also ridiculed "the cult-worship, the college-chair worship" of Shakespeare on college campuses (*WWC,* 1:135). Perhaps the poet's most penetrating remark on his relationship with literary professionals of his day was this, in 1888, to Traubel: "I do not value literature as a profession. I feel about literature what [General Ulysses S.] Grant did about war. He hated war. I hate literature. I am not a literary West Pointer" (*WWC,* 1:58). As to "formal-cut men in literature" comprehending *Leaves of Grass,* Whitman assumed the derisive tone of his withering "Did You Ask Dulcet Rhymes from Me?": "They like portions, beauties, what they would call 'gems'—do not see more. But it took more than that to compass *Leaves of Grass.* The thread connecting all was never penetrated by such men" (*WWC,* 7:391). Whitman's sentiments were returned: to his dying day *Leaves of Grass* was banned from the library of Harvard University.

Later revisions of the poem were almost entirely punctuational ("O Union!" in **l. 13** became "dread Mother"—her "Equal Brood" being of course the states). Section 3 was published separately in the *New York Tribune* on 19 February 1876 as "Ship of Democracy."

The Mystic Trumpeter

This stentorian paean to music—vaguely reminiscent of John Dryden's stately odes to music, "A Song for St. Cecilia's Day" and "Alexander's Feast"—first appeared individually in the

Kansas Magazine of February 1872. It became part of the *From Noon to Starry Night* group in 1881. In keeping with the generally minor nature of Whitman's revisions over his last three decades, the sole change in this poem was to remove "wild" from **l. 43.**

By Broad Potomac's Shore

The last poem in the *As a Strong Bird* pamphlet, it was moved to *From Noon to Starry Night* in 1881. The stanza numbers disappeared, and the **penultimate** line was deleted.

Two Rivulets (1876)

Eidólons

First published in the *New York Tribune* on 19 February 1876, this poem became, in 1881, one of the *Inscriptions* poems. There is a Whitman ms., "Notebook on Words," with this entry: "Ei-do-lon (Gr) phantom—the *image* of a Helen at Troy instead of real flesh and blood woman." Much later, Whitman explained to Traubel, "It is the custom everywhere to pronounce the word *ei*dolon: I always make it ei*do*lons: this is right, too. I make considerable use of the word" (*Comprehensive Reader's Edition,* p. 5). *Eidólon* can also be translated from the Greek as "ideal" or "concept." Later revisions of the poem were entirely in punctuation.

Prayer of Columbus

First published separately in *Harper's Magazine* of March 1874. Stating the very obvious, Whitman wrote to Ellen O'Connor, wife of his greatly admired friend William O'Connor, "as I see it now I shouldn't wonder if I have unconsciously put a sort of autobiographical dash in it" (*Correspondence*, 2:272). In January of 1873, Whitman had suffered a semiparalyzing stroke, and a few months later his beloved mother died. Whitman often remarked on this period being the darkest of his life, and the poem's mood clearly fits. The "Prayer" is linked in many respects with "Passage to India." After 1876, the long **prose introduction** was deleted. (Columbus in fact died in his mid-fifties, about Whitman's age when this poem was composed.) Also deleted was the parenthesis in **l. 31** and the separate stanza of **ll. 51–52.**

To a Locomotive in Winter

This poem first appeared, along with other poems, as a tantalizer for the publication of *Two Rivulets,* in the *New York Tribune* of 19 February 1876. It became a poem in the *From Noon to Starry Night* group in 1881 with no substantial revision. Among extensive mss. Whitman produced in writing the poem is this jotting about his intention: "The two ideas of Power & Motion (twins, dear to the modern) / Address the locomotive as personally inviting it / Ring the bell all through & blow the whistle."

Wandering at Morn

First published in the *New York Daily Graphic* of 15 March 1873 as "The Singing Thrush" (two prior ms. titles were entertained, "The Future Song" and "The Singing Bird"). It was moved to the *Autumn Rivulets* group in 1881.

With All Thy Gifts

First published in the *New York Daily Graphic* of 6 March 1873, this poem was moved, without the words capitalized in the last three lines, to *Autumn Rivulets* in 1881.

1881 Edition

The Dalliance of the Eagles

This poem appeared first in *Cope's Tobacco Plant,* November 1880. Mss. show Whitman worked strenuously on this poem, which was placed in the new, miscellaneous *By the Roadside* group.

Italian Music in Dakota

This poem was generated by Whitman's first trip to the West in 1879. He got as far as Colorado, but never set foot in the Dakotas. As elsewhere, he was not prevented from poetizing about a place he had never been. On the mention of the operas *Norma* and *La Sonnambula,* see the notes for **ll. 90 and 77** in "Proud Music of the Storm," above. *Poliuto* (1848) is an opera by Donizetti. When Whitman accompanied his young friend Peter Doyle from Washington on a trip to see the sights of New York many years before, they attended a performance of this opera, which Doyle recalled as *"Polyato."*

The Prairie States

The ms. of this poem, which Whitman dated 15 March 1880, was published in facsimile in *The Art Autograph* of May 1880. It became the last *Autumn Rivulets* poem.

A Riddle Song

First published in the Philadelphia *Forney's Progress* of 17 April 1880. What are the "two words" (ll. 21–22) of the riddle's answer? Whitman's close friend Richard Maurice Bucke wrote to suggest either "good cause" or "old cause." Traubel recorded the poet's unwillingness to offer an answer: "Horace, I made the puzzle: it's not my business to solve it" (*WWC,* 2:228). The poem was placed in the *From Noon to Starry Night* group in 1881.

Spirit That Form'd This Scene

The poem appeared in the *Critic* of 10 September 1881. It is another memorial of the 1879 trip to the West. In "An Egotistical Find" from *Specimen Days* (1882) is an eloquent prose complement to this poem: " 'I have found the law of my own poems,' was the unspoken but more-and-more decided feeling that came to me as I pass'd, hour after hour, amid all this grim yet joyous elemental abandon—this plenitude of material, entire absence of art, untrammel'd play of primitive Nature—the chasm, the gorge, the crystal mountain stream, repeated scores, hundreds of miles—the broad handling and absolute uncrampedness—the fantastic forms, bathed in transparent browns, faint reds and grays, towering sometimes a thousand, sometimes two or three thousand feet high—at their tops now and then huge masses pois'd, and mixing with the clouds, with only their outlines, hazed in misty lilac, visible" (Library of America, pp. 855–56).

A Clear Midnight

A ms. version of this poem says it was "for end of poems" (*Notes and Fragments,* p. 175). The apparently final ms. version (Library of Congress) is on the back of a letter dated 2 December 1880.

November Boughs (1888)

Mannahatta

First published in the *New York Herald* of 27 February 1888, without the italics. See note for l. 5 of "Proto-Leaf," above, for Whitman's 1889 comment on the Algonquian name for the island.

A Carol Closing Sixty-Nine

First published in the *New York Herald* of 21 May 1888 (Whitman discarded two prior ms. titles, "Carols at nearing Seventy" and "A Carol-Cluster at 69").

A Font of Type

non pareil . . . long primer (l. 3): Whitman lists four font sizes from six to ten points.

As I Sit Writing Here

First published in the *New York Herald* of 14 May 1888.

Queries to My Seventieth Year

First published in the *New York Herald* of 2 May 1888. One ms. contains these lines that Whitman chose not to publish: "Steep me in immobility / As we grow old we narrow on ourselves concentrating / Something to us unspeakably pensive in our own age—our sorrows—"

America

First published in the *New York Herald* of 11 February 1888.

After the Dazzle of Day

First published in the *New York Herald* of 3 February 1888.

Halcyon Days

First published in the *New York Herald* of 29 January 1888. Six months later, in private, Whitman gave the twenty-nine-year-old Traubel, who told Whitman he was feeling "well," a quite different definition of "halcyon" days: "It is so great—so superb—to be always well. However, these are your years to expect it—from eighteen to forty-five—halcyon days, sure enough" (*WWC,* 2:30).

Of That Blithe Throat of Thine

First published in *Harper's Monthly* of January 1885; Whitman received $30 for it.

Broadway

First published in the *New York Herald* of 10 April 1888. Whitman's beloved thoroughfare figures also in his orotund poem "A Broadway Pageant" (1860), written on the occasion of a parade down Broadway in honor of a visiting Japanese embassy. There is also an extant ms. poem of seven lines titled "Broadway, 1861" describing the city amid preparations for the Secession War (see *Comprehensive Reader's Edition,* p. 678). Also pertinent are Whitman's glowing prose reminiscences in *Specimen Days,* "Broadway Sights" and "Omnibus Jaunts and Drivers."

To Get the Final Lilt of Songs

First published in the *New York Herald* of 16 April 1888 as "The Final Lilt of Songs."

The Dead Tenor

First published in the *Critic* of 8 November 1884, this poem saluted the tenor Pasquale Brignoli, whose funeral had been held in New York City five days earlier. In 1889, Whitman had occasion to describe the powerful impact of Brignoli. A visitor to Mickle Street recalled attending Friedrich von Flotow's opera *Martha* with the poet more than three decades before: "Brignoli sang an aria [doubtless *M'appari*] which carried you away: you listened to it with your neck craned forward, drinking it in, dead, buried, and resurrected, till the last: then you sank back in your seat exclaiming: 'Lord! The voice of an angel and the manners of a codfish!' " Whitman declined to believe he had hurled such an insult: "I was a great lover of Brignoli: knew him, too, personally: I always stood up for him. These things, like that of the fish, were said often of him by others. I doubt if a singer ever lived, a tenor, with a sweeter voice than Brignoli had then. . . . I never thought of his manners when I heard him sing: they were not present: they were easy to forget" (*WWC,* 4:249–50). The eminent American soprano Clara Louise Kellogg, however, did recall Brignoli's stage manners as atrocious. During the tenor's first big aria in *Puritani,* he was thus observed by her: "Brignoli stood still in one spot and thrust first one arm out, and then the other, at right angles from his body, twenty-three times. I counted them." Brignoli also forbade colleagues to touch him onstage: "Imagine playing love scenes with a tenor who did not want to be touched!" Kellogg added (*Memoirs,* p. 41). —***Fernando's . . . Gennaro's*** (l. 8): For the mention of Fernando (the tenor hero of *La Favorita*) and Ernani (the tenor hero in Verdi's opera of the same name), see the notes to ll. 89 and 80 of "Proud Music of the Storm," above. Manrico is the principal tenor role of Verdi's *Il Trovatore* (1853). Gennaro is the principal tenor role in Donizetti's opera *Lucrezia Borgia* (1833).

Yonnondio

First published in the *Critic* of 26 November 1887.

Life and Death

First published in the *New York Herald* of 23 May 1888.

A Prairie Sunset

First published in the *New York Herald* of 9 March 1888.

Twilight

First published in the *Century,* December 1887. Whitman told Traubel he received several letters that suggested the poem's final word, "oblivion," subverted the Whitman ethos. Whitman's not very edifying response: "But *oblivion* as I use it there is just the word, both as furnishing sense and rhythm to the idea I had in mind" (*WWC,* 1:141).

Now Precedent Songs, Farewell

In *November Boughs,* Whitman added on the page with this and a short, four-line poem titled "An Evening Lull" the following note: "The two songs on this page are eked out during an afternoon, June, 1888, in my seventieth year, at a critical spell of illness. Of course no reader and probably no human being at any time will ever have such phases of emotional and solemn action as these involve to me. I feel in them an end and close of all."

After the Supper and Talk

First published in *Lippincott's Magazine,* November 1887, after the editor at *Harper's* had rejected it; a ms. has "So Loth to Depart" as a title.

1891–92 Edition

Good-Bye my Fancy

Whitman uses *fancy* in the Shakespearean sense of creative imagination or inspiration (for example, the Duke's opening speech in *Twelfth Night:* "So full of shapes is fancy / That it alone is high fantastical"). One might analogize this poem—and its near twin, "Good-Bye my Fancy!"—with Prospero's farewell to Ariel in the last speech of *The Tempest.*

On, on the Same, ye Jocund Twain!

eclaircissement (l. 6): French for "clarification."

The Pallid Wreath

First published in the *Critic* of 10 January 1891 (on the extant ms. Whitman wrote, "My friends, Can you use this in the Critic? The price is $5"). The ms. had "funereal" in the first line, and the misprinting of this as "funeral" began in the *Critic.*

To the Sun-Set Breeze

First published in *Lippincott's Magazine,* December 1890. In an unpublished ms. at Yale, Ezra Pound wrote, "And yet if a man has written lines like Whitman's to the 'sunset breeze' one has to love him."

A Twilight Song

First published in the *Century* of May 1890, with the subtitle "For unknown buried soldiers, North and South." Whitman worried this poem through at least five extant ms. drafts.

A Voice from Death
First published in the *New York World,* 7 June 1889, a week after the flood. Heavy rains caused the collapse of a dam, killing about 2,200 people.

"The Rounded Catalogue Divine Complete"
First published in *Good-Bye my Fancy.*

L. of G.'s Purport
First published in *Good-Bye my Fancy.*

Good-Bye my Fancy!
First published in *Good-Bye my Fancy;* on *fancy,* see note to poem of similar title above.

Poems in Appendix 1

The Love That Is Hereafter
This poem appeared in the *Long Island Democrat* of 19 May 1840. Two published poems are known to predate this one: "Young Grimes" (same periodical, 1 January 1840) and "The Inca's Daughter" (same periodical, 5 May 1840). For a full discussion of Whitman's pre-1855 poems, see the edition by Thomas Brasher, *The Early Poems and Prose Fiction* (1963), in *The Collected Writings*. This poem is significant as an early expression of Whitman's yearning for passionate connection.

Each Has His Grief
This poem is given as it appeared in the *New York New World* of 20 November 1841; at the time Whitman was a printer in the *New World* office. It had previously appeared, with minor variants and without the fourth stanza, as "We All Shall Rest at Last" in the *Long Island Democrat* of 14 July 1840. —**check** (l. 3): surely a typographical error for *cheek.*

A Sketch
This poem was identified as Whitman's by Jerome Loving as recently as 1994 *(Walt Whitman Quarterly Review,* pp. 116–22.). Signed "W." at the bottom, it appeared in the *New World* on 10 December 1842, a few weeks after Whitman's temperance novel, *Franklin Evans: or The Inebriate,* appeared in the same paper.

The Mississippi at Midnight
This appeared in the second issue of the *New Orleans Crescent,* 6 March 1848, during Whitman's brief tenure as one of its editors. A different version was published in the "Specimen Days and Collect" volume of Whitman's *Complete Prose Works* (1892), for which see Brasher, p. 42.

Resurgemus

This poem appeared in the *New York Tribune* of 21 June 1850, when the first line read, "Suddenly, out of its state and drowsy air, the air of slaves." The obvious typographical error of "state" for *stale* has been corrected. A thoughtful editor might have concluded that "air" worked better with the lightning image in the second line, but Whitman saw to it that the two words were changed to "lair" when, as the only previously published poem in the 1855 *Leaves,* it appeared, untitled, as "Suddenly out of its stale and drowsy lair . . ." (see note for that version, above).

Supplement Hours

Five years after Whitman's death another *Leaves* edition appeared with thirteen hitherto unpublished poems under the rubric *Old Age Echoes*. This poem and the two following are from this group. In "An Executor's Diary Note, 1891," Horace Traubel says the title for this group was devised by the poet himself.

Of Many a Smutch'd Deed Reminiscent

From *Old Age Echoes* (1897). Compare this confessional and love-professing poem with Leaves of Grass 13 of 1860.

A Thought of Columbus

From *Old Age Echoes* (1897). This was first published by Traubel as "Walt Whitman's Last Poem" in *Once a Week* (New York), 16 July 1892. —**éclaircissement** (l. 17): French for "clarification."

A Select Whitman Bibliography

OTHER EDITIONS AND WRITINGS BY WHITMAN

Democratic Vistas. Washington: 1871.

Specimen Days. Philadelphia: Rees Welsh, 1882–83.

Complete Prose Works. Philadelphia: David McKay, 1892.

Calamus: A Series of Letters Written During the Years 1868–1880. Ed. Richard Maurice Bucke. Boston: Maynard, 1897.

The Wound Dresser: A Series of Letters Written from the Hospitals in Washington. Ed. R. M. Bucke. Boston: Small, Maynard, 1898.

Notes and Fragments: Left by Walt Whitman. Ed. R. M. Bucke. London, Ontario: A. Talbot, 1899; rpt. 1972.

Letters Written by Walt Whitman to His Mother from 1866–1872. Ed. Thomas Harned. New York: Putnam's, 1902.

The Complete Writings of Walt Whitman. 10 vols. Ed. R. M. Bucke, Thomas Harned, Horace Traubel. New York: Putnam's, 1902.

An American Primer by Walt Whitman. Ed. Horace Traubel. Boston: Small, Maynard, 1904.

The Gathering of the Forces: Editorials, Essays, Literary and Dramatic Reviews . . . by Walt Whitman. 2 vols. Ed. Cleveland Rodgers and John Black. New York: Putnam's, 1920.

The Uncollected Poetry and Prose of Walt Whitman. 2 vols. Ed. Emory Holloway. New York: Doubleday, Page, 1921.

Walt Whitman's Workshop: A Collection of Unpublished Manuscripts. Ed. Clifton Furness. Cambridge: Harvard University Press, 1928; rpt. 1964.

I Sit and Look Out: Editorials from the BROOKLYN DAILY TIMES. Ed. Emory Holloway and Vernolian Schwarz. New York: Columbia University Press, 1932.

Walt Whitman and the Civil War: A Collection of Original Articles and Manuscripts. Ed. Charles Glicksberg. Philadelphia: University of Pennsylvania Press, 1933.

New York Dissected: A Sheaf of Recently Discovered Newspaper Articles by the Author of LEAVES OF GRASS. Ed. Emory Holloway and Ralph Adimari. New York: Wilson, 1936.

Faint Clews and Indirections: Manuscripts of Walt Whitman and His Family. Ed. Clarence Gohdes and Rollo Silver. Durham: Duke University Press, 1949.

A Concordance to Walt Whitman's LEAVES OF GRASS *and Selected Prose Writings*. Ed. Edwin Eby. Seattle: University of Washington Press, 1949–55.

Walt Whitman of the NEW YORK AURORA. Ed. Joseph Rubin and Charles Brown. State College, Pennsylvania: Bald Eagle, 1950; rpt. 1972.

Whitman's Manuscripts LEAVES OF GRASS *1860*. Ed. Fredson Bowers. Chicago: University of Chicago Press, 1955.

The Collected Writings of Walt Whitman. Gen. eds. Gay Wilson Allen and Sculley Bradley. New York: New York University Press, 1961–84. Includes *Comprehensive Reader's Edition; A Textual Variorum of the Printed Poems; Prose Works 1892; The Early Poems and the Prose Fiction; Notebooks and Unpublished Prose Manuscripts; Daybooks and Notebooks;* and *The Correspondence.*

Walt Whitman's Blue Book: The 1860–61 LEAVES OF GRASS. 2 vols. Ed. Arthur Golden. New York: New York Public Library, 1968.

Walt Whitman's Autograph Revision of the Analysis of LEAVES OF GRASS *(for Dr. R. M. Bucke's* WALT WHITMAN). Ed. Stephen Railton. New York: New York University Press, 1974.

Complete Poetry and Collected Prose. New York: Library of America, 1982.

Selected Letters of Walt Whitman. Ed. Edwin Haviland Miller. Iowa City: University of Iowa Press, 1990.

Walt Whitman: A Bibliography. Joel Myerson. Pittsburgh: University of Pittsburgh Press, 1993.

The Walt Whitman Archive. 6 vols. Ed. Joel Myerson. New York: Garland, 1993.

Major Authors on CD-ROM: Walt Whitman, Ed. Ed Folsom and Kenneth Price. Woodbridge, Conn.: Primary Source Media, 1997.

The Journalism, 1834–1846. Ed. Herbert Bergman. New York: Peter Lang, 1998.

WORKS ABOUT WHITMAN

Because the critical reception of Whitman has passed through several phases during the last century, the date of publication is significant; the following works are therefore arranged chronologically.

John Burroughs. *Notes on Walt Whitman as Poet and Person.* New York: American News, 1867.

Richard Maurice Bucke. *Walt Whitman.* Philadelphia: David McKay, 1883.

John Addington Symonds. *Walt Whitman, A Study.* London: Routledge, 1893; rpt. 1968.

Horace L. Traubel, Thomas B. Harned, and R. M. Bucke. *In Re Walt Whitman.* Philadelphia: David McKay, 1893.

John Burroughs. *Whitman: A Study.* Boston: Houghton Mifflin, 1896.

William Sloane Kennedy. *Reminiscences of Walt Whitman.* London: Gardner, 1896.

Henry Bryan Binns. *A Life of Walt Whitman.* London: Methuen, 1905.

Bliss Perry. *Walt Whitman, His Life and Work.* New York: Houghton Mifflin, 1906; rev. ed. 1908.

Edward Carpenter. *Days with Walt Whitman.* London: George Allen, 1906.

W. C. Rivers. *Walt Whitman's Anomaly.* London: George Allen, 1913.

Thomas B. Harned. *The Letters of Anne Gilchrist and Walt Whitman.* New York: Doubleday, Page, 1918.

Henry S. Saunders. *Parodies on Walt Whitman.* New York: American Library Service, 1923.

Emory Holloway. *Walt Whitman: An Interpretation in Narrative.* New York: Knopf, 1926.

Clara Barrus. *Whitman and Burroughs: Comrades.* Boston: Houghton Mifflin, 1931.

Frederik Schyberg. *Walt Whitman.* 1933; Eng. tr., New York: Columbia University Press, 1951.

Newton Arvin. *Whitman.* New York: Macmillan, 1938.

Henry Seidel Canby. *Walt Whitman, an American.* Boston: Houghton Mifflin, 1943.

Gay Wilson Allen. *A Walt Whitman Handbook.* Chicago: Packard, 1946.

Robert Faner. *Walt Whitman and Opera.* Carbondale: Southern Illinois University Press, 1951; rpt. 1972.

Roger Asselineau. *The Evolution of Walt Whitman.* 1954; Eng. tr., Cambridge: Harvard University Press, 1962.

Gay Wilson Allen. *The Solitary Singer: A Critical Biography of Walt Whitman.* New York: Macmillan, 1955; rpt. 1967.

Richard Chase. *Walt Whitman Reconsidered.* New York: Wm. Sloane, 1955.

Milton Hindus, ed. *LEAVES OF GRASS One Hundred Years After.* Stanford: Stanford University Press, 1955.

R. W. B. Lewis, ed. *The Presence of Walt Whitman.* New York: Columbia University Press, 1962.

James Edwin Miller. *Walt Whitman.* New York: Twayne, 1962.

Edwin Haviland Miller. *Walt Whitman's Poetry: A Psychological Journey.* New York: Houghton Mifflin, 1968.

Edwin Haviland Miller, ed. *A Century of Whitman Criticism.* Bloomington: Indiana University Press, 1969.

Gay Wilson Allen. *Walt Whitman: A Reader's Guide.* New York: Farrar Straus, 1970.

Milton Hindus, ed. *Walt Whitman: The Critical Heritage.* New York: Barnes & Noble, 1971.

Thomas Brasher. *Whitman as Editor of the BROOKLYN DAILY EAGLE.* Detroit: Wayne State University Press, 1972.

Joseph Jay Rubin. *The Historic Whitman.* University Park: Pennsylvania State University Press, 1973.

Floyd Stovall. *The Foreground of LEAVES OF GRASS.* Charlottesville: University of Virginia Press, 1974.

Gay Wilson Allen. *The New Walt Whitman Handbook.* New York: New York University Press, 1975.

Harold Aspiz. *Walt Whitman and the Body Beautiful.* Champaign: University of Illinois Press, 1980.

Justin Kaplan. *Walt Whitman: A Life.* New York: Simon & Schuster, 1980.

Jim Perlman, Ed Folsom, and Dan Campion, eds. *Walt Whitman: The Measure of His Song.* Minneapolis: Holy Cow, 1981; rev. ed. 1998.

Jerome Loving. *Emerson, Whitman and the American Muse.* Chapel Hill: University of North Carolina Press, 1982.

Paul Zweig. *Walt Whitman: The Making of the Poet.* New York: Viking, 1984.

Harold Bloom, ed. *Walt Whitman: Modern Critical Views.* New York: Chelsea House, 1985.

Louis Budd and Edwin Cady, eds. *On Whitman: The Best from AMERICAN LITERATURE.* Durham: Duke University Press, 1987.

Charley Shively, ed. *Calamus Lovers: Walt Whitman's Working Class Camerados.* San Francisco: Gay Sunshine, 1987.

Henry Christman, ed. *Walt Whitman's New York.* New York: New Amsterdam, 1989.

Betsy Erkkila. *Whitman the Political Poet.* New York: Oxford University Press, 1989.

M. Jimmie Killingsworth. *Whitman's Poetry of the Body.* Chapel Hill: University of North Carolina Press, 1989.

Edwin Haviland Miller. *Walt Whitman's "Song of Myself": A Mosaic of Interpretations.* Iowa City: University of Iowa Press, 1989.

Charley Shively, ed. *Drum Beats: Walt Whitman's Civil War Boy Lovers.* San Francisco: Gay Sunshine, 1989.

Michael Moon. *Disseminating Whitman.* Cambridge: Harvard University Press, 1991.

Joel Myerson, ed. *Whitman in His Own Time.* Detroit: Omnigraphics, 1991.

Byrne R. S. Fone. *Masculine Landscapes: Walt Whitman and the Homoerotic Text.* Carbondale: Southern Illinois University Press, 1992.

Robert K. Martin, ed. *The Continuing Presence of Walt Whitman.* Iowa City: University of Iowa Press, 1992.

Ed Folsom. *Walt Whitman's Native Representations*. New York: Cambridge University Press, 1994.

Ed Folsom, ed. *Walt Whitman: The Centennial Essays*. Iowa City: University of Iowa Press, 1994.

Geoffrey Sill, ed. *Walt Whitman of Mickle Street*. Knoxville: University of Tennessee Press, 1994.

David Reynolds. *Walt Whitman's America: A Cultural Biography*. New York: Knopf, 1995.

Gay Wilson Allen and Ed Folsom, eds. *Walt Whitman and the World*. Iowa City: University of Iowa Press, 1995.

Ezra Greenspan, ed. *Cambridge Companion to Walt Whitman*. New York: Cambridge, University Press, 1995.

Betsy Erkkila and Jay Grossman, eds. *Breaking Bounds: Whitman and American Cultural Studies*. New York: Oxford University Press, 1996.

Kenneth Price. *Walt Whitman: The Contemporary Reviews*. New York: Cambridge University Press, 1996.

Gary Schmidgall. *Walt Whitman: A Gay Life*. New York: Penguin Plume, 1997.

Joann P. Krieg. *A Whitman Chronology*. Iowa City: Iowa University Press, 1998.

J. R. LeMaster and Donald Kummings, eds. *Walt Whitman Encyclopedia*. New York: Garland, 1998.

Jerome Loving, *Walt Whitman: The Song of Himself*. Berkeley: University of California Press, 1999.

Index of Titles

All subsequent titles of poems included in this edition are also indexed; in each case the reader is referred to the poem's first title. Titles derived from a poem's first line are followed by ellipses.

After the Dazzle of Day.......389
After the Supper and Talk.......395
Ages and Ages Returning at Intervals, *see* Enfans d'Adam 12.......221
Ah Poverties, Wincings, and Sulky Retreats.......301
America.......388
Among the Multitude, *see* Calamus 41.......251
Are You the New Person Drawn toward Me?, *see* Calamus 12.......235
Artilleryman's Vision, The, *see* The Veteran's Vision.......281
As a Strong Bird on Pinions Free.......341
As Adam Early in the Morning, *see* Enfans d'Adam 15.......222
As I Ebb'd with the Ocean of Life, *see* Leaves of Grass 1.......195
As I Lay with My Head in Your Lap, Camerado.......302
As I Sit Writing Here.......388
As if a Phantom Caress'd Me, *see* I thought I was not alone . . . (Debris).......263
As Nearing Departure, *see* To My Soul.......263
As the Time Draws Nigh, *see* To My Soul.......263
As Toilsome I Wander'd Virginia's Woods.......283
Assurances, *see* Faith Poem.......153

Backward Glance O'er Traveled Roads, A.......377
Base of all Metaphysics, The.......334
Beautiful Women, *see* Women sit, or move to and fro . . . (Debris).......262
Beginners.......261
Beginning My Studies.......271
Behold This Swarthy Face, *see* Calamus 19.......239
Bodies of men and women engirth me . . . , The.......89
Boston Ballad, A, *see* Clear the way there Jonathan! 103
Broadway.......390
Bunch Poem.......155

Burial, *see* To think of time 75
Burial Poem, *see* To think of time 75
By Broad Potomac's Shore 348

Calamus Cluster 223–252
1 "In paths untrodden" 223
2 "Scented herbage of my breast" 223
3 "Whoever you are holding me now in hand" 225
4 "These I, singing in spring, collect for lovers" 227
5 "States!" 228
6 "Not heaving from my ribbed breast only" 230
7 "Of the terrible question of appearances" 230
8 "Long I thought that knowledge alone would suffice" 231
9 "Hours continuing long, sore and heavy-hearted" 232
10 "You bards of ages hence!" 233
11 "When I heard at the close of the day" 234
12 "Are you the new person drawn toward me?" 235
13 "Calamus, taste" 235
14 "Not heat flames up and consumes" 236
15 "O drops of me!" 237
16 "Who is now reading this?" 237
17 "Of him I love day and night" 238
18 "City of my walks and joys" 239
19 "Mind you the timid models of the rest" 239
20 "I saw in Louisiana a live-oak growing" 240
21 "Music always round me" 241
22 "Passing stranger!" 241
23 "This moment as I sit alone" 242
24 "I hear it is charged against me" 242
25 "The prairie-grass dividing" 243
26 "We two boys together clinging" 243
27 "O love!" 244
28 "When I peruse the conquered fame" 244
29 "One flitting glimpse" 245
30 "A promise and gift to California" 245
31 "What ship, puzzled at sea" 246
32 "What think you I take my pen in hand" 246
33 "No labor-saving machine" 247
34 "I dreamed in a dream" 247
35 "To you of New England" 248
36 "Earth! my likeness!" 248
37 "A Leaf for hand in hand" 249

38 "Primeval my love for the woman I love" 249
39 "Sometimes with one I love" 250
40 "That shadow, my likeness" 250
41 "Among the men and women, the multitude" 251
42 "To the young man, many things to absorb" 251
43 "O you whom I often and silently come" 252
44 "Here my last words, and most baffling" 252
45 "Full of life, sweet-blooded, compact" 252
Carol Closing Sixty-Nine, A 387
Carol of Occupations, *see* Come closer to me 66
Carol of Words, *see* Poem of The Sayers of The Words of The Earth .. 160
Chanting the Square Deific 299
CHANTS DEMOCRATIC CLUSTER 188–94
8 "Splendor of falling day" 188
10 "Historians! you who celebrate bygones!" 190
12 "To oratists—to male or female" 191
14 "Poets to come!" 192
18 "Me imperturbe" 193
19 "I was looking a long while" 194
20 "American mouth-songs!" 194
Child's Reminiscence, A, *see* A Word Out of the Sea 208
City of Orgies, *see* Calamus 18 239
City of Ships 275
Clear Midnight, A 374
Clear the way there Jonathan! 103
Clef Poem 151
Come closer to me 66
Come Up from the Fields Father 273
Crossing Brooklyn Ferry, *see* Sun-Down Poem 134

Dalliance of the Eagles, The 371
Dead Tenor, The 391
DEBRIS CLUSTER 262–63
Despairing cries float ceaselessly . . . (Debris) 262
Did You Ask Dulcet Rhymes from Me? 280
Dirge for Two Veterans 303
Dresser, The 271

Each Has His Grief 414
Earth, My Likeness, *see* Calamus 36 248
Eidólons 360
Elemental Drifts, *see* Leaves of Grass 1 195

ENFANS D' ADAM CLUSTER 214–22
1 "To the garden, the world" 214
2 "From that of myself" 215
3 *see* The bodies of men and women engirth me 89
4 *see* Poem of Procreation 149
5 *see* Bunch Poem 155
6 "O furious! O confine me not!" 217
7 "You and I—what the earth is, we are" 218
8 "Native moments!" 219
9 "Once I passed through a populous city" 220
10 "Inquiring, tireless, seeking that yet unfound" 220
11 "In the new garden, in all the parts" 221
12 "Ages and ages, returning at intervals" 221
13 "O hymen! O hymenee!" 222
14 "I am he that aches with love" 222
15 "Early in the morning" 222
Europe the 72[d] and 73[d] Years of These States, *see* Suddenly out of its stale and drowsy lair 101
and see Resurgemus 418
Excelsior, *see* Poem of The Heart of The Son of Manhattan Island 152

Faces, *see* Sauntering the pavement 95
Facing West from California's Shores, *see* Enfans d'Adam 10 220
Faith Poem 153
Farm Picture, A 278
Fast Anchor'd Eternal O Love!, *see* Calamus 38 249
Font of Type, A 387
For Him I Sing 333
For You O Democracy, *see* Calamus 5 228
From Pent-Up Aching Rivers, *see* Enfans d'Adam 2 215
Full of Life Now, *see* Calamus 45 252

Give Me the Splendid Silent Sun 279
Glimpse, A, *see* Calamus 29 245
Gods 331
Good-Bye my Fancy 402
Good-Bye my Fancy! 409
Great are the myths 108

Halcyon Days 389
Hand-Mirror, A 260

Have you learn'd lessons . . . (Debris) 262
Here the Frailest Leaves of Me, *see* Calamus 44 252
Hush'd Be the Camps To-day 284

I Am He That Aches with Love, *see* Enfans d'Adam 14 222
I celebrate myself 15
I Dream'd in a Dream, *see* Calamus 34 247
I Hear America Singing, *see* Chants Democratic 20 194
I Hear It Was Charged Against Me, *see* Calamus 24 242
I Saw in Louisiana a Live-Oak Growing, *see* Calamus 20 240
I Sing the Body Electric, *see* The bodies of men and women engirth me 89
I Sit and Look Out, *see* Leaves of Grass 17 199
I thought I was not alone . . . (Debris) 263
I understand your anguish . . . (Debris) 262
I wander all night in my vision 81
I Was Looking a Long While, *see* Chants Democratic 19 194
In Paths Untrodden, *see* Calamus 1 223
Inscription 307
Italian Music in Dakota 371

L. of G.'s Purport 408
Leaf for Hand in Hand, A, *see* Calamus 37 249
Leaf of Faces, *see* Sauntering the pavement 95
Leaf of Faces, A, *see* Sauntering the pavement 95
Leaves of Grass 1 "Elemental drifts!" 195
Leaves of Grass 2 "Tears! tears! tears!" 308
Leaves of Grass 13 "O bitter sprig!" 198
Leaves of Grass 17 "I sit and look out" 199
Leaves of Grass 21 "Now I make a leaf of Voices" 200
Leaves of Grass 22 "What am I, after all, but a child" 201
Leaves of Grass 24 "Lift me close to your face" 202
Lesson Poem, *see* Who learns my lesson complete? 107
Life and Death 392
Look Down Fair Moon 284
Love That Is Hereafter, The 413

Mannahatta ("I was asking for something specific") 258
Mannahatta ("My city's fit and noble name resumed") 386
March in the Ranks Hard-Prest, and the Road Unknown, A 277
Me Imperturbe, *see* Chants Democratic 18 193

MESSENGER LEAVES CLUSTER 253–58
Miracles, *see* Poem of Perfect Miracles 154
Mississippi at Midnight, The 417
Mother and Babe 276
My Legacy, *see* Souvenirs of Democracy 340
Mystic Trumpeter, The 345

Native Moments, *see* Enfans d'Adam 8 219
Night Poem, *see* I wander all night in my vision 81
No Labor-Saving Machine, *see* Calamus 33 247
Noiseless, Patient Spider, A 330
Not Heat Flames Up and Consumes, *see* Calamus 14 236
Not Heaving from My Ribb'd Breast Only, *see* Calamus 6 230
Not My Enemies Ever Invade Me 301
Not Youth Pertains to Me 285
Now Lift Me Close, *see* Leaves of Grass 24 202
Now List to My Morning Romanza, *see* A young man came to me 98
Now Precedent Songs, Farewell 394

O Captain! My Captain! 298
O Hymen! O Hymenee!, *see* Enfans d'Adam 13 222
O Living Always, Always Dying, *see* Calamus 27 244
O Tan-Faced Prairie-Boy 283
O You Whom I Often and Silently Come, *see* Calamus 43 252
Of Him I Love Day and Night, *see* Calamus 17 238
Of Many a Smutch'd Deed Reminiscent 421
Of persons arrived at high positions 260
Of That Blithe Throat of Thine 390
Of the Terrible Doubt of Appearances, *see* Calamus 7 230
On, on the Same, ye Jocund Twain! 403
On the Beach at Night Alone, *see* Clef Poem 151
Once I Pass'd Through a Populous City, *see* Enfans d'Adam 9 220
One Hour to Madness and Joy, *see* Enfans d'Adam 6 217
One Song, America, Before I Go 340
One's-Self I Sing 307
Out of the Cradle Endlessly Rocking, *see* A Word Out of the Sea 208
Over the Carnage Rose Prophetic a Voice, *see* Calamus 5 228

Pallid Wreath, The 404
Passage to India 315

Paumanok Picture, A, *see note for* Poem of Salutation 492
Picture, *see* Women sit, or move to and fro . . . (Debris) 262
Poem of a Few Greatnesses, *see* Great are the myths 108
Poem of Apparitions in Boston, the 78th Year of These States,
see Clear the way there Jonathan! 103
Poem of Faces, *see* Sauntering the pavement 95
Poem of Joys 201
Poem of Perfect Miracles 154
Poem of Procreation 149
Poem of Salutation 121
Poem of The Body, *see* The bodies of men and women
engirth me 89
Poem of the Child That Went Forth, *see* There was a child
went forth 105
Poem of the Daily Work of The Workmen and Workwomen of These
States, *see* Come closer to me 66
Poem of The Heart of The Son of Manhattan Island 152
Poem of The Poet, *see* A young man came to me 98
Poem of The Propositions of Nakedness 157
Poem of The Road 140
Poem of The Sayers of The Words of The Earth 160
Poem of Walt Whitman, An American, *see* I celebrate myself 15
Poem of Wonder at The Resurrection of The Wheat 130
Poem of You, Whoever You Are 132
Poems of Joy, *see* Poem of Joys 201
Poets to Come, *see* Chants Democratic 14 192
Prairie States, The 372
Prairie Sunset, A 393
Prairie-Grass Dividing, The, *see* Calamus 25 243
Prayer of Columbus 362
Promise to California, A, *see* Calamus 30 245
Proto-Leaf 177
Proud Music of the Storm 323

Queries to My Seventieth Year 388

Reconciliation 304
Recorders Ages Hence, *see* Calamus 10 233
Respondez!, *see* Poem of The Propositions of Nakedness 257
Resurgemus 418
see also Suddenly out of its stale and drowsy lair 101

Riddle Song, A 372
Roots and Leaves Themselves Alone, *see* Calamus 13 235
"Rounded Catalogue Divine Complete, The" 407
Runner, The 308

Salut au Monde!, *see* Poem of Salutation 121
Sauntering the pavement 95
Scented Herbage of My Breast, *see* Calamus 2 223
Sketch, A 416
Sleep-Chasings, *see* I wander all night in my vision 81
Sleepers, The, *see* I wander all night in my vision 81
Small the Theme of My Chant, *see* Inscription 307
So long! 264
Sometimes with One I Love, *see* Calamus 39 250
Song at Sunset, *see* Chants Democratic 8 188
Song of Joys, A, *see* Poem of Joys 201
Song of Myself, *see* I celebrate myself 15
Song of Occupations, A, *see* Come closer to me 66
Song of the Answerer, *see* A young man came to me 98
Song of the Open Road, *see* Poem of The Road 140
Song of the Rolling Earth, A, *see* Poem of The Sayers of
The Words of The Earth 160
Souvenirs of Democracy 340
Sparkles from the Wheel 330
Spirit That Form'd This Scene 374
Spontaneous Me, *see* Bunch Poem 155
Starting from Paumanok, *see* Proto-Leaf 177
Stronger Lessons, *see* Have you learn'd lessons . . . (Debris) 262
Suddenly out of its stale and drowsy lair 101
see also Resurgemus 418
Sun-Down Poem 134
Supplement Hours 420

Tears, *see* Leaves of Grass 2 308
Tears! tears! tears! *see* Leaves of Grass 2 308
Tests 261
That Music Always Round Me, *see* Calamus 2 223
That Shadow My Likeness, *see* Calamus 40 250
There was a child went forth 105
These I Singing in Spring, *see* Calamus 4 227
This Compost, *see* Poem of Wonder at The Resurrection of
The Wheat 130

This Dust was Once the Man........329
This Moment Yearning and Thoughtful, *see* Calamus 23........242
Thou Proud Mother with Thy Equal Brood, *see* As a Strong Bird on Pinions Free........341
Thought, *see* Of persons arrived at high positions 260
Thought 3, *see* Of persons arrived at high positions 260
Thought of Columbus, A........421
THOUGHTS CLUSTER........260
Three old men slowly pass . . . (Debris)........262
To a Cantatrice........257
To a Certain Cantatrice, *see* To a Cantatrice........257
To a Certain Civilian, *see* Did You Ask Dulcet Rhymes from Me?........280
To a Common Prostitute........254
To a Historian, *see* Chants Democratic 10........190
To a Locomotive in Winter........365
To a President........257
To a Pupil........255
To a Stranger, *see* Calamus 22........241
To a Western Boy, *see* Calamus 42........251
To Get the Final Lilt of Songs........391
To Him That was Crucified........253
To My Soul........263
To One Shortly to Die........254
To the East and the West, *see* Calamus 35........248
To the Garden the World, *see* Enfans d'Adam 1........214
To the Reader at Parting, *see* Leaves of Grass 24........202
To the Sayers of Words, *see* Poem of The Sayers of The Words of The Earth........160
To The States, *see* Walt Whitman's Caution........257
To The States, To Identify the 16th, 17th, or 18th Presidentiad........256
To the Sun-Set Breeze........404
To Thee, Old Cause!........333
To think of time 75
To You ("Let us twain walk aside")........258
To You ("Stranger! if you, passing")........258
To You, *see* Poem of You, Whoever You Are........132
Trickle Drops, *see* Calamus 15........237
Twilight........393
Twilight Song, A........405

Untold Want, The........332

Veteran's Vision, The 281
Vigil Strange I Kept on the Field One Night 276
Vocalism, *see* Chants Democratic 12 191
Voice from Death, A 406

Walt Whitman, *see* I celebrate myself 15
Walt Whitman's Caution 257
Wandering at Morn 366
We Two Boys Together Clinging, *see* Calamus 26 243
We Two, How Long We Were Fool'd, *see* Enfans d'Adam 7 218
What Am I After All, *see* Leaves of Grass 21 200
What Place Is Besieged?, *see* Calamus 31 246
What Ship Puzzled at Sea, *see* Calamus 31 246
What Think You I Take My Pen in Hand?, *see* Calamus 32 246
When I Heard at the Close of the Day, *see* Calamus 11 234
When I Peruse the Conquer'd Fame, *see* Calamus 28 244
When I Read the Book 309
When Lilacs Last in the Door-Yard Bloom'd 291
Whispers of Heavenly Death 329
Who learns my lessons complete . . . , ... 107
Whoever You Are Holding Me Now in Hand, *see* Calamus 3 225
With All Thy Gifts 367
Woman Waits for Me, A, *see* Poem of Procreation 149
Women sit, or move to and fro . . . (Debris) 262
Word Out of the Sea, A 208
Wound-Dresser, The, *see* The Dresser 271

Year That Trembled and Reel'd Beneath Me 281
Yet, Yet, Ye Downcast Hours, *see* Despairing cries float ceaselessly . . .
and I understand your anguish . . . (Debris) 262
Yonnondio 392
You Felons on Trial in Courts, *see* Leaves of Grass 13 198
Young man came to me . . . , A 98
Youth, Day, Old Age and Night, *see* Great are the myths 108
and see note 492

About the Editor

GARY SCHMIDGALL earned his doctorate in English from Stanford University and has taught at the University of Pennsylvania, New York University, The City University of New York, and Columbia University. Before turning to biography in recent years with well-received studies of Oscar Wilde and Walt Whitman (both published by Penguin Plume), he taught, lectured, and published extensively in the fields of Shakespeare and Renaissance literature, and literature and music. His principal previous works are *Shakespeare and the Courtly Aesthetic* (University of California), *Shakespeare and the Poet's Life* (University of Kentucky), *Literature as Opera* (Oxford), and *Shakespeare and Opera* (Oxford). He lives in Manhattan.